Warfare in
Tenth-Century Germany

WARFARE IN HISTORY

ISSN 1358-779X

Series editors
Matthew Bennett, Royal Military Academy, Sandhurst, UK
Anne Curry, University of Southampton, UK
Stephen Morillo, Wabash College, Crawfordsville, USA

This series aims to provide a wide-ranging and scholarly approach to military history, offering both individual studies of topics or wars, and volumes giving a selection of contemporary and later accounts of particular battles; its scope ranges from the early medieval to the early modern period.

New proposals for the series are welcomed; they should be sent to the publisher at the address below.

Boydell and Brewer Limited, PO Box 9, Woodbridge, Suffolk, IP12 3DF

Previously published volumes in this series are listed at the back of this volume

Warfare in Tenth-Century Germany

David S. Bachrach

THE BOYDELL PRESS

First published 2012
The Boydell Press, Woodbridge
Paperback edition 2014

ISBN 978-1-84383-762-6 hardback
ISBN 978-1-84383-927-9 paperback

The Boydell Press is an imprint of Boydell & Brewer Ltd
PO Box 9, Woodbridge, Suffolk IP12 3DF, UK
and of Boydell & Brewer Inc.
668 Mt Hope Avenue, Rochester, NY 14620-2731, USA
website: www.boydellandbrewer.com

A CIP catalogue record for this book is available
from the British Library

The publisher has no responsibility for the continued existence or accuracy of URLs
for external or third-party internet websites referred to in this book, and does not guarantee
that any content on such websites is, or will remain, accurate or appropriate

Typeset by www.thewordservice.com

This publication is printed on acid-free paper

Contents

List of Illustrations

Acknowledgments

A great many people have provided me with help in bringing this project to a conclusion. I would like to thank Charles Bowlus, Richard Abels, David Warner, Bernard Bachrach, Clifford Rogers, Kenneth Baldwin, Eric Goldberg, Thomas Noble, Jonathan Lyon, Patrick Geary, and the anonymous readers of several articles that prepared the way for this book, for their valuable suggestions, observations, and corrections, and for their generosity in reading portions or the entirety of this text in manuscript (in some cases several times). To the extent that this book helps to illuminate the history of the German kingdom in the tenth century, the community of scholars to which I have the privilege of belonging must take a great part of the credit. Naturally, the errors of commission and omission that remain in the text are mine alone. I also want to thank the library staff at the University of New Hampshire for obtaining the numerous scholarly works that I needed for my research, and the UNH Center for the Humanities whose generous support in providing a research leave made it possible to complete this text in a timely fashion. I owe a particular debt of thanks to my wife Elyse, and to my children Madeline, Rachel, and Henry who showed tremendous patience while daddy was locked away in his office. It is to them that I dedicate this book.

To my children Madeline, Rachel,
and Henry with all of my love.

Abbreviations

MGH	*Monumenta Germaniae Historica*
DA	*Die Urkunden Arnolfs*, ed. Paul Kehr, MGH *Diplomata regum Germaniae ex stirpe Karolinorum* vol. 3 (Berlin, 1940).
DK	*Die Urkunden Zwentibolds und Ludwigs des Kindes*, ed. Theodor Schieffer, MGH *Diplomata regum Germaniae ex stirpe Karolinorum* vol. 4 (Berlin, 1960).
DO I	*Die Urkunden Konrad I., Heinrich I. und Otto I.*, ed. Theodor Sickel, MGH *Diplomatum regum et imperatorum Germaniae* vol. 1 (Hanover, 1879–1884).
DO II	*Die Urkunden Otto des II und Otto des III.*, ed. Theodor Sickel, MGH *Diplomatum regum et imperatorum Germaniae* vol. 2 (Hanover, 1888–1893).
DO III	*Die Urkunden Otto des II und Otto des III.*, ed. Theodor Sickel, MGH *Diplomatum regum et imperatorum Germaniae* vol. 2 (Hanover, 1888–1893).
DH I	*Die Urkunden Konrad I., Heinrich I. und Otto I.*, ed. Theodor Sickel, MGH *Diplomatum regum et imperatorum Germaniae* vol. 1 (Hanover, 1879–1884).
DH II	*Die Urkunden Heinrichs II. und Arduins*, ed. Harry Bresslau, Robert Holtzmann and Hermann Reincke-Bloch, MGH *Diplomatum regum et imperatorum Germaniae* vol. 3 (Hanover, 1900–1903).
Capitularia	*Capitularia Regum Francorum*, ed. Alfred Boretius and Viktor Krause 2 vols. MGH *Capitularia*, Legum Sectio II (Hanover, 1883–1897).
Concilia	*Concilia*, Legum Sectio III, 3 vols. (Hanover, 1893–1984).
Epistolae	*Epistolae*, 8 vols. (Hanover, 1887, 1939).
Poetae Latini	*Poetae Latini Aevi Carolini*, 4 vols. (Hanover, 1881–1899).
SRG	*Scriptores rerum Germanicarum in usum scholarum separatim editi* (Hanover, 1871–).
SS	*Scriptores.* (Hanover, 1824–).
MIÖG	*Mitteilungen des Instituts für österreichische Geschichtsforschung*
PL	*Patrologiae Cursus Completus, Series Latina*, ed. J.-P. Migne, 221 vols. (Paris, 1841–1866).

Simplified Ottonian Genealogy

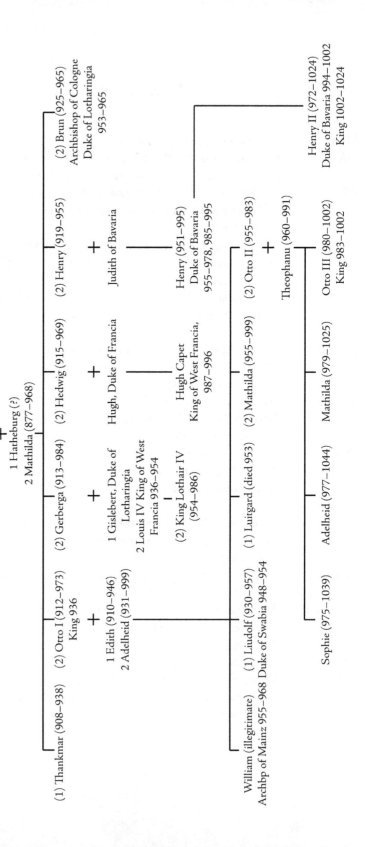

Simplified Carolingian Genealogy

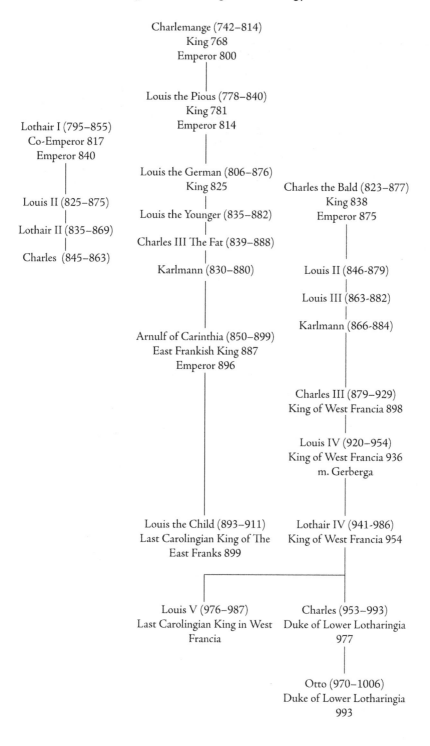

Charlemange (742–814)
King 768
Emperor 800

Louis the Pious (778–840)
King 781
Emperor 814

Lothair I (795–855)
Co-Emperor 817
Emperor 840

Louis the German (806–876)
King 825

Charles the Bald (823–877)
King 838
Emperor 875

Louis II (825–875)

Louis the Younger (835–882)

Lothair II (835–869)

Charles III The Fat (839–888)

Charles (845–863)

Karlmann (830–880)

Louis II (846-879)

Louis III (863-882)

Karlmann (866-884)

Arnulf of Carinthia (850–899)
East Frankish King 887
Emperor 896

Charles III (879–929)
King of West Francia 898

Louis IV (920–954)
King of West Francia 936
m. Gerberga

Louis the Child (893–911)
Last Carolingian King of The
East Franks 899

Lothair IV (941-986)
King of West Francia 954

Louis V (976–987)
Last Carolingian King in West
Francia

Charles (953–993)
Duke of Lower Lotharingia
977

Otto (970–1006)
Duke of Lower Lotharingia
993

Denmark

Baltic Sea

North Sea

Poland

England

Elbe

Weser

Saxony

Friesland

Magdeburg

Oder

Rhine

Merseburg

Cologne

Fritzlar

Thuringia

Meuse

Aachen

Bohemia

Lower
Lotharingia

Franconia

Mainz

Frankfurt

Laon

Trier

Rouen

Upper
Lotharingia

Metz

Worms

Rheims

Regensburg

Danube

Paris

Augsburg

Bavaria

Sens

Seine

Swabia

West
Francia

Burgundy

Kingdom of Italy

Milan

Hungary

Pavia

Adriatic
Sea

Ligurian
Sea

The Ottonian World
919–973

N

0   250 mi

Corsica

Rome

0   250 km

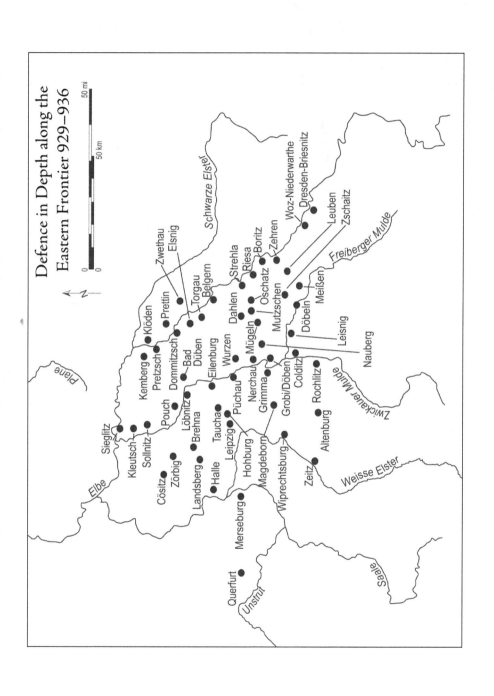

Defence in Depth along the
Eastern Frontier 929–936

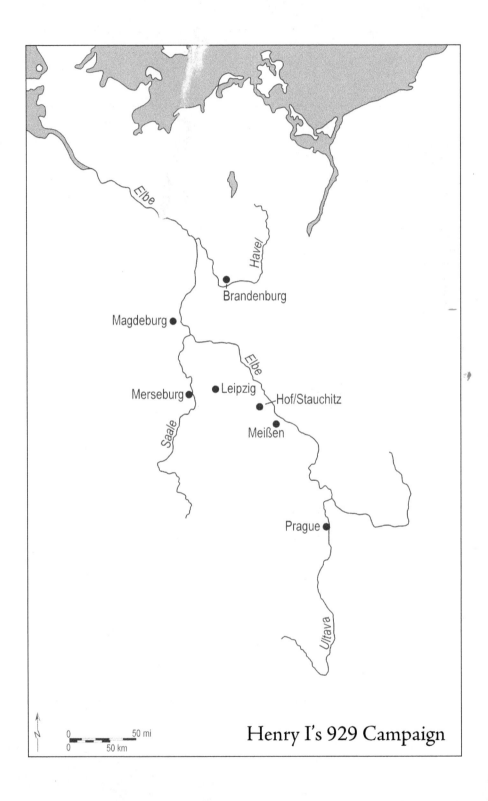

Henry I's 929 Campaign

Introduction

Over the course of half a century, the first two kings of the Saxon dynasty, Henry I (919–936) and Otto I (936–973), waged war across the length and breadth of Europe. Ottonian armies campaigned from the banks of the Oder in the east to the Seine in the west, and from the shores of the Baltic Sea in the north, to the Adriatic and Mediterranean in the south. In the course of scores of military operations, accompanied by diligent diplomatic efforts, Henry and Otto defeated Lotharingians, West Franks, Danes, Obodrites, Weleti, Sorbs, Bohemians, Hungarians, Lombards, and Byzantines, as well as triumphing in the internecine conflicts of East Francia. The end result of more than fifty years of consistent, if not absolute, military and diplomatic success was the establishment of an empire that rivaled in size, population, and wealth that of the great Charles (died 814).

This record of accomplishment, which is virtually unrivaled in both scope and duration from the early ninth to the early nineteenth century in Western Europe, was achieved through well planned and thoroughly organized campaigns that focused on the acquisition of territory over the long term. To achieve these conquests, the Ottonian kings undertook many scores of sieges, including sustained operations that were intended to capture great fortress cities of Roman origin, such as Mainz, Regensburg, Rheims, Senlis, Paris, Pavia, and Rome itself, as well as massive fortresses of more recent vintage that were constructed by various Slavic polities, including Prague, Levy Hradec, Vysehrad, Brandenburg, and Jana. In this respect, Ottonian military operations were consistent with warfare throughout the medieval millennium, which was dominated by sieges, particularly in the context of campaigns that were intended to conquer territory.[1]

Contrary to the long-established narrative that the Ottonian kings fielded small armies of a few hundred to a few thousand heavily armed mounted fighters (*Ritterkrieger*) led by warrior aristocrats, the siege operations that dominated warfare in the tenth century required very large armies, composed predominantly of foot soldiers.[2] Booty seeking magnates, who sought out riches

---

[1]   In this context, see Jim Bradbury, *The Medieval Siege* (Woodbridge, 1992); and Peter Purton, *A History of the Early Medieval Siege, c. 450–1200* (Woodbridge, 2010), and the enormous literature cited there. Cf. Guy Halsall, *Warfare and Society in the Barbarian West 450–900* (London, 2003), 215-227.

[2]   With regard to small armies, see the observations by Leopold Auer, "Mittelalterliche Kriegsge-schichte als Forschungsproblem," *Francia* 10 (1982), 449-463; and idem, "Formen des Krieges im abendländischen Mittelalter," in *Formen des Krieges vom Mittelalter zum "Low-Intensity-Conflict"*, ed.

to support their followers in a manner consistent with Beowulf's ring givers, had a limited role to play in extended wars of conquest.[3] Indeed, mounted fighting men had only a marginal role to play in the conduct of sieges generally as even the most gallant warhorse and fearless rider faces insurmountable challenges when attempting to charge over deep ditches and scale high walls. In a similar manner, a man on horseback could play only a very minor part in the defense of a fortress city or stronghold.

To raise, equip, and supply the large armies that were required to invest, besiege, and, in some cases, storm massive fortifications, the Ottonian kings required a concomitantly extensive logistical and administrative capacity. This conclusion is at odds with the dominant political narrative of the Ottonian kingdom which has its origins in the so-called "New Constitutional History" as practiced by historians including Theodor Mayer, Otto Brunner, and Walter Schlesinger from the 1930s to the 1970s, and still holds sway today.[4] This school sought to identify

Manfried Rauchensteiner and Erwin A. Schmidl (Graz, Vienna and Cologne, 1991), 17-43. Both of these studies draw heavily upon Auer's earlier essays on the military contingents provided to the Ottonian kings by ecclesiastical magnates, namely "Der Kriegsdienst des Klerus unter den sächsischen Kaisern," *Mitteilungen des Instituts für Österreichische Geschichtsforschung* 79 (1971), 316-407; and part 2 in *Mitteilungen des Instituts für Österreichische Geschichtsforschung*, 80 (1972), 48-70. In the English tradition, the main proponents of small armies have been Karl Leyser, "The Battle at the Lech, 955: A Study in Tenth-Century Warfare," *History* 50 (1965), 1-25, reprinted in idem, *Medieval Germany and its Neighbours: 900–1250* (London, 1982), 43-67; and Timothy Reuter, "Plunder and Tribute in the Carolingian Empire," *Transactions of the Royal Historical Society* 5 ser. 35 (1985), 75-94; idem, "The End of Carolingian Military Expansion," in *Charlemagne's Heir: New Perspectives on the Reign of Louis the Pious (814–840)*, eds. Peter Godman and Roger Collins (Oxford, 1990), 391-405; idem, "The Recruitment of Armies in the Early Middle Ages: What Can We Know?" in *Military Aspects of Scandinavian Society in a European Perspective, AD 1000–1300*, ed. A. Norgard Jorgensen and B. L. Clausen (National Museum, Copenhagen, 1997), 25-31 at 32-37; and idem, "Carolingian and Ottonian Warfare," in *Medieval Warfare: A History*, ed. Maurice Keen (Oxford, 1999), 13-35. Also see Halsall, *Warfare and Society in the Barbarian West 450-900*, who insists on small Carolingian armies, but does not venture into the tenth century.

Two important exceptions to this consensus are Karl Ferdinand Werner, "Heersorganisation und Kriegsführung im deutschen Königreich des 10. und 11. Jahrhunderts," *Settimane di Studio de Centro Italiano Sull'alto Medievo* 15 (1968), 791-843; and Charles R. Bowlus, *Franks, Moravians, and Magyars: The Struggle for the Middle Danube, 788–907* (Philadelphia, 1995); and idem, *The Battle of Lechfeld and Its Aftermath, August 955: The End of the Age of Migrations in the West* (Aldershot, 2006), whose studies have illustrated both the great scale and complexity of military operations carried out by the rulers of the Ottonian dynasty, as well as their East Carolingian predecessors.

3   For a thoughtful critique of the booty-centered warfare model that is based on a careful analysis of both written sources and material developed by archaeologists through excavations, see Eric J. Goldberg, *Struggle for Empire: Kingship and Conflict under Louis the German, 817–876* (Ithaca, NY, 2006), 119-146. With regard to the putative continuing importance of *Beowulf*, and *Beowulfian* type culture for understanding Carolingian and implicitly Ottonian government as well, including military affairs, see Reuter, "Plunder and Tribute," 91.

4   Regarding this tradition, see Hans-Werner Goetz, "Die Wahrnehmung von 'Staat' und 'Herrschaft' im frühen Mittelalter," in *Staat im frühen Mittelalter*, ed. Stuart Airlie, Walter Pohl, and Helmut Reimitz (Vienna, 2006), 39-58, here 39, where he describes the model established by the new constitutional school as emphasizing the aristocratic community of the king and nobility at the expense of institutional or territorially-based organizational principles; and Steffen Patzold, "Die Bischöfe im karolingischen Staat Praktisches Wissen über die politische Ordnung im Frankenreich des 9. Jahrhunderts," ibid, 133-162.

the specifically "Germanic" character of the early medieval state, and insisted on a state model (*Staatlichkeit*) based on the "Germanic" concept of lordship (*Herrschaft*), characterized by personal ties between the lord and his retainers, or the aristocratic association (*Herrschaftsverband*) of the king and the nobles.[5] Fundamental to this model, which still dominates the political history of the early German kingdom, is the view that the Ottonian kings, unlike their Carolingian predecessors, lacked a central administration, a concept of public authority, public offices, and the capacity for long-term planning.[6]

Such a conclusion rests on a largely assumed, and rarely tested, hypothesis that the eastern lands of the Carolingians enjoyed a lower level of political and administrative sophistication than was the case in the West, and that the eastern successor state of the Carolingians, i.e., the lands reassembled by Henry I, was marked by an even further decline in culture and administration. This political narrative of royal rule "without a state," to use the provocative title of Gerd Althoff's study of Ottonian kingship, is, however, untenable in light of the detailed analysis of the governments of Henry I and Otto I by scholars who focus on economic and administrative, as contrasted with purely political, history.[7] On the basis of investigations of the policies of Ottonian rulers regarding the management of

---

[5] For a clear restatement of this basic paradigm, which remains the orthodoxy among specialists in Ottonian political history, see Jan Brademann, "Der König und seine fideles: Zum Ausmaß ottonischer Königsherrschaft," in *Auf den Spuren der Ottonen III. Protokoll des Kolloquiums am 22. Juni 2001 in Walbeck/Hettstedt*, ed. Roswitha Jendryschik, Gerlinde Schlenker, and Robert Werner (Halle an der Salle, 2002), 47-60.

[6] See, for example, the studies by Otto Brunner, *Land und Herrschaft. Grundfragen der territorialen Verfassungsgeschichte Österreichs im Mittelalter*, 4th edn (Vienna, 1959); Hagen Keller, "Zum Charakter der 'Staatlichkeit' zwischen karolingischer Reichsreform und hochmittelalterlichem Herrschaftsausbau," *Frühmittelalterliche Studien* 23 (1989), 248-264; Timothy Reuter, *Germany in the Early Middle Ages 800–1056* (London, 1991), 89 and 211; John W. Bernhardt, *Itinerant Kingship and Royal Monasteries in Early Medieval Germany c. 936–1075* (Cambridge, 1993), 5; Gerd Althoff, *Die Ottonen: Königsherrschaft ohne Staat* (Stuttgart, 2000), 8; Henry Mayr-Harting, *Church and Cosmos in Early Ottonian Germany: The View from Cologne* (Oxford, 2007), 3.

[7] With regard to the Ottonian inheritance of royal administrative capacity from the late Carolingians, see the observations by Karl Glöckner, "Das Reichsgut im Rhein-Maingebiet," *Archiv für hessische Geschichte und Altertumskunde* new series 18 (1934), 195-216; F. J. Heyen, *Reichsgut im Rheinland. Die Geschichte des königlichen Fiskus Boppard* (Bonn, 1956); Karlheinz Mascher, *Reichsgut und Komitat am Südharz im Hochmittelalter* (Cologne, 1957); Rudolf Kraft, "Das Reichsgut von Oppenheim," *Hessisches Jahrbuch für Landesgeschichte* 11 (1964), 20-41; Marianne Schalles-Fischer, *Pfalz und Fiskus Frankfurt: Eine Untersuchung zur Verfassungsgeschichte des fränkischen-deutschen Königtums* (Göttingen, 1969); Michael Gockel, *Karolingische Königshöfe am Mittelrhein* (Göttingen, 1970), idem, "Die Bedeutung Treburs als Pfalzort," in *Deutsche Königspfalzen: Beiträge zur ihrer historischen und archäologischen Erforschung*, vol. 3 (Göttingen, 1979), 86-110; Peter Schmid, *Regensburg: Stadt der Könige und Herzöge im Mittelalter* (Kallmünz, 1977); and the collection of studies in *Le Grand domaine aux époques mérovingienne et carolingienne. Die Grundherrschaft im frühen Mittelalter*, ed. A. Verhulst (Ghent, 1985). Now also see the recent studies by Bernard S. Bachrach and David S. Bachrach, "Continuity of Written Administration in the Late Carolingian East c. 887–911: The Royal Fisc," *Frühmittelalterliche Studien* 42 (2008 appeared 2009), 109-146; David S. Bachrach, "Exercise of Royal Power in Early Medieval Europe: The Case of Otto the Great 936–973," *Early Medieval Europe* 17 (2009), 389-419; and idem, "The Written Word in Carolingian-Style Fiscal Administration under King Henry I, 919–936," *German History* 28 (2010), 399-423.

the royal fisc, that is the total economic resources of the government, it is clear that the first two Saxon kings maintained the administrative inheritance of the Carolingian empire, and had the capacity to mobilize massive financial, human, and material resources to sustain their far-flung military operations.[8] The present study, with its focus on military affairs, provides yet a further challenge to the traditional model of discontinuity with the Carolingian past.

It is my contention that in their effort first to reestablish the East Frankish kingdom, and then to renew the empire of Charlemagne, Henry I and Otto I drew heavily upon a massive inheritance from their Carolingian predecessors that included not only military institutions, and political models of highly developed royal power, but also crucial economic, cultural, and educational resources. To assume a priori – as much of the current scholarship dealing with the political culture of the tenth-century German kingdom does – that such an inheritance was unavailable to the Ottonians certainly flies in the face of the extensive scholarly tradition dealing with the economic history of German kingdom. Moreover, and perhaps even more importantly, it is contradicted by the massive physical evidence of continuity and expansion of roads, ports, cities, palaces, cathedrals, and fortresses undertaken by the Ottonians on the foundations of their Carolingian predecessors.[9]

This physical infrastructure, with its high quality stone buildings, that equaled, and even surpassed their ninth-century predecessors, had an equally impressive counter-part in the literary production under the Ottonians. As the diligent efforts of numerous specialists in the intellectual history of the Ottonian kingdom have demonstrated, not only did the tenth century inherit vast numbers of texts from the ninth, but the Ottonian century also saw the considerable copying of older works. Indeed, as Josef Fleckenstein observed, the tenth century did not require a new dedication to education, because the royal monasteries and bishoprics maintained the role that they had played under the Carolingians.[10] In addition, however, to these important elements of continuity in intellectual life east of the

---

[8]   Even scholars who once doubted the administrative capacity of the Carolingian government in both the East and the West have now come to understand that Charlemagne and his successors maintained a highly successful set of administrative institutions. See, for example, the observations by Matthew Innes, "Charlemagne's Government," in *Charlemagne: Empire and Society*, ed. Joanna Story (Manchester, 2005), 71-89, which can be contrasted with his argument that Carolingian and Ottonian royal power in the Rhineland was fundamentally weak, in *State and Society in the Early Middle Ages: The Middle Rhine Valley, 400–1000* (Cambridge, 2000).

[9]   Regarding the construction of numerous stone churches by the Ottonians see, for example, Gerhard Leopold, "Archäologische Ausgrabungen an Stätten der ottonischen Herrscher," *Herrschaftsrepräsentation im Ottonischen Sachsen* (1998), 33-76. The basic starting point for the construction of royal palaces under the Ottonians is now *Die deutsche Königspfalzen: Repertorium der Pfalzen, Königshöfe und übrigen Aufenthaltsorte der Könige im deutschen Reich des Mittelalters* vols. 1-4 (Göttingen, 1982–2000).

[10]   Josef Fleckenstein, "Königshof und Bischofsschule unter Otto dem Großen," *Archiv für Kulturgeschichte* 38 (1956), 38-62, reprinted in idem, *Ordnungen und formende Kräfte des Mittelalters: Ausgewählte Beiträge* (Göttingen, 1989), 168-192, here 178-192.

Rhine, the Ottonian kingdom also saw the development of vibrant new literary traditions, replete with new genres and a wide range of new texts.[11]

Consequently, Henry I and Otto I did not begin *de novo* to develop a military, administrative, and intellectual infrastructure for their kingdom and empire. They built upon the existing structures that they had inherited from their Carolingian predecessors. An argument for continuity should not, however, be confused with a claim for stasis. The Ottonians, just like their Carolingian predecessors, developed and refined their material, cultural, intellectual, and administrative inheritance in ways that fit their own time. It was the success of the Ottonians in molding the raw materials bequeathed to them into a formidable military machine that made possible the establishment of Germany as the preeminent kingdom in Europe from the tenth through the mid-thirteenth century. This achievement deserves recognition even if we no longer admire empire building and military success as ends in themselves.

Sources

The written sources of information for the Ottonian kingdom, as well as for the later ninth century in East Francia, present a significantly different profile than those of the eighth and early ninth centuries.[12] In the earlier period, there is an abundance of prescriptive legislation in the form of capitularies, much of which touches on military affairs.[13] However, comparatively few texts that provide descriptive information about the implementation of royal policies have survived. As a consequence, scholars are much better informed about how military institutions were intended to operate than how they actually functioned.

The situation is reversed for the tenth century. Early Carolingian legislation retained its legal force in the East Frankish kingdom, as well as in its Ottonian successor, but very little new legislation was issued by Louis the German, his Carolingian descendents, or the Ottonians, at least legislation that has survived or been identified by scholars.[14] However, a great wealth of descriptive informa-

---

[11]   Rosamond McKitterick, "Ottonische Kulture und Bildung," in *Otto der Große. Magdeburg und Europa*, ed. Matthias Puhle (Mainz, 2001), I: 209-224; and eadem, "Bischöfe und die handschrift-lichen Überlieferung des Rechts im 10. Jahrhundert," in *Mönchtum-Kirche-Herrschaft 750-1000. Josef Semmler zum 65. Geburtstag*, ed. Dieter R. Bauer, Rudolf Hiestand, Brigitte Kasten and Sönke Lorenz (Sigmaringen, 1998), 231-242.

[12]   See the observations on this point by Goldberg, *Struggle for Empire*, 18, 210, 228-9; and Bachrach and Bachrach, "Continuity of Written Administration in the Late Carolingian East c. 887–911: The Royal Fisc," 109-146; and Bachrach, "The Written Word," 409-410.

[13]   Regarding Carolingian military legislation, see F. L. Ganshof, "Charlemagne's Army," in *Frankish Institutiions under Charlemagne*, trans. Bryce Lyon and Mary Lyon (Providence, RI, 1968), 59-68 and 151-161.

[14]   Regarding the legal force of early Carolingian legislation in the East Frankish kingdom, see *Conventus apud Confluentes* in *Capitularia*, 2:156, cc 8-9; *Die Urkunden Ludwig des Deutschen, Karlomanns und Ludwigs des Jüngeren*, ed. Paul Kehr (Berlin, 1932-1934), n. 147 All citations to the charter collections of the Carolingian and Ottonian kings refer to charter numbers rather than to page numbers; and the discussion by Goldberg, *Struggle for Empire*, 229. The ongoing force of

tion about military matters has survived in a wide range of written sources. The conduct of military operations, battlefield tactics, the construction of fortifications, the deployment of siege engines, the establishment of garrisons, logistics, morale, strategy, and a host of other topics are illuminated in royal as well as private charters, letters, and variety of narrative texts including annals, saints' lives, episcopal *gestae*, and self-conscious works of history.

The bulk of these texts are contemporaneous with the events that they treat. However, this does not mean that these works can be read transparently as straightforward depictions of reality. Many of these texts were written by clerics who had an agenda or *parti pris* that led them to misrepresent information regarding military affairs. Consequently, it is important that historians seeking to use narrative texts to understand contemporary warfare evaluate not only an author's potential access to reliable or accurate information of a military nature, but also the likely reliability of the author in presenting information to which he had access.

In an important discussion of this process, Patrick Geary identified a number of the techniques that historians use when analyzing texts, and particularly narrative sources. These include identifying the audience for the text and the concomitant expectations within which the author was forced to work, and identifying the manner in which a particular text was used during the Middle Ages through a careful examination of its manuscript tradition.[15] Numerous scholars have used these techniques successfully to negotiate the complex relationship between narrative texts and the historical reality they purport to depict. Over the past fifteen years, however, the prominent specialist in Ottonian history, Johannes Fried, has

---

Carolingian legislation in the Ottonian period merits far more attention than it has received to date. At present, the bulk of the scholarship on this point has concerned the capitulary *de villis*, which is widely understood to have maintained its legal force throughout the tenth century. See the survey of the literature on this point by Bachrach, "The Written Word," 402-409. Intriguing in this context is the observation by King Henry II (1002–1024) in 1017 that he had inherited property in a manner that was consistent with the laws and capitularies that treated this matter, i.e. *legaliter et capitualiter*, indicating the ongoing force of Carolingian legislation into the eleventh century as well. *Die Urkunden Heinrichs II. und Arduins* ed,ed. Harry Bresslau, Robert Holtzmann and Hermann Reincke-Block(Hanover, 1900-1903), hereafter DH II, 39b.

Moreover, it should be noted that Ottonians continued to issue capitularies in their own names. For example, Otto I issued a capitulary in 938 or 939 regulating property exchanges involving monasteries that reinforced traditional Carolingian legislation on this issue. See *Die Traditionen des Hochstifts Freising: Band II 926-1283*, ed. Theodor Bitterauf (Munich, 1909, repr. Aalen, 1967), nr. 1118, 52-53; and the discussion of this legislation by Philippe Depreux, "The Development of Charters Confirming Exchange by the Royal Administration (Eighth–Tenth Centuries)," in *Charters and the Use of the Written Word in Medieval Society*, ed. Karl Heidecker (Turnhout, 2000), 43-62, who investigates the topic up through the reign of Louis the Child (died 911). Similarly, Caspar Ehlers, "Der helfende Herscher: Immunität, Wahlrecht und Königsschutz für sächsische Frauenstifte bis 1024," in *Essen und die sächsischen Frauenstifte im Frühmittelalter*, ed. Jan Gerchow (Essen, 2003), 45-58, here 52, identifies a capitulary issued by Otto I that limited royal power over immune convents. It is likely that further scholarship in this area will illuminate additional Ottonian legislation.

15   Patrick Geary, "Zusammenfassung," in *Historiographie im frühen Mittelalter*, ed. Anton Scharer and Georg Scheibelreiter (Vienna 1994), 539-542. Geary also emphasized the difficulties inherent in each of these approaches if pursued in isolation. He suggests, for example, that scholars must be wary of "constructing" the audience for the text on the basis of the text itself.

posed in a series of publications what he describes as a fundamental challenge to scholars who claim that they can write accurately about human affairs in the past.[16] It is Fried's contention that the epistemology of modern historians is fatally flawed because it depends on medieval writers having obtained and transmitted accurate information. Fried asserts that in dealing with medieval narrative works, historians confront texts that cannot, by their very nature, convey reality.[17]

From an epistemological perspective, Fried's claim represents a variation on the argument that the *parti pris* of the author creates an insurmountable barrier to historical research. Indeed, Fried makes this point when arguing in a study concerned with "memory" that early medieval writers were concerned with the "true" event rather than with the "real" event, that is with the way things should have been rather than the way that they were.[18] In making this claim, Fried echoes the arguments put forth a generation earlier by Amos Funkenstein and Roger Ray.[19] In sum, by denying that there were any outside controls on narrative sources because of the inability of anyone to remember, or rather to demonstrate a correct memory of the past, Fried attempts to exclude one of the most powerful tools of historical epistemology, namely an appeal to the rhetoric of plausibility that takes into account the knowledge and expectations of the audience of a text.[20]

Fried's position regarding the lack of controlling authorities on the production of Ottonian narrative texts has found few adherents, and has elicited considerable criticism from other leading specialists in the history of early medieval Germany. Gerd Althoff, for example, has emphasized that Ottonian writers did face the necessity of writing in a manner that conformed with the expectations of their patrons and audience, often composed of leading members of the Ottonian family and court. As Althoff makes clear, members of the Ottonian court were well informed about past events, and insisted that their view of the past be presented accurately.[21]

---

[16] Johannes Fried, "Die Kunst der Aktualisierung in der oralen Gesellschaft: Die Königserhebung Heinrichs I. als Exempel," *Geschichte in Wissenschaft und Unterricht* 44 (1993), 493-503; idem, "Die Königserhebung Heinrichs I. Erinnerung, Mündlichkeit und Traditionsbildung im 10. Jahrhundert," in *Mittelalterforschung nach der Wende 1989*, ed. Michael Borgolte (Munich, 1995), 267-318; idem, "Wissenschaft und Phantasie. Das Beispiel der Geschichte," *Historische Zeitschrift* 263 (1996) 291-316; idem, "Erinnerung und Vergessen. Die Gegenwart stiftet die Einheit der Vergangenheit," *Historische Zeitschrift* 273 (2001), 561-593; and idem, *Die Schleier der Erinnerung: Grundzüge einer historischen Memorik* (Munich, 2004). See the sustained critique of Fried's methodology and a model for analyzing narrative works to ascertain the value of the information that they provide regarding military affairs by David S. Bachrach, "Memory, Epistemology, and the Writing of Early Medieval Military History: The Example of Bishop Thietmar of Merseburg (1009–1018)," *Viator* 38 (2007), 63-90.

[17] Fried, "Wissenschaft und Phantasie," 296-7.

[18] Fried, "Erinnerung und Vergessen," 575.

[19] Amos Funkenstein, *Heilsplan und natürliche Entwicklung: Formen der Gegenwartsbestimmung im Geschichtsdenken des hohen Mittelalters* (Munich, 1965), particularly 70-77; and Roger D. Ray, "Medieval Historiography through the Twelfth Century: Problems and Progress of Research," *Viator* 5 (1974) 33-60, here 43-57.

[20] Regarding the importance of the rhetoric of plausibility in the understanding of medieval writers see the important contribution by Justin C. Lake, "Truth, Plausibility, and the Virtues of Narrative at the Millennium," *Journal of Medieval History* 35 (2009), 221-238.

[21] Gerd Althoff, "Geschichtsschreibung in einer oralen Gesellschaft. Das Beispiel des 10. Jahrhun-

In his effort to vitiate the value of narrative sources, it should be emphasized that Fried also disregarded the crucial controls on these texts that can be exercised by examining the material reality within which events occurred. The methods of *Sachkritik* were pioneered by Hans Delbrück in his multi-volume history of western warfare to test the statements made by classical authors about the size of armies that fought on particular battlefields.[22] Over time, specialists in military history have expanded the investigation of material reality to take account of a host of other factors that impinged upon the reality of warfare. In this study, a consideration of the brute facts of physical reality, e.g. the carrying capacity of horses, the speed of ox-drawn vehicles, or the range of missile weapons and to a lesser extent the material constraints imposed by institutional realities, provide yet another sound basis for the critique of information provided by written sources.[23]

Moreover, contrary to Fried's assertions, in addition to the external controls placed on the veracity of narrative accounts by the material reality of the tenth century as this has been developed through the work of archaeologists, it is also possible for the diligent scholar to identify controls placed on authors by the expectations of their audiences. For the most part, the historical works of the tenth century were written for audiences that were very familiar with the matters treated in these texts. Consequently, authors were constrained by the rhetoric of plausibility to avoid alienating their audiences.[24] As a practical matter, this meant that when writing about military affairs for an audience that included men knowledgeable about such matters, it was important to present an account that was plausible to them.

Nevertheless, even when taking advantage of these important controls on written sources, it is also necessary for every historian of the Ottonian period to be cognizant of the fact that the narrative works that treat the reign of Henry I were written at a remove of several decades from the events they are recounting. Thus, the depiction of a particular battle, for example, may have more to do with the realities of warfare in the 960s than fighting in the 930s. However, this problem of distance from the subjects treated by later tenth-century authors also is mitigated by several factors. First, the military technology available during the reign of Otto I was virtually identical with that of his father. This included both the arms used by individual fighting men and the fortifications that they were

derts," in *Ottonische Neuanfänge. Symposium zur Ausstellung 'Otto der Große, Magdeburg und Europa,'* ed. Stefan Weinfurter and Bernd Schneidmüller (Mainz, 2001), 151-169, here 154-159.

[22] Hans Delbrück, *Geschichte der Kriegskunst im Rahmen der politischen Geschichte*, 6 vols. (Berlin 1900-1936). The first three volumes, dealing with ancient and medieval warfare, are now available in English translation by Walter J. Renfroe as *History of the Art of War within the Framework of Political History*, vols. 1-3 (Westport, 1975–1982).

[23] With regard to the importance of *Sachkritik* in developing a sound appreciation of the realities of warfare, see the discussion by Bernard S. Bachrach, "Early Medieval Military Demography: Some Observations on the Methods of Hans Delbrück," in *The Circle of War in the Middle Ages*, ed. Donald J. Kagay and L. J. Andrew Villalon (Woodbridge, 1999), 3-20.

[24] This matter is treated in detail in chapter seven.

deployed to defend or assault. Consequently, we should not expect that there were significant developments in tactics in the absence of technological stimuli.

Second, a continuity in tactics between the reigns of Henry I and Otto I is also likely given the great similarities between the conduct of war by Otto and the wars of the later Carolingians, including Louis the German in the East, as these have been identified by scholars. It seems unlikely that if Henry I's reign did present a two-decade long anomaly in the conduct of war over the period 840–973, that such a phenomenon would remain utterly unnoticed by the authors of narrative sources, even if they were writing two or three decades after the events in question.

Finally, the authors of narrative works, such as Widukind of Corvey, Adalbert of Magdeburg, and Liudprand of Cremona, had access to considerable numbers of informants, who were present during the campaigns of Henry I, and who consequently could provide information about the battles in which they fought. Thus, despite the dangers inherent in the oral transmission of information, when the accounts of our independently composed narrative sources are consistent both with each other, and with the technology that archaeologists have demonstrated was available during Henry I's reign, we can proceed with reasonable confidence that these texts provide a solid foundation for understanding the conduct of war not only during the reign of Otto I but also during the first two decades of the Ottonian dynasty as well.

In addition to the considerable corpus of narrative sources that describe contemporary military affairs, it is necessary for the modern scholar to consult the texts regarding the proper conduct of war that were available to men in positions of military authority in the early Ottonian period. Warfare in the tenth century, as in all eras, was a highly complex and difficult business. It was necessary to train both officers and men in strategy and in tactics, as well as in the basic techniques of combat with sword, spear, and bow. In a manner consistent with specialists in other fields where a high level of technical knowledge was required, Henry I, Otto I, and their magnates patronized the production of a wide range of military manuals and handbooks, many of which were illustrated, as well as works of both biblical and secular history, which provided information about military leadership, operations, tactics, and training. A great many of these texts, including many tenth-century manuscripts, have survived and provide considerable insights into contemporary views about both military education and training.[25]

As will become clear throughout this study, the traditional view of Ottonian aristocrats as illiterates, who were incapable of making use of the written word, is entirely inconsistent with their military successes over the long term. Moreover, such an understanding of Ottonian lay society is at odds with the observations of contemporary writers. It is true that the authors of narrative sources in the tenth and early eleventh centuries are characterized by a penchant for ignoring the intel-

---

[25] This material is dealt with in detail in chapters four and five.

lectual attainments of secular men, particularly those who had military careers. Nevertheless, despite this bias against discussing the education of aristocrats, it is quite common to find references to their extraordinary learning with regard to *res militaris*. This praise was not related to physical skills with sword and bow, but rather to the command of men in the field, and particularly to the tactical and strategic skills of military officers. Moreover, in the case of some prominent aristocrats, contemporary authors even stressed the more general learning that such men attained in a wide range of matters, including both sacred scripture and profane law. This was the case, for example, with Margrave Gero (died 965), who was one of Otto I's leading commanders over the course of three decades, or Otto I's junior officer, Ansfrid of Huy (died 1010), who later in life became bishop of Utrecht (995–1010).[26]

Even though it is clear that many Ottonian secular aristocrats were well versed in military learning, and that at least some benefitted from a much broader liberal and religious education with the diffusion of information found in handbooks, histories, and other texts military utility did not depend ultimately on the ability of all, or even a majority of, Ottonian military commanders to read or even understand Latin. A ruler such as Otto I, or a great magnate such as Margrave Gero, did not sit alone in front of his hearth with a copy of Vegetius' *Epitoma* in his hand, perusing the text for useful information regarding tactics or the training of his men. As the native Frankish speaker Einhard made clear in his biography of Charlemagne, useful texts were read aloud in Latin to audiences composed of laymen whose native languages included both proto-Romance and a variety of German dialects.[27] There is absolutely no reason to believe that this practice ended during the Ottonian period. Moreover, for those men, who could not immediately understand a Latin work, there were a great many clerics, as well as other lay aristocrats, who could explain the points at issue. As Flodoard observed with regard to the synod of West Frankish and German bishops, which was held at the royal palace of Ingelheim in 948, a letter of Pope Agapetus II (946–956) first was read out in Latin, and then translated publicly into German.[28] The lessons learned from the written word in a great hall or palace could quite easily be transmitted in the course of a campaign, or on the training fields established by magnates for their military households.

Traditionally, historians investigating Ottonian warfare have limited their attention to written sources, and often a very narrow selection of these. However, of crucial importance for understanding both the nature and the scope of warfare in tenth-century Germany and its neighbors is the vast and continuously growing corpus of archaeological material dealing with fortifications, much of which has been available since the early twentieth century. Many hundreds of fortified sites, ranging from fortress cities to simple watch towers,

---

26 The education of Gero and Ansfrid is discussed below in chapter four.
27 Einhard, *Vita Karoli*, ch. 24.
28 Flodoard, *Annales, an.* 948.

have been excavated, including a very large number that do not appear in any surviving written sources.[29] The discoveries of archaeologists, including the size of fortifications, the nature of their defenses, their locations, and the techniques used to construct them, provide a sound material basis both to evaluate information provided by written sources, and to establish the scale of Ottonian military operations, particularly those that focused on the capture of fortified sites. In addition, the work of archaeologists has brought to light considerable information about the types of weapons used by both the Ottonians and their opponents, which provides yet another basis for evaluating information derived from written sources.

Scope of the Work

Current scholarship on the early Ottonians, with its emphasis on the politics centered on the royal court, has focussed on questions such as whether Henry I sought to establish a style of rule based on "friendship-alliances" or whether Otto I wished to establish greater vertical distance from his key subjects than was enjoyed by his father. The answers to such questions, although interesting – and problematic – in their own right, have very little to do with the "nuts and bolts" of the operations of the royal government, or with the conduct of war.[30] The rules of the political game, as Gerd Althoff, for example, has interpreted them, may help to explain how and why a particular magnate chose to weep at the feet of the king in a public setting.[31] But such theories regarding the organization of politics do not further our understanding of military training, tactics, the mobilization of the expeditionary levy, or the material reality involved in the siege of a massive fortified city. Moreover, the narrow focus in much of modern scholarship dealing with the Ottonians on particular types of court rituals and political relationships has tended to crowd out questions regarding the actual tasks undertaken by kings, including their conduct of war.[32] It is striking, for

[29]   For example, the written sources dealing with northern Bavaria in the period 700–1000 identify a total of thirty fortified places. Excavations in northern Bavaria by 1998 had unearthed some 250 fortified places built during the same period, providing an 800% increase in the fortified sites now known to scholars. See the discussion of this point by Peter Ettel, "Ergebnisse der Ausgrabungen auf der Burg Horsadal, Roßtal bei Nürnberg," in *Frühmittelalterliche Burgenbau in Mittel und Osteuropa*, ed. Joachim Henning and Alexander T. Ruttkay (Bonn, 1998), 127-136, here 127.

[30]   See the detailed discussion of this issue by Bachrach, "Exercise of Power," 389-419.

[31]   Gerd Althoff, *Spielreglen der Politik im Mittelatler. Kommunikation in Frieden und Fehde* (Darmstadt, 1997). But also see the warning issued by Philippe Buc, *The Dangers of Ritual: Between Early Medieval Texts and Social Scientific Theory* (Princeton, 2001), regarding the ability of modern scholars to "read" depictions of rituals to tease out rules to which participants adhered.

[32]   Indeed, the problem of getting German historians to ask questions about the administration of the medieval German kingdom and empire was noted as early as 1928 by Marc Bloch, "Un problem d'histoire comparée: la ministérialité en France et en Allemagne," *Revue historique de droit français et étranger* 7 (1928), 46-91, republished as "A Problem in Comparative History: The Administrative Classes in France and in Germany," in *Land and Work in Medieval Europe: Selected Papers by Marc Bloch*, trans. J. E. Anderson (Berkeley, CA, 1967), 44-81.

example, that just one monograph has been written in German on the military history of pre-crusade Germany since the second world war.[33]

This current study consequently fills a substantial lacuna in the modern historical treatment of a basic aspect of early medieval German history, namely war, preparation for war, and war's aftermath. In addition, however, the arguments made here about the size of Ottonian armies, their complexity, and the sophisticated nature of warfare in the tenth century, offer a fundamental challenge to the dominant political narrative concerning the archaic nature, to use the Weberian term, of the German kingdom as a whole.

In considering the issue of the complexity of the state it is helpful, for comparative purposes, to observe that the Roman Republic of the third century BC was less populous, poorer, and less heavily administered than the Ottonian kingdom of the tenth century. Yet the Roman state of this period regularly raised armies in the range of 40,000–50,000 combatants, and naval contingents whose crews and marines number 70,000 men.[34] Similarly in Africa in the nineteenth century, the Ashanti people, who inhabited the region of modern Ghana, were capable of mobilizing armies of as many 30,000 men for campaigns, albeit not for major siege operations, despite having nothing resembling an administrative system of the type employed by the Ottonians, or even the less developed Roman State of the third century BC.[35] As a consequence, when considering the ability of the Ottonian kings to mobilize large armies, and to manage a military infrastructure to support these troops in the field, it is illuminating to consider the capacities of far less sophisticated polities.

The first two chapters of this study provide a chronologically organized account of the successful efforts by Henry I and Otto I first to reestablish the East Frankish kingdom as it had developed under Arnulf of Carinthia (died 899), and then to forge a new empire that both rivaled and was constructed on the foundations of Charlemagne's *imperium*. This chronological account provides the basic framework for understanding the scale of the Ottonian achievement, and particularly the central role of siege warfare, with the need for concomitantly large armies that were mobilized by Henry I and Otto I.

The following six chapters are organized thematically to illuminate the military resources that Henry and Otto brought to bear over half a century of warfare. Chapter three is focused on the tri-partite nature of the military organization of

---

33   Bruno Scherff, *Studien zum Heer der Ottonen und der ersten Salier (919-1056)* (Bonn, 1985), who devotes much of his attention to the Salians rather than to the Ottonians.

34   Peter Brunt, *Italian Manpower 225 B.C.–A.D. 14* (Oxford, 1987), 44-90, 131-155, 391-434; and a useful synthesis regarding the size of armies deployed by the Roman Republic in this period by Jonathan P. Roth, *Roman Warfare* (Cambridge, 2009), particularly 39-72.

35   For the Ashanti armies, see Emmanuel Terray, "Contribution à une étude de l'armée assante," *Cahiers d'études africaines* 16 (1976), 297-356; and Étienne Renard, "La politique militaire de Charlemagne et la paysannerie franque," *Francia* 36 (2009), 1-33, here 2, who draws attention to the heuristic value of the Ashanti military capacity for understanding the greatly more sophisticated administrative capacities of the Carolingian empire.

the Ottonian kingdom, which provided large armies for offensive campaigns and maintained a highly militarized population for the common defense. Chapter four treats the military education of the men who led and commanded Ottonian armies in the field. The focus here is on learning from books in a manner consistent with the education of professionals throughout the early Middle Ages. In chapter five, the discussion turns to the arms and equipment used by fighting men, and the training that they received both in using their weapons, and in tactics. The latter included both combat in the field and in the far more common siege operations to capture enemy strongholds. Chapter six considers military morale, and the range of techniques used by Henry, Otto, and their military commanders to motivate their troops in the face of the drudgery and danger of life on campaign. The focus in chapter seven is on the tactics that Ottonian commanders actually used in the field, through a careful analysis of the descriptions provided by the authors of narrative sources. The final chapter deals with Ottonian campaign strategy, military planning, and the complexities of large-scale siege warfare as these are illuminated by the series of campaigns fought during the civil war of 953–954.

It has been traditional to describe warfare in the early Middle Ages, particularly in the post-Carolingian period, using archaicizing language, with terms such as war band, war path, and warrior playing a prominent role. These terms have tended to reinforce the image that warfare was small-scale, disorganized, or even unorganized, haphazard, and focused on the immediate gratification of a small group of warrior aristocrats whose support the king required to maintain his own position atop a putative pyramid of "feudal" oath-takers. In light of the scale of the campaigns launched by both Henry I and Otto I, it would be highly misleading to use such *Beowulfian* terminology to depict Ottonian armies. The men who led armies were military commanders, and the men who led individual units were officers, that is, they held the *officium* of command. Men who made a career and earned their livelihood through military service were soldiers. They were professionals, and were clearly denoted as such by the authors of contemporary narrative sources, who distinguished them from the men who served in various levies. Consequently, in this study I will use terminology that is appropriate to an understanding of the large and complex military institutions that were developed and maintained by the first two rulers of the Ottonian dynasty.

I

Restoring Francia Orientalis:
Henry I's Long Term Strategy

Introduction

When he took up his quill in 967 or 968 and considered the events of the past fifty years, the Saxon monk and historian Widukind expressed pride at the success of the first two kings of the Saxon dynasty, Henry I (919–936) and Otto I (936–973).[1] According to Widukind, Henry restored unity to the eastern kingdom, expanded his territory eastwards from the Saale to the Elbe river, established hegemony over the Danes, the trans-Elben Slavs, and the Bohemians, and also dominated affairs in the West Frankish kingdom as well as in the kingdom of Burgundy.[2] His son Otto, building upon the foundation established by Henry, conquered the Slavic lands between the Elbe and the Oder rivers, maintained a dominant position over the rulers of Burgundy and West Francia, and conquered Italy all the way south to Capua and Benevento.[3]

The military conquests through which the first two Saxon kings forged this empire resulted from the application of significant military resources in a focused manner in pursuit of medium- and long-term policy goals. Henry and Otto conceptualized strategic operations on the basis of a thorough understanding of contemporary political and military realities, as well as the Carolingian inherit-

---

[1] Widukind of Corvey, *Res gestae Saxoniae*, ed. and trans. Albert Bauer and Reinhold Rau in *Quellen zur Geschichte der sächsischen Kaiserzeit*, vol. 8 (Darmstadt, 1971). Widukind wrote the bulk of his *Res gestae* as a middle-aged man, c. 968, and then revised and augmented the text sometime after 973. Regarding the chronology of Widukind's composition of the *Res gestae*, see Helmut Beumann, *Widukind von Korvey: Untersuchungen zur Geschichtsschreibung und Ideengeschichte des 10. Jahrhunderts* (Weimar, 1950), 178, where Beumann deals with the older scholarly traditions concerning the compositional history of the text and concludes that the work was completed up to book III, chapter 69, which dealt with the death of the rebel magnate Wichmann in 967 or 968. Beumann's chronology, including the augmentation of the text by Widukind after Otto I's death in 973, generally has been accepted by scholars. In this regard, see Gerd Althoff, "Widukind von Corvey: Kronzeuge und Herausforderung," *Frühmittelalterliche Studien* 27 (1993), 253-272, here 258-259.
[2] Widukind, *Res gestae*, 1.40, for Widukind's summary of Henry I's accomplishments.
[3] Widukind, *Res gestae*, 3.75-6, for the summary of Otto's achievements at his death in 973.

ance upon which these were founded. Otto's long-term policies will be examined in the next chapter. Here, the focus is on Henry's career as ruler of East Francia.

Although he regularly faced the need to deal with immediate crises, Henry focused throughout his reign on two main policies. The first of these was to reestablish royal control within the frontiers of *Francia orientalis* as these had been constituted under Arnulf of Carinthia (887–899), the last adult Carolingian ruler in the eastern kingdom that emerged from the unified Carolingian empire.[4] Henry's second major policy was to protect the integrity of these frontiers against attacks from West Franks, Danes, Slavs, and Hungarians in the west, north, and east. It is in light of these two overriding objectives that the military campaigns of Henry's seventeen-year career are to be understood.

The Carolingian Inheritance

When Henry I became king in 919, the east Frankish kingdom had already been in existence for more than seventy years. According to the treaty of Verdun (843), which was established by Louis the Pious's sons, Lothair I (840–854), Louis the German (840–876), and Charles the Bald (840–877), the Carolingian empire was divided into three equal parts according to economic and demographic criteria.[5] Louis the German received *Francia orientalis*, which encompassed much of what today constitutes western and west-central Germany.[5] However, over the course of his lengthy reign, Louis worked diligently to expand his power.[6]

The main focus of Louis the German's efforts in the east was containing the rising power of the Moravian kingdom, which threatened traditional Carolingian dominance among the Slavic polities in the south-east.[7] Louis also maintained his father's policies of keeping the Slavic polities along the course of the Saale

---

4   With respect to the basic understanding of contemporaries about the natural unity of East Francia, as it had been constructed by Louis the German and expanded by his successors up to Arnulf, see the discussion by Paul Egon Hubinger, "König Heinrich I. und der deutsche Westen," *Annalen des historischen Vereins für Niederrhein, insbesondere das alte Erzbistum Köln* 131 (1937), 1-23; W. Eggert, *Das ostfränkisch-deutsche Reich in der Auffassung seiner Zeitgenossen, Forschungen zur mittelalterliche Geschichte* (Vienna, 1973), 15, 155; and Helmut Beumann, "Die Einheit des ostfränkischen Reiches und der Kaisergedanke bei der Königserhebung Ludwigs des Kindes," *Archiv für Diplomatik* 23 (1977), 142-163.

5   F. L. Ganshof, "Zur Entstehungsgeschichte und Bedeutung des Vertrages von Verdun (843)," *Deutsches Archiv* 12 (1956), 313-330, translated as "The Genesis and Significance of the Treaty of Verdun (843)," by Janet Sondheimer in F. L. Ganshof, *The Carolingians and the Frankish Monarchy: Studies in Carolingian History* (London, 1971), 289-302, remains basic. A useful guide also is provided by Rosamond McKitterick, *The Frankish Kingdoms under the Carolingians: 751–987* (London, 1983), 172-173, and Map 9. However, over the course of his lengthy reign, Louis the German worked diligently to expand his power in both the east and the west. The basic work on Louis the German is now Eric J. Goldberg, *Struggle for Empire: Kingship and Conflict under Louis the German, 817–876* (Ithaca, NY, 2006).

6   See Goldberg, *Struggle for Empire, passim.*

7   The basic study is now Charles R. Bowlus, *Franks, Moravians, and Magyars: The Struggle for the Middle Danube, 788–907* (Philadelphia, 1995).

and lower Elbe as clients.[8] It was in the west, rather than in the east, that Louis the German worked to expand the territory of his kingdom. Following the death of his brother Lothair I, and the latter's immediate heirs, Louis the German was able to secure control much of *Francia media* including the Rhineland, most of Lotharingia, and much of what today we consider Alsace, which he incorporated into *Francia orientalis*.[9] The process of integrating (880) Lotharingia into the eastern kingdom was completed by the treaty of Ribemont between the western Carolingian rulers Louis III (863–882) and Carloman II (866–884), and Louis the German's son, Louis the Younger (835–882).

After the death of his elder brothers, Louis the German's youngest son, Charles III, brought the entire Carolingian empire under the rule of a single king during the period 884–887.[10] However, the coup d'état against Charles by his illegitimate nephew, Arnulf of Carinthia, the son of Carloman (died 880), resulted in the renewed division of the empire into several kingdoms, of which East Francia emerged as the most powerful.[11] Arnulf established a hegemonic position among the Carolingian successor states and was crowned emperor in 896. The death of Arnulf in 899, and of his elder son Zwentibold, who had been established as king in Lotharingia (895–900), left the eastern kingdom under a regency government for Louis the Child (899–911).[12]

Following the death of Louis the Child in 911, the new king in *Francia orientalis*, Conrad of Franconia (d. 918), the first non-Carolingian king in the east, lost control of Lotharingia to the West Frankish ruler Charles III the Simple (898–923).[13] In the wake of Conrad's election, it was also the case that parts of Alsace began to act in an autonomous manner and east Frankish influence in Burgundy deteriorated.[14] In addition, during the last two years of Conrad's reign, in 917–918, the leaders of the southern *regna* of Bavaria and Swabia, Arnulf (907–937) and

---

8   See Goldberg, *Struggle for Empire*, 119-146.
9   Goldberg, *Struggle for Empire*, 236-237, 260-261, 295-298, 305-306, 313-314.
10   Regarding the career of Charles III, see Simon MacLean, *Politics in the Late Ninth Century: Charles the Fat and the End of the Carolingian Empire* (Cambridge, 2003).
11   The collection of articles published in Franz Fuchs and Peter Schmid, eds. *Kaiser Arnolf: Das ostfränkische Reich am Ende des 9. Jahrhunderts* (Munich, 2002), provide a good starting point for the reign of this last powerful Carolingian king in the east.
12   The events of this period are most thoroughly recounted by Regino of Prüm, *Reginonis abbatis Prumiensis Chronicon cum continuatione Treverensi*, ed. Friederich Kurze, MGH SRG (Hanover, 1890), hereafter *Chronicon*. Also see the new translation and detailed introduction to the text by Simon MacLean, *History and Politics in Late Carolingian and Ottonian Europe: The Chronicle of Regino of Prüm and Adalbert of Magdeburg* (Manchester, 2009). Regarding Zwentibold's rule in Lotharingia, see Martina Hartmann, "Lothringen in Arnolfs Reich. Das Königtum Zwentibolds," in Fuchs and Schmid, eds. *Kaiser Arnolf*, 122-142.
13   See Robert Parisot, *Le royaume de Lorraine sous les Carolingiens, 843-923* (Paris, 1899), 515-575; Auguste Eckel, *Charles le Simple* (Paris, 1899), 91-115; Heinrich Sproemberg, "Die lothringische Politik Ottos des Großen," *Rheinische Vierteljahrsblätter* 11 (1941), 1-101, here 15-20; Bernd Schneidmüller, "Französische Lothringenpolitik im 10. Jahrhundert," *Jahrbuch für westdeutsche Landesgeschichte* 5 (1979), 1-31, here 9-14.
14   See the brief survey by Thomas Zotz, "Das Elsass-Ein Teil des Zwischenreichs?" in *Lotharingia: Eine europäische Kernlandschaft um das Jahr 1000*, eds. Hans-Walter Herrmann and Reinhard

Burchard I (917–926), respectively, seized *de facto* control over their regions, and successfully repulsed royal military campaigns against them.[15]

Reestablishing the East Frankish Kingdom 919–925

On the eve of Henry I's election as king, therefore, the east Frankish kingdom, as it had been constructed by Louis the German, and maintained by his successors, was fractured. The southern *regna* of Bavaria and Swabia had withdrawn their allegiance from the royal authority, and Duke Arnulf of Bavaria (907–937) even declared himself to be king.[16] Lotharingia as well as Alsace were under the control of the West Frankish ruler Charles III. In the east, the traditional East Frankish hegemony over the Slavic polities along the lower Elbe and middle Saale, as well as in Bohemia and Moravia, was seriously threatened by the Hungarians, who had begun raiding into the East Frankish kingdom, and even further west at the beginning of the tenth century.[17]

Swabia

Henry's election as king took place in mid May 919 at Fritzlar, located on the north bank of the Eder river near the Franconian frontier with Saxony. Present at the assembly were the magnates (*principes et natu maioribus*) of Franconia,

Schneider (Saarbrücken, 1995), 49-70, here 65-66; and René Poupardin, *Le royaume de Bourgogne (888-1030)* (Paris, 1907), 30-33, respectively.
[15] For a detailed discussion of Bavaria in this period, see Ludwig Holzfurtner, *Gloriosus Dux. Studien zu Herzog Arnulf von Bayern (907-937)* (Munich, 2003), 32-100; and Martin Lintzel, "Heinrich I. und das Herzogtum Schwaben," *Historische Vierteljahresschrift* 24 (1927), 1-17, here 1-2.
[16] Holzfurtner, *Gloriosus Dux*, 122-132.
[17] In 907, the Bavarian regional levy had suffered a massive defeat at Pressburg (Bratislava) in the course of which Margrave Leopold of Bavaria (889–907), the father of Arnulf, was killed. Regarding the battle at Pressburg, see Adalbert of Magdeburg, *Continuatio Reginonis*, ed. F. Kurze, *Reginonis abbatis Prumiensis Chronicon cum continuatione Treverensi*, MGH SRG (Hanover, 1890), hereafter *Continuatio*, an. 907. For an analysis of the importance of the battle, see Charles R. Bowlus, *The Battle of Lechfeld and its Aftermath, August 955: The End of the Age of Migrations in the West* (Aldershot, 2006), 83-84; and R. Hiestand, "Preßburg 907: Eine Wende in der Geschichte des ostfränkischen Reiches?" *Zeitschrift für bayerische Landesgeschichte* 57 (1994), 1-20. Just three years later a substantial royal army, under the nominal command of Louis the Child, was defeated by the Hungarians at Augsburg. The western losses included the overall commander of Louis's army, Duke Gebhard of Franconia, a leading member of the powerful Conradine family, and uncle of the future King Conrad I (911–918). Regarding the battle at Augsburg, see Adalbert of Magdeburg, *Continuatio*, an. 910; *Liudprandi Cremonensis Opera Omnia: Antapodosis, Homelia Paschalis, Historia Ottonis, Relatio de Legatione Constantinopolitana*, ed. P. Chiesa (Turnhout, 1998), here *Antapodosis*, 2.3-4.
    For a useful synthesis of the Hungarian attacks during the first half of the tenth century, see Heinrich Büttner, "Die Ungarn das Reich und Europa bis zur Lechfeldschlacht des Jahres 955," *Zeitschrift für bayerische Landesgeschichte* 19 (1956) 433-458. The effort by Maximilian Georg Kellner, *Die Ungarneinfälle im Bild der Quellen bis 1150* (Munich, 1997) to minimize the importance and size of Hungarian raids in this period is largely unconvincing. See the detailed response to Kellner's arguments by Bernard S. Bachrach, "Magyar-Ottonian Warfare: *à-propos* a New Minimalist Interpretation," *Francia* 13 (2000), 211-230.

Saxony, and Thuringia, who composed, in the words of the Saxon historian Widukind, the army of the Franks (*exercitus Francorum*).[18] Immediately following the end of the assembly, Henry led these combined forces on his first campaign as king, which was directed against Duke Burchard of Swabia.[19]

Henry's decision to begin his efforts to reunify the east Frankish kingdom with an invasion of Swabia was recommended by two factors. First, Burchard had only recently been able to establish his control in the region following the execution of his main opponents, the brothers Erchanger and Berthold, by King Conrad I in early 917. Consequently, the duke's relationships with the Swabian magnates, and particularly the influential abbots and bishops, had not yet matured.[20] Second, Burchard was also heavily involved in a war with King Rudolf II of Burgundy (912–937). The latter had taken advantage of the death of Conrad I in 918 to invade Swabian territory in an effort to take control in the counties of Aargau and Thurgau, located in the north-east of modern Switzerland.[21]

Few details regarding Henry's Swabian campaign have survived. Widukind records simply that when Burchard received word that Henry had arrived with his entire army, the Swabian duke realized that he would not be able to resist the king's invasion. Consequently, he surrendered, placing all of his fortifications and his supporters (*urbes et populus*) under Henry's control.[22] Following Burchard's rapid capitulation, he and Henry came to an agreement that allowed the duke to retain his office, as well as *de facto* control over the church.[23] However, Burchard did formally recognize Henry's authority over royal fiscal property in Swabia.[24] Following Burchard's death in 926, Henry asserted tighter control in Swabia through the appointment of his *fidelis* Hermann as duke (926–947).[25] From this point onward, the king controlled not only fiscal lands in Swabia, but also the church.[26]

First Intervention in Lotharingia

In the immediate aftermath of Henry's invasion of Swabia, the king turned his attention west, where Count Gislebert (died 939) took the opportunity of a revolt

18   Widukind, *Res gestae*, 1.26.
19   Ibid., 1.27.
20   On Burchard's still tenuous control over Swabia, see Heinrich Büttner, *Heinrichs I. Südwest- und Westpolitik* (Stuttgart, 1964), 7; Lintzel, "Heinrich I. und das Herzogtum Schwaben," 1-2.
21   Büttner, *Heinrichs I. Südwest- und Westpolitik*, 8; Lintzel, "Heinrich I. und das Herzogtum Schwaben," 1-2.
22   Widukind, *Res gestae*, 1.27.
23   Regarding Burchard's continued control over the Swabian church, see Lintzel, "Heinrich I. und das Herzogtum Schwaben," 3. Cf. Wolfgang Giese, *Heinrich I.: Begründer der ottonischen Herrschaft* (Darmstadt, 2008), 72, who argues that Burchard's control over both the royal fisc in Swabia and the church were tightly regulated by Henry.
24   With regard to Henry's control over the fisc in Swabia after 926, see Karl Schmid, "Die Urkunde König Heinrichs I. für Babo aus dem Jahre 920," *Singener Stadtgeschichte* 2 (1990), 30-42, here 32-34; and the recent discussion by Bachrach, "The Written Word," 410-413.
25   For the appointment of Hermann, see Adalbert of Magdeburg, *Continuatio, an.* 926.
26   Lintzel, "Heinrich I. und das Herzogtum Schwaben," 9-10.

by Count Robert of Paris against the Carolingian king, Charles III, to declare himself king of Lotharingia in January 920.[27] Gislebert's father Reginar I (died 915) had held the dominant position in lower (northern) Lotharingia until his death, and played the leading role in inviting Charles III to take control in this *regnum* following the death of King Louis the Child in 911.[28] Henry I supported Gislebert's revolt, and then gave refuge to the count when King Charles succeeded in driving him out of Lotharingia.[29]

It is likely that Henry saw Gislebert's revolt as an opportunity to reassert eastern control in Lotharingia, which had been lost when Gislebert's father had transferred his loyalty to the western Carolingian, Charles III.[30] However, the immediate result of Henry's first intervention in Lotharingian affairs was the decision by King Charles to invade western Franconia, with the objective of capturing territories along both banks of the Rhine, including the important fortress city of Worms.[31] In response, Henry mustered a significant army at Worms itself, and Charles beat a hasty retreat rather than risk a battle. Nevertheless, Henry's forces did secure at least a minor victory, killing Count Erlebaldus of Chartres in a skirmish when the latter attempted to reach Charles's camp at Pfeddersheim, some six kilometers west of Worms.[32] Rather than continuing hostilities, the two kings, Charles and Henry, agreed through their representatives to a truce in early 921, which was to hold until 11 November.[33] The two rulers subsequently met later that same year on a ship anchored in the middle of the Rhine near Bonn on 7 November and agreed to a peace settlement (*pax*), whose terms included Charles recognizing Henry as east Frankish king, and Henry's acceptance of Charles's rule in Lotharingia.[34]

---

[27] For a valuable overview of events in Lotharingia in the period 920–925, with a focus on Henry's policies, see Büttner, *Heinrichs I. Südwest- und Westpolitik*, particularly, 6-42; and Schneidmüller, "Französische Lothringenpolitik im 10. Jahrhundert," 14.

[28] Sproemberg, "Die lothringische Politik Ottos des Großen," 22; Walter Mohr, *Geschichte des Herzogtums Groß-Lothringen (900-1048)* (Saarbrücken, 1974), 12.

[29] See the discussion of these events by Sproemberg, "Die lothringische Politik Ottos des Großen," 22; and the near contemporary observations by Richer, *Histoire de France, vol. 1, 888-954*, ed. Robert Latouche (Paris, 1930), 1.38, hereafter Richer, *Historiae*.

[30] Robert Holtzmann, *Geschichte der sächsischen Kaiserzeit*, 3rd edn (Munich, 1955), 75; and Sproemberg, "Die lothringische Politik Ottos des Großen," 21-22.

[31] Flodoard, *Annales, an.* 920. Adalbert of Magdeburg, *Continuatio*, misdates these events to 923. In the early tenth century, Bishop Tietlach of Worms (891–914) issued an ordinance regarding the maintenance of the city walls that required neighborhoods within the city, and also a series of villages in the region around Worms, to maintain specific sections of the wall. See the discussion by Heinrich Büttner, "Zur Stadtentwicklung von Worms im Früh-und Hochmittelalter," in *Aus Geschichte und Landeskunde. Forschungen und Darstellungen. Franz Steinbach zum 65. Geburtstag gewidmet von seinen Freunden und Schülern* (Bonn, 1960), 389-407, here 394. The text of the ordinance (*Mauerbauordnung*) is published in *Quellen zur Geschichte der Stadt Worms III: Annalen und Chroniken*, ed. Heinrich Boos (Berlin, 1893), 203.

[32] Flodoard, *Annales, an.* 920.

[33] Ibid., *an.* 921.

[34] Flodoard, *Annales, an.* 921. See the important discussion of the treaty of Bonn by Susanne Kaeding, Britta Kümmerlen and Kerstin Seidel, "Heinrich I. – ein 'Freundschaftskönig,'" *Concilium*

Bavaria

Henry's truce with Charles in early 921 now afforded him the freedom to undertake a campaign into Bavaria to force Duke Arnulf to acknowledge the Saxon's assumption of the royal office. Arnulf's position in Bavaria was significantly more secure in 921 than had been Burchard's in Swabia just two years earlier. At the forefront of the struggle against the Hungarians for more than a decade, Arnulf commanded significant numbers of battle-hardened troops. In addition, he maintained firm control over the church in Bavaria along with the substantial military resources that were commanded by the duchy's abbots and bishops.[35]

However, Henry had available a model for defeating Arnulf that had been provided five years earlier by Conrad I. In the spring of 916, Conrad marched into Bavaria and undertook a lengthy siege of Regensburg, which was well protected by a circuit of Roman walls.[36] Arnulf was able to escape just before the city fell to the east Frankish king, but was forced to take refuge among the Hungarians, with whom he had made a tribute agreement the previous year.[37]

Following in the footsteps of his royal predecessor, Henry also besieged Arnulf in Regensburg.[38] When Arnulf realized that he would not be able to hold the city, he surrendered.[39] The two men then came to a *modus vivendi*. In describing the agreement that Henry and Arnulf made, Widukind uses the term *amicus regis* to describe the Bavarian duke.[40] Here, the Saxon monk clearly is drawing upon the Roman imperial terminology of friendship to describe the relationship between the duke and the king.[41] Arnulf did not emerge as an independent ruler, and was

medii aevi 3 (2000), 265-326, who emphasize both the Roman and Frankish treaty-making traditions that were followed by Henry I and Charles III.

[35] Holzfurtner, *Gloriosus Dux*, 48-63.

[36] Regarding the Roman walls and for a synthesis of the archaeological investigations of Regensburg in the Roman and early medieval periods, see Carlrichard Brühl, *Palatium und Civitas: Studien zur Profantopographie spätantiker Civitates vom 3. bis 13. Jahrhundert*, vol. 2 (Cologne, 1990), 219-255, with a discussion of the Roman walls at 229.

[37] Holzfurtner, *Gloriosus Dux*, 117-122. Arnulf, however, returned shortly thereafter and successfully drove Conrad out of Bavaria.

[38] Widukind, *Res gestae*, 1.27. Cf. Liudprand, *Antapodosis*, 2.21, who indicates that the armies of Henry and Arnulf met in the field, but that the two commanders decided to conclude an arrangement rather than fight. The anonymous text of the *Fragmentum de Arnulfo duce Bavariae* (MGH SS 17, 570), records that Henry I invaded Bavaria without success, after being defeated by the inhabitants (*incoli*) of one city, which is almost certainly to be understood as Regensburg. If there was a failed invasion by Henry, it is not clear when this took place.

[39] Widukind, *Res gestae*, 1.27.

[40] Widukind, *Res gestae*, 1.27. Gerd Althoff, *Amicitia und pacta: Bündnis, Einung, Politik und Gebetsgedenken im beginnenden 10. Jahrhundert* (Hanover, 1992) postulates that Henry I developed a new style of rule based on a novel concept of friendship. This argument is largely unconvincing as demonstrated in the detailed analysis of the question by Kaeding, Kümmerlen and Seidel, "Heinrich I. – ein 'Freundschaftskönig,'" 265-326.

[41] Regarding the Roman tradition of making pacts of "friendship" with political inferiors, see

required to provide military aid to the king when called upon to do so, as we will see below. However, Arnulf did maintain full control over the Bavarian church, and was also able to undertake independent military operations.[42]

Henry I's Second Intervention in Lotharingia, 923

Immediately after describing Henry's settlement with Arnulf of Bavaria, Widukind observed, "After the king had unified the kingdom (regnum), which his predecessors had forged through both civil and external wars, and after he had brought peace from confusion on every side, he turned his banners toward Gaul and the kingdom of Lothair."[43] In the interval since Henry's peace agreement with Charles in November 921 open warfare had broken out in the West Frankish kingdom between the Carolingian ruler and Count Robert of Paris.[44] Henry openly sided with Robert, and met with him west of Cologne on the Roer river, a tributary of the Meuse, in the spring of 923, where the two men concluded a pact of friendship (amicitia) and exchanged gifts before departing.[45]

Subsequently, Robert, whose army was victorious on the field, was killed at the battle of Soissons on 15 June 923. Charles III, in the wake of his defeat at Soissons, was captured by the West Frankish magnate Heribert of Vermandois (died 943).[46] Henry used the ongoing conflict in the West Frankish kingdom to intervene directly in Lotharingia. The German king began operations with the capture of Saverne (German: Zabern), located in Alsace, which controlled the road from Strasbourg to the important episcopal city of Metz.[47] Henry left a substantial garrison there, and likely intended that this fortification would serve as rear-echelon staging area for operations against the fortress city of Metz, which was located approximately 100 kilometers to the north-west.[48]

Following the death of King Robert, the West Frankish magnates, joined by many secular and ecclesiastical principes in Lotharingia, chose Duke Raoul of Burgundy (died 936), the son-in-law of Robert, as king. Among these Lotharingian magnates was Bishop Wigeric of Metz (917–927) who sought the aid of the

Holtzmann, Geschichte der sächsischen Kaiserzeit, 73; and Kaeding, Kümmerlen and Seidel, "Heinrich I. – ein 'Freundschaftskönig'," 266-268 and 286-287.

[42] Concerning Arnulf's control over the Bavarian church, see Liudprand, Antapodosis, 2.23. Regarding Arnulf's intervention in Italy, and his effort to gain control of Verona, see Liudprand, Antapodosis, 3.49-52.

[43] Widukind, Res gestae, 1.27.

[44] For the turn of events in this period, see Flodoard, Annales, an. 923, with a detailed analysis by Sproemberg, "Die lothringische Politik Ottos des Großen," 21-26.

[45] Flodoard, Annales, an. 923. For a discussion of this agreement, see Schneidmüller, "Französische Lothringenpolitik im 10. Jahrhundert," 18; K. Schmid, "Zur Amicitia zwischen Heinrich I. und dem westfränkischen König Robert im Jahre 923," Francia 12 (1984), 119-147; and Kaeding, Kümmerlen, and Seidel, "Heinrich I. – ein 'Freundschaftskönig'," 293-295.

[46] Flodoard, Annales, an. 923.

[47] Ibid. Büttner, Heinrichs I. Südwest- und Westpolitik, 31 suggests that these were Swabian troops provided by Duke Burchard.

[48] Regarding Henry's capture of the Saverne, see Flodoard, Annales, 923.

new West Frankish king in besieging Saverne. Henry's troops held the fortification throughout the autumn of 923, but eventually capitulated when the German king failed to send reinforcements.[49] The Rheims historian Flodoard records that Bishop Wigeric then burned Saverne to the ground.[50]

In the meantime, however, Henry began his campaign against the Roman fortress city of Metz that boasted an urban defensive circuit of some 3,200 meters.[51] Adalbert of Magdeburg, who served as a court official under Otto I before assuming high ecclesiastical office, indicates that Henry, who had gained the support of both Count Gislebert and Archbishop Robert of Trier (915–930), forced Bishop Wigeric to accept his authority.[52] Flodoard describes the events somewhat differently, stressing Henry's ravaging of the region between the Rhine and Moselle, but concluding that the German king withdrew when he received word that Raoul had mobilized a large army to confront him.[53]

Despite the failure of Henry's campaign to gain direct control over the city of Metz, and also the loss of the fortification at Saverne, the German king's first offensive into Lotharingia did secure important positive results. Archbishop Robert of Trier and Count Otto of Verdun, who was the most powerful secular magnate in upper (southern) Lotharingia, committed themselves fully to Henry and accepted his rule over Lotharingia.[54]

Henry's Third Intervention in Lotharingia, 925

In 924, Henry's attention was fixed on Saxony and Thuringia, which were the victims of substantial raids by Hungarian forces.[55] That summer, however, a column of Hungarian troops was annihilated by detachments of the Saxon local levy, and an important Hungarian commander was captured and delivered to Henry at the fortified palace at Werla.[56] Henry used this opportunity to negotiate a nine-year peace agreement with the Hungarians, thereby giving him a free hand to intervene again in Lotharingia.[57]

---

49 Ibid.
50 Ibid.
51 Concerning the siege, see Adalbert of Magdeburg, an. 923; but cf. Flodoard, Annales, an. 923. Regarding the walls of Metz, see Brühl, Palatium und Civitas, II, 48; and for background, see Bernard S. Bachrach, "Fifth Century Metz: Later Roman Christian Urbs or Ghost Town?" Antiquité Tardive 10 (2002), 363-381.
52 Adalbert of Magdeburg, Continuatio, an. 923, "Eodem anno Heinricus rex adiunctis sibi Ruotgero archiepiscopo et Gisalberto duce Mittensem urbem obsedit et Witgerum, licet diu reluctantem, sibi obedire coegit."
53 Flodoard, Annales, an. 923.
54 Sproemberg, "Die lothringische Politik Ottos des Großen," 23.
55 Widukind, Res gestae, 1.32. See the discussion of these events by Bernard S. Bachrach and David S. Bachrach, "Saxon Military Revolution, 912–973?: Myth and Reality," Early Medieval Europe 15(2007), 186-222.
56 Widukind, Res gestae, 1.32.
57 Regarding the nature of this agreement as a peace settlement, see Bachrach and Bachrach, "Saxon Military Revolution?" 220-222, and the literature cited there.

As a consequence of events in Saxony, however, it was not until the spring of 925 that Henry again was able to undertake direct military operations in Lotharingia. The German king mobilized his army at Worms and then marched to the erstwhile Roman fortress of Zülpich, 220 kilometers to the north-west, which was held by troops loyal to Count Gislebert.[58] The latter had, during the course of previous year, again switched sides and given his allegiance to the recently elected West Frankish king Raoul.[59] Henry's troops captured Zülpich by storm.[60]

Following this show of force, the Lotharingian magnates en masse recognized Henry's authority. The German king was able to impose his own candidate, Bernuinus (925–939), as bishop of Verdun in place of Raoul's choice, Hugh.[61] Henry also received hostages from Gislebert who pledged his future loyalty to the German king.[62] As Flodoard of Rheims summed up the results of the campaign in 925, "All of the Lotharingians joined themselves to Henry."[63] This settlement was ratified in November 926 when King Raoul attended an assembly at Worms that had been summoned by Henry I.[64]

King Henry only found it necessary to lead military forces into Lotharingia one more time during the course of his reign, in 928. On this occasion, the German king personally led a large army to lay siege to the fortification (*castrum*) of Durofostum on the Meuse, which belonged to Count Boso of Pérthois, the brother of King Raoul.[65] Henry succeeded in forcing Boso to return properties he had seized from the bishops of Verdun and Metz, Bernuinus and Benno (927–929), both of whom had been installed with the support of the German king.[66]

Eastern Policy, 924–936

Defending the Frontier

Traditionally, scholars have seen Henry I's policy toward the trans-Saale Slavs, particularly the Sorbs, as maintaining basic continuity with his Carolingian predecessors and Conrad I.[67] This entailed imposing tribute on the numerous

---

[58] Flodoard, *Annales, an.* 925.

[59] Ibid.

[60] Ibid., "*Heinricus denique, Rhenum transiens, oppidum quoddam, nomine Tulpiacum, quod Gisleberti fideles tutabantur, vi cepit.*"

[61] Flodoard, *Annales, an.* 925.

[62] Ibid.

[63] Ibid., "*Heinrico cuncti se Lotharienses committunt.*"

[64] *Herimanni Augiensis Chronicon*, ed. G. H. Pertz, MGH SS 5, 113.

[65] Flodoard, *Annales, an.* 927.

[66] For the siege of Durofostum, see Flodoard, *Annales, an.* 928. Regarding Henry's installation of Benno as bishop of Metz in 927, see Flodoard, *Annales, an.* 927, who makes clear that Benno was the choice of Henry I, who imposed the prelate against the wishes of the people of the city.

[67] Scholars generally have seen Henry's policy with regard to the trans-Saale region as a basic continuation of Carolingian policy, which entailed the imposition of tribute upon the Slavic polities but not their conquest and integration into the eastern kingdom. In this regard see, for example, Walter Mohr, *König Heinrich I. (919-936): Eine kritische Studie zur Geschichtschreibung der letzten hundert Jahre* (Saarlouis, 1950), 54-55; Holtzmann, *Geschichte der sächsischen Kaiserzeit*, 93;

Slavic polities and undertaking punitive expeditions against them when the Slavs refused to pay. Certainly, Henry's father, Duke Otto of Saxony (880–912), and Henry himself, before his accession as king, sustained a policy of maintaining consistent pressure on the Slavs who lived beyond the frontiers of *Francia orientalis*. Widukind observed that Henry I campaigned in the Sorbian region of Daleminzia, located between the Saale river and the Lausatian mountain range, even before he succeeded his father as duke in 912, commanding a large army that included both professional soldiers (*milites*) and elements of the Saxon expeditionary levy (*exercitus*).[68] The intense pressure against the Slavic polities in these regions, reported by Widukind, is confirmed by the excavations of numerous Slavic fortifications. During the first three decades of the tenth century, Slavic rulers from the Saale eastwards undertook a massive program of improving and expanding their fortifications to meet the ongoing threat from the west.[69]

In addition to adhering to the traditional Carolingian policy of maintaining hegemony over the Sorbs, Duke Otto and Henry also expanded northwards the system of fortifications known as the Sorbian march. These new fortifications were intended to defend the lower Elbe frontier against the Hevelli, members of the large Weleti confederation of Slavic peoples who lived in the region between the lower Elbe and the Oder.[70] Slavic fortifications at Biederitz, Schartau, Burg, Grabow, and Dretzel, all of which were located within a day's march to the north and east of the important trading center of Magdeburg, on the Elbe, were captured and either replaced or rebuilt by the Saxons in the first decades of the tenth century.[71]

In addition to the complex of defensive works in the immediate vicinity of Magdeburg, Henry also developed a defensive line along the lower Elbe with

---

Josef Fleckenstein, *Early Medieval Germany*, translation of *Grundlagen und Beginn der deutschen Geschichte* by Bernard S. Smith (New York, 1978), 133-135; Giese, *Heinrich I.*, 114-115.

[68]   Widukind, *Res gestae*, 1.17.

[69]   With regard to fortifications at Havelberg and Spandau, see Joachim Henning, "Der slawische Siedlungsraum und die ottonische Expansion östlich der Elbe: Ereignisgeschichte-Archäologie-Dendrochronlogie," *Europa im 10. Jahrhundert: Archäologie einer Aufbruchszeit*, ed. Joachim Henning (Mainz, 2002), 131-146, here 132. Regarding the considerable increase in the number and size of fortifications in Lausatia during the first three decades of the tenth century, see idem, "Archäologische Forschungen an Ringwällen in Niederungslage: Die Niederlausitz als Burgenlandschaft de östlichen Mitteleuropas im frühen Mittelalter," in *Frühmittelalterliche Burgenbau in Mittel und Osteuropa*, ed. Joachim Henning and Alexander T. Ruttkay (Bonn, 1998), 9-29.

[70]   See the basic work on the Hevelli by Lothar Dralle, *Slaven an Havel und Spree. Studien zur Geschichte des hevellisch-wilzischen Fürstentums (6. bis 10. Jahrhundert)*, (Berlin, 1981). Regarding the broad division of Slavic peoples into three major confederations, the Weleti, Obodrites, and Sorbs, see the discussion by Gerhard Lebuda, "Zur Gliederung der slawischen Stämme in der Mark Brandenburg (10.-12. Jahrhundert)," *Jahrbuch für die Geschichte Mittel und Ostdeutschland* 42 (1994) 103-139, particularly, 103-111.

[71]   The Slavic fortifications at all of these sites were replaced by German fortifications early in the tenth century. See Joachim Herrmann and Peter Donat (eds). *Corpus archäologischer Quellen zur Frühgeschichte auf dem Gebiet der Deutschen Demokratischen Republik (7. bis 12. Jahrhundert)* (Berlin, 1973), 363, 371, 364, 366, 357, and 362. Also see Ernst Nickel, "Magdeburg in karolingisch-ottonischer Zeit," *Zeitschrift für Archäologie* 7 (1973), 102-142, here 104, who emphasizes that Magdeburg was already well established by 805.

fortifications at Tangermünde, Osterburg, and Walsleben.[72] This line was anchored at the confluence of the Havel with the Elbe by the two fortifications of Havelberg and Klietz.[73] These Ottonian fortifications marked the reestablishment under Henry I of the defensive line along the course of the lower Elbe that Charlemagne had organized during the final decade of the eighth and the first decade of the ninth century, the so-called *Limes Saxoniae*.[74]

A New Policy

However, the intensive raiding by the Hungarians against Saxony and Thuringia, which included major raids in 915 and in 924, made clear to Henry I that the traditional policy of maintaining hegemony over the Sorbs, and particularly the Daleminzi, who dwelled in the valleys of the Saale, Mulde, and middle Elbe, no longer was sufficient to safeguard the frontier against the new threat from the southeast.[75] Instead, he decided on a new policy, which was focused on extending eastwards the system of defense in depth that had been developed to hinder raiding by Sorbs, the *Limes Sorabicus*.[76]

---

[72] Regarding the fortifications at Tangermünde and Osterburg, see *Corpus archäologischer Quellen*, 175 and 189. For German control of Walsleben see Widukind, *Res gestae*, 1.36.

[73] Concerning the large fortification at Klietz that was controlled by Henry I, see Hubert Reimer, "Der slawische Burgwall von Klietz, Kreis Havelberg – ein Vorbericht," *Jahresschrift für mitteldeutsche Vorgeschichte* 75 (1992), 325-345, particularly 343 for the establishment there of a German garrison. With respect to the Slavic fortification at Havelberg, see Christian Popp, "Gründung und Frühzeit des Bistums Havelberg," *Mitteilungen des Vereins für Geschichte der Prignitz* 3 (2003), 6-82, here 18. Ultimately, a further fortification was constructed just three kilometers to the west of Klietz at Arneburg, which would become a major bulwark of German rule along this portion of the middle Elbe through the remainder of the tenth and early eleventh century. For the important role played by the fortress at Arneburg in securing this portion of the frontier, see Thietmar von Merseburg, *Chronik*, ed. and trans. Werner Trillmich, 8th edn (Darmstadt, 2002), hereafter *Chronicon*, 4.38 and 6.28. Also see the discussion of Arneburg by David S. Bachrach, "The Military Organization of Ottonian Germany, c. 900–1018: The Views of Bishop Thietmar of Merseburg," *Journal of Military History* 72 (2008), 1061-1088, here 1072-1073.

[74] See the detailed discussion of both the Carolingian and Ottonian frontiers along the lower Elbe in Matthias Hardt, "Linien und Säume. Zonen und Räume an der Ostgrenze des Reiches im frühen und hohen Mittelalter," in *Grenze und Differenz im frühen Mittelalter* (2000), 39-56; and idem, "Hesse, Elbe, Saale and the Frontiers of the Carolingian Empire," *The Transformation of Frontiers from Late Antiquity to the Carolingians*, ed. Walter Pohl, Ian Wood, and Helmut Reimitz (Leiden, Boston and Cologne, 2001), 219-232, particularly 223-226.

[75] Widukind, *Res gestae*, 1.20, records that before Henry's accession as king a Hungarian army (*exercitus*), which was guided by Slavs, inflicted considerable damage in Saxony before returning to Daleminzia. Adalbert of Magdeburg, *Continuatio, an.* 915, indicates that the Hungarians launched a major raid that caused damage in both Saxony and Thuringia, and even reached the monastery of Fulda. It is not certain that these two accounts refer to the same raid, but it seems likely in the absence of the discussion of other raids. Widukind records a second raid (1.32) that likely took place in 924, which saw two Hungarian columns cross the Saale, one heading north toward the Harz and the second heading south into Thuringia. Regarding the 924 date, see the discussion by Bachrach and Bachrach, "Saxon Military Revolution?" 199. For an overview of Hungarian raids into Saxony and Thuringia, see Büttner, "Die Ungarn das Reich und Europa," 441-442.

[76] Regarding the defensive system along the Saale, see Hansjürgen Brachmann, "Der Limes Sorabicus – Geschichte und Wirkung," *Zeitschrift für Archäologie* 25 (1991), 177-207; and Goldberg, *Struggle for Empire*, 127. The idea that Henry intended to use the trans-Saale region as a buffer against Hungarian attacks was first suggested by Franz Lüdke, *König Heinrich I.* (Berlin, 1936), 104-105. More

Defense in Depth

Defense in depth is a term coined by modern scholars to describe a multi-layered scheme that has the two-fold purpose, first, of protecting valuable human and agricultural assets against raiders and, second, of destroying raiding forces as they attempt to withdraw toward friendly territory.[77] Along the eastern frontiers of Saxony and Thuringia, as well as of Bavaria, as will be seen below, two types of fortifications were constructed as part of the defense in depth. The first of these consisted of large fortified refuges (German: *Fluchtburgen*), often located on easily defensible sites, where local populations could find protection for themselves, their tools, and their livestock in the face of enemy raids.[78] In addition to these larger sites, Henry, following in the tradition of his Carolingian predecessors, maintained or constructed large numbers of fortifications at choke points along major transportation routes, such as river fords, mountain passes, and along roads through swampy regions.[79]

When the system of defense in depth functioned effectively, the local populations took refuge in the *Fluchtburgen* after receiving word about an imminent attack.[80] At the same time, the military forces of the region took up their positions at the fortifications along the main roads. Raiders, who were denied easy access to supplies, were forced to break up into smaller groups in order to forage. At this point, the regional commander could concentrate his own forces and destroy the raiding army piecemeal. If the regional commander had sufficient forces at his disposal, as we will see below in the case of the battle of Riade in 933, he could mass his entire army and seek battle against a foe that was now exhausted by weeks of campaigning with inadequate supplies, and perhaps burdened with plunder and captives.

Defense in Depth East of the Saale

For the most part, the early tenth-century Sorbian march was based upon the defensive system that had been constructed originally by Charlemagne along the course of the Unstrut river and middle course of the Saale river. Comprising at

---

recently, Dralle, *Slaven an Havel und Spree*, 109, raised the possibility that Henry saw this region as a possible *"glacis"* that would protect the *"Festung"* of Saxony against Hungarian attack.

77   See Bowlus, *The Battle of Lechfeld*, 47-64, for a valuable description of the Ottonian system of defense in depth along the eastern frontier. Bowlus argues (47) that Henry modeled his defensive system on the scheme that was already in place along Bavaria's eastern frontier. I suggest, instead, that both the Bavarian and the Saxon-Thuringian defensive systems date back to earlier Carolingian roots.

78   Regarding the nature of *Fluchtburgen* in the Ottonian period as largely constructed by the royal government or by license from the royal government, see Michael Mitterauer, "Burgbezirke und Burgwerkleistung in der babenbergischen Mark," *Jahrbuch für Landeskunde Niederösterreich* 38 (1970), 217-231; and Reinhard Friedrich, "Ottonenzeitliche Befestigungen im Rheinland und im Rhein-Main-Gebiet," *Europa im 10. Jahrhundert*, 351-363.

79   These smaller fortifications are discussed in more detail below.

80   Ekkehard of St Gall described the system of fire signals that was in use in Swabia to alert local populations about the enemy attacks with specific reference to preparations for Hungarian depredations. See Ekkehard of St Gall, *Casus Sancti Galli*, ed. Hans F. Haefele (Darmstadt, 1980), 136.

least nineteen fortifications, this defensive system allowed Charlemagne, and his successors, including Louis the Pious (814–840), Louis the German, and Arnulf to project military forces across the Saale for offensive operations, and to interdict Slavic raids directed toward Erfurt in the south, and the eastern foothills of the Harz to the north.[81] The linchpins of this defensive system were the fortresses at Merseburg and Querfurt, which guarded the principal fords across the Saale.[82]

Early in his reign, and perhaps even before his accession as king, Henry had begun the process of pushing his defensive line east of the Saale. No later than 924, Henry had a strong fortification at Püchen, located on the west bank of the Mulde river, some 60 kilometers east of the Saale frontier.[83] The German king took refuge here when he was surprised by a superior Hungarian army while campaigning in the vicinity of Eilenburg.[84] This latter site was a crucial fording point over the Mulde, and eventually became an important point along the principal highway (Hohen Straße) from Merseburg to the upper Lausatian region and then into Silesia in modern Poland.[85] The final settlement of affairs in Lotharingia in 928, which followed upon the capitulation of Count Boso of Pérthois, freed Henry to undertake a major campaign that would substantially alter the political landscape along the erstwhile eastern frontier with the Slavs, and permit the king to implement his plan of expanding his system of defense in depth to the middle Elbe.

The Campaign of 928–929, Brandenburg

In the late winter of 928, Henry I began a three-stage offensive that led to the subjugation of Slavic polities along his entire eastern frontier. Henry's first main objective was to capture Brandenburg, the princely seat of the Hevelli, a Slavic polity centered on the Havel river.[86] To the south, the Hevelli princes ruled the hilly region today known as Fläming.[87] To the east, the Hevelli princes ruled both banks of the Havel river up to the major fortification at Spandau located 80 kilometers east of Brandenburg on an island in the Havel river.[88] The construc-

See the discussion by Walter Schlesinger, *Die Entstehung der Landesherrschaft, Teil I* (Dresden, 1941), 79; Paul Grimm, *Handbuch vor-und frühgeschichtlicher Wall-und Wehranlagen Teil I: Die vor-und frühgeschichtlichen Burgwälle der Bezirke Halle und Magdeburg* (Berlin, 1958), 44-46; Hardt, "Linien und Säume," 39-56; idem, "Hesse, Elbe, Saale and the Frontiers of the Carolingian Empire," 219-232; and Volker Herrmann, "Der 'Limes Sorabicus' und Halle im frühen Mittelalter," in *Siedlung, Kommunikation und Wirtschaft im westslawischen Raum: Beiträge der Sektion zur slawischen Frühgeschichte des 5. deutschen Archäologenkongresses in Frankfurt an der Oder* (2007), 133-143.

Grimm, *Handbuch*, 45.

Thietmar of Merseburg, *Chronicon*, 1.17

Ibid.

Regarding the route of the Hohen Straße, see Joachim Herrmann, "Lorenzkirche, Markt des Burgwards Strehla im Daleminzergau der Mark Meißen," *Herbergen der Christenheit: Jahrbuch für deutsche Kirchengeschichte* 19 (1993), 17-27, here 19.

Widukind, *Res gestae*, 1.35.

Joachim Herrmann, "Belizi 997-Beltz-Belzig: Von der Slawenburg zur kursächsischen Festung zwischen Havelland und Fläming. Eine archäologisch-historische Topographie," *Veröffentlichungen des brandenburgischen Landesmuseums für Ur-und Frühgeschichte* 28 (1994), 191-221, here 196

Adriaan von Müller, "Der Burgwall von Berlin Spandau," *Europas Mitte um 1000*, ed. Alfried

tion of the fortifications at both Brandenburg and Spandau dates to the decade preceding 928, and is indicative of the wide-ranging efforts by Slav rulers to ward off the increasing pressure imposed on them by the dukes of Saxony during the early tenth century.[89]

The princes of the Hevelli had strong ties to Bohemia. In 906/907, the Hevelli princess Drahomir was married to Duke Vratislav of Bohemia (died 921). Moreover, the familial relationship between the Hevelli ruling family and the Premyslids in Bohemia likely dated back to the ninth century.[90] As a consequence, the Hevelli were indirectly connected with the Hungarians, with whom the Bohemians had developed a *modus vivendi*.[91] It is in this context that the Bohemian rulers had permitted Hungarian armies to pass unmolested through their lands to launch raids into Thuringia and Saxony, most recently in 924.[92] As a consequence, Henry likely believed it would be necessary to neutralize the Hevelli before undertaking substantial military actions further south.

Widukind, who is our best source for this war, makes clear that Henry's campaign against the Hevelli involved several subsidiary military operations before the *urbs* at Brandenburg itself was captured. He stressed that the German forces wore out the Slavs in numerous battles (*multis preliis fatigans*) over a lengthy period.[93] It was only after he had sufficiently isolated Brandenburg that Henry deployed his army in a close siege of the fortress. Widukind draws attention to the fact that by the time Henry actually began direct operations against the Hevelli princely seat, the coldest part of the winter had arrived. As a result, the army was forced to camp on ice (*castris super glaciem positis*).[94] Ultimately, Henry captured Brandenburg by storm, after besieging the stronghold for some time.[95]

The Capture of Gana

Once Henry had secured his base of operations at Brandenburg, he marshaled his forces to begin the second phase of the campaign, which was directed against the important Daleminzi center at the "fortress called Gana," located approximately 180 kilometers south-south-east of Brandenburg.[96] There is considerable

Wieczorek and Hans Hinz (Stuttgart, 2000), 278-281, here 279.

89 Henning, "Der slawische Siedlungsraum," 132.

90 Lothar Dralle, "Zur Vorgeschichte und Hintergründen der Ostpolitik Heinrichs I.," in *Europa Slavica, Europa orientalis: Festschrift für Herbert Ludat zum 70. Geburtstag*, ed. Klaus-Detlev Grothusen and Klaus Zernack (Berlin, 1980) 99-126, here 115; and Bernhard Friedmann, *Untersuchungen zur Geschichte des abodritischen Fürstentums bis zum Ende des 10. Jahrhunderts* (Berlin, 1986), 180-181.

91 Friedmann, *Untersuchungen zur Geschichte des abodritischen Fürstentums*, 180-181.

92 Ibid.

93 Widukind, *Res gestae*, 1.35.

94 Widukind, *Res gestae*, 1.35. In describing the siege and capture of Brandenburg, Widukind alludes to Cicero's speech against Lucius Calpurnius Piso. Cicero, *In Pisonem*, 17 reads, "*exercitus nostri interitus ferro, fame, frigore, pestilentia.*" Here, Cicero was listing the causes for the casualties suffered by Piso's troops when he served as governor of Macedonia. Widukind paraphrases here listing only hunger, arms (literally iron), and cold as the causes for the casualties suffered by the defenders of Brandenburg.

95 Widukind, *Res gestae*, 1.35.

96 Widukind, *Res gestae*, 1.35, "*signa vertit contra Dalamantiam, adversus quam iam olim reliquit ei*

scholarly dispute regarding the exact location of this stronghold.[97] However, recent excavations at Hof/Stauchitz, just west of the Elbe in the valley of one of its left tributaries called the Jahna, have identified a massive complex that may be the site of fortress captured by Henry.[98]

Henry's army faced an exceptionally difficult challenge at Gana. According to Widukind, the operations here lasted for twenty days before the German troops successfully stormed the walls.[99] Likely as a result of substantial losses suffered during this action, Henry issued exceptionally harsh orders regarding the survivors. The king permitted his troops to slaughter the surviving male defenders before dividing up the young boys and girls among his professional soldiers (*milites*) as slaves.[100]

As a result of his victories at both Brandenburg and Gana, Henry was able to impose tribute payments on both the Hevelli and the Daleminzi. In addition, however, Henry also gained recognition as overlord of the Slavic polities whose lands were located east of the lower Elbe, including several of the peoples who comprised the Obodrite confederation and the Redarii, who were part of the Weleti confederation. The latter lived north and east of Havelland along the shores of the Baltic Sea east to the Oder river.[101]

Prague

After his capture of Gana, Henry began a 220-kilometer march south up the course of the Elbe toward Prague. While underway, the German king ordered the construction of a new fortification at Meißen, located 25 kilometers south-east of Gana, along the Elbe river. This fortification immediately became a linchpin in system of German defenses that were intended to control the middle Elbe region.[102] Dendrochronological dating of the wooden structures at Meißen,

---

pater militiam; et obsidens urbem quae dicitur Gana."

[97] Werner Radig, *Der Burgberg Meißen und der Slawengau Daleminzien* (Augsburg, 1929), 48, suggested two locations for the location of Gana, namely Burgberg near Zschaitz, and the Zöthener Schanze south of Lommatzsch. Werner Coblenz, "Archäologische Betrachtungen zur Gana-Frage im Rahmen der älterslawischen Besiedlung des Gaues Daleminzien," in *Beiträge zur Archivenwissenschaft und Geschichtsforschung*, eds. R. Groß and M. Kobuch (Weimar, 1977), 354-370, here 358, rejected these options and suggested instead a location in the valley of the Jahna river between Hof and Stauchitz. For an overview of the historiographical discussion regarding the location of Gana, see Judith Oexle and Michael Strobel, "Auf den Spuren der 'urbs, quae dicitur Gana', der Hauptburg der Daleminizier. Erste archäologischer Untersuchungen in der slawischen Befestigung von Hof/Stauchitz," *Arbeits und Forschungsberichte zur sächsischen Bodendenkmalpflege* 46 (2004), 253-263, here 253.

[98] Oexle and Strobel, "Auf den Spuren," 253-263.

[99] Widukind, *Res gestae*, 1.35.

[100] Ibid., "*Preda urbis militibus tradita, puberes omnes interfecti, pueri ac puellae captivitatai servatae.*"

[101] Widukind, *Res gestae*, 1.36. For an overview of the Slavic peoples who lived in the regions between the lower Elbe and the Oder, who are sometimes denoted as Polabian Slavs, see P. M. Barford, *The Early Slavs: Culture and Society in Early Medieval Eastern Europe* (Ithaca, 2001), 257-8.

[102] For the strategic significance of the fortress at Meißen, see Werner Coblenz, "Zur Frühgeschichte der meißner Burg: Die Ausgrabungen im meißner Burghof 1959/1960," *Meißner Heimat Sonderheft 1961*, 3-32. Thietmar of Merseburg, *Chronicon*, 1.16 noted that Meißen was carved out of virgin forest lands.

including barracks for the garrison, indicates that construction began in 929, which suggests that Henry detached men from his forces to build the fortress even as he continued his campaign toward Prague.[103]

When Henry arrived at Prague he was joined by a Bavarian army commanded by Duke Arnulf. The German king clearly intended to have sufficient forces to storm Prague, just as he had captured both Brandenburg and Gana by storm. However, the Bohemians declined to fight. Instead, according to Widukind, when Henry arrived *cum omni exercitu*, Duke Wenceslaus (921–935) surrendered, i.e. accepted Henry's *ditio*, rather than attempt to defend his well fortified capital.[104] It seems likely that Wenceslaus made this decision with the knowledge of what had just happened at both Brandenburg and Gana, namely the successful capture by storm of these two impressive fortifications. Instead, the Bohemian duke agreed to pay tribute to the German king.[105]

Restructuring the Frontier

After his capture of Brandenburg and Gana, and the capitulation of Wenceslaus at Prague, Henry was not content simply to impose tribute on the Sorbian peoples dwelling in the lands between the Saale and the Elbe, as he had done with the Slavs of the Weleti and Obodrite confederations, including the Hevelli. Instead, he worked diligently to establish close control over the valleys of the Saale, Mulde, and Elbe rivers in a manner consistent with his plan to establish a system of defense in depth that would protect Thuringia and Saxony from Hungarian raids (see map). In addition to the major new fortification at Meißen, Henry rebuilt or replaced a series of Slavic fortifications along the Elbe, where he installed garrisons. These include the fortifications at Auberg, Torgau, Fichtenberg, and Görzig.[106] The last named was replaced in 929 by the German fortification at Strehla, which protected a ford over the Elbe.[107] Henry also constructed a new fortification at Zehren, located on the left bank of the Elbe six kilometers north of Meißen, which replaced a nearby Slavic fortified site.[108]

---

[103] Regarding the dating of the earliest construction, see Arne Schmid-Hecklau, *Die archäologischen Ausgrabungen auf dem Burgberg in Meißen: Die Grabungen 1959-1963* (Dresden, 2004), 205.
[104] Widukind, *Res gestae*, 1.35.
[105] Ibid., 1.36.
[106] See, in this context, Gerhard Billig, "Mittelalterliche Burgen in Dommitzsch nördlich Torgau," *Landesgeschichte und Archivwesen: Festschrift für Reiner Gross zum 65. Geburtstag* (Dresden, 2002), 21-34, here 26; Grimm, *Burgwälle*, 113; and Heinz-Joachim Vogt, "Archäologische Untersuchungen im Altstadtbereich von Torgau," *Ausgrabungen und Funde* 37 (1992), 46-53; Günther Wetzel, "Der erste slawische Burgwall des Kreises Bad Liebenwerda in Fichtenberg bei Mühlberg," *Ausgrabungen und Funde* 22 (1977), 76-85, here 75; and Werner Coblenz, "Boleslav Chrobry in Sachsen und die archäologische Quellen," *Slavia Antiqua* 10 (1963), 249-285, here 274.
[107] Gerhard Billig, *Die Burgwardorganisation im obersächsisch-meissnischen Raum: Archäologisch-archivalisch vergleichende Untersuchungen* (Berlin, 1989), 68; and Herrmann, "Lorenzkirche," 18. For a general overview of the "Burgenkette" established by Henry along the course of the middle Elbe, see W. Rittenbach and F. Seifert, *Geschichte der Bischöfe von Meißen 968-1581* (Leipzig, 1965), 5.
[108] Werner Coblenz, "Der Burgberg Zehren, eine Befestigung aus der Zeit der ersten Etappe der deutschen Ostexpansion," in *Archäologische Feldforschungen in Sachsen: Fünfzig Jahre Landesmuseum*

In addition to establishing the middle Elbe as the new frontier with the Slavs, Henry also secured the route from the important military center of Merseburg on the Saale east to Meißen. The construction of a new fortification at Leipzig, which was located on the high east bank of the Elster river 30 kilometers due east of Merseburg, recently has been dated to c. 930.[109] At the mid-point along the 90-kilometer route between Leipzig and Meißen, Henry constructed a new fortification at Dahlen.[110] The three new fortifications at Leipzig, Dahlen, and Meißen were too far from each other for the garrisons to provide immediate assistance. Consequently, the German king also garrisoned the erstwhile Slavic fortifications at Grimma and Oschatz.[111] The first of these was located approximately halfway between Leipzig and Dahlen, and the second approximately halfway between Dahlen and Meißen. The line of fortifications Merseburg-Leipzig-Grimma-Dahlen-Oschatz-Meißen subsequently guarded the primary line of march for German armies traveling from the Saale to the Elbe for campaigns into Silesia and Poland.[112]

Henry further strengthened his hold on the lands of the Daleminzi through the establishment of garrisons all along the course of the Mulde river valley, including its two southern sources, the Zwickauer and Freiburger Mulde. Among the important fortifications in the lower Mulde valley were Zörbig and Cösitz.[113] These two erstwhile Slavic fortifications protected the only two fords over the Fuhne, a right tributary of the Saale, and one of the very few western flowing rivers in the entire northern plain of modern Germany and western Poland.

Further south along the middle course of the Mulde, the long-established Saxon outpost at Püchen was reinforced by fortifications at Pouch and Eilenburg.[114] The

für Vorgeschichte Dresden (Berlin, 1988), 373-77. Werner Coblenz, "Wallgrabung auf dem Burgberg Zehren," *Aufgrabung und Funde* 2 (1957), 41-45.

[109] Regarding the construction of the fortification at Leipzig, see Herbert Küas, "Die Leipziger Burg des 10. Jahrhunderts," *Arbeits und Forschungsberichte zur sächsischen Bodendenkmalspflege* 20/21 (1976), 299-332, with the confirmation of Küas's dating of the construction of Leipzig to the period of Henry's conquest of the region between the Saale and the Elbe by Friedemann Winkler, *Leipzigs Anfänge: Bekanntes, Neues, offene Fragen* (Beucha, 1998), 41. Some of Küas's arguments regarding the use of stone for the first phase of the construction at Leipzig have been contested in the recent literature. See, in this context, Thomas Westphalen, "Die frühen Burgen Leipizgs," in *Archäeologie und Architektur: Das frühe Leipzig*, ed. Wolfgang Hocquél (Leipzig, 2003), 43-50.

[110] Herrmann, "Lorenzkirche, Markt des Burgwards Strehla," 18.

[111] Regarding the fortifications at Oschatz, see Lutz Jansen, "Ausgrabungen in Oschatz und Altoschatz," *Archäologie aktuell im Freistaat Sachsen* 6 (1998), 176-179.

[112] Regarding the military highway from Merseburg to Meißen, see Schmid-Hecklau, *Meißen*, 12.

[113] Regarding the fortification at Zörbig, see Berthold Schmidt and Waldemar Nitzschke, "Untersuchungen in slawischen Burgen zwischen Saale und Fläming," *Ausgrabungen und Funde* 20 (1975), 43-51, here 48. For a discussion of the fortification at Cösitz, see Hansjürgen Brachmann, "Der slawische Burgwall von Cösitz, Kr. Köthen," *Ausgrabungen und Funde* 21 (1976), 162-3 and 244-247; and idem, "Der Limes Sorabicus," here 189-190. The fortification at Cösitz is identified as having been destroyed in a Frankish campaign in 839 by the *Annales de Saint-Bertin*, ed. Félix Grat, Jeanne Vieillard, and Suzanne Clémencet (Paris, 1964).

[114] Concerning the new Ottonian fortification at Pouch, see Willi Rittenbach, "Über die Grenzen des Bistums Meißen," *Jahrbuch für die Geschichte Mittel- und Ostdeutschlands* 19 (1970), 49-73, here 59; and Paul Grimm, *Tilleda: Eine Königspfalz am Kyffhäuser, Teil I: Die Hauptburg* (Berlin, 1968), 112.

latter quickly developed into an important stopping point along the Hohen Straße, which linked Merseburg to Silesia and then to Poland, passing over the Elbe at the newly constructed Ottonian fortification at Strehla.[115] The important fortified center at Colditz, located on the Zwickauer-Mulde just before it joins with its sister stream, the Freiburger Mulde, is also dated to Henry's conquest of the region in 929.[116] Just south of Colditz was the important Slavic fortification at Rochlitz, which also fell into Henry I's hands either during the campaign of 929, or shortly thereafter.[117] To the east, along the Freiburger Mulde and in the region between this river and the Elbe, Henry garrisoned the former Slavic fortifications at Döbeln, Zschaitz, and Mügeln, as well as Böritz, which was located just a few kilometers north of Zehren, noted above, and provided for the defense of a secondary Elbe crossing.[118]

Slavic Resistance, 929

The development of a system of mutually reinforcing fortifications in the region between the Saale and the Elbe appears to have moved forward with considerable speed and little if any resistance by the indigenous Sorbs.[119] By contrast, the effort by Henry I to impose tribute upon members of the Weleti confederation was met with a ferocious response. In July or early August 929, a major force of Redarii, one of the most prominent groups among the northern Weleti, launched an assault on the German fortress of Walsleben, located in the modern district of Stendal, approximately 22 kilometers west-south-west of the fortress at Havelberg.[120] The entire garrison, as well as the population of the surrounding area who had taken refuge at the fort, were slaughtered after the walls were stormed by an overwhelming force.[121]

In order to retaliate for this violation of the peace and tribute agreements that he had made earlier that year with the Slavic leaders, Henry dispatched a substantial army in late August to undertake the siege of Lenzen, located on the east bank of the Elbe, approximately 85 kilometers north-west of Walsleben. The fortification at Lenzen was the central seat of the Slavic people known as the Lionen, who were members of the Obodrite confederation. This stronghold

---

[115] Herrmann, "Lorenzkirche, Markt des Burgwards Strehla im Daleminzergau der Mark Meißen," 17.

[116] Karlheinz Blaschke, "Die Frühgeschichte der Stadt Colditz," *Sächsische Heimatsblätter* 2 (1965), 290-307, here 290.

[117] Udo Baumbach, "Zur Baufolge an der Burg Rochlitz," *Burgenforschung aus Sachsen* 3-4 (1994), 33-57.

[118] Grimm, *Burgwälle*, 25.

[119] There is no mention in the contemporary narrative sources of a revolt against German rule at this time. Indeed, even after the death of Henry I in 936 and the subsequent revolts by Slavic polities in the north-east and in the south-east, the region of Daleminzia appears to have remained quiet. In addition, excavations of the numerous fortifications that were established by Henry I in 929 and in the succeeding years have not identified evidence of destruction during the reigns of either Henry or Otto I.

[120] Widukind, *Res gestae*, 1.36.

[121] Ibid.

traditionally had served as an important mobilization point for operations by the Slavs against targets located west of the Elbe.[122] During the course of the siege, Henry's army achieved a crushing victory over a Slavic relief force, and then gained the submission of the fortification.[123] The victory at Lenzen was so complete that it appears that the trans-Elben Slavs did not contest German rule again for the remainder of Henry's reign.[124]

Defending the New Frontiers, 932–934

In 932 Henry undertook his first major campaign into the mountainous Lausatian (German: Lausitz) region, which comprises the lands between the Bobr, Kwisa, and Elbe rivers in parts of the modern states of Saxony and Brandenburg in Germany, the lower Silesian Voivodeship in western Poland, and the northern third of the Czech Republic.[125] During this, and several subsequent operations, Henry occupied numerous Slavic fortifications in the region and established garrisons there. This was the case, for example, with regard to the twin fortifications at Lübbenau and Groß Lübbenau, which were first constructed at the end of the ninth century by the Lausatians, and then substantially expanded in the early 920s as the threat from the German kingdom became more intense.[126] Henry's campaign in 932 appears to have been limited to lower Lausatia (northern region) which was separated from upper Lausatia (southern region) by the so-called Grenzwall, a district of dense forest lands that was largely uninhabited during the tenth century.

Two years later, in 934, Henry undertook his last campaign against the Slavs, on this occasion the Ukrani, another group within the Weleti confederation, who lived along the banks of the Ucker river, which flows north from its source in the modern region of Uckermark in Germany to the Baltic sea.[127] This was quite a daring campaign by the now aging Henry I, who turned 58 in 934. The heartland of the Ukrani was located some 180 kilometers north-east of Brandenburg, which Henry had captured in 929, and 230 kilometers from Magdeburg on the Elbe, a major base of operations for the German king. In addition to the great

---

[122] Heike Kennecke, "Forschung Burg Lenzen, Wo Slawen gegen Sachsen kämpften," *Archäologie in Deutschland* 22 (2006), 8-13, here 8.

[123] For a detailed discussion of this battle, see Bernard S. Bachrach and David S. Bachrach, "Early Saxon Frontier Warfare: Henry I, Otto I, and Carolingian Military," forthcoming in *Journal of Medieval Military History* 10, pp. 17–60

[124] At least there are no reports of rebellions in the narrative sources for the period 929–936, and archaeologists have not found, to date, evidence for the destruction of German fortifications during this time.

[125] For the campaign, see *Annales Hildesheimensis*, MGH SS 3, 54. For a discussion of the significance of the conquest of Lausatia for communications between Poland and Bohemia, see Rudolf Lehmann, "Zur Geschichte der Verkehrsstraßen in der Niederlausitz bis zum Ausgang des 18. Jahrhunderts," *Jahrbuch für brandenburgische Geschichte* 25 (1974), 49-93, who accepts 932 as the beginning of the German conquest of the region (49).

[126] Eberhard Kirsch and Andreas Mehner, "Der Schloßberg von Lübbenau, Lkr. Oberspreewald-Lausitz," *Veröffentlichungen zur brandenburgischen Landesarchäologie* 36/37 (2002-2003), 203-222.

[127] Adalbert of Magdeburg, *Continuatio*, an. 934.

distances involved in a campaign against the Ukrani, Henry's army also had to face an impressive network of at least seventeen mutually reinforcing Ukrani fortifications, each of which was supported by a large number of settlements whose inhabitants could take refuge within the walls of the *Fluchtburgen* and help in the defense of the walls.[128] This campaign by Henry does not appear to have brought any permanent results, however, and it was not until the 950s, as will be seen in the next chapter, that Otto I's military commanders were able to conquer the Ukrani.

In 934, Henry also undertook a significant military campaign against the Danes in order to control raiding by the latter into Frisia. Henry led an army against the Danish ruler Cnupa (Chnuba), who held, among other territories, the important trading center at Hedeby (German: Haithabu).[129] Widukind records that Henry won a victory over the Danes, forced them to pay tribute, and caused Cnupa to receive baptism.[130]

The *Agrarii Milites* and Riade (933)

Henry's successful effort to push his eastern frontier to the middle Elbe took place in the context of a peace agreement he reached with the Hungarians following their failed raid of 924. In addition to his offensive against the Slavs in 928–929, and the construction of numerous fortifications along the Mulde and Elbe rivers, Henry also improved the system of defense in depth within Saxony and Thuringia.

In describing events following the peace agreement with the Hungarians in 924, Widukind asserted:

> Henry wisely considered how he might defend the fatherland and defeat the barbarian nations. To describe everything that he did is beyond my ability, but it is not fitting that these matters should be left completely in silence. First, he selected every ninth man from among the *agrarii milites* to live in fortifications... He desired that all law courts, assemblies, and festivals should be held in the fortifications. They were to train in these fortifications day and night so that they would learn in times of peace what do to when faced by the enemy.[131]

Generations of scholars have made this brief passage bear unsustainable weight to support broad-gauged claims about the constitutional and social development of the German kingdom.[132] It is now clear that the men identified by

128 See the discussion by Volker Schmidt, *Drense: Eine Hauptburg der Ukrane* (Berlin, 1989), 55.
129 Widukind, *Res gestae*, 1.40.
130 Widukind, *Res gestae*, 1.40. See the discussion by Helmut Beumann, "Magdeburg und die Ostpolitik der Ottonen," *Die historische Wirkung der östlichen Regionen des Reiches: Vorträge einer Tagung zum vierzigjährigen Bestehen der Bundesrepublik Deutschland* (Cologne, 1989), 9-29, here 9-10.
131 Widukind, *Res gestae*, 1.35.
132 The survey of the literature by Edward J. Schoenfeld, "Anglo-Saxon 'Burhs' and Continental 'Burgen': Early Medieval Fortifications in Constitutional Perspective," *The Haskins Society Journal* 6 (1994), 49-66, is now indispensable. Also see, regarding specific arguments concerning the identity and meaning and social implications of the *agrarii milites*, D. Schäfer, "Die agrarii milites des Widukind," *Sitzungsberichte des königlichen preussischen Akademie der Wissenschaften*

Widukind were not the so-called king's freemen (German: *Königsfreien*), nor were they proto-ministerials, who, although unfree, would eventually comprise the lowest level of German nobility.[133] Rather, Henry I undertook a series of military reforms that were intended to provide garrison troops for large numbers of new and newly refurbished fortifications, men who could also play an active role in the strategy of defense in depth against the Hungarians.[134] The *agrarii milites*, whom Widukind mentions, were members of the local levies who were trained both to protect their own fortifications and, importantly, to serve in the field against the Hungarians and other raiders in conjunction with the professional soldiers of the royal military household, and of the military households of secular and ecclesiastical magnates as part of a system of defense in depth.[135]

Henry's essentially defensive military reforms were very successful. In 932, the king formally declared to the bishops of Germany that he intended to break the peace agreement that he had reached with the Hungarians eight years before.[136] Widukind, who worked diligently throughout his history to depict Henry I as acting in the manner of a Christian king who followed the dictates of just war theory, presented the king's decision as an effort to spare the church the burden of taxation that would go to enrich the Hungarians.[137] In fact, however, Henry was seeking to mobilize public opinion for an offensive war against the Hungarians, perhaps in the border regions between Bavaria and the Magyar core lands in the Carpathian Basin.[138] Henry first made his case to the secular magnates and prelates who had assembled for a synod at Erfurt in late May. The latter included the archbishops of Mainz, Trier, and Hamburg, as well as the bishops of Verden, Strasbourg, Constance, Paderborn, Augsburg, Halberstadt, Münster, and Minden, representing Saxony, Franconia, Lotharingia, and Swabia.[139] Just six weeks later, Duke Arnulf of Bavaria held a similar assembly

27 (1905), 569-577; Erich Sander, "Die Heeresorganisation Heinrichs I.," *Historisches Jahrbuch* 59 (1939), 1-26, here 6; Heinrich Büttner, "Zur Burgenbauordnung Heinrichs I," *Blätter für deutsche Landesgeschichte* 92 (1956), 1-17, here 4; Gerhard Baaken, *Königtum. Burgen und Königsfreien. Studien zu ihrer Geschichte in Ostsachsen* (Cologne and Stuttgart, 1961), 14-21 and 59-70; Josef Fleckenstein, "Zum Problem der *agrarii milites* bei Widukind von Corvey," in *Beiträge zur niedersächsischen Landesgeschichte zum 65. Geburtstag von Hans Patze im Auftrag der Historisichen Kommission für Niedersachsen und Bremen*, ed. Dieter Brosius and Martin Last (Hildesheim, 1984), 26-41; and Matthias Springer, "Agrarii Milites," *Niedersächsisches Jahrbuch für Landesgeschichte* 66 (1994), 129-166.

133 Regarding the scholarly rejection of the model of Königsfreien, see Timothy Reuter, "The End of Carolingian Military Expansion," 392-393; and Schoenfeld, "Anglo-Saxon *Burhs* and Continental *Burgen*," 53. With respect to the failure of the ministeriales model, see ibid., 54.

134 Bachrach and Bachrach, "Saxon Military Revolution?" 215-216.

135 Ibid.

136 Widukind, *Res gestae*, 1.36. See Bachrach and Bachrach, "Saxon Military Revolution?" 199 and 220-222.

137 Bachrach and Bachrach, "Saxon Military Revolution?" 220-222.

138 Regarding the core regions of the Hungarian territory, see Bowlus, *The Battle of Lechfeld*, 22-27.

139 *Die Konzilien Deutschlands und Reichsitaliens 916-1001: Teil I 916-960*, ed. Ernst-Dieter Hehl and Horst Fuhrmann (Hanover, 1987), 110, for the list of bishops who participated.

of bishops and secular magnates at Dingolfing on 16 July 932 where it is almost certain that Henry's ally (*amicus*) made clear his acceptance of the king's new bellicose stance against the Hungarians.[140]

The Hungarians, however, took the field first and in early 933 mobilized a large army for raids in force into both Thuringia and Saxony.[141] As the Hungarians made their way into the trans-Saale region, the Daleminzi, who now lived under close German rule, refused to provide them with any aid. This was in marked contrast to the situation before 929 when the Daleminzi had offered significant assistance to the Hungarians, even providing guides so that the raiders could bypass the system of fortifications along the Saale and Unstrut rivers.[142]

Once they reached the Saale, the Hungarians divided their forces into two raiding columns.[143] The western column, which headed into Thuringia, was systematically denied supplies when the inhabitants of this region sought refuge in *Fluchtburgen* along with their animals and possessions. While denying the raiders any easy means of re-supply, the local levies were mobilized. These local militia troops, likely supported by higher quality expeditionary levies and *milites* who lived in the area, successfully attacked, and destroyed the Hungarians in detail as the latter dispersed in a desperate search for food and fodder.[144] This is the essence of a successful system of defense in depth.

The eastern column attempted to capture a fortification in the region around Merseburg, whose lady, according to Widukind, was the illegitimate sister of Henry I.[145] It was near here, at Riade, that the German king stationed his army. On the morning of 15 March 933, Henry sent out contingents of lightly armed Thuringian mounted troops to draw the Hungarian army into a trap.[146] However, the Hungarians realized the danger before Henry was able to unleash his forces and retreated, abandoning both their camp and the prisoners they had taken.[147] Again, the system of defense in depth had been proven effective. The fortification besieged by the Hungarians served as the anvil against which the hammer of Henry's field forces struck the raiders.

Hegemony in the West, 925–936

Following his conquest of Lotharingia in 925, Henry assumed a dominant role in the affairs of the West Frankish kingdom. The ongoing struggle for power

---

[140] Regarding the assembly, see ibid., 120.
[141] Liudprand, *Antapodosis*, 2.28, 47-8; Widukind, *Res gestae*, 1.38.
[142] Widukind, *Res gestae*, 1.38.
[143] Ibid.
[144] Ibid.
[145] Ibid.
[146] The battle at Riade received enormous contemporary attention despite the fact that the fighting, itself, was inconclusive. See Flodoard, *Annales*, an. 933; Adalbert of Magdeburg, *Continuatio, an.* 934 (933); Liudprand, *Antapodosis*, 2.25; *Die Annales Quedlinburgenses*, ed. Martina Giese (Hanover, 2004), 458; Widukind, *Res gestae*, 1.38.
[147] Widukind, *Res gestae*, 1.38.

between King Raoul and his ally Hugh the Great (died 956), on the one hand, and Count Heribert of Vermandois on the other led to numerous diplomatic and military interventions in the west by Henry I or his surrogates.[148] Raoul visited Henry's court in 926, and Heribert came seeking aid in both 927 and 928, and again in 931.[149] In 930 and 932, Gislebert, who had been appointed by Henry as duke of Lotharingia in 928, led Lotharingian forces into the West Frankish kingdom at the order of the German king where he besieged, respectively the fortifications at Douai and Péronne.[150] Gislebert again invaded the West Frankish kingdom in 935 commanding both Lotharingian and Saxon forces pursuant to Henry's decision to aid Heribert of Vermandois against Hugh the Great. On this occasion, Gislebert's men besieged the fortress at St Quentin.[151] In June of this year, Henry oversaw a negotiated settlement between Heribert and Raoul, and then made a peace agreement (*pacta amicitia*) with King Raoul at Ivois on the Chiers river, a right tributary of the Meuse.[152] By the end of this year, both Raoul and King Rudolf II of Burgundy had become *amici* of the German king, indicating in the traditional Roman sense that they were his subordinate allies, and recognized Henry's hegemonic role north of the Alps.[153]

In light of this dominant position, it appears that Henry contemplated in 935, despite his advanced age, a campaign into Italy with the goal of being crowned emperor at Rome.[154] However, before plans for this expedition could be developed, Henry suffered serious injuries in a hunting accident at the royal palace at Bodfeld in the Harz mountains when he fell from his horse. In the spring of 936, the now weakened Henry held a royal assembly at Erfurt where he named his son Otto as heir.[155] The king then traveled to the royal palace at Memleben on the Unstrut river where he died on 2 July 936.

Henry I's Legacy

In the space of less than six years Henry was able to restore the frontiers of *Francia orientalis*. Just four years later, in 929, Henry firmly established the Elbe as his eastern frontier, at the same time bringing about the permanent incorporation of the populous and productive Sorbian polities into the German kingdom. By the end of his reign, Henry was also the dominant figure in the west, having won

---

[148] Regarding Henry's policy of intervention in the West Frankish kingdom to ensure the security of Lotharingia, see Sproemberg, "Die lothringische Politik Ottos des Großen," 28-35; Büttner, *Heinrichs I. Südwest- und Westpolitik*, 26-42.

[149] Flodoard, *Annales, ann.* 927, 928, 931.

[150] Ibid., *ann.* 930 and 932.

[151] Ibid., *an.* 935.

[152] Ibid.

[153] Holtzmann, *Geschichte der sächsischen Kaiserzeit*, 103-104.

[154] Widukind, *Res gestae*, 1.40. Cf. Gunther Wolf, "König Heinrichs I. Romzugsplan 935/936," *Zeitschrift für Kirchengeschichte* 103 (1992), 33-45.

[155] Liudprand, *Antapodosis* 4.15; Flodoard, *Annales, an.* 936; Adalbert of Magdeburg, *Continuatio, an.* 936.

recognition from the kings of both Burgundy and West Francia of his hegemonic status. After seventeen years on the throne the first Saxon king bequeathed to his son a kingdom in the east more powerful than that ruled by any of his Carolingian predecessors, including Louis the German and Arnulf of Carinthia. It was now up to the twenty-four year old Otto I to prove himself as Alexander to his father's Philip.

2

Forging a New Empire

When Otto I succeeded his father in 936, the horizon for conceptualizing his political and military policies was far broader than it had been for Henry. As a result of his father's conquests, the young king inherited an East Frankish/German realm that was larger and more powerful than any kingdom since the division of the Carolingian empire following the death of Louis the Pious in 840. Indeed, from the very beginning of his reign, Otto made clear that he saw himself as the natural successor of the great Charles, not least by having himself crowned at Aachen.[1]

When Otto formulated his medium and long-term strategy for maintaining the hegemonic position of the eastern kingdom, he chose to follow the reasoning that Henry pursued in the west. Thus, Otto limited his initiatives to a policy of intervening in the affairs of *Francia occidentalis* for the purpose of protecting Lotharingia from the revanchist designs of the Carolingian kings Louis IV (936–954) and Lothair IV (954–986), his brother-in-law and nephew respectively. Otto was content to play a dominant role in the political affairs of the western kingdom, often acting as an arbiter between the conflicting claims of the king and the West Frankish magnates, including Hugh the Great, who was also Otto's brother-in-law. When necessary, Otto also deployed military forces in the west, some of which comprised very large armies. But he did so only to establish an equilibrium of power there that was conducive to his long-term policy of maintaining the territorial integrity of the eastern kingdom, and particularly the integrity of Lotharingia under his control. Otto consistently avoided the temptation to pursue direct territorial aggrandizement in *Francia occidentalis*. In this manner, Otto would appear to have adhered to the policy not only of his father Henry, but also to the policy of Arnulf of Carinthia, who also was content to play the role of hegemon rather than of conqueror in the west. In this manner both Arnulf and Otto I were quite different from Louis the German, who had sought to reunify the entire Carolingian empire under his direct rule.[2]

---

[1]   Regarding the importance of Charlemagne as a model for Otto see, for example, Hagen Keller, "Entscheidungssituationen und Lernprozesse in den Anfängen der deutschen Geschichte: Die 'Italien und Kaiserpolitik' Ottos des Großen," *Frühmittelalterliche Studien* 33 (1999), 20-48.

[2]   This is the central argument of Goldberg, *Struggle for Empire*.

In the east, however, Otto developed a new imperial policy from the very beginning of his reign. Within a year of his elevation as king, Otto established and
richly endowed the monastery of St Maurice at Magdeburg, which was intended
to spearhead the Christian mission to the trans-Elben Slavs. This effort mirrored
Charlemagne's mission to the Saxons, and was tied to the view that the duty of
an emperor included bringing Christianity to the pagans.[3] The great synod of
Ingelheim, in 948, which was attended by the papal legate, Bishop Marinus of
Bomarzo, affirmed this mission, and established bishoprics at Brandenburg and
Havelberg, as well as three additional bishoprics in Danish Jutland, which were
to be under the authority of the archbishop of Bremen.[4]

From his accession until 955, Otto focused on maintaining the hegemonic position in the trans-Elben lands that his father had established. However, following a
major Slavic revolt in 955, Otto revised this policy, and worked to establish direct
control over all of the lands between the Elbe and the Oder. By the mid 960s,
Otto successfully established a seamless network of military districts throughout
this entire region, and subjected all of the Slavic peoples living there to his rule.

It was in Italy, however, where Otto's long-term policy of renewing Charlemagne's empire in the west was enunciated most clearly.[5] Otto launched an initial
invasion of Italy in 951 during which he captured the capital of the Lombard
kingdom at Pavia, but ultimately failed to secure a lasting peace. A second invasion of Italy commanded by Otto's son Liudolf in 956 also achieved considerable initial success. But this invasion also failed to bring about a final settlement
when Liudolf died in 957. Otto undertook a renewed invasion of Italy under his
direct command in 961, and conquered the entire peninsula south to Spoleto.
Upon his entrance to Rome on 2 February 962, Otto was crowned as emperor
by Pope John XII (955–964), an achievement that his father had not attained. At
his death in 973, Otto ruled directly fully two-thirds of the empire that Charlemagne had bequeathed to his heir Louis the Pious in 814, and he was recognized
as a superior by the West Frankish ruler Lothair IV and King Conrad II of
Burgundy (937–993), whose sister Adelheid (931–999) Otto married in 951. In

3   Otto I's efforts to expand Christianity among the Slavs has received enormous scholarly
attention, particularly in regard to the ruler's view that such work was an essential element of
imperial rule. See, for example, Carl Erdmann, "Der Heidenkrieg in der Liturgie und die Kaiserkrönnung Ottos I.," *MIÖG* 46 (1932), 129-142; F. Dvornik, "The First Wave of the Drang Nach
Osten," *Cambridge Historical Journal* 7.3 (1943), 129-145; Heinrich Büttner, "Die christliche Kirche
ostwärts der Elbe bis zum Tode Ottos I," in *Zur Geschichte und Volkskunde Mitteldeutschlands*, ed.
Walter Schlesinger (Vienna, 1968), 145-181; Herbert Ludat, "Böhmen und die Anfänge Ottos I.,"
Politik, Gesellschaft, Geschichtsschreibung: Giessener Festgabe für Frantisek Graus zum 60. Geburtstag
(Cologne, 1982), 131-164; and Beumann, "Magdeburg und die Ostpolitik der Ottonen," 9-29.
4   See the discussion by Johannes Laudage, *Otto der Grosse (912-973): Eine Biographie* (Regensburg, 2001), 164.
5   For Otto's Italian policy, Herbert Zielinski, "Der Weg nach Rom: Otto der Große und die
Anfänge der ottonischen Italienpolitik," in *Die Faszination der Papstgeschichte*, ed. Wilfrid Hartmann and Klaus Herkbers (Cologne, 2008), 97-107, is now the essential introduction.

addition, Otto brought German rule and Christianity to a vast swath of lands where Frankish rule earlier had been intermittent or non-existent.

The Revolts of 937–939

As is often the case when a new and untested king comes to power, Otto faced a series of challenges to his rule. In Saxony, Otto's decision in 936 to appoint the important magnate Hermann Billung as his new frontier commander along the lower Elbe led to political unrest as Hermann's older brother Wichmann saw himself excluded from this high office.[6] Following the death of Count Siegfried of Merseburg in 937, Otto selected Count Gero to serve as his new frontier commander (margrave) along the middle Elbe frontier. This decision alienated Otto's own illegitimate, elder brother Thankmar, who had expected to have this post because his mother Hatheburg was Count Siegfried's cousin.

The relationship between Otto and Duke Eberhard of Franconia (died 939), the younger brother of the late King Conrad I, also deteriorated rapidly after the Eberhard demanded an oath of loyalty and service from a Saxon magnate named Bruning. The latter commanded a fortification at Helmern, located in the eastern foothills of the Egge range, near the border between Franconia and Saxony. In describing these events, Widukind claimed that Bruning, filled with pride in his Saxon heritage, refused to serve anyone other than the king himself.[7] We need not accept Widukind's pro-Saxon *parti pris* to see that Duke Eberhard was testing the new king's hold on power by seeking to draw royal *fideles* into his own camp. When Bruning refused Eberhard's demands, the Franconian duke raised the ante by destroying the fortification at Helmern. In response, Otto took stern measures against Eberhard. In September 937, the young king condemned the Franconian duke's military commanders (*principes militum*), who had participated in the attack on Helmern, to the humiliating punishment of publicly carrying dogs on their shoulders on a lengthy march to the royal city of Magdeburg.[8]

In Bavaria, discontent with Otto developed when the newly established king used the death of Duke Arnulf in mid July 937 to reimpose direct royal control over both the royal fisc and the church within the duchy.[9] When Arnulf's son Eberhard refused to accept Otto's conditions for assuming office as *dux*, the king attempted to expel him with a rapid strike into Bavaria in early 938. But Otto was unable to settle matters at this time. The failure of Otto's initial foray into Bavaria was due largely to the fact that the king mobilized too small an army to

---

6   Regarding this episode, see Reuter, *Germany in the Early Middle Ages*, 152.
7   Widukind, *Res gestae*, 2.6.
8   See the discussion of this type of punishment by Bernd Schwenk, "Das Hundetragen. Ein Rechtsbrauch im Mittelalter," *Historisches Jahrbuch* 110 (1990), 289-308, who does not comment directly on this episode.
9   See the discussion by Schmid, *Regensburg*, 118, and 146-147; and the treatment of this topic by Bachrach, "Exercise of Royal Power," 411-413, and the literature cited there.

reduce the fortifications held by the rebels.[10] This error in judgment, which led to the failure of the campaign, was to have dangerous consequences for the new king when Duke Eberhard, Thankmar, and Wichmann, sensing weakness, broke into open revolt in both Franconia and Saxony.[11]

After taking stock of his initial failure, Otto moved methodically over the entire spring and summer of 938 to capture all of the fortifications that had been seized by the rebels in Saxony. At Eresburg, which long had served as a primary seat of the Saxon dukes, Otto's brother Thankmar was killed.[12] The other main instigator of the rebellion in Saxony, Wichmann, surrendered soon after and, treated mercifully, remained loyal to the king until his own death in 944.[13] Following the king's determined campaign in Saxony, Duke Eberhard of Franconia sued for peace, using Otto's younger brother Henry, whom he held as a captive, as an intermediary.[14]

When he had settled affairs in the north, Otto then undertook a second campaign into Bavaria in the autumn of 938.[15] This time, Otto succeeded in driving Eberhard and his supporters from Bavaria, and installed Berthold, the younger brother of Duke Arnulf, as duke (938–947).[16] As part of the new settlement, Otto seized direct control over the royal fisc in Bavaria, and assumed control over ecclesiastical appointments.[17] In doing so, Otto replicated his father's success in Swabia in 919.

The uneasy peace in the kingdom did not last long, however. In early 939, Otto's brother Henry rose in rebellion with the support of both Duke Eberhard of Franconia and Duke Gislebert of Lotharingia.[18] The rebels were aided by King Louis IV of West Francia who sought to use the conflict in Germany to regain control over portions of Lotharingia. During the next nine months Otto conducted numerous military operations, with a particular focus on sieges in Lotharingia, including the major fortresses at Breisach and Chièvrement. In addition, he defeated the rebels at Birten in March 939, and at Andernach on 2 October 939.[19] Otto's brother Henry was severely wounded at Birten, and Dukes Gislebert and Eberhard both were killed at Andernach, bringing the rebellion to a close.

---

[10]   Adalbert of Magdeburg, *Continuatio, an.* 938.

[11]   Regarding the revolt in Saxony, see Widukind, *Res gestae*, 2.11.

[12]   Widukind, *Res gestae*, 2.11.

[13]   Ibid.

[14]   Ibid., 2.12-13.

[15]   Adalbert of Magdeburg, *Continuatio, an.* 938; *Annales of Einsiedeln*, MGH SS 3, 141; *Herimanni Augiensis Chronicon*, 113; *Annales Magdeburgenses a. 1-1188*, ed. G. H. Pertz, MGH SS 16, 143.

[16]   Widukind, *Res gestae*, 2.34; Adalbert of Magdeburg, *Continuatio, an.* 938.

[17]   See Bachrach, "Exercise of Power," 411-413, and the literature cited there.

[18]   For an overview of these events, see Holtzmann, *Geschichte der sächsischen Kaiserzeit*, 122-129.

[19]   For the battle at Birten, see Adalbert of Magdeburg, *Continuatio, an.* 938; Liudprand, *Antapodosis*, 4.24; Widukind, *Res gestae*, 2.17. For the battle at Andernach, see Liudprand, *Antapodosis*, 4.29; *Annales Quedlinburgenses*, 462; Richer, *Historiae*, 2.19; and Widukind, *Res gestae*, 2.26.

The Eastern Frontier 936–954: Rebellion and Consolidation

Trans-Elben Regions

The widespread revolt against Otto's rule in the period 937–939 had a counterpoint among the Obodrites and Weleti in the north and the Bohemians in the south, who also sought to test the mettle of the new king. In 936, *legati*, who had been dispatched by Otto's illegitimate brother Thankmar, likely to collect tribute payments, were mistreated by the trans-Elben Slavs. In response, Otto, along with Hermann Billung, his new frontier commander in the north-east, undertook a punitive expedition.[20] Widukind indicates that the royal army inflicted significant damage on the rebellious Slavs and re-imposed tributary status on some of them.[21] However, this did not mark the end of the revolt.

The open warfare within the German kingdom in the period 937-939 again encouraged the trans-Elben Slavs to rebel against German rule. Gero, whose command encompassed the frontier along the middle Elbe, is reported to have used trickery to assassinate thirty Slavic leaders (*principes*) at a feast in an effort to break their resistance.[22] This effort failed, and the Obodrites, whose main area of settlement was between the lower Elbe and the Baltic Sea, openly rebelled. Gero dispatched an army under the command of a *dux* named Haica to deal with the Obodrites, but this army was annihilated and the commander himself was killed.[23] The failure of this expedition and the hard fighting against the Obodrites and the Weleti caused significant dissension among the professional soldiers (*milites*) in Gero's command, who wished to see him replaced. The difficult war was made even worse, from the stand-point of these soldiers, because the traditional tribute payments that provided salaries for the troops could not be collected from the rebels.[24] In the end, however, Otto refused to deprive Gero of his office and kept him as frontier commander for the next twenty-five years.

Otto's faith in his commander was repaid in 939 when Gero succeeded in establishing a loyal Hevelli prince named Tugumir at Brandenburg.[25] Tugumir killed his own nephew, who had gained the leading position among all of the *principes* in Havelland, and took control at Brandenburg. At this point Tugumir opened the city to a German garrison and proclaimed his loyalty to Otto, accepting the latter's *ditio*. Likely with considerable exaggeration, Widukind states that this success led to the reestablishment of tribute payments from all of the Slavic peoples between the Elbe and the Oder.[26]

---

[20] Widukind, *Res gestae*, 2.4.
[21] Ibid., 2.4.
[22] Ibid., 2.20.
[23] Ibid.
[24] Ibid., 2.30.
[25] Ibid., 2.21.
[26] Ibid.

Bohemia

By contrast with this relatively rapid success in reestablishing hegemony east of the middle and lower Elbe, the dominant German position in Bohemia was not easily restored. Duke Boleslav I (935–972) murdered his brother Wenceslaus in 935, and altered the pro-German orientation of Bohemia that had domi-nated ducal policy over the previous six years.[27] In response to a request for aid from anti-Boleslav elements in Bohemia, Otto dispatched two armies under the overall command of Count Asik to intervene on behalf of the magnates who opposed Boleslav's rule.[28] Despite an initial success by Asik in 936, Duke Boleslav was able to defeat in detail the two armies dispatched by Otto before they could join together.[29]

It would be another fourteen years before Otto was able to restore the *status quo ante* with the Bohemians.[30] In 950, however, the German king personally led an army into Bohemia with the goal of subjugating the Bohemians to German rule and reestablishing the position that had been enjoyed by Henry I from 929 to 936.[31] In July 950, Otto captured the fortress at Nimburg (Czech Nymburk) on the Elbe, approximately 40 kilometers west of Prague.[32] Otto then advanced to the Bohemian central seat, itself.[33] There, Boleslav, making the same decision as his brother Wenceslaus had made in 929, surrendered rather than face an assault on the city. According to Widukind, Boleslav made his decision because of the strength and enormous size of the German army (*innumera multitudo exercitus*).[34] As was his practice, Widukind used the term *exercitus* to denote the expeditionary levy, which he contrasted with the *milites* who were professional soldiers serving in the military households of magnates.[35] Otto's army, again as had been true of Henry I in 929, included both Saxon and Bavarian troops, the

---

[27]   Regarding the general conduct of Bohemian-Ottonian affairs in the period 936–950, see Ludat, "Böhmen und die Anfänge Ottos I.," 131-164; Jaroslav Panek and Oldrich Tuma (eds), *A History of the Czech Lands* (Prague, 2009), 72-75; and Klaus Zernack, "Otto der Große und die slawische Reiche," in *Otto der Große, Magdeburg und Europa* (Mainz, 2001), 517-524, particularly 519.

[28]   Ludat, "Böhmen und die Anfänge Ottos I.," 135.

[29]   Ibid.

[30]   See the observations by Widukind, *Res gestae*, 1.35 and 2.40; and the discussion by Ludat, "Böhmen und die Anfänge Ottos I.," 131-164.

[31]   Widukind, *Res gestae*, 3.8.

[32]   Ibid. While at Nimburg, Otto issued a charter on behalf of St Emmeram. See *Die Urkunden der deutschen Könige und Kaiser: Konrad I., Heinrich I. und Otto I.*, ed. Theodor Sickel (Hanover, 1879-1884), 207-208, hereafter DO I, 126.

[33]   Flodoard, *Annales*, an. 950, "*Otto rex qui quandam Wenedorum magnam obsederat urbem, nomine Proadem, regem ipsorum in subjectionem recipit.*"

[34]   Widukind, *Res gestae*, 3.8, "*Considerata itaque virtute Regis ac innumera multitudine exercitus.*" Adalbert of Magdeburg, *Continuatio*, an. 950, states that Otto put down a rebellion by the Bohe-mian *princeps* Boleslav with a *validissima manus*.

[35]   Regarding the standard meaning of *miles* as professional soldier, see the discussion by Bachrach, "Memory, Epistemology, and the Writing of Early Medieval Military History", 63-90. Concerning Widukind's distinction between the *exercitus* and *milites*, see Fleckenstein, "Zum Problem der *agrarii milites* bei Widukind von Corvey," 35.

latter now commanded by Henry, Otto's younger brother, whom the king had appointed as duke in 948.[36]

Hegemony in the West 940–954

The settlement of the rebellions within Germany, and the reestablishment of stability to the north-eastern frontier permitted Otto to focus his attention and military resources on the west. As a first order of business, in 940 Otto mobilized a large army, drawn from the entire German kingdom and an additional contingent provided by King Conrad II of Burgundy, for an invasion of West Francia.[37] This campaign was to serve two purposes. First, it was necessary to punish Louis IV for his intervention on behalf of the rebel dukes Gislebert and Eberhard in the previous year. Secondly, and more importantly, Otto needed to demonstrate to both the West Frankish king and the Lotharingian magnates that Lotharingia was an integral part of the eastern kingdom and that they would not be allowed to break away as had happened in 911.[38] Otto registered a significant political success in this campaign when King Louis' main opponents, Hugh the Great and Count Heribert of Vermandois, along with Count Roger of Laon, swore allegiance to the German ruler at Attigny in the Ardennes region of modern France.[39]

From this point onwards, Otto maintained a consistent policy of intervening on behalf of whichever side appeared to be losing ground in the ongoing struggle for power in the West Frankish kingdom. It is not entirely obvious whether Otto's efforts in this regard were helped or hindered by the fact that his sister Gerberga was married to King Louis IV, and his other sister Hadwig was married to Duke Hugh the Great. Thus, in 942, King Otto dispatched military forces under the command of Duke Otto of Lotharingia (940–944) to aid Hugh and Heribert.[40] The German ruler then oversaw the negotiation of a settlement among the major actors, following which he received Louis IV at Visé on the Meuse river where Otto affirmed his friendship (amicitia) with the west Carolingian king.[41]

In 944, Otto I again intervened in West Francia. On this occasion his effort was on behalf of Louis. Otto dispatched an army under the command of Duke Hermann of Swabia to besiege fortifications that were being held by the West Frankish king's erstwhile supporters Raoul and Reginar III of Hainaut (940–958), the nephew of Duke Gislebert, who had joined with Hugh the Great to

---

[36] Henry is identified in DO I, 126, as intervening with his brother, the king, on behalf of the monastery of St Emmeram, located in Regensburg.

[37] Flodoard, Annales, an. 940.

[38] This issue was particularly pressing as a number of Lotharingian magnates, including Count Isaac of Cambrai, Count Dirk of Holland, as well as the bishops of Toul, Metz, and Verdun swore loyalty to Louis IV when he invaded Lotharingia in 939. See Flodoard, Annales, an. 939, and the discussion by Sproemberg, "Die lothringische Politik Ottos des Großen," 32.

[39] Flodoard, Annales, an. 940.

[40] Ibid., an. 942.

[41] Ibid.

oppose the Carolingian ruler.[42] When Louis' position deteriorated even further, Otto personally commanded a full-scale invasion of the West Frankish kingdom in 946 to restore the *status quo ante*. Otto intended this army, which was drawn from throughout the German kingdom, to be very large (*magnus valde exercitus*) since the campaign was intended to capture a number of fortified cities that were being held by Louis' opponents.[43] During this campaign, Otto besieged the fortress cities of Rheims, Laon, and Rouen, forcing the first two of these to return their allegiance to Louis IV.[44] Otto also undertook limited operations against both Paris and Senlis, although he gave up the latter siege because, as Flodoard emphasized, the German king did not wish to accept the enormous casualties that an assault on the massive fortification would entail.[45]

Otto did not personally lead an army again into the West Frankish kingdom after 946. However, over the next six years, Otto repeatedly dispatched military forces under the command of Duke Conrad the Red of Lotharingia (945–953), his son-in-law, to intervene in West Francia. This includes two campaigns in 948, as well as expeditions in 949, 951, and 952.[46]

The Hungarians 937–950

In addition to internal rebellions, revolts by the Slavs, and his ongoing intervention in West Frankish affairs, Otto also had to contend with the continued threat of raids by the Hungarians, which by no means had been ended by Henry I's relatively bloodless victory at Riade in 933. Indeed, 937 saw a major raid by the Hungarians into eastern Franconia and an attempted raid into Saxony and Thuringia.[47] In the case of the latter attack, however, the ongoing improvements that Henry had made to the system of defense in depth beyond the Saale brought significant dividends. During their withdrawal from these *regna*, the greater part of the Hungarian army was destroyed when the raiders attempted to return along their invasion routes. As the *Annals* of Quedlin-

---

[42] Ibid., *an.* 944.

[43] Widukind, *Res gestae*, 3.2, gives a figure of 30 *legiones* for the army that invaded West Francia in 946. He described the army commanded by Otto on the Lechfeld as comprising just eight *legiones*. Widukind, *Res gestae*, 3.44, specifically identifies the *legiones* at the Lechfeld as comprising 1,000 each. Leyser, "The Battle at the Lech", 59, argues that the use of this round number is simply a topos, perhaps taken from Widukind's knowledge of the "ancient divisions of the Germanic peoples or the Old Testament." Leyser, does not, however, provide any evidence to support this contention. Concerning Leyser's misunderstanding of Widukind's text, and the likelihood that Widukind's depiction of *legiones* as units of 1,000 men was taken from the monk's understanding of contemporary Ottonian military organization, see Bachrach, "Magyar-Ottonian Warfare," 218-220. Widukind's contemporary, Adalbert of Magdeburg, *Continuatio, an.* 946, similarly observed the large size of the German army, describing it as a *manus valida*.

[44] Flodoard, *Annales, an.* 946; Adalbert of Magdeburg, *Continuatio,* 946; Widukind, *Res gestae*, 3.2-4.

[45] Flodoard, *Annales, an.* 946.

[46] See Flodoard, *Annales, ann.* 948, 949, 951, 952.

[47] Widukind, *Res gestae*, 2.5.

burg put it, "they died in the swampy areas and in other difficult locations."[48] It was precisely at choke points in the narrow passages through swamps, along narrow roads in wooded regions, and over rivers that defenders, in a system of defense in depth, were mobilized to take advantage of the terrain, and attack raiders who were now slowed down by carts and wagons carrying their booty.[49] Following the failure of the 937 raid there were no further Hungarian attacks against either Thuringia or Saxony during Otto I's reign.

The success against the Hungarians in the north was matched in 943 by Duke Berthold of Bavaria who inflicted a substantial defeat on a Magyar army at the battle of Wels in upper Austria.[50] Otto's brother Henry also was quite successful against the Hungarians during his reign as duke of Bavaria (948–955). In 948, Henry defeated the Hungarians near Floß on Entenbühl mountain, located in the Oberpfälzer Wald, along Bavaria's eastern frontier with Bohemia. Two years later, Henry won another victory over the Hungarians at Ticino (modern Switzerland).[51]

Otto's First Italian Campaign 951–952

As Otto settled in for the Christmas season in 950 at the royal palace at Memleben, located on the Unstrut river, he could feel confident that all of his frontiers were now relatively secure.[52] Bohemia was again a tributary of the German kingdom. Repeated Hungarian raids had been beaten back with heavy losses. Otto's role as the power broker in West Francia was unchallenged. King Conrad II of Burgundy and his kingdom stood under Otto's protection.[53] It was in this context that word reached Otto that the Lombard king, Lothar (948–950) had died on 22 November, and that Berengar II (died 966) and his son Adalbert (died c. 975) had been crowned as kings of Italy on 15 December at Pavia.[54]

Ten years earlier, in January 941, Berengar sought refuge at Otto's court along with his wife Willa.[55] Berengar had tried and failed to seize the Lombard crown from Hugh of Provence (928–945), who had ruled in Italy since 928, and paid for his failure with exile.[56] In 945, however, Berengar, who likely had continued to receive intelligence about affairs in Italy throughout his stay in Germany, decided,

48 *Annales Quedlinburgenses*, an. 937, "In eadem tempestate venientes Ungari vastaverunt Thuringiam, deinde in Saxoniam, ibique in paludibus caeterisque difficultatibus perierunt." *Annales Einsiedelnensis*, 141, dates this raid to 938, but concurs that "Interim magna pars Ungarorum a Saxonibus occisa est."
49 Regarding the system of defense in depth in Bavaria, and the importance of attacking raiders as they attempted to withdraw while loaded with booty, see Bowlus, *Lechfeld*, 47-60.
50 *Herimanni Augiensis Chronicon*, 113; *Annales Magdeburgenses*, 144; Widukind, *Res gestae*, 2.36.
51 *Annales Quedlinburgenses*, 465.
52 For Otto I's stay at Memleben, see DO I, 130.
53 Holtzmann, *Geschichte der sächsischen Kaiserzeit*, 141-146.
54 Giuseppe Sergi, "The Kingdom of Italy," in *The New Cambridge Medieval History volume III, c. 900 – c. 1024*, ed. Timothy Reuter (Cambridge, 1999), 346-371, here 355.
55 Liudprand, *Antapodosis*, 5.10.
56 Ibid., 5.10.

almost certainly with Otto's knowledge and permission, that the time was ripe for a renewed effort to topple Hugh. When Berengar arrived at Verona he was quickly joined by numerous opponents of the Lombard king. Support for Hugh rapidly dissipated, and he was forced to leave Italy altogether, transferring the royal office to his son Lothar.[57] Eventually Lothar, who still retained significant magnate support, was able to come to an agreement with Berengar, the terms of which left Lothar as king while Berengar received back his old lands and office in the march of Ivrea, and received official recognition as Lothar's "chief advisor."[58]

The death of Lothar in 950 quickly led to renewed hostilities in Italy. The partisans of Lothar's widow Adelheid, the sister of King Conrad II of Burgundy, maintained that Berengar was a usurper, and that Adelheid's next husband should be the Lombard king.[59] The German king, now thirty-eight, had been a widower since the death of his wife Edith in 946. The invitation by Adelheid's partisans for Otto to intervene in Italy on her behalf against Berengar was most welcome.[60] Obviously, Otto considered taking the widow as his new bride.

As the hegemonic figure north of the Alps, the only remaining piece of the Carolingian empire outside of Otto's direct or indirect control was the Lombard kingdom, and with it, Rome. Otto announced his plans to go to the eternal city at the Easter assembly at Aachen in 951, and ordered that preparations begin for a campaign into Italy that would take place late in the summer.[61] Widukind, Adalbert of Magdeburg, and Hrosvita of Gandersheim record that Otto's son Liudolf, whom the king had appointed to serve as duke of Swabia in 948, undertook a preliminary expedition into Italy early in the summer of 951.[62] Scholars have tended to view Liudolf's advance into Italy as an effort to steal a march on his uncle Henry, the duke of Bavaria, as part of the traditional rivalry between the dukes of Swabia and Bavaria over who would exercise greater control over affairs in the Lombard kingdom.[63]

The implication of this view is that Liudolf acted without either the knowledge or permission of his father Otto.[64] However, this interpretation owes too

---

57   Ibid., 5.26-27.
58   Ibid., 5.28.
59   Liudprand, *Historia Ottonis*, ch. 1-2.
60   Zielinski, "Der Weg nach Rom," 97-107, emphasizes the increasingly frequent communications between the German and papal courts throughout the 940s as evidence of Otto's interest in intervening in Italy. By contrast, Laudage, *Otto der Grosse*, 159-169, argues that Otto was too heavily committed in the east to be interested in Italian affairs, and that Otto did not plan to conquer Italy in 951, but rather only wished to demonstrate his hegemonic position in the west.
61   Regarding the assembly, see Flodoard, *Annales, an.* 950.
62   Widukind, *Res gestae*, 3.6; Adalbert of Magdeburg, *Continuatio*, an. 951; and Hrosvita, *Gesta Ottonis*, in *Hrotsvithae Opera*, ed. Paul von Winterfeld, MGH SRG 34 (Hanover, 1965), pp. 221-222, lines 607-623.
63   See the discussion of the literature on this topic by Käthe Sonnleitner, "Der Konflikt zwischen Otto I. und seinem Sohn Liudolf als Problem der zeitgenössischen Geschichtsschreibung," in *Festschrift Gerhard Pferschy zum 70. Geburtstag*, ed. Alfred Ableitinger (Graz, 2000), 615-625, here 615-616.
64   Keller, "Entscheidungssituationen und Lernprozesse," 36, points to a charter that Otto issued

much to hindsight regarding Liudolf's rebellion against his father in 953, and does not take into account the military realities that were involved in bringing an army over the Alps into Italy. There could be no doubt in Otto's mind that word of his invasion of Italy would reach Berengar long before the German king could mobilize the *innumeris multitudo ex omni regno suo*, which included forces from Lotharingia, Franconia, Bavaria, and Swabia, that he would command during his invasion.[65] This meant that Berengar would have the opportunity to deploy his forces in the *clusae* of the Alps to bar Otto's army from descending onto the Lombard plain through the Alpine passes, the long-established strategy that was employed frequently by Italian rulers against invaders from the north.

Hrosvita, who provides the greatest detail regarding Liudolf's preliminary foray into Italy, emphasizes that the Swabian duke mobilized his small force (*praepaucis sociis*) in secret (*secreto*).[66] Among the most common *topoi* in early medieval sources is the conceit that the army from the "home side" was very small, while the opponent's army was very large.[67] Consequently, it is not necessary to accept at face value that the duke of Swabia led a tiny force to secure the alpine passes. It is likely, however, that Liudolf's forces were dwarfed by the exceptionally large army that Otto was mobilizing for the main invasion. The most important point in Hrosvita's account is her emphasis on Liudolf's effort to move in secret, since this would provide him with the tactically important element of surprise as he moved to control the Alpine pass through which his father would march, most likely the Brenner. Hrosvita concludes her discussion of Liudolf's undertaking by emphasizing that Otto was very pleased when he received word of his son's success.[68]

When Otto's army had finally mobilized and began its crossing of the Alps, likely in early September, there was no resistance. Liudolf, who had cleared the passes and established his own Swabian expeditionary forces on the Lombard plain, rejoined his father and accompanied Otto over the Alps with the army.[69]

on 15 October 951 (DO I, 139) to Bishop Hartbert of Chur, transferring to him fiscal revenues from the *comitatus* of Chur away from the count, who at this time was Liudolf, as evidence of Otto's displeasure with his son. However, from an administrative standpoint it was important for the king to have a man in place who could coordinate the provision of supplies to the royal army as it marched toward and through the Alps. The diocese of Chur, which included a number of important royal monasteries as well as substantial fiscal resources, was pivotal in this regard. This is particularly true given that Chur controlled the alpine route from the upper Rhine over Splügen to Chiavenna, Lake Como, and on to Milan. That Otto decided Hartbert was the right man to oversee this logistical operation does not entail that the king was displeased with his son. Indeed, Otto likely had far more important tasks for his heir.

[65] For the description of the army, see *Annales Quedlinburgenses, an. 951.*
[66] Hrosvita, *Gesta Ottonis,* line 610.
[67] Delbrück, *History of the Art of War, Volume II: The Barbarian Invasions,* 227; and idem, *Numbers in History* (London, 1913), 11-12, and 14.
[68] Hrosvita, *Gesta Ottonis,* lines 614-616. Hrosvita suggests that it was only after hearing about Liudolf's success that Otto decided to invade Italy himself. This clearly was not the case because the plan for the invasion had been set in motion several months earlier during the assembly at Aachen.
[69] Widukind, *Res gestae,* 3.6.

Otto captured Pavia without opposition on 23 September and immediately began regulating matters in Italy in favor of his supporters.[70] Otto also married Adelheid, thereby securing the support of Lothar's erstwhile adherents for his own claims to rule in Italy.

Otto departed Italy in February 952 confident that matters were well in hand. He left behind Duke Conrad the Red of Lotharingia to deal with Berengar. The latter, realizing that he could not hope to prevail, came to an agreement with Conrad and accompanied him to Magdeburg, where Otto celebrated Easter in 952.[71] However, the German king did not accept the arrangements that Conrad had negotiated with Berengar, and ordered the latter to present himself at the royal assembly that was to take place on the Lechfeld, south of Augsburg, in August that same year. Augsburg was the traditional mobilization point for armies marching into Italy through the Brenner pass, and the clear implication of holding an assembly here was that Otto would invade Italy again if Berengar proved recalcitrant. At the royal assembly in August Otto imposed harsh conditions on the Lombard king, requiring him to transfer possession of the marches of Verona and Friuli, as well as Istria, to the Bavarian duke, which brought both ends of the Brenner pass under Duke Henry's control. Berengar also was required to recognize Otto's superior status in Italy, and to swear loyalty to the German king.[72]

After the assembly at Augsburg, Otto had good reason to believe that he had reaped the final fruits of the Italian campaign. However, he was to find that the new political arrangements, which favored his young wife Adelheid, as well as her potential children, and his brother Henry, would bring a much different harvest. Conrad the Red and Liudolf saw themselves increasingly excluded from the *Königsnähe* that they had enjoyed over the past decade, which led ultimately to a renewed round of rebellion against Otto's rule.[73]

The Rebellion of 953–955

The main participants in the rebellion against Otto were his son Liudolf and son-in-law Conrad the Red. They were supported in Franconia by Archbishop Frederick of Mainz (937–954). Several Saxon magnates, most prominently Wichmann the Younger and Eckbert One-Eye, the sons of Wichman the elder, joined the revolt. In Bavaria, the rebels were led by the palatine count Arnulf, one of Duke

---

70 DO I, 136-138. Berengar had fled and taken refuge at Montefeltro. See Liudprand, *Historia Ottonis*, ch. 6.

71 Adalbert of Magdeburg, *Continuatio*, an. 952.

72 Adalbert of Magdeburg, *Continuatio*, an. 952. Keller, "Entscheidungssituationen und Lernprozesse," 38, suggests that by the time he met Berengar at Augsburg, Otto had formally given up any claim to be king in Italy.

73 Regarding Liudolf's belief that he was going to be superseded by his step-mother Adelheid and her future children, and his subsequent decision to rebel against his father, see Gunther G. Wolf, "De pactis Ottonis I.," *Archiv für Diplomatik* 37 (1991), 33-48.

Arnulf's sons and also the brother-in-law of Duke Henry.[74] Finally, Berengar took the opportunity presented by the rebellion in Germany to reestablish his control over the marches of Verona and Friuli, and to renounce his loyalty to Otto.[75]

The initial plan of the two main conspirators, Liudolf and Conrad, was to capture Otto at the Easter assembly that was to be held at the royal palace at Ingelheim, and to force him to reestablish the preeminent position of the dukes among his advisors.[76] Otto received word of the plot, and set out for Mainz where he hoped to determine what position Archbishop Frederick intended to take with regard to the rebels.[77] Soon after Otto arrived at Mainz, Liudolf and Conrad rushed to the city, and there compelled the king to accept their terms, which likely included stripping Henry of his office as duke of Bavaria, securing Liudolf's status as Otto's successor, and restoring Conrad to his earlier status as chief among Otto's advisors.[78]

Within a few days, however, Otto had extricated himself from Liudolf and Conrad and was at Dortmund, where the king was joined by his brother Henry and their mother Mathilda.[79] Otto celebrated Easter Sunday at Dortmund on 3 April where he publicly rejected the agreement that had been reached at Mainz, which he insisted had been forced upon him.[80] Otto then summoned Liudolf, Conrad, and Archbishop Frederick to appear before him at a royal assembly to be held at Fritzlar.[81]

At the royal assembly, which took place in late April or early May, Otto stripped Frederick of his office as archchaplain, stripped Conrad of his ducal office in Lotharingia, and imprisoned two Thuringian counts, William of Weimar and Dedi of Hochseegau, who came to Fritzlar to beg for forgiveness for their part in the planned rebellion.[82] The king decided to postpone any decisions about Liudolf, and left his son as duke of Swabia for the time being.

Open War, 953

Despite his success in nipping in the bud any rebellion in Saxony, Otto did not achieve his main goal at the assembly at Fritzlar, namely ending the revolt by Conrad and Liudolf. In order to bring the rebellion in the west to a rapid conclusion, Otto used the same plan of action that he had successfully implemented in

---

74 For a detailed reconstruction of the events in 953–954, see Holtzmann, *Geschichte der sächsischen Kaiserzeit*, 152-162.

75 Regarding Berengar's reacquisition of the march of Friuli, see Adalbert of Magdeburg, *Continuatio, an.* 956, who depicts the Lombard king as in control of all of Italy before Liudolf's invasion that year.

76 Adalbert of Magdeburg, *Continuatio, an.* 953.

77 Ibid., and Widukind, *Res gestae,* 3.13-15.

78 See the discussion by Holtzmann, *Geschichte der sächsischen Kaiserzeit,* 154.

79 Widukind, *Res gestae,* 3.14-15.

80 Ibid.

81 For the proceedings at Fritzlar, see Flodoard, *Annales, an.* 953; and Adalbert of Magdeburg, *Continuatio, an.* 954 (misdated by a year).

82 Widukind, *Res gestae,* 3.16.

Saxony in 938. He led a substantial army, composed of both Saxon and Bavarian troops, into Lotharingia where he captured numerous fortifications that were held by garrisons loyal to the erstwhile Duke Conrad, including the fortress at Breisach.[83] Otto was aided by Count Reginar III of Hainault, who remained loyal to Otto during the rebellion of 953.[84] Following these successful operations in Lotharingia, Otto set out for Franconia, where he intended to capture the fortress city of Mainz, then being held by Liudolf and Conrad.[85]

Even as he maintained his aggressive siege of Mainz in the late summer of 953, Otto continued his efforts to work out a peaceful settlement with his son. However, despite a face-to-face meeting in the royal camp outside the walls of Mainz, these negotiations remained fruitless. The principal stumbling block was that Liudolf refused to hand over his main conspirators to Otto for judgment. The failure of the negotiations led to a substantial backlash in Otto's army as many of his magnates no longer wished to fight a civil war simply to maintain Henry as duke of Bavaria.[86] At the same time, the count palatine of Bavaria, Arnulf, rose in rebellion against Henry and drove out most of the duke's supporters in Bavaria, including his own sister Judith, Henry's wife.[87] Liudolf escaped during the confusion at Mainz, and made his way south to join Arnulf at Regensburg.

At this point, at the end of September 953, Otto decided that he was unlikely to capture, in the near term, the city of Mainz, which, despite the departure of Liudolf, was still defended by Conrad's household troops (*milites*), Archbishop Frederick's household troops (*milites*), and the urban population itself, which likely numbered in excess of 30,000 people.[88] Otto's army had now been in the field for almost five months. According to Widukind, the men were exhausted by their extended service.[89] As a consequence, the king dismissed the levies and permitted them to return home. He then began a campaign into Bavaria to pursue his son, accompanied by only his royal household troops.[90]

As he marched toward Bavaria, Otto sent riders ahead to summon his *fideles* to join the royal army, along with their military households. Among those who heeded Otto's call was Bishop Ulrich of Augsburg (923–973), whose diocese

---

83   Ibid., 3.18.

84   Flodoard, *Annales, an.* 953.

85   Flodoard, *Annales, an.* 953; Adalbert of Magdeburg, *Continuatio, an.* 953; Ruotger, *Vita Brunonis*, ed. Walter Berschin and Angelika Häse (Heidelberg, 1993), ch. 16; *Annales Quedlinburgenses, an.* 953; Widukind, *Res gestae*, 3.21

86   Widukind, *Res gestae*, 3.20.

87   Ibid.

88   For the *milites* of Conrad and Archbishop Frederick at Mainz, see Flodoard, *Annales, an.* 953; and Ruotger, *Vita Brunonis*, ch. 16. Regarding the population of Mainz, see Paul Bairoch, Jean Batou, and Pierre Chèver, *La population des villes européennes de 800 à 1850* (Geneva, 1988), 7.

89   Widukind, *Res gestae*, 3.21, "*exercitus diutino labore fatigatus.*"

90   Ibid., 3.26. Widukind's emphasis on the small size of the royal column that participated in this campaign is in marked contrast to his frequent emphasis on the very large armies that the king normally took on campaign. In describing Otto's invasion of Bohemia in July 950, for example, Widukind stressed that Duke Boleslav decided against attempting to hold the fortress of Prague against the German king because of the immense size of the German army. See Widukind, *Res gestae*, 3.8.

was located along the Swabian-Bavarian frontier.[91] Otto spent the next several months operating in Bavaria, but because of the small size of his army, and his lack of siege equipment, much of which had been destroyed during the siege of Mainz, he was unable to bring the Bavarians to heel.[92] As Widukind reports, "The Bavarians did not seek peace following the king's sudden advance, nor did they seek battle. Instead, enclosed behind their walls, they abandoned their lands and prepared to fend off the army."[93]

Otto withdrew from Bavaria in December 953 with Liudolf still ensconced at Regensburg. However, in Lotharingia the royalist forces continued to enjoy success. Brun, Otto's youngest brother and newly appointed archbishop of Cologne, was named as the Lotharingian duke in September. Conrad, who had departed Mainz at some point after Otto's withdrawal, had been unable to salvage his position, failing in an effort to capture and hold the city of Metz.[94]

The Final Stage of the Revolt, 954–955

Otto was poised for a major invasion of both Swabia and Bavaria in the spring of 954 when a major raid by the Hungarians changed the entire political calculus of the revolt.[95] Liudolf and Conrad were widely seen as having invited the Hungarians to intervene in Germany on their behalf, and even to have been responsible for providing guides so that raiders could pass safely through the defenses of Bavaria.[96] Ultimately, the Hungarian raids into Franconia and Lotharingia failed because the mounted archers had no way of dealing with the numerous fortified centers into which the populations retreated with their belongings.[97] However, political support for the rebels collapsed in light of their perceived alliance with the Hungarians. Conrad surrendered and sought Otto's forgiveness.[98] Otto's supporters in Swabia, led by Bishop Ulrich of Augsburg, gained the upper hand against Liudolf's loyalists after the bishop and his brother Count Dietpald inflicted a crushing defeat on the rebels at the battle of Mantahinga.[99] Even in Bavaria the political mood swung against the rebels, leaving Liudolf, Count Pala-

---

91   Gerhard of Augsburg, *Vita Sancti Uodalrici*, ed. Walter Berschin and Angelika Häse (Heidelberg, 1993), 1.10.

92   Widukind, *Res gestae*, 3.18.

93   Ibid., 3.26, "Boiarii repentino regis adventu nec ad pacem vertuntur nec bellum publicum presumunt, sed clausi muris grandem exercitui laborem suaeque regionis solitudinem parant."

94   Ruotger, *Vita Brunonis*, ch. 24.

95   Regarding the raids by the Hungarians, particularly in Franconia and Lotharingia, see *Gesta episcoporum Cameracensium Liber I. II. III. usque ad a. 1051*, ed. L. C. Bethmann, MGH SS 7, 428; Sigebert of Gembloux, *Vita Wicberti*, ed. W. Wattenbach, MGH SS 8 (Hanover, 1858), 513-514; and John of St. Arnoul, *Vita Iohannis Abbatis Gorziensis*, MGH SS 4, 355-356.

96   See in this context, Ruotger, *Vita Brunonis*, ch. 24.

97   *Gesta episcoporum Cameracensium Liber I.*, 428; Sigebert, *Vita Wicberti*, 513-514; and *Vita Iohannis Abbatis Gorziensis*, 355-356.

98   Widukind, *Res gestae*, 3.42.

99   Gerhard, *Vita Sancti Uodalrici*, 1.10.

tine Arnulf, and their most devoted followers, holding just Regensburg and a few fortifications in its environs.[100]

In mid June 954, the king led a large army to the Bavarian town of Langen-zenn, approximately 20 kilometers west of Nuremberg, to a pre-arranged meeting with the Bavarian magnates and Liudolf.[101] After failing to agree to terms Liudolf withdrew in the night and Otto pursued him, stopping first at the powerful fortress of Roßtal, located 20 kilometers south of Nuremberg, which was held by Liudolf's ally, the count of Hammerstein.[102]

After an initial assault on Roßtal failed to take the fortress by storm, Otto decided to bypass it, likely leaving a small force to keep the garrison there under surveillance, and then advanced to Regensburg.[103] Having absorbed the lessons of his failure the previous winter, Otto brought with him not only a large army, but also a substantial siege train to undertake his investment of the fortress city of Regensburg.[104] Liudolf and Arnulf used a variety of tactics to attempt to break the king's siege of the city, including a daring two-pronged assault against Otto's camp.[105] In the end, however, Liudolf and his supporters were forced to surren-der.[106] The city of Mainz surrendered in October 954 following intermittent siege operations of more than fifteen months.[107]

Otto, who had received word of serious disturbances along the lower Elbe frontier while conducting the siege of Regensburg in the summer of 954, then hurried back to Saxony, leaving his brother Henry in charge of the mopping up operations. Liudolf had agreed to his father's terms, but this entailed handing over his most devoted loyalists to royal justice. These men refused to accept Otto's conditions, and withdrew into the old city of Regensburg, which was protected by the Roman walls. It was not until April 955, when Otto returned to Bavaria with a large army and siege train, that he and Henry were able to compel these last holdouts to surrender.[108]

The Lechfeld Campaign

Following this final success at Regensburg in April 955, Otto was again called back to Saxony by continuing Slavic unrest, which was instigated in large part by Wichmann the Younger, who sought to undermine the position of his uncle Hermann Billung as the commander of the northern Saxon march

100 Widukind, *Res gestae*, 3.31-32.
101 Ibid.
102 Ibid., 3.35, for the assault on the fortress. Regarding the identity of the defending commander, see Peter Ettel, "Der Befestigungsbau im 10. Jahrhundert in Süddeutschland und die Rolle Ottos des Großen am Beispiel der Burg von Roßtal," *Europa im 10. Jahrhundert*, 365-379, here 373.
103 Widukind, *Res gestae*, 3.36.
104 Ibid.
105 Ibid.
106 Ibid., 3.38-41.
107 Ibid., 3.41.
108 Ibid., 3.43.

and royal viceroy in the Saxon regnum.[109] While Otto was listening to reports about attacks into German-controlled lands by the Slavs, and preparations that were being made for a larger Slavic uprising, he received word in July from his brother Duke Henry that the Hungarians had again launched a major raid into Bavaria.[110] The king quickly decided to march south with only a small force of Saxon troops, and issued orders for the mobilization of the Swabian, Bavarian, and Franconian, as well as the Bohemian expeditionary levies to join him as he prepared to meet the Hungarian army.[111]

This Hungarian invasion was unlike any previous raid, as the goal was the capture of a major fortified city rather than mere raiding for plunder.[112] The target of their invasion in 955 was Augsburg. To this end, the Hungarian army, for the first time, included both large numbers of men who were trained to fight on foot and a siege train.[113] One likely source for up-to-date technology and training would seem to have been the Byzantines with whom the Hungarians had a long, albeit often contentious, relationship.[114] Of particular interest to the Byzantines in the early 950s, of course, was Otto's invasion of Italy in 951–952, and his obvious interest in extending German power south, at least to Rome, and perhaps even into the Byzantine sphere of influence in Apulia and Calabria.[115] The commander of the Magyar army at Augsburg in 955, Bulcsu, had spent a considerable amount of time in Constantinople, and had even been given a high court office by Emperor Constantine VI (913–959).[116] The decision by Bulcsu to undertake a major change in strategy vis-à-vis the Ottonian kingdom may well have been developed in conjunction with the Byzantines.[117] The capture of Augsburg would

---

[109] Widukind, *Res gestae*, 3.44; and Thietmar, *Chronicon*, 2.9.

[110] Widukind, *Res gestae*, 3.44.

[111] Bowlus, *Lechfeld*, 108-112.

[112] See the discussion here by Bachrach, "Magyar-Ottonian Warfare," 224-230.

[113] Gerhard, *Vita Sancti Uodalrici*, 1.12, "*diversa ferens instrumenta ad depositionem murorum.*"

[114] The indigenous populations of Pannonia, which were ruled by the Hungarians, had had access to sophisticated siege technology since the later sixth century. See the discussion by Speros Vryonis Jr, "The Evolution of Slavic Society and the Slavic Invasions of Greece: The First Major Slavic Attack on Thessaloniki, A.D. 597," *Hespia* 50 (1981), 378-90; Jim Bradbury, *The Medieval Siege* (Woodbridge, 1992), 10-11, 16, 19, 29, 54-55; and W. T. S. Tarver, "The Traction Trebuchet: A Reconstruction of an Early Medieval Siege Engine," *Technology and Culture* 36 (1995), 136-167, here 144-145; with a synthesis by Bachrach, "Magyar-Ottonian Warfare," 224-225.

[115] Regarding Byzantine rule in Southern Italy during the 950s and 960s, see Barbara M. Kreutz, *Before the Normans: Southern Italy in the Ninth and Tenth Centuries* (Philadelphia, 1991), 94-102; and Graham Loud, "Byzantium and Southern Italy (876–1000)," *The Cambridge History of the Byzantine Empire c. 500–1492* (Cambridge, 2008), 560-582, here 562-565.

[116] Büttner, "Die Ungarn das Reich und Europa bis zur Lechfeldschlacht des Jahres 955," 150, observes that the Hungarian leader Bulcsu spent considerable time in Constantinople in the years before the Lechfeld campaign. Also see the observations of C. A. Macartney, *The Magyars in the Ninth Century*, 2nd edn (Cambridge, 1968), 114-116.

[117] Leyser, "The Battle at the Lech," 48, asserts that the Hungarians had no interest in territorial conquest. This claim, in light of the Hungarian conquest of Pannonia, is not tenable. Concerning the Hungarian conquest of Pannonia, and their defense of this region through the establishment of fortifications, see Sabine Felgenhauer-Schmiedt, "Herrschaftszentren und Burgenbau des 10.

give the Hungarians control over access to the Brenner pass, and facilitate their crossing of the Alps by this route.

Otto arrived with his army in the environs of Augsburg on 9 August 955 to find the city under close siege by the Hungarians. The German king decided to launch an attack on the Hungarian camp the next day, the tenth, in an effort to break the siege. The battle itself was a draw. The Hungarians enjoyed an initial success when one column launched an attack on Otto's baggage train, which was defended by a contingent of Bohemian troops, who had been sent by Duke Boleslav I in response to a summons by the German king. The Bohemians were quickly over-run, and the Hungarians also succeeded in defeating a contingent of Swabian troops. However, a counter-attack led by Conrad the Red, who had been received back into Otto's good graces, overwhelmed the Hungarians and drove them off.[118]

After the initial setback had been made good by Conrad's victorious cavalry charge, Otto launched a general assault on the main Hungarian army. Although very bloody – among the casualties was Conrad who was killed by an arrow that struck him in the throat – this main part of the battle also was a draw. The Hungarians withdrew in good order from the field, but abandoned their camp. It was in the aftermath of the battle that the Germans won their overwhelming victory.[119]

Bavaria, like Thuringia and Saxony, was protected by a well developed system of defense in depth, which had been expanded continually throughout the first half of the tenth century.[120] By 955, every significant river ford, forest road, swamp path, and mountain pass was protected by fortifications that were manned by both garrisons of professional soldiers and by local levies that were mobilized in times of war.[121] Thus, even under normal circumstances, the Hungarians would have faced significant difficulties in withdrawing from Bavaria once orders had been issued for the levies to mobilize and man their forts. However, the summer of 955 was particularly rainy, and all of the rivers in Bavaria, which normally

---

Jahrhunderts in Niederösterreich. Neue archäologische Forschungen im nördlichen Grenzgebiet," *Europa im 10. Jahrhundert*, 381-395.

[118] The most detailed accounts of the fighting are provided by Gerhard, an eyewitness to the battle, in his *Vita Uodalrici*, 1.12; and by Widukind, *Res gestae*, 3.53-4, and 3.56. The basic account of the battle is now Bowlus, *Lechfeld*, 104-129.

[119] Bowlus, *Lechfeld*, 131-162.

[120] Scholars have devoted considerable attention to various elements of this system of defense in depth, which dates back at least to the early tenth century, and likely to the last quarter of the ninth, as the threat from the Great Moravian kingdom became more acute. For the early development of fortifications along the Bavarian frontiers, see Mitterauer, "Burgbezirke und Burgwerkleistung in der babenbergischen Mark," 217-231; Leopold Auer, "Zum Kriegswesen unter den früheren Baben-bergern," *Jahrbuch für Landeskunde von Niederösterreich* 42 (1976), 9-25, particularly 10-15; Rudolf Büttner, "Die Wehrorganisation der frühen Babenbergerzeit im Einzelhofgebiet der Bezirke Melk und Scheibbs," *Verein für Landeskunde von Niederösterreich* 42 (1976), 26-37; and the synthesis of this scholarly tradition by Bowlus, *Lechfeld*, 82-85.

[121] The success of the Bavarian system of defense in depth is described in detailed by Bowlus, *Lechfeld*, 138-152.

might be forded in multiple places during typically dry summer months, were raging torrents. What began as an orderly retreat from the Lechfeld therefore turned into a rout as the Hungarian army fragmented into small groups of men who sought, in vain, to find a way home. Pressed from their rear by Otto's army, and hemmed in on all sides by local militia forces, the Hungarian army was virtually annihilated, its leaders captured, and then hanged in a public spectacle in Regensburg.[122]

Drive to the East 955–965

The Battle of Recknitz

Following his victory over the Hungarians, Otto hurried back to Saxony where he assumed direct control over a punitive expedition against the Obodrites that was intended to restore security to the lower Elbe frontier region. Over the past year there had been numerous Slavic raids into the northern march, some of which had been commanded by the rebel counts and brothers Wichmann and Eckbert One-Eye.[123] Hermann Billung, Otto's loyal military commander along the entire northern tier of the frontier, had succeeded in defeating these raids by his nephews, but a counter-raid by Count Thiadrich of the *pagus* of Norththuringia against the Obodrites was unsuccessful.[124] Further south and east, the frontier commander Gero had succeeded in inflicting significant losses on the Ukrani, a northern Weleti people, bringing back immense booty (*preda ingens*).[125]

Despite the successes by both Hermann Billung and Gero, when Otto arrived at Magdeburg, likely in the first week of September, and received reports there, he learned that a general revolt against German rule had broken out, led by two Obodrite princes named Nacco and Stoignew. Otto immediately mobilized a large army with the intention of bringing the uprising to a rapid conclusion by assaulting the heartland of the Obodrites in eastern Holstein and the western regions of the modern German state of Mecklenburg-Vorpommern.[126] From

---

[122] The triumph is recorded by Widukind, *Res gestae*, 3.48.

[123] Ibid., 3.50 and 3.52.

[124] Ibid., 3.45.

[125] Ibid., 3.42. See the discussion by Volker Schmidt, *Drense: Eine Hauptburg der Ukrane*, 55, regarding the system of defense-in-depth focused on fortified centers that had been constructed by the Ukrani.

[126] The basic work on the settlement areas of the Obodrites is Joachim Herrmann, *Siedlung, Wirtschaft und gesellschaftliche Verhältnisse der slawischen Stämme zwischen Oder/Neiße und Elbe* (Berlin, 1968). But also see the important study by Friedmann, *Untersuchungen zur Geschichte des abodritischen Fürstentums*, particularly 180-230, for Obodrite relations with Henry I and Otto I. A total of thirty-five Obodrite fortifications have been identified in eastern Holstein and western Mecklenburg-Vorpommern. See Torsten Kempke, "Bemerkungen zur Delvenau-Stecknitz-Route im frühen Mittelalter," *Hammaburg: Vor-und frühgeschichtliche Forschungen aus dem niederelbischen Raum* 9 (1989), 175-184, here 175. This accounts for approximately seventy percent of the fifty-three fortifications listed by the so-called Bavarian Geographer in the lands of the Obodrites from the mid-ninth century.

Magdeburg, it was a march of some 260 kilometers north-north-east, over Havelberg, to the valley of the Recknitz river. Here, on 15 October, at a ford located near the modern town of Ribnitz-Damgarten, Otto was confronted by an enormous Obodrite army (*ingens exercitus*) under the command of the two Slavic princes.[127] Otto ordered the deployment of archers as well as siege engines (*machinae*), which might have included both stone-throwing and spear-hurling equipment, to keep the attention of the Obodrites at the ford. He then dispatched a flying column under the command of Gero, which included both German troops and Slavic allies, to construct three bridges further downstream out of sight of the enemy.[128]

When Gero sent word back to the king that the bridges were completed, Otto dispatched his mounted forces, consisting largely of the military house-holds of his magnates (*milites*), to cross the bridge and launch a flank attack on the Slavs.[129] The Obodrite foot soldiers could not move quickly enough to stop Otto's mounted troops, and so were caught in a pincer of foot soldiers attacking across the ford, protected by their archers and engines, and the mounted forces attacking them from the flank. The Slavic army disintegrated during the attack, and their prince Stoignew was killed during the retreat.[130]

In the immediate aftermath of his victory on the Recknitz, Otto inflicted considerable damage through much of the Obodrite heartland. The reports of devastation found in Widukind's *Res gestae Saxoniae* have been confirmed through archaeological excavations.[131] A detailed study of the important cult and trading center at Groß Raden, approximately 70 kilometers south-west of the battle site, suggests that this place was sacked in 955.[132] Similarly, archaeologists also have been able to date to 955 the sudden, catastrophic destruction of the substantial fortification at Klempenow, some 80 kilometers, as the crow flies, south-east of the battlefield on the Recknitz.[133]

---

[127] Widukind, *Res gestae*, 3.53-55.

[128] Ibid., 3.54.

[129] Ibid.

[130] In this context, Widukind, *Res gestae*, 3.55, draws attention to the reward earned by a soldier named Hosed who was awarded 20 *mansi* by Otto I for killing Stoignew. DO I 133, issued on 27 July 951, similarly records a grant of property by Otto I to a *miles* named Walpert for his service against the Slavs.

[131] Widukind, *Res gestae*, 3.53.

[132] Regarding the temple site at Groß Raden, see Rolf Voss, "Der altslawische Tempelort Groß Raden in Mecklenburg," in *Europas Mitte um 1000*, ed. Alfred Wieczorek and Hans Hinz (Stutt-gart, 2000), 252-256. Concerning the fortification at Groß Raden, see *Corpus archäologischer Quellen*, 124. Regarding the important role played by Groß Raden in trade along the Baltic Sea, see Joachim Herrmann, "Reric-Ralswiek-Groß Raden. Seehandelplätze und Burgen an der südlichen Ostseeküste," *Lübecker Schriften zur Archäologie und Kulturgeschichte* 9 (1984), 91-96. Regarding the destruction of Groß Raden in 955, see idem, "Der Lutizenaufstand 983. Zu den geschichtlichen Voraussetzungen und den historischen Wirkungen," *Zeitschrift für Archäologie* 18 (1984), 9-17, here 16.

[133] Jens Ulrich, "Der Burgwall von Klempenow, Lkr. Demmin," *Archäologische Berichte aus Meck-lenburg-Vorpommern* 11 (2004), 28-38, here 33.

Drive to the Oder

Despite Otto's immense victory over the Obodrites on the Recknitz, and his subsequent devastation of the Obodrite heartland, he was not able to break completely Slavic resistance to German rule. According to Widukind, it was the arch-rebel Wichmann the Younger who again stirred up trouble, this time among the Redarii.[134] In both 957 and 958, Otto personally led campaigns against the Redarii, and compelled them to recognize his authority and to pay tribute.[135] In 960, Otto again led a campaign into Slavic lands that took him all the way to the Oder.[136] The destruction of the fortification at Reitwein, located on the modern frontier between Germany and Poland, is likely to be dated to this campaign.[137]

Fortress Districts (*Burgwarde*) in the Trans-Elben Lands

In order to intensify direct control over the lands of the Obodrites and Weleti, Otto introduced an extensive system of fortress districts in which garrisons were to be supported by taxes imposed on local Slavic populations.[138] The most intensive development of this system took place in the lands of the Hevelli. At least seventeen fortress districts, with substantial garrisons, were established along the valley of the Havel, east from Brandenburg toward the Oder.

Further to the south, in Fläming, Otto rebuilt or expanded numerous Slavic fortresses that had been captured earlier and provided them with German garrisons. In this context, the establishment of a German fortification over an earlier Slavic settlement at Luckenwalde, on the eastern slope of the Fläming hills, forty kilometers south of modern Berlin, also is likely to be connected with this period of consolidation of Ottonian rule up to the Oder.[140] Similarly, within the Fläming hills, Otto occupied and substantially rebuilt numerous Hevelli fortifications that originally were taken by Henry I in the context of his capture of Brandenburg in 929. Along the upper course of the Plane river these included Niemegk, Mörz and Fredersdorf.[141] Just to the east Otto garrisoned

---

134 Widukind, *Res gestae*, 3.58.

135 Ibid., and Flodoard, *Annales, an.* 958.

136 Adalbert of Magdeburg, *Continuatio, an.* 960.

137 Klaus Grebe, "Ein Wallprofil vom Burgwall Reitwein und seine Auswertung für die Geschichte der Anlage," *Ausgrabungen und Funde* 27 (1982), 274-275, here 274.

138 Joachim Herrmann and Richard Hoffmann, "Neue Forschungen zum slawischen und frühdeutschen Burgwall 'Räuberberg' bei Phöben, Kr. Potsdam Land," *Ausgrabungen und Funde* 4 (1959), 294-306.

139 With regard to the fortress districts in Havelland, see Billig, *Die Burgwardorganisation im obersächsisch-meissnischen Raum*, 15; and Herrmann and Hoffmann, "Phöben," 294-306.

140 Thomas Kersting, "Die Burg von Luckenwalde am Niederen Fläming, Brandenburg: Bodendenkmalpflege und Landesgeschichte," *Cum grano salis: Beiträge zur europäischen Vor- und Frühgeschichte: Festschrift für Volker Bierbrauer zum 65. Geburtstag* (Friedberg, 2005), 331-338.

141 Herrmann, "Belizi 997-Beltz-Belzig," 196.

the important fortress at Belzig.[142] These fortifications became the center of German fortress districts in the period after 955.[143]

Conquest of the Lusatia 963

In addition to rebellions, the main threat to German hegemony in the region between the lower Elbe and the Oder was the rising power of the incipient Polish state under the leadership of Miesco I (c. 960–992).[144] Miesco, who hoped to establish his power westwards up to the Oder river, imposed tributary status on a number of Slavic polities in the Lausatian region.[145] In 963, while Otto was fully engaged in Italy, Margrove Gero undertook a wide-ranging offensive against Miesco along the entire frontier between the Polish and German spheres of influence. Wichmann the Younger, in view of his long-established relationships with a number of Slavic princes, was recruited by Gero to enlist the Redarii to campaign against the Poles.[146] Wichmann, who was now operating with the full support of the German kingdom, defeated the Polish duke in two battles, and succeeded in capturing considerable booty as well as killing Miesco's brother. While Wichmann was leading attacks against the Poles from the north-west, Gero invaded Lausatia, where the local princes of two peoples, the Milceni and Lutizi, had recognized Miesco's authority.[147] The numerous Slavic fortifications in the district were neutralized, and many of them were then occupied by German troops.[148] Over the course of the 960s, the entire region subsequently was organized into fortress districts of the same type that Otto was also developing at that same time in the lands of the Hevelli.[149]

Lotharingia and the West Frankish Kingdom, 955–965

While Otto was devoting enormous energy and military resources to pacifying the trans-Elben Slavs, his brother Brun took the leading role in maintaining the hegemonic position of the German kingdom in the West. Otto's initial effort to establish his brother Brun as duke of Lotharingia faced serious challenges from some local magnates, particularly Count Reginar III of Hainault, who had

---

[142] Ibid.

[143] Ibid.

[144] Jerzy Strezelczyk, "Bohemia and Poland: Two Examples of Successful Slavonic State Formation," *Cambridge Medieval History vol. III c. 900–c. 1024*, 514-535, here 523-525.

[145] Adalbert of Magdeburg, *Continuatio, an.* 963; and Widukind, *Res gestae*, 3.66. See the discussion by Wolfgang Brüske, *Untersuchungen zur Geschichte des Lutizenbundes: Deutsch-wendische Beziehungen des 10.-12. Jahrhunderts* (Cologne, 1955), 29-31.

[146] Widukind, *Res gestae*, 3.66.

[147] Adalbert of Magdeburg, *Continuatio, an.* 963; and Widukind, *Res gestae*, 3.66.

[148] This was the case, for example, at Lübbenau, Lkr. Oberspreewald-Lausitz and Groß Lübbenau, Kr. Calau. See in this context, Kirsch and Mehner, "Der Schloßberg von Lübbenau", 203-222; and Horst Rösler, "Ein altslawischer Burgwall mit frühdeutscher Überbauung von Groß Lübbenau, Kr. Calau," *Ausgrabungen und Funde* 28 (1983), 85-90.

[149] With regard to the fortress districts established during Otto I's reign, see J. Huth, "Die Burgwarde der Oberlausitz," *Letopis B* 28.2 (981), 132-161.

hoped to gain the ducal office for himself.[150] As a consequence, during the period 955–957 Brun undertook a systematic campaign to destroy adulterine fortifications in Lotharingia, and succeeded in depriving his primary rival, Reginar, of his office as count.[151]

Despite these challenges, Brun still was able to mobilize the military forces of Lotharingia in the service of Otto I's policies in the West Frankish kingdom. In 957, Brun led a Lotharingian army through West Francia into the duchy of Burgundy, where he provided military aid to his nephew, the West Frankish King Lothair IV.[152] In 959, Brun again intervened in West Francia, on this occasion settling a dispute between King Lothair and Brun's other nephews, Hugh Capet, Odo and Odo-Henry, the sons of Hugh the Great, concerning the possession of fortifications in the duchy of Burgundy.[153] The very next year, Brun led a substantial Lotharingian army into Burgundy with which he aided Lothair in the siege of the fortress city of Dijon.[154]

Italy 957–965

Liudolf's Last Campaign, Italy 957

After initially settling affairs against the Obodrites in 955, Otto turned his attention again to Italy where Berengar was the last of the rebels of 953 who still maintained power. According to Adalbert of Magdeburg, it was Brun who suggested to his brother Otto that he send Liudolf to Italy to deal with the Lombard king, and restore German hegemony there.[155] The King's son was to be given a chance to redeem himself for the rebellion of 954–954. In September 956, Liudolf set out for Italy to seize power. As had been true of Otto's invasion five years earlier, Liudolf succeeded in driving Berengar and his son Adalbert out of Pavia and gaining recognition for his father's supremacy throughout most of northern Italy.[156] After almost a year in Italy, however, Liudolf succumbed to an illness, and died in September 957 at Pombia, south of Lake Maggiore.[157] Within a short period, word reached Otto, while he was campaigning against the Redarii, that his son had died and that Italy again had fallen out of his grasp.[158]

Conquest of Italy and Imperial Coronation 961–962

Otto was too heavily engaged in pacifying the region between the Elbe and

---

[150] Sproemberg, "Die lothringische Politik Ottos des Großen," 55-57.
[151] Flodoard, *Annales*, ann. 957, 959; Adalbert of Magdeburg, *Continuatio*, an. 958.
[152] Ibid., *an.* 958.
[153] Ibid., *an.* 959.
[154] Ibid., *an.* 960.
[155] Ruotger, *Vita Brunonis*, c. 36.
[156] This campaign was widely recorded. See *Annales Einsiedelnensis, an.* 956; Adalbert of Magdeburg, *Continuatio, an.* 956, Hrosvita, *Vita Ottonis,* lines 1142-1163; Flodoard, *Annales, an.* 957; and Widukind, *Res gestae,* 3.57.
[157] Hrosvita, *Vita Ottonis,* line 1164.
[158] Widukind, *Res gestae,* 3.58

the Oder to undertake any new initiatives in Italy up through the end of 960. However, Berengar's decision in 959 to attempt to extend his rule southwards over both the duchy of Spoleto and the papal state itself provided Otto with a renewed opportunity to intervene in the peninsula.[159] In face of this developing threat to his power in Rome, Pope John XII dispatched legates to the German king in the autumn of 960 begging for his aid.[160]

When the papal legates arrived in Germany and came to the Christmas court at Regensburg, Otto had just completed three years of heavy campaigning against the Slavs, during the course of which he successfully pacified the entire region between the Elbe and the Oder.[161] The king had reason to feel confident that he would have quiet along his eastern frontier, and among his Slavic tributaries. As a consequence, it would be possible for him to undertake a renewed offensive south of the Alps. It is in this context that Otto ordered a kingdom wide royal assembly (placitum regalis) to be held in May 961, where orders would be issued for the mobilization of an army for the invasion of Italy.[162]

The king left nothing to chance in this invasion. Several German prelates, as well as Otto's close military advisor Margrove Gero, had made numerous trips to Rome over the previous several years and almost certainly provided the king with detailed information about the military resources as well as the political factions, both in the eternal city, and in northern and central Italy more generally.[163] In order to deal with all of the possible threats, Otto ordered the mobilization of an enormous army with which to crush all opposition in Italy.[164] The assembly point was set for Augsburg, from where it was an easy march to the Brenner pass.[165] From the outset of this campaign, which began in the autumn of 961, the German army met little resistance all the way to Pavia.[166] Rather than face Otto, Berengar, his wife Willa, and his heir Adalbert, all took refuge in inaccessible fortifications in the eastern Appenine mountains hoping to wait out the German king as they had done in 951.[167]

---

[159] Regarding the opening provided to Otto by Berengar's southern campaign, see Zielinski, "Der Weg nach Rom," 102-103.

[160] Liudprand, Historia Ottonis, ch. 1; Adalbert of Magdeburg, Continuatio, an. 960.

[161] For the Christmas court at Regensburg, see Adalbert of Magdeburg, Continuatio, an. 960.

[162] Annales Sancti Nazarii, ed. C. L. Bethmann, MGH SS 17 (Hanover, 1861), an. 962; Adalbert of Magdeburg, Continuatio, an. 961.

[163] Regarding the frequent contact between Otto and the papal court, see Zielinski, "Der Weg nach Rom," 99-102.

[164] Regarding the observations of contemporary and near contemporary writers that Otto's army was enormous, see Rodulfi Glabri Historiarum Libri Quinque: Rodulfus Glaber Five Books of Histories, ed. and trans. John France (Oxford, 1989), 24, "Sed mox ut Otto hoc factum comperit, ira accensus cum permaximo exercitu Romam properavit"; Adalbert of Magdeburg, Continuatio, an. 961 " Rex in Italiam ire disponens maximam suorum fidelium multitudinem Wormatie coadunavit ..."; and Benedicti Sancti Andreas Chronicon, ed. G. Zucchetti (Rome, 1920) in Fonti per la Storia d'Italia 55, ch. 56, "tanta pene multitudo gentis in Italia, que sic impleverunt faciem terre." These forces included a substantial number of men from the expeditionary levy of Lotharingia whom Brun dispatched at his brother's command. See Vita Brunonis, ch. 41.

[165] Annales Sangallenses maiores, MGH SS 1 (Hanover, 1826), 79.

[166] Benedicti Sancti Andreas Chronicon, ch. 56; Liudprand, Historia Ottonis, ch. 2.

[167] Benedicti Sancti Andreas Chronicon, ch. 56.

This time, however, Otto had no intention of departing from Italy before completing its conquest and being crowned emperor. When Otto was established at Pavia, he appointed a raft of loyalists to important offices throughout Lombardy, including the historian Liudprand who received the bishopric of Cremona.[168] Otto then dispatched his trusted advisor, Abbot Hatto of Fulda (956–968), to make arrangements with Pope John XII for the German king to be received at Rome and crowned as emperor.[169]

Following these successful negotiations, Otto marched his army south to Rome and arrived in the environs of the city in late January, making his camp at Monte Mario, two kilometers north-west of the modern Vatican palace.[170] A few days later, on 2 February, Otto was crowned emperor. Over the next twelve days a synod of German and Italian bishops under the joint leadership of Otto and John XII worked out the details of the German king's establishment of a new archbishopric at Magdeburg, which was to be the metropolitan see over the eastern bishoprics of Brandenburg, Havelberg, and the soon to be established bishoprics at Meißen, Zeitz, and Merseburg, as well as the center for the Christian mission to the Slavs, both west and east of the Oder.[171]

Immediately after settling affairs at Rome, Otto departed for Pavia on 14 February to oversee mopping up operations against Berengar and his remaining adherents. Otto established sieges at a series of fortifications, including San Giulio in Lago di Orta (near Novara), where Willa had sought refuge, and San Leo de Montefeltre, south-west of San Marino, where Berengar himself was ensconced.[172] The last of the fortresses finally surrendered at the end of 963, and the erstwhile Lombard king along with his wife Willa and their daughters were sent into captivity north of the Alps at Bamberg.

The Problem of Rome 963–964

As it became clear that Otto intended his conquest of Lombardy to be permanent, Pope John began mobilizing all of the German king's opponents in a bid to ward off what he feared would be the imposition of direct German control over the papal state. To this end, the pope invited Berengar's son Adalbert to come to Rome, and swore to support him against Otto.[173] Otto reacted swiftly. With the surrender of Berengar at St Leo imminent in October 963, the German ruler

---

168 Otto's charters during this period provide good insight into his intervention in northern Italian affairs. See DO I, 234-35, and DO I, 237-249.

169 For the charter that Hatto received from Pope John XII on 10 December 961, see *Codex Diplomaticus Fuldensis*, ed. E. F. J. Dronke (Fulda, 1850, repr. Aalen, 1962), nr. 711, pp. 328-9; and Adalbert of Magdeburg, *Continuatio*, an. 961. Regarding the diplomatic service of the abbots of Fulda under Otto I, particularly in connection with the papacy, see Christian Lubeck, "Die Äbte von Fulda als Politiker Ottos des Großen," *Historisches Jahrbuch* 71 (1952), 273-304.

170 Liudprand, *Historia Ottonis*, ch. 2; and Adalbert of Magdeburg, *Continuatio*, an. 962.

171 Liudprand, *Historia Ottonis*, ch. 11.

172 Adalbert of Magdeburg, *Continuatio*, an. 962. Also see MacLean, *History and Politics in Late Carolingian and Ottonian Europe*, 262 n. 170.

173 Liudprand, *Historia Ottonis*, ch. 4; Adalbert. *Continuatio*, an. 963; and *Annales Magdeburgensis*, an. 963.

departed with the greater part of his army, and headed south again to Rome, where he established his siege camp at the beginning of November.[174] Adalbert fled rather than risk a battle against the emperor. The pope threw himself upon Otto's mercy.[175] On 6 November, a synod of German and Italian bishops began to hear charges against John XII, finally deposing him on 4 December with Otto's agreement and encouragement. Pope Leo VIII (963–965) was then elected with the emperor's support.[176] Otto remained in Rome to settle affairs in the city, where he received word that Berengar had finally surrendered.

After more than two years of steady campaigning, Otto believed that affairs in Italy were finally settled. Berengar, Willa, and their daughters were in captivity. Berengar's three sons, including Adalbert, were all in exile. A friendly pope was on the throne of St Peter, and the city of Rome had been pacified. Under these conditions, Otto sent his weary troops home to Germany for a well deserved rest.[177]

Otto's decision, however, led to a renewed revolt within the city of Rome on 3 January. The rebels, including the now deposed Pope John XII, sought to assassinate both the German ruler and Leo VIII.[178] Otto, whose court evidently had developed good sources of intelligence within the city, received word of the plot well in advance and was able to suppress the revolt very quickly. Otto demanded a large number of hostages to secure the good behavior of the Romans, and then marched south on 11 January to head off any effort by Adalbert to raise a revolt in the duchy of Spoleto.[179] At the request of Pope Leo, Otto freed the hostages before departing. This was to prove a major error.

As soon as Otto's, now reduced, army was on the march to Spoleto John XII again raised a revolt. Pope Leo was able to escape to his imperial benefactor, but Bishop Otger of Speyer, whom Otto had established as his governor in Rome, fell into the hands of the rebels and was severely mistreated. The two legates, whom John himself had dispatched to Otto's court in 960, were tortured even more, with the cardinal deacon John losing his tongue, nose, and two fingers from his right hand, and the notary Azo losing his right hand.[180] When these miserable creatures made their way to Otto's camp, the emperor immediately issued orders for a new army to be mobilized north of the Alps to deal with the Romans once and for all.[181]

Although John XII died in mid May 964, the Romans refused to accept Otto's choice of Leo VIII as pope. Instead, they demanded that the emperor recognize the cardinal deacon Benedict, who had the support of a number of important

---

[174] Liudprand, *Historia Ottonis*, ch. 8.

[175] Ibid., ch. 16.

[176] Ibid.

[177] Ibid., ch. 17.

[178] Ibid., ch. 17, and Adalbert of Magdeburg, *Continuatio, an.* 964.

[179] Liudprand, *Historia Ottonis*, ch. 17-18; Adalbert of Magdeburg, *Continuatio, an.* 964.

[180] Liudprand, *Historia Ottonis*, ch. 19.

[181] Adalbert of Magdeburg, *Continuatio, an.* 964; *Benedicti Sancti Andrea Chronicon*, ch. 57; and Liudprand, *Historia Ottonis*, ch. 17.

local magnates.[182] Otto, enraged by the intransigence of the Romans and their repeated rebellions, refused to negotiate. When new forces arrived from Germany, Otto began a close siege of the eternal city, hoping to starve the Romans into submission.[183] The city surrendered after just five weeks, and Otto made his third entrance into Rome on 23 June 964.[184] A few months later, the fortress at Isola Comacina, the last of the strongholds still held by Berengar's supporters, surrendered to Otto's troops. Northern Italy was now fully pacified. The emperor celebrated Christmas at Pavia, and in January 965 returned to Germany.

Otto's Return to Germany 965

Following his return to Germany, Otto undertook a series of administrative and personnel changes that were to shape the organization of the western and eastern frontiers for the remainder of his reign. In May 965, the renowned frontier commander and close royal advisor Gero died. Rather than replacing Gero with one man, Otto decided to promote six of Gero's long-time officers, each of whom was placed in command of his own march. From north to south, these were Thiadrich in the Saxon North March (later called the Altmark), Hodo in the Saxon East March, Gero's nephew Thietmar in Saxon Schwabengau around Aschersleben, Gunther in the Merseburg march, Wigger in the march of Zeitz, and Wigbert in the march of Meißen.[185] This division of Gero's old office into six parts remained in place for the remainder of Otto's reign.

In October 965, Otto's brother Brun died at age 40. He had held office as archbishop of Cologne and duke of Lotharingia for twelve years, loyally serving Otto in both capacities. In many respects, Brun was an irreplaceable loss for the emperor, having served as one of his closest, and certainly most loyal, advisors. Brun had maintained the peace in Lotharingia, securing the region for the German kingdom. He also had played a key role in maintaining Otto's preeminent position in the politics of the West Frankish kingdom, where Lothair IV relied on the aid provided by his Saxon uncles. Otto decided not to appoint a new duke in Lotharingia, but rather divided authority there between Frederick (959–978), who had already served in upper Lotharingia as Brun's lieutenant since 959, and Godfrey (965–969), who received the title of dux in lower Lotharingia.[186]

---

[182] Adalbert of Magdeburg, *Continuatio, an.* 964.

[183] *Benedicti Sancti Andrea Chronicon,* ch. 57; Adalbert of Magdeburg, *Continuatio, an.* 964; and Liudprand, *Historia Ottonis,* ch. 21.

[184] Liudprand, *Historia Ottonis,* ch. 22; and Adalbert of Magdeburg, *Continuatio, an.* 964.

[185] See the still useful discussion of these events by Holtzmann, *Geschichte der sächsischen Kaiserzeit,* 208.

[186] Sproemberg, "Die lothringische Politik Ottos des Großen," 53-65.

Italy 965–970

In the late spring of 965, while Otto was contemplating his restructuring of the eastern frontier, word arrived at the court that yet another revolt had broken out in Italy. Several Lombard magnates, including Count Bernhard of Pavia, Bishop Wido of Modena, and Bishop Sigolf of Piacenza, had invited Adalbert to return as king. Otto immediately ordered Duke Burchard II of Swabia (954–973) to take an army into Italy to crush the rebellion.[187] Adalbert of Magdeburg, who was personally acquainted with Burchard, recorded that the Swabian duke actively sought intelligence regarding the location of the rebel army.[188] When he learned of the rebels' location, Burchard, whose force consisted of the Swabian expeditionary levy as well as Lombards who remained loyal to Otto, traveled by ship down the Po, until he reached the point where the enemy was encamped. Adalbert, Berengar's son, decided to risk a fight against the Swabian duke and launched an attack as soon as he received word that the royal army had landed. In the ensuing battle, fought on 25 June, Burchard scored a major victory, in the course of which Wido, Adalbert's brother, was killed. Adalbert himself fled into the mountains to escape.[189]

However, events, which were moving along auspiciously for the German ruler, turned sour toward the end of the year. Pope Leo VIII died in March. His successor, John XIII (965–972), was elected on 1 October in the presence of Bishop Liudprand of Cremona and Bishop Otger of Speyer, whom Otto had sent as *missi* to Rome to ensure that the papal succession followed in the interests of the emperor.[190] However, Pope John, who was a member of the powerful Crescentius family, was attacked and imprisoned just before Christmas by rival magnates, but managed to send out a message to Otto to come to his aid. The stage was set for Otto's third Italian expedition.[191]

The German ruler held an assembly at Worms in August 966, where he had ordered his army to mobilize.[192] Otto faced virtually no resistance as he marched into northern Italy. By December, Otto was in Rome where he broke with his past policy of leniency toward the Roman population. Instead, he executed the commanders of the twelve traditional military districts in and around Rome. He also sent a large number of Roman magnates into exile in Germany.[193]

After settling affairs in Rome, Otto decided to secure the southern frontier of his new Italian possessions by establishing a military alliance with Pandulf Iron-

---

187 Adalbert of Magdeburg, *Continuatio, an.* 965.

188 Ibid., *an.* 965, "*Tunc imperator Burchardum ducem Alamannorum in Italiam misit; qui ad congrediendum ei, ubicumque inveniretur, cum Langobardis imperatoris fidelibus et Alamannis iusum per Padum navigavit et illis, ubi eum audierat esse, partibus navim applicuit.*"

189 Ibid., *an.* 965.

190 Ibid.

191 Ibid.

192 Ibid., *an.* 966.

193 Ibid.

head (944–981) and his brother Landulf (943–969), who ruled the independent principalities of Capua and Benevento. These territories formed a buffer between the lands of the papal state and the duchy of Spoleto, and the Byzantine ruled districts to the south. To this end, Otto traveled to Capua in February 967, where he received an oath of fidelity from the two brothers.[194] Otto remained in Italy for the rest of the year, securing final papal agreement for the establishment of Magdeburg as an archbishopric (20 April 967), and having his twelve-year-old son Otto II crowned as co-emperor in the Lateran palace on 24 December.[195]

However, Otto's ongoing presence in Italy, and especially the agreements that he reached with Pandulf and the latter's brother Landulf in early 967, had aroused Byzantine concerns about the western emperor's plans regarding southern Italy. Emperor Nikephoros II (963–969) sent troops to the region in 967, and may have been planning to dispatch a major army there.[196] Rather than waiting for the Byzantines, Otto decided to seize the tactical initiative. In early 968, he led an army to Capua and Benevento, and then crossed over into Byzantine Apulia in March, where he besieged the coastal fortress city of Bari.[197] Although the siege ultimately was unsuccessful, this round of fighting did lead to negotiations between the two emperors in which Liudprand of Cremona was to play a central role.[198]

However, Emperor Nikephoros refused to accept Otto's demands for an imperial princess as a bride for Otto II, as well as a settlement of southern Italian affairs in a manner that served Ottonian security interests for Spoleto and Rome. Consequently, the western emperor renewed his military offensive in southern Italy so as to secure a better bargaining position. In November 968, Otto again led an army into Calabria and Apulia, where he remained in direct command until May.[199] However, the initial stages of this campaign went poorly as Otto's ally Pandulf was defeated and captured in a battle outside the walls of Bovino, located near the frontier between Campania and Apulia.[200] Following this initial success, the Byzantine general Eugenius pressed his advantage by launching an invasion of Campania. He succeeded in capturing Avellino, some 30 kilometers to the south of Benevento.[201] Eugenius then led his army to Capua, 60 kilometers to the north-east, where he besieged the city for the better part of six weeks, deploying a wide range of siege equipment.[202] Here, Eugenius was joined by the

---

194 For a general overview of these events, see Kreutz, *Before the Normans*, 102-106; and Loud, "Byzantium and Southern Italy (876-1000)," 565-566.
195 Adalbert of Magdeburg, *Continuatio, an.* 967; Thietmar of Merseburg, *Chronicon*, 2.35.
196 Loud, "Byzantium and Southern Italy (876–1000)," 565.
197 *Anselmi Gesta Episcoporum Leodiensium*, MGH SS 7, 202, ch. 24. *Lupi Protospatarii annales*, ed. G. H. Pertz, MGH SS 5, 55, dates the campaign to 969.
198 Liudprand, *Relatio de legatione Constantinopolitana*.
199 DO I, 374, was issued on 20 May 969 at Conca in the Romagna, so Otto had returned from Calabria by that date.
200 Kreutz, *Before the Normans*, 105; and Loud, "Byzantium and Southern Italy (876–1000)," 565.
201 *Chronicon Salernitanum*, ed. U. Westerbergh (Stockholm, 1956), c. 172.
202 Ibid.

ruler of Naples, Marinus. However, when the Byzantines and their allies received word that a German army was coming to relieve the city they broke off the siege. Eugenius withdrew to Salerno, while Marinus led his troops back to Naples.[203]

The relief army, which included expeditionary levies from Saxony and Swabia, under the command of Margrave Gunther of Merseburg, along with troops from the duchy of Spoleto, then marched from Capua to Naples where the troops are reported to have captured considerable booty.[204] From here, the combined German-Italian army, which now included troops from Capua as well as Benevento, marched on the fortress at Avellino, which they succeeded in retaking from the Byzantines after a brief siege.[205] With Campania cleared of Byzantine troops, the Germano-Italian army then headed south into Apulia.[206]

Their goal was the Byzantine-held fortified town of Ascoli-Satriano on the frontier between Campania and Apulia. They were met by a Byzantine army under the command of the *patricius* Abdila. The German and Italian troops won a smashing victory over the Byzantines. The *Chronicle of Salerno* records that 1,500 Greek soldiers were killed, and that Abdila himself was wounded in the fighting. Even more important than the battle, however, was the murder of Emperor Nikephoros on 11 December 969 at Constantinople, which fundamentally changed the diplomatic situation in southern Italy, and between the western and eastern empires more generally.[207]

John Tzimiskes (969–976), Nikephoros' cousin and successor, almost immediately began negotiations with Otto. Pandulf was released, and German troops withdrew from Apulia. Otto, having settled affairs in Italy, returned home to Germany in August 970. Otto subsequently dispatched a high-level embassy to Constantinople under the leadership of Archbishop Gero of Cologne (969–976) in late 971. The German prelate was able to obtain a Byzantine princess, a niece of John Tzimiskes named Theophanu, as a bride for Otto II, and returned with her and a large Byzantine entourage from Constantinople in early 972.

Settled Frontiers

The negotiated settlement with John Tzimiskes left Otto in direct control of Italy south to the duchy of Spoleto. The western emperor's alliance with the princes of Capua and Benevento meant that he also had a buffer between German dominated lands and the Byzantine sphere of influence in Apulia and Calabria. When Otto returned from Italy in 972, the western frontiers of the German kingdom had been secure for more than three decades. Lotharingia was firmly within the

---

203 Ibid.
204 Ibid., ch. 173.
205 Ibid.
206 Ibid.
207 For an older treatment of these events from the perspective of the Ottonians, see B. A. Mystakides, *Byzantinische-deutsche Beziehungen in der Zeit der Ottonen* (Stuttgart, 1891), 37-38. Also see Kreutz, *Before the Normans*, 106.

eastern kingdom, and Otto maintained his hegemonic role in both the kingdom of Burgundy and in the West Frankish kingdom throughout his reign.

In the east, Otto decided, likely as early as 965 when he reorganized Gero's march, that the Oder was to serve as the permanent frontier of the German kingdom, much as the lower Elbe and middle Saale had served under Charlemagne. Otto did not authorize any campaigns against the nascent Polish state under Duke Miesco I after Gero's victories in 963.[208] Nor are there any reports that Miesco sought to raid west of the Oder. In part, the fixing of the frontier along the Oder was made easier by the fact that Miesco, having married Dobrava, the daughter of Duke Boleslav I of Bohemia, was baptized as a Christian in 965 or 966.[209]

Otto's policy regarding the Oder frontier is illuminated by the failed adventure of Margrave Hodo of the Saxon East March, who sought personal advantage by raiding over the Oder in the spring of 972.[210] The bishop and historian, Thietmar of Merseburg (died 1018), whose father took part in Hodo's raid, emphasized that the whole plan was misconceived and that the margrave had virtually no support.[211] Miesco overwhelmed the East Saxon column at the battle of Zehden on 24 June 972. Hodo and Thietmar's father, Siegfried, barely escaped with their lives. When Otto received word of the failed raid, he ordered both Hodo and Miesco to cease all hostilities, which they did.[212]

On 23 March 973, Otto held an enormous assembly at the convent and royal palace of Quedlinburg which was attended by representatives of the Danes, Bohemians, Poles, Russians, Bulgarians, Hungarians, Byzantines, the papacy, and the southern Italian principality of Benevento.[213] It was clear to everyone in both the Latin West and the Orthodox East that Emperor Otto I stood astride Europe like a colossus. After thirty-six years of almost continuous war, following upon Henry I's seventeen years of campaigns, Otto had largely reestablished Charlemagne's empire.

---

[208] Regarding the development of the Polish state, see Barford, *The Early Slavs*, 261-262; and Klaus Zernack, "Otto der Große und die slawische Reiche," in *Otto der Große, Magdeburg und Europa* (Mainz, 2001), 517-524, here 520-23.

[209] See the discussion by Beumann, "Magdeburg und die Ostpolitik der Ottonen," 16-17.

[210] Thietmar of Merseburg, *Chronicon*, 2.29.

[211] Ibid.

[212] Thietmar of Merseburg, *Chronicon*, 2.29. Also see the discussion by Zernack, "Otto der Große und die slawische Reiche," 523.

[213] Thietmar of Merseburg, *Chronicon*, 2.31.

3

Military Organization

The military campaigns of Henry I and Otto I, which focused largely on the capture and defense of fortifications, required the deployment of large armies over long periods. Concomitantly, protecting both the frontiers and internal regions with extensive networks of strongholds, including many fortress cities of Roman origin, required the mobilization of very large numbers of men for local defense. The core of the Ottonian armies on campaign consisted of the royal military household, and professional fighting men provided by lay and ecclesiastical magnates. However, the numerically preponderant element of these armies on campaign was provided by men of the expeditionary levy. The local defense was undertaken by all able-bodied men in a region, which included both professional soldiers in the area, and large numbers of men drawn from all walks of life, and every social status.

Writing from his vantage point in the early eleventh century, Bishop Thietmar of Merseburg presented contemporary military organization as comprising three separate elements: the general levy that was organized for local defense, the expeditionary/select levies of militia forces that were deployed beyond the boundaries of their local region, and the professional military households of ecclesiastical and secular magnates, including the royal military household.[1] Readers familiar with Carolingian military organization will note the similarity between this system and the military forces available to the rulers of the *regnum Francorum*.[2]

Thietmar's views regarding the military organization of the Ottonian kingdom were based upon his own broad experiences as an advisor to Henry II (1002–1024) and his service as a military commander under this king. Thietmar also collected information from numerous well informed sources, including his own father, uncles, and brothers, who served as military commanders in the armies of

[1]   Regarding Thietmar's treatment of military organization, see Bachrach, "The Military Organization of Ottonian Germany," 1061-1088.
[2]   Concerning the constitutional structure of the basic institutions of military organization in the *regnum Francorum*, see Bernard S. Bachrach and Charles R. Bowlus, "Heerwesen," in *Reallexikon der Germanischen Altertumskunde*, ed. Heinrich Beck et al. (Berlin and New York, 2000), 14, 122-136; Bernard S. Bachrach, *Early Carolingian Warfare: Prelude to Empire* (Philadelphia, 2001), 51-83, and 287-312; and Timothy Reuter, "The Recruitment of Armies in the Early Middle Ages: What Can We Know?" in *Military Aspects of Scandinavian Society in a European Perspective, AD 1000–1300*, ed. A. Norgard Jorgensen and B. L. Clausen (National Museum, Copenhagen, 1997), 25-31.

the Ottonian kings. Thietmar obtained considerable additional information from reading written sources. These latter included texts such as Widukind's *Gesta* of the Saxon kings as well as royal and private charters issued on behalf of the bishopric of Merseburg.[3]

Thietmar, who was a self-consciously proud Saxon, focused most of his attention on contemporary affairs close to home.[4] However, the broad range of narrative sources from the tenth and early eleventh century that were composed throughout the Ottonian kingdom, and indeed in the West Frankish and Italian kingdoms as well, sustain the bishop's assessment of the military organization that prevailed in Germany during the tenth and early eleventh century. So too do numerous royal charters and privileges that were issued on behalf of secular and ecclesiastical *fideles* of the king from the reign of Henry I onwards. In addition, the enormous and growing volume of information that is provided by the excavations of fortifications throughout the German kingdom and its neighbors provides considerable insights into the scale and complexity of the military organization described in the considerable body of written sources from this period.

Local Levies

When Henry I came to power in 919, he inherited a kingdom whose military topography was dominated by fortified cities, major fortifications, and lesser strongholds. In the west and south, the seats of economic and political power in the *regna* of Franconia, Swabia, and Bavaria were in fortified cities such as Mainz, Aachen, Worms, Ingelheim, Frankfurt, Würzburg, Augsburg, Chur, and Regensburg, many of which had their origins as Roman *urbes*. To the north and east in Thuringia and Saxony, fortified royal palaces and episcopal seats at Werla, Tilleda, Quedlinburg, Magdeburg, Erfurt, Paderborn, Hildesheim, and Hamburg, among many others, dominated economic and political affairs behind their massive walls.[5] The conquest of Lotharingia in 925 brought Ottonian control over the fortress cities of Cologne, Trier, Metz, Verdun, Cambrai, Toul, and Strabourg.

---

3   Regarding Thietmar's personal military service, role as royal advisor, and sources of information, see Bachrach, "Memory, Epistemology," 63-90.

4   The basic study of Thietmar's *Chronicon* remains Helmut Lippelt, *Thietmar von Merseburg: Reichsbischof und Chronist* (Cologne, 1973). Concerning Thietmar's audience and *parti pris*, and particularly his desire to immortalize his friends and relatives, see Lutz E. von Padberg, "Geschichtsschreibung und kulterelles Gedächtnis: Formen der Vergangenheitswahrnehmung in der hochmittelalterlichen Historiographie am Beispiel von Thietmar von Merseburg, Adam von Bremen und Helmold von Bosau," *Zeitschrift für Kirchengeschichte* 105 (1994), 156-177, here 158, and the literature cited there; and Bachrach, "Memory, Epistemology," 71-75.

5   The royal palace at Quedlinburg, for example, has received extensive attention from archaeologists, who emphasize both its substantial defensive works and major buildings, which were constructed during the reigns of both Henry I and Otto I. See, for example, Ulrich Reuling, "Quedlinburg: Königspfalz-Reichsstift-Markt," in *Deutsche Königspfalzen: Beiträge zu ihrer historischen und archäologischen Erforschung vierter Band: Pfalzen-Reichsgut-Königshöfe*, ed. Lutz Fenske (Göttingen, 1996), 184-247.

These fortified cities and palaces had their rural counterparts in vast numbers of so-called *Fluchtburgen* that provided refuge for local populations in times of foreign attack.[6] A great many of these fortifications also served as the administrative centers for local comital authority.[7] In addition, Henry I possessed systems of royal fortifications that had been established by Carolingian kings in order to provide a defense in depth of the frontier against the Danes in the north and west, and against the Slavs, and eventually, the Hungarians in the south and east.

As noted above, a system of defense in depth was based upon the reality that an invading force could not be stopped at the frontier, but must rather be met and defeated either while operating within one's own territory or during the return march. The strategic decision to develop a system of defense in depth postulated a matrix of mutually reinforcing fortifications, usually within a day's march of one another, to which local populations could flee when faced by raids or invasions. These fortifications also served as rallying points for defensive forces, and bases of operation for actions against invaders once field forces were to be mobilized in response to an invader.[8]

---

[6]   Regarding the *Fluchtburgen* in the lower and middle Rhineland, see Reinhard Friedrich, "Ottonenzeitliche Befestigungen im Rheinland und im Rhein-Main-Gebiet," *Europa im 10. Jahrhundert: Archäologie einer Aufbruchszeit*, ed. Joachim Henning (Mainz, 2002), 351-363. Concerning rural fortifications in Lotharingia, see Johnny de Meulemeester, "Comment s'est défendu au IXe siècle?" *Acta Archaeologica Lovaniensia* 8 (1995), 371-385. For the Carolingian and then Ottonian systems of rural fortifications in Austria, see Felgenhauer-Schmiedt, "Herrschaftszentren und Burgenbau des 10. Jahrhunderts in Niederösterreich," 381-395; and Mitterauer, "Burgbezirke und Burgwerkleistung," 217-231. Among the important studies treating *Fluchtburgen* in the east are Paul Grimm, "Der Burghagen bei Reifenstein: Zur Funktion frühgeschichtlicher Befestigungen," *Ausgrabungen und Funde* 15 (1970), 285-291; idem, "Drei Befestigungen der Ekkehardinger – Archäologische Beiträge zum Problem von Graf und Burg im 10. Jahrhundert," *Zeitschrift für Archäologie* 5 (1971), 60-80; idem, "Zu zwei Reichshöfen nahe der Pfalz Tilleda," *Ausgrabungen und Funde* 19 (1974), 266-273; idem, "Zu Burgenproblem des 8.-10. Jh. westliche der Saale," *Zeitschrift für Archäologie* 16 (1982), 203-210; and Günther Binding, *Deutsch Königspfalzen von Karl dem Großen bis Friedrich II (765-1240)* (Darmstadt, 1996), 166.

[7]   This point was made regarding the Ottonian kingdom as a whole by Werner Emmerich, "Landesburgen in ottonische Zeit," *Mainfrankisches Jahrbuch für Geschiche und Kunst* 16 (1964), 301-304, here 301; and by Fleckenstein, "Zum Problem der *agrarii milites* bei Widukind von Corvey," 30. The same conclusion was drawn in more focused studies of regional fortifications by Auer, "Zum Kriegswesen unter den früheren Babenbergern," 10; Friedrich, "Ottonenzeitliche Befestigungen im Rheinland," 361; Mitterauer, "Burgbezirke," 219; and Meulemeester, "Comment s'est défendu au IXe siècle?" 380.

[8]   This type of defensive strategy was adopted by the late Roman empire and by the Byzantine empire. See in this context Edward N. Lutwak, *The Grand Strategy of the Roman Empire* (Baltimore, 1976, repr. London, 1999); and John Haldon, *Warfare, State and Society in the Byzantine World 565–1204* (London, 1999). Regarding the development of a system of defense-in-depth in Bavaria during the late ninth and early tenth century, see Bowlus, *The Battle of Lechfeld*, 48-59.
    With regard to western fortifications, see, for example, Günther Binding, "Spätkarolingiche-ottonische Pfalzen und Burgen am Niederrhein," *Chateau Gaillard* 5 (1972), 23-35; and Friedrich, "Ottonenzeitliche Befestigungen im Rheinland," 351-363. With regard to eastern fortifications along the middle Elbe, Saale, Unstrut frontier, see Schlesinger, *Die Entstehung der Landesherrschaft*, 79; and Grimm, *Handbuch vor-und frühgeschichtlicher Wall-und Wehranlagen Teil I: Die vor- und frühgeschichtlichen Burgwälle der Bezirke Halle und Magdeburg, passim*; idem, "Zu Burgenproblem des 8.-10. Jh. westliche der Saale," here 206-7; and Brachmann, "Der Limes Sorabicus – Geschichte und Wirkung," 191.

In order to sustain and make effective this enormous military infrastructure Carolingian kings required that every able-bodied man within the *regnum Francorum* serve in defense of his home district. In doing so, the Carolingians built upon the military organization that they had inherited from their Merovingian and ultimately late-Roman predecessors.[9] The universal obligation for military service in defense of the local region, denoted in Carolingian capitulary legislation as *Lantwehr*, was intended to provide sufficient manpower to hold the walls of fortress cities and lesser fortifications against the determined attacks of enemy forces.[10]

In addition to active service in times of war, moreover, Carolingian kings also required the local population to provide labor to maintain the walls of the fortifications in which they were to take refuge. The best-known enunciation of this requirement in the west is set out in the Edict of Pîtres, issued by Charles the Bald in 864.[11] Here, the West Frankish king required that all those men who did not have sufficient wealth to serve in the expeditionary levy were to work on constructing fortifications and bridges, and to serve in defense of these fortifications according to *antiqua consuetudo*.[12]

A charter issued by King Arnulf to his *fidelis* and *ministerialis* Heimo in 888 illustrates that these *antiquae consuetudines* also were implemented in the Carolingian east.[13] In this privilege, Arnulf granted a judicial immunity from the local comital court to Heimo's dependants, including both free men (*ingenui*) and

9   Regarding the Roman and Merovingian background to the organization of local defenses in the Carolingian period, see Bernard S. Bachrach, *Merovingian Military Organization 481–751* (Minneapolis, 1972), 66; idem, "Grand Strategy in the Germanic Kingdoms: Recruitment of the Rank and File," in *L'Armée romaine et les barbares du IIIe au VIIe siècle*, ed. Françoise Vallet and Michel Kazanski (Paris, 1993), 55-63, here 58-9; and idem, *Early Carolingian Warfare*, 52-3. Cf. Innes, *State and Society in the Early Middle Ages*, 144, who makes the untenable claim that universal military obligation for local defense dates only to the first decade of the ninth century. In this context, Innes seems unaware not only of the tradition of universal military obligation for local defense dating back to the fourth century in Roman law, but also of the enormous requirements for defensive manpower to defend Frankish fortifications against both the Saxons and the Slavs from the seventh century onward. Major systems of fortifications in Thuringia, for example, included the Germar Mark and also the major grouping that has been identified in the context of the *Hersfelder Zehntverzeichnis*. With regard to these earlier systems of fortifications, see the discussion by Hardt, "Linien und Säume. Zonen und Räume," 39-56; idem., "Hesse, Elbe, Saale and the Frontiers of the Carolingian Empire," 219-232.
10   For this universal military obligation in the Carolingian period, which fell on free and unfree alike, see Helen Maud Cam, *Local Government in "Francia" and England* (London, 1912), 37; and Ganshof, "Charlemagne's Army," 59-61. Regarding the effective deployment of these defense forces, particularly against the Vikings, see the discussion by Charles R. Bowlus, "Two Carolingian Campaigns Reconsidered," *Military Affairs* 48 (1984), 121-125, here 123-4; and Simon Coupland, "The Carolingian Army and the Struggle against the Vikings," *Viator* 35 (2004), 49-70, here 69-70.
11   Capitularia II, nr. 273 c. 27. See the discussion of this text by Janet Nelson, *Charles the Bald* (London, 1992), 207.
12   Capitularia II n. 273 c. 27.
13   *Die Urkunden Arnolfs*, ed. Paul Kehr, MGH *Diplomata regum Germaniae ex stirpe Karolinorum* 3 (Berlin, 1940), 32, hereafter DA. Regarding Heimo's service under Arnulf, see the discussion by Bowlus, *The Battle of Lechfeld*, 290-299, with a discussion of this charter at 233-4. Schlesinger, "Burgen und Burgbezirke. Beobachtungen im miitteldeutschen Osten," 162, argues that Arnulf's charter on behalf of Heimo demonstrates that the regulations set out in the Edict of Pîtres also were enforced

unfree men (*servi*) who lived on his lands.[14] However, all of these dependants, both free and unfree, were required to provide labor service on fortifications at the discretion of the margrave (*terminalis comes*). In addition, they had an obligation to serve in defense of these fortifications when called upon to do so by the count.[15]

The ongoing use in the tenth century of the many hundreds of fortifications, and the continued centrality of siege warfare in campaigns of territorial conquest, are crucial factors in understanding the importance of continuity in military organization from the Carolingians to the Ottonians. With regard to the general levy, the Ottonians maintained the universal obligation for local defense, and also for the maintenance of fortifications at the direction of comital authorities.[16] To a greater degree than the Carolingians, however, the Ottonian kings transferred the authority and obligation to mobilize the local levies from counts to ecclesiastical authorities. This was particularly the case with regard to the dependants of abbots and bishops.

In 940, for example, Otto I issued a privilege on behalf of the monastery of Corvey in which he established Abbot Folkmar as a military immunist with authority over all of the dependants of the monastery within the districts (*pagi*) of Auga, Netga, and Huetgo. These *pagi* were located within the administrative jurisdictions (*comitatus*) of Counts Rethard, Dedi and Hamp, and Hermann. [17] This immunity, which gave the abbot the authority for the *Burgbann*, made Folkmar responsible for the organization of the corvée to maintain fortifications, and for the mobilization of the monastery's dependants to defend these fortifications in case of attack.[18] The inhabitants in these three *pagi*, who were not the dependants of the monastery of Corvey, were not included within the abbot's military immunity, and thus were subject to mobilization by the counts named in the charter.[19]

---

in the east. Also see Mitterauer, "Burgbezirke," 220-21, who connects the grant to Heimo by Arnulf with the Anglo-Saxon *trimodas necessitas*.

[14]   DA, 32.

[15]   Ibid., "*homines eius inde cum terminali comite, ubi ipse elegerit, urbem aedificerunt et, si quando necesse eveniat, ad semetipsos defendendos cum rebus suis illuc confugium faciant custodias cum caeteris more solito ad communem suae salvatoris vel circumspectionis contra inimicorum insidias tutelam vigilanter exhibentes.*" Also see the grant in 908 by Louis the Child to Bishop Erchanbald of Eichstätt in which the last east Carolingian king made the bishop responsible for mobilizing the local levy for the defense of fortifications that were to be erected against the Hungarian threat. *Die Urkunden Zwentibolds und Ludwigs des Kindes*, ed. Theodor Schieffer. MGH *Diplomata regum Germaniae ex stirpe Karolinorum* 4 (Berlin, 1960), nr. 58, hereafter DLC. In this case, the grant of a royal *licencia* is further demonstration of the public nature of fortifications, even when they were constructed by magnates.

[16]   Regarding the public nature of local defense during the Ottonian period, see Mitterauer, "Burgbezirke," 222; Wilhelm Berges, "Zur Geschichte des Werla-Goslarer Reichsbezirks vom neunten bis zum elften Jahrhundert," in *Deutsche Königspfalzen* vol. 1 (Göttingen, 1963), 113-157, here 138; and Bachrach, "Military Organization of Ottonian Germany," 22-27.

[17]   DO I, 27.

[18]   Ibid.

[19]   DO I, 27.

In 965, Otto granted a similar privilege to the monastery of Weißenburg so that its dependants, including several classes of unfree and semi-free men called *servi, lidi,* and *coloni,* as well as men who had the status of *fiscales* and *censuales,* wherever they lived, were not to be subject to the *Burgbann* of any magnate other than Abbot Erkanbert and his successors.[20] The privilege further specifies that this immunity from local military service to anyone other than the abbot was to be valid with regard to the monastery's dependants even if the latter have been granted as *beneficia* to other royal *fideles.*[21]

This last clause raises the specter of the precarial grant of monastic resources, *pro verbo regis,* to other royal *fideles.*[22] As will be seen below, the Ottonian kings regularly granted church lands as benefices to their *fideles* for military purposes. This charter indicates, however, that Otto I intended that the monastery of Weißenburg should have access to all of its dependants for military purposes, even if some of them were required to perform labor and other duties on behalf other of the king's *fideles* in times of peace.

The mobilization of the general levy for the local defense continued after the death of Otto I in 973. Otto II (973–983) issued a number of charters on behalf of abbots and bishops authorizing them to summon the men of their region for local defense. Soon after his accession, for example, Otto II made a grant to the bishopric of Merseburg with regard to the fortress district centered on the fortification at Zwenkau. The grant included a military immunity that made the bishop of Merseburg responsible for mobilizing the free men (*liberi homines*) living within the boundaries of the fortress district (*civitatis terminus et apper-tinentias positos*) for fortress work (*ad opus muri urbani faciendum*) and also for expeditionary military service (*ad ministrationem expeditionis tribuendam*).[23]

---

[20] DO I, 287, "*servi vel lidi vel coloni vel qui dicuntur fiscales vel censuales qui in proprietate beati Petri apostolorum principis in abbatia Wizinburg vel ubicumque commorantur et habitant, seu ad opus monachorum deserviant seu fidelibus nostris beneficiales existant, ad nullam aliam civitatem vel castellum muniendum ab aliquo cogantur vel distringantur nisi tantum ad idem praescriptum monasterium quod nos … in suam, ut ab antiquis fuit, dignitatem restituimus, ut illud muniant et custodient et ad iussum abbatis Erkanberti qui eidem monasterio modo praeesse videtur, vel successorum eius vel advocati aut ministrorum eius ad hoc opus moneantur et distringantur.*" Also see Karl Leyser, "Henry I and the Beginnings of the Saxon Empire," *The English Historical Review* 83 (1968), 1-32; reprinted in K. J. Leyser, *Medieval Germany and its Neighbours 900–1250* (London, 1982), 11-42, here 16, who notes the continued military obligation for local defense on the free and semi-free well into the tenth century.
[21] DO I, 187.
[22] Regarding the tradition of granting church lands to royal *fideles pro verbo regis,* dating back to the reign of Charles Martel, see Ganshof, *Frankish Institutions,* 148-149, n. 387; Bernard S. Bachrach, "Charles Martel, Mounted Shock Combat, the Stirrup and Feudalism," *Studies in Medieval and Renaissance History* 7 (1970), 49-75; reprinted with the same pagination in idem, *Armies and Politics in the Early Medieval West* (Aldershot, 1993); Herwig Wolfram, "Karl Martell und das fränkische Lehenswesen. Aufnahme eines Nichtbestandes," in *Karl Martel in seiner Zeit,* eds. Jörg Jarnut, Ulrich Nonn, and Michael Richter (Sigmaringen, 1994), 61-78; and Ulrich Nonn, "Das Bild Karl Martells in mittelalterlichen Quellen," in ibid., 9-21.
[23] See *Die Urkunden der deutschen Könige und Kaiser: Die Urkunden Otto des II und Otto des III.,* ed. Theodor Sickel (Hanover, 1888-1893), 89, hereafter DO II. The next clause in the immunity makes clear that the *ministratio* here is service rather than a payment, because in addition to mobilizing the

The charters granted to ecclesiastical magnates are evidence that the mobilization of the entire able-bodied male population for local defense was a living tradition. These charters dealt with events in real time, and do not represent fossilized
practices from an earlier era. Indeed, the ongoing importance of the general levy
for the Ottonian military system was significant enough to draw the attention of
foreigners. For example, Liudprand of Cremona, an Italian magnate and advisor
at the court of Otto I, observed in his work *Antapodosis* that Saxony had the
praiseworthy tradition of requiring all men to serve in the defense of their home
region.[24] In this context, local levies are also frequently mentioned in contemporary narrative sources both in the defense of fortifications and even operating in
the field within their home districts.[25]

   It should be emphasized, however, that as a militia comprising all able-bodied
men, many of whom possessed only rudimentary arms and training, the effectiveness of the local levy was greatly diminished when they were deprived of the
protection of their fortifications. This was particularly true when they faced experienced and well-equipped opponents. Regino of Prüm, an older contemporary of
King Henry I, deftly explained the disaster that could befall a poorly trained local
levy. In 882, a force of local men who lacked armor (*inermes*) and horses, i.e., they
were *pedites*, was mobilized from the nearby fields and agricultural settlements
(*ex agris et villis*) into a single unit (*unum agmen*) to engage the Vikings. When
this local levy, which Regino notes was very large (*innumera multitudo*), advanced
against the Vikings, the latter, although greatly outnumbered, did not retreat.
Rather, the Vikings recognized that the local militia lacked military training and
could be defeated by the smaller but more disciplined force. The result was a
major defeat and slaughter of the local levies at the hands of the Vikings.[26]

   When properly deployed and led, however, contemporary chroniclers note
the crucial role that local levies played in the successful defense of a region, and
even the defeat or destruction of enemy forces. Perhaps the best example of the

---

ministratio, the bishop is also made responsible for collecting the payments that are due to the royal fisc
(*quicquam ad fiscum pertinet dominicalem*). For further illustrations of the delegation of the authority
to mobilize the local levy for both fortress work and defense, see DO II, 204 and 214.

24   Liudprand, *Antapodosis*, 2.25, "*Validissimo igitur per quatriduum congregato exercitu, est enim
Saxonum mos laudandus atque imitandus quatinus annum post unum atque duodecimum nemini
militum bello deesse contingat, etsi corporis invalidus viribus, mentis tame vigore animatus, prout valuit
equum conscendit atque, collectis in unum copiis, huiusmodi est verbis ad pugnandi rabiem excitavit.*"

25   Regarding the deployment of local levies in defense of their home districts, both behind the
walls of fortifications and in the field, see, for example, Widukind, *Res gestae*, 1.38, 3.30-2, 3.36, 3.47;
Gerhard of Augsburg, *Vita Uodalrici*, 1.10, 1.12; Alpert of Metz, *De diversitate temporum*, in *Alpertus
van Metz: Gebeurtenissen van deze tijd en Een fragment over bisccop Diederik I van Metz*, ed. Hans
van Rij (Amsterdam, 1980), c. 8- 9; Ekkehard, *Casus Sancti Galli*, 114, 120-22,136-8, 170; Adalbert of
Magdeburg, *Continuatio*, *an.* 953; and Thietmar of Merseburg, *Chronicon*, 1.15, 4.37, 5.19, 5.21, 6.80,
7.23, 7.44, and 7.48.

26   Regino of Prüm, *Chronica, an.* 882. See the discussion of this battle by Franz Beyerle, "Zur
Wehrverfassung des Hochmittelalters," in *Festschrift Ernst Mayer zum 70. Geburtstag* (Weimar,
1932), 31-91, here 40, who concludes on the basis of Regino's account that this local levy should be
seen as representative of a general collapse in the fighting ability of militia forces, including expeditionary levies, throughout the *regnum Francorum*.

effective use of local levies occurred in the context of the Lechfeld campaign. As Charles Bowlus has demonstrated in his masterful account of the aftermath of the battle of the Lechfeld (955), the Hungarian army that faced Otto I on 10 August withdrew in good order from the field.[27] Over the next several days, however, the large Hungarian army was cut to pieces through the coordinated efforts of Otto's field army and the local levies. The latter had been mobilized for service when the Hungarians first crossed the Enns river in late July.[28]

Select Levies

Warfare under the Ottonian kings, particularly offensive warfare that was intended to conquer territory, focused on the capture and defense of fortifications. Indeed, this had been true of warfare in the Latin West for the better part of five centuries before Henry I came to power.[29] These military operations, as a consequence, required very large armies that were composed primarily of foot soldiers, which included those professionals who rode to war, but were trained to fight on foot. From the end of the late Roman empire onward, the bulk of these fighting men were drawn from expeditionary levies. In this context, the authors of contemporary narrative accounts regularly record the prominent role played by the select levies of the *regna* of the Ottonian kingdom in offensive military campaigns, particularly in the context of sieges.[30] When describing these fighting men, the writers diligently distinguished them from the professional soldiers who served in the military households of the secular and ecclesiastical magnates.[31] A

[27] Bowlus, *The Battle of Lechfeld*, 131.
[28] See Leyser, "The Battle at the Lech," 62, who stressed the importance of the attacks on the Hungarians after the battle as being decisive for achieving victory.
[29] For background regarding the domination of warfare by sieges from the late fifth century onward, see Bachrach, *Merovingian Military Organization, passim*; and Purton, *Early Medieval Siege, passim*.
[30] See, for example, Adalbert of Magdeburg, *Continuatio, ann.* 910, 944, 950, and 965, for Bavarian, Carantanian, Swabian, and Lotharingian expeditionary levies; Liudprand, *Antapodosis*, 1.20, for the Bavarian levy; Gerhard, *Vita Sancti Uodalrici*, 1.10 and 2.40 for the Bavarian and Swabian levies; *Annales Quedlinburgenses*, an. 997, for the Saxon levy; Adalbold, *Vita Heinrici II*, MGH SS 4, c. 6, c. 25, c. 28, c. 32, c. 40, c. 43, c. 46, for the Bavarian, Franconian. Lotharingian, Thuringian, Saxon, and Swabian levies; Flodoard, *Annales, ann.* 948, 949, 950; and Ruotger, *Vita Brunonis*, ch. 41 for Lotharingian levies; Widukind, *Res gestae*, 1.17, 1.21-2, 1.24, 1.35, 1.36, 1.38, 2.3, 2.22, 3.17, 3.23, 3.44, 3.68, for Saxon, Franconian, Thuringian, Swabian, and Bavarian levies; and Thietmar of Merseburg, *Chronicon*, 2.27, 3.7, 3.20, 5.12, 5.19, 5.24, 6.3, 6.5-7, 7.57 for Bavarian, Swabian, Saxon, Thuringian, Franconian, and Lotharingian levies. For an overview of this problem with specific reference to the role played by the select levies in capturing fortifications, see Bachrach and Bachrach, "Early Saxon Frontier Warfare".
[31] For an introduction to this practice, see the comments by Leyser, "Henry I," 23, with regard to the distinction drawn by Widukind between the *exercitus* and *milites*; Bernard S. Bachrach, "Dudo of St. Quentin as an Historian of Military Organization," *The Haskins Society Journal* 12 (2002), 165-185, here 171, concerning Dudo of St. Quentin's distinction between *milites* and the levy drawn from a particular region, e. g. *Frisones*, *Walgrenses*, who served in the select levy; and Bachrach, "The Military Organization of Ottonian Germany," 17-18, for the distinctions between professional soldiers and the men of the select levy drawn by Thietmar of Merseburg.

western writer, Flodoard of Rheims, who provides considerable information concerning the Lotharingian expeditionary levy that served both Henry I and Otto I, regularly denoted professional soldiers as *milites*. By contrast, Flodoard used ethnic or geographical designations for the levies.[32]

Flodoard's contemporary, Widukind of Corvey, also consistently used the term *milites* to denote professional fighting men. When discussing the service of the select levy, Widukind frequently described these men as the *exercitus* of a particular *regnum*, e.g. Saxony or Thuringia.[33] However, Widukind, like Flodoard, also used geographical designations to identify the expeditionary levies. In describing an army dispatched by Otto I in 939, for example, Widukind noted that the troops included a large contingent of men from the Hassegau (*validus manu Hassiganorum*), and an *exercitus* mobilized from Thuringia. Widukind subsequently described the men of the Hassegau as Saxons.[34] The anonymous author of the *Annals of Quedlinburg* similarly drew attention to a regional sub-group within the Saxon expeditionary levy, observing that the men of Westphalia served on campaign in the royal army, in this case under Otto III (983–1002).[35]

The obligation to provide men to serve in the expeditionary levy was based, in principle, on the wealth of an individual, or ecclesiastical institution, and not upon social status or even the capacity of a particular landowner to perform military service personally.[36] Carolingian legislation in the ninth century set out wealth requirements for different types of military service, with more and better equipment demanded of wealthier individuals. In the first decade of the ninth

---

32   Flodoard, *Annales, ann.* 922, 923, 930, 932, 934, 935, 938, 944, 948, 949, 952, and 958 for Lotharingian, Swabian, and Saxon expeditionary levies. In discussing fighting against the Vikings in 925, for example, Flodoard describes King Raoul's siege and capture of the *castrum* of Eu, held by the Northmen, see Flodoard, *Annales, an.* 925. The West Frankish king mobilized *milites* from the military household of the archbishop of Rheims as well as *Franci* who were to serve under the command of Count Arnulf. Crucially, in this context, the mobilization of the *Franci* followed the announcing of the royal *bannum*, i.e. the public authority of the king to raise the army. The objective of the royal campaign was a *praesidium* held by the Northmen. Rollo, the count of Rouen, dispatched 1,000 Northmen from his city to defend this place alongside the *inhabitatores oppidi*. Nevertheless, the *Franci* surrounded the *praesidium*, broke through the outer wall, and then breached the inner wall of the fortification, thereby demonstrating their effectiveness in siege warfare.
33   Regarding Widukind's practice of distinguishing between the *milites* and the *exercitus* see Fleckenstein, "Zum Problem der *agrarii milites* bei Widukind von Corvey," 35. Springer, "Agrarii Milites," 153, recognizes that Widukind drew this distinction between the two forces but argues, without any supporting evidence, that the *milites* were those who lived directly in the ruler's household and the *exercitus* consisted of those who lived in the countryside.
      Werner, "Heersorganisation und Kriegsführung im deutschen Königreich des 10. und 11. Jahrhunderts," 778-779, drew attention to the fact that in the Carolingian era armies were mobilized on the basis of the territorial divisions of the *regna*. He also observed (806) that bishops listed in the *indiculus loricatorum* were organized by their geographical position within the traditional Carolingian *regna*, and not according to their ecclesiastical provinces. From this, Werner concluded that the *regnum* remained the basic unit for the mobilization of military forces in the Ottonian kingdom as well.
34   Widukind, *Res gestae,* 2.3.
35   *Annales Quedlinburgenses, an.* 997.
36   This issue will be discussed in greater detail below.

century, Charlemagne revised upward the minimum wealth requirement for service on foot with a short sword and shield from one *mansus*, or its equivalent in income, to three or four *mansi*, or their income equivalent, depending upon how many men the government required for service from particular regions.[37] In light of considerable recent research, it is clear that the term *mansus*, when used by the Carolingian government, had come by the ninth century to mean a measurement of income derived from property rather than a physical description of the size of the property.[38] Wealthier individuals with twelve *mansi*, or their equivalent in income from other sources, were required to serve on *expeditio* with a coat of mail (*lorica*), a helmet, and shield, as well as a spear, long sword (*spatha*), and a short sword.[39]

Individuals who fell in between these wealth classes were required to come to war with equipment that was superior to that of a simple swordsman. However, their equipment was inferior to that of a man who came to war with a well equipped warhorse and all of the arms and armor that were stipulated for the "twelve-mansi men."[40] The lightly armed Thuringian mounted forces who took part in the battle of Riade in 933 may be seen to have been composed of men who fell into this middle category.[41]

Individuals and institutions that possessed in excess of twelve *mansi* were subject to providing armed men commensurate with their property and income.

[37] For the capitulary legislation regarding the economic basis for the obligation to serve in the expeditionary levy, see *Capitularia* I: no. 40 c. 2; no. 49 c. 2; no. 50 c. 1; n. 165 c. 6, II: n. 273 c 26-27. See the discussion of the implications of these charters for the mobilization of expeditionary levies by Reuter, "The End of Carolingian Military Expansion," 400; and Bachrach, *Early Carolingian Warfare*, 54-5. Innes, *State and Society*, 147, goes seriously off track here suggesting that a man named Gundhart, who had obligation to serve in the expeditionary levy on the basis of his property holdings, was a "professional" soldier. There is absolutely no basis for suggesting that Gundhard was a professional, that is a man who earned his living as a soldier either as member of a magnate's military household or as a man who offered to serve for pay in place of another landowner who was required to provide a man for service in the expeditionary levy. Indeed, as Innes himself shows, Gundhart was a free landowner who made his living cultivating his fields (147).

[38] Jean Durliat, "Le manse dans le polyptyque d'Irminon: nouvel essai d'histoire quantative," in *La Neustrie: Les pays au nord de la Loire de 650 à 850*, 2 vols., ed. Hartmut Atsma (Paris, 1989), 467-504, demonstrated that *mansi*, although of different sizes, were assessed the same *hostilitium*, that is the tax to support the army. On this basis, Durliat concludes that a *mansus* was a measurement of income/production rather than a measurement of size. Regarding the successful implementation of a standard *mansus* value throughout much of the *regnum Francorum*, see Christoph Sonnlechner, "The Establishment of New Units of Production in Carolingian Times: Making Early Medieval Sources Relevant for Environmental History," *Viator* 35 (2004), 21-48, here 45-8; and Walter Goffart, "Frankish Military Duty and the Fate of Roman Taxation," *Early Medieval Europe* 16 (2008), 166-190.

[39] See *Capitularia* I n. 44 c. 6; and the detailed discussion by Bachrach, *Early Carolingian Warfare*, 55, with the literature cited there.

[40] See the discussion of this point by F. L. Ganshof, "Benefice and Vassalage in the Age of Charlemagne," *Cambridge Historical Journal* 6 (1939), 147-175, here 160, with specific regard to the regulations set out in *Capitularia* I n. 77, c.9 and n. 75, concerning the service of men who held four *mansi*.

[41] Widukind, *Res gestae*, 1.38, refers to the Thuringian mounted forces at Riade as *inermes*, that is not armored.

Thus, for example, a layman who possessed 60 *mansi* might be called upon to provide fifteen foot soldiers for service in the expeditionary levy, five heavily armed mounted fighting men, or some combination of the two.[42] A similar relationship between wealth and the obligation to provide men for service in the expeditionary levy characterized the military organization of Anglo-Saxon England in the ninth and tenth centuries.[43] For comparative purposes, it is also worthy of note that urban militias in both Spain and Italy in the eleventh and twelfth century established obligations for service in expeditionary levies on the basis of both real property and income.[44]

If the Ottonian kings issued special legislation beyond what had been established by Charlemagne and his successors regarding the specific wealth requirements for service in the expeditionary levy, this has not survived. However, royal charters and privileges make clear that there was a selection mechanism for service in the expeditionary levy under both the late Carolingians and the Ottonians.[45] In addition, these charters suggest that the selection mechanism for service continued to be based on wealth requirements.

In 856, for example, Lothair II (855–869) issued a charter on behalf of a man named Winnibert and his sons, affirming that they were no longer responsible for undertaking military service with the royal army when it was on expedition.[46] Winnibert had given his property to the monastery of St Arnulf at Metz and, as a result, no longer had the personal economic wherewithal that would be make him subject to mobilization in the select levy.[47] Evidently, however, the local count had ignored the arrangement between Winnibert and St Arnulf, and tried to mobilize the former landowner. This charter, therefore, was to serve Winnibert as proof that he was not to be harassed any further by the local count, or by any other royal officials for taxes and services that were due from the property

---

42   See Bachrach, *Early Carolingian Warfare*, 56.

43   C. Warren Hollister, *Anglo-Saxon Military Organization* (Oxford, 1962), 26. With regard to the continuation of these wealth requirements well into the thirteenth century, see Michael Powicke *Military Obligation in Medieval England* (Oxford, 1962), 119 and 168.

44   With regard to the wealth requirements for expeditionary military service in Spain, see Elena Lourie, "A Society Organized for War: Medieval Spain," *Past and Present* 35 (1966), 54-76, here 57-8; and James F. Powers, *A Society Organized for War: The Iberian Municipal Militias in the Central Middle Ages, 1000–1284* (Berkeley and Los Angeles, 1988), 98 and 177. Concerning the wealth-based obligations for military service in the Italian city-states, see Daniel Waley, *The Italian City-Republics*, third edn (New York, 1988), 53; and Aldo A. Settia, "Infantry and Cavalry in Lombardy (11th-12th Centuries)," trans. Valerie Eads, *Journal of Medieval Military History* 6 (2008), 58-78.

45   Reuter, "Plunder and Tribute in the Carolingian Empire," 90-92, argues, against a strict reading of the capitulary evidence from the reigns of Charlemagne and Louis the Pious, that the mobilization of men on the basis of wealth requirements was a novelty introduced to put sufficient numbers of troops in the field for *defensio patriae*. The charter issued by Lothair II clearly indicates that the wealth requirements for service for *expeditionary duty* were still in place more than a decade after the death of Louis the Pious, and half a century after the putative reforms for defensive purposes proposed by Reuter.

46   *Die Urkunden der Karolinger dritter Band: Urkunden Lothars I. und Lothars II.*, ed. Theodor Schieffer (Berlin, 1966), 6.

47   Ibid.

now held by St Arnulf. While this charter was certainly issued well before the accession of Henry I in 919, or his conquest of Lotharingian in the early 920s, Lothair II's intervention in this case makes clear that Carolingian military legislation regarding the mobilization of the select levy was still being enforced more than forty years after the death of Charlemagne.

The ongoing connection under the Ottonian kings between property ownership and the duty to serve in the expeditionary levy is illustrated in a charter issued by Otto II in 979, in which the king confirmed a grant of a *villa* at Grabs in Raetia that Otto I had made to the monastery of Einsiedeln.[48] Among the resources that are explicitly identified as being attached to this *villa* are the tax payments levied on each hearth (*fiscum ordeum de accensis ignibus*). The charter connects these tax assessments to the expeditionary military service obligations on the *villa* (*adiutoria nostrae expeditionis*), as well as all of the other obligations that are owed to the imperial government (*cuncta ceteraque omnia ad imperiale ius pertinentia*).[49] As Walter Goffart has demonstrated with regard to the taxes levied by Charles the Bald (840–877) to finance payments to the Vikings, fiscal information for the purposes of levying taxes also provided the selection mechanism for the military obligations for service *in expeditio* that were based upon an individual's wealth.[50]

In this charter from early in Otto II's reign, therefore, it is possible to see the ongoing application of this same principle that tied together assessments of wealth and the obligation of an individual to perform military service on campaign. On this basis, it seems clear that a wealth-based selection mechanism for the mobilization of the expeditionary levy must have been firmly in place under Otto I. To suggest otherwise would require that the practice of mobilizing men on the basis of their wealth for service in the expeditionary levy died out some time after the death of Lothair II in 869, and was then revived after a substantial lacuna of more than a century under Otto II. Such a view certainly strains credulity.

The ongoing use of a selection mechanism based on wealth for service in the expeditionary levy similarly is evidenced in a charter issued by Otto III in 997 on behalf of a man named Siggo.[51] In this case, Otto III granted to Siggo in *proprium* a *mansus* in the *villa* of Diedenhofen. Siggo was freed from having to do any service for this *mansus* to the man who held this *villa* as a *beneficium* and he also was freed from the immunity held by this benefice holder for judicial matters (*bannum*). However, the benefice holder was denoted as Siggo's *senior*, and so it seems likely that for purposes of military service, Siggo was to serve in

---

48 DO II, 181.
49 Ibid.
50 Goffart, "Frankish Military Duty and the Fate of Roman Taxation," 166-190. Cf. Innes, *State and Society*, 153, who appears unaware of the sources that demonstrate the close connection between taxation and military service as outlined by Goffart.
51 See *Die Urkunden Otto des II. und Otto des III.* (Hanover, 1893), nr. 261, hereafter DO III.

the unit that was mobilized by the man who held the entire *villa* of Diedenhofen as an immunity.[52]

The mobilization of men to serve in the expeditionary levy generally was the responsibility of the count in whose *comitatus* landowners held property. In order to ascertain which men had sufficient property and/or income to be subject for service *in expeditio*, counts in the Carolingian empire were required to keep detailed, up-to-date lists of properties owners within their *comitatus*.[53] From the Carolingian period, we have legislation that requires the keeping of such lists. In the tenth century, we have records of court proceedings demonstrating that such lists actually were made, and used by comital courts (*mallum*).[54] As a consequence, rather than simply relying on information from prescriptive texts about how the government was intended to operate, for the Ottonians we can see how the government officials actually carried out their duties, and in particular their success in maintaining property lists.

It is important to note, however, that mobilizing men for service in the expeditionary levy was far more complex than simply having a list, and summoning the men to go on campaign. Not all property owners wished to go to war. A free property owner and dependant of the monastery of Fulda named Gunthart, for example, sought to avoid going on campaign with his count because the latter was his enemy. He sought instead to pay the fine for avoiding military service (*heribannum*), thus costing himself a considerable sum of money but also avoiding the danger of going to war in the company of a man who sought his death.[55]

Just as importantly, not all property owners could serve on campaign, either because they were too old, or too young, or physically impaired, or women, or monks, or priests. People in these categories had to find substitutes to serve

[52]   Regarding the obligation, in the Carolingian period, for every man to have a *senior* who was to be responsible for seeing that all men eligible for expeditionary military service did their duty when mobilized, see *Capitularia* II n. 71 c. 2 and 5. Regarding the importance of this legislation for the mobilization of armies by Louis the German, see Goldberg, *Struggle for Empire*, 124.

[53]   For the legislation regarding list-making for property owners, including the names of their *seniores*, see *Capitularia* I: n. 67 c. 4. Also see the *Annals of St. Bertin, an.* 869; and Frothar of Toul, letter 2, MGH *Epistolae* V, 277. With regard to the general practice of list-making by the Carolingians, see *Capitularia* II: n. 188 c. 5; n. 273 c. 27; n. 274 c. 14, and the discussion of these texts by Janet Nelson, "Literacy in Carolingian Government," in *The Uses of Literacy in Early Medieval Europe*, ed. Rosamond McKitterick (Cambridge, 1990), 258-296, here 279.

[54]   Regarding the role of the comital *mallum* in keeping track of allodial properties within the *comitatus*, see the discussion by Bachrach, "Exercise of Power," 408-9. Regarding the role of the count and his *vicarii* in verifying property transactions that included laymen in the Carolingian period in the east, see Katherine Bullimore, "Folcwin of Rankweil: The World of a Carolingian Local Official," *Early Medieval Europe* 13 (2005), 43-77. For the continuation of this practice in the tenth century see, for example, *Urkundenbuch der Abtei Sankt Gallen: Teil III 920-1360*, ed. Hermann Wartmann (St. Gall, 1882), nr. 788 p. 9-10.

[55]   Einhard, letter 42, in Einhard, *Epistolae*, ed. K. Hampe, MGH Epp. V (Berlin, 1899), 105-145, here 131. See the discussion of this text by Innes, *State and Society*, 147, who incorrectly asserts that Gundhart was a professional soldier. As the letter makes clear, Gundhart was to be mobilized for service with his count in a manner consonant with the obligations of wealthier members of society to serve in the expeditionary levy, that is as militia troops.

on their behalf, or pay the fine (*heribannum*) that greatly exceeded the cost of finding a substitute who would serve for pay.[56] Finally, a not insignificant number of landowners or land-holders already had military obligations that precluded them from serving in the expeditionary levy.

This last problem is illuminated by King Arnulf's privilege on behalf of the monastery of Corvey that was issued in 897.[57] In a circular letter, which was intended for recipients throughout Saxony, Arnulf forbade the bishops, abbots, counts, vicars and all office holders and magnates in Saxony from demanding military service from the *vassalli* of the abbot of Corvey.[58] The first section of the circular letter informed the various magnates that *vassalli* of the monastery of Corvey were living in their areas of jurisdiction, or area of local importance in the case of those *natu maioribus*, and that they were not to be summoned for military service in the expeditionary levy on the basis of the property that they owned or held in the particular locality. The second part of the circular letter informed these office holders and magnates that the *milites*, who are part of Corvey's military household, were under the monastery's military immunity, and were to serve *in expeditio* under the abbot's jurisdiction alone.[59] The implication of this charter is that comital authorities throughout Saxony kept lists of property owners in their jurisdictions, and would normally have the task of mobilizing these property owners for service on campaign, when ordered to do so by the king. However, Arnulf wished the abbot of Corvey to have the ability to summon all of his own *milites* for service in the royal army, and so had to alter the normal procedures for mobilizing landowners.

The bishopric of Halberstadt enjoyed a similar privilege, likely first issued under Otto I, which Otto III confirmed in 992. In this case, the bishops of Halberstadt possessed the delegated authority to mobilize men for war with jurisdiction over the "*milites liberos et servos eiusdem ecclesie.*"[60] Consequently, counts were not permitted to mobilize the bishop's troops for service in the expeditionary levy no matter how much property they possessed within their *comitatus*. It should be noted that the privilege covered both free and unfree (*servi*) fighting men, indicating that such *servi* were liable for service in the expeditionary levy.

In addition to having their own military retainers immune from mobilization by the count, some abbots (abbesses) and bishops received even broader military immunities for all of their dependants. In 937 Otto confirmed the immunity of the archbishop of Hamburg, and specifically included within this immunity all of

---

56 See the discussion of this point by Bachrach, *Early Carolingian Warfare*, 59.
57 *DA*, 155.
58 Ibid., "*episcopis abbatibus comitibus vicariis omnibusque in sublimitate positis et natu maioribus in Saxoniae partibus constitutis.*"
59 Ibid., "*Notum itaque generalitati vestre fieri volumus … quod sint inter vos qui militiam coenobii, quod vocatur Nova Corbeia, id est vassallos eiusdem abbatis, plus iusto in hostem ire compellant.*"
60 *DO* III, 104.

the monasteries held by the archbishopric.[61] The immunity contains the militarily significant clause that

> if any of the freemen should wish to become a *iamundling* or *litus* or even a *colonus* of the aforementioned monasteries with the consent of their co-heirs, they shall not be prohibited from doing so by any power, but rather they shall have license to do so with our authority. In addition, the aforementioned Adaldag and his successors as archbishop of the church of Hamburg shall have power over the free men and *iamundlingi* of the aforementioned monasteries whether on expeditionary service or going to the palace of the king.[62]

As this charter makes clear, the archbishop of Hamburg henceforth would be responsible for mobilizing his dependants for expeditionary military service, whether these men were members of the bishop's military household, or simply tenants holding land from the bishopric.[63]

A similar military privilege was issued to the bishopric of Worms by Otto I in 965.[64] In this case, the king forbade the local count to mobilize the dependants (*homines*) of the church for expeditionary service. However, the king then eviscerated this privilege by adding the clause, "unless the kingdom needed them."[65] Under these circumstances, the dependants were to go to war with their bishop, who would act in place of the counts in whose jurisdictions the bishop's dependants lived.[66]

These types of privileges for ecclesiastical magnates continued into the eleventh century. In 1003, for example, Henry II confirmed a grant of property made to the convent of Essen by Otto III and extended the convent's privileges, including its military immunity.[67] The privilege prohibits local counts from mobilizing the dependants of the convent, whether *servi*, *liti*, or *liberi* for service in the expeditionary levy. Rather this obligation now rested on the

---

[61]   DO I, 11.

[62]   Ibid., "*Si vero aliquis ex libertis voluerit iamundling vel litus fieri aut etiam colonus ad monasteria supradicta cum consensu coheredum suorum, non prohibeatur a qualibet potestate, sed habeat licentiam nostra auctoritate; habeat quoque potestatem praedictus Adaldag successoresque eius Hammaburgensis aecclesiae archiepiscopi super libertos et iamundilingos monasteriorum supradictorum in expeditionem sive ad palatium regis.*"

[63]   R. Wenskus, "Die soziale Entwicklung im ottonischen Sachsen im Lichte der Königsurkunsden für das Erzstift Hamburg-Bremen," in *Institutionen, Kultur und Gesellschaft im Mittelalter: Festschrift für Josef Fleckenstein zu seinem 65. Geburtstag*, ed. Lutz Fenske (Sigmaringen, 1984), 501-514, here 511, sees this charter as evidence that unfree property owners no longer served in the expeditionary levy. The charter does not say this. There is no limitation here, for example, on the count mobilizing the unfree dependants of the archbishop for service in the expeditionary levy. As will be seen below, unfree property owners in Saxony continued to be subject to service in the expeditionary levy into the eleventh century.

[64]   DO I, 310.

[65]   Ibid., "*vel quid exigere ullo umquam tempore praesumat, nec ab hominibus ipsius aecclesiae hostilis expeditio requiratur, nisi quando necessitas utilitati regum fuerit, simul cum suo episcopo pergant.*"

[66]   Similar privileges were held by the bishopric of Würzburg and the monastery of Hornbach. See DA, 67 and DO I, 117.

[67]   DH II, 39b.

abbess or her chosen advocate.[68] Thus, again we see the possibility that the free, semi-free, and unfree dependants of the convent might have sufficient wealth to make them subject to service *in expeditio*.[69] The charter specifically provides for the mobilization of those subject to service *in expeditio* outside the gates of the *civitas*.[70]

Professional Soldiers

Many property owners with an obligation to serve in the expeditionary levy might find themselves in a position where they had to find substitutes or pay the very heavy fine due for the failure to fulfill one's military obligations (*heribannum*). It seems likely that the Ottonians permitted many small to middling property owners to find either a male relative or even a dependant to serve on an *ad hoc* basis. Certainly, Carolingian legislation provided for the clubbing together of small-scale property owners who either had to pick one of their members, or someone else, to serve on behalf of the entire group.[71] Similar provisions were in effect in Anglo-Saxon England in the tenth century.[72] The situation, however, was more complex for substantial secular and ecclesiastical landowners who possessed hundreds, and in some cases, thousands of *mansi*.[73] Many of these very wealthy landowners chose to maintain a permanent military household, as seen above with regard to monasteries such as Corvey and bishoprics such as Hamburg, rather than attempting to mobilize substantial forces of well equipped men on an *ad hoc* basis.[74] Much ink has been spilled to justify the claim that *milites* of the Ottonian period were early members of

---

68 Ibid., "*aut homines ipsius ecclesiae servos litos vel liberos alios ad placitum vocare presumat aut in militiam sive hostem ire contingat nisi abbatissa vel advocatus quem abbatissa et congregatio eiusdem loci in hoc opus elegerit.*"

69 Regarding the service of unfree men as soldiers, see John B. Freed, "The Formation of the Salzburg Ministerialage in the Tenth and Eleventh Centuries," *Viator* 9 (1978), 67-102.

70 Ibid.

71 See, for example, *Capitularia* II n. 273 c. 27.

72 Hollister, *Anglo-Saxon Military Institutions*, 38-9.

73 Klaus Petry, "Die Geldzinse im Prümer Urbar von 893: Bemerkungen zum spätkarolingischen Geldumlauf des Rhein-Maas-und Moselraumes im 9. Jahrhundert," *Rheinische Vierteljahresblätter* 52 (1988), 16-42, here 19-20, notes that Prüm had 1,700 *mansi* at the end of the ninth century. Theoretically, the abbots of Prüm could be called upon to dispatch 142 heavily armed mounted fighting men, 570 armed men on foot, or some combination of the two for expeditionary military service.

74 The basic study regarding the military households of ecclesiastical magnates is Leopold Auer, "Der Kriegsdienst des Klerus unter den sächsischen Kaisern," 316-407; and idem, "Der Kriegsdienst des Klerus unter den sächsischen Kaisern," Part 2 48-70. John Nightingale, "Bishop Gerard of Toul (963–94) and Attitudes to Episcopal Office," in *Warriors and Churchmen in the High Middle Ages: Essays Presented to Karl Leyser*, ed. Timothy Reuter (London, 1992), 41-62, provides valuable insights regarding the military service of bishops in Lotharingia during the Ottonian period. For a later period also see Benjamin Arnold, "German Bishops and their Military Retinues in the Medieval Empire," *German History* 7 (1989), 161-183.

a juridical-social caste that would ultimately evolve into the dominant warrior nobility of medieval Europe.[75]

In this context, Karl Leyser made the quite influential argument that King Henry I was able to establish Saxony as the most powerful region in Germany, and subsequently to establish the hegemonic position of the German kingdom, by creating a powerful force of warrior nobles, each with a small group of armed retainers, who were able to overwhelm their less well trained and well equipped opponents both within Germany and beyond its frontiers.[76] In making this case, however, Leyser did not explain how relatively small numbers of mounted warriors were able to undertake wars of conquest that required the sieges of massive stone fortifications. Nor did he address the continued importance of expeditionary levies identified in numerous contemporary narrative accounts.

Certainly it is the case that many aristocrats served in war, either because they chose a military career or because they were summoned on the basis of their wealth in a manner consistent with other landowners. However, there is no basis for concluding that warfare, in itself, made a professional soldier noble in the tenth century. Indeed, privileges on behalf of the ecclesiastical institutions, noted above, make clear that semi-free and even unfree men (*servi*) continued to serve as *milites* into the eleventh century.[77] The case of the *miles* Wolfstein also is illuminating in this context. Wolfstein, who served as a professional soldier in the military household of Bishop Abraham of Freising (977–994), did not have the legal status of a completely free man in Bavaria, i.e. a *nobilis* according to Bavarian law.[78] Rather he was a semi-free dependant of the bishop. As a consequence, when he wished to dispose of his property, he required the supervision of an *advocatus*, as a legally impaired individual.[79] Wolfstein was but one of likely thousands of similar individuals who served as professional soldiers (*milites*), but who in no way could be considered noble or aristocratic.

---

[75]   This is the basic premise, for example, of Leyser, "Henry I and the Beginnings of the Saxon Empire," 11-42; and Franz-Reiner Erkens, "Militia und Ritterschaft: Reflexionen über die Entstehung des Rittertums," *Historische Zeitschrift* 258 (1994), 623-659. See the discussion of this problem by Bachrach and Bachrach, "Saxon Military Revolution?" 4-6; and Bachrach, "Memory, Epistemology," 90.

[76]   Leyser, "Henry I and the Beginnings of the Saxon Empire," 11-42.

[77]   The substantial number of fighting men from unfree backgrounds in the military household of the bishops of Freising, for example, has received detailed treatment by Günther Flohrschütz, "Die freisinger Dienstmannen im 10. und 11. Jahrhundert," *Beiträge zur altbayerischen Kirchengeschichte* 25 (1967), 9-79.

[78]   Regarding the juridical classes in early medieval Bavaria, see the discussion by Warren Brown, *Unjust Seizure: Conflict, Interest, and Authority in an Early Medieval Society* (Ithaca, NY, 2001), 13-14.

[79]   *Die Traditionen des Hochstifts Freising: Band II 926-1283*, nr. 1259 p. 157. Regarding the large number of unfree fighting men in the military household of the bishops of Freising, see Flohrschütz, "Die freisinger Dienstmannen," 9-79.

Military Households

The *indiculus loricatorum,* which is a record of the reinforcements (*supplementum*) of armored, mounted fighting men (*loricati*) who were summoned to Italy in 982 by Otto II on the eve of his campaign that ended in disaster at Cap Callone, sheds considerable light on the scale of the military households maintained by both secular and ecclesiastical magnates.[80] Just under 2,000 *loricati* were summoned for service in Italy to join those who had already been mobilized the previous year, with contingents of as many as 100 *loricati* required from the bishops of Strasbourg and Augsburg, and the archbishop of Cologne.[81] Several counts were required to lead as many as forty *loricati.*[82] It should be emphasized, moreover, that each of these heavily armed fighting men likely had three horses, i.e. a riding horse, pack horse, and war horse, as well as a batman to care for them.[83] In addition, these troops likely were accompanied by supply carts or wagons with support troops to maintain them.[84] In sum, therefore, the military contingents dispatched as reinforcements numbered significantly more than the 2,000 or so *loricati* listed in the *indiculus,* and the individual contingents consequently likely were larger than the 90 or 100 men listed in the document.

The example of Conrad the Red, Otto I's son-in-law and sometime duke of Lotharingia, also sheds light on the scale of the military households maintained by some lay magnates. Following his revolt in 953, Conrad was stripped of his public office with the concomitant loss of his authority to mobilize expeditionary levies for campaign.[85] The former duke was, however, an exceptionally wealthy man.[86] Conse-

---

[80] For the text of the *indiculus,* see *Constitutiones et acta publica imperatorum et regum 911-1197,* vol. 1, ed. Ludwig Weiland (MGH, Hanover, 1893), 632-3. Regarding the nature of the *indiculus loricatorum,* and particularly the fact that the surviving text refers to the reinforcements summoned by Otto II for the campaign in Italy, see Werner, "Heersorganisation und Kriegsführung im deutschen Königreich," 825.

[81] *Constitutiones et acta publica,* 633.

[82] Ibid.

[83] Regarding the regular practice of maintaining three horses to support a single heavily armored, mounted fighting man, see the discussion by Bernard S. Bachrach, "William Rufus's Plan for the Invasion of the Mainland in 1101," in *The Normans and Their Adversaries: Studies in Honor of C. Warren Hollister,* ed. Bernard S. Bachrach and Richard Abels (Woodbridge, 2001), 31-63. Liudprand of Cremona describes the batman of a professional soldier as a *miles,* i.e., the *miles militis.* See, in this context, Liudprand, *Antapodosis,* 2.62.

[84] The problem of logistics is considered below in chapters six–eight.

[85] Concerning Otto I's action to strip Conrad the Red of all of his public offices, see Adalbert of Magdeburg, *Continuatio, an.* 954, who observes that when Conrad sought forgiveness from the king, he was permitted to retain only his allodial properties.

[86] With regard to the wealth of Conrad the Red, see the exceptionally large donation that he made to the church of Speyer in 946 in *Urkundenbuch zur Geschichte der Bischöfe zu Speyer: Band I Ältere Urkunden,* ed. Franz Xavier Remling (Mainz, 1852, repr. 1970), nr. 13 p. 11-13. Concerning the importance of this grant to the bishopric, see E. Voltmer, "Von der Bischofsstadt zur Reichsstadt. Speyer im Hoch-und Spätmittelalter (10. Bis Anfang 15. Jahrhundert," in *Geschichte der Stadt Speyer,* ed. W. Eger (Stuttgart, 1982), 249-368, here 269.

quently, when he came to join Otto I's army at Augsburg in 955 he was accompanied by such a large force of mounted troops (*validus equitatus*) that the entire army took heart at their arrival.[87] These troops certainly included at least some of Conrad's *milites*, who had followed him into rebellion in 953 in Lotharingia.[88]

Both lay and ecclesiastical magnates supported their *milites* in a variety of ways. Many of these professional fighting men were maintained directly within the magnate's household, eating at his table, and sleeping in his hall.[89] Other fighting men were given benefices by their lords.[90] In addition, the Ottonian kings took a direct role in building up the military households of their magnates. One of the techniques that was adopted from the later Carolingians was to grant benefices directly to the *milites* of their magnates.

In 888, for example, King Arnulf granted to a *miles* named Engilger eight *hobae* at Völs that belonged to Arnulf before he became king.[91] Engilger, who served in the military household of Jezo, *comes* in the Zillertal in the Austrian Tyrol, was to have full possession and usufruct of these lands.[92] In a similar manner, in a

---

[87] Widukind, *Res gestae*, 3.44.

[88] See the observation by Flodoard, *Annales an.* 953.

[89] Regarding the distinction between *milites* who were sustained directly within the episcopal household and those who were provided with benefices, i.e. were *casati*, see Hincmar of Rheims, *Collectio de ecclesiis et capellis*, ed. Martina Stratmann (Hanover, 1990), 120. There are indications in several narrative sources of *milites* who were supported within the household. See, for example, Gerhard, *Vita Uodalrici*, 1.4, who notes that some *milites* were invited into the bishop's home to enjoy his hospitality alongside Ulrich's high-ranking guests (*hospites*). In a similar vein, Gerhard, *Vita Uodalrici*, 1.28, presents some of the bishop's *milites* as being part of the episcopal *familia*. Ruotger, *Vita Brunonis*, ch. 30, also presents some of the archiepiscopal *milites* as serving within Brun's household and receiving clothing from him. The anonymous author of the *gesta* of the bishops of Eichstätt presents Bishop Gunzo (died 1019), as taking advice from his household chaplains and *milites*. See *Anonymus Haserensis de episcopis Eichstetensibus a. 741-1058*, ed. L. C. Bethmann, MGH SS 7, c. 25. Ekkehard, *Casus Sancti Galli*, 262, differentiates between *milites* and men who hold *beneficia* with the implication that the *milites* were supported directly within the abbot's household rather than with benefices.

[90] Both narrative sources and charters are replete with information regarding the grants of *beneficia* to *milites* by abbots and bishops. See, for example, Gerhard of Augsburg, *Vita Sancti Uodalrici*, 1.28; *Gesta episcoporum Cameracensium Liber I* c. 88 and c. 92; *Liber II* c. 117; *Gesta Treverorum* ed. G. Waitz, MGH SS 8, c. 30-1; *Vita Iohannis Abbatis Gorziensis*, c. 36; Ekkehard, *Casus Sancti Galli*, 262; *Urkundenbuch der Stadt Strassburg; Erster Band Urkunden und Stadtrechte bis zum Jahr 1266*, ed. Wilhelm Wiegand (Strasbourg, 1879), nr. 52 p. 43-5; *Urkundenbuch zur Geschichte der jetzt die preussischen Regierungsbezirke Coblenz und Trier bildenden mittelrheinischen Territorien: Erster Band von den ältesten Zeiten bis zum Jahre 1169*, ed. Heinrich Beyer (Koblenz, 1860), nr. 217 p. 275; *Die Traditionen des Hochstifts Freising: Band I 744-926*, ed. Theodor Bitterauf (Munich, 1905, repr. Aalen, 1967), nr. 1080, p. 24-5; *Die Traditionen des Hochstifts Passau*, ed. Max Heuwieser (Munich, 1930, repr. Aalen, 1969), nr. 104 p. 88; *Hamburgisches Urkundenbuch*, ed. Johann Martin Lappenberg (Hamburg, 1907), nr. 48 pp. 52-55; and *Urkundenbuch der Reichsabtei Hersfeld* vol. I, ed. Hans Weirich (Marburg, 1936), nr. 77 pp. 146-7.

[91] DA, 17.

[92] Ibid., "*donavimus proprietatem recordantes crebri serviis nobis per illum facti, priusquam regium nomen acciperemus, hoc est in loco Fellis noncupato VIII hobas tales, quales in eisdem locis servi habere soliti sunt et XX mancipia ...*" In other charters, Arnulf, Louis the Child, Conrad I, Henry I, and Otto I granted property to the *vassalli* of their own *fideles* without specifying that these *vassalli* were fighting men. See DA, 14, 51, 52, 86, 98, 162, 173; DLC, 42, 76; DC I, 19, 27; DH I, 14; DO I, 279.

charter dated to 951, Otto I granted fiscal properties that were located within the *comitatus* of Margrave Gero to a *vir nobilis* and *strenuus miles* named Waltpert for his brave military service against the Slavs.[93] According to the charter, it was Gero who sought the grant of fiscal property on behalf of the *miles* Waltpert so that the latter probably was one of Gero's dependants, likely a senior member of his military household given his status as *nobilis*. The grant is quite substantial, comprising two *marcae*, a term that is used synonymously with *villae* in Otto I's charters. Consequently, it is likely that we are seeing here an effort by the king both to reward an outstanding soldier and to build up the military forces available to Gero by giving one of his lieutenants the wherewithal to recruit additional soldiers. In an early eleventh-century continuation of this practice, Henry II granted six royal *mansi* at Bubach to Gero, a *miles* of Bishop Henry of Würzburg in 1002.[94]

The Ottonians also made direct grants to their magnates to provide them with the resources to support larger military households. In 945, for example, Otto I granted four entire *villae* to the brothers Folcmar and Richbert, who were the sons of the royal *fidelis* Frederick.[95] These *villae* were in the immediate vicinity of the fortification of Zörbig that was constructed over the remains of a Slavic fortification that dated back to the ninth century.[96] The context of this very large grant, which likely comprised several hundred *mansi*, indicates that Folcmar and Richbert were to use these resources to recruit a garrison to serve under their command at Zörbig.[97]

The Ottonian kings also exchanged properties with their magnates so that the latter had a substantially increased economic presence in areas of potential military conflict. In 952, for example, Otto I granted five entire *villlae*, as well as a separate economic unit comprising forest lands with its administrative center (*caput*) at Steinbach, to his *vassallus* Hermann Billung, the military commander of the northern march against the Obodrites and Redarii.[98] A close examination of this charter

---

93 DO I, 133, "*quod strenuus miles et vir nobilis nomine Walpertus singulari fortitudine contra Slavos semper pugnaverit et rebelles eorum infrenaverit. Quia igitur regalis celsitudinis moris est fideles donis et honoribus honorare et sublimare, complacuit elementie nostre flagiationibus dilectissimi marchionis nostri Gero [obtemperantes] iam fato Walperto duas marcas in marchia predicti marchionis Geronis.*"

94 DH II, 4.

95 DO I, 69. This may be the same *comes* Frederick who witnessed a grant of property to Queen Adelheid in 957. See DO I, 325. The Fuhne is one of only two rivers, along with the Bruchgraben, that flows east–west in this region.

96 Berthold Schmidt and Waldemar Nitzschke, "Untersuchungen in slawischen Burgen zwischen Saale und Fläming," *Ausgrabungen und Funde* 20 (1975), 43-51, here 48.

97 *Die Traditionen des Hochstifts Freising: Band II 926-1283*, nr. 1125 p. 58, sheds light on the process by which Otto I could build up the resources of important dependants, who then used these resources to gain their own dependants. Here, Otto I granted property to his *fidelis* Aripo. Aripo then granted a portion of this property to the *nobilis vir* Engilhart.

98 DO I, 152. In April 953, Otto granted the properties that he had received from Hermann Billung to the monastery of St Maurice at Magdeburg. See DO, I 164.

reveals that the *villa* at Trotha included the fortification at Groitsch (Grodista), and the *villae* at both Uppin and Brachstedt included fortifications as well.[99]

Most of the properties granted to Hermann Billung were located in the immediate vicinity of Halle along the course of the Saale river, which had been the frontier up until Henry I's campaign of 928-929. The property at Steinbach and the *villa* of Scheidungen were, however, located along the Unstrut as it flows into the Saale. It is clear that Otto I wanted Hermann to have a vested interest in the region near the developing Saxon "capital" at Magdeburg, which was located several hundred kilometers south and west of the great magnate's main area of operations along the course of the lower Elbe. Among the fortresses for which Hermann now became responsible was the important stronghold of Barby.[100]

Six years later, in 958, Otto orchestrated another exchange of properties with Hermann Billung that led to the further expansion of the magnate's holdings along the lower Unstrut river.[101] In 961, Otto again added to Hermann's possessions east and southeast of the important fortress city of Halle through an exchange of properties that brought Asendorf, Dornstedt, and Lobitzch into the margrave's possession.[102]

The Ottonians, however, did not rely solely on fiscal property to enable their magnates to expand their military households. The government also made use of *precaria*, that is lands "borrowed" from the church to support royal policies.[103] For example, in 973, immediately after his accession as king, Otto II vowed to fulfill his father's promise to the monastery of St Maximin at Trier to return a considerable quantity of property that had been borrowed by the king in the Rhine-

99 DO I, 152. The identification of fortifications at these last two *villae* is to be found in DO I, 329.
100 Regarding the importance of the fortification at Barby, particularly for its role in the extended defensive screen for Magdeburg, see Dietrich Claude, "Der Königshof Frohse," *Blätter für deutsche Landesgeschichte* 110 (1974), 29-42, here 37. Barby was the center of a *Burgward* during Otto I's reign, and perhaps during the reign of his father Henry I as well. For the description of *Burgward* centered on Barby see DO I, 222b. Regarding the organization of this *Burgward*, see Brachmann, "Der Limes Sorabicus", 134.
101 DO I, 198.
102 DO I, 223. In a similar manner, Otto granted the Burgward of Tuchheim to Margrave Gero as a benefice. See DO I, 298. Tucheim is situated on a northern extension of the Fläming hills directly on the edge of the marshlands formed by the Fiener Bruch. There was a Slavic settlement at Tuchheim that was replaced by a German fortification, perhaps during the reign of Henry I. See the brief description of the fortification in *Corpus archäologischer Quellen*, 362.
    In an important change of policy, however, Otto I transferred all of the fortress districts granted to Hermann Billung and Gero first to the monastery of St. Maurice at Magdeburg, and subsequently the archbishopric of Magdeburg. See DO I, 222a-b; 230, 231, 278, 293, 296, 329, 387; and DO II, 12, and 270.
103 For a useful survey of this practice in the West during the Carolingian period, see Giles Constable, "Nona et Decima: An Aspect of Carolingian Economy," *Speculum* 35 (1960), 224-250. Constable did not identify this practice in the East. Janet Nelson, "The Church's Military Service in the Ninth Century: A Contemporary View?" *Studies in Church History* 20 (1983), 15-30; reprinted *Politics and Ritual in Early Medieval Europe* (London, 1986), 117-132, here 124-6, emphasizes that western bishops, including those such as Hincmar of Rheims who had very strong eastern connections, used *precaria*, at royal command, to support fighting men, but did not use this method exclusively.

land districts of Nahegau, Wormsgau, and Speyergau.[104] The lands, which were intended to provide prebends (*prebendariae*) for the monks at St Maximin, had been taken instead to establish benefices for the *milites* of Archbishop Rudbrecht of Mainz (970–975).[105] In this context, Otto II promised that neither he nor any of his successors as king and emperor would presume to borrow these lands again to establish such benefices.[106] However, Otto II did not fulfill his promise to return the lands as a charter issued by Otto III in 992 makes clear.[107] Otto III excused this delay in returning the properties as his father and grandfather had promised because of military necessity, a frequent refrain dating back to the early Carolingian period.[108] The charter goes on to note that the most recent beneficiary of these lands had been Count Heribert. Thus, lands that originally had been taken from St Maximin around 970 had yet to be returned more than two decades later because three kings had found use for them in supporting the military households of their prominent *fideles*.

In a similar vein, Otto I granted the monastery of St Peter, which belonged to the bishopric of Toul, to Duke Frederick of Upper Lotharingia, to be held until his death.[109] When Otto II issued a charter confirming the bishopric's properties in 973, the king drew attention to the fact that Duke Frederick was still in possession of the monastery of St Peter but that it would, in fact, ultimately be returned to Toul.[110]

Such grants generally were seen by contemporary churchmen as abuses, especially when the lands and incomes being "borrowed" belonged to them. Liudprand of Cremona comments on this distaste for *precaria* by presenting Otto I as taking a strong position against utilizing church lands for military purposes. After describing the treacherous withdrawal of Archbishop Frederick of Mainz from the siege of Breisach in 939, Liudprand states that a certain rich count (*comes praedives*), whom he leaves unnamed, attempted to use the departure of the archbishop to gain a favor from the king.[111] The magnate asked Otto I to give him the royal monastery of Lorsch in return for staying with the army. But the king refused this request and humiliated the count in the process. The count had claimed that if he had the monastery he could see to his own needs and those of his *milites* better.[112] Otto replied that he would not succumb to this blackmail and

---

104 DO II, 57.

105 Ibid. Regarding the distinction between the monks' property and the abbot's property for purposes of supporting the royal court and army, see the detailed discussion by John Bernhardt, *Itinerant Kingship*, 85-135.

106 DO II, 57, "nullusque successorum nostrorum, regum videlicet vel imperatorum, eas inde auferre vel in beneficium dare presumat."

107 DO III, 95.

108 Ibid., "sed variis bellorum aliorumque imperii negotiorum obstantibus causis effectum completionis non perceperunt."

109 This grant is a *perditum*.

110 DO II, 62.

111 Liudprand, *Antapodosis*, 4.28

112 Ibid., "Nuntiis itaque directis regi supplicat ut abbatiam quandam, Laresheim dictam, praediis ditis-

thereby incur God's wrath by taking away the *stipendia servorum Dei* and giving these *stipendia* to *militibus*.[113]

The Royal Military Household

The most important military household was that of the king himself. When Henry I came to power as duke of Saxony in 912, he already had a substantial military household that was capable of undertaking extended military operations beyond the frontiers of his duchy.[114] Following Henry's accession as king in 919, and over the ensuing decades, both he and Otto I gained ever greater control over the fiscal resources throughout the traditional boundaries of the eastern Carolingian kingdom in Franconia, Bavaria, Swabia, and Lotharingia.[115] Henry and Otto also garnered significant wealth through territorial conquest, tributes, and from the confiscation of properties from rebels.[116] These resources permitted the first two kings of the Ottonian dynasty to expand the numbers of *milites* in their employ.[117]

Henry and Otto, however, did not limit themselves to fiscal property when seeking resources to support the royal military household. As noted above with regard to Otto I's decision to "borrow" lands from St Maximin to support the military household of the archbishop of Mainz, ecclesiastical institutions provided considerable lands and income to the king as *precaria* whether or not they wished to do so.[118] Indeed, when lands that had been taken as *precaria* were returned to churches, the royal charters frequently included the polite fiction that these properties had been taken *iniuste* and that never again would the king or his

---

simam ei concedat, cuius possessionibus quod sibi deerat ac militibus suis ministrare praevalet."

113   Ibid.

114   See Widukind, *Res gestae*, 1.17.

115   Regarding royal control over the fisc, even in those regions that had been in rebellion against King Conrad I, see Schalles-Fischer, *Pfalz und Fiskus Frankfurt*; Gockel, *Karolingische Königshöfe am Mittelrhein*; Hans Constantin Faußner, "Die Verfügungsgewalt des deutschen Königs über weltliches Reichsgut im Hochmittelalter," *Deutsches Archiv* 29 (1973), 345-449; and Peter Schmid, *Regensburg*. 118 For the use of fiscal resources to support royal *milites*, see DO I, 111, 230; DO III, 43, 177; DH II, 2, 263.

116   Regarding the confiscation of property by the royal government, see DO I, 30, 32, 52, 59, 60, 78, 80, 107, 115, 135, 164, 171, 194, 195, 200, 204, 207, 217, 219, 226, 316, 320, 330, 331, 332, 333, 383, and 419a-b. With respect to tribute payments and their distribution to royal *fideles*, see DO I, 295 and 406. With regard to the administrative procedures that were set in train to confiscate properties, and general use of written documents by government officials in this process, see Bachrach, "Exercise of Royal Power," 389-419.

117   Widukind observed, for example, that following the efforts of Archbishop Hatto of Mainz (891-913) to foment unrest in Saxony at the behest of King Conrad I (911-918), Henry I, then duke, attacked Hatto's main supporters Burchard and Bardo. The latter were forced to give up their properties in Saxony and Thuringia, which Henry then divided up among his own *milites*. For the passage, see Widukind, *Res gestae*, I. 21. See the discussion of this episode by Bachrach and Bachrach, "Saxon Military Revolution?" 200.

118   For the use of church lands as *precaria* to support royal *fideles*, see, for example, DO I, 280; DO II, 97; DO III, 119 and 123; and DH II, 503.

successors ever give out lands from this church as *beneficia*.[119] Thus, for example, in the context of returning churches and tithe revenues to the monks of Stavelot-Malmedy in 966, Otto I promised that these lands would be reserved for the monks alone and that "*nullis umquam temporibus alicui in benefitium cedant*."[120]

The king's extensive military responsibilities entailed that the forces of the military household were designated for a wide variety of assignments within the Ottonian kingdom. An important contingent of royal *milites* travelled with the king.[121] In his 882 revision of Adalhard of Corbie's *De ordine palatii*, Archbishop Hincmar of Rheims (845–882) described *milites* such as these in the west Frankish military household as *expediti*, i.e. ready to move.[122] The *milites regis* serving at court provided the Ottonian kings with a rapid deployment force around which larger armies comprising both the *milites* of other magnates and expeditionary levies could be organized.[123]

A smaller unit drawn from among the *milites* who were attendant upon the king were employed as royal bodyguards. At Charlemagne's court, these men were denoted as *antrustiones*.[124] Widukind does not use a specific term to describe these picked men, rather denoting them as a unit (*manus*) of faithful soldiers (*fideles milites*) who protected the king day and night.[125] Thietmar of Merseburg uses the term *domestici regis* for Henry II's bodyguard.[126]

A second distinct group within the royal military household were young men who were being trained to serve as officers. Some of these men went on to hold command positions within the king's military household, while others returned to their families to accept command positions within the military households of secular and ecclesiastical magnates. The career of one such officer in training is described in some detail by Gerhard in his *Vita* of Bishop Ulrich of Augsburg (923–973)

Shortly after the death of Henry I and the accession of Otto I in 936, Ulrich sent his nephew Adalbero to study under the direction of a monk named Benedict, to whom Gerhard gives the honorific *doctissimus magister*.[127] Bishop Ulrich,

---

[119] Regarding the description of fiscal confiscations of ecclesiastical property as *iniuste*, see DO I 83, 93, 121, 157, 163, 176, 225, 367, 384, 419a, and 466. See the discussion of the royal confiscation or borrowing of ecclesiastical property in Bachrach, "Exercise of Royal Power," 389-419.

[120] DO I, 319.

[121] See, for example, Widukind, *Res gestae*, 1.39; Liudprand, *Antapodosis*, 4.24 and 4.27; Thietmar of Merseburg, *Chronicon*, 6.7.

[122] Hincmar of Rheims, *De ordine palatii*, ed. Thomas Gross and Rudolf Schieffer, MGH *Fontes iuris germanici antiqui in usum scholarum separatim editi* (Hanover, 1980), c.27.

[123] In this context, see the discussion by Liudprand, *Antapodosis*, 4.24, where Otto I's courtier observes the role played by the *milites regis* at the battle of Birten in 939.

[124] See the discussion by Bachrach, *Early Carolingian Warfare*, 68-71.

[125] Widukind, *Res gestae*, 2.31

[126] Thietmar of Merseburg, *Chronicon*, 5.19 and 6.7. Thietmar also records that one member of Otto II's bodyguard was a Slav named Zolunta who helped to save the king from the disaster at Cap Colone. See *Chronicon*, 3.21 and 3.23. Regarding the role of the royal bodyguard, see Bachrach, "Military Organization of Ottonian Germany," 1069.

[127] Gerhard, *Vita Uodalrici*, 1.3.

however, did not intend for Adalbero to have a career in the church, although the youth's study of the *scientia grammaticae* and *alia libra* certainly could have prepared him for this path. Rather, as Gerhard makes clear, when the young Adalbero had become educated (*doctus atque educatus*) in the foundations of both good knowledge (*bona scientia*) and training (*disciplina*), and had grown into his manly strength (*virile robur*), he was taken from school (*scola*) and presented by his uncle Ulrich to Otto I, whom Gerhard refers to anachronistically as *imperator*.[128] Ulrich recommended the young man for service in Otto's household (*regalis servitium*).[129]

Because of his training and background, Adalbero served the king for a period of time in both the secular and ecclesiastical spheres.[130] According to Gerhard, who was well acquainted both with Ulrich and with Adalbero himself, the young man did exceptionally well at the royal court (*curtis imperatoris*), "putting in a solid effort every day."[131] After receiving training as an officer at the royal court, Adalbero then returned to his uncle's household and assumed command of the Augsburg bishop's military forces (*militia episcopalis*).[132] In this role, Adalbero was able to bring "know-how" from the king's court back to his uncle's military household, which would prove quite valuable when the bishop's troops went on a royal campaign.

This type of military training and *cursus* from the royal court to the military households of the king's magnates marks an important element of continuity with Carolingian military tradition. Charlemagne and his successors had routinely recruited both high-ranking sons of aristocratic families, and also very talented *mediocres* to train at the royal court.[133] These youths and young men were described by Hincmar of Rheims as *discipuli* who were to be placed under the charge of a *magister*.[134] The training of future officers at the Ottonian court can be seen to parallel the training of young men in the royal chapel for future high office as abbots and bishops.[135]

Yet another component of the king's military household were units provided by magnates, at the request of the ruler, to serve for a period of time in the royal

128 Ibid., 1.3.
129 Ibid.
130 Ibid.
131 Ibid., "*certo sedulitate eius servitii cottidiani.*"
132 Ibid.
133 See the discussion of the training of officers at the Carolingian court by Bachrach, *Early Carolingian Warfare*, 71-75.
134 Hincmar, *De ordine palatii*, c. 28.
135 There is considerable controversy concerning the development of an official "policy" to use the royal chapel to train future bishops to serve the emperor. See the discussion by Timothy Reuter, "The 'Imperial Church System' of the Ottonian and Salian Rulers: A Reconsideration," *Journal of Ecclesiastical History* 33 (1982), 347-74; and the response by Josef Fleckenstein, "Problem und Gestalt der ottonisch-salischen Reichskirchen," in *Reich und Kirche vor dem Investiturstreit: Gerd Tellenbach zum achzigsten Geburtstag*, ed. Karl Schmid (Sigmaringen, 1985), 83-98, with a synthesis of the entire controversy by Bernhardt, *Itinerant Kingship*, 29-30. There is no question, however, that many clerics who had spent time in the royal chapel went on to hold high ecclesiastical office.

presence. Adalhard of Corbie had denoted these men as *pueri* and *vassalli*, who
were supported by their own lords, but actually served at court.[136] In his biography
of Bishop Ulrich, Gerhard observed that two of the prelate's nephews, named
Manegold and Hupold, had commanded military forces that were attached to
the royal court in the period before their uncle's death.[137] Their service under the
king brought them considerable advantages when Ulrich's successor as bishop
attempted to withdraw benefices from the men who were serving under Manegold and Hupold. The two magnates complained to their patrons at the royal
court, and were able to refuse the new bishop's demands.[138]

Royal Garrisons

The *milites* directly in the court, however, represent just a small part of the king's
overall military household. In aggregate, the largest number of the king's *milites*
were assigned to serve as garrison troops in royal fortifications that numbered
many score in active service at one time.[139] These fortifications were located
throughout the Ottonian kingdom, but particularly along threatened frontiers.
Throughout the reigns of Henry I and Otto I, the greatest concentration of royal
fortifications was located in the east.[140] In addition, Henry I maintained garrisons
in the west in the course of his efforts to reintegrate Lotharingia into the German
kingdom.[141] In response to repeated Danish aggression during the latter part of
Otto I's reign, Otto II also constructed a series of fortifications along the Danish
frontier in 974.[142]

In many cases, the royal *milites* serving as garrison troops held benefices within

---

[136] Adalhard, *De ordine palatii*, ch. 28. See the discussion of this *ordo* of fighting men by Bachrach,
Early Carolingian Warfare, 75-6.

[137] Gerhard, *Vita Uodalrici*, 1.28.

[138] Ibid., "*Ipsi autem quia episcopo sancto Uodalrico adhuc vivente ab eo missi saepe in auxilio imperatoris cum herili multitudine militum venerunt et in eius servitio voluntatem eius strenue in omnibus
adimplentes tamdiu permanserunt usque cum illius gratia muneribus honorati redire dimissi sunt.*"

[139] The system of fortress districts maintained by the Ottonian kings is dealt with in detail below.

[140] For a useful visual reference to the fortifications held by the king in the east, see Gerhard Billig,
Burgwardorganisation, appendix 1, with a map of the fortifications from the Ottonian period that
can be identified from written sources along the middle regions of the eastern frontier. A great
many of these fortifications were garrisoned by royal *milites*. See, in this context, the observation
by Schmid-Hecklau, *Meißen*, 205, concerning the construction of barracks at Meißen to house
the garrison at this royal fortress that was constructed by Henry I in 929. For a general introduction to the deployment of royal garrisons to fortresses throughout the east, see Grimm, *Burgwälle*,
46; Herrmann, "Belizi 997-Beltz-Belzig," 203; and Bachrach, "Military Organization of Ottonian
Germany," 1069-1070. For the later tenth and early eleventh century, see the discussion by Coblenz,
"Boleslav Chrobry in Sachsen und die archäologische Quellen," 249-285, who focuses on the role
played by both royal and magnate garrisons in defending the eastern frontier against the Polish
duke Boleslav Chrobry.

[141] See, for example, Flodoard, *Annales*, an. 923, who records the defense of the *castrum* at Saverne,
in Alsace, by Henry I's troops against the army of the west Frankish king, Raoul.

[142] See Thietmar of Merseburg, *Chronicon*, 3.6 and 3.24.

the fortress district where they served.[143] The royal *fidelis*, Wichart, for example, held the fortification at Rothenburg, on the Saale, along with its dependent properties, as a benefice.[144] Under his command were other royal *fideles* who held smaller benefices within the fortress district (*Burgward*).[145]

A charter issued by Otto II in 979 on behalf of Bishop Albuin I of Säben-Brixen (967–1005) sheds further light on the support of royal *milites* who served in garrisons.[146] In this charter, Otto II confirmed an earlier lifetime grant of the *curtis* of Villach to Bishop Albuin, a grant that likely had been issued during the reign of Otto I.[147] The *curtis* included a fortification (*castellum*) that was garrisoned by *milites*.[148] Before the lifetime grant to Albuin, both the *curtis* and its component *castellum* had been held by a royal *fidelis* named Henry who had received both payment and service (*tributum, servitium*) from the *milites* on the basis of the *beneficia* held by the latter.[149] As the details of the grant make clear, each of the men in the garrison held a benefice, properly to be understood as military lands, which were attached to the *castellum*.[150] The possessor of the larger administrative unit (*curtis*), to which the *castellum* and all of its appurtenances were subordinate, was to receive a portion of the revenues that each of the *milites* enjoyed.

Command Structure

Both the royal household, and the military households of the king's secular and ecclesiastical magnates were organized into sub-units under the command of officers, that is men who held an *officium*.[151] In garrisons, the commander

---

[143] The organization of these fortress districts is treated in detail below.

[144] DO I, 230.

[145] Ibid.

[146] DO II, 205.

[147] It is frequently the case that Otto II issued confirmations of grants made by his father.

[148] DO I, 205.

[149] Ibid., "*possideat et teneat et omne tributum et servitium quod Heinrico ad eadem curtem ex beneficio militum suorum persolvebatur.*" The charter does not identify Henry, and he is not accorded a title as *dux* or *comes*, so it remains unclear who he was.

[150] For an overview of the problem of lands held by soldiers from the government in the western tradition, see Bernard S. Bachrach, "Military Lands in Historical Perspective," *The Haskins Society Journal* 9 (1997), 95-122.

[151] It should be noted that *miles* was a standard term for soldier of whatever rank. In this regard, Liudprand, *Antapodosis*, 2.62, uses the term *miles* to indicate both the batman of a soldier and the soldier himself when describing the efforts of King Berengar I of Italy (887–915) to escape the Hungarians by pretending to be a simple soldier. Regarding the meaning of the term *miles* as soldier in tenth- and eleventh-century narrative sources, see the discussion by Bachrach, "Memory, Epistemology," 63-90. Also see Joachim Bumke, *Studien zum Ritterbegriff im 12. und 13. Jahrhundert*, second revised edition (Heidelberg, 1977), which maintains the same basic view regarding the use of the term *milites* as the first edition (Heidelberg, 1964). This work was translated into English as *The Concept of Knighthood in the Middle Ages*, trans. W. T. H. Jackson and E. Jackson (New York, 1982). The English text is cited here. In this context, Bumke, *Concept of Knighthood*, 38 demonstrates that that the term *miles* was not used as an indication of social standing, or as a synonym for vassal, but rather retained its basic meaning of soldier in pre-crusade Germany.

frequently was denoted as the *praefectus* of a particular fortification.[152] In the field, unit commanders usually were denoted as *principes*. In discussing the army that won a victory at Lenzen in 929, for example, Widukind notes that the overall command of the expeditionary levy (*exercitus*) was held by Bernhard.[153] He was accompanied by Thietmar, denoted as a *legatus*, who had command of a unit of *milites*.[154] Under Thietmar's command were the *principes* of the *milites* whom Widukind mentions returned along with Thietmar to Saxony following the successful battle against the Redarii.[155] The anonymous author of the *Gesta* of the bishops of Cambrai similarly described the officers in Otto I's army that invaded the west Frankish kingdom in 946 as *principes*.[156]

It is also possible to identify officers serving in the larger magnate military households. Widukind, for example, describes the officers serving under Duke Eberhard of Franconia as his *principes militum*.[157] In this case, Widukind notes that Otto I punished all of the duke's military officers (*principes militum*) who had participated in the assault on the royal garrison at Helmern.[158] Similarly, Gerhard identifies the officers who served in the military household of the bishops of Augsburg. In this case, it is the nephews of Bishop Ulrich, Manegold and Hupold, whom Gerhard identifies as *principes militum*.[159]

Fortress Districts

In addition to the bulk of the royal *milites*, who were stationed in garrisons rather than in attendance upon the king in person, a substantial number of *milites* in the military households of lay and ecclesiastical magnates also served as garrison troops in royal fortifications. They balanced these duties with guarding the fortifications that their lords held with a license from the king.[160] Among the earliest

---

[152] See, for example, Widukind, *Res gestae*, 2.8. Regarding the command structure of garrisons see, for example, Karl August Eckhardt, "Präfekt und Burggraf," *Zeitschrift der Savigny-Stiftung für Rechtsgeschichte. Germanistische Abteilung* 46 (1926), 163-205. The term *praefectus* had been used by the Carolingians to denote unit commanders, but not necessarily the commanders of fortifications. See the discussion by David S. Bachrach, *Religion and the Conduct of War c.300-c.1215* (Woodbridge, 2003), 43-45.

[153] Widukind, *Res gestae*, 1.36. See the discussion of this battle by Leyser, "Early Medieval Warfare," 36, who does not appreciate that the forces here included both members of the expeditionary levy and professional soldiers from the military households of the king and his magnates.

[154] Widukind, *Res gestae*, 1.36.

[155] Ibid.

[156] *Gesta episcoporum Cameracensium Liber I* c. 72. Also see the use of *principes* as military officers in *Arnulfi Gesta Archiepiscoporum Mediolanensium*, ed. C. L. Bethmann and W. Wattenbach, MG SS 8, c. 16.

[157] Widukind, *Res gestae*, 2.6.

[158] Ibid.

[159] Gerhard, *Vita Uodalrici*, 1.28.

[160] The topic of royal control over the construction and holding of fortifications would repay an in-depth study. The need to obtain such licenses is discussed in numerous narrative sources and royal charters. See, for example, *Gesta episcoporum Cameracensium Liber I* c. 112; *Ex Miraculis S. Wigberhti*, ed. G. Waitz, MGH SS 4, 224-228, c. 5; Ekkehard, *Casus Sancti Galli*, 44; *Vita Sancti*

detailed descriptions of the substantial fiscal revenues that were devoted to the maintenance of fortifications and their garrisons in the Carolingian period is the *Hersfelder Zehntverzeichnis* (HZV).[161] This document consists of a list of the tithe revenues, which originally had provided a substantial portion of the revenues (*ministerium*) of Counts Alberich and Markward in southern Hassegau in Saxony, that subsequently were granted by Charlemagne to the monastery of Hersfeld in 780.[162] Included in this list are 19 fortress districts (*urbes*) and 239 settlements that were established on royal property.[163] The fortifications comprised elements of a defensive system erected by King Pippin I (died 768) and Charlemagne along the Saale and Unstrut rivers to protect Thuringia from both Saxon and Slavic raids, the Sorbian march discussed in chapter one.[164] Many of the settlements listed in the HZV were subordinated to the *urbes* and provided them with revenues.

The fortress and fortified palace at Allstedt provides a good illustration of how the Carolingians and the Ottonians utilized income producing properties to support royal fortifications. During the course of the ninth and tenth centuries, many of the properties that had been used to support the fortification at Allstedt were granted in part or whole to the monastery of Hersfeld and subsequently to the monastery of Memleben.[165] Many of these grants are now lost (*perdita*). However, in the decade of the 990s, many of these properties came back into the hands of members of the royal family, and the charters for these transfers have survived. For example, in October 991, Otto III confirmed an exchange of properties between his grandmother Adelheid and Abbot Wunniger of Memleben.[166] The dowager empress was to receive lifetime usufruct of the tithes paid by eleven *villae*, all of which Memleben had received originally from the royal fisc, and all of which also appear in the HZV as paying their tithes to support the maintenance of royal fortifications.[167] The abbots of Memleben had been given the authority by Otto II and Otto III to maintain a series of fortresses, each of which was supported by numerous *villae*.[168] As a consequence, Otto III's charter on behalf

---

Bernwardi episcopi Hildesheimensis auctore Thangmaro, ed. Walter Berschin and Angelika Häse (Heidelberg, 1993), 282-4; DO I, 259, 265, 373, 374; DO II, 89, 204; DO III, 316; DH II, 259, 303. Regarding the service of the *milites* of secular and ecclesiastical magnates in royal fortresses, see the discussion by Bachrach, "Military Organization of Ottonian Germany," 1070-1075.

161 For the text of this documents, see *Urkundenbuch der Reichsabtei Hersfeld*, ed. Hans Weirich (Marburg, 1936), nr. 38.

162 The crucial initial study of this document is Walter Schlesinger, "Burgen und Burgbezirke. Beobachtungen im mitteldeutschen Osten," *Von Land und Kultur, Festschrift für Rudolf Kötzschke*, ed. Werner Emmerich (1937), 77-105; reprinted in idem, *Mitteldeutschen Beiträge zur deutschen Verfassungsgeschiche des Mittelalters* (Göttingen, 1961), 158-187, with additional discussion by idem, *Die Entstehung der Landesherrschaft, Teil I* (Dresden, 1941), 79

163 *Urkundenbuch der Reichsabtei Hersfeld*, nr. 37.

164 Grimm, *Handbuch vor-und frühgeschichtlicher Wall-und Wehranlagen Teil I*, 44-46.

165 Regarding this train of events, see Michael Gockel, "Allstedt," *Die deutschen Königspfalzen: Repertorium der Pfalzen, Königshöfe und übrigen Aufenthaltsorte der Könige im deutschen Reich des Mittelalters, vol. II Thüringen* (Göttingen, 2000), 1-38, here 27-33.

166 DO III, 75.

167 Gockel, "Allstedt," 27-33.

168 DO II, 139, 191; DO III, 75, 106, 142, 305.

of his grandmother makes clear that in the late tenth century the revenues from a large number of *villae* were still being used to support a series of fortresses that were constructed along the Saale and Unstrut rivers. These same fortresses and *villae* appear in the HZV, which dates back to the late eighth century. As a consequence, it is possible to see the overall continuity of this fortress district system throughout the tenth century, including during the reigns of Henry I and Otto I.

In addition to maintaining Carolingian-era fortification systems, the Ottonian kings also constructed large numbers of new fortifications to protect their conquests in the east and endowed these with dependent properties as well. As is true of most royal properties, information about these fortifications and their dependent *villae* is almost always to be found in the context of grants to royal dependants. This is the case, for example, with regard to Otto I's charter on behalf of the monastery of St Maurice at Magdeburg in April 961, which survives in three copies.[169] In this act, in a manner strongly reminiscent of the *modus operandi* seen in the HZV, Otto transferred to St Maurice the tithe revenues (*decima*) that were collected at Magdeburg, Frohse, Barby, and Calbe, all major fortifications, from the Slavic and German dependants of these places.[170] The charter specifically identifies these payments as part of a military tax, noting that the payment was owed by those who were supposed to take refuge in the aforementioned fortifications.[171]

Just three months later, in July 961, Otto I made an additional grant to St Maurice involving frontier fortifications, in this case the *Burgwarde* of Giebichenstein and Rothenburg, noted above.[172] Giebichenstein is denoted as the *caput* of a series of fortifications (*urbes*) each of which is identified as possessing both dependent properties and dependants, including Slavs and Germans.[173] The dependent properties of Rothenburg are denoted rather more generally as "everything that legally pertains to this fortification."[174]

A rather more detailed image of the fiscal appurtenances associated with royal fortresses can be seen in the case of the *castellum* of Grimschleben. In April 978, Otto II took under his protection the monastery of Nienburg, located 35 kilometers south of Magdeburg on the left bank of the Saale river.[175] The monastery that was constructed within this fortified site (*castellum*) had been founded nine

---

[169] DO I, 222a-c.

[170] DO I, 222b.

[171] DO I, 222a, "*omnes Sclavani qui ad predictas civitates confugium facere debent.*" The second extant version of the text, which the editor argues superceded the first version, leaves out this phrase, noting instead that the payment came from the "Theutonici" and the "Sclavi" who were dependants (*pertinentes*) to the five fortifications that are specifically denoted as the *capites* of fortress districts (*burgowardae*).

[172] DO I, 232a-b.

[173] DO I, 232a, "*Giviconsten cum salsugine eius ceterasque urbes cum omnibus ad eas pertinentibus aquis salsis et insulsis terris cultis et incultis mancipiis Teutonicis et Sclavanicis.*"

[174] Ibid.

[175] DO II, 174.

years earlier by Archbishop Gero of Cologne and his brother Thietmar.[176] Nienburg, which was located on the exceptionally important route along the Saale
between Magdeburg and Merseburg, served as an important stopping point for
royal officials and troops moving south to join the *Via Regia* (Hohen Straße) to
Meißen and then east to Lausatia, or south toward Bohemia.[177]

In the context of granting his protection (*mundiburdium*) to Nienburg, Otto
transferred royal *mansi* to the monastery which were drawn from three *villae* that
were dependent upon the royal *castellum* of Grimschleben, which was located just
a few kilometers to the east on the right bank of the Saale.[178] Excavations of this
site have identified a substantial fortification that was protected by a blended earth,
timber, and stone wall with a width of some eight meters. The wall rose approximately 4.5 meters above ground level and was protected by a two-meter wide ditch.[179]

Eleven months later, on 3 March 979, Otto II made a second grant to Nienburg of properties associated with Grimschleben.[180] The original grant, which is
still extant, was made at Dornburg some 40 kilometers north of Grimschleben,
and it is clear from the text that the scribe did not have access at that point to a
full account of the properties associated with the *castellum*, but rather only to a
partial list. The charter, therefore, includes the proviso that any of Grimschleben's
dependent properties that had been given to a third party by Otto I or by Otto
II were not included in this grant to Nienburg.[181] Sometime thereafter, however, a
second charter was drawn up on behalf of Nienburg that provided a full account
of the properties that had been delegated by the king to support the *castellum*
at Grimschleben. This charter, which survives in a fifteenth-century copy, lists
twenty *villae* by name.[182] Taken in sum, the series of grants to the monastery of
Nienburg makes clear that through the end of Otto I's reign, the fortification of
Grimschleben was supported by the revenues drawn from a minimum of twenty-
three *villae*. This is quite an extraordinary investment of resources, and gives a
sense of the enormous wealth that was required to maintain a system of scores
of fortresses along the eastern frontiers of the Ottonian kingdom.

---

[176] See the discussion of this act by Bernhardt, *Itinerant Kingship*, 170. Werner Hülle, *Westausbreitung und Wehranlagen der Slawen in Mitteldeutschland* (Leipzig, 1940), 82-83, suggested that Grimschleben was a bridgehead over the Saale and was part of a paired fortress system with Nienburg
that protected the important ford there.
[177] Regarding the development and route of the *via regia*, see Herrmann, "Herausbildung und
Dynamik der Germanisch-Slawischen Siedlungsgrenze in Mitteleuropa," 269; Bernd W. Bahn,
"Zscheiplitz im Netz alter Straßen," *Burgen und Schlösser in Sachsen-Anhalt* 1 (1999), 204-218, here
213; and Karlheinz Blaschke, "Straßen und Fernhandel im Mittelalter," *Leipzig, Mitteldeutschland
und Europa: Festgabe für Manfred Staube und Manfred Unger zum 70. Geburtstag* (Beucha, 2000),
263-273, here 264.
[178] DO II, 174.
[179] Hülle, *Westausbreitung und Wehranlagen der Slawen*, 82.
[180] DO II, 185a-b.
[181] DO II, 185a, "ac legaliter pertinens ad illud remansit non datum, ex toto et integro, excepto quod
genitor noster aut nos alicui antea per preceptum donavimus, modo eiusdem nostrae coniugis frequenti
ac assidua peticione ad predictum monasterium perpetualiter delegamus atque concedimus."
[182] DO II, 185b.

This system of supporting royal fortifications with revenues taken from royal *villae* continued on throughout the tenth century, and into the eleventh. Describing conditions in his own day, Bishop Thietmar of Merseburg observed that in 1006, Henry II rebuilt the fortress of Arneburg, located on the west bank of the Elbe about 10 kilometers north-east of the modern city of Stendal. As part of this process Henry II endowed the fort with the resources necessary to support a garrison there.[183] Henry was attempting to restore this stronghold to the state it had enjoyed in 997 when Otto III had strengthened it for defense against the Slavs.[184] In the intervening decade, according to Thietmar, the revenues that had been intended for the maintenance of the fortification and garrison had been misappropriated.[185] To give a sense of the scale of resources involved in this project, the single *villa* centered on the fortress at Arneburg itself comprised no fewer than 160 *mansi*, which was sufficient property to support 160 families for an entire year.[186]

Conclusion

The tri-partite military organization employed by the Ottonians drew heavily on Carolingian precedent and administration. In large part, this was the case because Henry I and Otto I faced the same challenges as did their predecessors. Warfare, which was dominated by sieges, required a very large levy of militarized civilians to garrison fortifications in the face of enemy attack. Conversely, capturing fortress cities and other major fortifications required large armies in the field. In the absence of a standing army numbering in the tens of thousands, the bulk of these fighting men had to be provided by the militia troops of the expeditionary levy. Nevertheless, continuous offensive warfare over a period of fifty years required a high degree of professionalization as well. The Ottonian king needed military commanders and fighting men who could serve year round, and provide important continuity in training and tactics to the larger forces of militiamen who were summoned for relatively brief campaigns in the summer and early autumn. In addition, it was these professional soldiers who garrisoned the king's fortifications, particularly in remote frontier regions where an insufficient number of loyal colonists had settled to provide for the local defense.

---

[183] Thietmar of Merseburg, *Chronicon*, 6.28, "*Arnaburch prius devastatam ob defensionem patriae renovavit, queque diu hinc iniuste ablata erant, restituit.*"
[184] Regarding Otto III's efforts to restore the fortification, see Thietmar of Merseburg, *Chronicon*, 4.38.
[185] Thietmar of Merseburg, *Chronicon*, 6.28.
[186] For the *villa* of Arneburg, see DH II, 111.

4

Military Education

Warfare was one of the major occupations and preoccupations of the secular elite in the Ottonian kingdom, as it had been under the Carolingians.[1] More surplus resources were devoted to the preparation for war, the conduct of war, and war's aftermath than to any other activity during the tenth century.[2] As a consequence, the formal education of would-be military commanders proceeded in a manner consistent with the training of other professionals whose occupations similarly benefitted from extensive expenditures by the royal government and magnates, including both secular and ecclesiastical *seniores*. Those receiving substantial support included master architects, surveyors, engineers, notaries, and estate managers. The education of these highly skilled professionals in the secular world can be compared to the education of clerics charged with the provision of pastoral care, and the administration of important institutions, including monasteries and bishoprics. Like other highly skilled professionals in both the secular and ecclesiastical spheres, military commanders required training in carrying out a wide range of tasks. These included, but were not limited to, strategy, logistics, constructing marching camps, constructing siege equipment, establishing a siege, defending against a siege, choosing a battlefield, battlefield formations, tactics involving foot soldiers, tactics involving mounted forces, providing leadership on

[1]   With regard to the cultural, political, and economic significance of war in the Carolingian and Ottonian empires, see the observations of Karl Leyser in "The Battle at the Lech" and "Early Medieval Warfare"; and Timothy Reuter in "Plunder and Tribute in the Carolingian Empire" and "Carolingian and Ottonian Warfare".

[2]   The enormous resources devoted to warfare are illuminated in a variety of ways in contemporary sources. The famous capitulary *de villis*, for example, makes clear that Charlemagne's government sought to maximize the production of royal estates largely for the support of the army on campaign. In this context, see the important studies by Klaus Verhein, "Studien zu Quellen zum Reichsgut der Karolingerzeit," part 1, *Deutsches Archiv für Geschichte des Mittelalters* 10 (1954), 313-394; and part 2, *Deutsches Archiv für Geschichte des Mittelalters* 11 (1955), 333-392; and Adriaan Verhulst, "'Karolingische Agrarpolitik': Das Capitulare de Villis und die Hungersnote von 792/93 und 805/6," *Zeitschrift für Agrargeschichte und Agrarsoziologie* 13 (1965), 175-189. Cf. Darryl Campbell, "The *Capitulare de Villis*, the *Brevium exempla*, and the Carolingian Court at Aachen," *Early Medieval Europe* 18 (2010), 243-264.

Another point of departure for considering the central economic importance of warfare during the early medieval period is the extent to which the revenues of ecclesiastical institutions were devoted to military matters. In the late ninth century, for example, Archbishop Hincmar of Rheims sought to limit this expenditure to 40 percent of ecclesiastical revenues. see Nelson, "The Church's Military Service in the Ninth Century".

the battlefield, maintaining military morale, training fighting men in the use of their arms, and training fighting men to form and maintain battlefield formations.[3]

It was once convenient for scholars wedded to the image of primitive Germans playacting as sophisticated Romans to characterize the Carolingian renaissance as an "optical illusion," and the secular elite of the Ottonian kingdom as illiterate to such an extent that royal administration was bereft of the use of writing for even the basic tasks of government.[4] This line of argument made it possible to bypass the necessity of grappling with the implications of a society that committed massive resources to an educational program, based on the written word, not only for its elite, but also for men with exceptional talent who were drawn from outside the elite.

Intensive scholarship over the past forty years, however, has demonstrated the enormous importance of "learning from books" and the practical application of this learning, not only at the height of the Carolingian power in the early ninth century, but also in the Carolingian successor states, both east and west of the Rhine. Moreover, this program of education was valued not only by clerics, but also by the secular elite that was engaged in the traditional pursuits of farming, legal disputes, and combat. As Rosamond McKitterick aptly has observed, these magnates "possessed essential handbooks for men of their class – law books and tracts on war and agriculture."[5]

Ottonian Education

In understanding education in the Latin West, including the education of wealthy and aristocratic sons in the Ottonian kingdom, it is important to draw a distinction between elementary study of the seven liberal arts in the *trivium* and *quadrivium* that was the focus of children between the ages of seven to fourteen (*pueritia*),

3   Cf. the suggestion by Guy Halsall, *Warfare and Society in the Barbarian West, 450–900* (London, 2003), 146; and Reuter, "Carolingian and Ottonian Warfare," 19-21, that important manuals for training future officers, such as Vegetius *Epitoma rei militaris* and Frontinus' *Strategemata* were of merely antiquarian interest to monks, and had no practical value in either the preparation for or the conduct of military affairs. Neither of these scholars provides any alternate explanation for the ways in which commanders were taught the myriad skills that were required to conduct military operations.

4   See, for example, Reuter, "Plunder and Tribute," 91, who argues specifically that the advanced and civilized nature of the Carolingian world is "probably an optical illusion." With regard to the lack of the use of the written word in the Ottonian kingdom, the observation by Keller, "Zum Charakter der 'Staatlichkeit' zwischen karolingischer Reichsreform und hochmittelalterlichen Herrschaftsausbau," 257, that "Despite the continuity of the idea of empire and the model of Charlemagne, everything that was of particular importance for high Carolingian imperial organization – centrality, office, law-giving, and writing – was absent in its successor states. Indeed they simply came to an end," is representative of the general thrust of scholarly opinion regarding the Ottonian state.

5   McKitterick, *The Carolingians and the Written Word*, 249. As the subsequent works by McKitterick and other authors, discussed below, make clear, this emphasis on lay learning was not restricted either to the lands west of the Rhine, nor to the ninth century.

and a more advanced training in specific fields that built upon this foundation.[6] With regard to the former, scholars have identified a great many late antique and even classical works that were diligently copied and updated by *magistri* for the purpose of teaching skills in reading, writing, and numeracy, including both simple arithmetic and more complex problems of geometry.[7] Crucially, the turn of the tenth century did not see any changes in this educational pattern. Rather, the schools of the Ottonian kingdom used the same works as those employed by their ninth-century predecessors, often the very same manuscripts, many of which have survived into the present.[8]

The late antique authors, whose works formed the core of this curriculum, include Cassiodorus, Isidore, Martianus Capella, Donatus, Victorius of Aquitaine, as well as the *corpus agrimensorum*, which was a late fifth- or early sixth-century compilation of Roman surveying texts.[9] In this context, Charlemagne's legislation leading to the vast expansion of the number of schools, principally in the *Admonitio generalis* and the *Epistola de litteris collendis*, led also to the production of a concomitantly large number of textbooks that served both monastic and cathedral schools throughout the Carolingian empire, including in East Francia, and consequently in the Ottonian kingdom as well.[10] From an Ottonian

6   Isidore of Seville's differentiation of the stages of life in *Liber differentiarum*, 2.19, in PL 83, col. 81, taken ultimately from Augustine, was widely copied by scholars during the early medieval period. Thus, for example, Rabanus Maurus, in his tract *De aetatibus hominis* (PL 111, col. 179), identified six stages of life, the first three of which were *infantia, pueritia,* and *adolescentia*. See the discussion of this text by Christoph Dette, "Kinder und Jugendliche in der Adelsgesellschaft des frühen Mittelalters," *Archiv für Kulturgeschichte* 76 (1994), 1-34, here 4.
7   Foundational to the modern understanding of early medieval education is Pierre Riché, *Education et culture dans l'Occident barbare, VIe-VIIIe siècles* (1962), translated by John Contreni as *Education and Culture in the Barbarian West, Sixth through Eighth Centuries* (Columbia, SC, 1976).
8   The great continuity in educational practices from the ninth to the tenth century is stressed by McKitterick, "Ottonische Kultur und Bildung," 209-224; and John J. Contreni, "The Tenth Century: The Perspective from the Schools," in *Haute moyen-age: culture, education et société. Études offertes à Pierre Riché*, ed. Michel Sot (Colombes, 1990), 379-387; reprinted with the same pagination in John J. Contreni, *Carolingian Learning, Masters, and Manuscripts* (Aldershot, 1992).
9   Regarding the importance of these authors for the basic curriculum in the liberal arts, see Wesley Stevens, "Compotistica et Astronomica in the Fulda School," in *Saints, Scholars, and Heroes: Studies in Medieval Culture in Honor of Charles W. Jones* (1979), 27-64, particularly 36-39; idem, "Field and Streams: Language and Practice of Arithmetic and Geometry in Early Medieval Schools," in *Word, Image, Number. Communication in the Middle Ages*, ed. John J. Contreni and Santa Casciani (Turnhout, 2002), 113-204, here 113; Menso Folkerts, "The Importance of Pseudo-Boethian *Geometria* during the Middle Ages," in *Boethius and the Liberal Arts: A Collection of Essays*, ed. Micahel Masi (Bern, 1982), 187-209, here 189; Detlef Illmer, "Arithmetik in der gelehrten Arbeitsweise des frühen Mittelalters: Eine Studie zum Grundsatz 'nisi enim nomen scieris, cognitio rerum perit,'" in *Institutionen, Kultur und Gesellschaft im Mittelalter: Festschrift für Josef Fleckenstein zu seinem 65. Geburtstag*, ed. Werner Rösener and Thomas Zotz (Sigmaringen, 1984), 35-58; Paul L. Butzer, "Mathematics in the West and East from the Fifth to the Tenth Centuries: An Overview," in *Science in Western and Eastern Civilization in Carolingian Times*, ed. P. L. Butzer and D. Lohrmann (Basel, 1993), 443-481, particularly 451-458; and Emily Albu, "Imperial Geography and the Medieval Peutinger Map," *Imago Mundi* 57 (2005), 136-148, here 138.
10   On the institutional significance of this legislation and the resulting proliferation of both monastic and cathedral schools throughout the Carolingian empire, see the discussion by John J. Contreni, "Learning in the Early Middle Ages," in idem, *Carolingian Learning, Masters and Manu-*

perspective, the monastic and cathedral schools of the nascent German kingdom possessed vast numbers of texts as part of their intellectual and material inheritance from the Carolingians. Moreover, in addition to their extensive use of these inherited books, it is clear that during the tenth century *magistri* in the eastern regions of the erstwhile Carolingian empire, as had been true of their ninth-century predecessors, developed their own teaching texts or handbooks (*libri manuales*) in which they collected works or passages from a variety of authors for use by their students.[11]

The practical use of both late antique and contemporary teaching texts in the classrooms of Ottonian schools is made clear not only by the enormous resources that were poured by the royal government and ecclesiastical centers into their production, but also in the very appearance of those manuscripts that have survived into the present.[12] Indeed, the diligent analysis of the manuscripts of these texts has elucidated the general pattern through which masters interacted with their students. As John Contreni has observed, teaching texts were organized so as to establish a dialogue between the master and the student, such that the preferred method of masters was "to present the essential material of grammatical, computistical and theological instruction as responses to questions."[13]

In this process, students took notes on wax tablets, which might over time then be transferred to parchment, as was the case, for example, with Walafrid Strabo (d. 849), who undertook his primary education at Fulda under the direc-

scripts (Aldershot, 1992), 1-21, here 10. Concerning the enduring influence of this legislation on the development of schools and the production of texts in the eastern portions of the erstwhile Carolingian empire under the Ottonian kings, see Fleckenstein, "Königshof und Bischofsschule unter Otto dem Großen," 168-192; Rosamond McKitterick, "Continuity and Innovation in Tenth-Century Ottonian Culture," in *Intellectual Life in the Middle Ages: Essays Presented to Margaret Gibson*, ed. Lesley Smith and Benedicta Ward (London, 1992), 15-24, and reprinted with the same pagination in Rosamond McKitterick, *The Frankish Kings and Culture in the Early Middle Ages* (Aldershot, 1995); and eadem, "Ottonische Kultur und Bildung," in *Otto der Große. Magdeburg und Europa*, ed. Matthias Puhle (Mainz, 2001), I: 209-224.

[11]   See the discussion on this point by Contreni, "Education and Learning in the Early Middle Ages," 21; and Joachim Ehlers, "Dom- und Klosterschulen in Deutschland und Frankreich im 10. und 11. Jahrhundert," in *Schule und Schüler im Mittelalter: Beiträge zur europäischen Bildungsgeschichte des 9. bis 15. Jahrhunderts*, ed. Martin Kintzinger (Cologne, 1996), 29-52, here 36.

[12]   Regarding the enormous number of texts that were produced by Carolingian and Ottonian *scriptoria*, see Bernhard Bischoff, "Über den Plan eines paläographischen Gesamtkatalogs der festländischen Handschriften des neunten Jahrhunderts," *Archivalische Zeitschrift* (1963), 166, who reports some 6,000 surviving manuscripts from the ninth century alone, as compared with just 1,811 manuscripts or fragments of manuscripts for the period before 800. With regard to this latter figure, see E. A. Lowe, *Codices Latini Antiquiores: A Palaeographical Guide to Latin Manuscripts Prior to the Ninth Century* in 11 volumes (Oxford, 1934–1971). Concerning the enormous production of manuscripts in the Ottonian kingdom, see Hartmut Hoffmann, *Buchkunst und Königtum im ottonischen und frühsalischen Reich*, MGH Schriften 30 (Stuttgart, 1986); and McKitterick, "Ottonische Kultur und Bildung," 209-224.

[13]   John J. Contreni, "Education and Learning in the Early Middle Ages: New Perspectives and Old Problems," *International Journal of Social Education* 4 (1989), 9-25; reprinted with the same pagination in idem, *Carolingian Learning, Masters and Manuscripts* (Aldershot, 1992), here 16.

tion of Rabanus Maurus.[14] Crucially, the native language of both of these men was German, which indicates that Latin was hardly a barrier to learning in the east. As Christophe Dette has demonstrated in his detailed analysis of the school at St Gall, the pattern of educational practice, as developed by the Carolingians in the ninth century, was diligently pursued among the German-speaking teachers and students of Ottonian schools of the tenth. Crucially for the present discussion of training future military commanders, this education was provided to the sons of lay aristocrats destined for a life in the world, as well as for future clerics and monks.[15]

After completing this preliminary education, the student at either a cathedral or a monastic school was, at the age of fourteen, both a competent reader of Latin texts and the master of basic arithmetic, but likely also, if he had any talent, able to compose some Latin prose, and to perform more advanced mathematical calculations. This was true whether the student was a native Romance speaker, or instead a native speaker of German. Moreover, as records from the monastery of St Gall make clear, the practical value of this education was recognized not only for sons of the nobility, but also for the dependants, including the unfree dependants, of both secular and ecclesiastical magnates. These unfree dependants subsequently served as priests in the private churches of the nobles and as stewards for their estates.[16]

Basic to the primary education of both aristocratic boys, and their specially chosen dependants, was practical literacy and numeracy. The practical skills that they learned including the making of *breves*, and other kinds of lists that were central to administrative control over estates.[17] Adalhard of Corbie's famous statutes for the administration of his monastery provide a reminder that practical literacy and numeracy, learned from books, were crucial for the administration of both monastic and secular estates.[18] Moreover, as Janet Nelson has observed, this

[14] Regarding the use of wax tablets and the specific case of Walafrid Strabo's early education, see Wesley M. Stevens, "Walafrid Strabo: A Student at Fulda," in *Historical Papers of the CHA for 1971*, ed. J. Atherton (Ottawa, 1972), 13-20; reprinted with the same pagination in idem, *Cycles of Time and Scientific Learning in Medieval Europe* (Aldershot, 1995), here 13.

[15] See the detailed treatment of this issue, with specific references to the education of aristocratic youth at the outer school of the monastery of St. Gall by Christoph Dette, "Schüler im frühen und hohen Mittelalter: Die St. Galler Klosterschule des 9. und 10. Jahrhunderts," *Studien und Mitteilungen zur Geschichte des Benediktinerordens und seiner Zweige* 105 (1994), 7-64.

[16] Ibid., 8-10.

[17] Ibid., 10.

[18] *Adalhardi abbatis Corbiensis Statuta seu Brevia*, ed. Joseph Semmler in *Corpus consuetudinum monasticum*, ed. Kassius Hallinger, vol. 1, *Initia consuetudines Benedictinae: Consuetudines saeculi octavi et noni* (Siegburg, 1963), 365-408, here 392: "*Per brevem tamen de singulis locis omni anno semper omnia suscipiat, ut si necesse fuerit cognosci possit, utrum ipsi ministri hoc fideliter peregissent.*" An English translation of this text is available in "Appendix II: The Customs of Corbie, Consuetudines Corbeiensis, a Translation by Charles W. Jones of the Directive of Adalhard of Corbie," in *The Plan of St. Gall*, ed. Walter Horn and Ernest Born, 3 vols. (Berkeley, CA, 1979), III: 101-120. See the detailed discussion of this text, with an emphasis on the importance of mathematical and engineering knowledge required by the abbot, by Dieter Hägermann, "Der Abt als Grundherr: Kloster und Wirtschaft im frühen Mittelalter," in *Herrschaft und Kirche: Beiträge zur Enstehung und Wirkungsweise episkopaler und monastischer Organisationsformen*, ed. Friedrich Prinz (Stuttgart, 1988), 345-385.

type of practical literacy was hardly limited to the west even in the ninth century. In his German translation of the *Book of the Evangelists*, written in the 860s, the East Frankish writer Otfrid used the term *breves* when translating the opening verses of Luke 2:1-7 regarding Augustus' decree that all the world was to be taxed, a clear indication that the term *breve* and the verb *imbreviare* had entered the vernacular of the East Frankish kingdom.[19]

It bears repeating that the turn of the tenth century did not mark a significant change in the ability of native German speakers to learn and utilize Latin.[20] Men, and some women, who held positions of power and influence were at least bi-lingual and may well have been poly-lingual.[21] Rosamond McKitterick has shown in her numerous studies that it is necessary to understand Latin texts as descriptive evidence of Frankish culture. In light of her substantial work in this area, one must agree with McKitterick that: "The Franks were thus a Germanic people who conducted their administrative, legal and intellectual affairs in Latin."[22] As the German-speaking inheritors of the East Carolingian kingdom, one can make the same observation regarding the Ottonians.

Advanced Education in the Ottonian Kingdom

The basic education provided by monastic and cathedral schools that focused on grammar and numeracy likely was sufficient for many men, both secular and ecclesiastical, who would go on to hold administrative positions in the Ottonian kingdom. However, in order to do highly specialized work, additional education was required. For men involved in fields such as engineering, architecture, medicine, and the law, this learning came from specialized handbooks, many of which were late antique in origin. In this context, the identification of the need to educate professionals in the applied sciences as contrasted with scholarly pursuits, particularly in the *quadrivium*, dates back to late antiquity and was central, for example, to Cassiodorus' view of the function of the state. Speaking in the name of King Theodoric, Cassiodorus focused on the practical application

Also see the observation of John J. Contreni, "Counting, Calendars, and Cosmology: Numeracy in the Early Middle Ages," in *Word, Image, Number. Communication in the Middle Ages*, ed. John J. Contreni and Santa Casciani (Turnhout, 2002), 43-83, here 48, that "some *pueri* who learned to work with numbers in the monasteries and cathedrals would put their numeric skills to other uses when charged with the collection of tithes and its divisions into fourths, or the calculations of harvests from fields, of rents from farmers, of tolls from merchants, and the increased minting and use of coins in the early medieval economy all presupposed a culture of counting."

[19]   See the discussion by Janet Nelson, "The Henry Loyn Memorial Lecture for 2006: Henry Loyn and the Context of Anglo-Saxon England," *The Haskins Society Journal* 19 (2007), 154-169, here 168.

[20]   For an overview of this problem, see Rosamond McKitterick, "The Written Word and Oral Communication: Rome's Legacy to the Franks," in *Latin Culture and Medieval Germanic Europe: Germania Latina I*, ed. Richard North and Tette Hofstra (Gröningen, 1992), 89-112; reprinted with the same pagination in Rosamond McKitterick, *The Frankish Kings and Culture in the Early Middle Ages* (Aldershot, 1995).

[21]   Ibid., 96,

[22]   Ibid., 99.

of mathematical skills, particularly geometry, for the work of engineers, surveyors, and architects, but also arithmetic skills for basic government functions such as minting coins, and establishing and maintaining market weights and measures.[23] Cassiodorus even noted in a letter to a surveyor (*agrimensor*) that the subject matter of the *quadrivium* was of a theoretical nature, and not subject to state support, while the work of surveyors was practical, and therefore did receive public support.[24]

The extensive efforts of modern paleographers and text editors have made clear that large numbers of late antique and even classical technical manuals were copied, annotated, and even updated by professional practitioners from the eighth through the eleventh century.[25] The pattern of surviving manuscripts indicates that some schools specialized in the production of certain genres of texts. For example, the monastery at Corbie under the direction of Charlemagne's cousin Adalhard produced large numbers of advanced mathematical works that had applications for surveying, engineering, architecture, and also agriculture.[26] Among these works were Cassiodorus' *Institutiones*, which had materials suitable both for elementary and advanced education in mathematics and applied science. This work contains Boethius' partial translation of Euclid, Columella's book on agriculture, and compilations of the *corpus agrimensorum*.[27] This collection of texts provided significantly more advanced instruction in mathematics than was available in Martianus Capella's more general work on the liberal arts.[28]

The pattern of specialization that took place in Carolingian schools also is

[23]   *Cassiodori Senatoris Variae*, ed. Theodor Mommsen and Ludwig Traube (Munich, 1894, repr, 1981), I, 10 and 45, III, 52, VII, 5. See the discussion by Riché, *Education and Culture*, 68.

[24]   Riché, *Education and Culture*, 68, and Cassiodorus, *Varia*, III, 52, for the passage. The texts of the Roman *agrimensores* works, which were transmitted in large part to the early Middle Ages, are now easily available in Brian Campbell, *The Writings of the Roman Land Surveyors: Introduction, Text, Translation and Commentary* (London, 2000).

[25]   A valuable survey of this material is provided by Bernhard Bischoff, "Die Überlieferung der technischen Literatur," in *Artigianato et tennica nella societa dell'alto medioevo occidentale, Centro italiano die studi sull'alto medioevo* (Spoleto, 1971), I: 267-297.

[26]   These texts are described in some detail by Folkerts, "The Importance of Pseudo-Boethian *Geometria* during the Middle Ages," 187-209.

[27]   Folkerts, "The Importance of Pseudo-Boethian *Geometria* during the Middle Ages," 190, takes the position, following the argument of B. L. Ullman, "Geometry in the Mediaeval Quadrivium," in *Studi dei bibliografia e die storia in onore di Tammaro de Marinis*, vol. 4 (1964), 263-285, that texts of the *agrimensores* were used solely to train monks in geometry as part of the quadrivium. This limited view of the value of these texts is not widely accepted by other specialists in mathematical education in the early medieval period, as will be seen below, and is based on Ullman's view (268) that bishops could not have had an interest in training their clerics, canons and acolytes in practical surveying. Obviously, the problem of settling property disputes through a proper delineation of boundaries, which is the focus of much of the *corpus agrimensorum*, was an important matter to bishops, such as Werner I of Strasbourg (1001–1028), cited by Ullman as obtaining an *agrimensores* manuscript for his cathedral school. In this context, it is not unreasonable to believe that such a manuscript could be used both for teaching geometry and for teaching the practical techniques of surveying.

[28]   Illmer, "Arithmetik in der gelehrten Arbeitsweise des frühen Mittelalters," 35; and Butzer, "Mathematics in the West and East," 451.

evident in schools of the tenth century. Scholars have identified a wide range of mathematical works that were produced at, and even exported from, a number of important monasteries in the Ottonian kingdom including those at St Gall, Reichenau, Lorsch, Einsiedeln, and Seligenstadt.[29] The productivity of these eastern schools was such that Paul Butzer was moved to describe the advances in mathematical knowledge over the course of the ninth, tenth and eleventh centuries as a "The Carolingian and Ottonian Renaissance."[30]

Advanced mathematical works provided a basis for understanding handbooks such as Vitruvius' *De architectura*, which were used by practicing architects such as the native German speaker Einhard and the anonymous "applied mathematician" who constructed Charlemagne's octagonal chapel at Aachen.[31] In addition to Vitruvius' handbook, which provided a considerable body of theoretical information, illustrated formularies also circulated in the East Frankish and subsequently Ottonian kingdom of the ninth and tenth centuries.[32] These formularies provided models for the construction of specific elements of buildings such as columns. Similar works dealing with the techniques for constructing buildings of wood also circulated. Some of these texts, which included new tenth-century compositions, also were illustrated so as to facilitate their use by craftsmen and builders.[33] In considering the practical value of these small pamphlet-sized works, it is useful to consider that the practice of combining knowledge from theoretical works and guidelines for the construction of specific architectural features in formularies dating back to late antiquity.[34]

In addition to architectural handbooks, another exceptionally important collection of practical manuals that circulated in tenth-century Germany consists of the wide range of texts that were grouped under the name *corpus agrimensorum.* In his pioneering work on science in late antiquity and the early medieval period, Otto Neugebauer emphasized that the body of texts, including the *agrimensores,* that were available in the Carolingian period represent a substantial increase rather than a decline in the study of the physical science as compared with earlier periods.[35] Neugebauer's findings in this regard have received considerable additional support from the tireless analysis of manuscript evidence by

29 Ilmer, "Arithmetik," 36.
30 Paul L. Butzer, "Die Mathematiker des Aachen-Lütticher Raumes von der karolingischen bis zur spätottonischen Epoche," *Annalen des historischen Vereins für den Niederrhein, insbesondere das alte Erzbistum Köln* 178 (1976), 7-30, here 10.
31 Regarding Einhard's use of Vitruvius, see Butzer, "Mathematics in the West and East," 453; and Bischoff, "Die Überlieferung der technischen Literatur," 274. For the description of this architect as an applied mathematician, see Butzer, "Mathematics in the West and East," 453, with the suggestion that he may have been Odo of Metz.
32 Bischoff, "Die Überlieferung der technischen Literatur," 276.
33 Ibid., 285.
34 See the discussion of one of these late antique formularies by V. Mortet, "La mesure des colonnes à la fin de l'époque romaine d'après un très ancien formulaire," *Bibliothèque de l'Ecole des Chartes* 57 (1896), 289, and the broader observation regarding the use of such texts by Riché, *Education and Culture,* 69.
35 Otto Neugebauer, *The Exact Sciences in Antiquity,* 2nd edition (Providence, RI, 1957), 146.

Wesley Stevens.[36] In this context, Stevens writes: "It was fortunate for engineers like Einhard, as well as surveyors who were assigned the duty of delineating boundaries between the kingdom of Lothaire, Charles the Bald and Louis the German, that instruction from such a *Corpus agrimensorum Romanorum* could be found in Carolingian schools."[37]

Here Stevens echoes the comments of A. P. Juschkewitsch and A. C. Crombie who wrote:

> The needs of building, trade, transport, commerce, financial institutions of noble and ecclesiastical as well as multiple royal households, instruments of credit, legal acts and records and so forth provided impetus for reflection concerning ratios and proportions, equations of first and second degree, similar configurations in discrete circumstances including the ancient theorem now bearing the name of Pythagoras, calculation of surface areas and of volumes, and so on.[38]

As Florentine Mütherich observed with regard to one compilation of *agrimensores* texts that this original sixth-century collection of practical field measurement texts was updated with contemporary materials in the ninth century.[39] Of exceptional importance for understanding advanced education in the Ottonian kingdom, monastic and cathedral schools in the tenth century not only continued to possess these mathematical, architectural and engineering works, but also updated them.[40]

Similar intellectual advances in the German-speaking eastern half of the Carolingian empire can be seen in the field of agriculture. Karl W. Butzer points out that texts composed by Virgil, Columella, Pliny, and Palladius were widely available to students, having been copied extensively by *scriptoria* that were based in Carolingian and subsequently Ottonian monasteries.[41] Walafrid Strabo, who, as noted above, received his basic education at the Thuringian monastery of Fulda, was intimately concerned with improving agricultural production, particularly in the area of medicinal herbs, and drew heavily upon both Virgil and Columella in his *Hortulus*, a poetic and pedagogical text dealing with farming.[42] This was true despite Strabo's own observation, echoing Augustine's comments in *De opere*

---

36   The collection of essays in Wesley Stevens, *Cycles of Time and Scientific Learning in Medieval Europe* (Aldershot, 1995), provides an invaluable introduction to the wide range of mathematical texts that were used and improved by Carolingian scholars.

37   Ibid., 39.

38   Ibid., and for the quotation, *Scientific Change: Historical Studies in the Intellectual, Social, and Technological Invention from Antiquity to the Present*, ed. A. C. Crombie (London, 1963), 294 and 319.

39   Florentine Mütherich, "Der karolingische Agrimensoren-Codex in Rom," *Aachener Künstblätter* 45 (1974), 59-74, here 59.

40   Butzer, "Die Mathematiker des Aachen-Lütticher Raumes," 16.

41   Karl W. Butzer, "The Classical Tradition of Agronomic Science: Perspectives on Carolingian Agriculture and Agronomy," *Science in Western and Eastern Civilization in Carolingian Times*, ed. Paul L. Butzer and D. Lohrmann (Basel, 1993), 539-596, here 573.

42   Ibid., 574.

monachorum, that experience gained through actual practical working was prefer-
able to gaining information from reading alone.[43]

Other writers, who were interested in the practical application of classical
knowledge to current problems of farming, updated the text of Apuleius with
plants that were indigenous to Reichenau and St Gall in Swabia, both of which
remained important centers of learning under both the eastern Carolingians and
the Ottonians.[44] In light of the extensive efforts to graft Carolingian agricultural
practices onto the classical tradition, preserved in books, Karl Butzer observed:
"systematic attempts to determine the equivalency of Latin and German plant
names were underway by 821, particularly in south-western Germany, and these
would have required both taxonomic skills and access to (and great familiarity
with) older descriptive works, preferably illustrated."[45] These herbs were primary
ingredients in the medicines used and developed by early medieval physicians.[46]

The additions made to herbal texts by German-speaking scholars in Swabia in
the ninth century had a corollary in manuscripts that provided information about
industrial applications. This was true, for example, in the exceptionally diverse
Mappae clavicula, which included a wide range of recipes for a many practical
fields, including dyeing, metal working, coloring glass, and annealing. A considerable number of these recipes were added from the eighth through the tenth
century, indicating a continuity of use over this period.[47] Moreover, a number of
recipe collections that contained information, derived from the *Mappae clavicula*,
also circulated separately from this text.[48]

In light of these literary traditions, which saw the copying and updating of
Latin treatises and handbooks in the predominantly German-speaking regions
of East Francia in the ninth century, and in the Ottonian kingdom of the tenth
century, it is necessary to concur with the observation by Giles Brown that:
"Wherever one looks there is continuity through the ninth century and beyond.

---

43 For Walafrid's comments in this regard, see Butzer, "Classical Tradition of Agronomic Science,"
574. In his *De opere monachorum*, Augustine argued in "reading good books, one grows more quickly
by putting into practice what one reads." See PL 40, col. 558-9 for the quotation.

44 Butzer, "The Classical Tradition of Agronomic Science," 575.

45 Ibid., 576.

46 The plan of St Gall, for example, includes a space for the *herbularius* with sixteen seed beds
located near the infirmary. Regarding this point, see Butzer, "The Classical Tradition of Agronomic
Science," 576.

47 The text of the *Mappae clavicula* has received considerable attention from scholars. See, for
example, the observations by Bischoff, "Die Überlieferung der technischen Literatur," 273-280;
and the detailed study and translation of the text by Cyril Stanley Smith and John G. Hawthorne,
"Mappae Clavicula: A Little Key to the World of Medieval Techniques," *Transactions of the American Philosophical Society* 64 (1974), 3-128. The authors point out (19) that many of the recipes in
the text indicate a corrupt translation of information from workshops of late antiquity to the early
medieval period, but that there are a significant number of additions from the eighth through
tenth centuries that do shed light on contemporary technical practice. In this context, painting and,
significantly for this essay, items of military significance were added to the original text during the
Carolingian and Ottonian periods. These latter include a number of recipes for producing incendiary devices.

48 Bischoff, "Die Überlieferung der technischen Literatur," 277-279, and 288.

This is especially true in the east where Ottonian culture is but late Carolingian culture under another name ..."[49] However, as in so many other areas of Ottonian history, continuity should not be confused with stasis. The intellectual elite of the Ottonian kingdom grafted new traditions onto old so that annotated and updated collections drawn from classical, late antique, and Carolingian sources were used side by side with new handbooks that were drawn from entirely contemporary or near contemporary works. In her discussion of Ottonian cultural production, for example, Rosamond McKitterick points out that the traditional Carolingian educational canon was supplemented by a wide variety of new texts including pontificals, handbooks for priests, musical handbooks, and legal collections.[50] With regard to the latter, McKitterick has demonstrated that large numbers of legal collections were composed for practical use by Ottonian bishops for specific short-term goals.[51]

As this brief survey indicates, elite education, including that of secular men, provided a basic understanding of Latin texts and numeracy, whether they were native Romance speakers or German speakers. Moreover, this was as true of the tenth century as it was for the ninth for the simple reason that the elite men of the Ottonian kingdom faced the same tasks and responsibilities as their grandfathers had faced in the ninth century when ruled by the Carolingians. For those men who entered careers in more specialized fields, additional education was necessary, and this was derived, at least in part, from classical, late antique, and contemporary books. To put this in rather obvious terms, when constructing a cathedral or palace in 950, it was just as important to have a detailed knowledge of architecture and engineering as it had been in 850, or in the heyday of the Carolingian empire in 800. It is in this context that continuity in the education of future military officers is to be understood.

Military Education

Early medieval writers, many of whom were clerics, generally were averse to praising secular learning.[52] Nevertheless, a particular narrative arc sometimes required that the learning of a military commander be described. The military commander Adalbero, discussed in the previous chapter, certainly benefitted from a liberal education, a point commented on by Gerhard of Augsburg in his

---

49   Giles Brown, "Introduction: The Carolingian Renaissance," in *Carolingian Culture: Emulation and Innovation*, ed. Rosamond McKitterick (Cambridge, 1994), 1-51, here 44.

50   McKitterick, "Ottonische Kultur und Bildung," 220-1.

51   Rosamond McKitterick, "Bischöfe und die handschriftlichen Überlieferung des Rechts im 10. Jahrhundert," in *Mönchtum-Kirche-Herrschaft 750-1000. Josef Semmler zum 65. Geburtstag*, ed. Dieter R. Bauer, Rudolf Hiestand, Brigitte Kasten and Sönke Lorenz (Sigmaringen, 1998), 231-242.

52   Regarding the hesitance of medieval writers, particularly those who were clerics or monks, to praise learning that was intended for secular purposes, see the discussion by Detlef Illmer, *Erziehung und Wissensvermittlung im frühen Mittelalter. Ein Beitrag zur Entstehungsgeschichte der Schule* (Kastellaun, 1979), 96; Butzer, "The Classical Tradition of Agronomic Science ," 580, and Dette, "Schüler im frühen und hohen Mittelalter," 11.

tenth-century *vita* of Bishop Ulrich of Augsburg. In this regard Adalbero was far from unique. Thus, for example, Asser, in his *De rebus gestis Aelfredi*, draws attention to the fact that King Alfred (871–899) recruited a Saxon named John to join his court, and eventually established him as an abbot, an office that certainly required much more than a passing acquaintance with "book learning." Of importance in the present context, however, is that Alfred recruited this Saxon because of the man's knowledge of military affairs.[53] Saxony, which at this point had been part of the *regnum Francorum* for the better part of three generations, clearly not only offered opportunities for advanced study of the military arts, but also had developed some reputation in this regard, if Alfred was advised to seek there for a man who could hold high office in the Anglo-Saxon kingdom.

A similar emphasis on advanced military training is evident in the *Gesta* of the bishops of Toul, in upper Lotharingia, whose author observes that Bishop Gauzelin (922–962), had a paternal half brother named Hardradus, who was highly trained in the study of military affairs.[54] Gauzelin is described by the author as having noble Frankish blood, and also as having been raised at the palace (*palatio*) among the king's magnates (*proceres*) before his elevation as bishop to replace Drogo.[55] In this context, it seems likely that Hardradus also received part of his training and education at the royal court, perhaps that of Charles the Simple, who was responsible for establishing Gauzelin as bishop.

Widukind of Corvey, whose *Res gestae Saxonicae* was commissioned by the royal court as a pedagogical text, also focused attention on the military learning of important Ottonian commanders. For example, in describing the successful defensive efforts of Henry I of Germany, while still duke of Saxony, to ward off an invasion by King Conrad I, Widukind emphasized the crucial role played by Count Thietmar in 915.[56] King Conrad, who was worried about Henry's increasing power, decided to take decisive action and summoned the expeditionary levies, i.e., *congregata omni virtute Francorum*, from all of the East Frankish kingdom for an invasion of the Saxon duchy.[57] Henry ensconced himself in the fortress of Grone (located near modern Göttingen) to await support from his *fideles*. Before the king could establish a siege, however, Thietmar, who commanded the duke's army on the eastern frontier, arrived at Grone where Conrad's envoys were trying to convince the Saxon ruler to make peace. Thietmar, who is characterized by

---

53 Asser, *De rebus gestis Aelfredi*, ed. W. H. Stevenson (Oxford, 1959), chs. 94-97, and specifically ch. 97 for the discussion of John's knowledge of the *belicosae artes*. See the discussion of this passage by Richard Abels, *Alfred the Great: War, Kingship and Culture in Anglo-Saxon England* (London, 1998), 223. It should be noted that Asser does not accord John an exceptional knowledge of the military arts, saying that he was *bellicosae artis non expers*, but I accept the basic thrust of Abels' implicit argument that Asser did not wish to overemphasize the secular aspects of John's career in Alfred's service.

54 *Gesta episcoporum Tullensium*, ed. Georg Waitz, MGH SS 8, 639, "*in militari studio vir quam maxime strenuous.*"

55 Ibid.

56 Widukind, *Res gestae*, 1.24.

57 Ibid., 1. 24.

Widukind as a man of very great experience in military matters (*vir disciplinae militaris peritissimus*) informed the envoys that he was bringing up a force of thirty units of professionals troops, i.e. *trigenti legiones*. Although this was a *ruse de guerre*, Conrad's envoys believed Thietmar, and the king's army retreated from Saxony.[58] Thietmar's enormous military skill, as identified by Widukind, is related directly to his successful use of strategy rather than to his physical skills with arms.

The opponent of Thietmar in this campaign, King Conrad I, also did not lack admirers of his military learning. When describing the elevation of Conrad in 911, Liudprand, an older contemporary of Widukind who also wrote for the Ottonian court, observed that the new king was a *"vir strenuus bellorumque exercitio doctus."*[59] It seems likely that Liudprand was aware of the victory gained by Henry I over King Conrad in 915, and that this description of the defeated Conrad as learned in war owed at least something to increasing the stature of Otto I's father. Nevertheless, the importance of being *doctus* in military matters clearly was appreciated as something desirable by the royal court in the 950s, when Liudprand was writing.

Otto I's military commander along the eastern frontier, Count Gero, also was singled out for praise as an exceptionally well educated officer. Widukind, who had access to a great many people who knew Gero personally, described him as *bellandi peritia*.[60] However, this knowledge of the military arts was not the count's only intellectual achievement. Widukind explains that Gero was also an important advisor to the king in civil affairs, that he was well spoken, and had a strong foundations in many areas of intellectual inquiry. Not least among these, from the Corvey monk's point of view, was Gero's dedication to God and to the church.[61]

Alpert of Metz, like his older contemporary Widukind, was particularly interested in military affairs and commented on the quality of the commanders who led forces into battle. In describing the defensive preparations made against raids by Scandinavian pirates up the Waal river in 1006, for example, Alpert observed that because the old military commander (*praefectus*) in the district had grown too feeble, a new man was chosen to lead the local defense.[62] This replacement was Count Hunerik (Unruoch) of Teisterbant (981–1010), who gained a substantial

---

58 Ibid. Widukind would appear to have borrowed this phrase from Caesar, *Comentarii de bello Gallico*, 1.21, where the Roman general described P. Considius as held to be a man *rei militaris peritissimus* in the armies of both Sulla and Crassus. This phrase was to have an active *Nachleben* taken up by a number of classical authors, including Lucius Ampelius, who used Caesar's description of P. Considius to describe King Pyrrus, whom he identified as the *"Omnium Graecorum sapientissimus et militaris disciplinae peritissimus fuit."* See Lucius Ampelius, *Liber Memorialis*, chapter 28.

59 Liudprand, *Antapodosis*, 2.17.

60 Widukind, *Res gestae*, 3.54.

61 Ibid., *"Erant quippe in Gerone multae artes bonae, bellandi peritia, in rebus civilibus bona consilia, satis eloquentiae, multum scientiae, et qui prudentiam suam opere ostenderet quam in ore, in adquirendo strennuitas in dando largitas et, quod optimum erat, ad cultum divinum bonum studium."*

62 Alpert of Metz, *De diversitate temporum*, ch. 8.

reputation as being skilled in military affairs while serving with Otto III in Italy.[63] Hunerik, who was born around 950, received the military education that would serve him so well under Otto III, during the reign of Otto I.

Alpert also emphasizes the military learning of commanders, who likely received their training during the reign of Otto II. When describing a campaign organized by King Henry II of Germany against Count Dirk III of Holland (993–1039), Alpert identifies the two commanders, Bishop Adalbold of Utrecht (1010–1026), and Duke Godfrey II of Lotharingia (1012–1023), as being learned to the highest degree in military affairs.[64] However, Alpert stresses that despite this fact, they were not knowledgeable about naval operations, thereby foreshadowing the difficulties that would ensue for the imperial army.[65] The author's observations on this point make clear that military education was quite complex and involved a wide range of topics, not all of which were learned by all prospective or even active military commanders.

Alpert, however, reserves his greatest praise for the learning of Bishop Ansfrid of Utrecht (995–1010), who became an ecclesiastic only after a very lengthy military career, which began during the reign of Otto I. Alpert observes that while holding office as count of Huy, Ansfrid: "investigated righteous legal decisions and spent so much time reading that he was mocked by some foolish people for living the life of a monk."[66] While it is certainly possible that Alpert exaggerated the extent to which Ansfrid was devoted to learning, and particularly to reading, it is impossible to escape the conclusion that this soldier and count had received an education during the reign of Otto I that permitted him to become a bishop renowned for his knowledge of both the law and sacred texts.

Alpert's observations regarding Ansfrid's learning are corroborated by his contemporary, Bishop Thietmar of Merseburg. The latter observed that Count Ansfrid received a thorough education in both temporal and ecclesiastical law from his paternal uncle, Archbishop Robert of Trier, who was the brother of Henry I's queen, Mathilda. Following this early education, another of Ansfrid's uncles, likewise named Ansfrid, sent the young man to study military matters (*res militaris*) with Archbishop Brun at Cologne. It was only after this broad-based liberal education, followed by a more focused military education, that the young Ansfrid was assigned to Otto I's personal military household.[67] This sequence recalls the career of Adalbero, noted above, who first received an extensive liberal education, and then learned how to be military officer at the court of Otto I.

It was not only high-ranking magnates who earned attention from contemporary writers for their military education. The author of the *Vita* of Burchard of Worms (1000–1025), for example, stressed the military learning of one of the

---

[63] Ibid., "*qui in exercitu tercii Ottonis imperatoris Italia in re militari opinatissimus habebatur.*"
[64] Ibid., 2. 21, "*adprime in re militari instructos.*"
[65] Ibid., "*navi nihil poterant.*"
[66] Ibid., 1.11.
[67] Thietmar of Merseburg, *Chronicon*, 4.31.

bishop's soldiers (*miles*) when describing the retreat of the army commanded by
the bishops of Würzburg, Worms, The archbishop of Mainz, and the abbot of
Fulda from Italy following the death of Otto III in 1002.[68] On their way back
home, the Germans were confronted by a large army mobilized by the city of
Lucca. In this context, the author observes that there was a certain *miles*, named
Thietmar, who "had the reputation of being most learned in military matters."[69]
So Burchard summoned Thietmar and asked him to develop a solution to the
tactical problem confronting the German army. Thietmar proposed a flanking
maneuver that proved successful, leading to a victory over the army of Lucca.[70]

As the examples illustrated here make clear, the depiction of a military officer
as *doctus* or *instructus in re militari* did not depend on his skill with a sword, lance,
or bow, but rather on his abilities as a commander in all aspects of a military
endeavor. In particular, the tactical skills of these officers appear to have been
especially praised. These abilities as tacticians were neither inborn, nor simply
matters of common sense. They had to be taught and learned.

Nevertheless, one certainly cannot conclude on the basis of the examples
provided here that all military commanders serving under Henry I and Otto I
had the same familiarity with literary works, and the same dedication to book
learning as Margrave Gero, Adalbero, or Ansfrid of Huy. It is possible, and
perhaps even likely, that some aristocrats who led men into battle could neither
read nor even understand Latin, despite the disadvantages this would cause them
in competing for high office, and administering their estates. This does not entail,
however, that the contents of military treatises, and other handbooks with military utility, were inaccessible to such men. The fast and ready translation into
Saxon, Frankish, or Swabian, of works by Vegetius and Frontinus, which were
composed in quite simple Latin, was certainly within the competency of clerics
employed by aristocrats, or even of fellow laymen whose fathers – such as those
identified by Christoph Dette in his investigation of lay aristocratic education –
thought that Latin learning was quite a good investment.[71]

Military "Schools"

In light of the crucial importance to Ottonian rulers, as had also been true of
their Carolingian predecessors, of properly organized military campaigns, it is not
surprising that more information survives regarding the actual *locus* of military
education than does, for example, regarding the training of engineers, architects,
or land surveyors. Adalhard of Corbie, in his handbook on the proper organization of a royal court, which was written to provide a model for the newly estab-

---

68   *Vita Burchardi episcopi*, ed. Georg Waitz, MGH SS 8 (Hanover, 1858). ch. 8.
69   Ibid., "*Inter quos erat quidam Thietmarus, miles episcopi Wormaciensis, vir strenuus et omni boni-
tate praecipuus, qui in hoc exercitu in militari re opinatissimus habetur.*"
70   Ibid.
71   Dette, "Kinder und Jugendliche," particularly 17-18.

lished government of Charlemagne's son Pippin in Italy (781–810), discusses the training of the future military officers, denoted as *discipuli*, who were assigned to individual *magistri* for their instruction.[72] This topic, it should be stressed, was not a matter of mere theoretical interest to Adalhard as the future abbot had undergone this same training at the court of King Pippin I in his youth alongside his older cousin Charles.[73]

These *discipuli* were designated by Adalhard as the second *ordo* of fighting men, who lived at the royal court alongside the permanent military household of the king (*expediti milites*), and the military households of the various magnates who were attached to the royal court for extended periods of time (*pueri et vasalli*).[74] Adalhard emphasizes that these *discipuli* were under the permanent direction of their *magistri* "whom they honored and by whom they were honored, each one in his own place, as opportunity provided, so that they might be encouraged by them (the *magistri*) when they saw the students and spoke with them."[75] In his updated version of Adalhard's text, which was composed no later than 882 for the court of the western Carolingian ruler Carloman II, Hincmar of Rheims (died 882) makes clear the continued relevance of the discussion of this court-based school for future officers, by including the passage about the education of this second *ordo* of *milites* in his own work.[76]

In this context, the famous story that Notker (died 912), a later contemporary of Hincmar and polymath monk at St Gall, tells about Charlemagne visiting the palace school after a long military campaign, may perhaps be better understood as more indicative of his understanding of education during the reign of Louis the German and the latter's sons, than during the early ninth century.[77] Charlemagne, it is reported, became very angry when he saw the sons of the nobility were wasting their time, but was quite pleased that the sons of lower-ranking

---

[72] For the text, see Hincmar of Rheims, *De ordine palatii*, ed. Thomas Gross and Rudolf Schieffer, MGH *Fontes iuris germanici antiqui in usum scholarum separatim editi* (Hanover, 1980), ch. 28. Among those scholars who sought to undermine the effectiveness and complexity of Charlemagne's rule, it was once argued that *De ordine palatii* had been "forged" by Archbishop Hincmar of Rheims (d. 882). For a detailed review of the historiography, see Bernard S. Bachrach, "Adalhard's *De ordine palatii*: Some Methodological Observations Regarding Chapters 29–36," *Cithara*, 39 (2001), 3-36. However, the modern consensus makes clear that the original work was, in fact, written by Adalhard, and was a description of Charlemagne's government. See, for example, Brigitte Kasten, *Adalhard von Corbie* (Düsseldorf, 1986), 72-84; P. Depreux, *Prosopographie de l'entourage de Louis le Pieux (781-840)*, Instrumenta I (Sigmaringen, 1997), 76-79; Janet Nelson, "Was Charlemagne's Court a Courtly Society?" in *Court Culture in the Early Middle Ages: The Proceedings of the First Alcuin Conference*, ed. Catherine Cubitt (Turnhout, 2003), 39-57, here 41; and Rosamond McKitterick, *Charlemagne: The Formation of a European Identity* (Cambridge, 2008), 142-157, and 271.

[73] Paschasius Radbertus, *Vita Sancti Adalhardi* = *Ex vita s. Adalhardi*, ed. G. H. Pertz, MGH SS 2 (Hanover, 1829), ch. 7.

[74] *De ordine palatii.*, ch. 28.

[75] Ibid., "qui a magistro suo singuli adhaerentes et honorificabant et honorificabantur locisque singuli suis, prout oportunitas occurebat, ut a domino videndo vel alloquendo consolarentur."

[76] Janet Nelson, *Charles the Bald* (London, 1992), particularly 75-85, for the education of the young Charles.

[77] Notker, *Gesta Karoli*, 1.3.

members of society were working hard. Charlemagne made clear to the former that they could expect no preferment from him in gaining high secular offices if they did not begin to work hard and stop wasting their time in *"luxurie ludo et inercie vel inanibus exercitiis."*[78] By contrast, the latter, if they continued on their present path, would gain preferment.

Obviously, not all young men destined for careers as military officers could be trained at the royal palace. Indeed, it seems likely that most such men, particularly those who were to command troops under the authority of one or another secular or ecclesiastical magnate, received their education under the direction of their principal.[79] Nevertheless, the information that is available regarding training of future officers in the households of kings likely also is pertinent to those men who learned their craft under the direction of lesser magnates.

It should be emphasized that the *discipuli* discussed by Adalhard, Hincmar, and Notker were not small boys learning the liberal arts, but rather youths above the age of fourteen, who had already been instructed in the *artes liberales*. Einhard, for example, makes the point that Charlemagne's sons were educated first in *"liberalibus studiis"* before undertaking their military training.[80] Thegan, in his discussion of the education of Louis the Pious, also emphasized that Charlemagne saw to it that his sons were taught both the *liberales artes* and secular law in the royal court in Aquitaine.[81] The so-called Astronomer recalled that Louis was not given his sword and belt, with the expectation that he would begin his formal military training, until he reached the age of thirteen.[82]

Louis the Pious gave the same education to his own sons. Lothair I was both an avid reader of a wide range of works, and also a writer.[83] So too was Louis the German, whom Regino of Prüm claimed was so well educated that he had a command of both the secular and ecclesiastical disciplines.[84] As Eric Goldberg has demonstrated, Louis was well versed in a wide range of biblical works and commentaries as well as classical texts before taking up his military training.[85] The latter stages of this education included the reading of Vegetius' *Epitoma rei militaris*.[86] Finally, Charles the Bald also received an extensive education in the *litterae studia*, before undertaking

---

[78] Ibid.

[79] See the observations in this regard by Pierre Riché, "Les bibiothèques de trois aristocrates laïcs carolingiens," *Le moyen âge* 69 (1963), 87-104, here 103.

[80] Einhard, *Vita Karoli*, ch. 19.

[81] Thegan, *Gesta Hludowici imperatoris*, ed. and trans. Ernst Tremp, MGH SRG 64 (Hanover, 1995), ch. 2.

[82] Astronomer, *Vita Hludowici imperatoris*, ed. and trans. Ernst Tremp, MGH SRG 64 (Hanover, 1995), ch. 6. Regarding the primary education in the liberal arts preceding military training, see Dette, "Kinder und Jugendliche in der Adelsgesellschaft des frühen Mittelalters," 17-18.

[83] See the observations by Mayke de Jong, "The Empire as *Ecclesia*: Rabanus Maurus and Biblical *Historia* for Rulers," in *The Uses of the Past in the Early Middle Ages*, ed. Yitzhak Hen and Matthew Innes (Cambridge, 2000), 191-226.

[84] Regino of Prüm, *Chronicon*, an. 876.

[85] Goldberg, *Struggle for Empire*, 32-46.

[86] Ibid., 42.

his own training in the military arts.[87] It was well understood by contemporaries that as the West Frankish king grew older, his palace was a school because "every day one might devote oneself to scholarly as well as to military exercise."[88]

The preparation of youths with a basic education in the liberal arts before sending them to the court to learn how to be officers can also be seen the careers of many aristocratic boys. For example, the young Witiza (747–821), who would go on in later life to gain fame as Benedict of Aniane, is reported by his biographer Ardo Smaragdus, to have been sent to the royal court of Pippin I by his father, where he was placed with the queen's personal military household (*scholares*) to be instructed.[89] Ardo, who knew Witiza personally, recorded that the young man was beloved by his fellow soldiers (*commilitiones*) for his energy and his leadership qualities.[90] After this period of military training, Witiza was given an office in the royal household with responsibilities for the provisioning of the royal court (*pincerna*), which points to the mathematical skills that he had acquired during his youth.[91] This office, however, comprised only part of his responsibilities, for he also served as a military officer in the armies both of Pippin, and after his death, of Charlemagne.[92] It was the death of Witiza's brother while they were both on campaign with Charlemagne in Italy in 773 or 774 that led him to give up his military career and become a monk.[93]

This Carolingian background, which makes clear the importance of military education at the royal court, clearly had its counterpart under the Ottonians. This is indicated by the story of Adalbero, the nephew of Bishop Ulrich of Augsburg, discussed in the previous chapter. As a young man, Adalbero received an extensive literary training, then, at the royal court, he learned how to be a military officer. After this military education, the now seasoned Adalbero returned to Augsburg to take up command of his uncle's military household. Ansfrid of Huy, also noted above, had a similar career, although he received his basic military training under Otto I's brother Brun, rather than directly at the royal court.

---

[87] Nelson, *Charles the Bald*, 75-85.
[88] Rosamond McKitterick, "The Palace School of Charles the Bald," in *Charles the Bald: Court and Kingdom*, ed. Janet L. Nelson and Margaret T. Gibson (Aldershot, 1990), 326-339; reprinted with the same pagination in Rosamond McKitterick, *The Frankish Kings and Culture in the Early Middle Ages* (Aldershot, 1995), 326, points out that in the preface to his *Vita Sancti Germani*, which he dedicated to Charles the Bald, Heiric of Auxerre noted that Charles' palace could be called a school because "every day one might devote oneself to scholarly as well as to military exercise." For the quotation, see *Vita sancti Germani* MGH Poet. III, p. 429, "*ita ut merito vocitetur scola palatium cuius apex non minus scholaribus quam militaribus consuescit cotidie disciplines.*"
[89] Ardo Smaragdus, *Vita Benedicti*, ed. W. Wattenbach, MHG SS 15.1, ch. 1, "*Hic pueriles gerentem annos prefatum filium suum in aula gloriosi Pipini Regis reginae tradidit inter scolares nutriendum.*"
[90] Ibid., "*qui mentis indole gerens aetatem, diligebatur a commilitonibus, erat quippe velox et ad omnia utilis.*"
[91] Ibid., "*Post haec vero pincernae sortitur offitium.*"
[92] Ibid., "*Militavit autem temporibus prefati Regis. Post cuius excessum cum regni gubernacula Karolus gloriosissimus rex potiretur, ei adaesit serviturus.*"
[93] Ibid., ch. 2, "*Tunc se voto Deo constrinxit seculo deinceps non militaturum.*"

Curriculum: Military Handbooks

As was true of other specialized secular fields that required a high degree of technical proficiency, such as surveying, engineering, and architecture, late antiquity bequeathed to the early Middle Ages several important handbooks that dealt with military science. The single most copied secular text in the West during the early Middle Ages was the *Epitoma rei militaris* composed by the fifth-century Roman bureaucrat Vegetius.[94] Accordingly, it will be valuable to illustrate just how practical military officers considered this text to be for illuminating important principles of command.

Charlemagne and his close advisor Alcuin were both very well acquainted with Vegetius' *Epitoma*. In fact, when writing to Charlemagne, Alcuin quoted from the text (*Praef.* bk. I) of Vegetius' work without even mentioning the author's name, making clear that Alcuin understood that his royal correspondent also knew the text very well.[95] In the mid ninth century, Rabanus Maurus, who served both as abbot of Fulda and archbishop of Mainz, in both of which capacities he had extensive military responsibilities, oversaw the composition of a revised version of Vegetius' handbook, which would only deal with those matters that were of value *"tempore moderno."*[96] He sent at least one copy of this text to the newly established Lothair II with whose father Rabanus had enjoyed a long and fruitful relationship. In a similar manner, Frechulf of Lisieux, royal chancellor of the West Frankish kingdom, provided King Charles the Bald with a specially revised edition of *Epitoma rei militaris.*[97] Moreover, according to Frechulf's surviving preface, this text was intended to provide guidance in both strategy and tactics when dealing with the Viking menace.[98] Charles the Bald's elder brother Louis the German also had a copy

---

94   Regarding the large number of Vegetius manuscripts in circulation during the early Middle Ages, see Michael D. Reeve, "The Transmission of Vegetius' *Epitoma Rei Militaris,*" *Aevum* 74 (2000), 243-354. For an alternative – though not in my view convincing – argument that manuscripts of Vegetius did not circulate widely in the Carolingian period, see Reuter, "Carolingian and Ottonian Warfare," 19-21.

95   Alcuin, *Epist.*, no. 257; and the discussion by L. Wallach, *Alcuin and Charlemagne: Studies in Carolingian History and Literature* (Ithaca, NY, 1959), 50-51. Although several of the manuscripts of Vegetius' text from the ninth century have survived, neither Alcuin nor Charlemagne's personal copies the handbook would seem be among the many exemplars that we still possess. See Philippe Richardot, *Végèce et la culture militaire au moyen âge (Ve-Xv siècle)* (Paris, 1998), 199-210. The disappearance of the copies possessed by such high-ranking members of society is an important illustration of just how much has been lost from this period, and casts yet more doubt on the arguments regarding the putative paucity of texts in circulation at any one time.

96   Rabanus Maurus, *De procinctu Romanae militiae*, ed. Ernst Dümmler, *Zeitschrift für deutsches Alterthum* 15 (1872), 443-451, here 450.

97   Rosamond McKitterick, "Charles the Bald (823–877) and His Library: The Patronage of Learning," *The English Historical Review* 95 (1980), 28-47; republished with the same pagination in Rosamond McKitterick, *The Frankish Kings and Culture in the Early Middle Ages* (Aldershot, 1995), here 31.

98   Ibid.

of Vegetius' handbook.[99] Outside the Carolingian royal family, Vegetius' text attracted the attention of King Odo of Francia (died 898), who acquired a copy of the handbook from the monastery of St Denis.[100] Further east, a ninth-century text of Vegetius' work also has been identified at the important royal monastery of Corvey, where Widukind wrote his history of the Saxon dynasty in the later tenth century.[101]

The Ottonians followed in the footsteps of their Carolingian predecessors with regard to the important role that they accorded to Vegetius' text. Of the eleven surviving manuscripts of the *Epitoma rei militaris* from the tenth century, six are from the Ottonian kingdom, including Lotharingia. This includes manuscripts composed at Freising, St Gall, Einsiedeln, and Ghent.[102] Liudprand of Cremona (died 972), who held an important position in Otto I's court as an advisor on Italian affairs and served as an envoy to the Byzantine imperial court, was familiar with the text, and cited it in his *Antapodosis*.[103] Henry II, the great-grandson of Henry I, brought back a manuscript of the *Epitoma* from Italy and gave it to the monastic library at Corvey.[104]

One of the difficulties in tracing out the practical value of texts such as Vegetius' *Epitoma* is making a solid connection between a particular event recounted in a narrative source, and a particular copy of a handbook. For this reason, the discussion of Ekkehard of St Gall (born c. 980) regarding the training regime for the military household employed by Abbot Engilbert of St Gall (925–933) is particularly important. Ekkehard, whose history of his monastery and region is based upon earlier narrative texts and administrative documents, describes in some detail the training of the *milites* who served the monastery.[105] Ekkehard notes, for example, that Engilbert had mock arms made for his *milites*, so that they could train for combat. These arms specifically included wicker shields with a heavy core of closely fitted wooden boards and felt armor for protection.[106] This is the specific kind of training called for by both Vegetius, and Rabanus in his revised version of the *Epitome*. In this context, it bears repeating that the monastic house at St Gall saw the production of one of the surviving tenth-century manuscripts of the *Epitoma*, so the inference certainly is permitted that Vegetius' suggestions with regard to training fighting men with double-weight arms were applied to the abbot's household troops.

The case of St Gall certainly does not entail that every military commander entrusted with the training of *milites* during the tenth century had to hand a copy

99   Goldberg, *Struggle for Empire*, 40-42.
100 Ibid.
101 See the discussion by Reeve, "Transmission," 287.
102 Richardot, *Végèce*, appendix 1.
103 Liudprand, *Antapodosis*, 4.20, p. 108.
104 Richardot, *Végèce*, 21, and appendix three, nr. 195; and Reeve, "Transmission," 280, although he misidentifies the king as Henry III rather than Henry II.
105 Ekkehard, *Casus Sancti Galli*, 114.
106 Ibid., "*piltris lorice*" and "*tabulis compactis et wannis scuta simulantur.*"

of Vegetius' text, and that he perused it in an effort to identify the best means for training each of his men. Nevertheless, it certainly would be rash to conclude, in the face of the efforts by important magnates in the Ottonian kingdom to produce, at great expense, new copies of Vegetius' *Epitoma*, that they intended these texts simply to adorn the book cases of their *scriptoria*. Rather, it is likely that Vegetius' views regarding the proper training of fighting men, as well as the proper deployment of troops in battle, found a ready audience, whether first hand through the reading or hearing of the text, or through oral transmission of these ideas.

In addition to Vegetius' work, Frontinus' *Strategemata* also found an audience in both the Carolingian and Ottonian empires. Readers likely were influenced by the Roman general and administrator's observation in the preface to his work that the knowledge gained from his text will help readers "to develop their own ability to think out and carry out operations successfully that are similar in nature [to those that they have studied]." Frontinus goes on to note that "the commander" who is so educated "will have an added benefit insofar as he will not be worried concerning the likelihood for the success of his plans because he has learned that similar plans already have worked in practice."[107]

The earliest surviving manuscript of *Strategemata* was copied in Francia during the second quarter of the ninth century.[108] Another copy was made of this text at Fulda at much the same time.[109] Otto I's brother Brun, who played a role in the education of numerous Ottonian aristocrats such as Ansfrid of Huy, gave a copy of Frontinus' text to the king as a gift.[110] In his dedicatory poem, Brun observes

---

[107] Frontinus, *Strategemata*, ed. Robert I. Ireland (Leipzig, 1999), 1.1.

[108] L. D. Reynolds, "Frontinus, *Strategemata*," in *Texts and Transmission: A Survey of the Latin Classics*, ed. L.D. Reynolds (Oxford, 1993), 171-174.

[109] Bernhard Bischoff, *Katalog der festländischen Handschriften des neunten Jahrhunderts (mit Ausnahme er wisigotischen)* 2 vols. (Wiesbaden, 1998-2004), II: 11.

[110] There is a general consensus among specialists that it was Archbishop Brun, who gave a copy of Frontinus' text to his brother Otto I. See the discussion by Josef Fleckenstein, "Bruns Dedikationsgedicht als Zeugnis der karolingischen Renovatio unter Otto d. Gr.: Zu Carl Erdmanns neuer und Wilhelm Wattenbachs alter Deutung," *Deutsches Archiv* 11 (1954-1955), 219-226; C. Stephen Jaeger, *The Origins of Courtliness: Civilizing Trends and the Formation of Courtly Ideals 939–1210* (Philadelphia, 1985), 119-121; and Hagen Keller, "*Machabaeorum pugnae*: Zum Stellenwert eines biblischen Vorbilds in Widukinds Deutung der ottonischen Königsherrschaft," in *Iconographia sacra: Mythos, Bildkunst und Dichtung in der Religions-und Sozialgeschichte Alteuropas: Festschrift für Karl Hauck zum 75. Geburtstag* (Berlin, 1994), 417-437, here 434. The effort by Johannes Fried, "Brunos Dedikationsgedicht," *Deutsches Archiv für Erforschung des Mittelalters* 43 (1987), 574-583, to overturn this consensus in favor of a later dating of the text to the reign of Otto III has not found adherents. Fried's argument (578-80) is that the period of blindness and destruction identified in the poem could not possibly refer to the reign of either Henry I or Otto I, because both were seen as a golden age by contemporaries. Thus, Fried claims that it was Brun of Querfurt who dedicated the poem to Otto III as part of his general effort to denigrate the reign of Otto II. However, this argument is highly problematic for two reasons. First, the early years of Otto I's reign were far from a golden age. Otto suffered significant military setbacks at the hands of pagan Slavs, i.e., the *barbari* identified in the poem. Second, if Brun of Cologne, as Fried contends, would have been hesitant to criticize the difficulties during the early part of his brother's reign, which were overcome, why would Brun of Querfurt believe that Otto III would be happy to see a denunciation of the failures of his father's reign, which were not overcome?

that the *res publica* had suffered the ravages of *barbaries seva*, but "where your right hand holds the scepter, the state enjoys safety provided by you."[111] Obviously, this dedication is appropriate for the gift of a military treatise from one experienced commander to another.[112]

The possession of the Vegetius and Frontinus texts by Carolingian and Ottonian rulers and their military commanders, and here it must be emphasized that only a tiny fragment of once circulating works are extant today, is certainly indicative of their perceived practical value for military commanders. In addition, however, the vast store of information provided by these texts likely also recommended them for use in teaching young men who were learning the military craft. In this context, the gift by Rabanus Maurus of a revised copy of Vegetius' *Epitoma* to the twenty-one year old Lothair II, which was designed to teach about military affairs *tempore moderno*, likely was intended for use by the youths at the latter's court, rather than for the regnant king himself. In light of the demonstrated presence of copies of military manuals by Vegetius and Frontinus at the royal courts, at least, of Charlemagne, Lothair I, Louis the German, Charles the Bald, Lothair II, and Otto I, we would seem to be on safe ground in asserting that these texts were available to instruct future military officers and were not simply of antiquarian interest to monks.

Curriculum: Histories

All too often, the discussion of military education in the early Middle Ages has turned solely on the question of military manuals. However, as both scholars and rulers in the Ottonian kingdom were aware, even if some modern historians are not, men destined for public office were supposed to be well versed in both biblical and secular history so as to prepare them for their duties. This, of course, included the public duty *par excellence*, that is attending to military matters. In this context, Isidore of Seville (d. 636) made it clear in his *Etymologies*, a handbook of unrivaled popularity in the early Middle Ages, that men who wished to be effective rulers should read history. He argued that these texts would help men in public life by allowing them to benefit from the experiences of the past.[113]

This same view was expressed by Frontinus, noted above, in describing the value of his own handbook, which was, at base, a compilation of examples of military tactics that were taken from historical works. Drawing on this tradition of promoting history as an important element in a ruler's education, Ardo Smaragdus (died 843), whose many works included the *Vita* of Benedict of Aniane noted above, observed that it was "the most ancient practice, customary

---

[111] MGH *Poetae latinae* V, 378, "*At tua dextra ubi sceptra tenet, Publica res sibi tuta placet.*"
[112] Fleckenstein, "Bruns Dedikationsgedicht," 219-226, interpreted the barbarism as invasions by foreign peoples, which would certainly fit the recurrent raids on the Ottonian kingdom by the Hungarians and Slavs.
[113] Isidore, *Origines*, bk. I, ch. xliii. See the discussion by Jacques Fontaine, *Isidore de Séville et la culture classique dans l'Espagne wisigothique* (Paris, 1959), 180-185, regarding Isidore's view of history.

for kings from then to now, to have deeds written down in annals for posterity to learn about."[114] In a similar vein, Lupus of Ferrières, who advised Charles the Bald regarding a wide range of issues, presented the Carolingian ruler with a "brief summary of the deeds of the emperors," indicating the scholar's view that reading histories, in the manner set out by Isidore of Seville, was important for conducting public affairs.[115]

The importance of histories to men in public affairs, moreover, was hardly a conceit of ambitious clerics who wished to gain preferment by dedicating historical texts to their principals. Charlemagne's interest in *historiae* and *res gestae antiquorum*, as sources of information about the past, was well documented in Einhard's popular *Vita Karoli*.[116] Indeed, when writing in 798 to Charlemagne, who was campaigning in Saxony, Alcuin addressed the king in the persona of Horace (Flaccus), a veteran soldier (*veteranus miles*), and reminded him of the importance of historical works when fighting wars.[117] Alcuin observed, "that it is very important for us to read in ancient books of history about the kind of strength that fighting men had so that the kind of wise temperament, which ought to be acted upon, shall guide and rule us in all things."[118] This is a lesson that was taken to heart by Charlemagne's descendents. In a letter to Rabanus Maurus, for example, Lothar I (died 955) made clear that he carried his works of history with him when he went on campaign.[119]

Hartmut Hoffmann, in his enormously important study of Ottonian *scriptoria*, has demonstrated fundamental continuities in the possession of Carolingian era works, including histories, the production of new copies of older works, and the writing of new texts.[120] The efforts of the Ottonian kings led to the establishment of a raft of new or newly expanded centers of learning, particularly in cathedral schools such as Cologne, Magdeburg, Würzburg, Trier, and Hildesheim, which meant that these texts became even more widely available throughout the king-

[114] Ardo Smaragdus, *Vita Benedicti abbatis Anianensis*; ed. O. Holder-Egger, MGH SS, 15.2 (Hanover, 1887), 201. See the discussion by de Jong, "The Empire as *Ecclesia*," 191-226, who suggests that Ardo was exaggerating the efforts by kings to commission contemporary works of history. It is not clear what definition of historical works de Jong is employing here, but there was certainly a profusion of royally sponsored history writing under both the Carolingian and Ottonian rulers. See, for example, Rosamond McKitterick, "Political Ideology in Carolingian Historiography," in *Uses of the Past*, 162-174; and Karl F. Morrison, "Widukind's Mirror for a Princess: An Exercise in Self-Knowledge," in *Forchungen zur Reichs-, Papst- und Landesgeschichte. Peter Herde zum 65. Geburtstag von Freunden, Schülern und Kollegen dargebracht*, 2 vols. ed. Karl Borchardt and Enno Bünz (Stuttgart, 1998), 49-71; McKitterick, "Charles the Bald (823-877) and His Library," 35.

[115] Lupus of Ferrièrres, 83, ed. Ernst Dümmler,MGH *Epistolae* vol. 6 (Berlin, 1925), 93, and the discussion by McKitterick, "Charles the Bald, (823–877) and his Library," 31.

[116] Einhard, *Vita Karoli*, ch. 24.

[117] Alcuin, *Epistolae*, 149, ed. E. Dümmler, MGH Epist. 4 (Berlin, 1895).

[118] Ibid., "*quod militantibus virtutis genus maxime necessarium esse in antiquis historiarum libris legimus, ut cuncta sapiens temperantia, quae agenda sint, regat atque gubernet.*"

[119] Rabanus Maurus, *Epistolae*, 49, ed. E. Dümmler, MGH Epist. 5 (Berlin, 1899), 503.

[120] Hartmut Hoffmann, *Buchkunst und Königtum im ottonischen und frühsalischen Reich*, MGH Schriften 30 (Stuttgart, 1986). Also see the observations by McKitterick, "Continuity and Innovation in Tenth-Century Ottonian Culture," 15-24.

dom.[121] It is in this context that Josef Fleckenstein emphasized that Otto I did not require a new "educational policy" along the lines of Charlemagne's *Admonitio generalis* and the *Epistola de litteris collendis*, because he could simply build upon the solid foundations that his dynasty had inherited from the Carolingians.[122]

Within the general compass of expansion on the Carolingian educational foundations, an analysis of the surviving manuscripts produced by Ottonian *scriptoria* makes clear the continued emphasis on historical works. New copies were made of classical and late antique works such as Livy,[123] Sallust,[124] Curtius Rufus,[125] Jordanes,[126] Prudentius,[127] Cassiodorus,[128] Statius,[129] Josephus,[130] Pseudo-Philo,[131] and Orosius.[132] So too were copies made of biblical historical works, including *Maccabees*[133] and independently circulating *Books of Kings*.[134] Illustrative of the importance of historical works to military education was the decision by the abbot of St Gall to bind his illustrated copy of *Maccabees* with a copy of Vegetius' *Epitoma*, the latter equipped with both Latin and German glosses.[135] In addition to this effort to expand their collections of ancient historical works, Ottonian *scriptoria* also copied early medieval historical works. These include Einhard's *Vita Karoli*,[136] Bede,[137] *Annales regni Francorum*,[138] Gregory of Tours,[139] Regino of Prüm,[140] and Ermoldus Nigelus.[141]

The Ottonian magnate cadre also adhered to the principle, enunciated by Ardo Smaragdus, that writing down contemporary events would provide valuable instruction to future rulers. Rosamond McKitterick has pointed to the important role that royal women played as patrons of historical works so as to maintain an

[121] Fleckenstein, "Königshof und Bischofsschule unter Otto dem Großen," 178-192.
[122] Ibid., 168-192.
[123] Hoffmann, *Buchkunst*, 164.
[124] Ibid,, 168, 198-9.
[125] Ibid., 208.
[126] Ibid., 220-21
[127] Ibid., 282
[128] Ibid., 432-3, 492.
[129] Ibid., 434.
[130] Ibid., 310-11.
[131] Ibid., 193.
[132] Ibid., 492.
[133] Ibid., 382.
[134] Ibid., 391.
[135] Ibid., 382. Regarding the dating of the text, see the observations by Keller, "*Machabaeorum pugnae*," 435, who sees the text as being composed in the context of Henry I's victory over the Hungarians at Riade in 933 or Otto I's victory over the Hungarians in 955; and Susanne Wittekind, "Die Makkabäer als Vorbild des geistlichen Kampfes: Eine Kunsthistorische Deutung des Leidener Makkabäer-Codex Perizoni 17," *Frühmittelalterliche Studien* 37 (2003), 47-71, here 47.
[136] Hoffmann, *Buchkunst*, 395, 221.
[137] Ibid., 155.
[138] Ibid., 221.
[139] Ibid., 224.
[140] Ibid., 337, 487.
[141] Ibid., 437-8.

official view of the past.[142] Hrosvita's *Gesta Ottonis* is a primary example of such an effort.[143] However, it should be emphasized that the royal court also patronized the writing of historical texts. Otto I, for example, commissioned or patronized several works of history that were intended to instruct future rulers, including Adalbert of Madeburg's continuation of Regino's *Chronicon*, Liudprand's *Liber de gestis Ottonis*, and finally Widukind's *Res gestae Saxonicae*.[144] The last-named text, in particular, was intended to provide a teaching guide for the royal princess Mathilda, who was to serve as regent in Germany during Otto I's absence in Italy.[145]

To these "royal" histories can be added a number of important *vitae* and *gestae* of bishops who were intimately connected with the Ottonian ruling house. These include Ruotger's *Vita Brunonis*, Gerhard's *Vita Uodalrici*, both which are noted above, and Thangmar's *Vita* of his student, Bishop Bernward of Hildesheim (993–1022).[146] To this corpus can be added the *Chronicon* of Thietmar of Merseburg, who was educated at the new Ottonian cathedral school at Magdeburg, which played a central role in shaping young clerics to serve the *res publica*. Consequently, it is hardly surprising that his history displays all of the hallmarks of a text that is intended to teach about proper and improper conduct of a ruler, including detailed discussions of military operations. In fact, the historical works adduced here all provided considerable information about military affairs, including discussions of errors made by military commanders in the field. As Widukind emphasized in the preface to his *Res gestae Saxoniae*, his work would give Otto I's daughter Mathilda, for whom he ostensibly wrote the text, "what you need to transform the best and most glorious into something even better and even more glorious."[147]

---

[142] McKitterick, "Ottonian Intellectual Culture in the Tenth Century," 67-71.

[143] *Hrotsvithae Opera*, ed. Paulus de Winterfried, MGH SRG 34 (1965).

[144] These works have received extensive scholarly and critical attention. With regard to Adalbert and Liudprand, see, for example, Wilhelm Wattenbach and Robert Holtzmann, *Deutschlands Geschichtsquellen im Mittelalter: Die Zeit der Sachsen und Salier: Das Zeitalter des ottonischen Staates (900-1050)*, part one, vols. 1-2, reedit. Franz-Josef Schmale (Cologne, 1967), II: 169; Dietrich Claude, *Geschichte des Erzbistums Magdeburg bis in das 12. Jahrhundert, Teil I: Die Geschichte der Erzbischöfe bis auf Ruotger (1124)* (Cologne, 1972), 114-135; Karl Hauck, "Erzbischof Adalbert von Magdeburg als Geschichtsschreiber," in *Festschrift für Walter Schlesinger* vol. 2, ed. Helmut Beumann (Cologne, 1974), 276-353; Michael Rentschler, *Liudprand von Cremona: Eine Studie zum ost-westlichen Kulturgefälle im Mittelalter* (Frankfurt am Main, 1981), 1-6; John M. Sutherland, *Liudprand of Cremona, Bishop, Diplomat, Historian: Studies of the Man and his Age* (Spoleto, 1988), 3-43; Karl Leyser, "Ends and Means in Liudprand of Cremona," *Byzantinische Forschungen* 13 (1988), 119-143, and reprinted in *Communications and Power in Medieval Europe: The Carolingian and Ottonian Centuries*, ed. Timothy Reuter (London, 1994), 125-142. All citations are to the second version. Wolfgang Maier-Bode, "Liudprand von Cremona," in *Weltbild und Realität: Einführung in die mittelalterliche Geschichtsschreibung*, ed. Ulrich Knefelkamp (Pfaffenweiler, 1992), 93-101; and Philippe Buc, "Italian Hussies and German Matrons: Liutprand of Cremona on Dynastic Legitimacy," *Frühmittelalterliche Studien* 29 (1995), 207-225.

[145] Morrison, "Widukind's Mirror for a Princess," 49-71; and Gerd Althoff, "Widukind von Corvey: Kronzeuge und Herausforderung," *Frühmittelalterliche Studien* 27 (1993), 253-272.

[146] For a positive appraisal of Thangmar's reliability in recounting the actions of his student Bernward, see the discussion by Martina Giese, *Die Textfassungen der Lebensbeschreibung Bischof Bernwards von Hildesheim* (Hanover, 2006), 2, 29, 37 and *passim*.

[147] Widukind, *Res gestae*, preface book I.

Curriculum: Other Manuals

Histories provide examples of tactics, strategies, and not least, mistakes made by earlier commanders. However, aspiring military commanders, as well as planners and strategists, also had to be prepared for a wide range of duties that required additional specialized technical training. When preparing for war, officers had to devote enormous attention to logistical matters. This included knowing how much food and drink men and beasts required on a daily basis, the means by which these supplies could be transported, the carrying capacity and speed of these various transportation resources, and ultimately the location and costs of both supplies and transportation. While on campaign, military commanders needed to know how to choose a campsite, how to organize the men within a specific area, and how to defend this camp against enemy assault. Marching through enemy territory might also require a commander to have a sufficient understanding of engineering to order the construction of temporary bridges. The siege of enemy fortifications brought an additional set of engineering challenges that had to be met by military officers. These included the construction of highly developed field fortifications, and building both siege ladders and engines.

Information regarding many of these problems was included by Vegetius in his *Epitoma rei militaris*. However, a wide range of additional manuals that contained information useful for solving these problems also were copied and circulated by both the Carolingians and Ottonians. Thus, for example, Vegetius drew attention to the critical importance of logistics emphasizing that "...armies are more often destroyed by starvation than by battle, and hunger is more savage than the sword."[148] He added, "... other misfortunes can in time be alleviated: fodder and grain supply have no remedy in a crisis except storage in advance."[149] However, the basic subject matter of logistics was the application of the principles of multiplication and division, often in very complex formulae, to the fundamental realities of feeding men and beasts, transporting food, and obtaining supplies whether through purchase, requisition, or foraging.

A basic element of schooling for both Carolingian and Ottonian students, namely Alcuin's *Propositiones ad acuendos juvenes*, provides a number of problems that clearly were designed to instruct students to think about logistical problems in a manner consistent with the needs of military campaigns.[150] *Propositio* 52, for example, entitled *Propositio de homine paterfamilias*, deals with the issue of trans-

[148] Vegetius, *Epitoma rei militaris*, ed. Alf Önnerfors (Stuttgart, 1995), 3.3. This translation is by N. P. Milner, *Vegetius: Epitome of Military Science* 2nd revised edn (Liverpool, 1996), 67.
[149] Ibid.
[150] For the text, see Alcuin, *Propositiones ad acuendos juvenes*, PL 101 cols. 1143-1160, 1-9. Regarding the considerable importance of this text for teaching purposes under both the Carolingians and Ottonians, see John J. Contreni, "Counting, Calendars, and Cosmology: Numeracy in the Early Middle Ages," in *Word, Image, Number. Communication in the Middle Ages*, ed. John J. Contreni and Santa Casciani (Turnhout, 2002), 43-83, 54; and Dette, "Schüler," 13-16.

porting food supplies over distances using animals that consume some of the supplies en route.[151] This problem provided students with the practical insight that not only was it necessary to obtain sufficient food supplies for their men and warhorses, but also that the packhorses and cart horses, which hauled food overland, had to be fed as well. *Propositio* 6, entitled *De porcis*, includes a detailed discussion of the differences in costs when buying pigs at different times of the year depending on whether food was available for them.[152] This *propositio*, as well as *propositiones* 5 and 43, also provided basic instruction in the nature of markets for food supplies, where prices fluctuated over the course of the year. Obviously, military planners also had to be cognizant of when and where supplies could be purchased, and the various costs that would be involved in these purchases.[153]

In addition to problems regarding the consumption of supplies by pack animals, and determining the cost of these foodstuffs for a specific number of men over a specific period, Alcuin also provided models for determining the carrying capacities of various types of standard vessels that would be used by military commanders. *Propositio* 8, for example, begins by explaining that there is a cask (*cupa*) that can hold 300 *modii*.[154] The text then denotes the number of *modii* by their constituent *sextarii*.[155] Alcuin draws attention to the problem of transporting loaded wagons and carts over rivers in *propositio* 19, in which he humorously explains that a man and his wife each weighed as much as a loaded wagon (*plaustrum*) while their two children each weighed the same as a cart (*plaustralum*). When attempting to cross a river, the only ship (*navis*) available could not carry the weight of two loaded vehicles. The task was to determine a way for all of the family to cross the river.[156]

In addition to learning how to solve the manifold problems involved in provisioning soldiers on the march or in garrison, a young would-be officer had to learn

---

[151]   For the text, see Alcuin, *Propositiones ad acuendos juvenes*, 1160. Also see the discussion by Contreni, "Counting, Calendars, and Cosmology: Numeracy in the Early Middle Ages," 55.

[152]   Alcuin, *Propositiones*, col. 1145. Alcuin, *Propositiones*, nr. 5 and 43, col. 1145 and 1157, also deals with the costs of pigs, identifying the different expense involved in purchasing boars, sows, and piglets. See the discussion of this problem by Dette, "Schuler," 17, who emphasizes the utility of this type of problem when instructing the sons of nobles who certainly were familiar with merchants, purchasing, and money; and Illmer, "Arithmetik in der gelehrten Arbeitsweise des frühen Mittelalters," 53, who emphasizes Alcuin's familiarity with a range of technical manuals, including texts of the *agrimensores*, and the general value of mathematical skills for supervising estates. Of course, these skills were transferable to the military sphere as well.

[153]   This kind of pricing information was widely understood and used by monastic estate managers to maximize their profits when selling surplus goods. See, for example, Jean-Pierre Devroey, "La céréaliculture dans le monde franc," in *L'ambiente vegetale nell'alto medioevo, Settimane di studio del Centro italiano di studi sull'alto medioevo* 37 (Spoleto, 1990), 221-253, reprinted with the same pagination in *Etudes sur le grand domaine carolingien* (Aldershot, 1993), 253; and Christophe Dette, "Die Grundherrschaft Weißenburg im 9. und 10. Jahrhundert im Spiegel ihrer Herrenhöfe," in *Strukturen der Grundherrschaft im frühen Mittelalter*, 2nd edn, ed. Werner Rösener (Göttingen, 1993), 181-196, here 194.

[154]   Alcuin, *Propositiones*, nr. 8, col. 1147.

[155]   Ibid.

[156]   Alcuin *Propositiones*, nr. 19, col. 1150.

the methods for moving his troops from point A to point B. In this context, two sets of problems had to be resolved. First was the basic problem of establishing an itinerary. Second was assuring that the line of march that had been chosen was safe, afforded accessible water supplies, and most importantly, could be traversed by a military force. In this context, an understanding of geography and particularly map-making was very important. The *tyrones* received an introduction to the basic concepts of geography through Martianus Capella's treatment of the subject, as an adjunct to his broader discussion of geometry.[157] Additional geographical knowledge could be obtained from a wide variety of sources, including historical texts as well as itineraries.[158]

When developing plans to march into unknown territories, or through enemy held lands, it was also important, however, to make use of scouts (*exploratores*).[159] A would-be military commander would have done well to heed the advice of Vegetius on this topic. In discussing the proper preparations to make before embarking on campaign, Vegetius emphasized regarding the commander that: "First, he should have itineraries of all regions in which war is being waged written out in the fullest detail, so that he may learn the distances between places in terms of the miles and quality of roads, and examine short-cuts, by-ways, mountains and rivers, accurately described."[160]

The young military officer then had to learn how to move his soldiers along the line of march that was developed in consultation with the appropriate geographical information drawn from texts and scouts. This generally required camping overnight, often in enemy territory. Here, it should be emphasized that establishing a military camp in a sound defensive location, with properly constructed defenses, is hardly a matter of simple common sense.[161] In choosing a campsite,

---

[157] Emily Albu, "Imperial Geography and the Medieval Peutinger Map," *Imago Mundi* 57 (2005), 136-148, here 138.

[158] Concerning maps, see Ernst Klebel, "Herzogtümer und Marken bis 900," *Deutsches Archiv für Geschichte des Mittelalters* 2 (1938), 1-53, who makes a compelling argument regarding their use by Charlemagne's armies.

[159] McKitterick, *Charlemagne*, 271, has observed that Charlemagne's "Campaigns were subjected to meticulous strategic planning ..." She notes, as well (217), that "Charlemagne's network of communications, with its great variety of means for acquiring knowledge of all kinds, underlay the remarkable success of Charlemagne's armies." Halsall, *Warfare and Society*, 147, argues against the grain of the evidence that he himself has adduced (148), that medieval military commanders rarely used scouts. See the criticism of Halsall's arguments on this point by Clifford R. Rogers, *Soldiers' Lives Through History: The Middle Ages* (Westport, CT, 2007), 83.

[160] Vegetius, 3.6, with the translation of this passage by Milner, *Vegetius*, 73.

[161] The notion of leaving decisions about military operations to the "common sense" of military leaders, in the manner suggested by Stephen Morillo, *Warfare under the Anglo-Norman Kings 1066-1135* (Woodbridge, 1994), 118, is not one that is endorsed by the officials charged with training officers to serve in the US army today. Rather, modern training manuals cover in detail a great many topics that might well seem to be common sense to someone who has not had the responsibility for leading men in the field. For example, the military manual FM 7-8: Infantry Rifle Platoon and Squad, 3.20, dealing with the topic "Point Ambush," emphasizes that the officer in charge is to instruct his men: "Take weapons off SAFE. Moving the selection lever on the weapon causes a metallic click that could compromise the ambush if the soldiers wait until the enemy is in the kill zone."

it was crucial for an Ottonian commander (and still is today!) to keep in mind a number of important principles, including assuring a good water supply, but at the same time not establishing his camp too close to streams, rivers, or even gullies that might be subject to a flash flood. This kind of balancing act was not always maintained, even by experienced military commanders, as the disaster suffered by Conrad III's army at Choirabacchoi outside Constantinople in 1147 as it traveled toward Asia Minor during the Second Crusade illustrates quite well.[162]

Second, a military commander, or someone on his staff, had to be able to calculate the physical area that would be required to house men, animals, and vehicles, while still leaving sufficient space for movement, cook fires, and latrines. Third, the officer in command had to understand the principles of constructing field fortifications, how much time it would take to dig a ditch and build a temporary palisade around his camp, and where to site the "gates" in these walls. Finally, the officer needed to know how many men to station for the defense of the camp at night, where to place them, what roles scouts should play in this defense, and where these scouts should be deployed.

The failure to take these precautions in times of war, even when in one's home territory, could be quite devastating. Thietmar of Merseburg, for example, observed in his discussion of Otto II's campaign in 976 against Duke Boleslav II of Bohemia (972–979) that a large force of troops from the Bavarian select levy was destroyed by a Bohemian raiding army because the Bavarians failed to take the basic precautions necessary for force protection while on campaign.[163] Thietmar specifically notes that the Bavarians did not fortify their camp or set guards while they marched to join Otto II's army in Bohemia. As a result, while many of the Bavarian troops were bathing in the early evening after a long day's march, a well-equipped Bohemian force – Thietmar describes them as armored (*loricati*) in contrast to the naked (*nudi*) Bavarians – assaulted the camp and slaughtered the hapless defenders, cutting them down in their tents and in the nearby fields as they attempted to flee.[164] By contrast, Widukind records that during the siege of Lenzen in 929, the Saxon commanders Thietmar and Bernhard established a regular fortified camp (*castra*) and posted guards to ensure that the Saxon troops would remain protected from assaults by the defenders of the fortification. They also posted scouts (*custodes exercitum*) to ensure that they would have warning of any effort to relieve the fortress.[165]

This was the same Thietmar whom Widukind praised as being *rei militaris peritissimus*. In light of the fact that Widukind was commissioned specifically

[162] *Ottonis episcopi Frisingensis et Rahewini gesta Frederici; seu rectius, cronica*, ed. Franz-Josef Schmale, 2nd edn. (Darmstadt, 1974), 222. During the march of the German forces toward Asia Minor to participate in the Second Crusade, King Conrad's army was struck by a flash flood. Since much of the army was encamped along the banks and in the flood plain of the Choirobacchoi river, near Constantinople, the Germans suffered substantial loss of life and equipment.
[163] Thietmar of Merseburg, *Chronicon*, 3.7.
[164] Ibid.
[165] Widukind, *Res gestae*, 1.36.

to write his history to provide guidance to Princess Mathilda, it seems reasonable to suggest that the initial description of this count as learned in military affairs would lead the perceptive student, who heard Widukind's text read aloud, to understand that taking proper precautions while on route included fortifying the camp and posting guards. When used in conjunction with a manual such as Vegetius' *Epitoma*, students would have this lesson reinforced when reading the observations of the *auctoritas* about making camp. Obviously, for less than perceptive students, the *magistri* could help to clarify these lessons through the type of question and response model noted above.

As was the case with logistical preparations and mapping out a line of march, Vegetius' text provides important guidance about establishing fortified camps. He emphasized that camps were crucial for an army on the march because they provided a place of refuge in case of enemy attack.[166] Among the guidelines that Vegetius sets out for identifying a proper campsite are choosing a location that was well provided with wood for fires, fodder for the horses, and water for the troops and animals. He also emphasized that the camp had to be of the right dimensions for the number of men, and their equipment, because too large a camp would be difficult to defend, while too small a site would cause overcrowding.[167] Vegetius then offers a detailed discussion of the kinds of fortifications that were appropriate for camps that were built in friendly territory, and those that were required when there was a danger of attack by enemy forces.[168] These latter fortifications included a ditch 9 to 12 feet wide, and 7 to 9 feet deep. The earth from the ditch was to be piled up on the interior side to form a fosse, and the latter was to be further reinforced with a palisade of sharpened stakes that were carried in the baggage train.[169]

The basic principles of establishing the area of a fortified camp with given lengths and widths, including those marked by broken ground, also were easily accessible to military *tyrones* in the works of the *agrimensores*, which were widely available to students in the Ottonian kingdom.[170] One work, which was part of this corpus, provided particularly useful information to future commanders. This was the illustrated text of Pseudo-Hyginus' *De munitionibus castrorum*.[171] The bulk of the text deals with the geometric problems of setting up camps of different sizes to house both men and horses along with their equipment. The end of the text, however, provides a number of maxims about the proper location to establish a camp, the need for a secure water supply, and the kinds of defenses

---

[166] Vegetius, *Epitoma*, 1.21.
[167] Ibid., 1.22.
[168] Ibid., 1.24.
[169] Ibid.
[170] Regarding the wide circulation of these texts, see Ullman, "Geometry in the Mediaeval Quadrivium," 263-285; Butzer, "Die Mathematiker des Aachen-Lütticher Raumes," 7-30; Stevens, "Compotistica," 38; and Illmer, "Arithmetik in der gelehrten Arbeitsweise des frühen Mittelalters," 53.
[171] For a detailed examination of one of these illustrated texts, see Mütherich, "Der karolingische Agrimensoren-Codex in Rom," here 67-8.

that should be erected to defend a camp, including the depth of the defensive ditches, and the types of ramparts that should be constructed, which depended on the nature of terrain and soil that was available. In addition, information is provided about the proper placement of artillery to defend the camp.[172]

The great value of the *agrimensores* for instructing students is further illustrated by their influence on Alcuin's *propositiones*, several of which appear to draw upon the agrimensores to provide examples of geometric problem solving to students.[173] *Propositio* 22, for example, concerns finding the area, measured in *arpentae*, of a slanting field (*campus fastigiosus*). *Propositiones* 23–25 detail, in turn, the techniques used to measure the areas of quadrangular, triangular, and circular fields.[174] Students who mastered these techniques would, as a consequence, be able to determine lengths, widths, and perhaps even the diameter, if they constructed circular camps, of the *castra* that would be required to house their men.

However, in order to make a calculation regarding the perimeter of the camp, the commander first had to make a series of calculations regarding the amount of space that was required by each tent, animal line, fire pit, latrine, wagon, and all of the other elements of an army on the march. This kind of calculation was taught in *propositio* 21, which begins by explaining that there is a field measuring 200 feet by 100 feet. The student is then told that a sheep requires an area 5 feet long and 4 feet wide. The problem to be solved concerns the maximum number of sheep that can be "packed" into this space.[175] An even more useful packing problem is provided in *propositio* 27, where the task is to determine how many houses measuring 40 x 30 feet can be fitted into a quadrangular *civitas* that has a measurement of 1100 feet by 600 feet.[176] Similar packing problems are then offered for triangular and circular *civitates* in *propositiones* 28 and 29.[177]

Perhaps the most technically challenging aspects of warfare facing aspiring military commanders, once they had absorbed lessons regarding feeding their men, plotting their line of march, and managing the troops on the road, involved the siege of enemy strongholds, particularly when this involved the deployment of engines. Aspiring military engineers could find much of value, not only in Vegetius' text, but also in the work of Vitruvius, and the *Mappae clavicula*. As noted above, the texts of both Vitruvius and *Mappae clavicula* were circulated in the Ottonian kingdom, in manuscripts copied during both the ninth and tenth century.[178]

---

[172] The text of Pseudo-Hyginus' *De munitionibus castrorum* is easily accessible in Catherine M. Gilliver, "The *De munitionibus castrorum*: Text and Translation," in *Journal of Roman Military Equipment Studies* 4 (1993), 33-48.

[173] See the discussion by Illmer, "Arithmetik in der gelehrten Arbeitsweise des frühen Mittelalters," 50.

[174] Alcuin, *Propositiones*, col. 1151.

[175] Ibid., nr. 21, col. 1150-1.

[176] Ibid., nr. 27, col. 1152.

[177] Ibid., cols. 1152-3.

[178] See Bischoff, *Katalog der festländischen Handschriften*, I: 153, II: 38, 115; and idem, Bischoff, "Die

Vitruvius, in book ten of his *De architectura*, provides considerable information, including illustrations, for constructing a range of engines.[179] The anonymous
author of *De rebus bellicis*, a copy of which was available at Speyer no later than
the eleventh century, also provided information about constructing spear-casting
engines, mantlets for protecting troops as they approached enemy fortifications,
and also for constructing pontoon bridges, using inflatable animal bladders.[180]
The *Mappae clavicula*, as it circulated in Ottonian kingdom, contained a number
of recipes, of recent origin, for the production of incendiaries to be used with a
variety of missile weapons, including self-bows, that is hand-held tension bows,
spear-shooting *ballistae*, and also stone-shooting engines that could discharge
unfired clay pots that were filled with incendiary materials.[181] The *Mappae clavicula* also has a detailed description of the construction of a battering ram.[182]

Of particular concern when constructing either assault ladders or siege towers
is determining the height of the wall to be assaulted. Ladders that are too short,
for example, will not reach the top of the wall, but ladders that are too long provide
an opportunity for defenders to push them away more easily. Helmuth Gericke,
in his investigation of mathematical learning in the Latin West, notes that illustrated *agrimensores* texts circulating in the tenth century provided detailed information about the use of the astrolabe and other surveying tools.[183] In describing
the value of these tools, Gericke points out that it is possible to measure the
height of a tower in the same manner that one measures the height of the sun.[184]
The height of towers also could be calculated using the techniques identified by
Bede, which were widely disseminated from the eighth century onwards.[185]

Überlieferung der technischen Literatur," 272; Smith and Hawthorne, "Mappae Clavicula," 3-14;
and Hoffmann, *Buchkunst*, 390-1.

[179] Vitruvius, *De architectura*, 10.1-12 for torsion powered stone throwers, and tension-powered
spear casters, as well as mobile siege towers.

[180] Anonymous, *De rebus bellicis*, ed. Robert I. Ireland (Leipzig, 1984), chs. 7 and 8 for a spear-
caster and a mantlet, and ch. 16 for a pontoon bridge. Regarding the manuscript tradition of this
work, see E. A. Thompson, "Introduction," in *A Roman Reformer and Inventor: Being a New Text of
the Treatise De rebus bellicis*, ed. E. A. Thompson (Oxford, 1952), 13; and "Anonymi Auctoris Libellus
de Rebus Bellicis: A Treatise by an Unknown Author on Military Matters," ed. and trans. Robert
Ireland in *De Rebus Bellicis part 2 BAR International Series* 63 (1979), 39-92, particularly 54, where
an eleventh-century copy is indicated.

[181] Smith and Hawthorne, "Mappae Clavicula," 68-9, for the recipes, and 19 for the discussion of
these recipes as recent additions to the text. Also see Bischoff, "Die Überlieferung der technischen
Literatur," 270.

[182] Smith and Hawthorne, "Mappae Clavicula," 68.

[183] Helmuth Gericke, *Mathematik im Abendland: Von den römischen Feldmessern bis zu Descartes*
(Berlin, 1990), 70.

[184] Ibid.

[185] See the discussion by Wesley M. Stevens, *Bede's Scientific Achievement: Jarrow Lecture, 1985*
(Jarrow, Durham, 1985); and idem, "Cycles of Time: Calendrical and Astronomical Reckonings in
Early Science," in *Time and Process: Interdisciplinary Issues, The Study of Time VII*, ed. J. T. Fraser
and Lewis Rowell (Madison, CT, 1993), 27-51.

Conclusion

Warfare in the early Middle Ages, as it is today, was a highly complex undertaking. It is simply impossible that the men responsible for mobilizing, supplying, and commanding large forces in the field for complex military operations hundreds or even thousands of kilometers from home acted simply through guess-work, or on the basis of some in-born talent for command. Rather, they required extensive training in a wide range of fields, which included not only a detailed knowledge of battlefield tactics, but also a command of logistics, geography, and often engineering as well. Like specialists in many other fields, much of this learning came from books, including both specialized military manuals, and texts that covered broader themes that were applicable to military affairs, including mathematics, geography, and engineering. We need not assume that every officer in the armies of Henry I and Otto I personally read these manuals in Latin in order for the lessons offered by a Vegetius to have had a direct and important impact on the conduct of war during the tenth century. Indeed, it is not even necessary that Henry I or Otto I, themselves, did so, although in the case of the latter, it seems clear that he was literate and sought out works of importance for military affairs.

However, as the observations by contemporaries regarding the learning of men such as Margrave Gero, Adalbero of Augsburg, and Ansfrid of Huy make clear, some Ottonian military commanders certainly did enjoy a liberal education, and had the ability, at least, to read the relatively simple Latin of Vegetius or Frontinus. For those who did not understand Latin, or who did not have direct access to such military manuals, it is very likely that this information was diffused through close contact both in war, and in the more common gatherings of aristocrats in social, legal, or religious events.

In a similar manner, information in technical works was complemented by a broad introduction to history, which provided a wealth of examples of proper leadership and tactics, as well as errors made by commanders in the past. Histories of all kinds were produced in large numbers in the Ottonian kingdom, which augmented the also large number of historical works that were inherited from the ninth century, and even earlier. These texts were widely understood as being important for the education of secular leaders, and were available to them both in the context of monastic schools, at the royal court, and perhaps in the households of learned secular aristocrats as well. Ultimately, this "book learning" was refined by personal experience in the field as the young would-be commanders gained practical experience of life on campaign under the direction of senior officers.

5

Arms and Training

Ottonian military commanders understood very well that effective military operations depended fundamentally on deploying men who had been trained in both combat techniques and tactics. The Bible, which formed a central part of education of men destined for service in either high ecclesiastical or secular office, provided numerous reminders that systematic and ongoing training was crucial for the conduct of war.[1] A number of psalms speak directly to the question of military training. Thus, for example, Psalm 18, echoing 2 Samuel 22:35, presents King David as thanking God for training his hands for battle so that he has the strength to draw his bow. Psalm 144:1 calls blessings upon God who teaches my hands for war and trains my fingers to fight. This particular psalm seems to have had particular resonance with military men. In the early eleventh century, the north Italian count, Ragenardus, had the text of this passage stitched into a battle flag (*vexillum*) that also featured images of the archangels Michael and Gabriel.[2]

Diligent readers and auditors of the Bible would also learn from 2 Samuel 1:18, which was understood by readers of the Latin Vulgate to be the second book of Kings, that David required the children of Judah be taught to use the bow. Perhaps the best known story, however, is that of David and Goliath, recounted in 1 Samuel 17, where David's lack of training as a soldier (17: 33, 39) is described, and used to explain both the concern that Saul had in sending him into battle, and David's inability to use the sword and armor that were provided to him. David, of course, was able to defeat Goliath despite his lack of formal military training, but that was because of his enormous skill with a sling, which he had developed over the course of his youth as a shepherd, and God's aid.

The information provided by the Bible regarding the importance of training for successful military operations was widely corroborated by contemporary narrative sources that provide insight into the thinking of military commanders

---

[1]   The vast numbers of *Eigenkirchen* that were established by secular magnates throughout the Ottonian kingdom provides a useful index of the availability of instruction in biblical matters to their proprietors. See the useful treatment of this topic, with the extensive literature gathered there, by Susan Wood, *The Proprietary Church in the Medieval West* (Oxford, 2006).

[2]   A reproduction of the image of this battle flag, formerly located in the cathedral of Cologne, can be seen in Ludwig Arnst, "Mittelalterliche Feldzeichen: Eine kunstgeschichtliche Studie," *Zeitschrift für christliche Kunst* 28 (1915), 164-180, here 175. See Bachrach, *Religion and the Conduct of War*, 92-95, for a discussion of this banner.

in two different ways. First, the authors of narrative works, particularly those who presented themselves as writing history in the Isidorean sense of recording events that actually happened in the past, worked under the burden of the rhetoric of plausibility.[3] Consequently, when authors wrote about warfare for an elite audience, their presentation of this topic had to be plausible to men who had experience of leading men on campaign.[4] This was particularly true regarding texts that were commissioned by the king for presentation at the royal court, such as Widukind's *Res gestae Saxonicae*.[5] Second, as was detailed in the previous chapter, works of history formed an important element in the curriculum of future military officers. As a consequence, the comments made by authors about the value of military training, or the difficulties that were posed when fighting men lacked military training, indicate the lessons that youthful would-be commanders were being taught by their elders.

In some cases, the observations by authors about the importance of training are made explicitly. Regino of Prüm, for example, famously claimed with regard to the local levy mobilized from the lands of his monastery that the men, who were drawn up in a phalanx (*in unum agmen conglobata*), were defeated by the Vikings in 882 because they lacked military training, i.e., *disciplina militari nudus*.[6] Widukind made a similar observation regarding the lack of training of a group of fighting men when discussing the success of Conrad the Red's attack against the Hungarians who had captured the baggage train of the royal army on the Lechfeld.[7] In this case, however, the ultimate result was positive for the Ottonian army. Widukind noted that many of the veteran professional soldiers (*veterani milites*), who had grown accustomed to military triumph in the service of Otto I, marveled at Conrad's triumph since he commanded a force of professional fighters (*milites*) who had barely any training at all, i.e., *fere bellandi ignaro*.[8]

---

[3]   Isidore of Seville, *Etymologiarum sive originum libri xx*, ed. W. M. Lindsay (Oxford, 1911, repr. 1957), 1.40. "*Historiae est narratio rei gestae, per quam ea, quae in praeterito fact sunt, dinoscuntur*." Concerning the importance of Isidore for medieval writers of history, see D. H. Green, *Medieval Listening and Reading: The Primary Reception of German Literature 800–1300* (Cambridge, 1994), 237-8; Leah Shopkow, *History and Community: Norman Historical Writing in the Eleventh and Twelfth Centuries* (Washington, DC, 1997), 20-1; and the exceptionally important study by Justin C. Lake, "Truth, Plausibility, and the Virtues of Narrative at the Millennium," *Journal of Medieval History* 35 (2009), 221-238.

[4]   This topic is discussed in detail in the previous chapter.

[5]   See, in this context, Karl F. Morrison, "Widukind's Mirror for a Princess: An Exercise in Self-Knowledge," in *Forchungen zur Reichs-, Papst- und Landesgeschichte. Peter Herde zum 65. Geburtstag von Freunden, Schülern und Kollegen dargebracht*, 2 vols. ed. Karl Borchardt and Enno Bünz (Stuttgart, 1998), 49-71; and Gerd Althoff, "Widukind von Corvey: Kronzeuge und Herausforderung," *Frühmittelalterliche Studien* 27 (1993), 253-272.

[6]   Regino, *Chronicon*, an. 882. Regino's *Chronicon* was widely copied in the Ottonian kingdom, with two copies surviving from the *scriptorium* at Reichenau alone, and another copy at Trier. See Hoffmann, *Buchkunst*, 331, 343, 347.

[7]   Widukind, *Res gestae*, 3.44.

[8]   Ibid. These were the men whom Conrad had been able to recruit to his military household after being forgiven by Otto I for the former duke's part in the rebellion of 954. As a consequence,

By contrast, Widukind drew specific attention to the highly trained forces that Henry I had available in 933. In his discussion of the battle of Riade, the Corvey monk observed that in leading his men against the Hungarians, the German king was confident because they were trained in mounted combat, i.e. *equestri prelio probatum*.[9] The emphasis by Widukind on mounted combat, as will be seen in chapter seven, referred specifically to the coordination of light and heavy cavalry, and the use of the feigned retreat.

Far more commonly, however, contemporary writers drew attention to specially trained fighting men who were given tasks commensurate with their elite status. Thus, for example, Liudprand of Cremona pointed out that Dukes Gislebert and Eberhard were protected only by their *electi milites*, who formed a rear-guard for the rebel army that was crossing the Rhine near Andernach in 939.[10] Duty in the rear-guard, particularly when undertaking a dangerous maneuver such as crossing a river when an enemy force was in the vicinity, is precisely the kind of task that would be given to highly trained fighting men. In a similar manner, Widukind describes Otto I as sending a select force of troops that was chosen (*electi*) from the entire army to attempt to capture the fortified settlement at Rouen (*urbs*) during his operations in the West Frankish kingdom in the campaign season of 946.[11] In many other instances, as will discussed in detail below, the authors of narrative texts describe fighting men maneuvering on the battlefield in a manner that necessarily required extensive training.

By contrast with the clear understanding among contemporary authors that training, as a general matter, was important for success in war, the specific nature of this training was not as frequently described in narrative texts. This reticence likely is to be understood as part of the general aristocratic *parti pris* of early medieval writers, who sought to educate, entertain, and flatter their noble patrons. Naturally, the latter were far less interested in "the other ranks" than in hearing about their friends and relatives.[12] Nevertheless, some glimpses of specific forms of training do come through in the sources, and these will be discussed in detail below.

As a consequence of the interests of the authors and audiences of narrative texts, the most valuable sources of information for gaining an appreciation of

---

at least some of Conrad's personal military establishment was new, and, by comparison with the veteran forces that Otto had assembled for the Lechfeld campaign, raw and inexperienced.

9   Widukind, *Res gestae*, 1.38.

10   Liudprand, *Antapodosis*, 4.29.

11   Widukind, *Res gestae*, 3.4, "*collecta ex omni exercitu electorum militum manu Rothun Danorum urbem adiit*."

12   With regard to the general pattern of playing to conceit of noble audiences, see the valuable observations of von Padberg, "Geschichtsschreibung und kulterelles Gedächtnis," 156-177. Regarding the specific tendency of medieval authors to over-emphasize the role and importance of elite figures in war, see Matthew Bennett, "The Myth of the Military Supremacy of Knightly Cavalry," in *Armies, Chivalry and Warfare*, ed. Matthew Strickland (Stamford, 1998), 304-316; reprinted in *Medieval Warfare 1000–1300*, ed. John France (Aldershot, 2006), 171-183. With regard to the aristocratic bias in sources that deal with Ottonian warfare, see Bachrach, "The Military Organization of Ottonian Germany, c. 900–1018," here 1067 and 1087.

the lengthy and detailed process of training that was required to produce effective fighting men are military handbooks such as Vegetius' *Epitoma rei militaris*. As seen in the previous chapter, Vegetius' work was widely available and highly desirable to military commanders in the Ottonian kingdom as it had been to their Carolingian predecessors. Moreover, we are fortunate to have available at least part of Rabanus Maurus' revised version of the text that he presented as being valuable in *tempore moderno* during the mid ninth century.[13] In the present context, Vegetius' *Epitoma* is particularly important because the text, and Hrabanus' revised edition, both include detailed instructions for training men in the handling of their arms, and in battlefield tactics.

Despite the enormous value of the *Epitoma*, care must still be taken when drawing insights from handbooks. They are prescriptive texts, and cannot be treated as a transparent description of military life. In this context, it is no more likely that Ottonian officers followed slavishly the precepts set out in military handbooks than did their Byzantine counterparts who certainly were trained in the techniques of command and drill, in part, through the use of treatises such as the *Strategikon*, ascribed to Emperor Maurice (582–602), the *Tactica* ascribed to Emperor Leo VI (886–912), the mid tenth-century *Sylloge taktikon*, the late tenth-century *Praecepta militaria*, and the eleventh-century *Tactica*.[14] Nevertheless, it would be highly imprudent, to say the least, to suggest that western rulers, including the Ottonians and their high ranking *fideles*, expended considerable resources to copy, and indeed, update military treatises out of mere antiquarian interest.[15]

Training the Infantry

The most common formation of foot soldiers in early medieval Europe was the phalanx. Charles Martel, for example, famously won his victory at the battle of Tours/Poitiers in 732 against an army of mounted Muslim troops through the effective deployment of a phalanx of foot soldiers who were armed with swords and shields.[16] Phalanxes of foot soldiers also were deployed by Charles the Bald against the Bretons in 851, by Louis the Younger (died 882) against his uncle Charles at Andernach in 876, and by Arnulf of Carinthia (died 899) in 891 at the battle of the Dyle against the Vikings.[17]

[13] Rabanus Maurus, *Epistolae*, nr. 57, for the prologue to his text.
[14] For a discussion of the value of these works for understanding the training and organization of the Byzantine army, see Haldon, *Warfare, State and Society*, 5 and *passim*.
[15] For the view that Vegetius' text was copied for mere antiquarian purposes by monks and not used by military commanders, see Halsall, *Warfare and Society in the Barbarian West*, 146; and Reuter, "Carolingian and Ottonian Warfare," 19-21.
[16] For the description of the Franks arrayed in a phalanx, see *Crónica mozárabe de 754*, ed. and trans. Eduardo López Pereira (Zaragoza, 1980), ch. 80.
[17] For these battles see Regino, *Chronica*, an. 860 (correctly 851); *Annales Fuldenses*, an. 876; and Regino, *Chronica*, an. 891. With regard to the deployment of the phalanx by Carolingian armies from Charlemagne onward, see the discussion by Erik Szameit, "Gedanken zum ostfränkischen

Indeed, the disciplined infantry phalanx was so effective in the field that its use was copied by the enemies of the Carolingians. The Northmen, for example, prepared for battle against a West Frankish army under the command of Count Odo of Paris by forming a phalanx since they believed that they could defeat their Frankish opponents by taking up a massed formation. Indeed, according to Richer, the Vikings believed that they would be able to defeat the Frankish forces *only* if they could maintain their battle formation (*acies*), as a unified force (*indivisi*).[18]

The phalanx was also the dominant military formation of foot soldiers in Anglo-Saxon England from the ninth to the eleventh century both in defense and on offense. At both the battle of Maldon (991) and at Hastings, the Anglo-Saxon army mustered in a phalanx. At Maldon, the Norse troops, like those who fought against Count Odo in West Francia, also were organized in a phalanx.[19] At the battles of Ashdown (871) and Sherston (1016) the Anglo-Saxon phalanx took the initiative by advancing against the Norse troops.[20] Even into the twelfth century, Anglo-Norman mounted troops were ordered by their commanders to dismount for battle and take position within the infantry phalanx.[21]

In light of the crucial tactical role of the phalanx in the armies of the Carolingians, the Ango-Saxons, and of their opponents, it is not at all surprising that foot soldiers also were deployed in this manner by both the Ottonians and their opponents. At the battle of Lenzen (5 September 929), for example, both a Saxon army and the Slavic Redarii were deployed in infantry phalanxes.[22] The Swabian levies fighting at the battle of Mantahinga in 953 also were organized in a phalanx, according to Gerhard, the biographer of Bishop Ulrich of Augsburg.[23] In describing a battle fought between two Slavic polities, Widukind records that Polish troops, under the command of Duke Miesco, deployed in a phalanx, while fighting against another group of Slavs, known to the Ottonian royal court as Wuloini.[24]

Kriegswesen des 9. und 10. Jahrhunderts," in *Schicksalsjahr 907: Die Schlacht bei Preßburg und das frühmittelaltertliche Niederösterreich* (St. Pölten, 2007), 67-76, here 71.

[18] See Richer, *Historiae*, 1.8, "*Nec minus et barbari acies ordinaverant ac indivisi adversarios excipere cogitabant.*"

[19] See the discussion of the poem and battle by Richard Abels, "English Tactics and Strategy in the Late Tenth-Century," in *The Battle of Maldon A.D. 991*, ed. D. G. Scragg (Oxford, 1991), 143-155, here 149.

[20] For the importance of the phalanx in Anglo-Saxon warfare, see Hollister, *Anglo-Saxon Military Institutions*, 131-134; and Nicholas Hooper, "The Anglo-Saxons at War," in *Weapons and Warfare in Anglo-Saxon England*, ed. Hawkes S. Chadwick (Oxford, 1989), 191-202, here 199-200. Cf. Abels, "Tactics, Strategy," 153 n. 17, with regard to the reliability of John of Worcester's account of the battles at Sherston and Ashdown. In his *vita* of King Alfred, Asser describes King Aethelred advancing with his men who were organized in a shield wall. See *Asser's Life of King Alfred*, ed. William Henry Stevenson (Oxford, 1959), ch. 38, and the discussion by Abels, "Tactics, Strategy," 154 n. 34.

[21] See the discussion by C. Warren Hollister, "Norman Conquest and Genesis of English Feudalism," *American Historical Review* 66 (1961), 641-663, here 655-6; and idem, *Anglo-Saxon Military Institutions*, 131.

[22] Widukind, *Res gestae*, 1.36.

[23] Gerhard of Augsburg, *Vita Sancti Uodalrici*, 1.10.

[24] Widukind, *Res gestae*, 3.69,

Hand-Held Arms

Of crucial importance in understanding the deployment and training of soldiers in the phalanx is their armament. Some writers, such as Regino of Prüm, observed that fighting men were equipped with swords (*gladii*). This all-purpose term, however, covers a wide variety of arms that fall under the rubric of *gladius*. These include the broad categories of long swords (*spatha*) and short swords (*sax*) that can be further subdivided according to the length and breadth of the blade, the size and shape of the pommel, whether or not the sword is fashioned of damascened metal, and the presence or absence of a stabbing point.[25]

Other writers, such as Widukind, tended toward circumlocutions, such as "they struck on the left and right with iron."[26] These iron weapons almost certainly included both swords and hand-held spears. The latter, which frequently were denoted in Carolingian legislation under the general rubric of *lancea*, also included a variety of types, some of which were intended for use by foot soldiers as a hand-held thrusting weapon, and others that were intended to be thrown as missile weapons.[27]

The most important source of information about all types of weapons actually used by fighting men consists of the material remains identified through excavations. Up to the early eighth century, the burial of arms remained a common practice in the Frankish lands with the concomitant possibility of close dating of weapons.[28] Over the course of the eighth century, however,

---

[25]   The basic work on the *spatha* up through the seventh century is Wilfried Menghin, *Das Schwert im frühen Mittelalter: Chronologische-typologischen Gräbern des 5. bis 7. Jahrhunderts* (Stuttgart, 1983). With regard to the wide distribution of the *spatha* throughout the regions that comprised the Ottonian kingdom, see the discussion by Herbert Westphal, *Franken oder Sachsen? Untersuchungen an frühmittelalterliche Waffen* (Oldenburg, 2002), 263-274. Various types of short swords, with their origins reaching back to the late Roman empire, also were widely distributed throughout the regions that would become the Ottonian kingdom no later than the early eighth century. See Westphal, *Franken oder Sachsen*, 266-72. The *sax* was much more commonly found during the early Middle Ages on the continent than in Anglo-Saxon England where, however, a range of these short swords have also been identified in weapons' burials. See the discussion by David A. Gale, "The Seax," in *Weapons and Warfare*, 71-84, here 71.
        Simon Coupland, "Carolingian Arms and Armor in the Ninth Century," *Viator* 21 (1990), 29-50, here 43, argues that the short sword fell out of use beginning in the early ninth century because of improvements in the long sword (*spatha*). In particular, Coulson points to improvements in the shape of the *spatha* that made it more maneuverable and therefore better for use in hand-to-hand combat, including on foot. Szameit, "Gedanken zum ostfränkischen Kriegswesen," 71, however, points to material drawn from excavations in Austria that suggest the continued use of short swords into the tenth century, which probably represent further developments of the late *sax*.

[26]   Widukind, *Res gestae*, 1.36, "*dextra laevaque ferro*".

[27]   The basic study of the hand-held lance from the late Roman through the Carolingian period is Dagmar Hüpper-Dröge, *Schild und Speer: Waffen und ihre Bezeichnungen im frühen Mittelalter* (Frankfurt, 1983), with a detailed discussion of Carolingian legislation regarding the requirement that soldiers come to muster with *lancea*, at 192-200.

[28]   With regard to the importance of burials of weapons for dating purposes, and the difficulty of dating individual weapons that have been excavated outside the context of burial sites, see the

Christian burial practices were revised to discourage the placement of burial goods within the *regnum Francorum*.[29]

Archaeologists have compensated in several ways for the general absence of burial goods from the lands of the *regnum Francorum* from the end of the eighth century onward. In both the northern lands and among the Slavs, the practice of arms burials continued unabated well into the tenth century. Excavations of these sites provide important information about the arms that were employed by the enemies of the *regnum Francorum* and its Ottonian successor state, and also shed continuing light on the arms that were used by Carolingian and Ottonian fighting men in the ninth and tenth centuries.[30]

In addition, chance finds of arms, particularly in rivers, have considerably expanded the corpus of arms that are available for study.[31] These latter finds are difficult to date closely because they are often found without any stratigraphic context.[32] However, manuscript illustrations, which frequently are very closely datable, have been used successfully by archaeologists and other specialists in the history of arms to track technological developments of individual weapons types, and also to identify the appearance of new types of arms.[33]

discussion by Alfred Geibig, "Die Schwerter aus dem Hafen von Haithabu," *Berichte über die Ausgrabungen in Haithabu: Bericht 33*, ed. Kurt Schietzel (Neumünster, 1999), 9-99, here 44.

[29] Concerning the difficulties in dating weapons that results from the ending of the practice of arms burials, see Herbert Westphal, "Zur Bewaffnung und Ausrüstung bei Sachsen und Franken: Gemeinsamkeiten und Unterschiede am Beispiel der Sachkultur" in *Kunst und Kultur der Karolingerzeit: Karl der Große und Papst Leo III. in Paderborn*, ed. Christoph Stiegemann and Matthias Wemhoff (Mainz, 1999), 323-327, here 323.

[30] In an overview of the state of the question regarding early medieval Slavic arms and fortifications, based upon grave-site excavations, Torsten Kempke, "Ringwälle und Waffen der Slawen in Deutschland," *Archäologie in Deutschland* 17 (2001), 24-27, here 24, observed that from the eighth century onward, weapons in the east were largely the same as those in the west. In this context, numerous studies of Slavic burial sites from the ninth and tenth centuries have shed considerable light on the transfer of both arms and arms-making technology from the *regnum Francorum* and the Ottonian kingdom to the east. See, for example, Alexander Ruttkay, "The Organization of Troops, Warfare and Arms in the Period of the Great Moravian State," *Slovenska archeologia* 30 (1982), 165-198, here 174-182; Zofia Kurnatowska, "The Organization of the Polish State—Possible Interpretations of Archaeological Sources," *Quaestiones Medii Aevi Novae* 1 (1996), 5-24, here 15; Janusz Górecki, "Waffen und Reiterausrüstungen von Ostrów Lednicki: Zur Geschichte des frühen polnischen Staates und seines Heeres," *Zeitschrift für Archäologie des Mittelalters* 29 (2001), 41-86; and Tomasz Kurasinski, "Waffen im Zeichenkreis. Über die in den Gräbern auf den Gebieten des frühmittelalterlichen Polen vorgefundenen Flügellanzenspitzen," *Sprawozdania Archeologiczne* 57 (2005), 165-196.

[31] Coupland, *Carolingian Arms*, 43, notes that despite the ending of the practice of burying arms within the *regnum Francorum* during the eighth century, a substantial number of individual weapons have been found in the east and north, where arms burials continued, and also in riverine mud.

[32] Geibig, "Die Schwerter aus dem Hafen von Haithabu," 44.

[33] Regarding the dangers of reading images of arms transparently, see the discussion by Bernard S. Bachrach, "A Picture of Avar-Frankish Warfare from a Carolingian Psalter of the Early Ninth Century in Light of the *Strategicon*," *Archivum Eurasiae Medii Aevi* 4 (1984), 5-27 (appeared in 1986); reprinted with the same pagination in *Armies and Politics in the Early Medieval West* (London, 1993); and Coupland, "Carolingian Arms," 31-2. Hüpper-Dröge, *Schild und Speer*, 192, emphasizes that illuminated manuscripts tend to confirm the image of the spear and shield combination that is attested in both excavations and legal sources.

The general consensus among specialists in the study of arms over the past thirty years is that spears and shields remained the primary weapons of foot soldiers in the *regnum Francorum*, the Ottonian kingdom, as well as their Danish and Slavic opponents through the end of the tenth century.[34] The most common type of spear is the so-called "winged lance" (Germ. *Flügellanzen*) that had its origins in the *regnum Francorum* in the eighth century.[35] It was rapidly diffused through trade and war into Scandinavia, England, and the Slavic east.[36] Close examination of winged lance-heads indicate a range of lengths from 150 to 250 cm.[37] These weapons were intended for hand-to-hand combat in the context of the infantry phalanx.[38]

There is no indication that Ottonian troops were deployed with spears to ward off attacks by heavily armed warriors who were engaged in the tactics of "mounted shock combat."[39] The winged lances employed by foot soldiers were insufficiently long to create a "hedgehog" formation to fend off men on horseback.

---

[34] The most common weapon combination used by foot soldiers in the armies of the Carolingians was the spear and shield. This continued into the tenth century. See Hüpper-Dröge, *Schild und Speer*, 190-192; and Szameit, "Gedanken zum ostfränkischen Kriegswesen," 71. With regard to the diffusion of western spears, particularly the so-called winged lance, into the Slavic world, and the continued use of the weapon into the eleventh century, see Górecki, "Waffen und Reiterausrüstungen von Ostrów Lednicki," 46-53; and Kurasinski, "Waffen im Zeichenkreis," 171-174.

[35] The first identifications of this lance as a Frankish weapon were in the nineteenth century by K. Koehler, "Geflügelte Lanzenspitzen," *Zeitschrift für Ethnologie* 29 (1897), 214-221; and P. Reinecke, "Studien über Denkmäler des frühen Mittelalters," *Mitteilungen der Anthropologischen Gesellschaft in Wien* 29 (1899), 35-52. See the discussion of this historiography in Kurasinski, "Waffen im Zeichenkreis," 171.

[36] See Kurasinski, "Waffen im Zeichenkreis," 172-173, and the literature cited there.

[37] For the shorter length spears with a range of 150–200 cm, see Erik Szameit, "Karolingische Waffenfunde aus Österreich Teil II: Die Saxe und Lanzenspitzen," *Archaeologia austriaca* 71 (1987), 155-171, here 155. A longer range of 200–250 cm was identified by H. Steuer, "Flügellanze," *Reallexikon der Germanischen Altertumskunde* volume 9 (Berlin, 1995), 251-254, here 252.

[38] This is the role envisioned by Szameit, "Karolingische Waffenfunde aus Österreich Teil II, "155. Szameit, "Gedanken zum ostfränkischen Kriegswesen," 71, in light of ongoing archaeological research, reiterated this view with regard to both the Carolingian period and the early tenth century. This is the same basic position taken by Coupland, *Carolingian Arms*, 47; and Kurasinski, "Waffen im Zeichenkreis," 173-174. Although tenth-century manuscript illuminations show mounted fighting men who are equipped with winged lances, there is no indication that this was intended to be used extensively in mounted combat. In this context, see the discussion by C. Steinacker, "Die Flügellanze der Karolingerzeit. Jagdspieß, Fahnenlanze oder Reiterwaffe?," in *Archäologie als Sozialgeschichte. Studien zu Siedlung, Wirtschaft und Gesellschaft im frühgeschichtlichen Mitteleuropa. Festschrift für Heiko Steuer zum 60. Geburtstag* (Rahden, 1999), 119-126, here 124-5.

[39] Lynn T. White, *Medieval Technology and Social Change* (Oxford, 1962), 1-38 and 135-153, argued for the role of the stirrup in making mounted shock combat possible. This view recently has been defended by J. F. Verbruggen, "The Role of Cavalry in Medieval Warfare," *Journal of Medieval Military History* 3 (2005), 46-71, here 62. White's thesis was effectively dismantled in three studies by R. H. Hilton and P. H. Sawyer, "Technological Determinism: the Stirrup and the Plough," *Past and Present* 24 (1963), 90-100; D. A. Bullough, "*Europae Pater*: Charlemagne and his Achievement in the Light of Recent Scholarship," *English Historical Review* 85 (1970), 59-105, here 84-90; and Bachrach, "Charles Martel, Mounted Shock Combat," 49-52. Concerning the general acceptance by specialists in military history of Bachrach's rebuttal of the Brunner-White thesis, see Kelly DeVries, *Medieval Military Technology* (Peterborough, 1992), 95-122.

Moreover, as will be discussed in greater detail below, there is no information in the surviving written sources or in the archaeological record to support the view that either the Ottonians or their opponents were equipped for cavalry charges with couched lances. Rather, the primary function of the winged lance was for use in the thrust and parry of hand-to-hand combat on foot.

Some foot soldiers of the Ottonian expeditionary levy, and even members of the local levy, may have been equipped with short swords (sax) either in place of or in addition to the spear.[40] However, the preponderance of men fighting on foot with swords very likely were dismounted professional soldiers (milites) and the wealthier members of the expeditionary levy.[41] Such men, who generally rode to war on horseback, were equipped with a doubled-edged long sword (spatha), that ranged in length from 90 to 100 cm.[42] In the eighth century, and earlier, the spatha had been intended almost exclusively for use on horseback as a slashing weapon, since it lacked a point and had a double edge.[43] The spatha, however, underwent substantial improvement over the course of the ninth century as sword smiths experimented with tapering blades from hilt to tip. The result was that the center of gravity of the weapon moved backward toward the hand-grip, making the weapon much more maneuverable for use in the cut, parry, and thrust of hand-to-hand combat.[44] As a consequence, the spatha, with its longer reach and increased maneuverability, made the sax redundant for use on foot.[45]

Most men serving in the phalanx, whether armed with swords or spears, were also equipped with shields. This was true both of the rank and file foot soldiers of the levy, of the dismounted professionals and of wealthier members of the expe-

[40] Szameit, "Gedanken zum ostfränkischen Kriegswesen," 71.

[41] As noted above with regard to the battle of the Dyle, it was by no means unusual for mounted fighting men to dismount and fight on foot. With regard to the general tendency of mounted men to serve on foot during battles, see Szameit, "Gedanken zum ostfränkischen Kriegswesen," 69. Rabanus Maurus, De procinctu Romanae miliciae, ch. 12, discusses the methods of training fighting men, who were armed for combat on foot, to mount their horses rapidly without hurting either themselves or their animals.

[42] Regarding the length of the spatha, see Coupland, "Carolingian Arms," 43. However, not all men who had horses were necessarily equipped with long swords. The Annales Fuldensis, an. 869, records, for example, that Count Gundacar, who was in the service of the Moravian prince Rastiz, after having betrayed his oath to Louis the German, was equipped with a shield (clypeus) and spear (hasta). Timothy Reuter, The Annals of Fulda (Manchester, 1992), 59, mistranslates the text as spear and sword.

[43] Regarding the technical improvements in the shape of the spatha, see Wilfrid Menghin, "Neue Inschriftenschwerter aus Süddeutschland und die Chronologie karolingischer Spathen auf dem Kontinent," in Vorzeit zwischen Main und Donau: Neue archäologische Forschungen und Funde aus Franken und Altbayern, ed. K. Spindler (Erlangen, 1980), 227-272, here 266-8; H. Jankuhn, "Ein Ulfberht-Schwert aus der Elbe bei Hamburg," in Festschrift für Gustav Schantes zum 65. Geburtstag, ed. K. Kersten (Neumünster, 1951), 212-229, here 212; and Coupland, "Carolingian Arms," 43.

[44] See the discussion by Coupland, "Carolingian Arms," 43.

[45] Coupland, "Carolingian Arms," 43; and Szameit, "Gedanken zum ostfränkischen Kriegswesen," 71. This transition also seems to have taken place among the Carolingians' enemies. James Graham-Campbell, Viking Artefacts: A Select Catalogue (London, 1980), 67-86, here 67, notes that the long sword was the dominant type, although short swords continued in use.

ditionary levy.[46] Underlining the importance of this piece of equipment, Ottonian kings, as had been true of their Carolingian predecessors, required that royal fiscal units and monasteries keep on staff shield makers who could produce these weapons for royal troops as well as for ecclesiastical contingents.[47] Moreover, there was sufficient demand for shields that private markets developed for the sale of this equipment, the most famous example of which is recorded in the *Annals of St. Bertin*. In this case, the shield vendors (*scuta vendentes*) followed Charles the Bald's army on its ill-fated march to the battle of Andernach.[48] The shields generally were constructed of wood that may have been reinforced with iron bands.[49]

Training with Sword and Spear

Within the broader didactic purpose of stressing the doctrine that constant training was crucial for fielding an effective army, Vegetius devoted considerable attention to training men to fight effectively in a phalanx.[50] In his revised version of Vegetius' *Epitoma*, which was specifically intended for use in contemporary times, Rabanus Maurus also focused on this topic. With regard to swords, Vegetius had emphasized the importance of training men to thrust with their weapons against posts called *pali*, that were designed to provide a target of the same proportion as an enemy combatant.[51] Rabanus edited this section of his text, giving it a new title: "How they are exercised with wicker shields and clubs."[52] Rabanus further augmented Vegetius's work by observing that it is the practice of individual soldiers to set up wooden posts in the ground so that they stand solidly at the

---

46   With regard to the general practice of equipping mounted fighting men and foot soldiers with shields, see Michael Müller-Wille, "Krieger und Reiter im Spiegel früh und hochmittelalterliche Funde Schleswig-Holsteins," *Offa: Berichte und Mitteilungen zur Urgeschichte, Frühgeschichte und Mittelalterarchäologie* 34 (1977), 40-74, here 51; Coupland, "Carolingian Arms," 35-38; Erik Szameit, "Fränkische Reiter des 10. Jahrhunderts," in *Otto der Große. Magdeburg und Europa. Katalog zur Austellung* 2, ed. Matthias Puhle (Mainz, 2001), 254-261, who argues (254) that Ottonian fighting men were equipped in the same manner as their Carolingian predecessors; and idem, "Gedanken zum ostfränkischen Kriegswesen," 69.

47   Regarding the requirement for Carolingian *villae* to have shield makers on staff, see capitulary *de villis*, c. 45. With regard to the production of shields at Ottonian monastic complexes and also royal palaces, see Paul Grimm, "Zu ottonischen Märkten im westlichen Mittelelbe- und Saalegebiet," *Vor- und Frühformen der europäischen Stadt im Mittelalter: Bericht über ein Symposium in Reinhausen bei Göttingen in der Zeit von 18. bis 24. April 1972 Teil I*, ed. Herbert Jankuhn, Walter Schlesinger, and Heiko Steuer (Göttingen, 1973), 332-337, here 335, for production at Fulda; and idem, "Fünf frühgeschichtliche Burgen bei Haina," *Studien aus Alteuropa* 2 (1965), 285-296, here 286, for a discussion of the production of shields at Haina on the basis of information provided in *Traditiones et antiquitates Fuldenses*, c. 43. The monastic plan of St Gall also includes a workshop for shield makers. See Walter Horn and Ernest Born, *The Plan of St. Gall*, 3 vols. (Berkeley, CA, 1979), I:347-348, II:191.

48   See *Annales Bertiniani, an.* 876 and the discussion by Coupland, "Carolingians Arms," 36.

49   Coupland, "Carolingian Arms," 37.

50   Vegetius, *Epitoma*, 1.3 and 3.26, for the crucial importance of regular training of troops, including men who already had been in military service for a considerable period.

51   Vegetius, *Epitoma*, 1.11.

52   Rabanus Maurus, *De procinctu Romanae miliciae*, ch. 6.

height of a medium-sized man, that is about six feet.[53] Then, the recruit (*tyro*) or
soldier (*miles*) was to rush against the post as if it were an enemy, thrusting first at
his face, and then at his side, then at his knee and lower leg.[54] While attacking the
post, the soldier or recruit was to practice lunging forward, stepping backward,
and thrusting upward. He was to take care, at all times, to cover himself with his
shield so as to avoid exposing himself to the enemy's weapon while moving in and
out on the attack.[55] In order that soldiers fight effectively under combat conditions, Rabanus followed Vegetius in emphasizing the importance of training with
double-weight practice weapons so that men would find their actual arms easier
to bear when faced with real opponents.[56] The swords were to be constructed of
wood, and the shields were to be made of wicker.[57]

It is clear that this practical advice actually was adopted for the training of
fighting men in the Ottonian kingdom. As noted in the previous chapter, Ekkehard of St Gall, in describing the training regimen put into practice for the
soldiers of the monastery's military household by Abbot Engilbert, draws attention to matters that clearly were inspired by, if not drawn directly from Vegetius.[58]
The abbot had mock arms made for his *milites*, including wicker shields with a
heavy core of closely fitted wooden boards and felt armor for protection. The
purpose of such double-weight weapons, as Vegetius emphasized, was to prepare
the men as well as possible for combat in the field, where normal weight weapons
would feel comparatively light.[59]

When fighting in a phalanx, it is exceptionally important to be aware not only
of the enemy to the front, but also of one's comrades on either side. Sloppily
delivered sword strokes have the potential to injure friend as much as the foe. In
this context, Rabanus emphasized that it was crucial to thrust with the sword
rather than slash with it.[60] The improved *spatha* of the ninth and tenth centuries,
discussed above, which was equipped with a point and with its center of gravity
moved back toward the hilt, lent itself to this thrusting motion in a manner
similar to that afforded by the standard issue Roman *gladius* of Vegetius' day.[61]

In addition to the importance of maintaining better control of the weapon in
a thrusting rather than slashing motion, the use of the point of a sword rather
than its edge was more likely to cause serious injury to the enemy. Rabanus
stressed that a slashing stroke would not have sufficient power to penetrate

---

53 Ibid.
54 Ibid.
55 Ibid.
56 Vegetius, *Epitoma*, 1.11; and Rabanus *De procinctu Romanae miliciae*, ch. 6.
57 Rabanus, *De procinctu Romanae miliciae*, ch. 6.
58 Ekkehard, *Casus Sancti Galli*, 114.
59 Ibid., "*piltris lorice*" and "*tabulis compactis et wannis scuta simulantur.*" Among the no longer
extant narrative sources upon which Ekkehard drew was the original *vita* of Wiborada. See Ekkehard, *Casus Sancti Galli*, 124.
60 Rabanus, *De procinctu Romanae miliciae*, ch. 7.
61 Coupland, "Carolingian Arms," 44.

a hauberk (*lorica*), but that a thrusting stroke will often prove fatal.[62] Just as importantly, a slashing stroke, as contrasted with a thrusting motion, opened up the right side of a soldier's body to the enemy, which substantially raised the risk of suffering a wound.[63]

Of crucial importance to the effective deployment of men equipped with both swords and spears in the phalanx was training them to use their shields effectively in combat. Vegetius instructed that men learning to thrust with swords at posts also were to hold their shields at the same time so that they could develop the skills necessary to protect their own bodies while striking at their opponents.[64] One can easily envision men training with spears being given the same instructions. In addition to these exercises against training posts, the soldiers also were to be trained through the staging of "mock battles" (*armatura*) in which the men were to be instructed to defend themselves with their shields while striking at the same time at their live opponents.[65]

Neither Vegetius' *Epitoma*, nor the portion of Rabanus' text that survives, includes chapters concerning the training of soldiers to serve in the phalanx with spears for use in hand-to-hand combat as thrusting weapons. Even in the absence of a specific discussion of training techniques for men equipped with spears, however, these manuals do provide important insights into the training of the majority of the men who served in the phalanx. In particular, it would require very little imagination to have men practice thrusting their spears at posts that also were used to train soldiers to thrust with the points of their swords.

Training the Phalanx for the Battlefield

At battles such as Lenzen and Mantahinga, Ottonian soldiers fighting on foot did far more than simply hold their ground in a shield wall in the face of enemy assault. They, like their Carolingian predecessors at the battle of the Dyle (891), advanced against enemy forces. In his discussion of the training of the phalanx to go on the attack, Vegetius repeatedly stressed the importance of maintaining order, keeping disciplined ranks, and of each man keeping his place in line.[66] Vegetius observed that when packed too closely together men lose the capacity to fight effectively. However, if they are spread out too thinly, they provide openings for the enemy to exploit.[67]

In order to maintain proper order in battle, Vegetius urged that troops regularly practice maintaining their positions as they participated in mock battles.[68] Here, Vegetius drew attention to the effectiveness of training men always to

---

62 Rabanus, *De procinctu Romanae miliciae*, ch. 7.
63 Ibid.
64 Vegetius, *Epitoma*, 1.11 and 2.23.
65 Vegetius, *Epitoma*, 1.13 and 2.23.
66 For a general statement of this point, see Vegetius, *Epitoma*, 1.9.
67 Ibid., 1.26.
68 Ibid., 2.23.

maintain their stations relative to their unit banners.[69] Apropos this point, in his discussion of the battle at Geule in 891, Regino of Prüm emphasizes that Frankish troops were organized in the phalanx by their commanders so that each man took his place under his own unit banner (*vexillum*).[70] Vegetius also provides specific guidelines for the spacing of men fighting men at three-foot (Roman feet) intervals in the same line, and six feet between lines.[71]

Training for Mounted Combat

In his description of the battle of Süntel (782), the author of the *Annales qui dicitur Einhardi* noted that when the enemy was in full retreat, mounted troops were in an ideal position to kill large numbers of enemy soldiers by catching them and stabbing them in the back.[72] In such an encounter, moving as fast as the horse can gallop has particular advantage. In most cases, however, even when facing a disorganized or unprepared opponent, maintaining unit cohesion remained important to ensure that the attacking force could be recalled or made aware of a new threat. Of particular importance in this context was training men and their horses to maintain their positions in line.

In his discussion of the battle of Riade (933), Liudprand of Cremona drew attention to this point when describing the final instructions given by Henry I to his heavy cavalry before the fighting had begun in earnest.[73] Liudprand was working from the reports of eye-witnesses to the battle, and claimed even to have seen a wall painting of the battle at Merseburg.[74] Nevertheless, it is possible that the depiction of events at Riade is reflective more of Ottonian battlefield tactics and training in the 950s, when Liudprand was resident at Otto I's court, than it was in the 933. Such a conclusion would require, however, that arms, tactics, and subsequently military training had substantially changed in the two decades at issue here.

In any event, Liudprand depicts King Henry as beginning the engagement by dispatching a unit (*legio*) of lightly armored Thuringian mounted troops to engage the Hungarians and draw them toward the main body of his army.[75] Henry's goal was to bring the fast and highly maneuverable Hungarian horsemen within range of his more heavily armored, mounted troops so that the latter could close with the mounted archers and bring their superior armament to bear in hand-to-hand combat. The Thuringians, in this context, can be understood to have been deployed in a type of feigned retreat.

---

[69] Ibid.

[70] Regino, *Chronica*, an. 891

[71] Vegetius, *Epitoma*, 2.23.

[72] *Annales qui dicitur Einhardi*, an. 782. See the discusson of the battle of Süntel mountain by Bowlus, "Two Carolingian Campaigns Reconsidered," 121-125.

[73] Liudprand, *Antapodosis*, 2.31.

[74] Ibid., 2.31.

[75] Widukind, *Res gestae*, 1.38, "*misit legionem Thuringorum cum raro milite armato, ut inermes prosequerentur et usque ad exercitum protraherentur.*"

While waiting for this stratagem to develop, Henry then, according to Liud-prand, issued a series of final directives to his heavy cavalry. First, he reminded the men that they were to maintain an ordered line. They were not to permit the faster horses to get ahead of the slower mounts. Second, the men were to cover themselves with their shields as they charged in an effort to catch the first shower of arrows. Finally, they were to close with the Hungarians as rapidly as possible so as to prevent the latter from getting off a second shot.[76] Liudprand insists that he had it on good authority that this is what Henry's *milites* actually did, referring to the painting of the battle that he saw on display in Merseburg, noted above.[77] Unfortunately for Henry I's troops, the Hungarians recognized the trap before it could be sprung and retreated, outrunning the more heavily armored *milites* before the latter could engage.[78]

The training that was required for both men and horses to carry out this type of precise control under battle conditions is discussed in some detail by Nithard, a cousin of Charles the Bald, and one of his military commanders.[79] After Charles the Bald and Louis the German had joined their armies together to face their elder brother Lothair I in 842, the two kings ordered their men to undertake a series of military exercises of the type that Nithard explained were quite common.[80] Equal numbers of Saxons, Gascons, Austrasians, i.e. East Franks, and Bretons were selected and placed at opposite ends of a large practice field. At a pre-arranged signal, both sides charged at each other with great speed.[81] Then, first one side, and then the other, wheeled around and pretended to flee, their backs protected by their shields.[82]

This type of training provided mounted fighting men with valuable experience in maintaining a serried front as they charged an enemy. In addition, the wheeling about in pretended flight described by Nithard provided fighting men with the kind of practice that was required to "sell" the feigned retreat to enemy forces. These military exercises, as described by Nithard, parallel the *armatura* called for by Vegetius for training fighting men under simulated battle conditions.

Hand-Held Missile Weapons

By the early ninth century, and perhaps even earlier, Carolingian armies in the field regularly included men equipped with bows.[83] Charlemagne issued capitu-

---

76   Liudprand, *Antapodosis*, 2.31.
77   Ibid.
78   Widukind, *Res gestae*, 1.38, "*sed nichilominus videntes exercitum armatum fugerunt.*"
79   Nithard, *Historiarum libri IV*, ed. R. Rau in *Quellen zur karolingischen Reichsgeschichte* (Darm-stadt, 1955), here 3.6.
80   Nithard, *Historiarum*, 3.6, "*Ludos etiam hoc ordine saepe causa exercitii frequentabant.*"
81   Ibid., "*alter in alterum veloci invicem ruebat.*"
82   Ibid., "*Hic pars terga versa protecti umbonibus ad socios insectantes evadere se velle simulabant, at versa vice iterum illos, quos fugiebant persequi studebant.*"
83   See the observations by Alessandro Barbero, *Carlo Magno, un padre dell'Europa* (Rome, 2000), trans. Allen Cameron as *Charlemagne: Father of a Continent* (Berkely, 2004), 253-4.

laries that required men of the expeditionary levy to bring bows, bowstrings, and a quiver of arrows on campaign.[84] It may be that Carolingian experience with the Avar mounted archers during the late eighth century convinced Charlemagne that it was important to have a sufficient number of archers to provide protection to his army when it faced an opponent with the capacity to strike from a distance.

Nevertheless, despite the considerable emphasis in contemporary legislation on the arming of troops with bows, and the substantial material evidence for the use of these bows, there is very little information in narrative sources about the deployment of archers on the battlefield by the Carolingians, as contrasted with their use in sieges.[85] Written sources from Anglo-Saxon England are somewhat more forthcoming. *Beowulf* describes the deployment of archers in conjunction with the phalanx, with the arrows arching over the men in the shield wall to strike the enemy.[86] Similarly, the poetic account of the battle of Maldon describes both the Danes and Anglo-Saxons formed in opposing phalanxes with archers showering the enemy with arrows.[87] Insofar as such epic poems were intended to provide a familiar setting within which to recount their stories, we can be confident that the intended audiences for both of these works were familiar with the use of bows on the battlefield.

Most of the battles fought by Henry I and Otto I, as had also been true of the Carolingian rulers of *Francia orientalis*, were against opponents who included large numbers of archers in their ranks. The main striking force of the Hungarians consisted of horse archers, whose effectiveness was widely reported in contemporary sources.[88] Moreover, material sources developed in the context of extensive excavations indicate that both the Slavic and Danish opponents of the Ottonians included numerous men equipped with bows.[89] However, as is true of Carolingian-period narrative sources, tenth-century texts provide little informa-

---

[84] Capitularia I: 75; 77 c. 9 and c. 17. See the discussion of this capitulary by Ganshof, *Frankish Institutions under Charlemagne*, 65 and 157 n. 42. Matthew Strickland and Robert Hardy, *From Hastings to the Mary Rose: The Great Warbow* (Stroud, 2005), 51-59, provide an overview of the use of bows in Anglo-Saxon England, by the Vikings, and also by the Carolingians in the early ninth century.

[85] See the discussion by Coupland, "Carolingian Arms," 49.

[86] *Klaeber's Beowulf and the Fight at Finnsburg*, ed. R. D. Fulk, Robert E. Bjork, and John D. Niles (Toronto, 2008), lines 3114-3118.

[87] *Battle of Maldon*, ed. Donald Scragg (Manchester, 1981), line 72. See the discussion by Manley, "Archer and the Army," 225; and Abels, "Strategy, Tactics," 149.

[88] Again, the most up to date and comprehensive treatment of this topic is now Bowlus, *Battle of Lechfeld*, 19-44.

[89] Numerous excavations of Slavic sites have identified bows and arrows. See, for example, *Corpus archäologischer Quellen*, 138; Müller-Wille, "Krieger und Reiter im Spiegel früh und hochmittelalterliche Funde Schleswig-Holsteins," 44; and Schmidt, *Drense: Eine Hauptburg der Ukrane*, 49-50. With regard to Danish and Viking use of bows, see Graham-Campbell, *Viking Artefacts*, 74; and Harm Paulsen, "Pfeil und Bogen im Haithabu," in *Berichte über die Ausgrabungen in Haithabu:Bericht 33*, ed. Kurt Schietzel (Neumünseter, 1999), 93-147, who provides considerable information about the bows and arrows that were available to the Danes and other northern peoples during the eighth through tenth centuries. Of particular importance is the identification of bows with a range of up to 200 meters (140).

tion about the deployment of archers in the field. One of the few exceptions is Widukind's description of Otto I's battle against the Obodrites at the Recknitz river in 955.[90] In this case, Otto is presented as deploying archers, as well as field artillery, against the Obodrites.[91]

In a similar manner, the throwing of javelins is not specifically attested in the context of battles during the reigns of Henry I and Otto I, although, as will be seen below, missile weapons of a variety of types were used by both attackers and defenders in the context of sieges. However, Liudprand of Cremona describes the equipping of light infantry, who were armed with both swords (*ensis*) and throwing spears (*pilum*) to deal with the Muslims operating out of the fortress of Fraxinetum in modern La Garde-Freinet near Saint-Tropez in Provence. [92] Archaeological finds also shed some light on this question, as the discovery of smaller lance heads suggests that some foot soldiers within the *regnum Francorum* and its Ottonian successor also may have been provided with javelins that were intended to be thrown as missile weapons.[93]

Both Vegetius and Rabanus' revised version of the *Epitoma* provide insights into the training of men to use both bows and javelins on the battlefield. The men were to be given regular practice throwing javelins at man-sized targets so that they would be well prepared for actual combat conditions. In this vein, Vegetius observed that using heavy-weight practice spears during training would have the same positive results in combat conditions as would be obtained using heavy weight shields and practice swords, noted above.[94] In his updated version of Vegetius' text, Rabanus also included a discussion of training fighting men to use heavy weight practice spears when they developed their skills throwing these missile weapons at targets.[95]

In discussing the training of soldiers to shoot arrows, Vegetius observed that only a quarter to a third of recruits would have an aptitude for this type of combat.[96] When these men were identified by their trainers, they were to be given regular exercise shooting at the same type of man-sized targets employed to train

---

90   Widukind, *Res gestae*, 3.53-5.

91   Ibid. 3.54, "*Imperator vero de nocte consurgens iubet sagittis et aliis machinis ad pugnam provocare, et quasi vi flumen paludemque transcendere velle.*"

92   Liudprand, *Antapodosis*, 2.49, "*Elige igitur iuvenes nimia quasi mobilitate volipedes, qui me imperatorem, praeceptorem, dominum aequanimiter audiant. Horum neminem aliquid praeter singulas parmas singulosque pilos ensesque singulos ac simplices vestes cum exiguitate obsonii habere permitto.*"

93   This is the view of Szameit, "Karolingische Waffenfunde aus Österreich Teil II," 155 which he reiterated some two decades later in "Gedanken zum ostfränkischen Kriegswesen," 71. Coupland, "Carolingian Arms," 47, relying on Regino's comment that Charles the Bald's troops were unfamiliar with the Breton tactic of throwing spears from horseback, argues that spears likely were not used for throwing. Coupland does, however, point out that the Carolingians possessed light throwing spears (47). Bachrach, *Early Carolingian Warfare*, 93, summarizes the archaeological and written sources regarding the use of throwing spears by fighting men who were trained to serve in the Carolingian phalanx.

94   Vegetius, *Epitoma*, 1.14.

95   Rabanus, *De procinctu Romanae miliciae*, ch. 8.

96   Vegetius, *Epitoma*, 1.15.

soldiers in the use of the javelin.[97] It is not clear from the written sources whether professional soldiers in the service of the Ottonian king and his secular and ecclesiastical magnates were regularly equipped with bows for combat in the field. It may be that archers generally were drawn from among the poorer members of the expeditionary levy. One of the few narrative sources that sheds light on this question is Thietmar of Merseburg's observation that Margrave Leopold of the Bavarian eastern march was mortally struck by an arrow, shot by a personal enemy, while engaged in a military training exercise with his *milites*.[98] This observation by Thietmar may permit the inference that part of the training exercise included archery practice.

One additional hand-held missile weapon, which is discussed by both Vegetius and Rabanus, is the sling. In his description of this weapon, Rabanus diverges considerably from the text of the *Epitoma*, and relying rather on the biblical account of David and Goliath (1 Sam. 17:31-54).[99] There are several references to the use of slings by Ottonian soldiers in contemporary narrative sources, although none that describe the use of this weapon in the field. Adalbert of Magdeburg does record that Otto's army included slingers during the siege of one of King Berengar of Italy's fortifications on the island of Garda in 961.[100] In addition, an image from a gospel book belonging to Otto III, commissioned in the period 998–1001, includes a depiction of two soldiers armed with slings who are participating in the siege of a city, meant to illustrate Jerusalem.[101] The concomitant depiction of soldiers armed with crossbows among both the defenders and attackers is highly significant here since the hand-held weapon illustrated in this manuscript is one of the very first pictoral references to the crossbow.[102] Consequently, it would appear that the artist who painted this picture was attempting to describe weapons that were currently in use in his day.

Equipment and Training for Siege Warfare

Siege operations, that is the capture and defense of fortifications, dominated Ottonian warfare. These included operations against massive fortress cities of late

97   Ibid.
98   Thietmar of Merseburg, *Chronicon*, 4.21, "*et comes … cum suis militibus ludens, ex uno foramina ab excecati amico sagitta valente vulneratus est … .*" Cf. *Annales Quedlinburgenses*, an. 994, where Leopold is depicted being shot from a window.
99   Rabanus, *De procinctu Romanae miliciae*, 10; and Vegetius, *Epitoma*, 1.16.
100   Adalbert of Magdeburg, *Continuatio*, an. 961, "*Tunc Willa inprimis hostiliter aditur et adempto omni de lacu exitu cotidianis fundibulariorum et sagittariorum aliorumque belli instrumentum impugnationibus fatigatur.*"
101   The image is in Bayerische Staatsbibliothek, Clm. 4452 f. 188v. which is the cover image for this volume. The text is discussed in some detail by Henry Mayr-Harting, *Ottonian Book Illumination: An Historical Study* (Oxford, 1991), 166. The image refers to Luke 19:41, commonly understood as Christ weeping over Jerusalem.
102   For an introduction to the development and use of the crossbow, see the discussion by David S. Bachrach, "The Origins of the English Crossbow Industry," *Journal of Medieval Military History* 2 (2003), 73-87, particularly, 73-4.

Roman origin in West Francia, Italy, and within much of the German kingdom.[103] These fortress cities were supplemented in Germany and its western neighbors by the construction of many hundreds of additional fortifications throughout the early medieval period.[104] By the mid ninth century, the Slavic polities centered in Moravia and Bohemia had thoroughly adopted western techniques of fortress construction.[105] By the end of the ninth century, the West Slavic polities established by the Obodrites, Redarii, Liutizi (Wilzi), Ukrani, Hevelli, Lusatians, and Daleminzi in the river valleys of the Havel, Saale, Mulde, Elster, Elbe, and Oder, as well as the upland areas of Lausatia had also developed advanced techniques for the construction of very large numbers of substantial fortifications.[106]

[103] For an overview of the survival and use of Roman fortifications throughout the West, the best introduction remains, Stephen Johnson, *Late Roman Fortifications* (Totowa, NJ, 1983); and *L'Architecture de la Gaule romaine. Les fortifications militaires, Documents d'archéologie française* 100, directed by Michel Reddé with the aid of Raymond Brulet, Rudolf Fellmann, Jan-Kees Haalebos, and Siegmar von Schnurbein (Paris and Bordeaux, 2006). The older works by Adrien Blanchet, *Les enceintes romaines de la Gaule* (Paris, 1897), 13-219; and Albert Grenier, *Manuel d'archéologie gallo-romaine*, 6 vols. (Paris, 1924-1934), 5, 281-361, are still of substantial value. Regarding continuity, see Jean Hubert, "Evolution de la topographie de l'aspect des villes de gaule du Ve au Xe siècle," *Settimane di Studio del Centro Italiano di studi sull'alto Medioevo*, VI (1959), 529-558; and Carlrichard Brühl, *Palatium und Civitas: Studien zur Profantopographie spätantiker Civitates vom 3. bis zum 13 Jahrhundert, I Gallien* (Cologne and Vienna, 1975); and II *Belgica I, beide Germanien und Raetia II* (Cologne and Vienna, 1990).

[104] The scholarship regarding these early medieval fortifications is vast. A good starting point for the German kingdom and its neighbors is the collection of articles in *Frühmittelalterliche Burgenbau in Mittel und Osteuropa*; and *Europa im 10. Jahrhundert: Archäologie einer Aufbruchszeit*. Still valuable are the surveys of fortifications in the territory of the old German Democratic Republic and its eastern neighbors in Paul Grimm, *Handbuch vor-und frühgeschichtlicher Wall-und Wehranlagen*; *Corpus archäologischer Quellen*; and Billig, *Die Burgwardorganisation im obersächsisch-meissnischen Raum*. The basic starting point for the fortified palaces of the Ottonian period is now *Die deutsche Königspfalzen: Repertorium der Pfalzen, Königshöfe und übrigen Aufenhaltsorte der Könige im deutschen Reich des Mittelalters* vols. 1-4 (Göttingen, 1982-2000). Additional insights, from archaeological, art historical, and architectural perspectives have been developed through the series *Deutsche Königspfalzen: Beiträge zu ihrer historischen und archäologischen Erforschung*, 7 vols. (Göttingen, 1963-2007).

[105] See the discussion of the development of the Bohemian and Moravian fortifications, and the effect that this had on the conduct of warfare by the Carolingians, by Goldberg, *Struggle for Empire*, 119-31. With regard to several of the major Moravian and Bohemian fortifications, see Ivana Bohácová, "Zum Befestigungssystem der Premyslidenburgen (am Beispiel der archäologischen Untersuchungen in der Prager Burg und in Stará Boleslav)," in *Frühmittelalterliche Burgenbau*, 37-47; Cenek Stana, "Prerov- eine Burg des Boleslav Chrobry in Mähren," in ibid., 49-69; Andrea Bartoskova, "Zur Stellung von Budec in der Struktur der böhmischen frühmittelalterlichen Burgwälle," in ibid., 321-327; Katerina Tomkova, "Die Stellung von Levy Hradec im Rahmen der mittelböhmischen Burgwälle," in ibid., 329-339; Ludek Galuska, "Die großmärischen Siedlungsagglomeration Staré Mesto-Uherské Hradisté und ihre Befestigungen," in ibid., 341-348; and Pavel Kouril, "Frühmittelalterliche Befestigungen in Schlesien und Nordmähren," in ibid., 349-358.

[106] Regarding the systems of Slavic fortifications that were developed to oppose first Carolingian and then Ottonian invasions, see, for example, K. W. Struve, *Die Burgen in Schleswig-Holstein* vol. 1 *Die Slawischen Burgen* (Neumünster, 1981); Torsten Kempke, "Bemerkungen zur Delvenau-Stockitz-Route im frühen Mittelalter," *Hammaburg* 9 (1989), 175-184; Schmidt, *Drense*; Günter Wetzel, "Neue Erkenntnisse zur Befestigung der Burg bei Gehren, Kr. Luckau," *Ausgrabungen und Funde* 35 (1990), 90-92; Markus Agthe, "Slawischer Burgwall mit Voburgsiedlung von Leuthen-Wintdorf, Niederlausitz," *Ausgrabungen und Funde* 38 (1993), 300-303; Felix Biermann, "Handel,

The most straight-forward type of assault that is attested in narrative sources regarding the capture of fortifications, including both Slavic princely seats and *urbes* of Roman origin, is storming the walls.[107] Even before a military commander could consider ordering such an assault, however, several important conditions had to be met. From a practical perspective, an appropriately large number of wooden ladders either had to be transported to the siege in the army's baggage train, or had to be constructed on site. In either case, it was necessary to construct ladders that were sufficiently tall to reach the top of the wall, but not so tall as to afford the defenders an opportunity to knock them over with too much ease. The techniques for judging the height of walls, as seen in the previous chapter, were well developed in the early medieval West, and Ottonian commanders had access to this information from a variety of sources, including Vegetius' *Epitoma*, from Bede, and also by using an astrolabe in a manner described in detail in manuscripts of the *agrimensores*.[108]

However, simply having ladders of the correct height did not permit an assault against a high wall that was surmounted by highly motivated fighting men. The soldiers who were to mount these ladders, carrying their shields, swords, and spears, while encumbered, if they were fortunate, with helmets and hauberks as well, required extensive training. This training was to assure both their physical ability to climb what might be a ten-meter, or even taller, ladder, and also the mental toughness to make this ascent knowing that mortal combat awaited them at the top.[109] Modern fire fighters, who have to face the dangers contingent upon entering a burning building, but not the danger of being sliced or jabbed by an armored soldier, require considerable and consistent training to prepare them for this challenge. And this is true despite the many modern safeguards that have been developed, including well constructed metal ladders and good climbing boots.[110] It should be emphasized that this type of training was not likely to be part of a man's normal work experience any place in the Ottonian empire.

Haus- und Handwerk in frühmittelalterlichen Burg-Siedlungskomplexen zwischen Elbe und Lubsza," in *Frühmittelalterliche Burgenbau*, 95-114; Berndt Wachter, "Dendrodaten zu frühmittel-lalterlichen Burgen im Hannoverschen Wendland," in *Frühmittelalterlichen Burgenbau*, 235-247; Joachim Henning, "Archäologische Forschungen an Ringwällen in Niederungslage: Die Nieder-lausitz als Burgenlandschaft des östlichen Mitteleuropas im frühen Mittelalter," in *Frühmittelal-terliche Burgenbau*, 9-29; idem, "Der slawische Siedlungsraum und die ottonische Expansion östlich der Elbe: Ereignisgeschichte –Archäologie-Dendrochronlogie," *Europa im 10. Jahrhundert: Archäol-ogie einer Aufbruchszeit*, ed. Joachim Henning (Mainz, 2002), 131-146; and Kersting, "Die Burg von Luckenwalde am Niederen Fläming," 331-338.

[107] See, for example, Liudprand, *Antapodosis*, 3.52; Widukind, *Res gestae*, 3.34-5; Flodoard, *Annales*, an. 922, and 952; and Richer, *Historiae*, 3.105.

[108] Vegetius, *Epitoma*, 4.30. See the discussion of these methods in Stevens, *Bede's Scientific Achieve-ment*; idem, "Cycles of Time: Calendrical and Astronomical Reckonings in Early Science," 27-51; and Gericke, *Mathematik im Abendland*, 70.

[109] For the Carolingian background on this topic, see Bachrach, *Early Carolingian Warfare*, 103-7.

[110] See the discussion of the challenges involved in training firemen to scale ladders, while loaded with equipment in *Essentials of Fire Fighting*, ed. Michael A. Wieder, Carol Smith, and Cinthia Brackage, third edn (Stillwater, OK, 1992), 241-89.

The dangers of scaling a ladder and fighting a determined foe on the parapet of a fortification were compounded by the need to cross a killing ground just to reach the foot of the wall that was to be assaulted. As Vegetius observed, the men going up these ladders were in considerable danger from defenders, unless the latter could be cleared from the top of the wall through concerted missile fire from bows, slings, and various types of engines.[111] Stone-throwing and spear-shooting engines that were mounted on the walls and towers of the fortification would begin to take a toll on the attackers at not less than 400 meters before they were in a position to raise their ladders.[112] Once the attackers came within 200 meters, they would begin to fall prey to archers stationed on the walls and towers of the fortification.[113] At 100 meters, slingers stationed on the wall would be able to pick out their targets.[114] At the last stages of the assault, defenders equipped with spears and even stones would be able to inflict casualties on attackers as they reached the base of the wall, and attempted to ascend their ladders.

One important technique that was available to attackers when attempting to storm the walls was to protect themselves in a formation that was sometimes denoted in the sources as a *testudo*. This was the term used, for example by Abbo of Saint-Germain-des-Prés (died after 896), to denote the formation deployed by the Vikings in their assault on Paris in 885–886.[115] Abbo made clear what he meant by this term, noting that the Vikings advanced with "painted shields held up above to form a life-preserving vault."[116]

In his account of the deeds of Alfred the Great, Asser (died c. 909) observed that Anglo-Saxon troops also made use of the *testudo* formation when attacking the Vikings at the battle of Ashdown. In this case, the Anglo-Saxons, under the command of Alfred, who had not yet succeeded his brother as king, faced a Viking army that held the high ground. As a consequence, they formed up in a

---

[111] Vegetius, *Epitoma*, 4.21.
[112] Regarding the ranges of wall-mounted torsion artillery of the type described in late antiquity as an onager, see the discussion by W. Marsden, *Greek and Roman Artillery: Historical Development* (Oxford, 1969), II: 254; and Carroll Gillmor, "The Introduction of the Traction Trebuchet into the Latin West," *Viator* 12 (1981), 1-8, here 4. The best survey of both late Roman and early Byzantine artillery is now Tracey Rihll, *The Catapult: A History* (Yardley, PA, 2007), particularly, 232-269, which updates and largely replaces Marsden, *Greek and Roman Artillery*.
[113] Archers who were equipped with even 50-pound bows, who were stationed at the top of a 10-meter wall or tower, could hit targets at 200 meters. See the discussion of this point by W. McCleod, "The Range of the Ancient Bow," *Phoenix* 19 (1965), 1-14; and the observations by Bachrach, *Early Carolingian Warfare*, 107. For Viking bows with ranges up to 200 meters, see Paulsen, "Pfeil und Bogen im Haithabu," 140.
[114] See the discussion of ranges by M. Korfmann, "The Sling as a Weapon," *Scientific American* 229 (1973), 35-42. For the use of the sling by Roman troops, see W. B. Griffiths, "The Sling and its Place in the Roman Imperial Army," in *Roman Military Equipment: The Sources of Evidence, Proceedings of the Fifth Roman Military Equipment Conference, 1988*, ed. C. van Driel-Murray (Oxford, 1989), 255-279.
[115] See Abbo of Saint-Germain-des-Prés, *Bella parisiacae urbis*, ed. and trans. Nirmal Dass (Paris, 2007), line 302.
[116] Ibid., line 296, with the translation by Dass.

tight *testudo* formation, and then immediately began their assault on the enemy.[117] One might conjecture that the Viking forces that operated at Paris may well have learned the technique of protecting men in a *testudo* in the context of fighting against the Anglo-Saxons.

This tactical formation also was used by soldiers from East Francia during the later ninth century. Liudprand of Cremona, who it should be remembered wrote for an audience at Otto I's court, depicted Arnulf of Carinthia's East Frankish troops assaulting the walls of Rome in 896, while protecting themselves in a manner consistent with the *testudo* formation, although the future bishop of Cremona does not use this term.[118] According to Liudprand, the Germans advanced against the walls of Rome unit by unit (*catervertim*), with each group gaining protection not only from their shields (*clipei*) but also from specially constructed wicker screens (*crates*).[119]

It is clear that the tradition of deploying soldiers in this formation was maintained under the Ottonians in the tenth century. For example, Richer, in his discussion of Conrad the Red's deployment of Lotharingian troops at Senlis in 949, noted that the Lotharingians suffered extensively from the crossbow fire of the town militia (*urbani*).[120] In response, according to the Rheims historian, the attackers formed up in a *testudo* using their overlapping shields to protect themselves as they withdrew from the assault.[121] In a similar vein, Richer observed that Lotharingian troops who were holding the fortress of Verdun against an attack by the Carolingian ruler Lothair IV in 984, ordered the local craftsmen

---

[117] Asser, *De rebus gestis Aelfredi*, ch. 38-39. Cf. the suggestion by Richard Abels and Stephen Morillo, "A Lying Legacy? A Premiminary Discussion of Images of Antiquity and Altered Reality in Medieval Military History," *The Journal of Medieval Military History* 3 (2005), 1-13, here 11-12, that Asser was referring here to a "shield wall," and that "we ought not imagine that Alfred found a copy of Vegetius or Frontinus's *Strategemata* … and revived the Roman 'tortoise' formation." It should be emphasized here first that neither Frontinus nor Vegetius deal with the *testudo* in their extant works. Second, as Asser makes clear, Alfred's troops, far from standing still in a shield wall, advanced uphill against the Vikings. For a detailed treatment of the arguments made by Morillo and Abels regarding the value of narrative sources for understanding the reality of warfare in early medieval Europe, see Bernard S. Bachrach, "'A Lying Legacy' Revisited: The Abels-Morillo Defense of Discontinuity," *The Journal of Medieval Military History* 5 (2007), 154-193.
[118] Liudprand, *Antapodosis*, 1.27.
[119] Abbo, *Bella parisiacae urbis*, bk. 1 line 220, also notes the use of *crates*, in this case by the Vikings who were attacking the walls of Paris.
[120] Richer, *Historiae*, 2.92.
[121] Ibid,, "*Belgae vero, quia ab urbanis nimium arcobalistis impetebantur, resistere quiescunt. Nihil enim contra nisi tantum scutorum testitudine utebantur.*" In his commentary on the text, the editor, Robert Latouche (*Richer*, 282) suggests that the author was inspired in writing this section by Sallust's, *Jugurthine War*, ch. 94, where Marius is described as forming up his men in a *testudo* as they advanced against a Numidian held fortification. It is true that Sallust's text circulated widely during the early medieval period. See L. D. Reynolds, "Sallust" in *Texts and Transmission: A Survey of the Latin Classics*, ed. L. D. Reynolds (Oxford, 1983), 341-349. Nevertheless, it must be stressed that Richer operated within the context of writing for an audience that was familiar with warfare, and therefore was bound by the conventions of the rhetoric of plausibility. In this context, see the important observations by Lake, "Truth, Plausibility," 221-238, who focuses on this question with regard to Richer's claims to be writing about events that truly happened.

to construct shields (*clipei*) so that they could be used when they had to establish a *testudo*.[122]

As was true of an advancing phalanx, each man in a *testudo* had to keep his place in formation. He had to do so, moreover, while under concerted attack by enemies equipped with missile weapons. In addition, each soldier was responsible for holding his shield in the correct position so that the unit as a whole would be protected from enemy fire. Consequently, use of the *testudo* formation must be understood, *ipso facto*, as demonstrative of a high degree of military training.

Engines

Siege engines of a variety of types were in continuous use from the fifth through the ninth century in the regions that would become the Carolingian empire.[123] Similarly, the east Roman/Byzantine empire maintained an important poliorcetic component in its armies throughout the same period.[124] The enemies of both the Byzantines and the Franks, including the Avars, Arabs, and Vikings also acquired the technological expertise to operate and even to build their own siege engines.[125]

---

[122] Richer, *Historiae*, 3.103, "*clipeos quoque habendae testudini ordinandos instituerunt.*"

[123] The early scholarly controversy between G. Köhler, *Die Entwicklung des Kriegswesens und der Kriegführung in der Ritterzeit von Mitte des II. Jahrhunderts bis zu den Hussitenkriegen* vol. 3 (Breslau, 1890), 139-211, and Rudolf Schneider, *Die Artillerie des Mittelalters* (Berlin, 1910), 10-16, turned on the question of continuity or discontinuity in the use of artillery in the early Middle Ages. Köhler maintained that artillery of a variety of types, including torsion-powered engines, remained in use throughout the Merovingian and Carolingian period. Schneider held that these early medieval polities were simply too primitive to maintain a poliorcetic element in their armed forces. The weight of scholarly opinion has sided overwhelmingly with Köhler's view that artillery continued in use, although his views regarding the continued employment of torsion engines has engendered considerable further controversy. Regarding the state of the question concerning continuity or discontinuity in the deployment of siege engines in the early Middle Ages, see Paul E. Chevedden, "Artillery in Late Antiquity: Prelude to the Middle Ages," in *The Medieval City under Siege*, ed. Ivy A. Corfis and Michael Wolfe (Woodbridge, 1995), 131-173, here 131-134.
    Among the important works that treat the continued deployment of artillery during the early Middle Ages, see the observations by D. H. Hill, "Siege-craft from the Sixth to the Tenth Century," in *De rebus bellicis Part II*, ed. M. W. C. Hassall (Oxford, 1979), 111-117. With regard to the use of a variety of siege engines by the Merovingian kings, see Bernard S. Bachrach, *The Anatomy of a Little War: A Diplomatic History of the Gundovald Affair (568–586)* (Boulder, CO, 1994), 132-142. Concerning the use of artillery by the Carolingians in the eighth century, see idem, *Early Carolingian Warfare*, 107-118. For the use of siege engines by the later Carolingians, see Gillmor, "Traction Trebuchet," 1-8.

[124] With regard to the use of artillery by the Byzantine army during the early Middle Ages, see Haldon, *Warfare, State and Society*, 134-138. The best survey of both late Roman and early Byzantine artillery is Rihll, *The Catapult*, particularly 232-269.

[125] Regarding the use of siege engines by the Avars against Byzantine cities, see Rihll, *Catapult*, 263; Bachrach, *Early Carolingian Warfare*, 117; and Haldon, *Warfare, State, and Society*, 188, for the development of artillery by both the Avars and Arabs. With regard to the use of artillery by the Vikings, see Abbo, *Bella parisiacae urbis*, bk 1, lines 87 and 364-6. Also regarding the use of artillery by the Vikings, see Bernard Rathgen, *Das Geschütz im Mittelalter* (Berlin, 1928), 601.

So too did the Hungarians, who employed engines during their siege of Augsburg in 955.[126]

In light of this continuity in the use of engines, it is not at all surprising that authors of contemporary narrative sources record that Ottonian armies also deployed large numbers of engines in the course of besieging fortifications. Flodoard, for example, notes that in 952 Duke Conrad of Lotharingia, in command of elements of the Lotharingian expeditionary levy, was dispatched by Otto I to aid Hugh the Great to undertake a siege of the *munitio* of Mareuil.[127] In the course of this siege, Conrad's Lotharingian troops and Hugh's men built a large number of siege engines (*multae machinae*) that were deployed in the subsequent assault on the fortification.[128]

Widukind of Corvey also regularly noted the use of engines by Ottonian troops in the course of several siege operations. In his discussion of Otto I's siege of Mainz in 953, for example, Widukind referred to the large number of engines (*multae machinae*) that were deployed against the walls of the city.[129] He made similar observations about the deployment of engines by both Otto, and his younger brother Henry, in sieges of Regensburg in 954 and 955.[130]

Liudprand of Cremona also comments on the use of engines by Otto I, focusing on the critical role that they played in the emperor's siege of Rome in July 964.[131] In November of the previous year, Otto had imposed a settlement on the city, deposing Pope John XII and replacing him with Leo VIII. After part of the imperial army had been sent home, however, John's supporters rose in revolt.[132] Otto I then returned and established a regular siege of the entire city. In this context, Liudprand comments that the emperor used both famine and siege engines (*machinae*) as his weapons.[133]

Otto I's successors also deployed considerable artillery trains. In his *vita* of Bishop Bernward of Hildesheim, for example, Thangmar, who was present at the siege, observed that Otto III deployed numerous *machinae* and many other *instrumentae* against the walls of Tivoli in 1001. Some of these engines were transported there, and others were constructed (*paratae*) on site.[134] Henry II also

---

[126] Gerhard of Augsburg, *Vita Uodalrici*, 1.12, "*exercitus ungrorum inenarrabili pluritate ex omni parte ad expugnandam civitatem circumcinxit diversa ferens instrumenta ad depositionem murorum.*"

[127] Flodoard, *Annales, an.* 952.

[128] Flodoard, *Annales, an.* 952, "*Hugo comes cum suis super Maternam fluvium venit; cui occurrit dux Chonradus cum quibusdam Lothariensibus, obsidentque pariter munitionem apud Maroilum, quam Ragenoldus comes cum hominibus Artoldi praesulis intra ipsum fluvium nuper construxerat, instructisque multis undique machinis, fortiter opprimunt, tandemque non sine suorum damno capiunt atque succendunt.*"

[129] Widukind *Res gestae*, 3.18, "*Multae machinae muris admotae, sed ab urbanis destructae vel incensae.*"

[130] Widukind, *Res gestae*, 3.36 and 3.43.

[131] Liudprand, *De Ottone Rege*, 21.

[132] Ibid., 17.

[133] Ibid., 21, "*Quo audito, imperator urbem vallavit, neminem qui non membris truncaretur, exire permisit, machinis et fame usque adea afflixit, donec Romanis nolentibus urbem reciperet.*"

[134] *Vita Sancti Bernwardi episcopi Hildesheimensis auctore Thangmaro*, ed. Walter Berschin and Angelika Häse (Heidelberg, 1993), 316.

deployed siege engines during his campaigns. In 1008, for example, Henry II took materials from houses in the city of Trier to construct *machinae* with which he could assault the fortified archiepiscopal palace.[135] In 1022, Henry II fully invested the fortress of Troia in southern Italy and deployed *machinae*, so that he could "capture the city by force," in the words of Raoul Glaber.[136]

Mantlets

Some engines were designed to facilitate the movement of men to the walls of a fortification and to minimize casualties before the final assault. Thus, in addition to the use of the *testudo* formation, noted above, soldiers attacking a wall also could gain protection through the construction and deployment of large wood screens with an overlay of leather or fire retardant mats, which were carried on wheels. These protective engines had a variety of names, including *plutei* and *vinea*.[137] Vegetius provides a brief overview of the value of these engines and their means of construction in the context of describing the ways in which soldiers can attack city walls in greater safety.[138]

The practical deployment of these engines is described by several early medieval historians. For example, the anonymous author of the *Vita Hludowici* noted that Louis the Pious' troops made extensive use of mantlets (*vinea*) during his successful investment and siege of Tortosa in 808.[139] Similarly, the Vikings made use of these protective engines during their siege of Paris in 885–886.[140] Richer also describes the construction of a device of this type by Louis IV during his siege of Laon in 938.[141] According to Richer, this engine, which is described as providing protection to twelve men, was rolled up to the city, and allowed the men to begin the process of undermining the wall.[142] There is no specific mention of *vinea* or *plutei* being deployed by Ottonian troops. However, given the wide diffusion of information about this engine, not only among the Franks but also their opponents, it is certainly plausible that the *multae machinae* that accompanied Ottonian armies on campaign included mantlets as well.

---

135 *Gesta Treverorum*, ed. G. Waitz, MGH SS 8, ch. 30.
136 Raoul Glaber, *Historiarum*, 3.4
137 See Abbo, *Bella parisiacae urbis*, bk. 1 line 218-220, and the observation by Dass, nn. 47-48 at p. 111.
138 Vegetius, *Epitoma*, 4.15.
139 Anonymous, *Vita Hludowici*, ed. Ernst Tremp (Hanover, 1995), ch. 15.
140 Abbo, *Bella parisiacae urbis*, bk. 1 line 218-220.
141 Richer, *Historiae*, 2.10.
142 Flodoard, *Annales*, an. 938, records only that Louis was able to undermine the walls *"multis machinis"*. In providing additional detail here Richer is going beyond his source text, but also likely is providing information that would be understood and appreciated by his audience. In this context, see Lake, "Truth, Plausibility."

Rams

The weakest point of any fortification is its gate, where the circuit of the walls necessarily is broken to permit ingress and egress. A basic tool for exploiting this weakness was the battering ram (*arietes*), which was widely used in the Latin West during the early medieval period.[143] In addition to information provided about the use of battering rams in a range of historical works, such as Gregory of Tours and the anonymous *Vita* of Louis the Pious, Ottonian military commanders also had the opportunity to learn about the construction and deployment of these engines in manuals.[144] Vegetius describes, for example, a timber frame construction, covered with fire retardant hides and mats that provided a protective covering for the operating crew of the beam while they repeatedly rammed the gate.[145] This covering served a function similar to the frame of the mantlet, discussed above. The text of the *Mappae clavicula* also provides a description for the construction of a ram, although the surviving texts appears as if it were intended to serve as a set of rubrics for an experienced builder rather than as a blueprint for constructing the engine.[146]

Of importance in considering the texts of Vegetius and the *Mappae clavicula* is that they provide different instructions for protecting the housing in which the ram and operators worked. Whereas Vegetius suggested the use of animal skins and fire retardant mats, the *Mappae claviculae* indicates that alternating layers of felt, leather and sand are to be used.[147] The text then provides a strategy for defeating battering rams that were protected in this manner, indicating that first the outer layers of felt and leather must be burned off using an incendiary delivered in an unfired pot. Then, stones are to be thrown down onto the protective housing to knock off the sand, which will not burn. Once the sand has been removed, another incendiary pot is to be launched at the housing, which has been stripped down to flammable leather and wood.[148]

Abbo provides a detailed description of the construction and deployment of a ram by the Vikings at Paris, making clear that this was a wheeled device that was protected by a wooden housing of the type described by both Vegetius and the *Mappae claviciula*.[149] He recorded that the Vikings constructed a number of

---

[143] Regarding the wide use of the ram in the early medieval period up through the eighth century see Bachrach, *Early Carolingian Warfare*, 116.

[144] Detailed references to the deployment of rams can be found, for example, in Gregory of Tours, *Historiae*, 7.37; and Astronomer, *Vita Hludowici*, ch. 15, both of which, as seen in the previous chapter, were copied in Ottonian *scriptoria*, thereby making their information available to Ottonian audiences.

[145] Vegetius, *Epitoma*, 4.14.

[146] Smith and Hawthorne, "Mappae Clavicula," 68-9, provide a translation of the text, and note that the passage is "more than usually obscure."

[147] Ibid.

[148] Ibid., 69.

[149] Abbo, *Bella parisiacae urbis*, bk. 1 lines 205-12.

very large wheels (*monstra rotis*) from heavy oak, which were grouped together in threes.[150] The large size of the wheels meant that when they were connected together within a frame, the battering ram would be able to swing freely rather than drag on the ground. These wheeled engines were protected by a rectangular housing (*cubante domate sublimi cooperto*).[151] Abbo then notes that the battering rams had a crews of 60 men, each of whom was further protected by a helmet (*galea*).[152]

Artillery

Both defenders and attackers in sieges sought to strike the enemy at the greatest possible distance. For defenders, increasing the length of the "killing field" meant fewer men would be able to reach the parapet of the wall. Conversely, the attackers hoped to clear the walls while advancing against the enemy stronghold. Crucial to both defenders and attackers, therefore, was artillery that could hurl deadly projectiles up to twice the distance of a self-bow.

The two methods of propelling projectiles that were available from classical antiquity up through the early Middle Ages were tension and torsion. For the most part, tension engines, which drew their power from the potential energy stored in the bow of the weapon, fired long "sharps" that looked like spears.[153] These engines, often denoted as *ballistae* in the early medieval period, had the appearance of very large crossbows, and could be aimed and held cocked until the artilleryman had picked out his target.[154] Tension engines were ideal anti-personnel weapons for both attackers and defenders in sieges. They were relatively easily transportable in wagons, and could also be mounted on walls.[155] They also had a considerable advantage in range over hand-held self-bows, so that the operators of these engines were relatively free to pick their targets without worrying about being struck by opposing archers.[156]

Torsion artillery in the Roman imperial period frequently comprised complex two-armed engines. Some of these engines fired stones and others were designed

---

[150] Ibid., lines 206-7.
[151] Ibid., line 208.
[152] Ibid., line 210.
[153] Large tension-powered artillery that fired long sharps, and also hand-held tension-powered bows that were equipped with a lock and trigger mechanism (crossbow), generally were denoted in classical Latin sources as "scorpions." See Rihll, *Catapult*, 68. The term *ballista* in Vegetius' *Epitoma rei militaris*, 3.3, 4.9, and 4.22, referred to a torsion engine. See the discussion by Rihll, *Catapult*, 252-3.
[154] Abbo, *Bella parisiciae urbis*, bk. 1 lines 213-214, emphasizes the accuracy and power of the spear-casting engines employed by the defenders of Paris.
[155] For the transportability of engines, see Widukind, *Res gestae*, 3.54.
[156] A tension-powered spear caster had a theoretical maximum range of 450 meters, although the effective range likely was rather less. See the discussion by Marsden, *Greek and Roman Artillery*, 91; and Rihll, *Catapult*, 228-30. Nevertheless, spear-casting tension engines likely had better than twice the range of self-bows, including even the long bows in use by the Vikings in the ninth century, the latter having a range of 200 meters. With regard to the range of the viking bows, see Harm Paulsen, "Pfeil und Bogen im Haithabu," 140.

to cast spears.[157] These weapons fired their payloads in a horizontal trajectory.[158] By the Late Antique period, however, the two-armed stone-throwing engines had given way to the much simpler design of the one-armed engine that fired its payload of stone in a high arc.[159] The one-armed torsion engine, known as the onager or wild ass, was relatively easily transportable in ox-carts.[160] In addition, this type of artillery could be mounted on a wall for the defense of a fortification.[161] The maximum range of these weapons, firing a two to four kilogram stone was about 450 meters.[162] Like the spear-caster, this torsion engine was primarily an anti-personnel weapon.[163]

By the sixth century, the one-armed torsion engine had been joined by the early medieval lever or traction engine, which appears to have been used for the first time by the Avars against Byzantine cities.[164] The traction engine employed a lever principle, and was essentially a long beam fixed to a fulcrum. The shorter end of the beam faced the target, and the longer end had a sling attached into which the projectile was set. Energy was generated by the rapid descent of the target end and the concomitant rapid rise of the projectile end. The power for this descent was provided by a well trained crew of pullers, who pulled down in unison on ropes attached to the target end of the engine's central beam. Because of its design, the traction engine was much larger than contemporary torsion artillery. In particular, it required a very long beam and space along its sides for the crews of pullers.[165] Given a sufficiently large traction engine with a very long

---

[157]   Regarding the development of the two-armed torsion engine, see Rihll, *Catapult*, 76-80.

[158]   Rihll, *Catapult*, 77.

[159]   For a discussion of the transition to the simpler one-armed torsion engine, see the discussion by E. W. Marsden, *Greek and Roman Artillery: Technical Treatises* (Oxford, 1971), 249-265; and Rihll, *Catapult*, 77 regarding the difference in trajectories of two-armed and one-armed torsion engines. The one-armed engine often was denoted in Late Antique sources as an onager, or wild ass. The *locus classicus* of this term is Ammianus Marcellinus, *Historiae* 23.4 lines 4-7. See the critical treatment of Ammianus' understanding of siege engines by Rihll, *Catapult*, 244-48.

[160]   See the observation by Vegetius, *Epitoma*, 2.25, that Roman troops were accustomed to bringing their torsion engines with them on campaign fully assembled in a two-wheeled cart (*carpentum*).

[161]   Vegetius, *Epitoma*, 4.22.

[162]   See the discussion of the ranges by Gillmor, "Traction Trebuchet," 4; and Marsden, *Greek and Roman Artillery*, II:254.

[163]   In this context, W. T. S. Tarver, "The Traction Trebuchet: A Reconstruction of an Early Medieval Siege Engine," *Technology and Culture* 36 (1995), 136-167, here 149-150, conflates the one-armed torsion powered onager with the two-armed torsion powered engine, suggesting that the former, which he sees as heavy artillery, could only be maintained in Roman imperial workshops. Marsden, *Greek and Roman Artillery: Technical Treatises*, 249-265, argues for the continued use of one-armed torsion engines well into the Middle Ages. He is followed by Bachrach, *Anatomy of a Little War*, 134-5.

[164]   Regarding the use of siege engines by the Avars against Byzantine cities, see Rihll, *Catapult*, 263; Bachrach, *Early Carolingian Warfare*, 117; and Haldon, *Warfare, State, and Society*, 188, for the development of artillery by both the Avars and Arabs.

[165]   Tarver, "The Traction Trebuchet," 154, describes his reconstruction of a 16-foot (5 meter) rotating arm on a traction trebuchet that had the very limited range of just 100 meters with a payload of four kilograms. Obviously, the much larger payloads that were necessary to break stone walls required much larger engines with concomitantly longer rotating arms.

rotating arm, this engine could be deployed as heavy artillery that hurled large stones with sufficient power to smash stone walls and towers.[166]

Ottonian military commanders clearly had available tension-powered spear casters and torsion-powered stone throwers, both for the defense of fortifications and for offensive siege operations. With regard to tension-powered weapons, Abbo of Saint Germain-dés-Pres, in his late ninth-century account of the siege of Paris, repeatedly described the use of *ballistae* that were deployed on the walls and towers of the city.[167] The author of the *Gesta* of the bishops of Cambrai recorded that the defenders of the episcopal city were able to drive off a Hungarian assault in 954 with all manner of missile weapons (*telae*), which almost certainly includes those fired from spear casters.[168] In his description of the siege of Laon in 946 by Otto I, who had come to the aid of Louis IV, Richer also draws attention to the *telae* as well as the *lapides* that fell among both the attackers and the defenders in such numbers they seemed to be a hailstorm.[169] Widukind, as noted above, observed that Otto I deployed *machinae* at the battle of the Recknitz which likely consisted of tension-powered spear casters, although the possibility cannot be ruled out that some of them were stone throwers as well.[170]

Debates concerning the type of propulsion employed in stone-throwing engines have turned largely on the question of the terms used by contemporary authors to denote these weapons.[171] What has been missing from this discussion has been an assessment of the deployment of these engines, and particularly a recognition that traction engines, with their long rotating beams and teams of pullers, simply could not have been stationed atop walls or towers. As a consequence, when the authors of narrative texts describe the placement of engines in this manner, it is *ipso facto* clear that we are dealing with a small torsion-powered stone-thrower rather than a traction engine.[172] Thus, for example, when Abbo

---

[166] Rihll, *Catapult*, 263-265, discusses the introduction of this engine in the sixth century. Regarding the greater power of the traction engine, as contrasted with the one-armed torsion engine, see Chevedden, "Artillery in Late Antiquity," 164.

[167] Abbo, *Bella parisiacae urbis*, bk 1 lines 57-8, 87, 213, bk 2 lines 238-242

[168] *Gesta episcoporum Cameracensium Liber I. II. III. usque ad a. 1051*, ed. L. C. Bethmann, MGH SS 7, 1.75.

[169] Richer, *Historiae*, 2.54, "*In quo tela ac lapides tam dense ferebantur quam densa grando quandoque dilabitur.*"

[170] The identification of these *machinae* as spear-casters is suggested by Widukind's decision to list them alongside bows as the weapons used by Otto's troops at the ford. By contrast, Widukind does not mention *lapides* in this context.

[171] See, for example, the illuminating discussion by Randal Rogers, *Latin Siege Warfare in the Twelfth Century* (Oxford, 1992), 254-274.

[172] Two basic assumptions have buttressed the argument that one-armed torsion engines disappeared in the West during Late Antiquity, neither of which is founded upon the surviving source material. The first of these assumptions is that an "advanced" technology such as torsion power could not have been maintained by the barbarians who conquered the West. See, for example, Erich Sander, "Der Verfall der römischen Belagerungskunst," *Historische Zeitschrift* 149 (1934), 457-467; Friedrich Lammert, "Die antike Poliorketik und ihr Weiterwirken," *Klio* 31 (1938), 389-411; and Tarver, "Traction Trebuchet," 139-140. This thesis of overall technological decline simply cannot be

notes the deployment of *catapultae* on the towers at Paris, the necessary conclusion is that these were torsion engines.[173] In a similar manner, Widukind's poetic observation that in 938 both the attackers and defenders at the fortress of Laer cast stones as well as spears at each other indicates that mural artillery was being deployed here as well, with the concomitant requirement that the engines could fit atop the walls.[174]

The description in the *Gesta Treverorum* of Henry II's siege of the fortifications within the city of Trier in 1008 sheds additional light on the deployment of torsion-powered stone-throwers by the Ottonians.[175] The author of the *Gestae Treverorum* emphasized that the defenders made extensive use of engines in defense of the archiepiscopal palace, firing stones (*lapides*) out from this strong point (*arx*), at the royal troops (*caesariani milites*) as the latter launched an attack.[176] The limited space within the archiepiscopal palace and the use of the artillery specifically to target attacking troops indicates that the stone-throwers were smaller rather than larger, and designed as anti-personnel weapons. Both of these considerations point to the deployment of torsion rather than traction engines.

By contrast with the relatively light payload of the torsion engine, traction engines had the capacity, if they were sufficiently large, to throw very heavy stones. Abbo, for example, describes engines that he says are called *mangana* by his contemporaries that stand out because of the *saxa ingentia* that they can throw.[177] These are in marked contrast to the various *catapultae* that were deployed by both the

---

sustained in the face of the enormous technical and engineering skills displayed in Rome's western successor states.

The second assumption made by some scholars, such as Traver, "The Traction Trebuchet," 144-5, is that the development of the less expensive and simpler traction engine in the sixth century obviated the need for the continued use of Roman torsion engines. This argument presupposes, however, that early medieval decision makers would not deploy traction and torsion engines side by side, or that these two types of engines might serve different purposes. There is, however, no basis for such assumptions on the basis of surviving information about military decision makers. Rihll, *The Catapult*, 46-76, demonstrates in detail the great profusion of catapult types that were in use at the same time, making clear that a wide range of factors came into play when military leaders made decisions about what types of engines to construct. During the late twelfth and early thirteenth century, moreover, it is clear that a succession of English kings from Henry II to Henry III deployed both torsion and traction stone-throwing engines side by side for more than fifty years. In this context, see David S. Bachrach, "English Artillery 1189–1307: The Implications of Terminology," *English Historical Review* 121 (2006), 1408-1430.

[173] Abbo, *Bella parisiacae urbis*, bk 1 line 535.

[174] Widukind, *Res gestae*, 2.11, "*Illi autem urbis profecto auctore acriter resistentes lapides lapidibus, tela telis obicere non cessabant.*"

[175] The basic political events are set out in *Gesta Treverorum*, ch. 30.

[176] *Gesta Treverorum*, ch. 30, "*missis ex arce lapidibus, alios occiderunt, alios sauciaverunt.*" Regarding the use of the palace as the major defensive point within the city, and especially within the archiepiscopal compound, see Brühl, *Palatium und Civitas*, 87-88.

[177] Abbo, *Bella parisiacae urbis*, bk 1 line 365. In this context, Gillmor, "Traction Trebuchet," 1-8, is correct that Abbo's account of the siege of Paris is a clear demonstration of the use of the traction engine in the West. However, she is incorrect in asserting that this engine was necessarily deployed by the Vikings. If Abbo was consistent in his use of terminology, then the *catapultae* that were deployed by the Vikings were the same torsion engines as those mounted by the Franks on the towers and walls of the city of Paris. i.e. they could not be traction engines.

Franks defending Paris, and the Vikings who were attacking the city.[178] The latter were used, for example, to throw pots of burning lead rather than large stones.[179] A traction engine deployed from within the walls of a fortification had to be used in a manner similar to that of a modern mortar, i.e. without direct line of sight to the enemy.[180] It is certainly possible, and perhaps even likely, that Ottonian military commanders deployed traction engines in the sieges of erstwhile Roman fortress cities such as Mainz, Regensburg, Rheims, Senlis, and Rome. However, without the specific mention by a contemporary author that the engines deployed by the Ottonians threw particularly heavy payloads, it is not possible distinguish between traction and torsion engines simply on the basis that stones were thrown.

Mobile Siege Towers

Mobile towers were a regular feature of siege warfare during late Antiquity, and were deployed both by the Romans and their opponents. Ammianus Marcellinus, for example, noted that Julian deployed siege towers during his siege of Aquileia in 361.[181] Similarly, Procopius recorded that the Ostrogothic King Vittigis deployed mobile siege towers at Rome in 536–537.[182] Their deployment, and some aspects of their construction are also discussed by Vegetius and by Vitruvius in book ten of his *De architectura*.[183]

The most detailed treatment of the construction of a mobile siege tower during the Ottonian period comes from the pen of Richer of Rheims.[184] He describes the construction by King Lothair IV of a two-tiered mobile siege tower during his 984 siege of Verdun, which was being held by Lotharingian magnates loyal to the infant King Otto III. Richer reports that the tower was constructed of oak, which was taken from newly felled trees.[185] The base of

---

[178]   Abbo, *Bella parisiacae urbis*, bk 1 lines 227 and 525. It should be noted that Abbo uses the term *funda*, i.e. sling, as a metonymy for the entire stone-throwing engine.

[179]   Ibid., bk 1 line 227.

[180]   A late twelfth-century Italian manuscript of Petrus de Ebulo, *Liber ad honorem Augusti*, Burgerbibliothek Bern, ms. 120, fol. 109r, depicts the defenders of a fortification deploying a traction engine from within the walls of Naples, a fortified city rather than a modest fortification or tower. See Tarver, "The Traction Trebuchet," 157, for the image and citation.

[181]   Ammianus Marcellinus, *Res gestae*, 21.12.9-10.

[182]   *Procopii Caesariensis opera omnia*, ed. J. Haury and G. Wirth, 4 vols., second edn (Leipzig, 1962–1964), *De bello Gothico*, 1.21.3-4.

[183]   Vegetius, *Epitoma*, 4.17; and Vitruvius, *De architectura*, 10.13.4-5.

[184]   Richer, *Historiae*, 3.105. Edgard Boutaric, *Institutions militaries de la France avant les armées permanents* (Paris, 1863), 95-6, accepted Richer's account as accurate, and saw the tower constructed by Lothair's engineers as part of a continuity of siege technology that dated back to the late Roman period. John France, *Victory in the East*, 47-8, identified Richer's siege tower at Verdun as an early medieval precursor to the more advanced siege towers deployed in France during the mid-eleventh century, and in the campaign to Jerusalem at the end of the century. Cf. Sander, "Belagerungskrieg," 104-5, who, consistent with his view that early medieval Europe lacked siege engines of all types, works assiduously to deny the value of Richer's account despite describing the report as "sehr genau."

[185]   Richer, *Historiae*, 3.105, "*Quercus proceras radicitus succisas ad machinam bellicam extruendam advexerunt.*"

the tower was constructed of four 30-foot beams, which were fastened to each other so as to create an internal space of 100 square feet, i.e. 10 feet on each side. As Richer explains, "The length and width which was enclosed within these beams was ten feet. In a similar manner, the length of the beams that extended beyond the enclosed space was also ten feet on each side."[186] Four 40-foot beams were then fastened perpendicularly at each of the corners of the base.[187] These four perpendicular beams were then reinforced with 10-foot cross-beams that were fastened horizontally to the perpendicular beams at their mid-point and then at the top. A total of eight reinforcing beams were used.[188]

The next stage of the construction, according to Richer, was the attachment of four beams from the apex of the structure to the base. Two beams were used on each of two opposite sides. The purpose of these external supports was to keep the tower from wobbling or tipping over.[189] Each of these beams formed the hypotenuse of a right angle, the other two sides of which were the 40-foot perpendicular beams, and the 10-foot section of the base beams that extended beyond the central core of the structure.[190] Once the structure of the tower was completed, Richer reports the builders added two floors, consisting of planks, and additional wicker-work to provide protection to the men who would be stationed in the tower.[191]

In order to advance the tower toward the wall, Richer describes a pulley system that was powered by oxen. Four large posts were driven into the ground near to the walls of the fortification. Metal spikes then were driven into the posts in such a manner that ropes could be looped through them.[192] These same ropes were then run through pulleys attached to the tower, and then carried beyond the tower to a team of oxen, which were then hitched to the ropes.[193] The system

[186] Ibid., "Longitudinis et latitudinis spatium, quod intra commissuras earum tenebatur, decem pedum erat. Quidquid etiam a commissuris extra projectum erat, simili modo decem pedibus distendebatur."

[187] Ibid., "Transposueruntque bis per quatuor latera, festucas decem pedum, in medio scilicet et in summo, quae traductae, sublicas sibi fortiter annecterent."

[188] Ibid.

[189] Ibid., "A capitibus vero trabium, quibus sublicae nitebantur, quatuor trabes educate, et pene usque ad festucas superiors obliquatae, sublicis jungabantur, ut sic ex eis machina extrinsecus firmata, non titubaret."

[190] I thank my colleague Kenneth Baldwin, professor of engineering at the University of New Hampshire, for pointing out that the engine described by Richer would have been particularly stable and not at all prone to tipping over.

[191] Richer, Historiae, 3.105, "Super festucas quoque quae in medio et in summo machinam conectebant, tigna straverunt. Quae etiam cratibus contexerunt, super quas dimicaturi stantes et eminentiores facti, adversarios deorsum jaculis et lapidibus abruerunt."

[192] Ibid., "Dictabant enim quatuor stipites multae grossitudinis, terrae solidae mandandos, decem pedibus in terra defossis, octo vero a terra ejectis. Qui etiam transpositis per quatuor latera repagulis vehementissimis solidarentur. Repagulis quoque transmissis funes inserendos."

[193] Ibid., "Sed funium capita ab hostibus abducta, superiora quidem machinae, interiora vero bobus annecterentur. At interiora longius superioribus protenderentur. Superiora vero breviore ductu machinam implicitam haberent, ita ut inter hostes et boves machina staret."

was designed so that as the oxen pulled away from the walls of Verdun, the tower would be moved forward.[194]

Otto I's grandson, Otto III, deployed mobile towers in 998 during his siege of Castel Sant' Angelo where Crescentius had taken refuge following his deposition of Pope Gregory V.[195] Among the *omnae belli machinae* were towers that were constructed of tall fir trees.[196] After the towers were completed, they were pushed up to the walls of the Castel Sant' Angelo, and the imperial troops stormed into the upper levels of the fortress.[197]

Engineers and Crews

The construction of siege engines required considerable expertise not only in carpentry, and smith work, but also in complex engineering. Certainly a man who constructed wagons in peacetime would have available a significant body of practical information that was relevant to the building of mobile battering rams and mantlets. However, additional specialized training was required to know how to suspend a battering ram within a protective wooden frame in a manner that provided space for the crew.[198] The construction of a wooden tower was certainly a task with which carpenters would be familiar, but to provide it with the capacity to move was again a skill that was peculiar to warfare. The construction of artillery, including *ballistae*, one-armed torsion engines, and traction engines also required considerable specialized training and expertise beyond that required of craftsmen in the normal course of their civilian occupations.[199] Indeed, Karl Leyser, who was committed to the notion that mounted warriors dominated warfare in the tenth

---

194 Ibid., "Unde et fieret, ut quanto boves ab hostibus trahendo discederent, tanto machina hostibus attracta propinquaret."

195 Raoul Glaber, *Historiarum*, 1.12, "Sed mox ut Otto hoc factum comperit, ira accensus cum permaximo exercitu Romam properavit. Quod cum cognovisset Crescentius illum scilicet urbem propinquare, conscendens cum suis turrim que sita est extra civitatem trans Tiberim, ob altitudinem sui Inter Celos vocatam, vallavit eam defensurus pro vita."

196 *Arnulfi Gesta: Archiepiscoporum Mediolanensium*, ch. 12, for the characterization of Otto III's siege train. For the use of fir trees, see Raoul Glaber, *Historiarum*, 1.12, "Interea, iubente imperatore, consruuntur in giro machine ex lignis celsarum abietum nimium artificiose composite."

197 Raoul Glaber, *Historiarum*, 1.12, "At imperatoris exercitus a foris urgendo impellens machinas, paulatimque euntes applicate sunt turri. Sicque pugne inito certamine, dumque alii desuper contendentes intrare, alii prorupere ad ostium turris illudque concidentes evellunt, sursumque certatim gradients ad turris superiora pervenerunt."

198 See the discussion by Bernard S. Bachrach, with Rutherford Aris, "De Motu Arietum (On the Motion of Battering Rams)," in *Differential Equations, Dynamical Systems, and Control Science: A Festschrift in Honor of Lawrence Markus*, ed. K. D. Elworthy, W. Norrie Everitt, and E. Bruce Lee (New York and Hong Kong, 1993), 1-13, regarding the training that was necessary to operate a battering ram.

199 In the twelfth and thirteenth century, the kings of England employed highly trained *ingeniatores* to construct their siege engines who generally were paid at a rate two to three times that earned by master carpenters and smiths. See the discussion by David S. Bachrach "The Royal Arms Makers of England 1199–1216: A Prosopographical Survey," *Medieval Prosopography* 25 (2004, appearing 2008), 49-75.

century, observed that "the growth in the scale of equestrian warfare preceded, if only by a little, the equally important developments of siege technology and the new demands now made upon the skills of experts in siegecraft."[200]

Moreover the men who operated battering rams and artillery also required specialized training. The pulling of the ropes on a traction engine's rotating arm had to be synchronized very closely so as to maximize the energy that was transferred to the sling and payload. Similarly, the crew of a battering ram, who were operating under exceptionally dangerous circumstances, had to be able to coordinate their strokes so as to maximize the force being delivered to a gate or wall. The men commanding the stone-throwing artillery also required considerable practice in aiming and adjusting their engines so as to hit their targets. This was particularly difficult in the case of traction engines that were stationed within the walls of a fortification where fire had to be directed by a spotter who was stationed up on a wall or tower with the ability to see the enemy.

Conclusion

As Rabanus observed in his revision of Vegetius' handbook for use in *tempore moderno*, the root meaning of *exercitus* is to practice or to train.[201] Combat was not only a dangerous and frightening business, it was complex and difficult as well. The Tacitean or *Beowulfian* image of the Germanic warrior charging in a berserker rage across the battlefield is useful grist for Hollywood. But the commanders and officers of the armies of Henry I and Otto I were well aware from personal experience, reading histories, and not least, learning from military handbooks, that their men had to be drilled both in the use of their arms, and in battlefield deployments, if they were to be used effectively in war. This preparation entailed regular and effective exercises with double-weight weapons so that the soldier could build up his muscles and endurance with the result that regular arms in combat would feel light. It also required training the men to keep their places in line, whether in the infantry phalanx or on horseback, and exercising men at the targets with bows and spears. As Heiric of Auxerre observed in a letter to Charles the Bald c. 875, making a claim for the value of education within the heavily martial world of the royal palace, "every day one might devote oneself to scholarly as well as to military exercise."[202]

---

200 Karl Leyser, "Early Medieval Canon Law and the Beginning of Knighthood," in *Institutionen, Kultur und Gesellschaft im Mittelalter. Festschrift für Josef Fleckenstein zu seinem 65. Geburtstag*, eds. Lutz Fenske, Werner Rösener, and Thomas Zotz (Sigmaringen, 1984), 549-66; reprinted in *Communications and Power in Medieval Europe: The Carolingian and Ottonian Centuries*, ed. Timothy Reuter (London and Rio Grande), 51-71, here 69.

201 Rabanus, *De procinctu Romanae miliciae*, ch. 13, "Exercitus ab exercitio nomen accepit."

202 Heiric of Auxerre, *Vita sancti Germani*, MGH *Poetae Latini Aevi Carolini*, vol. 3, ed. Ludwig Traube (Berlin, 1896), 429, "ita ut merito vocitetur scola palatium cuius apex non minus scholaribus quam militaribus consuescit cotidie disciplinis." For the dating of the letter, see McKitterick, "The Palace School of Charles the Bald," 326.

The complexities of the battlefield were multiplied in the sieges that thoroughly dominated Ottonian warfare. Commanders had to ensure that their men were trained not only for combat in the field, but also to carry out the even more dangerous and terrifying task of storming enemy fortifications. Advancing in a phalanx was made even more difficult by the need to deploy shields in a defensive *testudo*. Once the wall was reached, the men had to climb ladders of ten meters or more in height, and then fight a determined foe on the parapet.

To make these exceptionally difficult tasks just a bit less deadly, Ottonian commanders deployed a range of engines, including artillery, covered rams, mant-lets and siege towers. However, the construction and operation of these *machinae* brought their own set of challenges, each of which had to be prepared for in advance through training. Ultimately, as the Carolingian commander Nithard observed in a historical work known to the Ottonians, it is not the larger army that prevails but the one that is better trained.[203]

---

[203] See Nithard, *Historiarum libri IV*, ed. Reinhold Rau (Darmstadt, 1955),1.5, and the additional observations on this passage by Goldberg, *Struggle for Empire*, 126.

6

Morale

Ottonian military commanders understood quite well that maintaining a high level of morale was crucial for success in combat.[1] From their first introduction to the Bible, stories such as those of Gideon and his 300 men in Judges 7 made clear that the side that is more confident and committed to victory would have an advantage in battle. But there were many challenges to maintaining high morale in an army. Early medieval warfare, like its ancient and modern counterparts, was characterized by long spans of tedium and drudgery interspersed with short periods of intense emotion, most notably fear. A lengthy campaign during which soldiers undertook long marches under the blazing sun or in pouring rain, and then dug a fortified camp every night, could wear down even the most dedicated fighting men. As Widukind of Corvey observed, when Otto I wished to pursue his rebellious son Liudolf into Bavaria during the civil war of 953, the king's army begged to be allowed to return home because the soldiers were exhausted by their long campaign.[2] Recognizing that these troops could not be pushed any further, Otto discharged them, and advanced south to Bavaria with a much smaller army than he had intended, ultimately failing to achieve any success there.

The anxiety, fear, and even terror of the night before battle could strike even veteran soldiers. Angelbert, a soldier in the army of Lothair I at Fontenoy (842), referred to the "terrors of the night" before going into combat.[3] At Lenzen, in 929, Widukind observed that as the Saxon troops waited for battle, some men

---

[1] For a basic understanding of morale, see J. T. MacCurdy, *The Structure of Morale* (Cambridge, 1943); and Carl von Clausewitz, *On War*, ed. and trans. M. Howard and P. Paret (Princeton, 1984), 100-14, and 184-5. Concerning morale in medieval armies, see J. F. Verbruggen, *The Art of Warfare in Western Europe during the Middle Ages from the Eighth Century to 1340*, 2nd edn, trans. S. Ward and R. W. Southern (Woodbridge, 1997), 37-54. The most comprehensive study of military morale for the early medieval period is B. S. Bachrach, *Early Carolingian Warfare: Prelude to Empire* (Philadelphia, 2001), 132-159. On the role played by religion in maintaining military morale from Late Antiquity to the high Middle Ages, see D. Bachrach, *Religion and the Conduct of War c. 300–1215*.

[2] Widukind, *Res gestae*, 1.21, "*Porro exercitus diutino labore fatigabus missionem petit et accipit.*"

[3] Writing about the dawn of the battle of Fontenoy, the poet Angelbert described the terrors of the night that had just passed. See Peter Godman, *Poetry of the Carolingian Renaissance* (London, 1985), 48-50, for the poem, and Bachrach, *Early Carolingian Warfare*, 131-135, for a discussion of the implications of this poem for understanding the fear that fighting men felt on the night before the battle, and once the battle began.

were excited, but others were taken by despair. As the Corvey monk put it, "the warriors turned first to hope and then to fear, each according to his own nature."[4]

Henry I and Otto I, following in a long tradition of western warfare, utilized a wide range of techniques to maintain a high level of morale among their men. The drudgery of life on campaign could be alleviated by the hope of material gain. Ottonian commanders sought to instill confidence in their men before battle by reminding them of the long tradition of martial success of which they were a part. Finally, fear of death in battle could be mitigated by a panoply of religious rites and ceremonies that made clear God was on their side, and would protect Ottonian troops, either physically in battle, or through assurance of a place in heaven.

Rewarding Service

Plunder was rarely sufficiently abundant to cover the costs of large-scale military campaigns that were directed at the capture of fortifications and the conquest of territory.[5] The enormous regular expenditures that were required to maintain a large military household, which was well equipped with armor, arms, and warhorses, simply could not be made good through the occasional capture of some cattle, a few gold trinkets, and a handful of slaves. In this context, Archbishop Hincmar of Rheims, who was among the strongest defenders of ecclesiastical privileges in the West Frankish kingdom, sought to limit military expenditures to forty percent of ecclesiastical revenues.[6]

The expenditure of a large proportion of ecclesiastical revenues on military affairs remained common well into the Ottonian period and beyond. For example, in his Gesta of the bishops of Liège, the canon Anselm (1008–1056) looked back fondly to the pontificate of Notker (972–1008), when the prelate, by wise counsel (prudens consilium), had been able to divide the revenues of the bishopric into three equal parts, one of which was to support his military household (militia).[7] Indeed, the heavy burden on ecclesiastical magnates continued well into the twelfth century. In the 1160s, Emperor Frederick I Barbarossa imposed penalties of 50 percent of the annual revenue of a bishopric if the prelate failed to serve

---

4   Widukind, Res gestae, 1.36, "et pro qualitate morum inter spem metumque versabantur bellatores."
5   A major exception, of course, is represented by the capture of the Avar treasure hoard by Charlemagne. Cf. Reuter, "Plunder and Tribute in the Carolingian Empire," 75-94, who attempts to make the case for war as a profit-making enterprise. See the criticism of Reuter's argument, with specific reference to the enormous costs associated with siege warfare by Goldberg, Struggle for Empire, 120 n. 4.
6   Hincmar of Rheims, Collectio de ecclesiis et capellis, 119-20. See an illuminating discussion of this text by Janet Nelson, "The Church's Military Service in the Ninth Century, 117-132.
7   Anselmi Gesta Episcoporum Leodiensium, MGH Scriptores 7, ch. 29, "Idem prudenti consilio praedia aecclesiae in tres aequas porciones divisit, quarum unam suis et successorum usibus, alteram Deo servientibus per aecclesias et per monsteria, terciam his qui miliciam exercerent concessit."

in person on campaign with the king in Italy.[8] Secular magnates bore exceptionally heavy military burdens of their own, with the obligation not only to keep a substantial military household for deployment on campaign, but also, as seen in chapter three, to provide garrison troops to serve in royal fortifications.[9]

Even if major magnates, including the king, could not hope to profit directly from war, many professional soldiers (*milites*) and even members of the expeditionary levy were rewarded, sometimes quite generously, for good service. One of the primary ways in which a military commander could reward his men was by providing benefices to his *milites* so that they became *casati*, i.e. were granted homesteads of their own, or the income from estates. For example, in 915, while he was still duke of Saxony, Henry I was able to secure control over the Thuringian properties of Archbishop Hatto of Mainz, as well as two magnates named Burchard and Bardo, who were allied with King Conrad I.[10] Rather than keep these lands in his own hands, Henry divided them among the members of his military household.[11]

Henry's broad-based grant to his *milites* can be understood as his effort to distribute the wealth that he obtained through the overall success of his military household. But it is also possible to see rewards that were granted to individuals because of their own remarkable feats of arms. Widukind, for example, records a substantial grant of 20 *mansi*, which, following Carolingian military obligations, could require the service of a heavily armed mounted fighting man and two heavily armed foot soldiers, that Otto I made to a *miles* named Hosed in 955.[12] The latter had gained considerable praise for tracking down and killing Prince Stoignew of the Obodrites following Otto's victory at the battle of Recknitz.

Surviving evidence from charters suggests that this type of largess on behalf of successful soldiers was far from uncommon. In 951, for example, Otto granted two full estates (*marcae*) to a *miles* named Walpertus, who "had always fought with singular bravery against the Slavs and bridled their (sic) rebels."[13] Both the

---

[8]   See the discussion of the military obligations of prelates in Staufen Germany by Karl-Friedrich Krieger, "Obligatory Military Service and the Use of Mercenaries in Imperial Military Campaigns under the Hohenstaufen Emperors," in *England and Germany in the High Middle Ages*, ed. Alfred Haverkamp and Hanna Vollrath (Oxford, 1996), 151-167, here 151 for the heavy penalties imposed on bishops who failed to provide the proper military service.

[9]   Some insight into the size of secular military households is provided by the *indiculus loricatorum*, which was drawn up by the chancery of Otto II in 982 to summon reinforcements from both ecclesiastical and secular magnates in Germany for service in Italy. Many counts were required to send reinforcements of 30 to 40 *loricati*, which meant, in practice, upwards of 100 men and horses. This was in addition to their initial contributions of forces for Otto II's campaign.

[10]   Widukind, *Res gestae*, 1.22. See the discussion by Leyser, "Henry I and the Beginnings of the Saxon Empire," 34.

[11]   Widukind, *Res gestae*, 1.22, "*terra cederent eorumque omnem possessionem suis militibus divideret.*" The use of the term *possessio* here may indicate that Henry gave full ownership of these properties to his *milites*, and not simply usufruct.

[12]   Widukind, *Res gestae*, 3.55. For the military obligations inherent in such a large property, see the detailed discussion by Bachrach, *Early Carolingian Warfare*, 54-59, and the literature cited there.

[13]   DO I, 133, "*singulari fortitudine contra Slavos semper pugnaverit et rebelles eorum infrenaverit.*"

size of the grant, and the naming of Walpertus as a *nobilis vir*, indicate that he was an officer. It is highly unlikely, for example, that he was simply a nobleman who had ridden to war as a *loricatus*, when summoned to do so by the king on the basis of landed estates. Rather, the identification of Walpertus in the charter as a *miles* is *prima facie* evidence that he was a professional soldier, that is a man who earned his primary livelihood by fighting.[14] The location of the grant in Gero's march (*marchia predicti marchionis Geronis*) suggests that Walpert was expected to use a substantial portion of the revenues of his newly acquired estates to establish or expand his own military household in this frontier region.

These grants of property to soldiers were paralleled by the distribution of booty among fighting men following successful military actions. Following the battle of Birten on 2 October 939, where Otto I's vanguard succeeded in defeating a Lotharingian army under the command of Duke Gislebert, the royalist troops captured the enemy's camp and baggage train.[15] Otto then rewarded his victorious troops by dividing up all of the spoils among them.[16] This was similar to Henry I's decision in 929 to distribute to his *milites* the *preda urbis* that was captured at Gana.[17]

Even when the king was not present, in person, to oversee the distribution of bonuses to the troops, Ottonian military commanders took it upon themselves to reward the soldiers for good service on campaign. When Hermann Billung, Otto's march commander along the northern frontiers of Saxony, captured a fortress held by rebels loyal to Wichmann the Younger, he granted a large portion of the spoils to the *milites* under his command.[18] Indeed, the military commanders who opposed the Ottonians also used the same techniques of rewarding service in order to maintain high morale and motivation among their own men. For example, when Count Palatine Arnulf of Bavaria threw in his lot with Liudolf in 953 and joined the rebellion against the king, he seized the ducal treasury in Bavaria, and divided all of the money (*pecunia*) that was stored there among his own household troops.[19]

The positive incentive offered by financial rewards clearly motivated many men to fight harder. As Widukind observed with regard to Otto I's capture of Eresburg during the rebellion of 939, the king's men were eager to continue the campaign against the rebels in Saxony, not least because they were avid for booty (*preda*).[20] The lack of sufficient rewards could also lead to a substantial loss of morale among fighting men, especially professional soldiers who did not have

---

[14]   Regarding the strict sense in which Ottonian writers used the term *miles* to designate professional soldiers as contrasted with men of the levies, see Bachrach, "Memory, Epistemology," 63-90, and the literature cited there.

[15]   Widukind, *Res gestae*, 2.17.

[16]   Ibid., "*sarcinae omnes et omnis hostium suppellex inter victores divisa.*"

[17]   Widukind, *Res gestae*, 2.35.

[18]   Widukind, *Res gestae*, 3.68.

[19]   Ibid., 3.20.

[20]   Ibid., 2.11.

other sources of income. During the early years of Gero's command along the eastern frontier, for example, his troops had to undertake a great many difficult military actions against the Slavs with very little booty to show for their efforts.[21] It should be recalled that the Slavic polities in this region had well developed systems of fortifications so that any substantial gains of spoils could only come through difficult, dangerous, and time-consuming siege warfare.[22] The lack of financial rewards led to a great deal of anger and even hatred toward Gero.[23]

A good military commander also knew that allowing his men to focus too much on the spoils of war could cause problems other than low morale, and even lead to military disaster. Early in Otto's reign, for example, the young king dispatched Count Asik with a substantial army to punish Duke Boleslav I for killing his brother Wenceslaus and other members of the pro-German party in Bohemia.[24] Asik, who led a combined force of Saxons and the so-called Merseburg legion, won an initial victory over the Bohemians. However, rather than securing the field, and keeping a careful watch, Asik allowed his troops to plunder the enemy dead and gather up spoils. As a consequence, Boleslav was able to launch a counter-attack that caught the Saxons completely by surprise, and inflicted very heavy casualties on them.[25] By contrast, when Otto invaded Bohemia in 950 and captured the fortress of Nimburg, he is reported to have decided "after receiving good counsel" to put off fighting a battle against Duke Boleslav "so that his soldiers would not incur any danger while attempting to seize spoils from the enemy."[26]

Leadership

As Otto I prepared his army to break the Hungarian siege of Augsburg in the second week of August 955, a certain mood of foreboding had overtaken his camp, which continued despite the arrival of substantial reinforcements from Franconia and Bavaria.[27] However, soon after Conrad the Red, erstwhile duke of Lotharingia, arrived with a powerful force of mounted troops (*validus equitatus*), the spirits of the entire royal army were lifted. The now enthusiastic troops (*erecti milites*) no longer wished to delay going into battle against the Hungarians.[28] It was not only the additional forces that cheered these soldiers, but also the pres-

---

[21] Ibid., 2.30, "*eo tempore bellum barbarorum fervebat. Et cum milites ad manum Geronis presidiis conscripti crebra expeditione attenuarentur et donativis vel tributaries premiis minus adiuvari possent ... .*"
[22] With regard to the difficulties and expense of siege warfare against the Slavs, see the observations by Goldberg, *Struggle for Empire*, 120-2, which are as valid for the Ottonian period as they are for the later ninth century.
[23] Widukind, *Res gestae*, 2.30, "*seditioso odio in Geronem exacuuntur.*"
[24] Ibid., 2.3.
[25] Ibid.
[26] Ibid., 3.8, "*prudenti rex consilio diremit prelium, ne miles in rapiendis hostium spoliis aliquod periculum incideret.*"
[27] Widukind, *Res gestae*, 3.44.
[28] Ibid., "*cuius adventu erecti milites iam optabant non differre certamen.*"

ence of their commander, Conrad, whom Widukind described as a man, "who by nature had an audacious spirit, but also was wise when making decisions, which is very rare among the bold. Whether on foot or on horseback, when he attacked the enemy, he was an indefatigable warrior, but he also demonstrated his concern for his fellows, both at home and in war."²⁹ In short, Conrad exhibited the qualities of *conmilitio*, that is caring for his men, suffering alongside them, all the while demonstrating proper leadership on the field of battle.³⁰

The men in Otto's camp were inspired by Conrad's reputation as a good leader. He vindicated this trust in him by leading a successful counter-attack against the Hungarians during the initial stages of the battle of the Lechfeld after the latter had captured the German baggage train. As the Hungarians were busy looting the wagons, Conrad overwhelmed them with a mounted attack, killing many of the raiders and driving the remainder into full retreat.³¹

Care for one's troops could be demonstrated in a variety of ways, including rewarding them for good service, noted above, and providing a stirring example on the battlefield, as Conrad did at the Lechfeld. Of primary importance for a commander, however, was making clear to his men that he valued their lives, and would not waste them in thoughtless action, or in an act of venality simply to gain glory. In this context, Otto I had a reputation as a commander who worked diligently to conserve the lives of his men, and to avoid battles or sieges where the losses in lives would outweigh whatever tactical or material gains that might ensue. For example, the contemporary historian Flodoard of Rheims, who was hardly a supporter of the Ottonian royal family, observed that in 946 Otto moved his army against the fortress city of Senlis as part of his overall campaign in the West Frankish kingdom on behalf of Louis IV.³² When he arrived there, Otto examined the extensive defenses of this very heavily fortified (*munitissima*) city, and realized that his men would suffer heavy casualties if he were to undertake an assault. Instead, to spare his men, Otto withdrew his army, and continued his march westward into Normandy.³³

Otto's desire to avoid battle and to spare his men whenever possible is visible in several other campaigns as well. Before committing his army to a battle against the Obodrite princes Stoignew and Nacco on the Recknitz river in October 955, for example, Otto sent his trusted lieutenant Margrave Gero to negotiate a settlement.³⁴ In this case, Otto's army was in a tactically disadvantageous situation,

---

29   Ibid., "*Nam erat natura audacis animi et, quod rarum est audacibus, bonus consilii et, dum eques et dum pedes iret in hostem, bellator intolerabilis, domi militiaque sociis carus.*"

30   The values of *conmilitio* are discussed by Verbruggen, *The Art of Warfare in Western Europe*, 51-52, who emphasizes the respect that a commander earned by suffering the same dangers as his men.

31   Widukind, *Res gestae*, 3.44.

32   Flodoard, *Annales, an.* 946. Regarding Flodoard's less than favorable depiction of the Ottonians, and particularly Henry I, see the discussion by Kaeding, Kümmerlen and Seidel, "Heinrich I. – ein 'Freundschaftskönig,'" 293-297.

33   Flodoard, *Annales, an.* 946, "*ut viderunt munitissimam, nec eam valentes expugnare caesis quibusdam suorum, dimiserunt.*"

34   Widukind, *Res gestae*, 3.53.

needing to cross a river in the face of an entrenched enemy. Consequently, the king's decision to negotiate first and fight second can be understood as resulting from practical considerations beyond simply safeguarding the lives of his men. By contrast, in 950, during his campaign in Bohemia, Otto actively sought a negotiated settlement with Duke Boleslav, despite having a significant military advantage.[35] Widukind described Otto's army as an *innumera multitudo exercitus*, which so frightened the Bohemian duke that he gave up any hope of defending his capital at Prague, and submitted himself to Otto's authority.[36] Nevertheless, as seen above, Otto, following good advice, according to the Corvey monk, did not seek battle because he did not want his men to suffer any losses.[37]

Inspiration

In addition to preserving the lives of their men whenever possible, good commanders also inspired their troops for battle with rousing orations.[38] Widukind, who wrote for an audience that was familiar with the events of the Lechfeld, put into the mouth of Otto I a speech that contained several elements designed to inspire his men to fight bravely. The king began by stressing the bonds between himself and his men, emphasizing, "my soldiers, it is necessary that we be in good spirits in this time of need."[39] He then went on to remind his men of their victorious tradition, emphasizing, "Up until this point, I have conquered my empire gloriously with your indefatigable hands and always unconquerable arms."[40] Otto added, "I realize that we are overmatched in numbers, but not in strength, and not in arms."[41] He then stressed further the advantages of his soldiers, "we know that most of them lack any armor at all, and, which is more, they lack our greatest consolation, that is the help of God." [42] Warming to this theme, Otto added, "their only protection is their bravery, but we have hope of divine protection."[43] The king

---

35   Ibid., 3.8.
36   Ibid., "*Considerata itaque virtute Regis ac innumera multitudine exercitus, Bolizlav urbe egressus maluit tantae maiestati subici quam ultimam perniciem pati.*"
37   Ibid.
38   Battlefield orations have a very long tradition in western warfare. Important in this context are the studies by John R. Bliese, "Rhetoric and Morale: A Study of Battle Orations from the Central Middle Ages," *Journal of Medieval History* 15 (1989), 201-226; "When Knightly Courage May Fail: Battle Orations in Medieval Europe," *The Historian* 53 (1991), 489-504; and "Rhetoric Goes to War: The Doctrine of Ancient and Medieval Military Manuals," *Rhetoric Society Quarterly*, 24 (1994), 105-130. Regarding the heuristic value of reports of battlefield orations in narrative sources, also see David S. Bachrach, "Conforming with the Rhetorical Tradition of Plausibility: Clerical Representation of Battlefield Orations against Muslims, 1080–1170," *International History Review* 26 (2004), 1-19.
39   Widukind, *Res gestae*, 3.44, "*opus esse nobis bonorum animorum in hac tanta necessitate, milites mei.*"
40   Ibid., "*hactenus enim inpigris manibus vestries ac armis semper invictis gloriose usus extra solum et imperium meum ubique vici.*"
41   Ibid., "*superamur, scio, multitudine, sed non virtute, sed non armis.*"
42   Ibid., "*maxima enim ex parte nudos illos armis omnibus penitus cognovimus et, quod maximi est nobis solatii, auxilio Dei.*"
43   Ibid., "*illis est sola pro muro audatia, nobis spes et protectio divina.*"

then reaffirmed that they were all in the battle together, tying his fate to that of his men, claiming "It is better in war, if this is the end that awaits, my soldiers, that we die gloriously rather than live a life of servitude subject to these enemies, and be freed from the torture of these evil beasts."[44] In concluding, Widukind has Otto draw a specific connection between his oration and the morale of his men, with the command, "I would talk longer, my soldiers, if I knew that I could increase your strength or the bravery of your spirit with words. But now it is better that we begin this conversation with our swords rather than with our tongues."[45]

Widukind described a similar oration in his account of the battlefield preparations made by Henry before the battle at Riade.[46] The king made three points in his brief speech to the troops. First, God was on their side, and they should place their hope of victory in His divine clemency. If they did so, God would help them on this day, as He had aided them in the past.[47] Second, Henry stressed that the Hungarians were the common enemy of everybody and that the soldiers should bend all of their efforts to protecting their fatherland and their families.[48] Finally, the king assured his troops that if they fought bravely, they would have victory.[49]

It was not always the commanding general, however, who delivered an oration to the troops on campaign. On occasion, this task was delegated to another inspirational speaker. In his *Gesta* of the bishops of Liège, for example, the canon Anselm recorded that Bishop Eraclius (959–971) addressed Otto I's troops during his 968 campaign in Calabria after an eclipse of the sun had spread fear among the emperor's soldiers.[50] In his oration, Eraclius stressed the victorious tradition of the Ottonian armies, and made the case that the eclipse was nothing that should frighten such successful soldiers. According to Anselm, Bishop Eraclius said in part:

> O bravest warriors, you who have won famous victories through a thousand dangers by your distinguished name, rise up, I urge you, rise up and fear nothing. Take up your manly strength, and cast aside this unseemly torpor. It would be shameful to fear the natural changes of the elements. There is nothing here to endanger life. No one is dripping blood from a wound received by an enemy. Harmless shadows are wrapped around the sky. After a short time, you see the light returning. Everything else is safe.[51]

44   Ibid., "*melius bello, si finis adiacet, milites mei, gloriose moriamur, quam subiecti hostibus vitam serviliter ducamus aut certe more malarum bestiarum strangulo deficiamus.*"
45   Ibid., "*plura loquerer, milites mei, si nossem verbis virtutem vel audatiam animis vestris augeri. Modo melius gladiis quam linguis colloquium incipiamus.*"
46   Widukind, *Res gestae*, 1.38.
47   Ibid., "*Rex vero postera die producens exercitum exhortatus est, ut spem suam divinae clementiae committerent divinum sibi auxilium quemadmodum in aliis preliis adesse non dubitarent ...*"
48   Ibid., "*communes omnium hostes esse Ungarios; ad vindictam patriae parentumque solummodo cogitarent.*"
49   Ibid., "*si viriliter certando persisterent.*"
50   *Anselmi Gesta Episcoporum Leodiensium*, ch. 24.
51   Ibid., "*fortissimi, inquit, bellatores, qui per mille periculorum facies tociens egregio vestro nomini*

Overwhelming Force

Confidence in their commander and confidence in their victorious tradition were important elements in maintaining high morale among soldiers in the field. But just as important was the understanding that the army as a whole was well prepared for battle, and overmatched the enemy. The highly influ-ential military historian Hans Delbrück famously observed that the authors of medieval narrative sources regularly minimized the size of the "home side" and exaggerated the size of the opposing army so as to make victories more glorious and to be able to explain away defeats.[52] Delbrück sought to use this insight to minimize the size of the armies identified in narrative sources as part of his overall thesis that medieval armies were small, ill-trained, and poorly equipped.[53] On occasion, authors favorable to the Ottonians indulged in this type of rhetoric. Widukind, for example, claimed that following the victory at Riade in 929, Henry's court, which was gathered at Quedlinburg, gave thanks because "with the favor of divine clemency a small force was able to gain victory over a great multitude."[54]

Far more often, however, the armies of the early Ottonians were character-ized by the authors of narratives sources on the "home side" as quite substantial. The terms used include "an exceptionally large force of the best soldiers" (*magna valde multitudo optimorum militum*),[55] "an exceptionally large army" (*magnus valde exercitus*),[56] "an enormous army beyond count" (*innumera multitudine exercitus*),"[57] "an exceptionally large army that filled the entire land,"[58] "an enormous multitude" (*maxima multitudo*),[59] and an "exceedingly large army" (*permaxima exercitus*).[60] These descriptions are matched by authors who were not fond of the Ottonians,

---

insignes rapuistis victorias, surgite quoeso, nil timentes surgite, virile robur, quod turpiter dormitantes amisistis, resumite. Pudeat naturales elementorum vices horrere. Nil de vitae periculo agitur, nullus de inflicto cum hostili dextra cruor stillat vulnere; innoxiae tantum hunc aerem involvere tenebras, quas paululum post cernetis illuscere redintegrato lumine; ceterum in tuto sunt omnia."

52 Delbrück, *History of the Art of War, Volume II,* 227; and idem, *Numbers in History,* 11-12, and 14.

53 See the detailed critique of Delbrück's methods by Bachrach, "Early Medieval Military Demog-raphy: Some Observations on the Methods of Hans Delbrück".

54 Widukind, *Res gestae,* 1.36, "*qui parvis copiis divina favente clementia magnificam perpetraverint victoriam.*"

55 Gerhard of Augsburg, *Vita Uodalrici,* 1.12.

56 Widukind, *Res gestae,* 3.2.

57 Ibid., 3.8.

58 *Benedicti Sancti Andreas, Chronicon,* 175, "*tanta pene multitudo gentis in Italia, que sic impleverunt faciem terre*"; *Annales Quedlinburgenses,* an. 951, "*Otto rex perrexit in Italiam et cum eo eius filius Ludolfus pius et Conradus audacissimus, gener ipsius regis, atque Fridericus, archiepiscopus Moguntia-censis ecclesiae, caeterorumque innumerabilis multitudo ex omni regno suo.*"

59 Adalbert of Magdeburg, *Continuatio,* an. 961, "*Rex in Italiam ire disponens maximam suorum fidelium multitudinem Wormatie coadunavit ... .*"

60 Raoul Glaber, *Historiarum,* 1.12, "*Sed mox ut Otto hoc factum comperit, ira accensus cum permaximo exercitu Romam properavit.*"

such as Flodoard of Rheims who described various Ottonian armies as a "multitude" (*multitudo*),[61] and a "huge army" (*ingens exercitus*).[62]

There is a similar pattern in the description of the armies of the later Ottonians. Raoul Glaber, who despite living in the French kingdom was very positive toward the Ottonian dynasty, stresses that Otto II's invasion force, which reached Paris in 978, included 60,000 men.[63] The *Gesta* of the bishops of Cambrai goes so far as to identify the royal military forces as exceptionally large (*innumerabilis multitudo*), even when King Henry II's military commander, Duke Godfrey of Lower Lotharingia, was defeated in 1018 by the Frisians under the leadership of Count Dirk of Holland.[64] Alpert of Metz similarly described Godfrey's forces as a *multitudo*.[65] This is quite the opposite of Delbrück's observation that most authors on the home side exaggerate the size of the enemy's army, and diminish the size of the army on the "home side," particularly when the favored side lost the battle. Many more examples can be adduced.[66]

On more than one occasion, the very large size of an Ottonian army led the enemy to surrender without a struggle. When Henry I arrived at Prague in 929, for example, with his entire army (*omnis exercitus*), which included substantial contingents provided by Duke Arnulf of Bavaria, the Bohemian Duke Wenceslaus surrendered, i.e. accepted Henry's *ditio* rather than attempt to defend his capital.[67] Wenceslaus's decision here was so striking, given the strength of the defenses at Prague, that Widukind attributed the victory to some kind of miracle.[68] In a similar vein, as noted above, in describing Otto's invasion of Bohemia in July 950, for example, Widukind stressed that Duke Boleslav decided against attempting to hold the fortress of Prague against the German king because of the immense size of the German army.[69]

---

61 Flodoard, *Annales, an.* 925.
62 Ibid., *an.* 944.
63 Raoul Glaber, *Historiarum*, 1.7, for the number, and 3.1 for his positive assessment of the German kings.
64 *Gesta episcoporum Cameracensium Liber I.* ch. 10
65 Alpert of Metz, *De diversitate temporum*, ch. 21.
66 See, for example, *Annales Quedlinburgenses, an.* 986; *Annales Ottenburani* MGH SS 5, 1-9, *an.* 986; Adalbold, *Vita Heinrici II*, MGH SS 4, 679-695, here ch. 7; and Giovanni Diacono, *La cronaca Veneziana*, ed. G. Zucchetti (Rome, 1890), 167.
67 Widukind, *Res gestae*, 1.35, for the description of Henry's army as *omnis exercitus*. Regarding Arnulf's participation in the Prague campaign, see *Annales Ratisponenses*, ed. W. Wattenbach, MGH SS 17, 583, "Heinricus Boemiam vicit cum Arnolfo." Also see *Auctarium Garstense*, MGH SS 9, 565, "Hainricus rex cum Arnolfo duce Boemanos vicit."
68 Regarding the massive defenses at Prague in this period, see Boháčová, "Zum Befestigungssystem der Premyslidenburgen (am Beispiel der archäologischen Untersuchungen in der Prager Burg und in Stará Boleslav)," 37-47; and Frolik, "Prag und die prager Burg im 10. Jahrhundert," 161-169. Widukind, *Res gestae*, 1.35, observed with regard to Wencelaus's decision to surrender that "*de quo quaedam mirabilia predicantur.*"
69 Widukind, *Res gestae*, 3.8, "*Considerata itaque virtute Regis ac innumera multitudine exercitus, Bolizlav urbe egressus maluit tantae maiestati subici quam ultimam perniciem pati.*"

Supply

The proverb, often attributed to Napoleon, that "c'est la soupe qui fait le soldat," i.e. an army travels on its stomach, has its early medieval counterpart in the widely read observation by Vegetius that "... armies are more often destroyed by starvation than by battle, and hunger is more savage than the sword."[70] He added, "... other misfortunes can in time be alleviated: fodder and grain supply have no remedy in a crisis except storage in advance."[71] Soldiers with full bellies are not guarantied to have high morale, but soldiers who do not have enough to eat are almost certain to be unhappy, and, over time, a lack of food will lead to poor performance in battle. As a consequence, the timely provision of supplies to the troops was of paramount importance to Ottonian military commanders. This problem was particularly acute when the army in question was an *innumerabilis multitudo*, *permaxima*, or even just *ingens*.

In general, the supply of a large army, particularly during the course of a lengthy campaign that culminated in a siege, as was very common in Ottonian warfare, could not rely upon foraging or ravaging the countryside.[72] Certainly, Ottonian military commanders used, on occasion, the technique of harrying the enemy's resources in order to gain a political or military advantage. Flodoard observed, for example, that in 923 Henry I ravaged the lands between the Rhine and the Moselle, plundering large herds of cattle and even taking young boys as prisoners.[73] But, significantly, there are no accounts in narrative sources of Ottonian armies plundering friendly territories, even when the army was *ingens* or *permaxima*. Indeed, in his description of Otto II's invasion of West Francia in 978, Richer, echoing the *Gesta* of the bishops of Cambrai, even claims that the German army refrained from attacking churches in enemy territory, instead concentrating their efforts on taking plunder from the royal fisc.[74]

To facilitate the transportation of food and other supplies, the Ottonian kings devoted considerable resources to the maintenance of roads, which were used by the court, by the army, and by merchants.[75] Among the more obvious additions to

[70] Vegetius, *Epitoma*, 3.3. I am quoting the translation of this passage by N. P. Milner, *Vegetius* 67.
[71] Ibid.
[72] Cf. Reuter, "The Recruitment of Armies in the Early Middle Ages: What Can We Know?" here 36; and Halsall, *Warfare and Society in the Barbarian West*, 129, who argue that large armies moving around the countryside would leave enormous swathes of destruction everywhere. This argument is thoroughly criticized by Renard, "La politique militaire de Charlemagne et la paysannerie franque," 1-33, particularly 1-8, who draws attention, among other examples, to the work of Terray, "Contribution à une étude de l'armée assante," 297-356, where it is demonstrated that at the beginning of the nineteenth century, the Ashanti, who dominated an area about the size of modern Ghana, mobilized armies of from 20,000 to 40,000 fighting men, despite the fact that they possessed a primitive infrastructure and an "intendance déficiente".
[73] Flodoard, *Annales*, an. 923.
[74] Richer, *Historiae*, 3.74; *Gesta episcoporum Cameracensium Liber I*, ch. 97.
[75] See, for example, the discussion by Thomas Szabo, "Der Übergang von der Antike zum Mittel-

180   WARFARE IN TENTH-CENTURY GERMANY

the well established Roman road network, which was extant not only within the western portions of the German kingdom but also extended to the east beyond the Elbe, are the so-called corduroy roads, which were constructed to permit travel through particularly swampy regions, and the sunken roads which were cut through dense forests.[76] During the course of military campaigns, these roads were traveled by numerous supply trains, which were described in some detail by the authors of contemporary narratives sources.[77]

However, given the relative difficulty of transporting supplies by land, the Ottonian kings also devoted considerable resources to the development of a wide range of riverine assets. These facilitated the movement of both men and supplies when the army was able to march along rivers, or carried out sieges of fortifications that were located on or near rivers.[78] The river boats employed by the Ottonian kings likely were either of the Utrecht type, which used a hollowed out and expanded oak trunk for a keel, or flat-bottomed barges.[79] The Utrecht

alter am Beispiel des Straßennetzes," in *Europäische Technik im Mittelalter 800 bis 1400: Tradition und Innovation, Ein Handbuch*, ed. Uta Lindgren, 4th edn. (Berlin, 1996), 25-43, here 26.

76   With regard to Roman period roads that extended into the Slavic lands east of the Elbe, see H. Lies, "Baggerfunde der Jahre 1974/75 von Magdeburg-Fermersleben," *Ausgrabungen und Funde* 21 (1976), 137-244, particularly 237. Concerning the construction of corduroy roads, see Wilhelm Unverzagt and Ewald Schuldt, "Ausgrabungen in den frühgeschichtlichen Burgwällen von Teterow und Behren-Lübchen im Lande Mecklenburg," in *Römisch-Germanische Kommission des deutschen Archäologischen Instituts* (ed.) *Neue Ausgrabungen in Deutschland* (Berlin, 1958), 564-568; Hajo Hayen, "Zwei hölzerne Moorwege aus dem Fundgebiet Ipwegermoor B, Kreis Ammerland," *Neue Ausgrabungen und Forchungen in Niedersachsen* 1 (1963), 113-131; Herbert Küas, "Wehrtürme und Wohntürme auf ausgegrabenen deutschen Burgen zu Leipzig, Meißen und Groitzch," *Sächsische Heimatblätter* 19 (1973), 145-155, here 148; and Ernst Nickel, "Magdeburg in karolingisch-otton-ischer Zeit," *Zeitschrift für Archäologie* 7 (1973), 102-142, here 108. Concerning the construction of so-called sunken roads, particularly in heavily forested areas, see Karl Riehm, "Vom Solquell zum Solbrunnen: Eine topographische Studie zur Gründungsgeschichte der Stadt Halle," *Jahresschrift für mitteldeutsche Vorgeschichte* 57 (1973), 197-209, here 207; Grimm, "Drei Befestigungen der Ekke-hardinger – Archäologische Beiträge zum Problem von Graf und Burg im 10. Jahrhundert," 64; and Bahn, "Frühe Verkehrslinien im Dreieck Memleben-Merseburg-Dornburg," 248.

77   For the discussion of supply trains, see Widukind, *Res gestae*, 2.17, 3.44; Flodoard, *Annales, an.* 923; Adalbert of Magdeburg, *Continuatio, an.* 939; Gerhard, *Vita Uodalrici*, 1.10; Liudprand, *Antapodosis*, 2.49; Alpert of Metz, *De diversitate temporum*, 2.10; Richer, *Historiae*, 3.93; Thietmar of Merseburg, *Chronicon*, 6.5, 6.15, 627.

78   Ottonian military commanders routinely made use of ships, particularly riverine shipping, during military campaigns. In this context, see, for example, Adalbert of Magdeburg, *Continuatio, an.* 939; Liudprand, *Antapodosis*, 4.24; and Widukind, *Res gestae*, 3.36.

79   The Utrecht ship, uncovered in 1930, which gives its name to the basic river boat type, has received extensive scholarly attention. In this context, see Johannes P. W. Philipsen, "The Utrecht Ship," *Mariner's Mirror* 51 (1965), 35-46; Aleydis Van de Moortel, "A New Look at the Utrecht Ship," in *Boats, Ships, and Shipyards. Ninth International Symposium on Boat and Ship Archaeology, Venice 2000*, ed. C. Beltrame (Venice, 2003), 183-189; idem, "The Utrecht Type: Adaptation of an Inland Boatbuilding Tradition to Urbanization and Growing Maritime Contacts in Medieval Northern Europe," in *Between the Seas: Transfer and Exchange in Nautical Technology*, ed. Ronald Bockius (Mainz, 2009), 321-327; and "The Utrecht Ship Type: An Expanded Logboat Tradition in its Historical Context," in ibid., 329-336. Regarding barges, see the discussion by D. Ellmers, "Post-Roman Waterfront Installations on the Rhine," in *Waterfront Archaeology in Britain and Northern Europe: A Review of Current Research in Waterfront Archaeology in Six European Countries Based on*

type river boat had a cargo capacity of about 6.5 metric tons. The largest barges had a cargo capacity of approximately 15 metric tons.[80]

A great quantity of the supplies carried along both roads and rivers came from the resources of the royal fisc. The Ottonians, following the models established by their Carolingian predecessors, maintained very strict oversight over the production on their estates, and kept detailed records of the supplies that were in storage for use by the army.[81] To facilitate the organization of supplies, many royal palaces were established as the administrative centers of networks of fiscal estates to manage the collection of supplies over a broad area.[82] In addition, the Ottonians, again following the precedent established by their Carolingian predecessors, placed substantial fiscal assets under the control of secular and ecclesiastical magnates along the main routes to the frontier regions, and along the frontiers, so that supplies would be pre-positioned for use by armies going on campaign.[83]

Considerable additional supplies were provided to the royal army by ecclesiastical magnates. In his *vita* of Bishop Ulrich of Augsburg, for example, Gerhard indicates that bishops regularly were given the task of supplying royal troops on campaign. As a general rule, Ulrich was generous to all of the strangers who came to Augsburg. However, according to Gerhard the bishop reserved his greatest generosity for the *vasalli* of the emperor (*imperator*) whom he received with the highest honor (*summus honor*), and provided with exceptional quarters.[84] Moreover, when the king's men left Augsburg, the bishop provided them

---

Papers Presented to the First International Conference on Waterfront Archaeology in Northern European Towns, ed. Gustav Milne and Brian Hobley (London, 1981), 88-95, here 88-91.

[80]   I thank Professor Van de Moortel for this information, which she provided to me before the publication of her study, "Medieval Boats and Ships of Germany, The Low Countries, and Northeast France: Archaeological Evidence for Shipbuilding Traditions, Timber Resources, Trade and Communications," in *Settlement and Coastal Research in the Lower North Sea Region* (Köthen, 2011), 67-105.

[81]   Regarding the central role of the royal fisc for the supply of the army, see Klaus Verhein, "Studien zu Quellen zum Reichsgut der Karolingerzeit," part 1, *Deutsches Archiv für Geschichte des Mittelalters* 10 (1954), 313-394; and part 2, ibid. 11 (1955), 333-392; and Adriaan Verhulst, "Karolingische Agrarpolitik: Das Capitulare de Villis und die Hungersnote von 792/93 und 805/6," *Zeitschrift für Agrargeschichte und Agrarsoziologie* 13 (965), 175-189; Bernard S. Bachrach, "Are They Not Like Us? Charlemagne's Fisc in Military Perspective," in *Paradigms and Methods in Early Medieval Studies (The New Middle Ages)*, eds. Celia Chazelle and Felice Lifshitz (New York, 2007), 319-343. Concerning the use of the royal fisc to supply Ottonian armies, see David S. Bachrach, "Feeding the Host: The Ottonian Royal Fisc in Military Perspective," *Studies in Medieval and Renaissance History*, third series, forthcoming.

[82]   There is broad agreement that both the Carolingians and Ottonians maintained a series of autonomously administered fiscal units that had obligations to deliver supplies to a central palace. See, for example, Schmid, *Regensburg*, 251; Schalles-Fischer, *Pfalz und Fiskus Frankfurt*, 326; and Schmitz, *Pfalz und Fiskus Ingelheim*, 382.

[83]   For the use of this system by the eastern Carolingians, see the important study by Bowlus, *Franks, Moravians, and Magyars*, 25-32. Regarding the use of this system by the Ottonians, see Bachrach, "Feeding the Host," pp.

[84]   Gerhard of Augsburg, *Vita Uodalrici*, 1.3, "vasalli autem imperatoris ab eo pergentes vel ad eum redeuntes summo honore suscepti et in tantum sunt opulentati ut in nullo eos aut iumenta eorum ulla indigentia fatigaret."

with all of the supplies (*necessaria*) that they required, so that they were happy (*laeti*) when they began their journeys anew.[85]

A charter issued by Otto II on behalf of the bishopric of Lorch-Passau in 977 indicates that Gerhard's emphasis on this issue was due to the enormous burden that supplying the army could impose on an episcopal see.[86] In the case of Passau, Otto II granted a royal property at Ennsburg and ten *hobae* at Lorch to the bishopric in order to compensate Bishop Pilgrim (971–991) for the *gravis* that was inflicted upon the city of Passau while it supplied (*sustentatio*) the royal army (*exercitus nostri*).[87]

This grant to Passau can be understood as an effort to reward good service. In other cases, however, the Ottonian kings, following the precedents set by their Carolingian predecessors, systematically granted properties to churches along important routes in order to facilitate the provision of supplies by these same churches to the army.[88] The monastery of Hersfeld, for example, acquired numerous properties along the major road systems, including the so-called "Long Hessen Road" from Mainz over Treysa to the lower Hessen basin, along the "Lower Hessen Road" from Mainz to Hersfeld and then further to Erfurt and the Saale, and the "Thuringian Road" that passed through the monastery of Rohr and then to Ohrdruf.[89] Wolfgang Metz argued in an investigation of king's itinerary that monasteries such as these provided supplies to the royal court, and frequently served as stopping places for the royal court in preference to minor royal fiscal units that were located in the same regions.[90]

In a similar manner, the Ottonian kings continued the practice of their Carolingian predecessors of making substantial grants to monasteries and bishoprics along the routes to the Alpine passes both north and south of the mountains.[91] Numerous monasteries received fiscal property including Altötting, St Gall, Reichenau, St Emmeram, Benedictbeuern, Scharnitz-Schlehdorf, Frauenchiemsee, Tegernsee, and St Mang at Füssen, which sat astride the Ottonians' preferred route into Italy through the Brenner pass.[92] Bishoprics also

---

[85] Ibid.

[86] DO II, 167.

[87] Ibid. These properties had originally been obtained from the bishopric of Passau by the royal fisc in an exchange carried out during the reign of Otto I. However, the exchange itself is a *perditum*.

[88] Regarding this practice in the late Carolingian east, see the important discussion by Bowlus, *Franks, Moravians, and Magyars*, 25-32

[89] See the discussion by Wolfgang Metz, "Tafelgut, Königsstraße und Servitium Regis in Deutschland, vornehmlich im 10. und 11. Jahrhundert," *Historisches Jahrbuch* 91 (1971), 257-291, here 271; and by John Bernhardt, *Itinerant Kingship and Royal Monasteries in Early Medieval Germany, c. 936–1075* (Cambridge, 1993), 240-1.

[90] Metz, "Tafelgut, Königsstraße und Servitium Regis," 257-291.

[91] On this point, see the detailed discussion by Wilhelm Störmer, "Zur Frage der Funktionen des kirchlichen Fernbesitzes im Gebiet der Ostalpen vom 8. bis zum 10. Jahrhundert," in *Die transalpinen Verbindungen der Bayern, Alemannen und Franken bis zum 10. Jahrhundert*, ed. Helmut Beumann and Werner Schröder (Sigmaringen, 1987), 379-403.

[92] Störmer, "Zur Frage der Funktionen des kirchlichen Fernbesitzes," 395-403, and particularly 385

received fiscal properties both north and south of the Alps, including Salzburg, Freising, Regensburg, Brixen, and later Bamberg during the reign of Henry II.[93]

Military Religion

Well fed and paid soldiers, who enjoyed the benefits of good leadership in a powerful army, could still suffer from low morale when facing the possibility of dying in battle. For the more introspective among them, the need to kill another person, especially a fellow Christian, could impose a significant additional burden of guilt that had the potential to undermine a soldier's effectiveness in battle. These fears and feelings of guilt were even more difficult to manage when soldiers did not believe that they were fighting for a just cause, or that God was not on their side. As a consequence, the Ottonians, following century old traditions, developed and maintained a wide range of religious rites and ceremonies that were intended to relieve the anxiety of soldiers by offering the promise of divine support in battle, and God's love to those who died in combat.

Armies of the Christian Roman empire and its western successors were accompanied into the field by small cadres of bishops and their attendant priests.[94] Christian priests had the task of invoking divine support on behalf of the army. This entailed caring for sacred relics on campaign, the celebration of intercessory masses, leading the soldiers in prayers to God, and preaching to the troops in order to encourage them to be worthy of divine aid.[95] These army-wide rites were mirrored by the mobilization of public religious rites on the "home front" that also were intended to gain God's support for the army in the field.[96]

Individual pastoral care for soldiers was not generally an element of army religion in either the late Roman Empire or in its early successor states. The ancient Christian practice of once in a lifetime confession, usually made on one's deathbed, was still in force in most of the Latin West through the end of the sixth century.[97] Consequently, there was no prescribed ritual through which soldiers

---

for Füssen. Also see, for example, the grants by Otto I in DO I, 25, 29, 83, 90, 99, 116, 119, 126, 203, 219, 277, and 380.

[93]   Störmer, "Zur Frage der Funktionen des kirchlichen Fernbesitzes," 395-403.

[94]   For the practice of deploying priests in Roman army units, see A. H. M. Jones, "Military Chaplains in the Roman Army," *The Harvard Theological Review* 46 (1953), 239-240. With regard to the provision of military chaplains to Arian troops in the Roman army, see Ralph W. Mathisen, "Barbarian Bishops and the Churches 'in barbaricis gentibus' During Late Antiquity," *Speculum* 72 (1997), 664-697.

[95]   See the discussion of these religious practices by Bachrach, *Religion and the Conduct of War*, 11-24.

[96]   The basic work on public ceremonies of all types from the late Roman Empire through the early Middle Ages is Michael McCormick, *Eternal Victory: Triumphal Rulership in Late Antiquity, Byzantium, and the Early Medieval West* (Cambridge, 1986). Regarding the mobilization of public prayers on behalf of the army, see Michael McCormick, "The Liturgy of War in the Early Middle Ages: Crisis Litanies, and the Carolingian Monarchy," *Viator* 15 (1984), 1-24; and idem, "Liturgie et guerre des carolingiens à la première croisade," in *'Militia Christi' e Crociata nei secoli XI-XIII: miscellanea del centro di studi medioevali* 13 (1992), 209-40; and Bachrach, *Religion and the Conduct of War*, 18-19.

[97]   Regarding the basic problem of once in a lifetime confession and the military life during the

could purge themselves of sin, and still remain in the secular world. The necessary consequence of this penitential system was that soldiers risked death in battle with the stain of homicide still on their souls. A number of contemporary sources indicate that the lack of remedial penance that would allow soldiers to remain active in the world caused considerable stress on fighting men who risked eternal damnation simply for carrying out their duties.[98]

The solution to this problem was the gradual development of a regime of repeatable confession whereby sinners could confess their sins as often as necessary and receive penances that could be carried out while still living in the secular world.[99] First in Ireland, and then in England, monastic houses developed penitential manuals that listed sins and appropriate penances for these sins. These so-called tariff books then spread rapidly throughout the Latin West.[100] The development and rapid spread of these penitential manuals is both a product of and evidence for the enormous demand among lay people for a means to reconcile themselves with God without having to forsake the secular world for a life of penitential seclusion in a monastery or hermitage.[101]

The development of repeatable confession saw a concomitant rethinking regarding the sinfulness of homicide. Until the middle of the fifth century, all homicides were treated in canon law as equally sinful.[102] In the sixth century, some distinctions began to be drawn between *homicidio* and *homicidio* that had been committed voluntarily (*sponte*).[103] Penitential manuals of the eighth century and later developed an entire hierarchy of penances for killing, the least sinful of which was the killing of an enemy soldier in the course of a publicly sanctioned war (*bellum publicum*).[104]

The institutionalization of the provision of pastoral care to fighting men is first visible in 742 when the *Concilium Germanicum*, which was held under the direction of Carloman, Carolingian Mayor of the Palace (741–747) and the English

early medieval period, see Bachrach, *Religion and the Conduct of War*, 24-30.
[98] Ibid., 26-28.
[99] See the discussion by Bernard Poschmann, *Penance and the Anointing of the Sick*, trans. and rev. Francis Courtney (New York, 1968), 122-131; Cyrille Vogel, "Les rituals de la penitence tarifée," in *Liturgica opera divina e umana, studi offerti à S. E. Mons A. Bugnini: Bibliotheca 'ephemerides liturgicae' subsidia* 26 (Rome, 1982), 419-427; Philippe Rouillard, *Histoire de la penitence des origins à nos jours* (Paris, 1996), 43-48; and a synthesis of this problem with regard to fighting men by Bachrach, *Religion and the Conduct of War*, 28-30.
[100] On the spread of these penitential manuals see, Rosamond Pierce (McKitterick), "The 'Frankish' Penitentials," *Studies in Church History* 11 (1975), 31-39; and Rob Meens, "The Frequency and Nature of Early Medieval Penance," in *Handling Sin: Confession in the Middle Ages*, ed. Peter Biller and A. J. Minnis (York, 1998), 35-63.
[101] This is the basic argument of David S. Bachrach, "Lay Confession in the *regnum Francorum*: The Evidence Reconsidered," *The Journal of Ecclesiastical History* 54 (2003), 3-22, with the literature cited there.
[102] Bachrach, *Religion and the Conduct of War*, 24.
[103] This distinction was drawn, for example, by the bishops at the council of Arles in 541. See *Concilium Aurelianense*, ed. F. Maassen, MGH *Concilia Aevi Merovingici* (Hanover, 1893), 93.
[104] The basic study of penances imposed on soldiers in the early Middle Ages is Raymond Kottje, "Die Tötung im Kriege: Ein moralisches und rechtliches Problem im frühen Mittlelalter," *Beiträge zur Friedensethik* 11 (1991), 1-21. See the discussion by Bachrach, *Religion and the Conduct of War*, 29-30.

missionary Boniface (martyred 754), established a sweeping new requirement for the recruitment of military chaplains (*capellani*). The assembled prelates imposed the obligation, in the second canon of the council, on every unit commander (*praefectus*) in the army to have on his staff a priest capable of hearing confessions and assigning penances to the fighting men under his care.[105]

As had been true of their Carolingian predecessors, pre-battle preparations of Ottonian armies included, as a matter of course, the celebration of mass and reception of the eucharist with the concomitant obligation to confess one's sins to a priest.[106] In the early morning hours of 5 September 929, for example, the men of the Saxon *exercitus* heard mass and received the eucharist, before entering battle against the Redarii.[107] When describing the morning before the battle of the Lechfeld (10 August 955), Thietmar of Merseburg focused his attention on the confession of Otto I himself.[108] Thietmar emphasized that Otto prostrated himself on the ground and confessed his sins directly to God. Only then did the king receive the host from his chaplain.[109] Just a few days earlier, during the Hungarian assault on the city of Augsburg, Bishop Ulrich celebrated a public mass and then had each of the soldiers receive communion. Gerhard, Ulrich's trusted aide, described this ceremony in a very particular manner, insisting that the bishop had brought all of his men back to life through the sacred *viaticum*.[110] This term is important here because by the tenth century the word *viaticum* had taken on two very specific meanings in the liturgy celebrated in the Ottonian kingdom. It could either signify a health-bringing rite designed for those who were ill, or it could be used to describe the consecrated bread and wine that was taken when an individual was about to die and after he had made his last confession.[111] In either case, the potential value of receiving communion for the morale of soldiers going into battle is clear. Indeed, Gerhard himself commented that

---

[105] *Concilium Germanicum*, ed. A. Werminghoff, MGH Concilia 2.1 (Hanover, 1906), 3, "*et unus-quisque praefectus* [*habeat*]*unum presbiterum, qui hominibus peccata confitentibus iudicare et indicare poenitentiam possint.*" Regarding this text, see Albert Michael Koeniger, *Die Militärseelsorge der Karolingerzeit: Ihr Recht und ihre Praxis* (Munich, 1918), 18-24; Carl Erdmann, *The Origin of the Idea of Crusade*, [orig. *Die Entstehung des Kreuzzugsgedankens*] (Stuttgart, 1935), trans. Marshall W. Baldwin and Walter Goffart (Princeton, 1977), 16; and B. Bachrach, *Early Carolingian Warfare*, 49-50. The text of the canons issued by the council was quickly reissued by Carloman as a capitulary in 742. On this point, see *Capitularia I* 24-26, where the entire collection of canons from the council was reissued as a capitulary. The most recent treatment of this topic is Bachrach, "Lay Confession in the *regnum Francorum*: The Evidence Reconsidered," 11-12.

[106] Concerning the connection between confession and receiving the host, see the discussion by Bachrach, *Religion and the Conduct of War*, 48-62. Regarding the synodal statutes that treat confession and reception of the eucharist, see Bernhard Poschmann, *Buße und letzte Ölung* (Freiburg 1951), 71-77; and Julia M. H. Smith, "Religion and Lay Society," in *The New Cambridge Medieval History: Volume 2 c. 700–900*, ed. Rosamond McKitterick (Cambridge 1995), 654-78.

[107] Widukind, *Res gestae*, 1.36, "*et primo diluculo data signo sacramentoque accepto.*"

[108] Thietmar of Merseburg, *Chronicon*, 2.10.

[109] Ibid.

[110] Gerhard of Augsburg, *Vita Uodalrici*, 1.12, "*Ministerio sacro peracto, viatico sacro omnes recreavit ...*"

[111] See Frederick S. Paxton, *Christianizing Death: The Creation of a Ritual Process in Early Medieval Europe* (Ithaca, NY, 1990), 192-5.

following the reception of communion the men were prepared both *"interius"* and *"exterius"* for battle.[112]

After hearing the confessions of soldiers and celebrating mass, priests serving with the army provided additional encouragement to the troops by carrying onto the battlefield sacred and consecrated objects as a material reminder of the support provided by God and His saints. The consecrated objects that are identified most frequently in the narrative sources were banners *(vexilli)* that had been blessed for service in battle. The consecration of *vexilli* dates back to the early Middle Ages.[113] The continuity of this practice under the Ottonian kings is illuminated in a late tenth-century Romano-German pontifical from Mainz that includes a blessing for a battle flag *(benedictio vexilli bellici)*. This blessing asks God to respond to the humble prayers of his supplicants and to sanctify with the holy blessings of heaven a *vexillum*, which has been prepared for use in war *(quo bellico usui preparatum est)*.[114] According to the prayer, the battle flag would aid the Christian people against their enemies. It would also inspire those who trust in God and offer a firm promise of victory *(victoriae certa fiducia)*.[115] This blessing is also found in a number of other tenth- and eleventh-century pontificals, indicating the widely recognized importance of consecrated banners for the conduct of war in this period.[116]

At the battle of Riade, Henry I's troops were preceded by a very large banner bearing the image of the Archangel Michael. According to Widukind, after Henry finished offering words of encouragement to the troops, they all looked up to the king, and took note of the angel, that is the banner, that was flying before him. As Widukind emphasized: "For the great banner was marked with the angel's name and image. They took great comfort and resolve from this."[117]

The positive impact of these consecrated *vexilli* on the morale of fighting men is similarly illustrated in a story told by Thietmar of Merseburg regarding Bishop Ramward of Minden (996–1002). In August 997, Ramward took part in a battle against the Slavs in the region of Bardengau on the lower Elbe.[118] In the initial stages of the fighting, the bishop, without a care for his own safety, took up a

---

[112]   Gerhard, *Vita Uodalrici*, 1.12.

[113]   For the blessings of crosses and battle flags, see *Le liber ordinum en usage dans l'église wisigothique et mozarabe d'Espagne du cinquième siècle*, ed. Marius Férotin, *Monumenta ecclesiae liturgica* 5 (Paris, 1904), cols. 149-153, new edition, Anthony Ward and Cuthbert Johnson (Rome, 1996).

[114]   *Le pontifical Romano-Germanique du dixième siècle*, ed. Cyrille Vogel and Reinhard Elze (Vatican, 1963), 378.

[115]   Ibid., *"ut contra adversarios et rebelles nationes sit validum tuoque munimeque circumseptum, sitque inimicis christiani populi terribile atque in te confidentibus solidamentum et victoriae certa fiducia."*

[116]   Blessings for battle flags can be found in numerous manuscripts, including Bamberg öffentliche Bibliothek, cod. Lit. 53, fol. 137v; Bamberg öffentliche Bibliothek, cod. Lit. 54, fol. 3 v; Episcopal archives of Eichstätt, the pontifical of Bishop Gondekar II of Eichstätt, fol. 139 v; Munich, Staatsbibliothek, Cod. lat. 6425 (Cod. Frising. 225), fol. 259 v; Paris, Bibliothèque nationale, Cod. lat. 1817 (Vienne 1817), fol. 134 r; and Wolfenbüttel, Landesbibliothek, Cod. lat. 4099 (Weissenburg. 15), fol. 39 r..

[117]   Widukind, *Res gestae*, 1.38.

[118]   Thietmar of Merseburg, *Chronicon*, 4.29.

cross in his hands and rode out ahead of the troops. He was then followed by the standard bearers (*signiferi*). According to Thietmar, the visible presence of Ramward on the battlefield with his cross, accompanied by the men with the banners, gave tremendous encouragement to the men, who went on to win a major victory over the Slavs.[119]

In addition to the encouragement offered to individual soldiers through confessions, and the personal feelings of being strengthened by the reception of the eucharist, Ottonian commanders also organized army-wide rites that were intended to obtain God's support for victory in battle. One common practice was fasting, through which soldiers made clear that they were penitent on the eve of battle and deserved divine aid. Ruotger, the biographer of Otto I's youngest brother Brun, observed that on the night before the battle on the Lechfeld, the German king ordered an army-wide fast to take place to honor the vigil of the feast of Saint Lawrence (9 August). Otto then begged the saint to intervene with the Lord on behalf of himself and his army in the forthcoming struggle against the pagan Magyars.[120] Widukind similarly associated the army's fast on the eve of the Lechfeld battle with Otto's order for his men to prepare themselves for combat.[121]

Prayers for saints to intervene on behalf of the army, such as Otto I's prayer to Saint Lawrence, were also a regular element in preparations for battle. At the battle of Birten (939), for example, the advance guard of Otto I's army had crossed the Rhine and was attacked by a numerically superior force of rebels. Liudprand of Cremona, a confidant of the king, observed in his account of this battle that when Otto realized that he would not be able to bring his forces across the river in time to join the battle, he remembered the example of the Israelites who were aided by the prayers of Moses when they were fighting against the Amelekites.[122] Consequently, Otto dismounted from his horse and went down on his knees, praying for victory, alongside all of his men, to God and Jesus Christ.[123] Widukind, commenting on the same events, recorded that Otto prayed, "O God, creator and ruler of the universe, look to your people over whom you have wished

<hr/>

119   Ibid., "*In illo certamine Ramwardus Mindensis episcopus fuit, qui socios, arrepta in manibus cruce sua, sequentibus signiferis precessit et ad hec facienda potenter consolidavit.*"
120   Ruotger, *Vita Brunonis*, c. 35, "*Imperator indici sanxit ieiunium ipsa, que tunc erat, in vigilia sancti Laurentii martyris, per cuius interventum sibi populoque suo ipsum Deum poposcit esse refugium.*" The importance of the feast of Saint Lawrence in the tenth-century German church is discussed by L. Weinrich, "Laurentius-Verehrung in ottonischer Zeit," *Jahrbuch für die Geschichte Mittel-und Ostdeutschlands* 21 (1972), 45-66.
121   Widukind, *Res gestae*, 3.44, "*Ieiunio in castris predicato, iussum est omnes in crastino paratos esse ad bellum.*"
122   Liudprand, *Antapodosis*, 4.24, "*Rex denique tantam suorum constantiam non sine divino instinctu esse considerans, quoniam fluvio intercedente corporali praesentia subvenire suis non poterat, recordatus populi Domini, qui repugnantes sibi Amalechitas orationibus Moysi servi Dei devicerat.*" See the relevant passage in Exodus 17.8-14.
123   Liudprand, *Antapodosis*, 4.24, "*protinus de equo descendit seseque cum omni populo lacrimas fundens ante victoriferos clavos, manibus domini et salvatoris nostri Iesu Christi adfixos suaeque laneae interpositos, in orationem dedit.*"

me to rule, so that secured from their enemies, all of the peoples shall know that no mortal can stand against your wishes, you who are all powerful, and who live and rule for eternity."[124]

Pastoral care for individual soldiers, and army-wide rites on campaign helped to assure fighting men that they individually were reconciled with God, and that the army as a whole merited divine aid. The Ottonian kings also utilized a range of techniques to mobilize public religious rites on the "home front" on behalf of the army with three overall purposes in mind. First, by making the case that they were fighting just wars, the Ottonians sought to convince families who had lost sons, brothers, husbands, and fathers, that their suffering was not in vain. Second, the mobilization of prayers by the kingdom as a whole on behalf of the army was intended to give soldiers an even greater sense of confidence that God would aid the army in war. Finally, by giving public thanks to God after victories, the Ottonians identified themselves directly as the beneficiaries of divine aid, i.e., having achieved victory *auxilio divine*. This clear identification of the Ottonian dynasty as being favored by God had obvious benefits for the morale of the men under their command over the long term.

Fundamental to Ottonian rule, as it had been for all rulers in the western tradition before them, was God's support for their government. Thus, in all of their public acts, the Ottonian kings emphasized that they ruled by the grace or with the aid of God, i.e. *auxilio divinei, gratia dei*. This emphasis on God's aid was given even fuller expression in a program of intercessory masses that were composed for times of war. For example, the Romano-German pontifical of Mainz, mentioned above, includes the text *praebe domine*.[125] This prayer calls on God to support the military operations of the army (*opus exercitui*) and to give aid to the soldiers just as He had aided the Israelites fleeing from Egypt.[126] Similar prayers for victory and the strength of king in war are to be found in royal *ordines*, such as the mass for the emperor (*missa pro imperatore*) written (c. 960) for the coronation of Otto I.[127] This intercessory mass includes the prayers for God to give "triumph to Your servant our emperor," and "let us have the power to rule which Joseph had in the armed camp, and which Gideon held in battle."[128] Here, the use of references to the military leaders of the Israelites makes clear the desire to obtain divine support for Otto's campaigns.

Particularly common are intercessory masses that were intended to obtain

---

124 Widukind, *Res gestae*, 2.17, "*Deus, inquit, omnium rerum auctor et rector, respice populum tuum, cui me preesse voluisti, ut, ereptus ab inimicis, sciant omnes gentes ullum mortalium tuae dispositioni contrare non posse, qui omnia potes et vivis et regnas in aeternum.*"
125 The late tenth-century version can be found in the *Le pontifical Romano-Germanique*, 380.
126 Ibid., 380.
127 *Die Ordines für die Weihe und Krönung des Kaisers und der Kaiserin*, ed. Reinhard Elze, MGH Fontes Iuris Germanici Antiqui 9 (Hanover, 1960), 5, and the discussion by Hagen Keller, "*Machabaeorum pugnae*": 418.
128 Elze, *Ordines*, 5-6, "*da servo tuo imperatori nostro triumphum*," and "*Sit nobis regendi auctoritas, qualem Iosue in castris, Gedeon sumpsit in proeliis.*"

divine support for the king in wars against the heathens.[129] One mass prayer begged "may the Lord conserve King Otto and his army, let us pray that Otto and his army be protected here and there, we pray that the savage sword and the pagan people be destroyed by us, please deign to conserve lord emperor Otto and the army of the Christians."[130] By drawing the clear connection between the king and the army in the context of a war against the heathens, this mass prayer makes the case that Otto was leading his army in a just war on behalf of the entire Christian people.

Once victory was achieved, the Ottonian kings took great care to give credit to God and the saints as publicly as possible for success in battle. In this manner, the Ottonians were able to demonstrate ongoing divine support for their rule, and also build continued public support for future military undertakings. In the aftermath of his important victory over the Hungarians at Riade in 933, for example, Henry I publicly accorded all of the honor for the victory to God.[131] Widukind, in describing these events, recorded that Henry also made extensive gifts to churches for the express purpose of giving alms to the poor as part of the overall celebration of the victory.[132]

In a similar manner, Otto I made a series of donations to churches in Italy to give thanks to God for his victory over King Berengar, and also for making possible his acclamation as emperor in 962. At the end of July 962, for example, Otto granted properties to the canons of St Giulio d'Orta expressly to give thanks to God for His support of the German king's military operation.[133] The royal charter reads, in part, "we [are] not unmindful of the good works of the three-fold majesty that has always supported us in our weakness, and which especially now mercifully has given us victory".[134]

Perhaps the most well known series of public offerings of thanks for a victory in battle came in the aftermath of Otto I's major victory over the Hungarians on the Lechfeld. Churches throughout Bavaria, which had the most to fear from a successful Hungarian invasion in 955, were dedicated, or rededi-

---

[129] Carl Erdmann, "Der Heidenkrieg in der Liturgie und die Kaiserkrönnung Ottos I.," *MIÖG* 46 (1932), 129-142, here 133.
[130] The text of this prayer was originally published by H. Hirsch, "Der mittelalterliche Kaisergedanke in den liturgischen Gebeten," *MIÖG* 44 (1930), 1-20, here 9, "*ut Ottonem regem et eius exercitum dominus conservet ... ut rex noster Otto et eius exercitus hinc et inde servetur oramus ... ut saeviens gladius et paganus populus depellatur a nobis oramus.*" Finally, "*ut domnum Ottonem imperatorem et exercitus Christianorum conservare digneris.*" Hirsch argues that the prayer was composed for for Otto I and his army. P. E. Schramm, *Die deutschen Kaiser und Könige in Bildern ihrer Zeit*, vol. 1 (Berlin, 1928), images 64, 74, 77, argues that the contemporary images associated with this prayer are of Otto II and Otto III. Erdmann, "Der Heidenkrieg," 130, is not certain whether this prayer should be associated with Otto I, Otto II, or Otto III.
[131] Widukind, *Res gestae*, 1.39.
[132] Ibid., "*divino cultui mancipavit et largitionibus pauperum deservire constituit.*"
[133] DO I, 243.
[134] Ibid., "*nos non immemores beneficiorum trinae insecabilisque maiestatis quae semper circa nostrae imbecillitatis fragilitatem operatur, specialiter tamen ideo quod misericorditer nobis victoriam tribuens ...*"

cated to Saint Lawrence on whose feast day (10 August) the battle took place.[135] Moreover, according to Thietmar of Merseburg, Otto I promised on the day of battle itself that if he were victorious he would establish a bishopric in Merseburg whose special patron was Saint Lawrence.[136] This bishopric eventually was established in 967.[137]

The tradition of honoring God for victories in battle even penetrated to the level of the local levies who served as a home guard for their own districts. In 924, for example, following their defeat of a Hungarian invasion into the region of Frickgau in Swabia, the local levy under its leader Irminger refused to keep for themselves the booty that had been captured from the Hungarians. Instead, the militia men took all of their spoils and placed them in a local church.[138]

The final element in the public religion of war was the care for those fighting men who fell in battle and on campaign. By memorializing and honoring those who had died, military commanders reinforced the sense that their deaths had not been in vain. In addition, these public memorials gave a sense to the remaining soldiers that they too would be remembered if they fell in battle. This concern for the ultimate fate of the souls of fighting men killed in combat is discussed by Thietmar of Merseburg in the context of describing Duke Boleslav Chrobry's victory over a German force under the command of Archbishop Gero of Magdeburg in 1015.[139] After recalling the deaths of several magnates and 200 fighting men, Bishop Thietmar stepped out of his role as narrator and called directly on God in a prayer to have mercy when considering the fate of their souls. He wrote, "please let all powerful God look with mercy on their names and their souls."[140] In addition, Thietmar asked God to have mercy on the souls of those still living for having caused this disaster through the sinfulness of their lives, and to protect them from ever suffering such a tragedy again.[141]

In order to ensure that prayers for these fighting men would continue to be said, their names were often included in so-called memorial books (libri memoriales). These texts listed the names of individuals under the day of the year on which they died so that their names could be included in intercessory masses for that day. The men who fell in the battle against Boleslav Chrobry, for example,

---

135 Regarding the (re)dedication of churches in Bavaria to St Lawrence in the aftermath of the Lechfeld campaign, see Bowlus, The Battle of Lechfeld, 143-4.

136 Thietmar of Merseburg, Chronicon, 2.10, "si Christus dignaretur sibi eo die tanti intercessione preconis dare victoriam et vitam, ut in Merseburgiensi episcopatum in honore victoris ignium construere domumque suimet magnam noviter inceptam sibi ad aecclesiam vellet edificare."

137 Thietmar, as the bishop of Merseburg, may be forgiven for tying the foundation of his see to the enormously important victory on the Lechfeld. However, it is important to note that when the see was established in 967 the cathedral was dedicated to St Lawrence.

138 Ekkehard, Casus Sancti Galli, 136, "At Irminger cums suis spolia in facie hostium collecta basilice triumphans intulit et per omnes circumquaque munitiones dispertivit." Irminger was not a count or officeholder but rather simply a land owner in the region.

139 Thietmar of Merseburg, Chronicon, 7. 21.

140 Ibid., "quorum nomina et animas Deus omnipotens misericorditer respiciat."

141 Ibid., "et nos quorum culpa hii tunc oppetiere, sibi per Christum reconciliet et, ne quid tale ulterius paciamur, clemens custodiat."

were subsequently included in the *Liber memorialis* of Merseburg so that their souls could receive the benefit of an annual remembrance and prayers.[142]

Before their entry into the memorial books, however, many fallen soldiers were given honorable and public burials so that their heroic deeds could be proclaimed and remembered. Following the battle of Mantahinga (954), for example, Bishop Ulrich of Augsburg had the body of Count Adalbert, who had died in the victory over a rebel army, carried thirty kilometers to Augsburg, where he was buried with honor (*honorifice*) in the cathedral church.[143] Similarly, following the battle of the Lechfeld, Ulrich went out among the fallen soldiers to look for his brother Dietpald and Reginald, the son of the bishop's sister. Once he located their remains, Ulrich had them brought back into the city and buried them together in a single grave before the altar of St Waldpurgis in the cathedral church.[144]

In order to memorialize even further those soldiers who had died in the king's service, some wealthy families went so far as to establish religious houses in memory of their departed relatives. In 960, for example, Margrave Gero, one of Otto I's closest military advisors, established the convent of Gernrode in memory of his son Siegfried, and installed the latter's widow Hathui as its first abbess.[145] In other cases, men even arranged on their own behalf to make major donations to religious houses in the event of their possible death in battle. For example, a charter issued in 982 by Otto II on behalf of the monastery of Gorze, records that one of the king's officers, a count named Conrad, had requested publicly that if he were to die fighting against the Saracens, all of his property be given to Gorze.[146] Otto, of course, acceded to this request noting that it was in his own interest to aid the efforts of his *fideles* to support the church for the benefit of their souls.[147] As events took place, Conrad was killed in the battle of Cap Callone (982), so that his considerable property all came into the hands of the monks at Gorze.[148]

---

[142] *Die Totenbücher von Merseburg, Magdeburg und Lüneburg*, ed. Gerd Althoff and Joachim Wollasch, MGH Libri Memoriales et Necrologia n.s. 2 (Hanover, 1983), fol. 5r., p. 11, "*Gero et Vuolcmar comites cum sociis*." For a similar commemoration of fallen soldiers, in this case from the battle of Cap Callone in 982, see *Annales necrologici Fuldenses*, ed. Georg Waitz, MGH SS 13, 205.

[143] Gerhard of Augsburg, *Vita Uodalrici*, 1.10.

[144] Ibid., 1.13.

[145] See the discussion of this event by Thietmar of Merseburg, *Chronicon*, 2.19; and the royal charter confirming the establishment of this house, DO I, 229.

[146] DO II, 280, "*Cunradus filius Ruodolfi quondam comitis in die belli quod fuit inter nos et Sarracenos, sub fanone nostro, hoc est imperiali vexillo, legali ritu tradendum nobis commendavit omne predium suum quod habuit in regno Lothariensi, rogavitque in conspectu totius exercitus nostram dominationem humiliter, ut hoc totum parvum cum magno ad monasterium sancti Gorgonii martyris in loco Gorzia vocato constructum nostra perceptione, si ea die moreretur, sicut fecit, traderemus*."

[147] Ibid., "*Si peticiones fidelium nostrorum quas pro usu et statu ecclesiarum ac remedio animarum suarum in conspectu imperii nostri fundunt, pia devotione compleverimus, id procul dubio ad presentis vite statum et eterne beatitudine premia capessenda nobis proficere confidimus*."

[148] Ibid.

Conclusion

The long-term military success of the first two kings of the Ottonian dynasty over more than half a century depended on a number of factors. Important among them was the fact that their soldiers were highly motivated, and expected victory. This was far from accidental. Henry and Otto devoted considerable resources and energy to maintain high morale among their men. Soldiers who served well could expect economic benefits, and might even receive very substantial rewards that would establish them as magnates in their own right. The fighting men also knew that their commanders, although committed to victory, would not waste their lives needlessly in the vain pursuit of glory. Indeed, the efforts of the Ottonians to mobilize very large armies often meant that the enemy surrendered rather than fight, saving further lives. While on campaign, Ottonian soldiers also benefited from a well-organized logistical system that provided adequate supplies on a timely basis. As a consequence, whether they were marching to the frontier, or in enemy territory, fighting men had full bellies at night.

In addition to securing the physical well-being of their soldiers, to the extent that this was possible in the inherently dangerous business of war, Henry and Otto, like all of their royal predecessors in the western military tradition, worked diligently to provide for the spiritual well-being of their men, and to secure divine support for their wars. Ottonian armies were regularly accompanied into the field by priests who heard confessions, celebrated mass, and distributed the eucharist among the troops. As a consequence, the soldiers could feel confident that they had purified their souls before battle, and would benefit from God's protection during the fighting. These individual pastoral efforts were reinforced by army-wide religious rites, which included fasts and prayers. The religious rites of the army were paralleled by public ceremonies that called upon God's aid for the army in battle, thanked God for victory, and memorialized the men who had died in combat. These public ceremonies, in aggregate, served to reinforce the image of Ottonian wars as just conflicts, which helped to alleviate concerns about the morality of fighting and also to ameliorate the feelings of loss among the families of soldiers who fell.

7

Tactics on the Battlefield

The preparation of men for battle and their deployment on the field for combat are the focus of tactics. The successful military commander is one who is able to use most effectively knowledge of the tactics that are appropriate in a given situation and has available soldiers who have been trained to carry out his orders. As Frontinus explained in his well appreciated *Strategemata*, the proper education of commanders is one that allows them to apply on contemporary battlefields models of troop deployments that were derived from examples taken from history.[1] The education of Ottonian military commanders and the training of their men to use a wide range of arms in numerous tactical situations were the focus of chapters four and five. The present chapter considers the ways in which fighting men were deployed by Henry I, Otto I, and their military commanders to defeat the enemy on the battlefield.

For the most part, information about the range of battlefield tactics that were available to Ottonian military commanders is provided by authors of contemporary narrative sources and, to a more limited extent, military manuals such as Vegetius' *Epitoma rei militaris* and Frontinus' *Strategemata*. It is clear that many of the authors of contemporary historical works had a *parti pris* that led to the misrepresentation of information about military matters in a variety of ways.[2] Nevertheless, the historian also has available a variety of methods to

---

1   Frontinus, *Strategemata*, ed. Robert I. Ireland (Leipzig, 1999), 1.1, "*ita enim consilii quoque et providentiae exemplis succinti duces erunt, unde illis excogitandi generandique similia facultas nutriatur; praeterea continget ne de eventu trepidet inventionis suae,qui probbatis eam experimentis comparabit.*" The value of this text to Ottonian military commanders is strongly indicated by Archbishop Brun of Cologne's decision to give a copy to his elder brother Otto I and to dedicate it to him as a man who had protected his fatherland from the invasions of enemies. See the observations by C. Stephen Jaeger, *The Origins of Courtliness: Civilizing Trends and the Formation of Courtly Ideals 939–1210* (Phildalphia, 1985), 119-21; and Keller, "*Machabaeorum pugnae*: Zum Stellenwert eines biblischen Vorbilds in Widukinds Deutung der ottonischen Königsherrschaft," 434. Scholars have not given a specific date to Brun's dedication poem, and hence the gift of the text of Frontinus to Otto I. However, in light of the reference to needing a leader to defeat the barbarians, who are threatening the *res publica*, it seems likely that the gift was made sometime in the 930s or early 940s, when the pagan Slavs posed the greatest threat to the Ottonian kingdom.
2   For the general problem of clerical biases in the writing of military history, see Verbruggen, *The Art of Warfare in Western Europe*, 11. For the more specific question of clerical biases in depicting warfare during the early medieval period, see Bernard S. Bachrach, "Gregory of Tours as a Military Historian," in Kathleen Anne Mitchell and Ian N. Wood eds., *The World of Gregory of Tours*

escape the "prison" of the text, to use Patrick Geary's evocative phrase, including
identifying authorial intention through an analysis of the author's biography,
identifying the audience for the text and the concomitant expectations within
which the author was forced to work, and identifying the manner in which a
particular text was used during the Middle Ages through a careful examination
of its manuscript tradition.[3]

As the discussion in chapter four regarding the education of Ottonian
officers makes clear, both historical works and military handbooks circulated
widely within the Ottonian kingdom. Contemporary authors, including Widukind, Gerhard of Augsburg, and Alpert of Metz, praised individual military
commanders not only for their extensive learning in military matters, but also
their broader study in other fields, including theology and law. In light of the
enormous numbers of texts that were patronized by noble families as well as
the royal government through their support of both monastic and cathedral
schools, and the evidence for magnates sending their sons to monastic schools,
it is hard to escape the conclusion that these Latin works, including military
manuals, technical manuals, and histories, were known and used by Ottonian
military commanders.

In addition, it bears repetition that historical works, such as those written by
Widukind, Liudprand of Cremona, and Gerhard of Augsburg were composed
for an audience that had a detailed knowledge and understanding of warfare. As
a consequence, in order to avoid alienating his audience, the author was bound
to provide an account that was plausible in a military sense to informed listeners,
even if some of the details had been changed in consonance with a broad narrative arc within the text as a whole.[4] Indeed, as scholars working with a nuanced
understanding of the epistemology of historical knowledge have made clear, in
the pursuit of rhetorical plausibility, it is in the author's interest to provide a

(Leiden 2002), 351-363; Thomas Scharff, *Die Kämpfe der Herrscher und der Heiligen: Krieg Und
historische Erinnerung in der Karolingerzeit* (Darmstadt, 2002); and Bachrach, "Memory, Epistemology," 63-90.

3   See the useful discussion of these points by Geary, "Zusammenfassung," 539-42, with specific
reference to the need to reconnect historiography to history. Geary also emphasized the difficulties
inherent in each of these approaches if pursued in isolation. He suggests, for example, that scholars
must be wary of "constructing" the audience for the text on the basis of the text, itself.

4   The classic work on the continuation of ancient rhetorical tradition in the Middle Ages is
Richard McKeon, "Rhetoric in the Middle Ages," *Speculum* 17 (1942), 1-32. See also, Nancy F.
Partner, "The New Cornificius: Medieval History and the Artifice of Words," in *Classical Rhetoric
and Medieval Historiography*, ed. E. Breisach (Kalamazoo, 1985), 5-60. For the particular applica-
tion of the tenets of rhetorical plausibility in medieval narrative works for modern understanding
of the audience, see Alexander Murray, "Religion among the Poor in Thirteenth Century France:
The Testimony of Humbert of Romans," *Traditio* 30 (1974), 285-324; A. Squire, *Aelred of Rievaulx*
(Kalamazoo, 1981), 78; M. Chibnall, *The World of Orderic Vitalis* (Oxford, 1984), 197-8; Roger Ray,
"Rhetorical Scepticism and Verisimilar Narrative in John of Salisbury's *Historia Pontificalis*," in
Classical Rhetoric and Medieval Historiography, ed. E. Breisach (Kalamazoo, 1985), 61-102, here 84;
John Bliese, "Aelred of Rievaulx's Rhetoric and Morale at the Battle of the Standard, 1138," *Albion* 20
(1988), 543-556, here 203; and now Lake, "Truth, Plausibility, and the Virtues of Narrative," 221-238.

context of accurate information precisely in those places in his narrative where he hopes to persuade an audience to accept his *parti pris*.[5]

These methods of critical analysis are powerful tools, but it is also possible to test the accuracy of a text by reference to the physical reality within which an author places his narrative. In this context, the methods of *Sachkritik* pioneered by Hans Delbrück in his multi-volume history of western warfare are of particular value.[6] Delbrück was interested particularly in using the physical realities of battlefields to criticize the numbers of soldiers reported in ancient and medieval narrative texts.[7] However, this methodology can be expanded to test an author's claims about the role that terrain or fortifications of a specific size and shape played in a campaign through the deployment of information developed in the course of archaeological investigations. For example, Thietmar of Merseburg's report that Henry I constructed a new fortification during the course of his campaign in Daleminzia in 929 has been confirmed through dendrochonological dating of wood samples taken from the oldest layers of the stronghold at Meißen.[8]

Nevertheless, despite the range of tools that are available to the historian to control for the *parti pris* of narrative sources, the danger remains that an author could describe the effective deployment of soldiers by a commander to show he had made the "correct" tactical decisions as a means of praising his patron or the patron's friends and relatives. This is particularly the case when an author specifically praises a commander for following the advice found in one or another historical text or handbook.[9] The historian must be particularly careful when it is clear that both the author of a text and his audience had access to the same historical works and handbooks that presented techniques for defeating an enemy force in a given tactical situation. Of course, such praise would also then be indicative of the understanding among military men in the audience of what the "correct" option had been on the battlefield.

For example, in his description of the death of the arch-rebel Wichmann, Widukind of Corvey provided a detailed description of the battle between the Wuolini, who were led by Wichmann, and the combined forces of Duke Boleslav I of Bohemia and the latter's son-in-law Duke Miesco of Poland.[10] Miesco, according to Widukind, deployed his foot soldiers in a phalanx in a position

---

5   This point has been made recently with respect to Carolingian sources specifically dealing with military matters by Scharff, *Die Kämpfe der Herrscher*, 42. Also see in this regard, Bachrach, "Dudo of St. Quentin as an Historian of Military Organization," 165-185; and Bachrach, "Memory, Epistemology," 63-90.

6   Delbrück, *History of the Art of War*, vols. 1-3, passim.

7   Regarding Delbrück's work in this area, and a critique of his methods as they concern the numbers of soldiers in medieval armies, see Bachrach, "Early Medieval Military Demography," 3-20.

8   Thietmar of Merseburg, *Chronicon*, 1.16. Regarding the dating of the earliest construction, see Arne Schmid-Hecklau, *Die archäologischen Ausgrabungen auf dem Burgberg in Meißen: Die Grabungen 1959-1963* (Dresden, 2004), 205.

9   Regarding this methodological difficulty, see the discussion by Bernard S. Bachrach, "The Practical Use of Vegetius' *De re militari* during the Early Middle Ages," *The Historian* 47 (1985), 239-255.

10   Widukind, *Res gestae*, 3.69.

that was, apparently, intended to block Wichmann's advance. When the Wuolini advanced against the Polish foot soldiers, Miesco ordered his men to withdraw at a slow pace so as to draw Wichmann's forces further away from the safety of their fortified camp.[11] When Miesco judged that the Wuolini were fully engaged and sufficiently distant from their *castra*, the Polish duke gave the pre-arranged signal for his Bohemian mounted forces, on loan from Boleslav, to attack the rear of Wichmann's army. At the same time, Miesco ordered his foot soldiers to go on the attack.[12] The result was a complete annihilation of the Wuolini.[13]

In composing his *Res gestae Saxonicae*, it is likely that Widukind had access not only to informants at Otto I's court but also to books in the royal library, including Frontinus' *Strategemata*.[14] Frontinus, in chapter three of the second book of his text, provided a number of examples of generals deploying their men so as to lure the enemy into a trap. Frontinus notes, for example, that Metellus was able to defeat Hirtuleius in Spain (78 BC) by withdrawing his center, and ultimately enveloping the enemy force when Hirtuleius advanced without taking due precaution to protect his own flanks.[15] Even more apropos, Frontinus describes Hannibal's withdrawal of the center at Cannae (216 BC), and subsequent double envelopment and destruction of the Roman army with his mounted forces.[16] As a consequence, when Widukind described Duke Miesco's foot soldiers "forgiving" the center so as to lure the enemy into a trap that was sprung by mounted troops, both he and his audience likely were aware that Hannibal had deployed this tactic with devastating success at Cannae.

It should be noted that certainly Widukind, and likely members of the royal court as well, were familiar with Hannibal's tactics at Cannae not only from Frontinus' brief synopsis but also from Livy's famous description of the battle in *Ab condite urbe*.[17] In addition, it is likely that both Widukind and the members of the Ottonian royal court also were familiar with the tactic of forgiving the center in order to draw the enemy into a trap from much more contemporary sources. For example, in his description of the battle of Andernach (876), the author of the *Annals of Fulda* describes in detail Louis the Younger's deployment of Saxon foot soldiers who withdrew in the face of Charles the Bald's army.[18] When the West Frankish troops were fully committed, Louis executed

---

11   Ibid., "*Cumque contra eum Wichmannus duxisset exercitum, pedites primum ei inmisit. Cumque ex iussu ducis paulatim coram Wichmanno fugerent, a castris longius protrahitur.*"

12   Ibid., "*equitibus a tergo inmissis, signo fugientes ad reversionem hostium monet.*"

13   Ibid.

14   For the possession of the text of Frontinus by both Archbishop Brun of Cologne and Otto I, see the discussion by Jaeger, *The Origins of Courtliness*, 119-21; and Keller, "*Machabaeorum pugnae*," 434.

15   Frontinus, *Strategemata*, 2.3.5.

16   Ibid., 2.3.7.

17   Livy, *Ab condite urbe*, 22.4-7. Regarding Widukind's familiarity with Livy, see Helmut Beumann, *Widukind von Korvey: Untersuchungen zur Geschichtsschreibung und Ideengeschichte des 10. Jahrhunderts* (Weimar, 1950), 222. Regarding the influence of Livy on the thinking of Brun at Cologne, see Mayr-Harting, *Church and Cosmos in Early Ottonian Germany*, 136.

18   *Annales Fuldenses*, an. 876. For an overview of the manuscript tradition of this text, see *The*

a double envelopment of his uncle's army by deploying mounted forces that had been held in reserve on both flanks.[19]

In evaluating Widukind's description of the tactics employed by Duke Miesco, and indeed, the account in the *Annals of Fulda* regarding Louis the Younger's deployment of his forces at Andernach, it is clear that both authors had a favorable opinion of the military commanders. Widukind describes Miesco as an *amicus imperatoris*, by which he meant a friendly client king.[20] The *Annals of Fulda* in the period c. 865–888 were produced under the leadership of Archbishop Liutbert of Mainz (863–889), who served as chancellor for Louis the Younger until the latter's death in 882.[21] Consequently, the positive depiction of their victories in a manner consistent with the great military commanders of the past does signal the need for caution. In neither case, however, is the commander specifically praised for using the tactics that he had learned from books. Moreover, neither commander is specifically compared with a Metellus or a Hannibal, to take the two examples used by Frontinus. The proper conclusion in evaluating the descriptions of battle by the authors of the annals of Fulda and Widukind is that the tactic of forgiving the center was known to the authors of historical works and their audiences not only through handbooks and historical accounts of past battles but also through practical experience on the battlefield.

As discussed in chapter four, it is clear that at least some Ottonian military commanders, such as Margrave Gero, were well read. However, when arguing for the transmission of information from texts such as Frontinus' *Strategemata*, or the histories such as *Ab urbe condita* or the *Annals of Fulda*, it is by no means necessary to conclude that all Ottonian officers, or even King Henry I, dutifully sat down to read, in Latin, the enormous range of historical and technical manuals that were available to them, whether in their own libraries, or in the libraries of monasteries and convents that they established and supported. The information about military matters provided in these texts could just as easily, perhaps even more easily, be transmitted orally either by clerics or by laymen who were versed in Latin and had a literate education.

This chapter will consider tactics in the context of four set-piece battles fought by Ottonian armies in the field. Two, at Lenzen and Recknitz, saw the victory of royal armies over Slavic opponents, the Redarii and Obodrites, respectively. The battle at Riade saw the deployment of Ottonian forces against the Hungar-

---

Annals of Fulda, translated and annotated by Timothy Reuter (Manchester, 1992), 1-9.

[19] See the discussion of this battle by Bachrach and Bachrach, "Saxon Military Revolution?" 210-211. Cf. Leyser, "Henry I and the Beginnings of the Saxon Empire," 26, who did not appreciate the difficulty of the task that Louis the Younger had assigned to his Saxon troops and takes at face value the negative presentation of the Saxons by the author of the *Annals of Fulda* despite the latter's demonstrated anti-Saxon *parti pris*.

[20] Regarding Widukind's use of the term *amicus* to denote a diplomatic relationship reminiscent of Roman relations with client kings, see Kaeding, Kümmerlen and Seidel, "Heinrich I. – ein 'Freundschaftskönig,'" 282-290.

[21] Regarding Liutbert's oversight of the production of the *Annals of Fulda*, see Goldberg, *Struggle for Empire*, 14-15.

ians. A fourth battle, at Mantahinga, saw two German armies pitted against each other during the civil war of 953–955. The final section will focus on the tactics used by Ottonian military forces as part of the strategy of defense-in-depth that protected the eastern frontier from Carantania to the Baltic Sea. The primary focus here will be on the aftermath of the confrontation on the Lechfeld (955), as it was on the second and third days after the battle that the Hungarian army was destroyed.

Lenzen, 929

On 30 June 929, Henry I was at Nabburg, some 55 kilometers north-north-east of Regensburg, where he had come with his army after the surrender of Prague in the previous month.[22] From Nabburg, Henry began his 400-kilometer journey northward toward the royal convent of Quedlinburg, where he planned to celebrate the marriage of his son Otto to Edith, the daughter of King Edward the Elder of Wessex (died 924), in September.[23] While on this march northward, which required the better part of a month for travel time alone, Henry I received a report that the frontier fortification at Walsleben had been sacked. In addition, the garrison as well as the population from the surrounding area that had taken refuge at the fortification, had been slaughtered by the Redarii, one of the peoples that had sworn earlier in the year to pay tribute to the German kingdom.[24]

Walsleben, in the modern district of Stendal, was located some 13 kilometers north-west of the Elbe fortification at Arneburg and 22 kilometers west-south-west of the fortress at Havelberg, and was an important element of Henry's newly established defensive line along the lower Elbe which stretched north from the important trading center at Magdeburg.[25] The strike at Walsleben, therefore, likely was understood by Henry as a substantial threat to the *pax* that he had established along the stretch of the lower Elbe, which was to be maintained by his fortified march. Moreover, the rebellion by the Redarii, from Henry's point of view, also threatened to disrupt the flow of tribute that he had imposed on Slavic peoples who were settled between the lower Elbe and the Oder rivers, and perhaps disrupt trade relations as well.[26] According to Widukind, the success of the Redarii attack had convinced a number of other Slavic polities to attempt to reverse Henry I's success against the Hevelli, which had culminated in the

---

[22] It is a march of some 600 kilometers from Prague to Nabburg along the route Prague-Pilsen, Domazlice-Furth-im-Walde-Nabburg, which would require at least twenty, and more likely thirty days for a very large force such as that commanded by Henry I and Duke Arnulf of Bavaria. See the discussion of the invasion routes into Bohemia from Bavaria by Bowlus, *Franks, Moravians, and Magyars*, 59.

[23] Widukind, *Res gestae*, 1.36.

[24] Barford, *The Early Slavs: Culture and Society in Early Medieval Eastern Europe*, 257-258.

[25] Hardt, "Linien und Säume. Zonen und Räume," 39-56; and idem, "Hesse, Elbe, Saale and the Frontiers of the Carolingian Empire," 223-226.

[26] Widukind, *Res gestae*, 1.35-36.

capture of their princely seat at Brandenburg. He writes, likely with some exaggeration, that "all of the barbarian nations dared to rise up in revolt again."[27]

Consequently, Henry and his advisers settled on a campaign strategy that was intended to reestablish the *status quo ante*. Consistent with his practice of securing control over territory by eliminating enemy strongholds and replacing them with his own fortifications, the king decided that he had to capture a major Slav stronghold and, moreover, one that was somewhat beyond the established frontier of his kingdom.[28] Henry chose as his target the fortress at Lenzen, the principal seat of the Lionen, which was constructed on the east bank of the Elbe, some 45 kilometers south-east of the important Ottonian trading center at Lüneburg.[29] Lenzen had served in the past as a base for Slav military operations into Saxon lands west of the Elbe.[30]

In evaluating Henry's decision to direct his retaliatory campaign against Lenzen, it is important to emphasize that the king was not operating on a "gut feeling" about the location and strength of this fortress. Rather, in order to assemble an army of sufficient size to prosecute a successful siege and also defend against a large Slav army that was already in the field, Henry and his advisors required a considerable body of detailed information. This included the size of Lenzen and the likely strength of its garrison, and the routes by which Lenzen could be reached from the west and south, as well as from the east and north, i.e. the direction from which a relief army likely would approach.

In this context, it should be recalled that the rulers of East Francia had long made a habit of collecting military intelligence regarding the fortifications of the Slavic polities to the east. A report commissioned by King Louis the German sometime between 846 and 862, the *Descriptio civitatum et regionum ad septentrionalem plagam Danubii*, provides a detailed description of the number of fortifications that had been constructed by the Carolingian king's opponents, and potential opponents, in the Slavic lands between the North Sea and the Danube.[31] According to the author of the report, sometimes referred to anachronistically as the Bavarian Geographer, the Obodrites in the far north had 53 *civitates*, the Wilzi to their south 95, the Hevelli 8, the Sorbs 50, the Daleminzi 14, the Bohemians 15, and the Moravians 11 *civitates*.[32] Extensive archaeological work over the past fifty years has identified large numbers of these fortifications dating to the

---

[27] Ibid., 1.36.

[28] Henry I's policy of replacing Slavic fortifications with his own strongholds has been established through extensive archaeological excavations. This topic is dealt with in detail in chapter one.

[29] For discussion of the historical role of Lenzen and its position as the main seat of the Lionen, see Kennecke, "Forschung Burg Lenzen, Wo Slawen gegen Sachsen kämpften," 8-13. For the decision to target Lenzen specifically, see Widukind, *Res gestae*, 1.36.

[30] Regarding Lenzen's use as a base of operations for campaigns west of the Elbe, see Kennecke, "Lenzen," 8.

[31] The report survives in one copy, Bayerische Staatsbibliothek, Clm 560, fols. 149v-150r. The text is discussed in detail by Goldberg, *Struggle for Empire*, 135-7.

[32] See ibid., 136.

mid ninth century.[33] King Henry, who by 929 had been campaigning against the Slavs for more than two decades, undoubtedly recognized the importance of the regular updating of this type of information.

Once he had chosen a target for the campaign, Henry issued orders for the mobilization of a substantial army, which included the military households of numerous Saxon magnates. Among the latter were the counts of Stade and Walbeck, and many other *nobiles viri*.[34] The overall command was assigned to Count Bernhard, whom Henry had promoted to oversee relations with the Redarii.[35] To provide additional support, the king assigned Count Thietmar, who likely was the same commander who had rescued Henry from Conrad I at Grone in 915, to join Bernhard as his *collega*.[36] Each of these counts and other *nobilies viri* commanded military households that included men who were equipped to fight on horseback as well as on foot. However, the bulk of Bernhard's force, in consonance with a campaign that was intended to capture a significant fortification, consisted of men from the Saxon expeditionary levy (*exercitus*) most of whom were equipped and trained to fight on foot in an infantry phalanx.

Widukind does not provide information regarding the line of march taken by the Saxon taskforce, but in light of the participation by the counts of Stade and Walbeck, whose principal seats were located approximately 120 kilometers north-west and 110 kilometers south-east of Lenzen, respectively, one likely mobilization point was the centrally located Lüneburg. Located a hard two days' march to the west of Lenzen, Lüneburg boasted both an important fortification and a substantial trading center that had developed around the local salt works.[37] As the main seat of the Billunger family and the location of the important monastery of St Michael, Lüneburg also possessed the infrastructure to mobilize food supplies and transportation resources that would be required for a substantial army. The most important source of these supplies likely was Hamburg, whose bishops enjoyed a series of immunities from both Henry I and Otto I which gave them jurisdiction over the resources not only of the bishopric but also a number of dependent monasteries for use in the service of royal *expeditiones*.[38]

By late August, the Saxon army had been fully mobilized, and Bernhard led his force to Lenzen, arriving there on Monday, the 30th of the month. The Saxon commander, following the standard military procedure suggested in military handbooks such as those by Vegetius and Pseudo-Hyginus, established a fortified

33   For example, Kempke, "Bemerkungen zur Delvenau-Stockitz-Route," 176, points out that at least 35 of the 53 Obodrite fortifications identified in the *Descriptio* have been excavated by archaeologists and dated to the early Slavic period.

34   Widukind, *Res gestae*, 1.36.

35   Ibid., 1.36., "*exercitus cum presidio miltiari Bernhado, qui ipsa Redariorum provinica erat sublegata.*"

36   Ibid., 1.36, and ibid., 1. 24 for Thietmar's service in 915.

37   In 956, Otto I granted the toll revenues that were derived from this salt works to the monastery of St Michael at Lüneburg. See DO I, 183.

38   See DO I, 11, which is a reconfirmation of this immunity, which dates back not only to the reign of Henry I, but also to the Carolingian period as well.

camp (*castra*).[39] Bernhard also dispatched scouts (*custodes*) to provide advance warning of enemy forces in the area. This was particularly important because Bernhard was well aware, as a result of the sack of Walsleben, that a substantial Slav army had been operating in the region that summer.

On the fifth day of the siege (3 September), scouts reported to the Saxon commanders that a large force of Slavs was located nearby. They also reported that the Slavs planned a night attack on the fortified Saxon camp.[40] One might surmise here that the scouts obtained this information through the vigorous interrogation of prisoners. In response, Thiatmer and Bernhard sent out additional scouts who were able to confirm the information brought by the first group of *custodes*. Once they obtained confirmation of the disposition of the Slav army, Bernhard and Thietmar held a conference with the other officers, and then ordered that the camp be put on alert in case the enemy attempted to attack that night.[41]

Widukind, who was well versed in the thinking of soldiers, commented on the feelings of the men as they waited for dawn. Some were taken by despair while others were excited. Some of the men were afraid of the coming battle while others were looking forward to it. As Widukind put it, "the warriors turned first to hope and then to fear, each according to his own nature."[42] This range of emotions is certainly what one would expect of any group of fighting men on the eve of battle. This is even more true when so many of the men were not professional soldiers, but rather members of the expeditionary levy who only occasionally were called upon to go to war.

That night there was a major rainstorm, but the morning dawned clear and bright. At first light, the Saxon troops went to hear mass, and received the host. Then each of the commanders stepped forward before the troops and swore to do his duty in the battle. Following this ceremony, the men also swore, each man to his neighbor, that he would serve bravely in battle.[43] This type of trust-building exercise was crucial to maintaining cohesion in a phalanx, where every man depended on his fellow soldier to keep his place in line, and fight in a coordinated fashion. The army then marched out of the camp following their banners (*signa*).[44]

The Slav army was drawn up in a massive phalanx facing the Saxon camp. Their force was composed primarily of foot soldiers, with only a very small number of mounted men. In the first stage of the battle, Bernhard drew up his own foot soldiers

39   Widukind, *Res gestae*, 1.36, observes that the Saxon force was protected by its *castra*. Regarding the importance of establishing a fortified camp, particularly when in enemy territory, see Vegetius, *Epitoma*, 1.21-24. For the observations by Pseudo-Hyginus, see Catherine M. Gilliver, "The *De munitionibus castrorum*", 33-48.
40   Widukind, *Res gestae*, 1.36, "et quia nocte contigua inpetum in castra facere decrevissent."
41   Ibid., "eadem hora collega dictante precepit, ut per totam noctem parati essent, ne qua forte irruptio barbarorum in castra fieret."
42   Ibid., 1.36, "et pro qualitate morum inter spem metumque versabantur bellatores."
43   Ibid., 1.36, "et primo diluculo data signo sacramentoque accepto, primum ducibus, deinde unusquisque alteri operam suam sub iuramento promittebat ad presens bellum."
44   Ibid., "erectis signis procedebant castris."

in a phalanx but did not commit them immediately to battle. Instead, he sought to test the training and discipline of the Slavs by deploying his mounted forces using the tactic of the feigned retreat. The goal of such an attack was to lure the enemy out from a strong defensive position by attacking, and then pretending to flee. An undisciplined force would then pursue, in the process losing the unit cohesion that was necessary to mount a successful defense against mounted troops. Once the enemy was sufficiently extended, the ostensibly fleeing mounted force would then wheel about, and inflict heavy losses on the now disorganized foe.

In 910, the Hungarians successfully used the tactic of the feigned retreat on the plain of the Lech near Augsburg against a large army composed of contingents from Swabia and Franconia under the nominal command of Louis the Child.[45] The Hungarians launched an early morning attack on the East Carolingian army with long-range weapons. When the Carolingian troops responded, the Hungarians engaged in a feigned retreat.[46] At first, this tactic was not successful, and the Frankish and Swabian troops did not pursue the enemy. However, at dusk, the Hungarians engaged in a final feigned retreat and successfully led many of the Franks and Swabians into a prepared ambush where the mounted archers inflicted very heavy casualties on the Carolingian forces.[47]

In his discussion of the fighting tactics of the Magyars, Regino of Prüm drew attention to the fact that their tactics of mounted combat were similar to those of the Bretons.[48] He emphasized that both of them presented difficulties to other peoples who were unfamiliar with their manner of fighting, a point that he had raised in the context of Charles the Bald's defeat at the hands of the Bretons in 851.[49] The Bretons provoked Charles' foot soldiers to break formation in the phalanx and pursue the Breton mounted troops, with disastrous results. The one important difference between the Bretons and Hungarians pointed to by Regino was that the latter employed bows and arrows (sagittae) while the Bretons relied on hurling javelins (misiliae).[50]

At Lenzen, however, the ground was too wet for the mounted soldiers to maneuver properly, and they were unable to draw the Slavs out from their phalanx to follow the withdrawing Saxons.[51] In describing this first round of fighting,

---

45   The fullest details regarding this battle are from Liudprand, *Antapodosis*, 2.3-5.
46   Liudprand, *Antapodosis*, 2.4, "Prius itaque ac Titoni croceum linqueret Aurora cubile, Hungariorum gens, necis sitiens, belli avida, hos, videlicet Christianos, adhuc opprimit oscitantes; nonnullos namque spicula priusquam clamores evigilarunt, alios vero cubilibus confossos neque strepitus neque vulnera exitarunt; citius enim ab iis spiritus recessit atque somnus. Gravis itaque hinc indeque oritur pugna, versique terta ceu in fugam Turci directis acriter boelis plurimos sternunt."
47   Liudprand, *Antapodosis*, 2.4, "Iam septimam descendens Phoebus occupaverat horam, et serenus adhuc Hulodoici partibus Mars favebat, cum Turci sicut non incallidi, positis ex adverso insidiis fugam simulant. Quos dum regis populus doli ignarus impetu validissimo sequeretur, omni prodeunt ex parte insidiae et quasi victi ipsi victores interimunt."
48   Regino of Prüm, *Chronicon*, an. 889.
49   Ibid., "Quorum pugna, quo ceteris gentibus inusitata, eo et periculosior."
50   Ibid.
51   Widukind, *Res gestae*, 1.36, "peditum vero innumerabilem multitudinem et nocturna pluvial in tantum impeditam ut vix ab equitibus coacti ad pugnam procederent."

Widukind emphasized that the Redarii did not have a large mounted force with them, but rather an "innumerable multitude of men on foot."[52] He pointed to this factor as having as much an effect on the failure of the feigned retreat as the wet and slippery ground. Widukind's observation on this point provides insight into the tactical thinking of Bernhard, and perhaps also the Slav commander, regarding the deployment of mounted forces alongside a phalanx.

Either through a direct acquaintance with the book, or through conversation with those who knew it, Bernhard may have had access to Vegetius' suggestions regarding the deployment of mounted forces on the wings so as to harass the enemy during an attack, and also the crucial importance of maintaining a reserve force so that a pincer movement could be executed on the battlefield.[53] Consequently, Bernhard's deployment of his mounted forces in the first stage of the battle may have been intended to force the opposing commander to commit his own cavalry at an early stage of the engagement and to show his hand regarding the forces that had been held in reserve.

From the perspective of the Slav commander, the lack of a significant mounted contingent narrowed his options for fighting the Saxons. Obviously, he hoped to force Bernhard to break off the siege of Lenzen. When he lost the element of surprise after the Saxon *custodes* found his army, the Slav leader's only real choice was to form up his army, which would force Bernhard either to depart and break off the siege or to fight a battle. In the latter case, the Slavs would enjoy the benefits of the tactical defensive, forcing the enemy to advance against a fixed position.[54]

The most important factor for the Slav commander was to maintain his phalanx no matter the tempting opportunities that might seem to present themselves on the battlefield. His ability to keep the foot soldiers in formation following the initial mounted assault therefore speaks to the Slav commander's understanding of his tactical situation. No less importantly, it points to the high level of training and discipline among the rank and file of his army, who kept their positions in the face of the ostensibly fleeing enemy troops. This is more than can be said for Charles the Bald's men, for example, in their battle against the Bretons in 851, noted above.

As the sun rose higher in the sky and the heat of the summer day rapidly dried the ground, affording better footing for his men, Bernhard gave the order for a general rapid advance of his infantry phalanx against the Slavs.[55] This maneuver

---

[52] Ibid., *"non plures haberent equites, peditum vero innumerabilem multitudinem."*

[53] Vegetius, *Epitoma,* 3.16-17.

[54] The long durée advantage of seizing the tactical defensive in a battle is made clear by Clifford J. Rogers, "The Offensive/Defensive in Medieval Strategy," *XII Congreß der Internationalen Kommission für Militärgeschichte* (Vienna, 1997), 158-171; idem, "Edward III and the Dialectics of Strategy, 1327-1360," *Transactions of the Royal Historical Society* 6.4 (1994), 265-283, both reprinted with the same pagination in idem, *Essays on Medieval History: Strategy, Military Revolutions and the Hundred Years War* (Burlington, VT, 2010).

[55] Widukind, *Res gestae,* 1.36, "*Igitur dato signo et exhortante legiones legato cum clamore valido irrunt in hostes.*"

required a high degree of training and discipline to carry out effectively.[56] In order that the entire front of the phalanx hit the enemy at the same moment, each soldier had to move at the same speed. In his treatment of this topic, Rabanus Maurus, in his *epitome* of Vegetius' text for use in *tempore moderno*, emphasized that the failure to keep formation during the attack often led to great danger.[57] To assure that fighting men kept the proper formation in battle, Rabanus urged that they be trained to charge, i.e., *rapido cursu*, with each man keeping his place in rank.

Despite the obvious preparation and training of the Saxon phalanx, the first attack on foot failed as well. The Saxons were not able to break the great strength and depth of the Slav infantry formation.[58] The fighting was fierce, and many men were killed on each side in the press of the battle. The Redarii were able to maintain their lines in the face of the Saxon onslaught despite the heavy losses that they endured. Their endurance in this battle is again a testament to the training and discipline of the Slav troops.

It seems unlikely that the leaders of the Redarii learned directly about such training methods from works such as Vegetius' *Epitoma*. Nevertheless, the constant military pressure imposed upon the Slavs by the Carolingians and their Ottonian successors, who employed the techniques set down in military manuals of the types enumerated above, almost certainly played a role in the development by the Redarii and other Slavs of tactics and concomitant training to deal with this ongoing threat. Indeed, learning of such military techniques from the enemy is hardly an unlikely scenario. As extensive excavations of fortifications east of the Elbe and Saale from the late ninth and early tenth century have made clear, it is certainly the case that western building techniques for the construction of fortifications made their way east, and led to the steady improvement in Slavic strongholds.[59]

Finally, however, Bernhard saw what he had been waiting for. A gap appeared in the flank of the enemy phalanx. The Saxon commander immediately signaled Thietmar, who was in command of the mounted forces that had been held in reserve for just this moment. With an initial squadron of fifty heavily armed mounted troops (*armati*), Thietmar led a charge into the flank of the Redarii. This surprise assault, after a hard day of fighting, utterly disrupted the enemy phalanx and threw the Slavs into a panic, leading very rapidly to a rout.[60]

56 Regarding the necessity of maintaining disciplined cohesion in phalanx warfare, with specific reference to the Anglo-Saxon context, see Guy Halsall, "Anthropology and the Study of Pre-Conquest Warfare and Society: The Ritual of War in Anglo-Saxon England," in *Weapons and Warfare*, 155-177, here 166.

57 Rabanus Maurus, *De procinctu Romanae miliciae*, ch. 5.

58 Widukind, *Res gestae*, 1.36, "Cumque nimia densitate iter pertranseundi hostes non pateret."

59 See, for example, the observations by Günter Wetzel, "Neue Erkentnisse zur Befestigung der Burg bei Gehren, Kr. Luckau," *Ausgrabungen und Funde* 35 (1990), 90-92, here 92.

60 Widukind, *Res gestae*, 1.36, "Ille vero prefectum cum quinquaginta armatis lateri hostili inmisit et ordines conturbavit; ex hoc caedi fugaeque tota die hostes patebant." In this discussion of the battle of Lenzen, Leyser, "Henry I and the Beginnings of the Saxon Empire," 31, leaves the misleading impression that a mere fifty mounted fighting men dominated the battlefield, arguing, "it is possible

As was the case in many medieval battles, the deaths on the field were dwarfed by the losses suffered when the losing side turned and fled. Mounted forces were in an ideal position to attack the fleeing men and stab them in the back. Thietmar's horsemen chased the enemy soldiers through fields, or drove them into a nearby lake where they drowned. Widukind records, likely with some exaggeration, that none of the enemy foot soldiers survived the battle, and just a handful of their mounted troops did so.[61] After the slaughter had ended and with dusk falling, Bernhard recalled his troops and celebrated the victory in camp. The next morning, the fortress of Lenzen surrendered.[62]

The plan of battle employed by Bernhard at Lenzen demonstrates his understanding of the value of having available troops with the training and equipment that enabled them to carry out a range of battlefield tactics. During the initial stages of the battle, the Saxon mounted forces permitted Bernhard to test the Slav phalanx without committing the bulk of his troops to battle. When it became evident that the Redarii would not move from their positions, Bernhard could have confidence in ordering his own infantry phalanx to advance because his flanks and rear were protected by the cavalry force that was held in reserve under the command of Thietmar against a sortie by the garrison at Lenzen, or from the arrival of fresh Slav troops. Finally, when the Saxon foot soldiers succeeded in creating a gap in the lines of the Redarii, Bernhard was able to deploy his mounted reserves in a shattering flank attack that won the battle. By contrast, the Slav commander's lack of cavalry meant that he could not counter this threat to his own flank, nor could he pose a serious threat to turn the flank of the Saxon phalanx as it advanced against his own forces.

Battle of Riade, 933

Sometime in the spring of 932, Henry met with envoys of the Magyar Khan at a royal assembly. This embassy would seem to have been intended to work out some serious difficulties that had arisen since the peace that Henry had imposed upon the Magyars in 924. Whatever the objective of the Magyar embassy, it failed. Widukind signals this by emphasizing the fact that the envoys went home without the *munera* that a great ruler traditionally provides to successful envoys, and which the Magyars were accustomed to receive when peaceful relations were the norm.[63] Henry subsequently held an assembly in late May 932, making clear

---

to detect once more the difference between the mass of warriors and a small élite of *armati* on horseback in the army which defeated the Redarii ... The Slavs had very few horsemen; the Saxons forced a decision with only fifty." It must be emphasized that Widukind does not say that only fifty men participated in the charge, but that Thietmar led a unit of fifty men. In light of the presence at the battle of at least four counts, and numerous other *nobiles viri*, the cavalry force available to Bernhard was substantially larger than fifty men.

61 Widukind, *Res gestae*, 1.36, "nec peditum ullus superfuit, equitum rarissimus."
62 Ibid.
63 Widukind, *Res gestae*, 1.38.

to his magnates that he was intent on war with the Hungarians.[64] Six weeks later, Duke Arnulf of Bavaria held a similar assembly with the magnates of his duchy to emphasize his own commitment to a renewed struggle against the Hungarians.[65] The latter struck first, however, and invaded Thuringia at the beginning of the campaign season in 933.[66]

The Magyar army, moving from the south-east, crossed the frontier into Thuringia and the invaders are reported to have inflicted considerable damage on the countryside. After this initial stage of the campaign, the Magyar commanders decided to divide their forces into two columns. One column moved west and tried to attack Saxony from the south. However, according to Widukind, a Saxon force joined with Thuringians and attacked the invaders, killing the leaders, and the remainder of this Magyar column scattered across the entire region.[67] As a consequence, according to Widukind, some Magyars were killed outright in battle, some were taken prisoner, some died of exposure in the countryside, and still others died of hunger.[68] In effect, this Magyar force suffered more or less the same fate as the contingent defeated in 924.[69]

The second Magyar column, which had remained in the east, obtained intelligence that a sister of King Henry, who had married the Thuringian noble Wido, lived in a fortress in the area of Riade, and that its treasury was filled with gold and silver. The Magyars attempted to capture the fortress by storm but failed to do so before night fell. While in camp, the Magyars, who clearly made effective use of scouts, learned that the other Magyar column had been destroyed and that King Henry was approaching with a very strong army (*validus exercitus*) to relieve the fortress.[70] As a consequence, the Magyars recalled, using various fire and smoke signals, their sub-units that had scattered to plunder the countryside, thereby reforming what Widukind describes as their enormous army (*ingens agmen*).[71]

Henry, who almost certainly deployed his own scouts, quickly realized that he had lost the overall element of surprise, and would not be able to catch the Hungarians scattered and unaware of his presence. Nevertheless, the German king hoped to set a trap for the invaders which would permit him to inflict heavy losses on their eastern column commensurate with the destruction of the column that had had penetrated further west into Thuringia proper. The fundamental tactical problems that Henry faced were the speed of the Hungarian horsemen, and their ability to inflict heavy casualties on his troops at a distance with their

64 *Die Konzilien Deutschlands und Reichsitaliens 916-1001: Teil I 916-960*, 110.
65 Ibid., 120.
66 Liudprand, *Antapodosis*, 2.28; and Widukind, *Res gestae*, 1.38.
67 Widukind, *Res gestae*, 1.38.
68 Ibid., 1.38.
69 Ibid., 1.35.
70 Widukind, *Res gestae*, 1.38. Liudprand, *Antapodosis*, 2.29, explicitly states that the Hungarians both interrogated prisoners and sent out scouts to learn the whereabouts of Henry's relief army.
71 Widukind, *Res gestae*, 1.38.

bows. Henry's plan, therefore, had to negate these two advantages of the enemy, while still giving the Hungarians sufficient enticement to commit to a battle.

As a result, Henry conceived a *ruse de guerre* so that his heavily armed mounted troops could engage the Magyars, and bring to bear their better weapons and armament in hand to hand combat. At the first stage of the battle, therefore, the German king sent out a force of unarmored (*inermes*) Thuringian horsemen together with a handful of armored (*armati*) cavalry to attack the Hungarians, and then retreat, giving the impression that they had been defeated by the enemy. This is the essence of the tactic of the feigned retreat. The objective was to bring the Hungarians within range of the mass of the German *armati*, who had been concealed at some distance from the rest of Henry's *exercitus*, which did not consist of mounted troops. Once, the Hungarians had reached a position that was sufficiently close to the heavy cavalry, the *milites* were to launch a charge against the enemy, and strike them before the mounted archers could take flight.[72]

Both the feigned retreat by the Thuringian light cavalry, and the charge by the heavy cavalry required a high degree of coordination that depended on extensive training. The Thuringians had to make a very good show of launching an attack against the Hungarians, and then "selling" their retreat as real, so that the latter did not detect the trap that had been set for them. The *armati*, who were waiting to engage the Hungarians, had to maintain a serried line as they charged so that the impact would be even across the entire front of the enemy line.[73] A piecemeal charge would provide numerous openings, as Vegetius observed, for the enemy to inflict losses on the attackers.[74]

As the situation developed, the Thuringian light horse attracted the attention of the Magyars. Then, before permitting the latter to engage them in hand to hand combat, the Thuringians executed a feigned retreat that was intended to lead the Magyars within easy range of the *armati*.[75] Unfortunately for Henry, the Magyars caught sight of the Saxon heavily armored horse and, realizing that a trap had been set, they fled. Widukind reports that Henry's force pursued the Magyars for a distance of about eight miles before the latter escaped largely unhurt.[76] The Saxons, having relieved the siege, took control of the Magyar camp, freed the prisoners held there, and recaptured the booty that had been taken.[77] In morale terms, this was a great Saxon victory. In light of Henry's tactical aims, however, it was less than satisfying.

Riade is one of the few battles fought by the Ottonians in which mounted forces played the dominant role. The foot soldiers in Henry's *exercitus* could not move with sufficient rapidity to engage the fleet Hungarian mounted archers

---

72 Widukind, *Res gestae*, 1.38.

73 This point is emphasized by Liudprand, *Antapodosis*, 2.31. Also see the discussion in chapter five.

74 Vegetius, *Epitoma*, 1.9 and 1.26.

75 Saxon troops also had attempted to use the tactic of the feigned retreat at the battle of Lenzen in 929, four years before Riade. See Widukind, *Res gestae*, 1.36.

76 Widukund, *Res gestae*, 1.38. Also see Liudprand, *Antapodosis*, 2.25-31.

77 Widukind, *Res gestae*, 1.38.

while the latter were in the field. The deployment of the unarmored Thuringian mounted forces by Henry to draw the Hungarians into a trap is reminiscent, however, of the use of the feigned retreat at the battle of Lenzen four years earlier. As had been true in that earlier conflict, the use of forces with complementary tactical abilities provided the Ottonians with considerable flexibility in designing a battle plan that would obviate the greatest strength of the enemy. At Lenzen, Bernhard hoped to disrupt the solid Slav phalanx. At Riade, Henry wished to take away the mobility of the Hungarian mounted archers by forcing them into the cut and thrust of a close order cavalry battle.

Battle of Mantahinga, 954

Following Liudolf's escape from Mainz in the summer of 953 and his flight to Bavaria, discussed in chapter two, Otto I broke off his siege of the fortress city, and led his army south, mobilizing loyal magnates with their military households along the line of his march. Among those who answered the king's summons was Bishop Ulrich of Augsburg, who left a small force to hold Augsburg, and hurried to join the king with all of the men whom he could raise, which likely included both his military household and some elements of the expeditionary levy.[78] After three months of campaigning, Otto ended his Bavarian campaign for the year, and returned to Saxony. When Ulrich finally returned to his diocese, after taking his leave of King Otto, he found the situation there had become untenable.

During Otto's offensive against the rebels in Bavaria, Arnulf, count palatine of Bavaria, launched a counter stroke south and west into Swabia. Arnulf's raid was intended to show Otto's loyalists that the king could not protect them, and to encourage them to ally themselves with their erstwhile duke, Otto's son Liudolf. Although Arnulf did not succeed in capturing Augsburg, itself, he did cause significant damage, including capturing a number of Ulrich's soldiers (milites).[79] Of more importance, however, was the fact that Arnulf's raid convinced a number of erstwhile royalist supporters to back Liudolf rather than Otto.[80]

As a consequence, when Ulrich returned to his episcopal seat, he faced a situation in which, according to Gerhard, "some of his soldiers (milites) had been captured, some had left his side because of their unworthy fears, and some had been reduced to poverty by the attacks [of Arnulf]."[81] Rather than attempting to defend the inadequate walls of Augsburg with his depleted forces (multitudo parva), Ulrich withdrew to a fort (castellum) called Mantahinga, located in modern Schwabmünchen

---

[78] Gerhard of Augsburg, *Vita Uodalrici*, 1.10.
[79] Ibid.
[80] Ibid. Gerhard observed that "almost the entire diocese was divided up as a *beneficium* among strangers by Liudolf and his followers." This meant, in effect, that the extensive revenues and resources of the diocese were now available to the rebels rather than to the king.
[81] Ibid.

some 25 kilometers south-south-west of Augsburg. He then issued a summons for all men who were still loyal to the Otto I to join him there.[82]

When Ulrich arrived, the stone shell of the fortification at Mantahinga was still standing, but it lacked any wooden buildings either inside or outside its walls. To combat the cold of winter, Ulrich ordered his men to set up their tents (*tabernaculae*), and to find sufficient supplies in the surrounding area to construct wooden huts (*tugurii*). The bishop then began the task of strengthening the ruins through the construction of a new wooden palisade that completely surrounded the *castellum*.[83]

When Arnulf received word that Ulrich had withdrawn to Mantahinga, he sent messengers to the bishop offering him a peace settlement if the prelate would agree to accept Liudolf's authority, and immediately cease the refortification of the *castellum*.[84] In order to gain more time to complete his defensive preparations, and to organize the royalist supporters in Swabia, Ulrich made a pretense of listening to Arnulf's offer. As his friend and biographer Gerhard observed, the bishop was able to turn the count palatine away from his plan of attacking the unfinished fortification with a "variety of promises and humble responses."[85] Ulrich even agreed to an exchange of hostages to assure the integrity of the ongoing negotiations.[86]

It is a testament to the bishop's skill as a diplomat that he was able to keep Arnulf at bay for a lengthy period. However, the basic principle of concealing one's plans from the enemy for as long as possible, and even feeding misinformation to the enemy, was central to the conduct of warfare as it was taught in military handbooks such as Frontinus' *Strategemata*. The first book of his text included an entire chapter on the topic of concealing one's plans (*de occultandis consilii*).[87] This idea clearly was part of a living tradition in western war, as Hincmar of Rheims, who was well aware of the nature of military planning and warfare, emphasized that it was crucial to keep plans a secret in his revised version of Adalhard of Corbie's text on the administration of the royal court.[88]

In the meantime, however, the bishop continued to strengthen the physical defenses of Mantahinga, restoring the walls of the *castellum* and completing the new palisade to the extent that he now deemed them defensible by the forces that he had available.[89] Then, when it was no longer possible to keep up the pretense of negotiating, Ulrich broke off talks with the rebels and publicly reaffirmed his support of King Otto.[90]

---

82 Ibid.

83 Ibid.

84 Ibid.

85 Ibid., "*diversis promisionibus et humillimis responsibus.*"

86 Ibid.

87 Frontinus, *Strategemata*, I.I.

88 Hincmar of Rheims, *De ordine palatii*, ch. 15. Regarding the recognized need for secrecy in military planning in the Carolingian period, see the discussion by Bachrach, *Early Carolingian Warfare*, 204.

89 Gerhard of Augsburg, *Vita Uodalrici*, 1.10, "*donec aedificatio castello vallisque renovatis.*"

90 Ibid., "*tunc manisfeste confessus est se sicut coepit in voluntate regis velle perdurare.*"

In response, Arnulf, Liudolf's Bavarian ally, mobilized a large force (*multitudo*) that consisted of two different elements. The first part was made up of levies whom Arnulf had mobilized in Bavaria and had led in his raid of the Augsburg diocese. Gerhard makes clear his distaste for these men of lower social status by describing them as "undesirables" (*infausti*).[91] The second part of Arnulf's force consisted of the *obsequia* of magnates in whose aid (*auxilium*) Arnulf placed his trust, including his own brother Hermann.[92] Arnulf then deployed this force to besiege the *castellum* of Mantahinga in an effort to compel Ulrich and his remaining supporters to go over to Liudolf.[93]

In this context, Gerhard goes out of his way to emphasize the lengths to which Ulrich went to avoid bloodshed. The prelate offered a large sum of money to the rebels to go home in peace. The rebels rejected this offer. The bishop also warned the rebels not to disturb any of the properties in the diocese dedicated to St Mary, the patron of Augsburg, under threat of excommunication. The rebels, according to Gerhard, not only ignored this injunction, they began to seize church properties and commenced the siege of Mantahinga on the Sunday before Lent.[94]

Arnulf did not feel time pressure to launch a direct assault on Mantahinga. He believed that all of Swabia, other than Ulrich's last force of holdouts, had come to support his ally, Liudolf.[95] Consequently, the Bavarian count palatine settled in for a siege, hoping to end Ulrich's resistance by starving him into submission. However, as Gerhard observed in his account, Arnulf's overconfidence regarding the strategic situation in Swabia led him to make a number of important tactical errors. The most important of these was to leave his siege camp unprepared for an assault by a relief force, i.e. they were *inparati ad bellum*.[96] Such a basic error illustrates the fallacy of assuming that military commanders simply knew what to do while on campaign. Officers had to be taught proper procedure, and these lessons had to be reinforced.

In the meantime, however, Ulrich, maintaining the strictest secrecy, had been organizing a relief army that was commanded by his brother Dietpald, and another count named Adalbert. As was true of the besiegers, the relief force also consisted of two elements.[97] Both Adalbert and Dietbald held office as *comites* and commanded personal military *obsequia* of *milites*. The main body of the relief force, however, consisted of local levies from the two counts' *pagi* denoted by

91 Ibid.
92 Ibid.
93 Ibid.
94 Ibid. Gerhard observes, with some exaggeration, that the only supporters remaining to Ulrich were his brother Dietpald and Count Adalbert. However, Arnulf's actions do indicate that he believed Swabia was firmly in the rebels' camp.
95 Ibid.
96 Ibid.
97 Ibid., "*nullus in regis aduitorio remanebat, nisi Adalpertus comes cum suis subditis, et Dietpaldus frater religiosi episcopi.*"

Gerhard as a *phalanx populi*.[98] Gerhard's use of this term indicates that these fighting men, as contrasted with professional *milites*, likely did not have horses and both marched and fought on foot. The men serving in the *phalanx* likely included both members of the expeditionary levy and the local levy since the military engagement took place within the diocese of Augsburg and, therefore, was a matter of local defense.

As Gerhard makes clear, Dietpald and Adalbert brought their force within striking distance of Arnulf's siege camp, and were able to remain undetected through the night. In contrast to Bernhard's sound preparations at Lenzen, noted above, Arnulf clearly did not post a sufficient number of scouts (*custodes*) to provide warnings about an approaching enemy force. This failure of command is another clear indication that military education was not simply a matter of common sense, but rather required the rigorous application of important principles of the type set out in military handbooks, and also discussed in historical works that were used to instruct future officers.

By contrast, Dietpald and Adalbert succeeded in bringing up a sizeable force without giving away their location to the enemy. This required the acquisition of very good field intelligence so that none of Arnulf's men would be in a position to run across the relief force in the course of gathering supplies, or carrying out any of the other daily duties that are associated with maintaining a siege camp. In addition, the night before the battle, Dietpald and Adalbert had to keep their men quiet so that they would not be heard by the enemy. Finally, and importantly in the context of launching a surprise attack early in the spring when it is still quite cold in southern Germany, the army had to maintain its readiness for battle without any of the comforts of camp, including a hot meal or camp fires of any sort, in order to hide its presence. Their success in maintaining camp discipline is a clear indication of the command skills of Dietpald and Adalbert, particularly since a large element of their force consisted of men from the local levies, i.e. the *populi*, many of whom likely lacked advanced military training.

After a cold night out in the field, Adalbert and Dietbald led their men against the besiegers in a surprise attack at dawn.[99] Gerhard, who likely was present at Mantahinga with Ulrich, and certainly had access to numerous participants in the battle when obtaining information about what had happened, used the term *phalanx* to denote the force that the two loyal counts led against Arnulf's camp.[100] This term, which was used widely in the classical texts, such as Vergil and Livy that were copied and read in Ottonian schools, meant specifically a military force that was drawn up in close order, that is the phalanx. It is likely, therefore, that Gerhard meant for his audience, which included members of Ulrich's military household who had served at Mantahinga, to understand that

---

98 Ibid.
99 Ibid., *"mane diliculo castra inimicorum invaserunt."*
100 Ibid.

Dietpald and Adalbert deployed their men in the same type of phalanx that Widukind described at the battle of Lenzen.

The surprise was complete, as Arnulf had not prepared his camp for the contingency of an enemy assault. The Bavarian troops were overcome immediately by fear and collapsed into a rout, leaving behind all of their possessions in the camp in an attempt to flee from the Swabians.[101] However, in a demonstration of the good discipline of their force, and the close command and control that Dietpald and Adalbert maintained, the Swabians, including not only the professional soldiers of the counts' military households but also the men of the local levy, maintained their pursuit of the enemy rather than stopping to loot the siege camp.[102] In many battles, the initial success of an attacker was reversed when the commander lost command and control and his men began looting before the enemy was completely defeated.[103] Indeed, in 955, a bit over a year after the events at Mantahinga, Conrad the Red was able to salvage the German position at the Lechfeld by launching an assault on the Hungarians who had stopped to loot Otto's baggage train rather than continue their attack.[104]

The Swabian victory at Mantahinga was absolute. A large part of the Bavarian army was cut down. Arnulf made his escape, but his brother Hermann was captured as were all of the supplies and equipment that had been transported to maintain the siege of Mantahinga. The Swabians suffered relatively light casualties in the assault, but Count Adalbert was wounded by a Bavarian officer named Egilolfus, who subsequently was killed by one of Adalbert's own men named Liutpert. Although Adalbert's wound appeared to be minor (*modicum vulnus*), it became infected and ultimately killed the count.[105] Gerhard records that even the Bavarians who survived the battle faced a difficult time gaining safety because the cold weather did not give them any opportunity to regain their strength, particularly those who had suffered wounds in the fighting.[106]

Ultimately, the battle at Mantahinga turned on better command decisions made by Adalbert and Dietplad as contrasted with Arnulf. The Bavarian count palatine made the classic error of assuming that the enemy was defeated, and did not take the types of precautions that were preached not only in military manuals such as Vegetius' *Epitoma*, and Pseudo-Hyginus' *De munitionibus castrorum*, but also in numerous historical works that circulated widely in the Ottonian kingdom. By contrast, the two Swabian counts took full advantage of the enemy's lack of care by bringing up their force under the cloak of darkness and launching a dawn assault against the unprepared Bavarian camp. Furthermore, Dietpald

---

101   Ibid., "*et repentino timore perculsi relictis spoliis fuga inimicis evadere studuerunt.*"
102   Ibid., "*illis autem eos sequentes.*"
103   For a general observation on this problem, see Bachrach, *Early Carolingian Warfare*, 177.
104   Widukind, *Res gestae*, 3.44.
105   Gerhard of Augsburg, *Vita Uodalrici*, 1.10.
106   Ibid., "*Paucissimi autem eorum ictibus contunsi ac diversis modis vulnerati periculum tamen mortis aequis eorum eos asportantibus eo die vix evaserunt quidam vero eorum gelu miserabiliter astringente nudi in desperatione vitae proprias mansiunculas repetierunt.*"

and Adalbert succeeded in maintaining the discipline of their men after the initial success, and continuing the pursuit of the enemy rather than losing cohesion in the looting of the siege camp. The result was a crushing victory, and the restoration of royal power in Swabia.

Recknitz, 955

Following his victory on the Lechfeld in August, Otto rapidly returned to Saxony and received a detailed report regarding the ongoing struggle against the Obodrites and other Slavic peoples in the region between the lower Elbe and the North Sea.[107] He was particularly concerned about the part played by the rebel Saxon nobles Wichmann the Younger and Eckbert, who led a number of raids against frontier fortifications, including the sack of the frontier fortress of "Cocarescemorium" and the slaughter of the garrison and population that had taken refuge there.[108] Hermann Billung, the commander of the northern march, reported his success in driving off these raiders, but also the failure of Count Thiedrich of Norththuringia's counterstroke against the Obodrites.[109] Gero, whose military command bordered that of Hermann Billung to the south and east, reported on his own successful raid against the Ukrani, one of the neighbors of the Obodrites. [110]

During this period of deliberation, Otto's court was visited by a legation sent by the rulers of the Obodrites who offered a peace agreement to the German king. They would pay the tribute that they customarily owed if, in turn, Otto would guarantee their domination of the regions along the Baltic coast.[111] Such an agreement would be similar to one reached by Charlemagne with the Obodrites during the late eighth century as part of his effort to contain the expanding power of the Danish kings.[112] The leader of the legation added, however, that if Otto would not agree to these terms, the Obodrites would "take up arms to preserve their liberty."[113] Widukind reports that Otto would not accept this offer of peace unless the Obodrites made good all of the losses that they had inflicted on his lands and people, a stipulation that the Obodrites refused to meet.[114]

It is 240 kilometers north-north-east from Magdeburg to the Recknitz river, which rises near Güstrow in Mecklenburg-Vorpommern, and empties into the

---

[107] Widukind, *Res gestae*, 3.53.

[108] Ibid.

[109] Ibid., 3.45. As a result of their participation, these two brothers were condemned as enemies of the *res publica*. See Widukind, *Res gestae*, 3.53.

[110] Ibid., 3.42.

[111] Ibid., 3.53, "Aderat et legatio barbarorum tributa socios ex more velle persolvere nuntians, caeterum dominationem regionis velle tenere."

[112] Regarding Charlemagne's effort to establish the Obodrites as the hegemonial power east of the Elbe as part of a diplomatic strategy to isolate the Danes, see Werner Budesheim, "Der 'limes Saxoniae' nach der Quelle Adams von Bremen, insbesondere in seinem südlichen Abschnitt," in idem (ed.), *Zur slawischen Besiedlung zwischen Elbe und Oder* (Neumünster, 1994), 28-41, here 29-31.

[113] Widukind, *Res gestae*, 3.53, "alioquin pro libertate armis certare."

[114] Ibid.

Baltic sea.[115] As was the case with regard to Henry I's campaign against Lenzen, Otto's march into Obodrite lands required considerable intelligence gathering well before the final decision was made to invade in the summer of 955. The Obodrite lands were well protected by networks of fortifications, many of which were quite massive. The so-called Bavarian Geographer identified no fewer than 53 *civitates* in the lands of the Obodrites in the mid ninth century, more than half of which have been identified to date through archaeological investigations.[116]

A great many of these fortifications were expanded and made more powerful as the population and wealth of the region grew over the course of the ninth and tenth centuries. At Klempenow, for example, archaeologists have located a series of three fortifications that were intended to protect both the salt works that developed at the convergence of the Tollense and Peene rivers, and also the river fords in the region.[117] The central fortification, which had a fortified perimeter of 400 meters, that was further protected by a ditch 10 meters wide, was destroyed in the mid tenth century. A recent excavation has uncovered large numbers of war arrows as well as spears on the site, and its sudden destruction very likely is to be understood the context of Otto's campaign in 955.[118]

In addition to the danger posed to the German line of communications by the numerous Obodrite fortifications, and their garrisons, Otto's staff had to solve the basic problem of finding a suitable line of march for a large army through lands that were both heavily forested and watered by numerous rivers and lakes. Lake Müritz, for example, which is fed by the Elde river, has a surface area of 117 square kilometers, and poses a major barrier to north-south travel. Moreover, the numerous water sources also created extensive swampy or marshy areas through which an army encumbered by an extensive supply train simply could not maneuver.

During Otto's march north, the Obodrites took full advantage of the terrain to harass the German army. One favorite tactic, commented on by Widukind, was the cutting down of trees across the tracks that had been made through forest lands for travel and trading purposes.[119] These makeshift barricades then provided cover for archers who engaged in hit and run tactics against the German army.[120] The use of this type of defensive barrier, known in Old High German as a *Mannhagen*,

---

[115] Ibid., *"Omniaque vastando et incendendo per illas regiones duxit exercitum."* A starting point from Magdeburg is suggested by a number of factors. First, it was the seat of Ottonian administration in the east, and Otto's palace there provided a useful base of operations for the royal court. Second, and just as importantly, Magdeburg was at the hub of a major logistical system with important transportation links to the fiscal resources of the Harz mountain region. Regarding Magdeburg's location at the nexus of a number of important transportation and trading routes, see Henry Mayr-Harting, "The Church of Magdeburg: Its Trade and Its Town in the Tenth and Early Eleventh Centuries," in *Church and City 1000-1500: Essays in Honour of Christopher Brooke*, ed. David Abulafia, Michael Franklin, and Miri Rubin (Cambridge, 1992), 129-150.

[116] Kempke, "Bemerkungen zur Delvenau-Stockitz-Route," 176.

[117] Ulrich, "Der Burgwall von Klempenow, Lkr. Demmin," 29. The fortifications at Klempenow continued to have military significance into the eighteenth century.

[118] For the sudden, catastrophic destruction of the fortification, see ibid., 33.

[119] Widukind, *Res gestae*, 3.53, "a tergo namque [via] arborum robore obstruitur."

[120] Ibid., "eademque armatorum manu vallatur."

was very old, and indeed, numerous place names from the ninth century and later indicate the location of a regulated passage through these man-made barriers.[121]

After several weeks of vigorous campaigning, during the course of which Otto's army inflicted enormous damage on a wide range of Obodrite assets, including the destruction of several fortifications, the Germans arrived at the Recknitz river near the modern town of Ribnitz-Damgarten. Here, they were confronted by a huge army (*ingens exercitus*) commanded by the princes Nacco and Stoignew.[122] The Obodrites had established their fortified camp at the one available ford over the Recknitz. The surrounding areas were made impassable by a large marsh.[123] To make matters even more difficult for Otto's army, the Obodrite commanders had issued orders to fell trees along the route taken by Otto's army so as to prohibit supplies from reaching them.[124]

The German king ordered the establishment of a fortified camp near the banks of the Recknitz, and took several days to prepare his army for what looked like a major battle. In the meantime, however, he dispatched his trusted commander, Margrave Gero, on a diplomatic mission to the Obodrite princes in an effort to broker a peace agreement before committing himself to the dangers of a battle.[125] In taking this tack, Otto was adhering to the Vegetian dictum that battles should be avoided whenever possible, and particularly when the enemy was in a stronger position.[126] Otto's goal was to have Stoignew as an *amicus*, that is, as a client king, which was the basic offer made by the Obodrites earlier in the summer before the campaign had begun.[127] Now, however, the situation was somewhat different. Otto had inflicted considerable damage on the Obodrites, thereby taking just vengeance for their attacks on his frontier fortifications. But the German army was also in a rather difficult situation, at the end of an extended and tenuous supply line, and faced with a determined enemy force that was in a strong defensive position. Negotiations for a peace settlement were now the prudent and acceptable option when the alternative was to risk battle under less than optimal conditions.

Gero, who died in 965 and was very well known at the royal court when Widukind was commissioned to write his history, is described by the corvey monk as

---

[121] Mathias Hardt, "The *Limes Saxoniae* as part of the Eastern Borderlands of the Frankish and Ottonian-Salian Empire," in *Borders, Barriers, and Ethnogenesis: Frontiers in Late Antiquity and the Middle Ages*, ed. Florin Curta (Turnhout, 2005), 35-50, here 44. Also see Franz Engel, "Die Mittelalterliche 'Mannhagen' und das Problem des Limes Saxoniae," *Blätter für deutsche Landesgeschichte* 88 (1951), 73-109.

[122] Widukind, *Res gestae*, 3.53.

[123] Ibid., "*fluvius fluvioque contigua palus.*"

[124] Ibid.

[125] Ibid., "*mittitur ad principem barbarorum, qui dicebatur Stoinef, Gero comes, quatinus imperatori se dedat: amicum per id adepturum, non hostem experturum.*"

[126] Vegetius, *Epitoma*, 3.9.

[127] Widukind, *Res gestae*, 3.53, says explicitly that Otto sent Gero to Stoignew to gain him as an *amicus*. As seen above, Widukind used this term, when describing the relationships among rulers, to denote the Roman idea of a client.

particularly apt for this diplomatic mission. The frontier commander was a man of many parts, learned in war, well schooled in public affairs, well spoken, knowledgeable on many subjects, and apt to demonstrate his prudence through actions rather than words.[128] Gero's task was either to make an arrangement that would lead to a *pax*, or to provoke the enemy to give up its strong defensive position and meet at a designated place for a battle. When it became clear that Stoignew understood the strength of his position, Gero withdrew.[129]

After Gero had made his report, and it was clear that Otto either had to fight a battle against a foe that was ensconced in a strong defensive position, or attempt to withdraw in the face of consistent enemy harassment, while being followed by a large enemy force. Neither choice was a good one. The dangerous tactical situation was the result of two factors. First, Otto's decision to inflict the maximum possible damage on the Obodrites had caused him to lead the army to the end of a tenuous line of communications. Secondly, the Obodrite princes had been able to take advantage of their knowledge of the terrain to mobilize a large army at the right place to establish a very strong tactical position. The battle of the Recknitz ultimately was made necessary because the Obodrites had obtained and put to use better intelligence than had the Germans.

Otto and his commanders understood that the current situation was untenable. The army would soon run out of supplies if it remained in place, blockaded both to the front and rear. They also decided that retreating in the face of the Obodrite army posed greater dangers than would attacking the enemy force and driving them off. The problem would be devising a plan that would mitigate or even eliminate the enormous advantage that the Obodrites had as long as they remained on the tactical defensive, protecting a relatively narrow ford across the river and swamp.

Frontinus, in his *Strategemata*, a copy of which Otto had received from his brother Brun, dealt explicitly with the issue of "leading the army through an area occupied by enemy forces."[130] One major category consisted of examples of generals who had been able to maneuver around an enemy force that occupied a strong defensive position along the army's line of march. This included several examples of crossing a river in the face of an enemy that occupied the opposite bank.[131]

The basic principle indicated by these historical examples is that the attacking force requires an element of misdirection so that the defenders focus their attention on the wrong place, while the attacking army effects its river crossing. Frontinus explains, for example, that when Alexander the Great was blocked from crossing a river by the Indian king Porus, the Macedonian general had his men undertake several mock crossings in the face of the Indians. The repeated

---

128 Widukind, *Res gestae*, 3.54, "*bellandi peritia, in rebus civilibus bona consilia, satis eloquentiae, multum scientiae, et qui prudentiam suam opere ostenderet quam ore.*"
129 Ibid., 3.54, "*irrisit Geronem imperatoremque et omnem exercitum, sciens eum multis molestiis aggravatum.*"
130 Frontinus, *Strategemata*, 1.4. the title of which is "*De transducendo exercitu per loca hosti infesta*".
131 Ibid., 1.4.8-10.

false attacks led the defenders to concentrate their forces along the part of the bank where Alexander had stationed his decoy forces. Once the Indians were committed, Alexander led a different column of troops to make a rapid crossing away from the Indian army.[132]

Obviously, no tactical situation is exactly identical to another, and students of Frontinus' text would not be able to look through it to find a precise set of procedures to solve a particular tactical problem. However, as Frontinus himself pointed out in the introduction to his *Strategemata*, by reading what other commanders had done in the past, the intelligent commander would be able to develop his own techniques that drew upon the principles that were illustrated in earlier successful operations. It is in this context that Widukind's description of Otto's plan of action is to be understood.

First, Otto ordered the deployment of his archers and artillery (*ingenia*) at the ford opposite the Obodrite host. They were to assault the enemy from a distance with two objectives in mind. If possible, Otto hoped to provoke the enemy to launch an attack across the ford against his own fortified encampment.[133] If this tactic were successful, the Obodrites would give up the tactical advantage of remaining on the defense, accepting heavy casualties as they advanced across the narrow ford, and then being forced to assault Otto's strong defensive position. However, even if the Obodrites remained disciplined, and refused Otto's gambit, the German king hoped that by deploying his own forces as if he were intending to launch his own attack, he would lead the Obodrites to focus their attention on the ford.[134] As it turned out, the Obodrites did not break their own defensive formation, but they were completely fooled by Otto's feigned attack, keeping all of their forces stationed directly across the river from the German camp.[135]

As he had planned, Otto then dispatched Gero with a substantial force, which included Slavic allies, the Ranen, a mile up-river from the ford, to construct three pontoon bridges that could be used to effect an uncontested crossing to obviate the Obodrites' defensive position.[136] The rapid construction of these bridges by Gero points to the important role that the combat engineers played in the battle of the Recknitz. It is highly unlikely that Gero's force cut down hundreds of trees, securely bound them together, and deployed them with the appropriate stabilizing elements to permit the rapid crossing of a river by men mounted on horses. First, such a construction project would have taken a considerable amount of time, and almost certainly would have been discovered by the Obodrites before being completed. Second, the physical act of cutting down hundreds of trees would have made an enormous amount of noise, which simply could not have been hidden from the enemy army located just a mile distant.

[132] Ibid., 1.4.9.
[133] Widukind, *Res gestae*, 3.54.
[134] Ibid., "*et quasi vi flumen paludemque transcendere velle.*"
[135] Ibid., "*iter totis viribus defendentes.*"
[136] Widukind, *Res gestae*, 3.54.

Rather, it is clear that Otto's army was equipped with a substantial quantity of pre-fabricated materials for the construction of pontoon bridges that were designed for rapid deployment. The preparation of these kinds of materials for campaigns is well attested in narrative sources, and also is described in considerable detail in the military handbooks that were copied by the Carolingians and Ottonians for the education of future officers. The author of the *Vita* of Louis the Pious, for example, noted that when the young king was preparing for a campaign against Barcelona, his advisors suggested that boats be constructed which would be cut into four pieces so that each piece could be carried over land in carts. When the army came to a river, the boats could be reassembled rapidly, and allow the troops to cross even when no bridges, fords, or local shipping could be located.[137]

The author of the military handbook *De rebus bellicis*, which was copied at the Carolingian court during Charlemagne's reign, emphasized the importance of bringing animal bladders, and bags made of animal skins, to make flotation devices that were necessary for the construction of pontoon bridges.[138] Vegetius emphasized that military forces should carry with them hollowed out logs (*scaphae*), as well as large quantities of rope and even chains. After binding together these prefabricated supports, it would be a simple matter, as Vegetius emphasizes, for the army to secure planks or logs across the top, and create a bridge that could be crossed safely by both foot soldiers and cavalry.[139] Finally, it should be noted that capitulary *de villis*, whose requirements for the management of estates exerted considerable influence on Ottonian fiscal resources, required that each royal estate have on hand wagons (*basternae*) which were specially constructed for war. Of the utmost importance was that they be made watertight so that they could be swum across rivers.[140]

Once Gero had succeeded in constructing the three pontoon bridges, he sent a messenger back to Otto to let him know that the operation to cross the river could now proceed. Otto then dispatched a large force of mounted troops who sped as rapidly as possible to the bridges to cross the river. Stoignew, who had taken up his position in a command post on a high hill that overlooked the river valley, immediately realized that Otto had tricked him and had found another

---

[137] Astronomer, *Vita Hludowici*, ch. 15.

[138] Anonymous, *De rebus bellicis*, ed. Robert I. Ireland (Leipzig, 1984), ch. 16.

[139] Vegetius, *Epitoma*, 2.25.

[140] Capitularia n. 32 ch. 64, "*Ut carra nostra quae in hostem pergunt basternae bene factae sint, et operculi bene sint cum coriis cooperti, et ita sint consuti, ut, si necessitas evenerit aquas natandum, cum ipsa expensa quae intus fuerit transire flumina possint, ut nequaquam aqua intus intrare valeat et bene salva causa nostra, sicut diximus, transire possit.*" On the influence of the capitulary *de villis* on the management of both East Frankish and Ottonian fiscal properties during the ninth and tenth centuries, see the discussion by Carlrichard Brühl, *Fodrum, Gistum, Servitium Regis: Studien zu den wirtschaftlichen Grundlagen des Königtums in Frankenreich und in den fränkischen Nachfolgestaaten Deutschland, Frankreich und Italien vom 6. bis zur Mitte des 14. Jahrhunderts* vol. 1 (Cologne and Graz, 1968), 68; Gockel, *Karolingische Königshöfe am Mittelrhein*, 27; Wolfgang Metz, *Zur Erforschung des karolingischen Reichsgutes* (Darmstadt, 1971), 21; and the recent synthesis of the scholarship on this topic by Bachrach, "The Written Word," 399-423.

point at which to cross the river. He dispatched troops to counter Otto's forces, but since the majority of the Obodrites were on foot (*pedites*) and the Germans were mounted, the Slavs were not able to match the speed of the German troops. As a consequence, Gero's bridgehead was reinforced by a substantial number of Otto's best trained *milites* before the Obodrites arrived, tired out and disorganized from their run. The subsequent battle at the pontoon bridges was brief, as Otto's mounted troops defeated the Obodrite foot soldiers and routed them. During this retreat, a large number of the Obodrites were cut down from behind.[141] Otto then advanced across the ford and captured the enemy camp.[142]

The aftermath of the battle was very bloody, as Otto determined that it was necessary to inflict a massive punishment on the enemy in a manner consistent with his execution of the Hungarian leaders following the battle on the Lech. Stoignew, who attempted to flee with his bodyguards once he realized that the battle had been lost, was tracked down by an officer named Hosed, who killed him. Hosed then decapitated the Obodrite prince and received a magnificent reward of twenty *mansi* from Otto for his service.[143] Following the capture of the Obodrite camp, Otto ordered the execution of 700 prisoners, and Widukind records that the killing went on far into the night. In addition, Otto ordered that Stoignew's advisors have their eyes and tongues ripped out, and then be tossed onto the pile of the dead.[144] The ultimate result of this victory was the subjugation of the Obodrites for the next 27 years, and the imposition of a network of Ottonian fortifications and garrisons throughout their lands. The establishment in 968 of the bishopric of Oldenburg, 90 kilometers south-east of the battle site, over the Obodrite settlement of Stargard, was an exceptionally clear signal of the overwhelming nature of Otto's victory.[145]

The plan used by Otto at the battle of the Recknitz again make clear the vital importance of having available forces with a variety of tactical capabilities. Obviously, the siege equipment (*ingenia*) and engineers who served in the army played an important role during the campaign in destroying the Obodrite infrastructure of fortifications. However, at the battle itself, the engineers not only provided crucial help in establishing an alternative crossing point for the army, but also helped to fix the attention of Stoignew on the ford through the deployment of their *ingenia* while the pontoon bridges were being constructed. The mounted forces deployed by Otto also played an important role in the battle, as their relatively greater speed over men on foot over short distances gave Gero a decisive advantage during the battle at the bridgehead. Finally, Otto's forces at the ford,

---

[141] Widukind, *Res gestae*, 3.54, "*Pedites barbarorum dum longiorem viam currunt et certamen ineunt, fatigatione dissoluti militibus citius cedunt; nec mora, dum fugae presidium quaeerunt, obtrunctantur.*"

[142] Ibid., "*eo die castra hostium invasa.*"

[143] Ibid., 3.55.

[144] Ibid.

[145] Regarding the establishment of the bishopric at Oldenburg, see Dietrich Kurze, "Christianisierung und Kirchenorganisation zwischen Elbe und Oder," *Jahrbuch des Diözesangeschichtsvereins Berlin* 30/31 (1990-1991), 11-30, here 14.

which appear to have consisted largely of foot soldiers, served as an important decoy during the initial stages of the battle, and then provided the manpower that was necessary to capture the enemy's fortified camp (*castra*).

The Tactics of Defense in Depth

As Charles Bowlus has demonstrated in his masterful account of the aftermath of the battle of the Lechfeld (955), the Hungarian army that faced Otto I on 10 August withdrew in good order from the field.[146] Over the next several days, however, the large Hungarian army was cut to pieces through the coordinated efforts of Otto's field army and the local levies, the latter having been mobilized for service when the Hungarians first crossed the Enns river in late July.[147] When word spread of the Hungarian advance across the Danube's right tributaries, including the Inn and Isar, local defense forces now behind the enemy army poured into *Fluchtburgen* and also fortifications that sat astride the Hungarian line of communications.[148] Many of these fortifications had served the Bavarian system of defense in depth since the late ninth century during the ongoing conflicts with the Moravians.[149]

On the evening of 10 August, the day of the battle, torrential rains began to fall and lasted for several days. The rivers that the Hungarians had crossed rather easily on their advance to Augsburg were now swollen and their routes home were severely constrained. They could only travel along narrow paths that were located above the level of the river floodplains. These were precisely the areas where the Carolingian kings, Bavarian dukes, and subsequently Ottonian kings had developed and maintained their systems of rural fortresses.[150] The Hungarian troops, now suffering from cold and wet, and being pursued by Otto's army, were forced to run a gauntlet of fortifications, filled with local men of the levies. As Gerhard of Augsburg, who was an eyewitness to the battle on the Lech observed, immediately after the battle was over, Otto sent out additional orders to keep a close guard on the fords and ferry crossings, and to kill any Hungarians who attempted to cross.[151]

---

[146] Bowlus, *The Battle of Lechfeld*, 131. Gerhard of Augsburg, *Vita Uodalrici*, 1.12, observed that despite the heavy losses suffered by the Hungarians in the battle against Otto, so many remained that the soldiers watching from the walls of Augsburg thought that they had not been in a battle at all, i.e. *non pugna lacessatos eos redire astimaverunt*.

[147] See Leyser, "The Battle at the Lech," 62, who stressed the importance of the attacks on the Hungarians after the battle as being decisive for achieving victory.

[148] Ekkehard of St Gall described the system of fire signals, using lamps, that were in use in Swabia to alert local populations about the enemy attacks with specific reference to preparations for Hungarian depredations. See Ekkehard, *Casus Sancti Galli*, 136.

[149] Auer, "Zum Kriegswesen unter den früheren Babenbergern," 10-13.

[150] See the discussion in Bowlus, *The Battle of Lechfeld*, 76-88, for the military topography of Bavaria. Regarding the numerous fortifications that were constructed to serve in the Bavarian system of defense in depth, see Mitterauer, "Burgbezirke und Burgwerkleistung," 217-231; Büttner, "Die Wehrorganisation der frühen Babenbergerzeit im Einzelhofgebiet der Bezirke Melk und Scheibbs"; and Auer, "Zum Kriegswesen unter den früheren Babenbergern," 10-13

[151] Gerhard of Augsburg, *Vita Uodalrici*, 1.12.

In his account of these events, Widukind emphasized that some of the Hungarians, whose horses were worn out, attempted to take refuge in nearby villages the evening after the battle, but were then cut down by armed men of the local militia, or burned alive in the buildings in which they took refuge.[152] In the days following the battle, many more the Hungarian troops were killed in battles at the fortifications they had to pass along the routes back to Pannonia.[153] Still others drowned attempting to cross the swollen rivers while avoiding the fords that were held against them.[154] The end result was the virtual annihilation of an army that had retreated in good order from the field of battle, having fought Otto the Great to a draw on the field.

In the north-east, the system of defense in depth that protected Thuringia and eastern Saxony scored similar successes. As noted above in the context of the Riade campaign of 933, one column of Hungarian troops was annihilated by local levies during a failed raid into Thuringia. In a similar manner, at the beginning of Otto's reign, in 937, the system of defense in depth, that had been developed by Henry I in the region between the Saale and Elbe scored a similar victory over the Hungarians.[155] The Hungarian attack, which was intended to test the mettle of the young king, was an utter failure. As the annals of Quedlinburg put it, "they [the Hungarians] died in the swampy areas and in other difficult locations.[156] The author of the *Annals of Einsiedeln* concurred, although he dated the raid to 938, emphasizing that a large number of Hungarians were killed by the Saxons.[157]

Ekkehard of St Gall, who drew upon much earlier but no longer extant narrative sources, provides a detailed image of the defense of the region around his monastery against the Hungarians in 924 that sheds considerable light on the tactics use by local levies that made the Ottonian system of defense in depth so effective.[158] Ekkehard emphasized that when the Hungarians arrived in the region of St Gall, the local population took refuge in fortifications.[159] These *Fluchtburgen* posed a substantial problem for the Hungarians, who lacked sophisticated siege engines, or often even simple siege ladders, until their campaign against Augsburg in 955. The danger for the Hungarians was particularly acute when large numbers of people had taken refuge within the walls, providing a robust defense force equipped not only with simple pole weapons, but bows as well. However, simply protecting the population was not sufficient to inflict heavy losses on the mounted archers.

---

[152] Widukind, *Res gestae*, 3.46.
[153] Ibid., "*secundo die ac tertio a vicinis urbibus reliqua multitudo in tantum consumpta est, ut nullus aut rarus evaderet.*"
[154] Ibid.
[155] Widukind, *Res gestae*, 2.5.
[156] *Annales Quedlinburgenses, an. 937,* "*In eadem tempestate venientes Ungari vastaverunt Thuringiam, deinde in Saxoniam, ibique in paludibus caeterisque difficultatibus perierunt.*" *Annales Einsiedelnensis,* 141, dates this raid to 938, but concurs that "*Interim magna pars Ungarorum a Saxonibus occisa est.*"
[157] *Annales Einsiedelnensis* MGH SS 3, 141.
[158] Ekkehard, *Casus Sancti Galli,* 120-122.
[159] Ibid.

While the non-combatants were protected in fortifications, local men gathered at predetermined locations, and prepared to launch attacks on the Hungarians when the opportunity permitted. The local defenders were aided not only by their knowledge of the local terrain, but also by a well developed communications system. In the region around St Gall, the locals (*villani*) pre-positioned both oil lamps and operators to provide information about the location of the enemy, and to summon fighters to mobilize.[160]

In describing the tactics used by the local defense forces against the Hungarians, Ekkehard mentions specifically a man named Irminger living in Frickgau who took a leading role in the events of 924.[161] He was not a magnate (*vir non adeo praepotens*), but he was brave and strong, leading Ekkehard to compare him to Mathathias and his six sons, including Judah the Maccabee.

Irminger recognized that the Hungarians, who had come to attack the island monastery of Säckingen, were separated from the main force.[162] He realized that his men could not hope to defeat the Hungarians in a direct confrontation. Instead, he relied on his familiarity with the local region to keep close watch on the invaders without allowing his own forces to be seen. Irminger then struck when there was an opportunity to inflict losses on the enemy with the least possible danger to his own men. During their raiding, the Hungarians had acquired a considerable quantity of booty, including wine. One night, when the raiders were drunk, Irminger organized his force into three groups, and launched an attack on the Hungarian camp on three sides. They killed almost all of the Hungarians except those who succeeded in swimming across the Rhine.[163] Irminger and his men then took the spoils they had taken and triumphantly placed them in the local church and made a progress through all of the local forts to show what they had accomplished.[164]

Irminger even took the offensive beyond his local region, seeking to attack the Hungarians on the other side of the Rhine. Knowing that all of the ships along his stretch of the river had been taken for the defense of the island of Reichenau, he called up his neighbors to bring their own ships and build a bridge so that he could lead the men to the other side, and defeat the Hungarians.[165] In the meantime, however, the Hungarians, who had been worn down by the locals, gathered numerous ships on their side of the Rhine, and advanced into Alsace. There,

---

[160] Ibid., 136, "Nam et villani quidam praedocti, ollis prunes in proximo monte paratas habentes, tumulto audito faces accensas levabant et ut discretionem sociorum et hostium nossent, quasi perlustrium fecerant."
[161] Ibid.
[162] Ibid.
[163] Ibid.
[164] Ibid., 136-8, "At Irminger cums suis spolia in facie hostium collecta basilice triumphans intulit et per omnes circumquaque munitiones dispertivit."
[165] Ibid. ,138, "Et quia naves praeter eius urbis defensaculo subductas nullas in Rheni viciniis sciverat, suadebat urbanis navibus ipsis pontibus iunctis armadas legiones transponere, se duce, qui illorum mores in armis iam nosset, quantocius confligere."

they were confronted by Liutfrid, a *potentissimus* of the region, and won a bloody victory over his forces in a set-piece battle.[166]

The men of the local militia in 924 were augmented by professional military forces that were deployed by local magnates. One of the *Fluchtburgen* that the Hungarians came upon during their raid was manned, in part, by household troops of Abbot Engilbert of St Gall.[167] The abbot, monks, and entire household of St Gall had withdrawn to a forest stronghold (*castellum*) when scouts (*exploratores*) had brought word that an overwhelming force of Hungarians was coming near.[168] The Hungarians did sack the monastery, and then sent out scouts of their own to locate the local population, and particularly the high value abbot and monks. In short order, the Hungarian scouts located the *castellum* in the forest, but realized that assaulting the stronghold would cost far too many casualties. The well designed gate could only be approached along a narrow path that was protected by a wall of the *castellum*. In addition, the garrison was very large. Consequently, as long as the defenders were well supplied with food, the Hungarians had no hope of capturing the site.[169]

When the Hungarians withdrew Engilbert ordered his scouts to shadow them, and to provide information to the remainder of the garrison that followed along behind. At opportune moments during the pursuit Engilbert's troops attacked the Hungarian rear-guard, killing some of them, and even taking a prisoner for questioning.[170] When the Hungarians realized that they were being pursued by a substantial force, their commander ordered the entire column to halt in an open field and construct a makeshift fortification of their own with vehicles, and other equipment that they had brought with them or captured during their raid.[171] Rather than press the attack against the Hungarians, Engilbert was content to have driven them from his lands, and to dispatch most of his troops back to the *castellum*, while he went back to the monastery of St Gall to inspect the damage there.[172]

The Hungarian raid in 924 was quite destructive, but the efforts of the Hungarians to take very large numbers of captives were blunted by the effective defense of *Fluchtburgen*. In addition, the Hungarians suffered significant casualties from the hit and run tactics employed by both local levies, and the professional soldiers who were employed by regional magnates such as Abbot Engilbert

---

[166] Ibid., "*Dum hec sataguntur, navibus Ungri de Swarzwalde multis paratis in Alsatiam ipsi priores suas legiones transponunt et a Liutfrido quodam, terre illius potentissimo, bello suscepti plurimo dampno sui tandem cruentam victoriam sunt adepti.*"

[167] Ekkehard, *Casus Sancti Galli*, 120-2, "*Castellum cum armatis legionibus obfirmatum.*"

[168] Ibid., 116.

[169] Ibid., 120, "*locum autem longo collo et artissimo impugnantibus maximo damno certoque periculo adibilem, tutores eius sue multitudini, dum victualia haberant, modo viri sint, nunquam cessuros.*"

[170] Ibid., 122, "*quosdam occidunt, unum autem vulneratum captum aveunt.*"

[171] Ibid., 122, "*alacriter instruentes vehiculis et ceteris impedimentis circumpositis noctem vigiliis partiuntur.*"

[172] Ibid., "*At Engilbertus, hostium invasionis primicerius, castellum repetere ceteris dimissis, cum paucis aeque audacibus monasterium vitabundus inambulat.*"

of St Gall. The major difference between the relative success of the Hungarians in 924 and their annihilation in 955 was the presence in the field of a major royal army, which crushed the mounted archers like a hammer against the anvil of the local system of defense in depth. In 924, Henry I was fighting off a Hungarian invasion of Thuringia, and could not provide support to the Swabian defense efforts. By contrast, Otto I not only broke the Hungarian siege of Augsburg, but pursued his enemy relentlessly after the battle on the Lech.

Conclusion

For the most part, Ottonian armies engaged in battles in the field only in the context of siege warfare. At Lenzen, Riade, and Mantahinga, the battles were the result of an effort to force the end of a siege. Similarly, Prince Stoignew's army on the Recknitz river was intent on ending Otto's campaign of destruction against the Obodrite infrastructure, including fortifications that were captured and burned by the Otto's army. As a consequence of the strategic importance of siege warfare, Ottonian armies were dominated numerically by foot soldiers, who were required in large numbers whether an enemy stronghold was to be taken by direct assault, or starved into submission.

However, Henry I, Otto I, and their military commanders were well aware of the importance of maintaining tactical flexibility in case a battle in the field became necessary or desirable. For this reason, Ottonian armies, including those that were deployed specifically to carry out siege operations, included contingents of mounted forces. At Lenzen, these mounted troops played a crucial part in the defeat of the Redarii by exploiting an opening in the enemy's flank and wrecking the cohesion of the enemy's infantry phalanx. Similarly at the battle on the Recknitz, the speed of the mounted troops provided a crucial advantage against the Obodrites who lacked a significant cavalry component. At Riade, the cavalry played the central role in the inconclusive fighting against the Hungarians.

It was the combination of well trained mounted troops and foot soldiers that made the Ottonian armies effective in battle. The successful cavalry charge at Lenzen was made possible by an infantry phalanx that was able to advance against an enemy that was established in a strong defensive position. Similarly, the deployment of a flying column of mounted troops on the Recknitz was made possible by both the infantry phalanx that held the Obodrite attention at the ford, and also a skillful team of combat engineers who rapidly constructed three pontoon bridges. Even at Riade, Henry I's plan depended upon combining the swiftness of the Thuringian light cavalry with the close order effectiveness of his heavily armed *loricati*.

The tactical flexibility that was the hallmark of Ottonian field armies also can be seen in the context of the system of defense-in-depth that was organized in Bavaria, Swabia, Thuringia and Saxony, which were subjected to intensive raiding by the Hungarians. Here, local levies, which did not have sufficient arms or training to defeat the Hungarians on their own, utilized guerilla tactics to wear down the invaders. However, when a substantial royal army was in the vicinity, as in 955, these same local levies garrisoned numerous fortifications and inflicted heavy casualties on the Hungarians as the latter sought to escape. The well armed and trained professional forces of the king and his magnates, for their part, depended on the local levies to herd the fast-moving Hungarians into killing zones, where they would be forced to fight.

8

Campaign Strategy: The Civil War of 953–954

Fundamental to Ottonian campaign strategy over the long term, particularly in the context of territorial conquest, was the capture and defense of fortifications. Of the dozens of major military operations undertaken by Henry I, Otto I, and their commanders over a period of half a century, a bare handful took place outside the context of a siege.[1] The civil war of 953–954 is particularly illuminating regarding the strategic thinking of Ottonian leaders because the leaders on both sides shared a common understanding of the nature of warfare. In particular, a close analysis of the campaigns over this two-year period will make clear the fundamental appreciation by Otto, his brothers Brun and Henry, his son Liudolf, son-in-law Conrad the Red, and Arnulf, count palatine of Bavaria, that control over major fortifications, and denying these assets to the enemy were fundamental to achieving their strategic goals.

Siege warfare, even more so than battles in the field, required the deployment of very large armies. In order to storm a strongly held enemy fortress an attacker required four to five men for every defender.[2] The military planners who were responsible for developing the garrison strengths in Alfred the Great's Wessex (died 899) concluded that the optimal ratio was one defender for approximately 1.3 meters of wall.[3] In light of the fundamental continuity in military technology between the late ninth and tenth century, as well as the broad diffusion of all types of weapons on both sides of the English Channel, it is very likely that Ottonian military planners came to the same basic conclusions. An effort will be made in this chapter, therefore, to calculate the size of the armies deployed by Otto I during his sieges of the great fortress cities of Mainz and Regensburg.

---

[1] See Appendix.

[2] A detailed analysis of the required ratios of attackers to defenders, which takes into account the volume of fire provided by both long-range projectile weapons, and hand- held arms, is provided by Bernard S. Bachrach and Rutherford Aris, "Military Technology and Garrison Organization: Some Observations on Anglo-Saxon Military Thinking in Light of the Burghal Hidage," *Technology and Culture* 31 (1990), 1-17; reprinted in Bernard S. Bachrach, *Warfare and Military Organization in Pre-Crusade Europe* (London, 2002), with the same pagination.

[3] For a useful introduction to many of the questions regarding the origin, size, and organization of the defensive scheme described in the Burghal Hidage, see the collection of essays in David Hill and Alexander R. Rumble, eds. *The Defence of Wessex: The Burghal Hidage and Anglo-Saxon Fortifications* (Manchester, 1996).

The deployment of large armies to undertake sieges brought concomitantly large logistical requirements, and the necessity for detailed military planning to assure that troops received sufficient quantities of food in a timely manner. As seen in the previous chapter, in wars beyond the frontiers of the Ottonian kingdom, it was necessary to develop information about the location and quality of roads, potential water routes, natural obstacles, and enemy fortifications. By contrast, in the case of the civil war of 953-954, this information was readily available to both sides through direct experience of, for example, the royal itinerary, or from informants who could be summoned quite easily to court. So too was information about the location and quantities of food and fodder that were stored on both royal fiscal estates, and church lands.

The Road to War

Otto I's invasion of Italy in 951 brought considerable initial military success. When he left the peninsula in February 952, it appeared that Conrad the Red, Otto's son-in-law and duke of Lotharingia, would be able to complete the conquest of Italy without much difficulty.[4] However, the defeat of the Italian King Berengar II, and Otto's decision to marry Adelheid, the sister of King Conrad of Burgundy, led to a significant rupture in the amicable relationships among Otto, his son Liudolf, and Conrad the Red. The latter two saw themselves as threatened by a new axis at the royal court, turning on Adelheid, whatever male offspring she might bear to the thirty-eight year old Otto, and Henry, the king's younger brother and duke of Bavaria.[5] The decisive point motivating Liudolf and Conrad to challenge Otto I may have been the decision by the king at his Easter court in 952 to reject the peace agreement that the duke of Lotharingia had arranged with Berengar. The scuttling of this agreement was largely seen as the work of Duke Henry of Bavaria, who hoped to gain control of the trans-alpine march of Verona and Aquileia.[6] Conrad saw Henry's intervention as fundamentally usurping his own role as the king's leading advisor.[7] Liudolf, for his part, was threatened not only by Henry's gains in Italy, at the expense of his own interests as duke of Swabia, but also by his uncle's efforts to promote the forthcoming children of Adelheid, who was now pregnant, as Otto's heirs.[8]

Nevertheless, in the initial stages of their conspiracy against Otto I's government, it is clear that Liudolf and Conrad the Red hoped to reach a peaceful

---

4   Adalbert of Magdeburg, *Continuatio, an.* 952.
5   Regarding Liudolf's belief that he was going to be superseded by his step-mother Adelheid and her future children, and his subsequent decision to rebel against his father, see Wolf, "De pactis Ottonis I". This view is based largely on the statement by Flodoard, *Annales, an.* 953, that Otto I had his magnates swear an oath of loyalty to his newborn son with Adelheid, a boy named Henry.
6   This was the interpretation of Adalbert of Magdeburg, *Continuatio, an.* 952, who was part of the royal court and had access to many of the key decision makers in the king's entourage.
7   Adalbert of Magdeburg, *Continuatio, an.* 952.
8   Wolf, "De pactis Ottonis I.," 33-48.

resolution of their grievances, and to convince the king to change his policies without resorting to war.[9] When Otto came to Mainz in late March to confer with Archbishop Frederick, the two dukes quickly brought considerable military forces into the city and presented the king with their demands.[10] Otto felt compelled to agree, but was then permitted to depart, indicating that Liudolf and Conrad had no interest in overthrowing the king, but rather were motivated by a desire to remove Duke Henry's influence at court.[11]

Nevertheless, as several contemporary chroniclers make clear, both Conrad and Liudolf took considerable precautions to ensure that the fortifications that they held through their ducal offices in Lotharingia and Swabia were garrisoned and provisioned.[12] Conrad also saw to the strengthening of the fortifications that were constructed on the lands that were owned by his family. This included the fortress that the Conradine family long had maintained within the city of Worms.[13] As Otto's actions during the rebellions of 938–939 had made clear, if war were to come, the dukes were aware that the king would focus his efforts on capturing all of the rebels' strongholds.

Despite his apparent acceptance of the demands made by Conrad and Liudolf at Mainz, Otto had no intention of bending to the wills of his son and son-in-law. Otto first made a brief trip to Aachen. Widukind records that Otto went to Aachen with the royal court, but did not stay there to celebrate Easter because nothing had been prepared for him.[14] This observation is quite important in the context of military logistics, as it illuminates the need for advance preparation even at a site such as Aachen, which was enormously well endowed with fiscal income.[15]

Following the diversion to Aachen, Otto led the court to the royal estate of Dortmund in Saxony, where he was joined by his mother Mathilda and his brother Henry.[16] Undoubtedly, this journey was preceded by instructions for the estate managers at Dortmund to prepare for a large gathering. Otto celebrated Easter at Dortmund on 3 April, and ordered that preparations be made for an assembly to be held at the royal estate of Fritzlar. Before traveling to Fritzlar, however, Otto made a very rapid trip to the royal convent of

---

9   Helmut Naumann, "Rätsel des letzten Aufstandes gegen Otto I. (953-954)," *Archiv für Kulturge-schichte* 46 (1964), 133-184, here 150.

10   Widukind, *Res gestae*, 3.13; Adalbert of Magdeburg, *Continuatio, an.* 953.

11   Widukind, Res gestae, 3.13; Adalbert of Magdeburg, *Continuatio,* an. 953.

12   Regarding Conrad's efforts to secure his strongholds, see Ruotger, *Vita Brunonis,* ch. 10; and Adalbert of Magdeburg, *Continuatio, an.* 953.

13   Regarding Conrad's possession of Worms as late as January 954, see Widukind, *Res gestae,* 3.30. The Conradine fortification at Worms remained in the family's possession, despite Conrad the Red's rebellion in 953, until the episcopate of Burchard of Worms in the early eleventh century. See *Vita Burchardi episcopi,* ch. 7.

14   Widukind, *Res gestae,* 3.14.

15   At this date, the church of St Mary at Aachen received one-ninth of the revenues of 50 royal estates. See DH I, 23 and DO I, 323. Also see the discussion by Bachrach, "The Written Word," 413-16.

16   Widukind, *Res gestae,* 3.14.

Quedlinburg, some 300 kilometers to the east of Dortmund, where he issued a charter on 21 April on behalf of Bishop Baldric of Utrecht.[17] During his journey to Quedlinburg, and while there, Otto likely issued additional orders for the assembly to take place at Fritzlar, and also orders for the mobilization of Saxon, and perhaps Thuringian forces in case it became necessary to take military action against Liudolf and Conrad.

From Quedlinburg, Otto, who was accompanied by his brother Brun, traveled some 180 kilometers south-west to Fritzlar, where his father had been raised as king in 919.[18] At the Fritzlar assembly, which could not have taken place much earlier than the last week of April given the distance that the king had to travel from Quedlinburg, Otto secured the loyalty of his Saxon, Thuringian, and Franconian magnates, and removed Conrad as duke of Lotharingia.[19] The die was now cast, and the civil war was about to begin.

Lotharingia: Spring of 953

Once Otto had made his decision to depose Conrad, a number of very important stratego-political issues came to the fore. In 939, during the revolt by Dukes Gislebert and Eberhard of Lotharingia and Franconia, as well as Otto's brother Henry, King Louis IV of West Francia had intervened on behalf of the rebels, going so far as to bring an army into Lotharingia.[20] Louis clearly hoped on that occasion to use the civil war in Germany to bring the ancestral Carolingian lands under his control just as his father, Charles *Simplex*, had done in 911. It was only the fortuitous, from Otto's standpoint, death in battle of dukes Gislebert and Eberhard at Andernach that ended the rebellion and blunted Louis's efforts. The political situation had changed considerably since 939. Louis was now married to Otto's sister Gerberga, and the German king had saved Louis's throne in 946. However, from Otto's perspective, the danger of Louis's intervention either on behalf of Conrad, or in his own direct interest remained a clear threat.[21]

This concern might have seemed particularly urgent as Conrad had developed a strong working relationship with Louis IV over the previous five years. It was Conrad, as duke of Lotharingia, who had commanded the Lotharingian expeditionary levies that were dispatched to aid Louis against Hugh the Great in 948 and 949.[22] In 950, Conrad again led the Lotharingian expeditionary levy into West Francia, now working with both Louis and Hugh the Great against rebels in the region of Rheims. The next year, in 951, Conrad, again working in

[17]   DO I, 164.
[18]   Widukind, *Res gestae*, 3.16.
[19]   Widukind, *Res gestae*, 3.16.
[20]   Flodoard, *Annales, an.* 939.
[21]   Widukind, *Res gestae*, 1.29, made this point when he observed that, up the time when he was writing, i.e. the late 960s, there was still conflict between the Carolingians and the rulers of East Francia regarding control over Lotharingia.
[22]   Flodoard, *Annales, ann.* 948 and 949.

conjunction with Louis, banned Lotharingian magnates, who also held lands in West Francia, from constructing fortifications in the latter kingdom without the license of the Carolingian king.[23]

After the assembly at Fritzlar stripped Conrad of his ducal office, Otto intended to break the erstwhile duke's rebellion in Lotharingia, and eliminate the potential for mischief by Louis IV. This was to be done by securing control over all of the fortifications and fortress cities in Lotharingia. The German king also intended to seize Conrad's family possessions in Franconia. This strategy was consistent with what might be termed the Ottonian military doctrine that wars of conquest necessarily involved gaining control over fortifications as a first step in pacifying the surrounding regions. Otto, like his father Henry, had followed this strategy in dealing with the Slavs, the West Franks, and the Italians over a period of three decades, with noteworthy long-term success. The king's first step was to travel from Fritzlar to Cologne, a distance of 200 kilometers as the crow flies, with a large force (*multitudo*) of Saxon, Thuringian, and Franconian troops whom he had mobilized in April.[24]

On his journey to Cologne, Otto issued orders for all of his loyal magnates in Lotharingia to join him there. This assembly would have a clarifying effect for all of the major political figures in the *regnum* regarding the state of the rebellion, and it is unlikely that Otto would have issued the summons for a public assembly unless he were confident that a majority of magnates remained loyal to him rather than to their erstwhile duke. Of particular concern to Otto was the position that Bishop Adalbero of Metz (929–964) intended to take in the current conflict.[25] The latter had acquiesced in, if not openly aided, Louis IV's invasion in 939, and certainly had supported Gislebert's rebellion.[26] By appearing at Cologne, however, Adalbero made clear that he supported the king, and would not aid the now deposed Conrad the Red, or Louis IV.[27]

During this Cologne assembly, Otto organized a detailed plan of action to capture the strongholds that remained loyal to Conrad. It is very likely during this assembly that the king made clear his intention of naming Brun to succeed the now visibly ailing Archbishop Wigfried of Cologne (died 9 July 953), and thus to take a leading role in pacifying Conrad's rebellion.[28] Among the regional magnates upon whom Otto relied to carry out these plans was

23 Ibid., *an.* 951.
24 For Otto's journey to Cologne from Fritzlar, see Adalbert of Magdeburg, *Continuatio, an.* 953.
25 Ibid.
26 Ibid., *an.* 939.
27 Ibid., *an.* 953, observed that Conrad and Liudolf had placed a great deal of hope in gaining the support of Adalbero of Metz, but in vain.
28 Brun was consecrated as archbishop of Cologne between 11 and 20 August, about five weeks after the death of Wigfried, indicating that that all of the logistical and political obstacles had been resolved well before this date. On 11 August, Brun intervened in a charter on behalf of Lorsch and was identified simply as Otto's dear brother. By contrast, on 20 August, Brun is identified in a charter issued on behalf of the convent of Oeren at Trier as *archiepiscopus*. See DO I, 166 and 168. For a description of Brun's consecration as archbishop, see Ruotger, *Vita Brunonis*, ch. 11.

Reginar III, the scion of the powerful Regnarid family, who was the nephew of Duke Gislebert.[29]

After dismissing his adherents at Cologne, Otto returned briefly to Saxony where he almost certainly met with his two frontier commanders, Hermann Billung and Gero, to discuss ongoing operations against the Slavs, and to check any possible uprising in favor of Liudolf, Otto's son.[30] While in Saxony, Otto also oversaw the final mobilization of forces that he planned to lead into Lotharingia and Franconia to bring the overall rebellion to an end. This mobilization included a substantial siege train that the king organized against the potential need to besiege the fortress city of Mainz, where Liudolf appears to have remained ensconced since the meeting with his father there in late March.

While Otto traveled back to Saxony, his regional commanders in Lotharingia put into effect the plans that had been developed at Cologne. A snapshot image of these efforts is provided by Flodoard of Rheims, who had obtained considerable information about the activities of Count Reginar. During May and the first half of June, Reginar worked diligently to capture one of Conrad's important strongholds along the Meuse river, where the Regnarid family's possessions also were concentrated.[31] Conrad, who hoped to break the siege, mobilized his personal household forces (*manus militum*), and marched to relieve his stronghold.[32] It is noteworthy in this context that Flodoard, who up to this point had always described Conrad as leading the Lotharingians (*Lotharienses*) to war, now describes him commanding only his own *milites*. This decision by Flodoard suggests that Otto's act of stripping Conrad of his ducal office had limited the ability of the latter to mobilize men of the expeditionary levy, who owed their service to the duke of Lotharingia, but not to Conrad personally.

Nevertheless, Conrad still commanded a formidable force, and had sufficient confidence in his troops that he was prepared not only to threaten Reginar's lines of communication, but even to fight a battle.[33] Widukind observed that Conrad had the advantage in this battle because he commanded exceptionally well equipped and well trained men, which is what one might expect of an erstwhile duke's military household.[34] Reginar's forces, which almost certainly included men of the local levy as well as the count's own military household, were not nearly as formidable individually as Conrad's soldiers. However, as Widu-

---

[29]   Reginar was also personally hostile to Conrad as the latter had forced the count to give up one of his family's fortifications, and besieged several others in 952. Conrad's action may be understood as part of his general duty to keep the peace in Lotharingia, as he also deprived several important magnates in the Verdun region of their *honores* this same year. For these events, see Flodoard, *Annales, an.* 952.

[30]   Adalbert of Magdeburg, *Continuatio, an.* 953, observes that Otto returned to Saxony to arrange matters there, but does not describe these efforts in detail.

[31]   For the location of the siege and subsequent battle near the Meuse, see *Annales Lobienses*, ed. Georg Waitz, MGH 13 (Hanover 1881), 224.

[32]   Flodoard, *Annales, an.* 953.

[33]   Flodoard, *Annales, an.* 953; Widukind, *Res gestae*, 3.17; and *Annales Lobienses*, 224.

[34]   Widukind, *Res gestae*, 3.17, "*illi fortissimo subpeditante fortium militum manu.*"

kind explained, Reginar regularly received reinforcements over the course of the long battle, which lasted from noon until evening.[35] Both Flodoard and Widukind agree that the fighting was both bloody and inconclusive, but that Conrad withdrew in the night, fleeing with his remaining troops to join his confederate Liudolf at Mainz.[36]

Mainz, July–September 953

Receiving reports from his brother Brun that matters were well in hand in Lotharingia, Otto marched south and west from Saxony, likely through Thuringia, into Franconia in late June and early July, capturing a number of Conrad's family holdings along the way.[37] The ultimate goal of this campaign was to secure the surrender of the great fortress city of Mainz, which was protected by a massive stone wall just under 4,000 meters in length, enclosing an area of 98 hectares.[38] In the mid tenth century, the population of Mainz itself was at least 30,000, and probably substantially greater.[39] This does not include the large numbers of people settled in Mainz's densely populated *suburbia*.[40]

Along with the inhabitants of the city proper, the populations of these *suburbia* and even more distant rural settlements had specific military obligations in the face of a siege.[41] In fact, Mainz had a system of defense for its walls that was similar to the one set out in the Anglo-Saxon Burghal Hidage under Alfred the

---

[35] Ibid., "*adverso exercitui dum novus semper additur, a meridie usque in vesperum protrahitur bellum.*"

[36] Flodoard, *Annales*, an. 953; and Widukind, *Res gestae*, 3.17.

[37] Widukind, *Res gestae*, 3.18, "*Rex autem circa Kalendas Iullii moto exercitu armis filium generumque quaerere temptavit; obvias urbes partis adversae aut armis cepit aut in deditionem accepit, quousque Mogontiam perveniret.*" There were several very well traveled roads between Saxony and Franconia that passed through Thuringia, and which were well equipped with both royal and ecclesiastical estates that provided supplies to the royal court and army. See the discussion by Metz, "Tafelgut, Königsstraße und Servitium Regis," 271; and by Bernhardt, *Itinerant Kingship*, 240-241.

[38] Brühl, *Palatium und Civitas*, II: 99-100.

[39] The population of the city of Mainz experienced rapid expansion over the course of the ninth century. The growth was so great that by the early tenth century it was necessary to expand the walls of the city. See the observation by Ludwig Falck, *Mainz im frühen und hohen Mittelalter (Mitte 5. Jahrhundert bis 1244)* (Düsseldorf, 1972), 73-4, that the early tenth century saw the massive expansion of the city walls by Archbishop Hatto to protect the rapidly growing commercial district located along the Rhine. The professional demographers Paul Bairoch, Jean Batou, and Pierre Chèver, *La population des villes européennes de 800 à 1850* (Geneva, 1988), 7, estimate the population of Mainz c. 1000 at 30,000 compared with 20,000 c. 800. These data published by the Centre d'histoire économique internationale de l'université de Genève, were developed prior to the consensus by economic historians, e.g., Adriaan Verhulst, "Economic Organization," in *The New Cambridge Medieval History, c. 70–c. 900*, II, ed. Rosamond McKitterick (Cambridge, 1995), 481-509; idem, *The Rise of Cities in North-West Europe* (Cambridge, 1999); and Michael McCormick, *The Origins of the European Economy: Communications and Commerce, A.D. 300–900* (Cambridge, 2001), 10-11, that posits a rapid expansion of the populations in the old Carolingian heartland during the ninth century.

[40] See the basic work by Falck, *Mainz*, 75-78, 82-83; and David Nicholas, *The Growth of the Medieval City from Late Antiquity to the Early Fourteenth Century* (New York, 1997), 69.

[41] For the defensive obligations of the local rural and suburban populations, see the discussion by Nicholas, *The Growth of the Medieval City*, 55.

Great and his immediate successors. Certain *cives* at Mainz, some of whom were merchants, made agreements with the archbishop to keep in repair and to defend with their retainers a particular segment of the wall called a *Zinnen*. Each segment measured approximately three meters and thus each contract holder would have to provide at least three men to defend the relevant portion of the wall if the city came under attack. In return for this service, the merchants, who contracted to repair and to defend the walls, were freed from paying tolls in the city market, which was controlled by the archbishop.[42]

In 953, the urban and suburban militia forces at Mainz were heavily reinforced by the substantial military households of the rebel dukes Liudolf and Conrad, as well as the household forces of Archbishop Frederick.[43] Liudolf, who was the king's son and heir, held office as duke of Swabia, and also controlled the family estates of the Conradine family in Swabia through marriage to the daughter of Duke Hermann. As a consequence, he had enormous resources to raise troops for his own military household. The large scale of Conrad's military household is indicated by Widukind's observation regarding the arrival of the former duke at Otto's camp just before the battle of the Lechfeld in August 955. At this time, even after he had been stripped of his ducal office and had lost much of his political influence and power, Conrad was still able to mobilize a powerful force of mounted troops (*valida equitatus*).[44] The scale of Conrad's family lands also is indicated by a gift that he made in 946 to the bishop of Speyer, including all of the lands that he held within the city itself, tolls and trading licenses, agricultural properties, mills, and slaves.[45] It is also pertinent here that the count of the Wormsgau, the office held by Conrad before the rebellion against Otto, had overall responsibility for the defense of Mainz.[46]   'Conrad had lots of power

Finally, the archbishops of Mainz maintained one of the largest military households among the ecclesiastical magnates in Germany. The *indiculus loricatorum*, which summoned reinforcements to join Otto II in Italy in 982, required that the current archbishop of Mainz dispatch a supplementary force of 100 *loricati* to join those already dispatched by the archbishop to serve in the king's army.[47]

---

[42] Falck, *Mainz* , 74-75; and Nicholas, *The Growth of the Medieval City*, 69. This system of defense was very similar to the one established in the early tenth century at Worms. In the early tenth century, Bishop Tietlach of Worms (891–914) issued an ordinance regarding the maintenance of the city walls that required neighborhoods within the city, and also a series of villages in the region around Worms, to maintain specific sections of the wall. See the discussion by Büttner, "Zur Stadtentwicklung von Worms im Früh- und Hochmittelalter," 394. *Quellen zur Geschichte der Stadt Worms III:* , 203.

[43] Ruotger, *Vita Brunonis*, ch. 16, observed that although Archbishop Frederick departed the city, he left behind his *milites*, who continued to stand guard there under the direction of Liudolf and Conrad.

[44] Widukind, *Res gestae*, 3.44.

[45] *Urkundenbuch zur Geschichte der Bischöfe zu Speyer*, nr. 13 p. 11-13. See the discussion of this text by Voltmer, *Von der Bischofsstadt zur Reichsstadt*, 269.

[46] See the observations by Falck, *Mainz*, 33.

[47] *Constitutiones et acta publica imperatorum et regum 911-1197*, 632-3.

In using this number to evaluate the overall size of the archbishop's household forces, it must first be observed that Otto II was hardly likely to summon all of Mainz's *loricati*, much less the archbishop's entire military household, for service 1000 kilometers from home in 982. Instead, the original force of *loricati*, and the additional force of 100 *loricati*, as well as their support troops, must be seen as comprising just a part of the military forces permanently maintained by the archbishops of Mainz.

After taking into account the considerable military forces that were available to defend the massive walls of Mainz, one need not think in terms of modern "total war" to understand the various options that were available to Otto I as he marched toward the fortress city. As events at Regensburg the next year (discussed below) show, it was hardly a certainty that a negotiated settlement could be reached between the sides without substantial bloodshed. Otto, as was only prudent, had to ensure that he had available the military resources that would be necessary to overawe the defenders of Mainz, or, *in extremis*, to carry out a successful assault on the city. As made clear by the battle at Andernach in 939 where Dukes Gislebert and Eberhard were killed, and the two battles fought at Regensburg in 954, during which Liudolf's main Bavarian ally Count Arnulf was killed, Otto I would do what was necessary to assure his hold on power.

In order to capture a fortification of any significance, it was necessary to deploy large numbers of men prepared to fight on foot. As noted above, a ratio of four or five attackers to each defender was required in order to establish a credible threat to storm the walls effectively.[48] This was particularly true when the walls were defended by men who were equipped with both hand-held missile weapons and artillery, particularly *ballistae*, which had a range of up to 400 meters.[49]

The perimeter wall at Mainz, with a length of 3,850 meters, would need some 3,000 men equipped with missile weapons to defend the city, at least against a single determined assault by a force that outnumbered the defenders by less than four to one.[50] However, using population models for pre-modern societies, with a population of some 30,000, Mainz would, in fact, have had a force in the neighborhood of 9,000 able-bodied men between the ages of 15 and 55 living within the walls,[51] This does not include the substantial populations living in the city's *suburbia* and nearby settlements. A combination of militia forces, i.e. the men of the local and select levies, and the *obsequia* of the bishop and his *fideles* with their military households, as well as the military households of Liudolf, Conrad, and their *fideles*, could easily reach 10,000 men to defend the walls.[52]

---

48   Bachrach and Aris, "Military Technology and Garrison Organization," 1-17.

49   Artillery, including defensive engines, is discussed in detail in chapter four.

50   Bachrach and Aris, "Military Technology and Garrison Organization," 1-17.

51   Concerning the age groups, see Ansley Coale and Paul Demeny, *Regional Model Life Tables and Stable Populations* (Princeton, 1966); and S. H. Preston, A. McDaniel, and C. Grushka, "A New Model Life Table for High-Mortality Populations," *Historical Methods* 26 (1994), 149-159.

52   In this context, it is important that the author of the *Vita Brunonis altera*, ed. Georg Waitz, MGH SS 4 (Hanover, 1841), ch. 8, observed that Liudolf and Conrad were supported at Mainz

It is in this context that Otto mobilized an exceptionally large army to besiege Mainz. Adalbert of Magdeburg, who was a member of Otto's court during the siege of the city, observed that the king had substantial contingents from Saxony, Franconia, and Lotharingia with him, and that his brother Henry also brought a large force of Bavarians to the siege.[53] Widukind noted that Otto brought to bear a large number of siege engines (*multae machinae*).[54] These engines likely included long range missile weapons, which could cast stones and spears, as well as mantlets and perhaps covered rams, which could be used to protect Otto's troops as they attempted to gain access to the city's gates.

In order to feed this very large army, Otto benefited from his location astride one of the most important traffic arteries in the entire kingdom, namely the Rhine and the old Roman imperial highway that ran along the west bank of the river.[55] This road connected Mainz to Würzburg and then to Regensburg in the south. This road also connected Mainz to the so-called central transit zone from the Rhineland to Thuringia and from here along the Hellweg to the dense cluster of royal estates in the Harz mountains to the northeast.[56] In addition, Mainz was a major river port and center of trade, which meant that Otto's army also could be supplied by ships traveling along the Rhine.[57]

Supplies for Otto's army at Mainz could be drawn from the very large fiscal complexes at Frankfurt, just 40 kilometers upstream on the Main, and at Ingelheim, which was located just 20 kilometers downstream from Mainz on the Rhine.[58] To give a sense of the scale of the supplies that had to be brought into Otto's camp, 1,000 men would require approximately one metric ton of food per

---

by a *prevalida conspiratione civium*, i.e. the urban population that was required in large numbers to defend the walls. The author of this later life, which was composed in the twelfth century, was fully aware that in order to defend the circuit of Mainz's walls, it was necessary to mobilize the population of the city.

[53] Adalbert of Magdeburg, *Continuatio, an.* 953.

[54] Widukind, *Res gestae*, 3.18.

[55] Falck, *Mainz* with discussion of the Roman highway at 52. Regarding the military highway along the Rhine, see Josef Hagen, *Römerstrassen der Rheinprovinz*, 2nd edn (Bonn, 1931); Johannes Ramackers, "Die rheinischen Aufmarschstrassen in den Sachsenkriegen Karls des Grossen," *Annalen des historische Verein Westfallen* 142-143 (1943-1951), 1-27; and Dieter Berger, "Alte Wege und Strassen zwischen Mosel, Rhein und Fulda," *Reinische Vierteljahrsblätter* (1957), 176-192.

[56] For the connection to Regensburg, see Franz Petri, "Der Rhein in der europäischen Geschichte und den europäischen Raumbeziehungen von der Vorzeit bis zum Hochmittelalter," *Das 1. Jahrtausend, Textband 2* (Düsseldorf, 1964), 567-615, here 608. For the connection to the Hellweg through the Rhineland and Thuringia, see Bernhardt, *Itinerant Kingship*, 68.

[57] Regarding the status of Mainz as a major river port in the tenth century, see Falck, *Mainz*, 51.

[58] Concerning the general importance of the royal palaces at Ingelheim, Frankfurt, Aachen, Regensburg, and Worms as administrative centers for the mobilization of supplies for royal armies, see the discussion by Schmid, *Regensburg*, 262-3. Regarding the specific use of the Ingelheim palace as an administrative center by both the Carolingian and Ottonian kings, see H. Schmitz, *Pfalz und Fiskus Ingelheim* (Marburg, 1974); and Franz Staab, "Zur Organisation des Früh- und Hochmittelalterlichen Reichsgutes an der Unteren Nahe," *Geschichtliche Landeskunde* 21 (1980), 1-29. The most detailed discussion of the fiscal administration under the direction of the royal palace at Frankfurt is Schalles-Fischer, *Pfalz und Fiskus Frankfurt*. She argues (265) that

day.[59] For every 1,000 horses, an additional five metric tons of grain and fodder would be required on a daily basis.[60]

In light of the enormous defenses at Mainz, Otto required an army of 20,000–25,000 men at a bare minimum to have any hope of capturing the city by storm. It is evident from his decision to mobilize an extensive artillery train that the king intended to give himself the option of undertaking a major assault on the walls of the city. Siege engines would not have been required had Otto wished simply to negotiate a settlement, or to blockade the city. Moreover, as will be seen below, Otto did eventually give the order for a general assault on the walls of Mainz. In order to gain an advantage of four to one, Otto required 20,000 men if Liudolf and Conrad could muster just 5,000 men to defend the walls of Mainz. In light of the resources possessed by the rebels, this latter figure seems likely to underestimate quite considerably the number of men that the rebel dukes had available.

Nevertheless, if the minimum estimate of 20,000 men is used, the royal army required on a daily basis twenty metric tons of food for the soldiers. If the army had, in aggregate, 5,000 warhorses as well as pack animals, then an additional twenty-five metric tons of grain and fodder would be required per day as well. While an army of 20,000 men and their mounts certainly required a very large quantity of supplies, and a concomitantly large supply of transportation resources, such a logistical effort was well within the capacity of the royal government.

To put this matter in some perspective, the West Frankish monastery of Saint-Germain-des-Prés, which had middling holdings for a royal house, possessed in 825 no fewer than twenty-five dependent estates (*villae*), comprising 1,700 *mansi* and several thousand dependants.[61] Just one of these estates, named *Villa*

---

the Ottonians controlled all of the fiscal lands in the Frankfurt region that had been held by the Carolingians.

59   Fighting men require approximately 3,000 calories a day to maintain their effectiveness on campaign. In this context, see Jonathan P. Roth, *The Logistics of the Roman Army at War (264–335)* (Leiden, 1999), 7-55; and Bernard S. Bachrach, "Crusader Logistics: From Victory at Nicaea to Resupply at Dorylaion," in *Logistics of Warfare in the Age of the Crusades*, ed. John H. Pryor (Aldershot, 2006), 43-62. For relatively brief campaigns of just a few weeks, fighting men could be supplied with a rough and ready diet of hard-baked biscuit or bread and some dried or smoked meat or fish, with approximately one kilogram per man of these foodstuffs providing 3,000 calories. See the obervations by Franz Stolle, *Der Römische Legionär und sein Gepäck ('Mulus Marianus'): eine Abhandlung über den Mundvorrat, die Gepäcklast und den Tornister des römischen Legionärs* (Strasbourg, 1914), 28; and Roth, *The Logistics of the Roman Army*, 43, 51-52, 70-71, with a synthesis by Bachrach, "Crusader Logistics," 54-56. Kathy L. Pearson, "Nutrition and the Early-Medieval Diet," *Speculum* 72 (1997), 1-32, here 8, identifies some of the ways in which meat and fish were processed so that they would not spoil.

60   Regarding the feeding of horses, see Bernard S. Bachrach, "*Caballus et Caballarius* in Medieval Warfare," in *The Story of Chivalry*, eds. H. Chickering and T. Seiler (Kalamazoo, 1988), 173-211; reprinted with the same pagination in Bernard S. Bachrach, *Warfare and Military Organization in Pre-Crusade Europe* (London, 2002), here 179-180.

61   These properties are discussed in detail by Konrad Elmshäuser, "*Facit Navigium*: Schaffahrt auf Seine, Marne, Mosel und Rhein in Quellen zur frühmittelalterlichen Grundherrschaft," in idem (ed.) *Häfen, Schiffe, Wasserwege: Zur Schiffahrt des Mittelalters* (Bremerhaven, 2002), 22-53, here 28-33. By comparison, the monastery of St Martin at Tours possessed no fewer than 20,000 slaves, c. 800. This information is discussed by Bishop Elipandus of Toledo in a letter Alcuin in 799. See

supra Mare, produced a surplus of twenty metric tons of grain that was to be shipped to the vicinity of Paris for use by the monastery or sold in local markets.[62] Taking this estate as an average for Saint-Germain's holdings, this one monastery produced around 500 metric tons of grain, which would be enough to support the entire royal army at Mainz for just under two weeks.

The royal fiscal complexes centered on Frankfurt and Ingelheim, in the immediate neighborhood of Mainz, were very large, and likely provided a great many hundreds of tons of supplies to the army. Ingelheim was a very wealthy center, as evidenced by the numerous large building projects that were undertaken there, and the very frequent use of the palace by both Carolingian and Ottonian rulers.[63] The fiscal complex centered on Frankfurt included no fewer than eighteen *villae*, several of which, such as Falkenstein, Königstein, and perhaps Homburg, also supported royal fortifications.[64]

Moreover, if supplies were required from further afield, the major concentration of royal fiscal estates north and south of Mainz along the Rhine could be accessed very easily by river boat or barge.[65] These included, for example, the royal palace and fiscal complex at Trebur, located just twenty kilometers from Mainz, which remained a crucial fiscal center for the Ottonians into the early eleventh century.[66]

Alcuin, Epistolae, vol. 2, nr. 182, p. 302, where Elipandus writes "*viginti millia servorum habere dinoscris.*" Alcuin admits to the accuracy of the figure ("*multitudinem servorum usque viginti millia*", nr. 200, p. 332).

[62] Elmshäuser, "*Facit Navigium*," 31.

[63] The wealth of the Ingelheim complex is attested by the substantial building projects undertaken there, including an enormous palace and church. See the discussion by Holger Grewe, "Die bauliche Entwicklung der Pfalz Ingelheim im Hochmittelalter am Beispiel der Sakralarchitektur," in *Deutsche Königspfalzen: Beiträge zu ihrer historischen und archäologischen Erforschung* vol. 7: *Zentren herrschaftlicher Repräsentation im Hochmittelalter, Geschichte, Architektur und Zeremoniell*, ed. Caspar Ehlers, Jörg Jarnut and Matthias Wemhoff (Göttingen, 2007), 101-120. Ingelheim was also one of the most visited of the royal palaces during the reign of Otto I, with twelve attested stays, including the celebrated synod of 948. The basic work on the royal fiscal center at Ingelheim is Hans Schmitz, *Pfalz und Fiskus Ingelheim* (Marburg, 1974), who emphasizes (326-384) the great wealth and size of the fiscal resources, while acknowledging that in the absence of an *Urbar*, it is not possible to provide an idea of the specific size of the complex at any one time. Also see the discussion by Staab, "Zur Organisation des früh-und hochmittelalterlichen Reichsgutes," 1-29, who discusses Ingelheim's far-flung resources.

[64] Regarding the fiscal resources in the Frankfurt region, see the discussion Schalles-Fischer, *Pfalz und Fiskus Frankfurt*, 265-291. With respect to the size and wealth of the royal fiscal complex at Frankfurt see *Die deutsche Königspfalzen: Repetorium der Pfalzen, Königshöfe und übrigen Aufenhaltsorte der Könige im deutschen Reich des Mittelalters: 1.2 Eschwege (Schluß) – Frankfurt (Anfang) – 1.3 Frankfurt (Fortsetzung) – 1.4 Frankfurt (Schluß)– Fritzlar (Anfang)*, ed. Michael Gockel and Karl Heinemeyer (Göttingen, 1986), 131-456.

[65] Regarding the enormous number of fiscal properties along the Rhine that were gained by Henry I when he became king in 919, see the discussion by Gockel, *Karolingische Königshöfe*, particularly 82, where he discussed continuity of administrative practices between the Carolingians and Ottonians. The considerable importance of Rhenish palace complexes for the Ottonians had earlier been observed by Walter Schlesinger, "Die Pfalzen im Rhein-Main-Gebiet," *Geschichte in Wissenschaft und Unterricht* 16 (1965), 487-504.

[66] Gockel, "Die Bedeutung Treburs als Pfalzort," 86-110.

The movement of supplies from these fiscal centers by road likely was accomplished by carts that, in the tenth century, were much the same as those employed
by the late Roman empire, as well as the Roman successor states in the West. It
was not until the rigid shoulder collar for horses, developed in the ninth century,
was combined with the development of the pivoted axle for wagons in the twelfth
century that there was a significant increase in the carrying capacity of vehicles.[67]
Carts which were drawn by two horses or mules could carry a load of approximately 500 kilograms.[68] Thus, in order to supply 20,000 men and 5,000 horses,
ninety carts had to reach the army each and every day of the campaign. Over the
course of Otto's two-month siege, therefore, the army required, at a minimum,
5,400 cart loads of food and fodder.[69] Of course, the royal army could be reached
easily by river along both the Main and Rhine. One barge, of the type typically
used for transportation on these rivers during the mid tenth century, could carry
up to fifteen tons of supplies, or the equivalent of 60 cart loads.[70]

In this context, Otto possessed considerable riverine assets along the Rhine.
Following his tense meeting at Mainz with Liudolf and Conrad, for example,
the king and royal court had traveled by river down to Cologne, before heading
north-east to celebrate Easter at Dortmund.[71] In addition to these royal ships,
moreover, Otto had access to a wide range of shipping assets owned by monasteries that held properties in the Rhineland. The monastery of Weißenburg, for
example, which owned an estate at Westhofen near Worms, required its dependants there to provide transportation by ship for goods to the royal palace and
fiscal center at Frankfurt, which meant that these ships necessarily had to pass
by Mainz.[72] Weißenburg's dependants on its estate at Weinolsheim near Oppenheim, in addition to their obligations to provide transportation by river, also had
to deploy their own carts to carry goods between Mainz, Frankfurt, and Worms.[73]

Naturally, if Otto wished to reserve the production of the royal fisc for other
purposes, he also had the option of levying supplies from monasteries and bish-

67   With regard to the slow diffusion of the rigid shoulder harness for horses after its initial development, see Paul Gans, "The Medieval Horse Harness: Revolution or Evolution? A Case Study
in Technological Change," in Villard's Legacy: Studies in Medieval Technology, Science, and Art in
Memory of Jean Gempel, ed. Marie-Thérèse Zenner (Aldershot, 2004), 175-188. Concerning the
development of the pivoted axle during the twelfth century, see Marjorie Nice Boyer, "Medieval
Pivoted Axles," Technology and Culture 1 (1960), 128-138; which is placed within a broader context
by John Langdon, Horses, Oxen and Technological Innovation: The Use of Draught Animals in English
Farming from 1066 to 1500 (Cambridge, 1986).
68   Regarding the carrying capacity of carts, see the basic studies by R. Lefebvre des Noëttes,
L'attelage et le cheval de selle à travers les âges, 2 vols. (Paris, 1931); and Albert Leighton, Transportation
and Communication in Early Medival Europe (New York, 1972).
69   Regarding the length and conduct of Otto I's siege of Mainz in 953, see Flodoard, Annales, an.
953; and Widukind, Res gestae 3.18.
70   See, in this context, Aleydis van Moortel, "Medieval Boats and Ships of Germany," 67-105.
71   This journey is mentioned by Adalbert of Magdeburg, Continuatio, an. 953.
72   See the discussion of this obligation by Elmshäuser, "Facit Navigium," 37.
73   Ibid., 38.

oprics as part of their *servitium regis*.[74] Given Archbishop Frederick of Mainz's erratic behavior, from the king's point of view, it is likely that Otto drew heavily upon the archbishopric's estates to supply his forces, not least to penalize the prelate for his dalliance with the rebel dukes. However, other ecclesiastical centers also likely were called upon to aid in the royal campaign, including the monastery of St Alban, located just outside the walls of Mainz, which had received a generous grant from Otto out of the royal fiscal resources of Ingelheim in 937.[75] Indeed, it is possible that Otto even made his headquarters at St. Alban, given its location south of Mainz on a promontory that overlooked the city.

Once Otto's army was in position, he launched a massive assault against Mainz's gates in an effort to capture the city and end the rebellion at a stroke. However, Liudolf and Conrad led a spirited defense. Many of the king's engines (*machinae*) were destroyed, as Widukind claimed, through the efforts of the urban militia.[76] Nevertheless, Otto continued his attacks, with much of the fighting taking place near Mainz's massive gates.[77] Indeed, Otto summoned additional troops from Saxony so that he could continue the siege.[78]

After two months, however, both sides recognized that they were at a stalemate. Liudolf and Conrad could not hope to persuade the king to change his policy with regard to the children produced by his new wife, or favoring Duke Henry, while they were bottled up in Mainz. For his part, Otto realized that although he probably could starve the defenders of Mainz into submission, there was little appetite among his leading magnates for a long drawn-out siege. Moreover, continued assaults against the mighty walls of the well defended city would cost far more lives than either the king or his supporters were prepared to endure. Consequently, Otto offered a truce to his son Liudolf to come into the royal camp and discuss terms for ending the hostilities.

These negotiations led to widespread joy in the royal camp, as the fighting men hoped that they would soon end this bitter war.[79] However, this joy soon turned to despair as the negotiations between Otto and Liudolf collapsed. Contemporary sources agree that there were two sticking points in resolving the conflict. First, Liudolf did not wish to offer up his principal supporters to Otto to be

---

[74] The basic work on *servitium regis* is Carlrichard Brühl, *Fodrum, Gistum, Servitium Regis.* See the valuable discussion of the use of resources of monasteries by the royal court under the Ottonians by Bernhardt, *Itinerant Kingship, passim.*

[75] See DO I, 9.

[76] Widukind, *Res gestae,* 3.18, "*Multae machinae muris admotae, sed ab urbanis destructae vel incensae.*"

[77] Ibid., "*crebrae ante portas pugnae.*"

[78] Widukind, *Res gestae,* 3.23, notes that Hermann Billung dispatched a *novus exercitus* from Saxony to join the king at Mainz, but it was ambushed by forces loyal to Conrad and Liudolf, and suffered such heavy losses that the men returned home.

[79] Widukind, *Res gestae,* 3.18, "*Ingens interea oritur laetitia in castris, et a castris circumquaeque fama diffusa.*"

punished. Second, both Liudolf and Conrad still wished to see the influence of Henry diminished at the royal court.[80]

Many of the magnates in Otto's camp blamed Duke Henry for the collapse of the negotiations. Ruotger, a partisan of Henry's brother Brun, wrote:

> Even among those in the royal camp, it was not uncommon to find those who praised the strength of those on the other side and proclaimed their lack of guilt, because they had been forced unwillingly to undertake this labor. Moreover, hardly anyone among the enemy was found to be so crazed that he cursed his royal majesty. Rather, they placed all of the guilt on Henry, his brother, the duke of Bavaria.[81]

Widukind presents Henry as cursing his nephew during the negotiations, demanding, "If I am accused of some wrong, if I am guilty, why don't you lead your legions against me? Advance your banners against me."[82]

The result of the failed negotiation was a crisis in the royal camp. Patience for continuing the war was exhausted, and many of Otto's troops pleaded with him to allow them to go home. Some were worn out by a long summer's campaign, but others could no longer bear fighting a war simply to keep Henry in his position of power.[83] This major setback to Otto's plans was transformed into a potential catastrophe when word arrived that Arnulf, count palatine of Bavaria and Henry's brother-in-law, had revolted and seized control of Regensburg.[84] Liudolf, using the confusion caused by the upheaval in the royal camp and perhaps aided by the Saxon magnates Wichmann the Younger and Eckbert, snuck out of Mainz with his troops and headed south to join his newfound ally Arnulf.[85]

The political situation was now transformed. In July, when the siege of Mainz began, it appeared that a political dispute among members of Otto's innermost circle would be resolved quickly. Lotharingia was largely pacified through Otto's rapid action in capturing all of Conrad's strongholds during the late spring. Swabia, where Liudolf held the ducal office, had not seen any fighting, and could be ignored safely so long as the king's son was trapped in Franconia. Saxony and Bavaria were calm. The revolt of Arnulf, and Liudolf's escape meant that the war would now move south, and engulf not only Bavaria, but likely Swabia as well.

[80]   Widukind, *Res gestae*, 3.18; Adalbert of Magdeburg, *Continuatio, an.* 953; and Ruotger, *Vita Brunonis*, ch. 17.

[81]   Ruotger, *Vita Brunonis*, ch. 17, "*Audire hoc erat frequentius, etiam ab eis, qui in castris regalibus militabant, laudare adverse partis fortitudinem, preferret in eisdem innocenciam causae quod coacti et nimis inviti hunc sibi laborem assumerent. Et quandoquidem nec inter hostes quisquam tam demens inventus est, qui maiestatem regiam blasphemaret, in Heinricum, fratrem eius, Bauwariorum ducem, … culpam omnem et malitiam retorquebant.*"

[82]   Widukind, *Res gestae*, 3.18, "*Ipse ergo si accusor reus criminis, si culpabilis existo, quare non contra me legiones ducis? Signa adversum me move.*"

[83]   Widukind, *Res gestae*, 3.22; and Adalbert of Magdeburg, *Continuatio, an,* 953.

[84]   Widukind, *Res gestae*, 3.20-22.

[85]   Regarding the treason by the brothers Wichmann and Eckbert at Mainz, see Widukind, *Res gestae*, 3.19 and 3.24.

Bavaria and Swabia, Autumn and Winter 953–954

Otto now faced a difficult choice. Should he continue the siege of Mainz and try to capture or negotiate a settlement with Conrad the Red from a now weakened military and political position, or should he pursue his son into Bavaria? Ultimately, following the advice of his brother Henry, Otto decided in early September to lead a relatively small army (*cum paucis*) south-east to Regensburg to attempt to salvage the situation in Bavaria. He left his brother Brun, whom he now appointed as duke of Lotharingia, to manage affairs in the west, just as Hermann Billung and Gero were overseeing the political and military situation in Saxony and along the eastern frontier.

In making his decision to go to Bavaria with relatively few troops, Otto apparently was convinced by Henry that Arnulf had only limited support and could be rooted out in a swift campaign. In giving this advice to his brother, Henry may well have been placing his own desire to be restored as duke above the king's interests. Nevertheless, there is some indication that Henry was receiving intelligence from Bavaria that the political situation was still fluid, and that Arnulf had not yet firmly established himself against his brother-in-law. In particular, Archbishop Herold of Salzburg (939–958) gave the impression to Henry, and through him to Otto, that he was loyal to his king and duke. And, indeed, Otto rewarded Herold for his support during the autumn of 953 with two grants, issued on 29 November and 10 December of that year.[86]

As he marched south, Otto issued a summons for loyal magnates in Franconia and Swabia to join his army.[87] The Bavarian magnates, who were loyal to Henry, were already with the royal army as it departed from Mainz.[88] Gerhard, whose friend and patron Bishop Ulrich of Augsburg heeded the royal summons, illuminates the difficulties that this surprise campaign posed to his principal. Because Augsburg was located in the border region between Swabia and Bavaria, Ulrich had to worry about attacks on his city by Liudolf's Swabian supporters coming from the west, and from Bavarian supporters of Arnulf and Liudolf coming from the east. As a result, he left a garrison, commanded by a number of his *vasalli*, to defend Augsburg. He then mobilized as many of his other *vasalli* as possible to join the royal army.[89]

However, as Liudolf's flight into Bavaria had been unexpected, Otto had not been able to give much warning to Ulrich to prepare for the campaign. Moreover, the king intended his march into Bavaria to be very fast so that Ulrich also had to move quickly to join the royal army. As a result, according to Gerhard, Ulrich did not bring with him wagonloads of supplies (*omisso vehiculo carpenti*), as he

---

86 DO I, 170 and 171.
87 Gerhard of Augsburg, *Vita Uodalrici*, 1.10.
88 Ibid.
89 Ibid.

normally would have done. Instead, he mounted his men and rode off with whatever *res* that they had been able to collect at short notice.[90] The upshot of these
rushed preparations, according to Gerhard, was that as the campaign dragged on
(*carmula prolongata*), Ulrich found it difficult to return to Augsburg because he
lacked sufficient supplies for his men once he left the royal army.[91]

Otto's objective was the fortress city of Regensburg, which was located some
350 kilometers as the crow flies to the south-east of Mainz.[92] His likely route
followed the course of the Main river, 150 kilometers eastward to the episcopal
city of Würzburg.[93] Bishop Poppo I of Würzburg (941–961) had benefited from
Otto's generosity when first chosen to fill his seat, receiving a charter granting
freedom of election, and a confirmation of all the previous grants made to the
bishopric by Otto I and his predecessors. In addition, the king had orchestrated
a favorable exchange of properties with Poppo.[94] Among the earlier grants and
privileges enjoyed by Würzburg were revenues from dozens of royal *villae*, and
immunity for the properties and revenues received by Würzburg from any
interference by royal officials at the local level.[95] As a consequence, Poppo was
in a position to provide extensive logistical support for Otto's army as the king
marched east along the Main.

From Würzburg, Otto likely led his forces south-east some 70 kilometers
further along the Main to Bamberg, near the confluence of the Main with
the Regnitz. At Bamberg, Otto's army likely turned south along the Regnitz,
and then to the Rednitz, whose headwaters rise in the region of Weissenburg
(Bavaria), some 25 kilometers north-west of the episcopal city of Eichstätt,
whose bishop was Starchand (933–966).[96] From Eichstätt, Otto's army was
able to follow the valley of the Altmühl for 60 kilometers to its confluence
with the Danube at Kelheim, some 20 kilometers west of Regensburg. It is
possible that Otto's confirmation of Eichstätt's possession of the monastery
of Herrieden, and the confirmation of Eichstätt's immunity for its property at
Heidenheim are to be dated to this campaign.[97] Naturally, Bishop Starchand
of Eichstätt would have been obligated to provide substantial logistical support
to Otto's forces.

[90]   Ibid., "*dimissa parte in augusta civitate vasallorum suorum caeterisque rebus collocatis cum quibus potuit, omisso vehiculo carpenti, aequitandi in servitium regis in regionem noricorum sagaciter venit.*"
[91]   Ibid.
[92]   Adalbert of Magdeburg, *Continuatio, an.* 953, says explicitly that Otto attempted to capture the city.
[93]   For the Mainz to Regensburg route over Würzburg, see Petri, "Der Rhein," 608.
[94]   DO I, 44.
[95]   DA, 66-69; and DH I, 5-7.
[96]   Regarding this route, see the discussion by Ettel, "Der Befestigungsbau im 10. Jahrhundert in Süddeutschland," 369.
[97]   DO I, 127, 128. In discussing these passages, Theodor Sickel, ibid., 208, postulated a date of 950 because of Otto's known campaign to Bohemia in that year. However, given Otto's likely route from Mainz to Regensburg, it is just as possible that Bishop Starchand asked for the confirmations as Otto marched past his city.

When the royal army arrived in the vicinity of Regensburg, it quickly became clear, contrary to the expectations of Henry and Otto, that any hope for a rapid conclusion of the campaign was illusory. Arnulf not only held the fortress city, but also enjoyed broad support within the duchy as a whole.[98] Arnulf refused to leave his stronghold to meet Otto in battle, and the king lacked sufficient forces to attempt to capture Regensburg by storm.[99] Moreover, even if Otto had wished to attempt to mount such as assault, his siege train had been badly damaged at Mainz, and, as a result, he did not have the equipment that would have been necessary for such an attack. Nevertheless, Otto remained with his forces in Bavaria for three months, and apparently had complete freedom of movement, as he issued charters from the region around Regensburg, including surviving charters at Aufhausen and Schierling in November and December 953, noted above.[100]

Otto obtained supplies for his army, in part, by seizing food and fodder from the rebels in Bavaria.[101] He also likely obtained considerable supplies from Archbishop Herold of Salzburg, whom the king rewarded with a formal confirmation of properties that had been obtained from the papacy, and also with the grant of additional properties that had been confiscated from the rebels.[102] It is not clear whether Otto obtained supplies from other ecclesiastical magnates, either through their voluntary assistance or by force, although Bishop Starchand of Eichstätt, as noted above, did likely provide a considerable quantity of supplies. Widukind cryptically reports that the bishops in Bavaria were slow to take any action during the campaign, as some favored one side, and others favored the other side. As a consequence, they sometimes helped the king and at other times the rebels.[103] Certainly, this was the case with Archbishop Herold, who, after aiding Otto during the autumn campaign of 953, switched sides, and actually took part in the battle of Mühldorf in 955 against Duke Henry.[104] In addition to supplies from various ecclesiastical magnates, Otto's army could draw

---

[98] Gerhard of Augsburg, *Vita Uodalrici*, 1.10, observed that Arnulf was able to gain control of Regensburg with a great multitude of supporters (*multitudo populi*), and also controlled numerous other strongholds, again with the ready support of the population (*et cum frequentia populorum*).

[99] Widukind, *Res gestae*, 3.26, observed that the Bavarians refused to come out from behind their walls, stating, " *nec bellum publicum presumunt, sed clausi muris grandem exercitui laborem suaeque regionis solitudinem parant.*"

[100] DO I, 170, 171. Regarding the length of Otto's campaign in Bavaria, Widukind, *Res gestae*, 3.28, says that he was there for three full months, which corresponds with Otto's charter issued from Schierling on 10 December. Adalbert of Magdeburg, *Continuatio, an.* 953, says that Otto was in Bavaria until almost Christmas.

[101] Widukind, *Res gestae*, 3.26, states that Otto's army "*omnia vastabat.*"

[102] DO I, 170, 171.

[103] Widukind, *Res gestae*, 3.27, "*Non minima quoque caeteris pontificibus cunctatio erat in Boioaria, dum favent partibus, nunc regi assistendo, nunc alienas partes adiuvando, quia nec sine periculo alienabantur a rege nec sine sui detrimento ei adhaerebant.*"

[104] See Adalbert of Magdeburg, *Continuatio, an.* 954; *Auctarium Garstense*, MGH SS 9, 566; and *Annales Sancti Rudberti Salisburgenses*, MGH SS 9, 571.

supplies from the royal fisc, which possessed a considerable number of estates in Bavaria, as well as from the estates of Henry's ducal fisc.[105]

After three months of campaigning, Otto demobilized his forces and began his return to Saxony just before Christmas to plan his next steps in dealing with the civil war that now affected Bavaria, as well as Swabia, Lotharingia, and parts of Franconia. The king's son remained at Regensburg. However, the count palatine Arnulf now took the fight into Swabia on behalf of Liudolf. Raiders dispatched by Arnulf had already been active in the region around Augsburg during the autumn. As Bishop Ulrich returned to his episcopal seat, he found that Arnulf was preparing to drive out all of the king's remaining supporters in Swabia, or to convince them to change sides. Realizing that he could not hold Augsburg against a determined siege, Ulrich, as was discussed in the previous chapter, withdrew to the abandoned fortress of Mantahinga, and began to rally royalist supporters.

Arnulf spent much of the winter of 953–954 in the region of Augsburg, working to consolidate Liudolf's position there, and negotiating, or so he thought, with Ulrich to gain the latter's submission.[106] Ulrich, for his part, spent these months busily strengthening the defenses of Mantahinga and secretly mobilizing support on behalf of the king. As the spring campaigning season drew near, and it became clear to Arnulf that the bishop of Augsburg would not change his allegiance, the Bavarian count palatine began to besiege Mantahinga at the beginning of Lent, in early February.[107] Even during the siege, Ulrich continued to coordinate the royalist forces in Swabia, and his brother Dietpold successfully mobilized an army to attack Arnulf's Bavarians at Mantahinga. The battle, which took place on 15 February, was a decisive victory for Dietpold. Arnulf's brother Hermann was captured, and the Bavarians were routed. This marked the end of major military operations in Swabia.[108]

Lotharingia, Autumn 953

After departing from his brother at Mainz, Brun, who was now both archbishop of Cologne and duke of Lotharingia, summoned an assembly of Lotharingian magnates to take place at Aachen.[109] Here, Brun accepted their oaths of loyalty to himself and to the king, and authorized them to keep order in the face of the continuing threat posed by Conrad the Red.[110] In particular, Brun ordered the

---

[105] Otto recovered significant fiscal holdings in Bavaria following the death of Duke Arnulf in 937. Regarding this *Revindikationspolitik* see Faußner, "Die Verfügungsgewalt des deutschen Königs über weltliches Reichsgut im Hochmittelalter," 409; and Schmid, *Regensburg*, 118, 148, 230. Also see the discussion by Bachrach, "Exercise of Royal Power," 411-12.

[106] Gerhard of Augsburg, *Vita Uodalrici*, 1.10.

[107] Easter in 954 fell on 26 March.

[108] This battle is described in detail in the previous chapter.

[109] Ruotger, *Vita Brunonis*, ch. 21.

[110] Ibid., "*Ibi principes regni quorum id intererat, convenit, eos variis multisque modis instruxit.*"

establishment of a territorial peace, with specific provisions for the protection of ecclesiastical property.[111] Brun then departed for Cologne to celebrate on 25 September his formal consecration as archbishop.[112]

After Otto and Brun abandoned the siege of Mainz, it is likely Conrad realized that although he was safe behind the walls of the archiepiscopal city, at least for the present, he would not be able to advance his cause by remaining there. He needed substantial additional support, and the withdrawal of Liudolf to Bavaria meant that the only remaining potential actor was King Louis IV of West Francia. However, in order to gain the latter's aid, Conrad desperately needed to demonstrate that intervening was worth the risk of a counter-stroke by Otto, and this meant achieving a noteworthy military or political success.

To this end, Conrad led his forces 225 kilometers west to the fortress city of Metz.[113] This city, along with Verdun and Toul, was crucial to the control of upper Lotharingia, and if he had been able to capture and hold Metz, Conrad would have been in a strong position to negotiate a settlement with King Louis.[114] However, it is likely that capturing the city by storm or through a protracted siege was not within Conrad's military capabilities, now that he had been stripped of his ducal office and the concomitant authority to mobilize the select levies of Lotharingia for expeditionary duty. Metz boasted an urban defensive circuit at this time of 3,200 meters, which was further protected by mural and gate towers, and it would have required a large and well supplied army to undertake a siege.[115]

Nevertheless, despite the powerful defenses at Metz, Conrad had an important initial success when, despite Bishop Adalbero's public affirmation of loyalty to Otto earlier in the year, the erstwhile Lotharingian duke was able to gain control over the city briefly when he secretly introduced his forces within the walls.[116] Very quickly, however, Conrad was forced to withdraw when it became clear that he did not have the support of either the urban population or the local rural magnates. In fact, it is likely that Abbot Agenoldus of Gorze (933–967), who in addition to his standing as a major political figure in the Metz region also had considerable spiritual authority, played the crucial role in forcing Conrad to depart from the city.[117]

While Conrad was in upper Lotharingia trying to gain control over Metz, Brun marched 110 kilometers south-west from Cologne to Liège to establish Rather, earlier bishop of Verona, as prelate there.[118] He was joined by the archbishop of

---

[111]   Ibid., "regiae maiestati et suae ipsorum fidei pollicitationes nullas preponerent, spondens se ante tempus et in tempore sempter paratum forae, ut pacem ecclesiae violatam, si sic necesse esset, vitae etiam suae periculo reformaret."

[112]   Ibid., ch. 21.

[113]   Ruotger, Vita Brunonis, ch. 24; and Flodoard, Annales, an. 953.

[114]   These cities in upper Lotharingia were the targets of Louis IV's son, Lothair IV, in the period 983–984.

[115]   Regarding the walls of Metz, see Brühl, Palatium und Civitas, II: 48.

[116]   Flodoard, Annales, an. 953.

[117]   Ibid.

[118]   Ruotger, Vita Brunonis, ch. 38.

Trier, and the bishops of Utrecht, Münster, Osnabrück, Cambrai, and Verdun.[119] When he received word that Conrad had marched west from Mainz and had tried to establish himself at Metz, Brun set off in pursuit with a army of loyal Lotharingian troops, many of whom were provided from the military households of the bishops who had been present at Rather's consecration.[120]

Brun forced a confrontation with Conrad the Red in mid October at the *villa* of Reimlingen, which was located in the Bliesgau, between modern Saarbrücken and Zweibrücken.[121] Ultimately, however, Conrad refused battle, because, Adalbert of Magdeburg suggests, the former did not want to act against the king.[122] It is just as likely, however, that Conrad realized a defeat in the field far from any hope of relief or safe refuge would mean disaster, and perhaps the wholesale slaughter of his supporters and troops, and perhaps even his own death. Brun, for his part, now held a dominant position in Lotharingia, and it was not in his interest at this point to risk a battle that might reverse the strategic situation.

As a consequence of the calculations made by both Conrad and Brun, the two armies withdrew from the field without shedding any blood. As the autumn rainy season was fast approaching, both commanders decided to take up permanent quarters and wait on events, particularly Otto's ongoing campaign in Bavaria. It is likely that Brun went to Cologne, while Conrad withdrew completely from Lotharingia and traveled to his family's stronghold at Worms where he remained throughout the remainder of 953 and into the early months of 954.[123]

The Hungarians, Winter 954

Even as Otto was campaigning in Bavaria during the autumn of 953, Arnulf and Liudolf established contact with the Hungarians to discuss obtaining military support for their revolt. The rebels likely saw obtaining aid from the Hungarians as even more pressing following the defeat of Arnulf's army at Mantahinga in mid February 954 at the hands of Otto's Swabian loyalists. It is more than 900 kilometers from the Alföld, the great Hungarian plain east of Budapest,

---

119 This list is provided by Rather in his text, *Phrenesis* ch. 1, in *Ratherii Veronensis Opera, Fragmenta, Glossae*, ed. Peter L. D. Reid, François Dolbeau, Bernhard Bischoff, and Claudio Leonardi, *Corpus Christianorum, Continuatio Mediaevalis* 46 (Turnhout, 1984), 199-200.

120 In a letter to his successor at Liège, Baldric, Rather observed that following his consecration, he went on campaign with Brun, mobilizing his own *militia* for service against the king's enemies. See *Die Briefe des Bischofs Rather von Verona*, ed. Fritz Weigle, MGH, *Die Briefe der deutschen Kaiserzeit* vol. 1 (Weimar, 1949), nr. 10, pp. 49-50.

121 Adalbert of Magdeburg, *Continuatio, an.* 954, places this event in 954, but does not give a specific date. Naumann, "Rätsel des letzten Aufstandes gegen Otto I. (953-954)," 180, suggests that Adalbert misdated the conflict, placing it immediately before the Hungarian raid into Lotharingia. Instead, Naumann suggests a date of October 953 for the confrontation for the two armies. This date certainly fits the chronology of Brun's participation in Rather's elevation at Liège in late September or early October.

122 Adalbert of Magdeburg, *Continuatio, an.* 954.

123 Conrad was at Worms when the Hungarians arrived there on Palm Sunday, 19 March 954. See Widukind, *Res gestae*, 3.30.

to Worms. Even mounted forces would require at least five weeks to travel this distance, if they did not stop for raiding or plundering along the way. This means that in order to reach Worms by 19 March, when their presence is attested by Widukind, the Hungarians must have set out on their raid by early February, at the latest. Given this time frame, it seems likely that Arnulf and Liudolf began their negotiations with the Hungarian leaders before 953 came to an end. It should be recalled that, despite the recurring hostilities between the Hungarians and their western neighbors, Arnulf's family had a long tradition of dealing with the steppe nomads. Indeed, Arnulf's father, Duke Arnulf, had once taken refuge with the Hungarians when driven from Regensburg by King Conrad I in 916.[124]

It is in this context that a large force of Hungarian raiders was permitted to enter Bavaria, and then was provided with guides by Liudolf so that they could pass through Franconia.[125] The Hungarian forces reached Worms in mid March, where they were welcomed by Conrad, who publicly distributed gifts of gold and silver to the mounted raiders before sending them westwards into lower Lotharingia.[126] In light of Liudolf's effort to guide the Hungarians away from Bavaria and into Franconia, it seems likely that the rebels saw the Rhineland and Lotharingia as the crucial battlegrounds in the next stage of the revolt. If Brun, and especially Otto, could be forced to devote their attention to the west, then Arnulf and Liudolf would have an opportunity to fortify their position in Bavaria, and perhaps also to reclaim the initiative in Swabia. Conrad, for his part, desperately needed a new tool to overturn Brun's dominant position in Lotharingia, and also to weaken Brun's principal allies in lower Lotharingia, including Count Reginar III.

Flodoard of Rheims, who had particularly good sources of information regarding affairs in lower Lotharingia, emphasized that Conrad made an arrangement with the Hungarians specifically to attack the lands of Reginar, as well as to attack Brun.[127] The Hungarians, however, did not limit themselves to attacks on Conrad's political enemies, but also sought booty and captives throughout the region, including a lengthy assault on Cambrai, before making their way into West Francia and then into Italy before wending their way back home.[128]

Their lack of siege equipment meant, however, that the Hungarian raiders were not able to capture any fortifications in the Ottonian kingdom. As a consequence, although the Hungarians did extensive damage, they failed to alter in any appreciable manner the military situation as it had existed in the late autumn of 953.

---

[124] See the discussion by Holzfurtner, *Gloriosus Dux*, 117-122.

[125] With regard to Liudolf's role in providing guides, see Widukind, *Res gestae*, 3.30.

[126] Ibid., 3.30, "*Dominica ante pascha Wormatiae eis est publice ministratum et muneribus auri et argenti plurimum donatum.*"

[127] Flodoard, *Annales, an.* 954.

[128] The attacks by the Hungarians are recorded in a large number of local chronicles, including Heriger, *Translatio S. Landoaldi sociorumque*, MGH SS 15, ch. 9; John of St Arnulf, *Vita Iohannis Abbatis Gorziensis*, ch. 136; Sigebert of Gembloux, *Vita Wicberti*, 14; Folcuin, *Gesta abbatum Lobiensium*, MGH SS 4, 25; and *Gesta episcoporum Cameracensium*, liber I, chapter 75.

Swabia was still lost to the rebels, as was Lotharingia. Arnulf and Liudolf were still ensconced in Bavaria. However, the political situation had changed dramatically. As the contemporary chroniclers make clear, the rebels were held fully responsible for the Hungarian raid, and whatever sympathy Conrad and Liudolf may have enjoyed among the magnates following the failure of negotiations at Mainz in August 953 was fully dissipated.[129] Conrad, recognizing the new political reality, gave up the struggle and sought Otto's forgiveness.[130] Otto was now positioned to invade Bavaria for a second time and bring an end to the rebellion.

Bavaria, Spring 954

In mid June 954, the king led a large army to the Bavarian town of Langenzenn, approximately 20 kilometers west of Nuremberg, to a pre-arranged meeting with the Bavarian magnates and Liudolf.[131] As he marched south from Saxony, Otto likely took a route over Erfurt and then Bamberg before heading south-southwest to Langenzenn. In this manner, he was able to take advantage of the well established royal fiscal centers on this principal north-south artery.[132] The meeting itself, was peaceful, but the two sides failed to agree to terms. Otto permitted his son to withdraw, and then pursued him to Regensburg.[133]

During the first day's march, Otto's army reached Roßtal, located 20 kilometers south of Nuremberg, which was held by Liudolf's ally, the count of Hammerstein.[134] The fortress, originally constructed by Charlemagne around 800, is built on a plateau west of the Rednitz river and encloses an area of some five hectares.[135] It was protected by massive walls comprising a mortared stone surface approximately 2 meters thick that protected an earthen and timber wall 7 meters wide. The wall was protected further by a 5.5 meter berm, and two ditches. The inner ditch was 15 meters wide and 3.5 meters deep.[136] Not wishing to waste any time in his pursuit of Liudolf, Otto decided against investing the fortress and beginning what might be a lengthy siege. Instead, he ordered an assault on the walls that lasted all day long.[137] When it became clear that he would not be able to capture the fortification quickly, Otto decided it was not worth the time to remain at

---

[129] See Widukind, *Res gestae*, 3.30; Flodoard, *Annales*, an. 954; Ruotger, *Vita Brunonis*, ch. 24; Adalbert of Magdeburg, *Continuatio*, an. 954; and John of St Arnoul, *Vita Iohannis Abbatis Gorziensis*, ch. 136.

[130] Adalbert of Magdeburg, *Continuatio*, an. 954.

[131] Widukind, *Res gestae*, 3.31-32.

[132] See Schlesinger, *Die Entstehung der Landesherrschaft*, 45, who describes Erfurt as a focal point of royal power on par with Würzburg and Büraburg.

[133] Widukind, *Res gestae*, 3.31-32.

[134] Widukind, *Res gestae*, 3.35, for the assault on the fortress. Regarding the identity of the defending commander, see Ettel, "Der Befestigungsbau im 10. Jahrhundert in Süddeutschland," 373.

[135] Regarding the defenses at Roßtal, see Ettel, "Der Befestigungsbau im 10. Jahrhundert in Süddeutschland," 373-378.

[136] Ibid.

[137] Widukind, *Res gestae*, 3.35.

Roßtal any longer, and so ordered the advance to continue to Regensburg, a march of three days.[138] Although Widukind does not mention this, it is likely that Otto left a force at Roßtal to prevent the garrison there from harassing his lines of communication.

Once the king arrived at Regensburg, he established elaborate siege camps around the city with a principal aim of blocking access to the major gates built into the eastern and western walls.[139] Regensburg was constructed on the south side of the Danube as a Roman legionary camp, and the imperial walls of the city, rebuilt in the fourth century, were still in use in 954. They comprised a rectangle with a circuit measuring 2,000 meters, enclosing an area of 24.5 hectares. These walls were built of mortared stone that ranged in width from 2.2 to 3 meters.[140] Between 920 and 936 the walls of Regensburg were massively expanded to the west by Duke Arnulf to enclose both the merchant district and the monastery of St Emmeram. The new fortification measured approximately 3,000 meters and enclosed an additional 40 hectares.[141] The entire circuit of exterior walls, therefore, was approximately 4,500 meters in length. It is likely that the walls of the western extension, which Otto faced in 954, were built of earth and timber, with perhaps a stone face.[142] The new walls also were protected by a substantial ditch. It is not known, however, whether this was filled with water diverted from the Danube.[143]

Otto initially intended to deploy his refurbished siege train (*machinae*) in an assault against the city. In light of the scale of the walls at Regensburg, which were 25 percent larger than those at Mainz, Otto had to plan for a defensive force of well in excess of 5,000 men, including both the local levies, and the military households of Liudolf, Arnulf, and their *fideles*. Arnulf, in particular, had used the ducal treasury at Regensburg to enhance his military forces.[144] Consequently, a royal army in the range of 20,000–25,000 men must be taken as a minimum figure.

[138] Ibid., 3.36. It is about 100 kilometers from Roßtal to Regensburg, indicating a marching speed of approximately 33 kilometers per day. This is likely an exaggeration of the speed of the entire force, which included a substantial siege train. However, it is possible that forward elements of Otto's army reached Regensburg in three days. Regarding the marching rates of medieval armies, see J. W. Nesbitt, "Rate of March for Crusading Armies in Europe: A Study in Computation," *Traditio* (1963), 167–182.

[139] Widukind, *Res gestae*, 3.36-37, "*Castrorum loca occupata munitionibus circumsepta.*" He notes that attacks were made against the king's *castrum* facing the west gate, and against Gero's *castrum* that faced the east gate.

[140] Regarding the Roman walls and a synthesis of the archaeological investigations of Regensburg in the Roman and early medieval periods, see Brühl, *Palatium und Civitas*, II: 229.

[141] Ibid., 239-241.

[142] This type of blended fortification, with a mortared stone front, was typical of fortifications built throughout Germany during the tenth century. Regarding these techniques, see Friedrich, "Ottonenzeitliche Befestigungen im Rheinland und im Rhein-Main-Gebiet," 353.

[143] Regarding the construction of the western expansion of Regensburg's walls, see Brühl, *Palatium und Civitas*, 241. Brühl notes, ibid., that this earth and timber wall likely was replaced by a stone wall around 1000.

[144] See the observation by Widukind, *Res gestae*, 3.20.

As had been true at Mainz, Otto benefited in supplying this large army from his location at a major transportation node. At Regensburg, the royal army could receive shipments of food and fodder by cart and wagon along the well established road network within Bavaria. Supplies also could be transported by boat or barge along the Danube and its many tributaries. As the rebels were now largely confined behind the walls of Regensburg, itself, there was little to hinder the requisitioning of supplies from Bavaria's bishops and abbots, as well as from royal estates within the duchy. However, if a longer siege became necessary, Otto could also summon supplies from royal estates in both western and eastern Franconia, which also could be transported by ship or barge most of the way to Regensburg along the Rhine, Main, Regnitz, and Rednitz rivers. From here, it was necessary to carry out a short overland passage before finally reaching the Danube.

Once Otto had brought his entire army up to Regensburg, it became clear that an assault on the walls, even with his reconstructed siege train, was not an attractive option. Widukind, our primary source for this siege, suggests that Otto was not able to bring his siege engines to bear against the walls.[145] He does not elaborate here about the specific reasons why Otto could not deploy his *machinae*. However, the presence of a substantial defensive trench beyond the western extension of the city's walls and the very large number of defenders meant that enormous firepower could be directed at the attacking forces as they tried to maneuver the siege engines into position.[146] Under these circumstances, the casualties suffered by the attackers would be catastrophic. Consequently, Otto settled in for a lengthy siege, hoping either to starve the defenders into submission, or to force them to fight a battle outside the walls against his numerically superior force.[147]

Liudolf and Arnulf, realizing that they could not expect any relief effort to break the siege, decided to launch an attack on Otto's forces rather than slowly starve. However, in order negate somewhat Otto's numerical advantage, the two rebel commanders decided to focus their attack on just one of the two main siege camps. In addition, rather than offering a set-piece battle outside the walls, they prepared a daring two-pronged assault on the royal camp built facing the western gate of the city. One force, comprising the mounted troops based within Regensburg, launched a direct attack against Otto's camp that was constructed in front of the west gate. A second force, dispatched from the northern waterfront of the city, was to travel west on the Danube by ship, and then attack the royal

---

[145] Ibid., 3.36, "*Sed cum multitudo machinas muris adplicari non sineret, satis dure interdum ab utrisque pugnatum pro muris.*"

[146] Regarding the very heavy casualties that attackers would suffer in attacking a fortification while advancing over level ground, see Bachrach and Aris, "Military Technology and Garrison Organization," 1-17. These casualties would certainly have been much higher for troops attempting to advance over substantial ditches, or trying to fill in these ditches so as to bring siege towers to bear.

[147] Widukind, *Res gestae*, 3.36, notes that rather than face starvation Liudolf ordered an attack on the king's camp that had been constructed facing the western city gate.

camp after landing on the river bank behind it.[148] If they were successful, Liudolf and Arnulf hoped to rout the king's troops and, if they were very fortunate, to capture Otto, himself.

As the defenders of Regensburg began to pour out of the city's western gate, Otto dispatched a significant force of mounted troops to meet them in the fields between his camp and the wall. However, he also left behind a substantial garrison to provide a secure base in case the battle went against him. As a result, rather than finding an empty camp, Liudolf's men came up from the river bank to face a well prepared and protected force of heavily armed men (*armati*).[149] The morale of the Bavarians collapsed when they realized that they had lost the element of surprise, and they beat a hasty retreat back to their river boats. However, the loss of command and control at the tactical level among the attackers led to the virtual annihilation of this water-borne force as Otto's troops advanced rapidly from the camp in good order and cut them down from behind.[150]

Following the failed assault, Liudolf, Arnulf, and their commanders decided to sue for peace, but the negotiations broke down when the rebels refused to accept King Otto's terms. Liudolf and Arnulf then attempted to change the dynamic of the siege with a renewed assault on Otto's forces, this time directed against the camp, under the command of Margrave Gero, which was located opposite the eastern gate of the city.[151] The fighting on this occasion was very bloody, lasting for three hours from mid-morning until noon. Among the dead was Arnulf.[152] In the end, the rebels were forced to retreat back into the city.[153]

After the failure of this assault and the death of his chief ally, Liudolf again sued for peace, this time acceding to his father's demands.[154] According to the terms of the agreement, the defenders withdrew from the "new city" (*nova urbs*), comprising the walled area that had been built by Duke Arnulf (died 936), and Liudolf, along with some of his followers, departed from Regensburg completely. A meeting was set for Liudolf to make a public request for forgiveness at the royal hunting lodge at Thangelstedt in Thuringia, some 300 kilometers north of Regensburg and about 30 kilometers southeast of Erfurt.[155] It was here that Liudolf publicly cast himself down before his father as a penitent and begged for forgiveness. Otto, accepting as genuine Liudolf's tears of contrition, lifted up his son and received him again into his grace.[156]

---

[148] Ibid.

[149] Ibid., "*Exilientesque de navibus irruunt in castra, offendentesque armatos ... .*"

[150] Ibid., "*dum trepidi fugae consulunt, circumfusi undique caeduntur. Alii naves ingredi nisi, timore perculsi deviantes, flumine absorbentur; pauci de pluribus superessent.*"

[151] Ibid., 3.37.

[152] Ibid., "*a tertia hora usque in nonam acriter pugnatum; ante portam urbis equo cadente ascensor Arnulfus armis exutus iliocoque telis perfossus occubuit.*"

[153] Ibid.

[154] Ibid., 3.38.

[155] Ibid., 3.40.

[156] Gerhard of Augsburg, *Vita Uodalrici*, 1.12, suggests that Bishop Ulrich was the principal figure

Epilogue

Conrad the Red, who had made his peace with the king earlier that spring, was permitted to keep his family lands. As part of the process of political rehabilitation, Conrad led his personal military household to fight against the Ukrani along the southern shore of the Baltic under the command of Gero.[157] The next year, in 955, Conrad was one of the heroes of the battle on the Lechfeld before being killed by an arrow as the Hungarians were withdrawing from the field.[158]

In Bavaria, Otto's peace agreement with Liudolf did not immediately bring about an end to hostilities. A substantial garrison refused to leave the old city at Regensburg, which was protected by the Roman walls.[159] Otto, who had been receiving ominous reports about Slavic activity in the north-east and about unrest in Saxony, could no longer remain in Bavaria. He left his now reinstated brother Henry in command and departed, meeting with his son Liudolf at Thangelstedt, as noted above. Henry, who spent the remainder of 954 reestablishing his authority throughout Bavaria, was unable to drive out the garrison at Regensburg itself.

Consequently, Otto returned to Bavaria with an army in April 955. On this occasion, the king was able to deploy his siege engines against the Roman fortifications of the old city of Regensburg.[160] The garrison recognized that they would not be able to maintain their defense of the walls, and surrendered to Otto. The commanders (*principes*) of the defending forces received the rather lenient punishment of exile, while the mass of the troops in the garrison (*reliquae multitudini*) were spared and allowed to return home.[161] A few weeks later, on 1 May, Henry defeated the remaining Bavarian rebels at the battle of Mühldorf, where he captured Archbishop Herold of Salzburg and had him blinded.[162]

Conclusion

The military commanders on both sides of the conflict of 953–954 understood that achieving their strategic goals required the capture or defense of fortress cities and lesser fortifications. Indeed, fundamental to Ottonian military strategy over the long term was the establishment and maintenance of fortifications as the

---

in negotiating the settlement between Liudolf and Otto, and that the final meeting between the two took place in Swabia rather than in Thuringia.

[157] Adalbert of Magdeburg, *Continuatio*, an. 954, notes that Conrad was permitted to retain his family's estates. Widukind, *Res gestae*, 3.42, observes that Conrad was dispatched by Otto to serve under Gero in the campaign against the Ukrani.

[158] Widukind, *Res gestae*, 3.44 and 3.46.

[159] Ibid., 3.39 and 3.43.

[160] Widukind, *Res gestae*, 3.43, "*Proximum agens rex pascha cum fratre, ducit post haec exercitum contra Rainesburg, iterum armis machinisque urbem torquens.*"

[161] Ibid.

[162] See *Auctarium Garstense*, 566; *Annales Sancti Rudberti Salisburgenses*, 571.

foundation of territorial conquest. During the campaigns of 953 and 954, Otto had to mobilize very large armies, numbering in the range of 20,000–25,000 men, at a minimum, to besiege the great fortress cities of Mainz and Regensburg. He also deployed large siege trains to provide protection for his troops as they assaulted the walls. Crucial to these military operations was the effective management of supplies. To this end, the Ottonians maintained close control over the agricultural production not only of the estates of the royal fisc, but also of ecclesiastical magnates who were required to provide supplies (*servitium regis*) for the maintenance of the court and army.

The considerable detail that is provided by contemporary sources regarding the civil war of 953–954 illuminates the broader pattern of campaign strategy that informed Ottonian warfare over more than half a century. Henry I, Otto I, and their military commanders undertook scores of military campaigns that culminated in substantial sieges and the expansion of royal control, both within East Francia and beyond its traditional borders. The long-term success of these operations is *prima facie* evidence for the ability of the first two Saxon kings to mobilize large armies, and concomitantly large quantities of supplies. Just as importantly, these successful campaigns point to the diligent collection of intelligence regarding road systems and water supplies, as well as the location and strengths of enemy military assets.

Conclusion

During their combined fifty-four years of rule, Henry I and Otto I used war as a basic tool of government in the pursuit of their medium and long-term policy objectives. War, for the early Ottonian kings, was not a pastime, nor was it primarily a means to provide their magnates with access to booty and plunder. The consistent, although not absolute, success of Ottonian armies against the West Franks, Danes, Slavic polities east of the Saale and Elbe rivers, Bohemians, Hungarians, Lombards, Byzantines, and within East Francia/Germany itself led to a fundamental reorientation of political authority throughout the Latin West. Henry I successfully resuscitated the East Frankish kingdom of Arnulf of Carinthia and Louis the German, raising it to a hegemonic status among the successor states of the Carolingian empire. He also extended his power eastwards into lands that never were incorporated into the *regnum Francorum*.

Otto I, building on the political and military achievements of his father, maintained the hegemonic role of the eastern kingdom in the affairs of both West Francia and Burgundy. He also gained control of the Lombard kingdom, as well as the papal state, and lands even further south up to the frontiers of Calabria and Apulia. In so doing, Otto re-established Charlemagne's empire, and justified both politically and militarily his claim to have brought about a *renovatio imperii*. Moreover, Otto went even further than his Carolingian model, and established direct military control over the vast swath of lands between the lower Elbe and the Oder river.

The wars of conquest by the Ottonians, as well as those in the defense of their own lands against both foreign and internal foes, were dominated by sieges. Henry, Otto, and their military commanders undertook scores of siege operations, many of which were directed against massive fortified sites, and even great fortress cities of Roman origin, including the eternal city itself. To undertake these campaigns, the Ottonians required large armies, sometimes reaching the tens of thousands of troops. This conclusion is based on a critical examination of the physical reality (*Sachkritik*) of the defenses of great fortresses, such as Mainz and Regensburg, and the technological capacity of both offensive and defensive weapons that were available to the Ottonians and their opponents. The great scale of Ottonian military forces, which has been illuminated through the excavations of fortified sites, also is frequently commented upon by contemporary writers. This is true despite the common practice among historians throughout the medieval period, including the tenth century, to downplay the size of the "home side" in an effort to give greater glory in victory, and to offer a means of explanation in the face of defeat.

In order to field large armies for campaigns that were directed toward the capture of fortresses, the Ottonians required more men than were available in the royal military household and the military households of secular and ecclesiastical magnates. The great majority of fighting men participating in the offensive campaigns undertaken by Henry and Otto were militia troops provided by the expeditionary levies. The service of these types of fighting men, which was required on the basis of their wealth, can be traced back to the late Roman empire, and is consistently attested throughout the early medieval period and, indeed, well into the fourteenth century in many parts of Europe.

Henry and Otto, in a manner consistent with their Carolingian predecessors, recognized that in order to field effective armies it was necessary to have well trained officers who understood how to lead men in war. To this end, both the Ottonian rulers and their magnates worked diligently to develop a curriculum for the training of future officers that drew on military handbooks, such as Vegetius' *Epitoma rei militaris*, and Frontinus' *Strategemata*, that provided important insights into many of the technical aspects of waging campaigns, including logistics, scouting, establishing camps, tactical formations, equipment, battlefield tactics, and strategy. Future officers also had access to a wide array of classical, biblical, as well as more contemporary historical works that offered numerous examples of the proper conduct of war, and, just as importantly, errors made by military commanders in the past. The use of history to train future leaders had, as the Ottonians knew well, a long pedigree in the Latin West, one that had been highly touted by Isidore of Seville, whose texts formed a central part of the curriculum for all educated men during the entirety of the early Middle Ages. The military manuals and historical works, which were copied assiduously in Ottonian *scriptoria*, were complemented by a range of additional technical works, such as the widely available *agrimensores* and Vitruvius' *De architectura*, which offered information about the laying out of military camps, organizing the proper supply of the troops, as well as the construction of siege equipment.

Military manuals, such as Vegetius' *Epitoma rei militaris*, also provide important insights, alongside the observations by contemporary writers, regarding the actual training of Ottonian soldiers. Ottonian commanders used the phalanx as the basic deployment of foot soldiers in the relatively few battles fought in the field. Even on the defensive, when fighting men are positioned as part of a "shield wall," serving in a phalanx required considerable training in the effective use of shield, spear, and sword. Soldiers had to be conditioned, through extensive practice, to thrust with their weapons, while holding a shield to protect their bodies, rather than slashing at the enemy. The thrusting stroke was not only more powerful, as Rabanus Maurus observed in his revision of Vegetius' *Epitoma* for use in *tempore moderno*, but also exposed less of the body to a counter-stroke by the opponent, and was less likely to harm a fellow soldier standing alongside in the phalanx.

Much more extensive training was required to prepare men to advance in a phalanx. Men had to learn to keep step, even at a run, with the other soldiers in their line so that all of the men would strike the enemy at the same time. In the course of sieges, in which most Ottonian soldiers found themselves deployed, men had to advance while protecting themselves with their shields in a tortoise formation, which also required extensive additional practice and coordination. Once they arrived at the base of the wall of a stronghold, the men often had to mount ladders, burdened with their arms, in the face of the active resistance of the enemy. This too was a skill that had to be learned through training and repetition.

Mounted fighting men also trained extensively in a number of combat techniques, which included not only the use of swords and spears while on horseback, but also tactical formations. The men and animals had to learn to advance in a line, and to wheel about in unison. This latter skill was exceptionally important in the feigned retreat, which the Ottonians, as well as their opponents, used as a *ruse de guerre* to convince an enemy to give up a strong defensive position.

The deployment of large, well trained armies, to be effective, also required that the soldiers be highly motivated to fight. Recognizing that hungry soldiers rarely enjoy high morale, the Ottonians assured the regular supply of their troops with food and equipment through the extensive logistical apparatus of the royal fisc, as well as through exactions imposed on numerous monasteries and bishoprics that owed *servitium regis*. To motivate their men to excel in the field, Henry and Otto, and their commanders offered generous rewards, both to individuals who had done remarkable deeds, and to the army as a whole when plunder was gained in successful military operations. In addition to the material well being of their men, the Ottonians also sought to secure the spiritual welfare of the troops. They established a broad array of religious rites and ceremonies extending from the battlefield to the home front that were intended to show that God was on their side, would protect them in battle, and would care for them in heaven if they died on campaign.

The enormous complexity and scale of Ottonian warfare, with the concomitant mobilization of financial, human, and material resources, should now be clear. The nature of warfare in this period, moreover, has important implications for the ongoing scholarly debates regarding the very nature of early medieval polities, including their political, administrative, social, and economic structure. The major wars of conquest by Henry I and Otto I could not have been sustained by a primitive society that lacked administrative institutions. The mobilization of the enormous resources for the construction and maintenance of hundreds of fortifications and garrisons could not be accomplished by an archaic polity or, to use Gerd Althoff's expression, a *Königsherrschaft ohne Staat*. Rather, Henry I and Otto I, building upon the inheritance of their Carolingian predecessors, and ultimately that of the late Roman empire, possessed an extensive and well organized administration, and indeed, bureaucracy, which mobilized the resources that were necessary for the successful conduct of war.

Appendix: Major Military Operations by Henry I, Otto I, and Their Commanders

The following information is drawn from narrative sources and is intended to illuminate both the large number of military operations undertaken by Ottonian armies, and the predominance of siege operations as contrasted with battles in the field. However, it is to be emphasized that a great many military operations, particularly sieges, are not discussed in surviving narrative works, and can only now be known through the excavation of fortified sites.

Sieges

919 The surrender of all of Duke Burchard of Swabia's *urbes* to Henry I.[1]
921 Henry I's siege of Regensburg.[2]
923 Siege and defence of the *castrum* of Saverne in the *pagus* of Alsace[3].
923 Defense of Worms against King Charles the Simple.[4]
923 Henry I's siege of Metz.[5]
c. 924 Defense of Püchen against the Hungarians.[6]
925 Henry I's siege of the fortification (*oppidum*) at Zülpich.[7]
926 Defense of Werla against the Hungarians.[8]
928 Henry I's siege of Durofostum.[9]
928-9 Henry I's capture of Brandenburg.[10]
928-9 Henry I's capture of Jahna (Gana).[11]
928-9 Siege of Lebusa.[12]

---

[1]   Widukind, *Res gestae*, 1.27.
[2]   Liudprand, *Antapodosis*, 2.21; *Annales Magdeburgenses*, 142; Widukind, *Res gestae*, 1.27.
[3]   Flodoard, *Annales, an.* 923.
[4]   Adalbert of Magdeburg, *Continuatio, an.* 923.
[5]   Adalbert of Magdeburg, *Continuatio, an.* 923.
[6]   Thietmar of Merseburg, *Chronicon*, 1.15.
[7]   Flodoard, *Annales, an.* 925.
[8]   Widukind, *Res gestae*, 1.32.
[9]   Flodoard, *Annales, an.* 928.
[10] *Annales Magdeburgenses*, 142; Widukind, *Res gestae*, 1.35.
[11] Widukind, *Res gestae*, 1.35.
[12] Thietmar of Merseburg, *Chronicon*, 1.16.

929 Henry I's siege of Prague.[13]

929 Defense of Walsleben against the Redarii.[14]

930 Siege of Douai by Duke Gislebert of Lotharingia.[15]

932 Siege of Péronne by Duke Gislebert of Lotharingia.[16]

933 Defense of unnamed fortress in region of Merseburg.[17]

935 Siege of St Quentin by Duke Gislebert of Lotharingia.[18]

936 Otto I's siege of unnamed *urbs hostium*.[19]

937 Defense of the fortress of Helmern by Bruning.[20]

938 Defense of the fortress of Belecke.[21]

938 Siege of the *castrum* of Pierrepont by Duke Gislebert of Lotharingia.[22]

939 Defense of Eresburg.[23]

939 Siege of the fortress of Laer by Otto I's commander Dedi.[24]

939 Siege of Eresburg by Otto I.[25]

939 Second siege of Laer by Otto I.[26]

939 Otto I's siege of Chièvrement.[27]

939 Otto I's siege of Breisach.[28]

939 Siege of Montreuil by Count Arnulf of Flanders.[29]

939 Defense of Montreuil against Northmen and Count Erluin.[30]

939 Otto I's siege of Immo in unnamed fortress[31]

944 Duke Hermann of Swabia's sieges of *castella* held by King Louis IV's *fideles* Reginar and that latter's brother Raoul.[32]

946 Otto I's sieges of Laon, Rheims, Rouen, and numerous other fortifications.[33]

13   Adalbert of Magdeburg, *Continuatio*, an. 929; Widukind, *Res gestae*, 1.35.
14   Widukind, *Res gestae*, 1.36; Thietmar of Merseburg, *Chronicon*, 19.
15   Flodoard, *Annales*, an. 930.
16   Flodoard, *Annales*, an. 932.
17   Liudprand, *Antapodosis*, 2.28, 2.47-8; Widukind, *Res gestae*, 1.38.
18   Flodoard, *Annales*, an. 935
19   Widukind, *Res gestae*, 2.4.
20   Widukind, *Res gestae*, 2.6.
21   Liudprand, *Antapodosis*, 4.20; Widukind, *Res gestae*, 2.11.
22   Flodoard, *Annales*, an. 938.
23   Widukind, *Res gestae*, 2.11.
24   Widukind, *Res gestae*, 2.11.
25   Widukind, *Res gestae*, 2.11; Thietmar of Merseburg, *Chronicon*, 2.2.
26   Widukind, *Res gestae*, 2.11.
27   Adalbert of Magdeburg, *Continuatio*, an. 939; *Herimanni Augiensis Chronicon*, 113; *Annales Magdeburgenses*, 144; Widukind, *Res gestae*, 2.22.
28   Adalbert of Magdeburg, *Continuatio*, an. 939; Liudprand, *Antapodosis*, 4.27; *Annales Einsiedelnensis* 141; *Herimanni Augiensis Chronicon*, 113; *Annales Magdeburgenses*, 144; Widukind, *Res gestae*, 2.24.
29   Flodoard, *Annales*, an. 939.
30   Flodoard, *Annales*, an. 939.
31   Widukind, *Res gestae*, 2.27.
32   Flodoard, *Annales*, an. 944.
33   Flodoard, *Annales*, an. 946; Adalbert of Magdeburg, *Continuatio*, an. 946; *Gesta episcoporum Cameracensium Liber I*, 426; *Annales Magdeburgenses*, 144; Widukind, *Res gestae*, 3.3.

947 Siege of Aquileia by Duke Henry of Bavaria.[34]

948 Siege of Mouzon by Duke Conrad the Red of Lotharingia, accompanied by Archbishop Robert of Trier, and Bishop Adalbero of Metz, in aid of Louis IV.[35]

948 Siege of Montaigu by Duke Conrad the Red of Lotharingia in aid of King Louis IV.[36]

949 Sieges of Laon and Senlis by Duke Conrad the Red of Lotharingia in aid of King Louis IV.[37]

950 Otto I's siege of Nimburg on the Elbe.[38]

950 Otto I's siege of Prague.[39]

951 Duke Conrad the Red's siege of a *munitio* held by Count Reginar III of Hainault.[40]

951 Otto I's siege of Pavia.[41]

952 Duke Conrad the Red of Lotharingia's siege of the *munitio* of Mareuil in aid of Hugh the Great.[42]

953 Siege by Count Reginar III of a *castrum* held by Conrad the Red.[43]

953 Otto I's siege and capture of numerous fortifications held by Conrad the Red in Lotharingia.[44]

953 Otto I's siege of Mainz.[45]

953 Otto I's siege of Regensburg.[46]

954 Defense of Mantahinga by Bishop Ulrich of Augsburg.[47]

954 Defense of Cambrai against the Hungarians.[48]

954 Defenseof Lobbes against the Hungarians.[49]

954 Defense of Metz against the Hungarians.[50]

954 Otto I's siege of Roßtal.[51]

954 Otto I's siege of Regensburg.[52]

---

34 Widukind, *Res gestae*, 2.36.
35 Flodoard, *Annales*, an. 948; Richer, *Historiae*, 2.83.
36 Flodoard, *Annales*, an. 948; Richer, *Historiae*, 2.84.
37 Flodoard, *Annales*, an. 949; Richer, *Historiae*, 2.92.
38 Widukind, *Res gestae*, 3.8.
39 Flodoard, *Annales*, an. 950; Adalbert of Magdeburg, *Continuatio*, an. 950.
40 Flodoard, *Annales*, an. 951.
41 *Benedicti Sancti Andrea Chronicon*, 175; Widukind, *Res gestae*, 3.10.
42 Flodoard, *Annales*, an. 952.
43 Flodoard, *Annales*, an. 953.
44 Widukind, *Res gestae*, 3.18.
45 Flodoard, *Annales*, an. 953; Adalbert of Magdeburg, *Continuatio*, an. 953; Ruotger, *Vita Brunonis*, ch. 16-17; *Die Annales Quedlinburgenses*, 466-467; Widukind, *Res gestae*, 3.18, 21, 28; Thietmar of Merseburg, *Chronicon*, 2.6.
46 Adalbert of Magdeburg, *Continuatio*, an. 953; Thietmar of Merseburg, *Chronicon*, 2.6.
47 Gerhard of Augsburg, *Vita Sancti Uodalrici*, 1.10; *Herimanni Augiensis Chronicon*, 114.
48 *Gesta episcoporum Cameracensium Liber I*, 428.
49 Sigebert, *Vita Wicberti*, 513-4.
50 John of St. Arnoul, *Vita Iohannis Abbatis Gorziensis*, ch. 67.
51 *Die Annales Quedlinburgenses*, 466-7; Widukind, *Res gestae*, 3.34-35.
52 Adalbert of Magdeburg, *Continuatio*, an. 954; Widukind, *Res gestae*, 3.36; Thietmar of Merse-

954-955 Duke Hermann of Saxony's siege of *urbes* by the rebels Wichmann and Ekbert in Saxon marches.[53]

955 Duke Hermann of Saxony's siege of the Abodrite fortress of Suithleiscranne.[54]

955 Defense of an unnamed Saxon fort against the Slavs.[55]

955 Otto I's siege of Regensburg.[56]

955 Bishop Ulrich's defense of Augsburg against the Hungarians.[57]

955 Margrave Thiadric's siege of an unnamed Slavic fortress.[58]

956 Liudolf's siege of Pavia and other fortifications in northern Italy.

959 Duke Brun of Lotharingia destroyed adulterine fortifications.[59]

960 Duke Brun of Lotharingia's sieges of Namur and Chièvrement.[60]

960 Duke Brun of Lotharingia aided King Lothair IV in the siege of Troyes.[61]

960x964 Duke Hermann of Saxony's siege fortress held by the rebel Wichmann's troops.[62]

961 Otto I's siege of Montefeltro.[63]

962-963 Otto I's siege of Monte Sancti Leonis.[64]

963 Otto I's siege of the *civitas* of Verim.[65]

964 Otto I's siege of Rome.[66]

969 Sieges of Naples, Avellino, and Bari by Swabian and Saxon troops accompanied by Beneventans.[67]

Battles

929 Lenzen[68]

933 Defeat of Hungarian army by Saxon and Thuringian forces.[69]

burg, *Chronicon*, 2.8.

53   Widukind, *Res gestae*, 350.

54   Widukind, *Res gestae*, 3.51.

55   Widukind, *Res gestae*, 3.52.

56   Widukind, *Res gestae*, 3.43.

57   Gerhard of Augsburg, *Vita Sancti Uodalrici*, 1.12; Widukind, *Res gestae*, 3.44; Thietmar of Merseburg, *Chronicon*, 2.9.

58   Widukind, *Res gestae*, 3.45.

59   Flodoard, *Annales*, an. 959.

60   Flodoard, *Annales*, an. 960.

61   Richer, *Historiae*, 3.12.

62   Widukind, *Res gestae*, 3.68.

63   Adalbert of Magdeburg, *Continuatio*, an. 961; Liudprand, *De Ottone Rege*, ch. 6.

64   Adalbert of Magdeburg, *Continuatio ann.* 963-963; *Chronicon Salernitanum*, 553-4; *Arnulfi Gesta Archiepiscoporum Mediolanensium.* ch. 7; Widukind, *Res gestae*, 3.63; Thietmar of Merseburg, *Chronicon*, 2.13.

65   *Chronicon Salernitanum*, 554.

66   Adalbert of Magdeburg, *Continuatio*, an. 964; *Herimanni Augiensis Chronicon*, 115; *Othloni Vita S. Wolfkangi*, ch. 9; *Benedicti Sancti Andrea Chronicon*, 181; Thietmar of Merseburg, *Chronicon*, 2.13.

67   *Chronicon Salernitanum*, ch. 173; *Lupi Protospatarii annales*, 55; Widukind, *Res gestae*, 3.72.

68   *Die Annales Quedlinburgenses*, 456; *Annales Magdeburgenses*, 142; Widukind, *Res gestae*, 1.36; Thietmar of Merseburg, *Chronicon*, 1.9.

69   Widukind, *Res gestae*, 1.38.

933 Riade.[70]

939 Birten.[71]

939 Defeat of a German army under the command of Haika by the Slavs.[72]

939 Andernach[73]

944 Battle of Wels[74]

948 Battle between Hungarians and Bavarians at Floß.[75]

950 Battle between Hungarians and Bavarians at Ticino.[76]

953 Battle between Conrad the Red and Count Reginar on the Meuse.[77]

954 The battle of Regensburg.[78]

955 Mühldorf.[79]

955 Lechfeld.[80]

955 Recknitz.[81]

964 Battle at Rome.[82]

965 Battle between Duke Burchard of Swabia and Adalbert, the son of Berengar.[83]

969 Battle of Ascoli between Swabian and Saxon troops and Byzantines.[84]

972 Defeat of Bavarians by Hungarians.[85]

972 Battle of Zehden.[86]

[70]   Flodoard, *Annales, an.* 933; Adalbert of Magdeburg, *Continuatio, an.* 934 (933); Liudprand, *Antapodosis*, 2.25; *Die Annales Quedlinburgenses*, 458; Widukind, *Res gestae*, 1.38.

[71]   Adalbert of Magdeburg, *Continuatio, an.* 939; Liudprand, *Antapodosis*, 4.24; Widukind, *Res gestae*, 2.17.

[72]   Widukind, *Res gestae*, 2.20.

[73]   Liudprand, *Antapodosis*, 4.29; *Die Annales Quedlinburgenses*, 462; Richer, *Historiae*, 2.19; Widukind, *Res gestae*, 2.26; Thietmar of Merseburg, *Chronicon*, 2.34.

[74]   *Herimanni Augiensis Chronicon*, 113; *Annales Magdeburgenses*, 144; Widukind, *Res gestae*, 2.36.

[75]   *Die Annales Quedlinburgenses*, 465; Widukind, *Res gestae*, 2.36.

[76]   *Die Annales Quedlinburgenses*, 465; Widukind, *Res gestae*, 2.36.

[77]   *Annales Lobienses*, 234; Widukind, *Res gestae*, 3.23.

[78]   Widukind, *Res gestae*, 3.36.

[79]   *Auctarium Garstense*, 566; *Annales Sancti Rudberti Salisburgenses*, 571

[80]   Flodard, *Annales, an.* 955; Adalbert of Magdeburg, *Continuatio, an.* 955; Liudprand, *Antapodosis*, 4.29; Ruotger, *Vita Brunonis*, ch. 35; *Die Annales Quedlinburgenses*, 467-8; *Herimanni Augiensis Chronicon*, 114-5; Richer, *Historiae*, 2.82; Widukind, *Res gestae*, 3.44; Thietmar of Merseburg, *Chronicon*, 2.9.

[81]   Flodoard, *Annales, an.* 955; Adalbert of Magdeburg, *Continuatio, an.* 955; *Die Annales Quedlinburgenses*, 467-8; Widukind, *Res gestae*, 3.53; Thietmar of Merseburg, *Chronicon*, 2.9.

[82]   Liudprand, *De Ottone Rege*, ch. 17.

[83]   Adalbert of Magdeburg, *Continuatio, an.* 965; *Herimanni Augiensis Chronicon*, 115.

[84]   *Chronicon Salernitanum*, ch. 173; *Lupi Protospatarii annales*, 55; Thietmar of Merseburg, *Chronicon*, 2.15.

[85]   Thietmar of Merseburg, *Chronicon*, 2.29.

[86]   Thietmar of Merseburg, *Chronicon*, 2.29.

Bibliography

Primary Sources

Abbo of Saint-Germain-des-Prés, *Bella parisiacae urbis*, ed. and trans. Nirmal Dass (Paris, 2007).

Adalbert of Magdeburg, *Continuatio Reginonis*, in *Reginonis abbatis Prumiensis Chronicon cum continuatione Treverensi*, ed. F. Kurze, MGH SRG 50 (Hanover, 1890).

Adalhardi abbatis Corbiensis Statuta seu Brevia, ed. Joseph Semmler in *Corpus consuetudinum monasticum*, ed. Kassius Hallinger, vol. 1, *Initia consuetudines Benedictinae: Consuetudines saeculi octavi et noni* (Siegburg, 1963), 365-408.

Adalhard of Corbie, "Appendix II: The Customs of Corbie, *Consuetudines Corbeienses*. A Translation by Charles W. Jones of the Directive of Adalhard of Corbie," in *The Plan of St. Gall*, ed. Walter Horn and Ernest Born, 3 vols. (Berkeley, CA, 1979), III: 101-120.

Adalbold, *Vita Heinrici II*, ed. D. G. Waitz, MGH SS 4 (Hanover, 1841).

Ademar de Chabannes, *Chronique*, ed. Jules Chavanon (Paris, 1897).

Alcuin, *De virtutibus et vitiis*, in *Patrologiae Cursus Completus, Series Latina*, ed. J.-P. Migne, vol. 101 (Paris, 18XX).

——— *Epistolae*, ed. Ernst Dümmler, MGH Epistolae *Karolini aevi*, vol. 2 (Hanover, 1895).

——— *Propositiones ad acuendos juvenes*, in *Patrologiae Cursus Completus, Series Latina*, ed. J.-P. Migne, vol. 101 (Paris, 18XX).

Alpert of Metz, *De diversitate temporum* in *Alpertus van Metz: Gebeurtenissen van deze tijd en Een fragment over bisccop Diederik I van Metz*, ed. Hans van Rij (Amsterdam, 1980).

Annales Einsiedelnensis, ed. G. H. Pertz, MGH SS 3 (Hanover, 1849).

Annales Fuldenses sive annales regni Francorum orientalis, ed. Friedrich Kurze, MGH SRG 7 (Hanover, 1891).

Annals of Fulda, trans. Timothy Reuter (Manchester, 1992).

Annales Hildesheimensis, ed. G. H. Pertz, MGH SS 3 (Hanover, 1849).

Annales Lobienses, ed. Georg Waitz, MGH SS 13 (Hanover, 1881).

Annales Magdeburgenses a. 1-1188, ed. G. H. Pertz, MGH SS 16 (Hanover, 18XX).

Annales necrologici Fuldenses, ed. Georg Waitz, MGH SS 13 (Hanover, 1881).

Annales Ottenburani, ed. G. H. Pertz, MGH SS 5 (Hanover, 1845).

Die Annales Quedlinburgenses, ed. Martina Giese, MGH SRG 72 (Hanover, 2004).

Annales Ratisponenses, ed. W. Wattenbach, MGH SS 17 (Hanover, 1861).

Annales de Saint-Bertin, ed. Félix Grat, Jeanne Vielliard, and Suzanne Clémencet (Paris, 1964).

Annales Sancti Nazarii, ed. C. L. Bethmann, MGH SS 17 (Hanover, 1861).

Annales Sancti Rudberti Salisburgenses, ed. G. H. Pertz, MGH SS 9 (Hanover, 1851).

The Annals of St Bertin, trans. Janet Nelson (Manchester, 1991).

Annales Sangallenses maiores, ed. G. H. Pertz, MGH SS 1 (Hanover, 1826).

Anonymus Haserensis de episcopis Eichstetensibus a. 741-1058, ed. C. L. Bethmann MGH SS 7 (Hanover, 1846).

Anselmi Gesta Episcoporum Leodiensium, ed. B. Koepke, MGH SS 7 (Hanover, 1846).

Ardo Smaragdus, *Vita Benedicti abbatis Anianensis*, ed. O. Holder-Egger, MGH SS 15.2 (Hanover, 1887),

Arnulfi Gesta Archiepiscoporum Mediolanensium, ed. C. Bethmann and W. Wattenbach, MG SS 8 (Hanover, 1848).

Asser, *De rebus gestis Aelfredi*, ed. W. H. Stevenson (Oxford, 1959).

Astronomer, *Vita Hludowici imperatoris*, ed. and trans. Ernst Tremp, MGH SRG 64 (Hanover, 1995).

Auctarium Garstense, ed. Wilhelm Wattenbach, MGH SS 9 (Hanover, 1851).

Augustine, *De opere monachorum*, in *Patrologiae Cursus Completus, Series Latina*, ed. J.-P. Migne, vol. 40 (Paris, 18XX).

Battle of Maldon, ed. Donald Scragg (Manchester, 1981).

Benedicti Sancti Andreas Chronicon, ed. G. Zucchetti in *Fonti per la Storia d'Italia* 55 (Rome, 1920).

Capitularia Regum Francorum, ed. Alfred Boretius and Viktor Krause, 2 vols., MGH *Capitularia*, Legum Sectio II (Hanover, 1890–1897).

Cassiodori Senatoris Variae, ed. Theodor Mommsen and Ludwig Traube, MGH (Munich, 1894, repr, 1981).

Chronicon Salernitanum, ed U. Westerbergh (Stockholm, 1956).

Codex Diplomaticus Fuldensis, ed. E. F. J. Dronke (Fulda, 1850, repr. Aalen, 1962).

Codex Laureshamensis 3 vols., ed. Karl Glöckner (Darmstadt, 1929–1936).

Concilium Aurelianense, ed. F. Maassen, MGH *Concilia Aevi Merovingici* (Hanover, 1893).

Concilium Germanicum, ed. A. Werminghoff, MGH *Concilia* 2.1 (Hanover, 1906).

Constitutiones et acta publica imperatorum et regum 911-1197, vol. 1, ed. Ludwig Weiland, MGH (Hanover, 1893).

Crónica mozárabe de 754, ed. and trans. Eduardo López Pereira (Zaragoza, 1980).

De rebus bellicis, ed. Robert I. Ireland (Leipzig, 1984); and "Anonymi Auctoris Libellus de Rebus Bellicis: A Treatise by an Unknown Author on Military Matters," ed. and trans., Robert Ireland in *De Rebus Bellicis. Part 2. BAR International Series* 63 (1979), 39-92.

Einhard, *Vita Karoli Magni*, ed. Oswald Holder-Egger MGH SRG 25 (Hanover, 1911, repr. 1965).

Ekkehard of St Gall. *Casus Sancti Galli*, ed. Hans F. Haefele (Darmstadt, 1980).

Epistolae Karolini Aevi vol. 3, ed. Ernst Dümmler, MGH (Berlin, 1899).

Flodoard, *Les Annales de Flodoard*, ed. Ph. Lauer (Paris, 1905).

———. *The Annals of Flodoard of Rheims 919–966*, trans. and ed. Steven Fanning and Bernard S. Bachrach (Peterborough, Ontario, 2004).

Folcuin, *Gesta abbatum Lobiensium*, ed. Georg Waitz, MGH SS 4 (Hanover, 1841).

Fragmentum de Arnulfo duce Bavariae, ed. Ph. Jaffé, MGH SS 17 (Hanover, 1861).

Frontinus, *Strategemata*, ed. Robert I. Ireland (Leipzig, 1999).

Gerhard of Augsburg, *Vita Sancti Uodalrici*, ed. Walter Berschin and Angelika Häse (Heidelberg, 1993).

Gesta episcoporum Cameracensium Liber I. II. III. Usque ad a. 1051, ed. L. C. Bethmann MGH SS 7 (Hanover, 1846).

Gesta episcoporum Tullensium, ed. Georg Waitz, MGH SS 8 (Hanover, 1858).

Gesta Treverorum, ed. G. Waitz, MGH SS 8 (Hanover, 1858).

Giovanni Diacono, *La cronaca Veneziana*, ed. G. Zucchetti, *Fonti per la Storia d'Italia* 9 (Rome, 1890).

Hamburgisches Urkundenbuch, ed. Johann Martin Lappenberg (Hamburg, 1907).

Heiric of Auxerre, *Vita sancti Germani*, ed. Ludwig Traube, MGH *Poetae Latini Aevi Carolini*, vol. 3 (Berlin, 1896).

Heriger, *Translatio S. Landoaldi sociorumque*, ed. O. Holder-Egger, MGH SS 15.2 (Hanover, 1888).

Herimanni Augiensis Chronicon, ed. G. H. Pertz, MGH SS 5 (Hanover, 1845).

Hincmar of Rheims, *Collectio de ecclesiis et capellis*, ed. Martina Stratmann (Hanover, 1990).

———. *De ordine palatii*, ed. Thomas Gross and Rudolf Schieffer, MGH *Fontes iuris germanici antiqui in usum scholarum separatim editi* (Hanover, 1980).

Hrotsvithae Opera, ed. Paulus de Winterfeld, MGH SRG 34 (Hanover, 1965).

Isidore of Seville, *Etymologiarum sive originum libri xx*, ed. W. M. Lindsay (Oxford, 1911, repr. 1957).

John of St Arnoul, *Vita Iohannis Abbatis Gorziensis*, MGH SS 4.

Klaeber's Beowulf and the Fight at Finnsburg, ed. R. D. Fulk, Robert E. Bjork, and John D. Niles (Toronto, 2008).

Die Konzilien Deutschlands und Reichsitaliens 916-1001: Teil I 916-960, ed. Ernst-Dieter Hehl and Horst Fuhrmann (Hanover, 1987).

Le liber ordinum en usage dans l'église wisigothique et mozarabe d'Espagne du cinquième siècle, ed. Marius Férotin, *Monumenta ecclesiae liturgica* 5 (Paris, 1904) revised edition Anthony Ward and Cuthbert Johnson (Rome, 1996).

Liudprand of Cremona. *Liudprandi Cremonensis Opera omnia: Antapodosis, Homelia paschalis, Historia Ottonis, Relatio de legatione Constantinopolitana*, ed. P. Chiesa (Turnhout, 1998).

———. *The Complete Works of Liudprand of Cremona*, ed. and trans. Paolo Squatriti (Washington, DC, 2007).

Lupi Protospatarii annales, ed G. H. Pertz MGH SS 5 (Hanover, 1845).

Ex Miraculis S. Wigberhti, ed. G. Waitz, MGH SS 4 (Hanover, 1841).

Nithard, *Historiarum libri IV*, ed. R. Rau, in *Quellen zur karolingischen Reichsge-schichte* (Darmstadt, 1955).

Die Ordines für die Weihe und Krönung des Kaisers und der Kaiserin, ed. Reinhard Elze, MGH *Fontes iuris germanici antiqui* 9 (Hanover, 1960).

Othloh von St. Emmeram, *Vita sancti Wolfkangi episcopi*, ed. Georg Waitz, MGH SS (Hanover, 1841).

Ottonian Germany: The Chronicon of Thietmar of Merseburg, ed. and trans. David A. Warner (Manchester, 2001).

Ottonis episcopi Frisingensis et Rahewini gesta Frederici; seu rectius, cronica, ed. Franz-Josef Schmale, 2nd edn (Darmstadt, 1974).

Paschasius Radbertus, *Vita Sancti Adalhardi* = *Ex vita s. Adalhardi*, ed. G. H. Pertz, MGH SS 2 (Hanover, 1829).

Petrus de Ebulo, *Liber ad honorem Augusti*, Bern, Burgerbibliothek, ms. 120, fol. 109r.

Le pontifical Romano-Germanique du dixième siècle, ed. Cyrille Vogel and Rein-hard Elze (Vatican, 1963).

Procopii Caesariensis opera omnia, ed. J. Haury and G. Wirth, 4 vols., 2nd edn (Leipzig, 1962–1964).

Quellen zur Geschichte der Stadt Worms III: Annalen und Chroniken, ed. Heinrich Boos (Berlin, 1893).

Rabanus Maurus, *De aetatibus hominis*, in *Patrologiae Cursus Completus, Series Latina*, ed. J.-P. Migne, vol. III (Paris, 1800)..

–––. *De procinctu Romanae militiae*, ed. Ernst Dümmler, *Zeitschrift für deutsches Alterthum* 15 (1872), 443-451.

–––. *Epistolae*, ed. E. Dümmler, MGH *Epistolae* 5 (Berlin, 1899).

Rather of Verona, *Phrenesis*, in *Ratherii Veronensis Opera, Fragmenta, Glossae*, ed. Peter L. D. Reid, François Dolbeau, Bernhard Bischoff, and Claudio Leon-ardi, *Corpus Christianorum, Continuatio Mediaevalis* 46 (Turnhout, 1984).

–––. *Die Briefe des Bischofs Rather von Verona*, ed. Fritz Weigle, MGH, *Die Briefe der deutschen Kaiserzeit*, vol. I (Weimar, 1949).

Recueil des chartes de l'abbaye de Saint-Benoît-sur Loire, eds. Maurice Prou and A. Vidier, 2 vols. (Paris, 1900–1907).

Regino of Prüm, *Chronicon*, ed. Friedrich Kurze, MGH SRG 50 (Hanover, 1890).

Richer, *Histoire de France (888-995)*, vol. I (888–954), ed. Robert Latouche (Paris, 1930).

Richer, *Histoire de France (888-995)*, vol. 2 (954–995), ed. Robert Latouche (Paris, 1937).

Rodulfi Glabri Historiarum Libri Quinque: Rodulfus Glaber Five Books of Histories, ed. and trans. John France (Oxford, 1989).

Ruotger, *Vita Brunonis*, ed. Walter Berschin and Angelika Häse (Heidelberg, 1993).

Scriptura Minora, ed. R. Hercher (Leipzig, 1885).

Sedulius Scotus, "Hartgarius Episcopus ad Eberhard", ed. Ludwig Traube, in MGH *Poetae Latini Aevi Carolini*, vol. 3, (Berlin, 1896).

Sedulius Scottus, *Collectaneum Miscellanum*, ed. Dean Simpson, *Corpus Christianorum, Continuatio Mediaevalis*, 67 (Turnhout, 1988).

Sigebert of Gembloux, *Vita Wicberti*, ed. W. Wattenbach MGH SS 8 (Hanover, 1858).

Thegan, *Gesta Hludowici imperatoris*, ed. and trans. Ernst Tremp, MGH SRG 64 (Hanover, 1995).

Thietmar of Merseburg, *Chronik*, ed. and trans. Werner Trillmich, 8th edn (Darmstadt 2002).

Die Totenbücher von Merseburg, Magdeburg und Lüneburg, ed. G. Althoff and J. Wollasch, MGH *Libri Memoriales et Necrologia* n.s. 2 (Hanover, 1983).

Traditiones et antiquitates Fuldenses, ed. E. F. J. Dronke (Fulda, 1844).

Die Traditionen des Hochstifts Freising: Band I 744-926, ed. Theodor Bitterauf (Munich, 1905, repr. Aalen, 1967)

Die Traditionen des Hochstifts Freising: Band II 926-1283, ed. Theodor Bitterauf (Munich, 1909, repr. Aalen, 1967).

Die Traditionen des Hochstifts Passau, ed. Max Heuwieser (Munich, 1930, repr. Aalen, 1969).

Die Urkunden Arnolfs, ed. Paul Kehr. MGH *Diplomata regum Germaniae ex stirpe Karolinorum* vol. 3 (Berlin, 1940).

Die Urkunden Heinrichs II. und Arduins ed. Harry Bresslau, Robert Holtzmann and Hermann Reincke-Bloch, MGH *Diplomatum regum et imperatorum Germaniae* vol. 3 (Hanover, 1900–1903).

Die Urkunden der Karolinger dritter Band: Urkunden Lothars I. und Lothars II., ed. Theodor Schieffer, MGH *Diplomatum regum et imperatorum Germaniae* vol. X (Berlin, 1966).

Die Urkunden Konrad I., Heinrich I. und Otto I., ed. Theodor Sickel, MGH *Diplomatum regum et imperatorum Germaniae* vol. 1 (Hanover, 1879–1884).

Die Urkunden Ludwig des Deutschen, Karlomanns und Ludwigs des Jüngeren, ed. Paul Kehr, MGH *Diplomatum regum et imperatorum Germaniae* vol. X (Berlin, 1932–1934).

Die Urkunden Otto des II und Otto des III., ed. Theodor Sickel, MGH *Diplomatum regum et imperatorum Germaniae* vol. 2 (Hanover, 1888–1893).

Die Urkunden Zwentibolds und Ludwigs des Kindes, ed. Theodor Schieffer. MGH *Diplomata regum Germaniae ex stirpe Karolinorum*, vol. 4 (Berlin, 1960).

Urkundenbuch der Abtei Sanct Gallen: Teil III 920-1360, ed. Hermann Wartmann (St Gall, 1882).

Urkundenbuch zur Geschichte der Bischöfe zu Speyer: Band I Ältere Urkunden, ed. Franz Xavier Remling (Mainz, 1852, repr. 1970).

Urkundenbuch zur Geschichte der jetz die preussischen Regierungsbezirke Coblenz und Trier bildenden mittelrheinischen Territorien: Erster Band von den ältesten Zeiten bis zum Jahre 1169, ed. Heinrich Beyer (Koblenz, 1860).

Urkundenbuch der Reichsabtei Hersfeld, ed. Hans Weirich vol. I (Marburg, 1936).

Urkundenbuch der Stadt Strassburg; Erster Band Urkunden und Stadtrechte bis zum Jahr 1266, ed. Wilhelm Wiegand (Strasbourg, 1879).

Vegetius, *Epitoma rei militaris*, ed. Alf Önnerfors (Stuttgart, 1995).

Vegetius: Epitome of Military Science, trans. N. P. Milner, 2nd revised edn (Liverpool, 1996).

Vita Brunonis altera, ed. Georg Waitz, MGH SS 4 (Hanover, 1841).

Vita Burchardi episcopi, ed. Georg Waitz, MGH SS 8 (Hanover, 1858).

Vita Sancti Bernwardi episcopi Hildesheimensis auctore Thangmaro, ed. Walter Berschin and Angelika Häse (Heidelberg, 1993).

Vita sancti Germani, ed. Ludwig Traube, MGH *Poetae Latini Aevi Carolini*, vol. 3 (Berlin, 1896).

Widukind of Corvey, *Res gestae Saxoniae*, ed. and trans. Albert Bauer and Reinhold Rau in *Quellen zur Geschichte der sächsischen Kaiserzeit*, vol. 8 (Darmstadt, 1971).

Scholarly Works

Abels, Richard. "English Tactics and Strategy in the Late Tenth Century," in *The Battle of Maldon AD 991*, ed. D. G. Scragg (Oxford, 1991), 143-155.

---. *Alfred the Great: War, Kingship and Culture in Anglo-Saxon England* (London, 1998).

Abels, Richard, and Morillo, Stephen. "A Lying Legacy? A Preliminary Discussion of Images of Antiquity and Altered Reality in Medieval Military History," *The Journal of Medieval Military History* 3 (2005), 1-13.

Agthe, Markus. "Slawischer Burgwall mit Voburgsiedlung von Leuthen-Wintdorf, Niederlausitz," *Ausgrabungen und Funde* 38 (1993), 300-303.

Albu, Emily. "Imperial Geography and the Medieval Peutinger Map," *Imago Mundi* 57 (2005), 136-148.

Alföldi-Rosenbaum, E. "The Finger Calculus in Antiquity and in the Middle Ages: Studies on Roman Game Counters I," *Frühmittelalterliche Studien* 5 (1971), 1-9.

Alston, Richard. "Review of J. H. W. G. Liebeschuetz, *Decline and Fall of the Roman City*," *Journal of Roman Studies* 92 (2002), 406-407.

Althoff, Gerd. *Amicitia und pacta: Bündnis, Einung, Politik und Gebetsgedenken im beginnenden 10. Jahrhundert* (Hanover, 1992).

---. "Widukind von Corvey: Kronzeuge und Herausforderung," *Frühmittelalterliche Studien* 27 (1993), 253-272.

---. *Spielreglen der Politik im Mittelatler. Kommunikation in Frieden und Fehde* (Darmstadt, 1997).

---. *Die Ottonen: Königsherrschaft ohne Staat* (Stuttgart, 2000).

---. "Geschichtsschreibung in einer oralen Gesellschaft. Das Beispiel des 10. Jahrhunderts," in *Ottonische Neuanfänge. Symposium zur Ausstellung 'Otto der Große, Magdeburg und Europa,'* ed. Stefan Weinfurter and Bernd Schneidmüller (Mainz, 2001), 151-169.

Arnold, Benjamin. "German Bishops and their Military Retinues in the Medieval Empire," *German History* 7 (1989), 161-183.

Arnst, Ludwig. "Mittelalterliche Feldzeichen: Eine kunstgeschichtliche Studie," *Zeitschrift für christliche Kunst* 28 (1915), 164-180.

Auer, Leopold. "Der Kriegsdienst des Klerus unter den sächsischen Kaisern," *MIÖG* 79 (1971), 316-407.

———. "Der Kriegsdienst des Klerus unter den sächsischen Kaisern," *MIÖG* 80 (1972), 48-70.

———. "Zum Kriegswesen unter den früheren Babenbergern," *Jahrbuch für Landeskunde von Niederösterreich* 42 (1976), 9-25.

———. "Mittelalterliche Kriegsgeschichte als Forschungsproblem," *Francia* 10 (1982), 449-463.

———. "Formen des Krieges im abendländischen Mittelalter," in *Formen des Krieges vom Mittelalter zum "Low-Intensity-Conflict"*, ed. Manfried Rauchensteiner and Erwin A. Schmidl (Graz, Vienna and Cologne, 1991), 17-43.

Baaken, G. *Königtum. Burgen und Königsfreien. Studien zu ihrer Geschichte in Ostsachsen* (Cologne and Stuttgart, 1961).

Bachrach, Bernard S. "Charles Martel, Mounted Shock Combat, the Stirrup and Feudalism," *Studies in Medieval and Renaissance History* 7 (1970), 49-75, reprinted with the same pagination in idem, *Armies and Politics in the Early Medieval West* (Aldershot, 1993).

———. "The Feigned Retreat at Hastings," *Mediaeval Studies* 33 (1971): 344-347 and reprinted in Stephen Morillo (ed.), *The Battle of Hastings* (Woodbridge, 1996), 190-193.

———. *Merovingian Military Organization 481–751* (Minneapolis, 1972).

———. "A Picture of Avar-Frankish Warfare from a Carolingian Psalter of the Early Ninth Century in Light of the *Strategicon*," *Archivum Eurasiae Medii Aevi* 4 (1984), 5-27.

———. "The Practical Use of Vegetius' *De re militari* during the Early Middle Ages," *The Historian* 47 (1985), 239-255.

———. "*Caballus et Caballarius* in Medieval Warfare," in *The Story of Chivalry*, ed. H. Chickering and T. Seiler (Kalamazoo, 1988), 173-211; reprinted with the same pagination in Bernard S. Bachrach, *Warfare and Military Organization in Pre-Crusade Europe* (London, 2002).

———. "Grand Strategy in the Germanic Kingdoms: Recruitment of the Rank and File," in *L'Armée romaine et les barbares du IIIe au VIIe siècle*, ed. Françoise Vallet and Michel Kazanski (Paris, 1993), 55-63.

———. *The Anatomy of a Little War: A Diplomatic History of the Gundovald Affair (568–586)* (Boulder, CO, 1994).

———. "The Education of the 'Officer Corps' in the Fifth and Sixth Centuries," in *La noblesse romaine et les chefs barbares du IIIe au VIII siècle*, in quarto, ed. Françoise Vallet and Michel Kazanski (Paris, 1995), 7-13.

———. "Military Lands in Historical Perspective," *The Haskins Society Journal* 9 (1997), 95-122.

–––."Early Medieval Military Demography: Some Observations on the Methods of Hans Delbrück," in *The Circle of War in the Middle Ages*, ed. Donald Kagay and L. J. Andrew Villalon (Woodbridge, 1999), 3-20.

–––. "Magyar-Ottonian Warfare: *à-propos* a New Minimalist Interpretation," *Francia* 13 (2000), 211-230.

–––. *Early Carolingian Warfare: Prelude to Empire* (Philadelphia, 2001).

–––. "William Rufus's Plan for the Invasion of the Mainland in 1101," in *The Normans and their Adversaries: Studies in Honor of C. Warren Hollister*, ed. Bernard S. Bachrach and Richard Abels (Woodbridge, 2001), 31-63.

–––."Adalhard's *De ordine palatii*: Some Methodological Observations Regarding Chapters 29–36," *Cithara*, 39 (2001), 3-36.

–––. "Fifth Century Metz: Later Roman Christian *Urbs* or Ghost Town?" *Antiquité Tardive* 10 (2002), 363-381.

–––. "Dudo of St. Quentin as an Historian of Military Organization," *The Haskins Society Journal* 12 (2002), 165-185.

–––."Gregory of Tours as a Military Historian," in Kathleen Anne Mitchell and Ian N. Wood eds., *The World of Gregory of Tours* (Leiden, 2002), 351-363.

–––. "Crusader Logistics; From Victory at Nicaea to Resupply at Dorylaion," in *Logistics of Warfare in the Age of the Crusades*, ed. John H. Pryor (Aldershot, 2006), 43-62.

–––."Are They Not Like Us? Charlemagne's Fisc in Military Perspective," *Paradigms and Methods in Early Medieval Studies (The New Middle Ages)*, ed. Celia Chazelle and Felice Lifshitz (New York, 2007), 319-343.

–––. "'A Lying Legacy' Revisited: The Abels-Morillo Defense of Discontinuity," *Journal of Medieval Military History* 5 (2007), 154-193.

Bachrach, Bernard S. and Aris, Rutherford. "Military Technology and Garrison Organization: Some Observations on Anglo-Saxon Military Thinking in Light of the Burghal Hidage," *Technology and Culture* 31 (1990), 1-17; reprinted in Bernard S. Bachrach, *Warfare and Military Organization in Pre-Crusade Europe* (London, 2002), with the same pagination.

Bachrach, Bernard S. and Aris, Rutherford,"*De Motu Arietum* (On the Motion of Battering Rams)," in *Differential Equations, Dynamical Systems, and Control Science: A Festschrift in Honor of Lawrence Markus*, ed. K. D. Elworthy, W. Norrie Everitt, and E. Bruce Lee (New York and Hong Kong, 1993), 1-13.

Bachrach, Bernard S. and Bachrach, David S.,"Continuity of Written Administration in the Late Carolingian East c. 887–911: The Royal Fisc," *Frühmittelalterliche Studien* 42 (2008 appeared 2009), 109-146.

Bachrach, Bernard S. and Bowlus, Charles R. "Heerwesen," in *Reallexikon der Germanischen Altertumskunde*, ed. Heinrich Beck et al. (Berlin and New York, 2000), 14, 122-136.

Bachrach, David S. *Religion and the Conduct of War c.300–c.1215* (Woodbridge, 2003).

–––. "The Origins of the English Crossbow Industry," *Journal of Medieval Military History* 2 (2003), 73-87.

–––. "Lay Confession in the *regnum Francorum*: The Evidence Reconsidered," *The Journal of Ecclesiastical History* 54 (2003), 3-22.

–––. "The Royal Arms Makers of England 1199–1216: A Prosopographical Survey," *Medieval Prosopography* 25 (2004, appearing 2008), 49-75.

–––. "Conforming with the Rhetorical Tradition of Plausibility: Clerical Representation of Battlefield Orations against Muslims, 1080–1170," *International History Review* 26 (2004), 1-19.

–––. "English Artillery 1189–1307: The Implications of Terminology," *English Historical Review* 121 (2006), 1408-1430.

–––. "Memory, Epistemology, and the Writing of Early Medieval Military History: The Example of Bishop Thietmar of Merseburg (1009–1018)," *Viator* 38 (2007), 63-90.

–––. "The Military Organization of Ottonian Germany, c. 900–1018: The Views of Bishop Thietmar of Merseburg," *Journal of Military History* 72 (2008), 1061-1088.

–––. "Exercise of Royal Power in Early Medieval Europe: The Case of Otto the Great 936–973," *Early Medieval Europe* 17 (2009), 389-419.

–––. "The Written Word in Carolingian-Style Fiscal Administration under King Henry I, 919–936," *German History* 28 (2010), 399-423.

–––. "Feeding the Host: The Ottonian Royal Fisc in Military Perspective," *Studies in Medieval and Renaissance History*, third series, forthcoming.

Bachrach, David S. with Bachrach, Bernard S. "Saxon Military Revolution, 912–973?: Myth and Reality," *Early Medieval Europe* 15 (2007), 186-222.

Bachrach, David S. and Bachrach, Bernard S. "Early Saxon Frontier Warfare: Henry I, Otto I, and Carolingian Military Institutions," *Journal of Medieval Military History*, 10 (2012) 17–60

Bahn, Bernd W. "Zscheiplitz im Netz alter Straßen," *Burgen und Schlösser in Sachsen-Anhalt* 1 (1999), 204-218.

Bairoch, Paul, Batou, Jean, and Chèver, Pierre. *La population des villes européennes de 800 à 1850* (Geneva, 1988).

Barbero, Alessandro. *Carlo Magno, un padre dell'Europa* (Rome, 2000), trans. Allen Cameron as *Charlemagne: Father of a Continent* (Berkeley, CA, 2004).

Barford, P. M. *The Early Slavs: Culture and Society in Early Medieval Eastern Europe* (Ithaca, NY, 2001).

Bartoskova, Andrea. "Zur Stellung von Budec in der Struktur der böhmischen frühmittelalterlichen Burgwälle," in *Frühmittelalterliche Burgenbau*, 321-327.

Baumbach, Udo. "Zur Baufolge an der Burg Rochlitz," *Burgenforschung aus Sachsen* 3-4 (1994), 33-57.

Bennett, Matthew. "The Myth of the Military Supremacy of Knightly Cavalry," in *Armies, Chivalry and Warfare*, ed. Matthew Strickland (Stamford, 1998), 304-316; reprinted in *Medieval Warfare 1000–1300*, ed. John France (Aldershot, 2006), 171-183.

Berger, Dieter. "Alte Wege und Strassen zwischen Mosel, Rhein und Fulda," *Rheinische Vierteljahrsblätter* 22 (1957), 176-191.

Berges, Wilhelm. "Zur Geschichte des Werla-Goslarer Reichsbezirks vom neunten bis zum elften Jahrhundert," in *Deutsche Königspfalzen* vol. 1 (Göttingen, 1963), 113-157.

Bernhardt, John. *Itinerant Kingship and Royal Monasteries in Early Medieval Germany, c. 936–1075* (Cambridge, 1993).

Beumann, Helmut, *Widukind von Korvey: Untersuchungen zur Geschichtsschreibung und Ideengeschichte des 10. Jahrhunderts* (Weimar, 1950).

———. "Die Einheit des ostfränkischen Reiches und der Kaisergedanke bei der Königserhebung Ludwigs des Kindes," *Archiv für Diplomatik* 23 (1977), 142-163.

———. "Magdeburg und die Ostpolitik der Ottonen," *Die historische Wirkung der östlichen Regionen des Reiches: Vorträge einer Tagung zum vierzigjährigen Bestehen der Bundesrepublik Deutschland* (Cologne, 1989), 9-29.

Beyerle, Franz. "Zur Wehrverfassung des Hochmittelalters," in *Festschrift Ernst Mayer zum 70. Geburtstag* (Weimar, 1932), 31-91.

Biermann, Felix. "Handel, Haus- und Handwerk in frühmittelalterlichen Burg-Siedlungskomplexen zwischen Elbe und Lubsza," in *Frühmittelalterliche Burgenbau* , 95-114.

Billig, Gerhard. *Die Burgwardorganisation im obersächsisch-meissnischen Raum: Archäologisch-archivalisch vergleichende Untersuchungen* (Berlin, 1989).

———. "Mittelalterliche Burgen in Dommitzsch nördlich Torgau," *Landesgeschichte und Archivwesen: Festschrift für Reiner Gross zum 65. Geburtstag* (Dresden, 2002), 21-34.

Binding, Gunther. "Spätkarolingiche-ottonische Pfalzen und Burgen am Niederrhein," *Chateau Gaillard* 5 (1972), 23-35.

———. *Deutsche Königspfalzen von Karl dem Großen bis Friedrich II (765-1240)* (Darmstadt, 1996).

Bischoff, Bernhard. "Über den Plan eines paläographischen Gesamtkatalogs der festländischen Handschriften des neunten Jahrhunderts," *Archivalische Zeitschrift* (1963), 166.

———. "Die Überlieferung der technischen Literatur," in *Artigianato et tennica nella societa dell'alto medioevo occidentale, Centro italiano die studi sull'alto medioevo* (Spoleto, 1971), I: 267-297.

———. "Die Hofbibliothek unter Ludwig dem Frommen," in *Mediaeval Learning and Literature. Essays presented to R.W. Hunt*, ed. M. T. Gibson and J. J. G. Alexander (Oxford, 1976), 3-22.

———. *Katalog der festländischen Handschriften des neunten Jahrhunderts (mit Ausnahme er wisigotischen)* 2 vols. (Wiesbaden, 1998–2004).

———. *Manuscripts and Libraries in the Age of Charlemagne*, trans. and ed. Michael Gorman (Cambridge, 1994).

Blanchet, Adrien. *Les enceintes romaines de la Gaule* (Paris, 1897).

Blaschke, Karlheinz. "Die Frühgeschichte der Stadt Colditz," *Sächsische Heimatsblätter* 2 (1965), 290-307.

———. "Straßen und Fernhandel im Mittelalter," *Leipzig, Mitteldeutschland und*

Europa: Festgabe für Manfred Staube und Manfred Unger zum 70. Geburtstag (Beucha, 2000), 263-273.

Bliese, John R. "Aelred of Rievaulx's Rhetoric and Morale at the Battle of the Standard, 1138," *Albion* 20 (1988), 543-556.

———. "Rhetoric and Morale: A Study of Battle Orations from the Central Middle Ages," *Journal of Medieval History* 15 (1989), 201-226.

———. "When Knightly Courage May Fail: Battle Orations in Medieval Europe," *The Historian* 53 (1991), 489-504.

———. "Rhetoric Goes to War: The Doctrine of Ancient and Medieval Military Manuals," *Rhetoric Society Quarterly*, 24 (1994), 105-130.

Bloch, Marc. "Un problem d'histoire comparée: la ministérialité en France et en Allemagne," *Revue historique de droit français et étranger* 7 (1928), 46-91; republished as "A Problem in Comparative History: The Administrative Classes in France and in Germany," in *Land and Work in Medieval Europe: Selected Papers by Marc Bloch*, trans. J. E. Anderson (Berkeley, CA, 1967), 44-81.

Bohácová, Ivana. "Zum Befestigungssystem der Premyslidenburgen (am Beispiel der archäologischen Untersuchungen in der Prager Burg und in Stará Boleslav)," in *Frühmittelalterliche Burgenbau in Mittel und Osteuropa*, ed. Joachim Henning and Alexander T. Ruttkay (1998, Bonn), 37-47.

Boutaric, Edgard. *Institutions militaires de la France avant les armées permanents* (Paris, 1863).

Bowlus, Charles R. "Two Carolingian Campaigns Reconsidered," *Military Affairs* 48 (1984), 121-125.

———. *Franks, Moravians, and Magyars: The Struggle for the Middle Danube, 788–907* (Philadelphia, 1995).

———. *The Battle of Lechfeld and its Aftermath, August 955: The End of the Age of Migrations in the West* (Aldershot, 2006).

Boyer, Marjorie Nice. "Medieval Pivoted Axles," *Technology and Culture*, 1 (1960), 128-138.

Brachmann, Hansjürgen. "Der slawische Burgwall von Cösitz, Kr. Köthen," *Ausgrabungen und Funde* 21 (1976), 162-3 and 244-247.

———. "Der Limes Sorabicus – Geschichte und Wirkung," *Zeitschrift für Archäologie* 25 (1991), 177-207.

Bradbury, Jim. *The Medieval Siege* (Woodbridge, 1992).

Brademann, Jan. "Der König und seine fideles: Zum Ausmaß ottonischer Königsherrschaft," in *Auf den Spuren der Ottonen III. Protokoll des Kolloquiums am 22. Juni 2001 in Walbeck/Hettstedt*, ed. Roswitha Jendryschik, Gerlinde Schlenker and Robert Werner (Halle an der Salle, 2002), 47-60.

Brown, Giles. "Introduction: The Carolingian Renaissance," in *Carolingian Culture: Emulation and Innovation*, ed. Rosamond McKitterick (Cambridge, 1994), 1-51.

Brown, Warren. *Unjust Seizure: Conflict, Interest, and Authority in an Early Medieval Society* (Ithaca, NY, 2001).

Brühl, Carlrichard. *Fodrum, Gistum, Servitium Regis: Studien zu den wirtschaftli-*

chen Grundlagen des Königtums in Frankenreich und in den fränkischen Nachfolgestaaten Deutschland, Frankreich und Italien vom 6. bis zur Mitte des 14.
Jahrhunderts, vol. 1 (Cologne and Graz, 1968).

———. Palatium und Civitas: Studien zur Profantopographie spätantiker Civitates vom
3. bis 13. Jahrhundert, 2 vols. (Cologne, 1975, 1990).

Brunner, Otto. Land und Herrschaft. Grundfragen der territorialen Verfassungsgeschichte Österreichs im Mittelalter, 4th edn (Vienna, 1959).

Brunt, Peter. Italian Manpower 225 B.C.–A.D. 14 (Oxford, 1987).

Brüske, Wolfgang. Untersuchungen zur Geschichte des Lutizenbundes: Deutsch-
wendische Beziehungen des 10.-12. Jahrhunderts (Cologne, 1955).

Buc, Philippe. The Dangers of Ritual: Between Early Medieval Texts and Social
Scientific Theory (Princeton, NJ, 2001).

———, "Italian Hussies and German Matrons: Liutprand of Cremona on Dynastic
Legitimacy," Frühmittelalterliche Studien 29 (1995), 207-225.

Budesheim, Werner. "Der 'limes Saxoniae' nach der Quelle Adams von Bremen,
insbesondere in seinem südlichen Abschnitt," in idem (ed.), Zur slawischen
Besiedlung zwischen Elbe und Oder (Neumünster, 1994), 28-41.

Bullimore, Katherine. "Folcwin of Rankweil: The World of a Carolingian Local
Official," Early Medieval Europe 13 (2005), 43-77.

Bullough, D. A. "Europae Pater: Charlemagne and his Achievement in the Light
of Recent Scholarship," English Historical Review 85 (1970), 59-105.

Bumke, Joachim. Studien zum Ritterbegriff im 12. und 13. Jahrhundert, 2nd revised
edn (Heidelberg, 1977).

———. The Concept of Knighthood in the Middle Ages, trans. W. T. H. Jackson and
E. Jackson (New York, 1982).

Büttner, Heinrich. "Die Ungarn das Reich und Europa bis zur Lechfeldschlacht
des Jahres 955," Zeitschrift für bayerische Landesgeschichte 19 (1956) 433-458.

———. "Zur Burgenbauordnung Heinrichs I," Blätter für deutsche Landesgeschichte
92 (1956), 1-17.

———. "Zur Stadtentwicklung von Worms im Früh-und Hochmittelalter," in Aus
Geschichte und Landeskunde. Forschungen und Darstellungen. Franz Steinbach
zum 65. Geburtstag gewidmet von seinen Freunden und Schülern (Bonn, 1960),
389-407.

———. Heinrichs I. Südwest- und Westpolitik (Stuttgart, 1964).

———. "Die christliche Kirche ostwärts der Elbe bis zum Tode Ottos I," in Zur
Geschichte und Volkskunde Mitteldeutschlands, ed. Walter Schlesinger
(Vienna, 1968), 145-181.

Büttner, Rudolf. "Die Wehrorganisation der frühen Babenbergerzeit im Einzelhofgebiet der Bezirke Melk und Scheibbs," Verein für Landeskunde von
Niederösterreich 42 (1976), 26-37.

Butzer, Karl. "The Classical Tradition of Agronomic Science: Perspectives on
Carolingian Agriculture and Agronomy," Science in Western and Eastern
Civilization in Carolingian Times, ed. P. L. Butzer and D. Lohrmann (Basel,
1993), 539-596.

Butzer, Paul L. "Die Mathematiker des Aachen-Lütticher Raumes von der karolingischen bis zur spätottonischen Epoche," *Annalen des historischen Vereins für den Niederrhein, insbesondere das alte Erzbistum Köln* 178 (1976), 7-30.

———. "Mathematics in the West and East from the Fifth to the Tenth Centuries: An Overview," in *Science in Western and Eastern Civilization in Carolingian Times*, ed. P. L. Butzer and D. Lohrmann (Basel, 1993), 443-481.

Cam, Helen Maud. *Local Government in "Francia" and England* (London, 1912).

Campbell, Brian. *The Writings of the Roman Land Surveyors: Introduction, Text, Translation and Commentary* (London, 2000).

Campbell, Darryl. "The *Capitulare de Villis*, the *Brevium exempla*, and the Carolingian Court at Aachen," *Early Medieval Europe* 18 (2010), 243-264.

Chadwick Hawkes, S., ed. *Weapons and Warfare in Anglo-Saxon England* (Oxford, 1989).

Chevedden, Paul E. "Artillery in Late Antiquity: Prelude to the Middle Ages," in *The Medieval City under Siege*, ed. Ivy A. Corfis and Michael Wolfe (Woodbridge, 1995), 131-173.

Chibnall, M. *The World of Orderic Vitalis* (Oxford, 1984).

Claude, Dietrich. *Geschichte des Erzbistums Magdeburg bis in das 12. Jahrhundert, Teil I: Die Geschichte der Erzbischöfe bis auf Ruotger (1124)*, (Cologne, 1972).

———. "Der Kónighof Frohse," *Blätter für deutsche Landesgeschichte* 110 (1974), 29-42.

Clausewitz, Carl von. *On War*, ed. and trans. M. Howard and P. Paret (Princeton, NJ, 1984).

Coale, Ansley, and Demeny, Paul. *Regional Model Life Tables and Stable Populations* (Princeton, 1966).

Coblenz, Werner. "Wallgrabung auf dem Burgberg Zehren," *Ausgrabung und Funde* 2 (1957), 41-45.

———. "Zur Frühgeschichte der meißner Burg: Die Ausgrabungen im meißner Burghof 1959/1960," *Meißner Heimat Sonderheft* 1961, 3-32.

———. "Boleslav Chrobry in Sachsen und die archäologische Quellen," *Slavia Antiqua* 10 (1963), 249-285.

———. "Die christliche Kirche ostwärts der Elbe bis zum Tode Ottos I," in *Zur Geschichte und Volkskunde Mitteldeutschlands*, ed. Walter Schlesinger (Vienna, 1968), 145-181.

———. "Archäologische Betrachtungen zur Gana-Frage im Rahmen der älterslawischen Besiedlung des Gaues Daleminzien," in *Beiträge zur Archivenwissenschaft und Geschichtsforschung*, eds. R. Groß and M. Kobuch (Weimar, 1977), 354-370.

———. "Der Burgberg Zehren, eine Befestigung aus der Zeit der ersten Etappe der deutschen Ostexpansion," in *Archäologische Feldforschungen in Sachsen: Fünfzig Jahre Landesmuseum für Vorgeschichte Dresden* (Berlin, 1988), 373-77.

Constable, Giles. "Nona et Decima: An Aspect of Carolingian Economy," *Speculum* 35 (1960), 224-250.

Contreni, John J. "Education and Learning in the Early Middle Ages: New Perspectives and Old Problems," *International Journal of Social Education* 4 (1989), 9-25: reprinted with the same pagination in idem, *Carolingian Learning, Masters and Manuscripts* (Aldershot, 1992).

———. "Learning in the Early Middle Ages," in idem, *Carolingian Learning, Masters and Manuscripts* (Aldershot, 1992), 1-21.

———. "Counting, Calendars, and Cosmology: Numeracy in the Early Middle Ages," in *Word, Image, Number. Communication in the Middle Ages*, ed. John J. Contreni and Santa Casciani (Turnhout, 2002), 43-83.

Coupland, Simon. "Carolingian Arms and Armor in the Ninth Century," *Viator* 21 (1990), 29-50.

———. "The Carolingian Army and the Struggle against the Vikings," *Viator* 35 (2004), 49-70.

de Jong, Mayke. "The Empire as *Ecclesia*: Rabanus Maurus and Biblical *Historia* for Rulers," in *The Uses of the Past in the Early Middle Ages*, ed. Yitzhak Hen and Matthew Innes (Cambridge, 2000), 191-226.

Delbrück, Hans. *Geschichte der Kriegskunst im Rahmen der politischen Geschichte*, 6 volumes (Berlin, 1900–1936).

———. *Numbers in History* (London, 1913).

———. *History of the Art of War within the Framework of Political History*, 3 vols., trans. Walter J. Renfroe (Westport, CT, 1975–l982).

Depreux, P. *Prosopographie de l'entourage de Louis le Pieux (781-840), Instrumenta I* (Sigmaringen, 1997).

———. "The Development of Charters Confirming Exchange by the Royal Administration (Eighth–Tenth Centuries)," in *Charters and the Use of the Written Word in Medieval Society*, ed. Karl Heidecker (Turnhout, 2000), 43-62.

Dette, Christoph. "Die Grundherrschaft Weißenburg im 9. und 10. Jahrhundert im Spiegel ihrer Herrenhöfe," in *Strukturen der Grundherrschaft im Frühen Mittelalter*, ed. Werner Rösener, 2nd edn (Göttingen, 1993), 181-196.

———. "Kinder und Jugendliche in der Adelsgesellschaft des frühen Mittelalters," *Archiv für Kulturgeschichte* 76 (1994), 1-34.

———. "Schüler im frühen und hohen Mittelalter: Die St. Galler Klosterschule des 9. und 10. Jahrhunderts," *Studien und Mitteilungen zur Geschichte des Benediktinerordens und seiner Zweige* 105 (1994), 7-64.

Devries, Kelly. *Medieval Military Technology* (Peterborough, Ontario, 1992).

Devroey, Pierre. "La céréaliculture dans le monde franc," in *L'ambiente vegetale nell'alto medioevo, Settimane di studio del Centro italiano di studi sull'alto medioevo* 37 (Spoleto, 1990), 221-253; reprinted with the same pagination in *Etudes sur le grand domaine carolingien* (Aldershot, 1993).

Die deutsche Königspfalzen: Repertorium der Pfalzen, Königshöfe und übrigen Aufenthaltsorte der Könige im deutschen Reich des Mittelalters, vols. 1-4 (Göttingen, 1982-2000).

Deutsche Königspfalzen: Beiträge zu ihrer historischen und archäologischen Erforschung, 7 vols. (Göttingen, 1963–2007).

Dralle, Lothar. "Zur Vorgeschichte und Hintergründen der Ostpolitik Heinrichs I.," in *Europa Slavica, Europa orientalis: Festschrift für Herbert Ludat zum 70. Geburtstag*, ed. Klaus-Detlev Grothusen and Klaus Zernack (Berlin, 1980) 99-126.

———. *Slaven an Havel und Spree. Studien zur Geschichte des hevellisch-wilzischen Fürstentums (6. bis 10. Jahrhundert)* (Berlin, 1981).

Durliat, Jean. "Le manse dans le polyptyque d'Irminon: nouvel essai d'histoire quantative," in *La Neustrie: Les pays au nord de la Loire de 650 à 850*, 2 vols., ed. Hartmut Atsma (Paris, 1989), 467-504.

Dvornik, F. "The First Wave of the *Drang Nach Osten*," *Cambridge Historical Journal* 7.3 (1943), 129-145.

Eckel, Auguste. *Charles le Simple* (Paris, 1899).

Eckhardt, Karl August. "Präfekt und Burggraf," *Zeitschrift der Savigny-Stiftung für Rechtsgeschichte. Germanistische Abteilung* 46 (1926), 163-205.

Eggert, W. *Das ostfränkisch-deutsche Reich in der Auffassung seiner Zeitgenossen, Forschungen zur mittelalterliche* (Vienna, 1973).

Ehlers, Caspar, "Der helfende Herscher: Immunität, Wahlrecht und Königsschutz für sächsische Frauenstifte bis 1024," in *Essen und die sächsischen Frauenstifte im Frühmittelalter*, ed. Jan Gerchow (Essen, 2003), 45-58.

Ehlers, Joachim. "Dom und Klosterschulen in Deutschland und Frankreich im 10. und 11. Jahrhundert," in *Schule und Schüler im Mittelalter: Beiträge zur europäischen Bildungsgeschichte des 9. bis 15. Jahrhunderts*, ed. Martin Kintzinger (Cologne, 1996), 29-52.

Ellmers, Detlef. "Post-Roman Waterfront Installations on the Rhine," in *Waterfront Archaeology in Britain and Northern Europe: A Review of Current Research in Waterfront Archaeology in Six European Countries Based on Papers Presented to the First Internatioanl Conference on Waterfront Archaeology in Northern European Towns*, ed. Gustav Milne and Brian Hobley (London, 1981), 88-95.

Elmshäuser, Konrad. "*Facit Navigium*: Schaffahrt auf Seine, Marne, Mosel und Rhein in Quellen zur frühmittelalterlichen Grundherrschaft," in idem (ed.) *Häfen, Schiffe, Wasserwege: Zur Schiffahrt des Mittelalters* (Bremerhaven, 2002), 22-53.

Emmerich, Werner. "Landesburgen in ottonische Zeit," *Mainfrankisches Jahrbuch für Geschiche und Kunst* 16 (1964), 301-304.

Engel, Franz. "Die Mittelalterliche 'Mannhagen' und das Problem des Limes Saxoniae," *Blätter für deutsche Landesgeschichte* 88 (1951), 73-109.

Erdmann, Carl. "Der Heidenkrieg in der Liturgie und die Kaiserkrönnung Ottos I.," *MIÖG* 46 (1932), 129-142.

———. *The Origin of the Idea of Crusade (Die Entstehung des Kreuzzugsgedankens*, Stuttgart, 1935), trans. Marshall W. Baldwin and Walter Goffard (Princeton, NJ, 1977).

Erkens, Franz-Reiner. "Militia und Ritterschaft: Reflexionen über die Entstehung des Rittertums," *Historische Zeitschrift* 258 (1994), 623-659.

Ettel, Peter. "Ergebnisse der Ausgrabungen auf der Burg Horsadal, Roßtal bei Nürnberg," in *Frühmittelalterliche Burgenbau in Mittel und Osteuropa*, ed. Joachim Henning and Alexander T. Ruttkay (Bonn, 1998), 127-136.

———. "Der Befestigungsbau im 10. Jahrhundert in Süddeutschland und die Rolle Ottos des Großen am Beispiel der Burg von Roßtal," *Europa im 10. Jahrhundert: Archäologie einer Aufbruchszeit*, ed. Joachim Henning (Mainz, 2002), 365-379.

Falck, Ludwig. *Mainz im frühen und hohen Mittelalter (Mitte 5. Jahrhundert bis 1244)* (Düsseldorf, 1972).

Faußner, Hans Constantin. "Die Verfügungsgewalt des deutschen Königs über weltliches Reichsgut im Hochmittelalter," *Deutsches Archiv* 29 (1973), 345-449.

Felgenhauer-Schmiedt, Sabine. "Herrschaftszentren und Burgenbau des 10. Jahrhunderts in Niederösterreich. Neue archäologische Forschungen im nördlichen Grenzgebiet," *Europa im 10. Jahrhundert: Archäologie einer Aufbruchszeit*, ed. Joachim Henning (Mainz, 2002), 381-395.

Fleckenstein, Josef. "Königshof und Bischofsschule unter Otto dem Großen," *Archiv für Kulturgeschichte* 38 (1956), 38-62, reprinted in idem, *Ordnungen und formende Kräfte des Mittelalters: Ausgewählte Beiträge* (Göttingen, 1989), 168-192.

———. *Early Medieval Germany*, translation of *Grundlagen und Beginn der deutschen Geschichte*, trans. Bernard S. Smith (New York, 1978).

———. "Zum Problem der *agrarii milites* bei Widukind von Corvey," in *Beiträge zur niedersächsischen Landesgeschichte zum 65. Geburtstag von Hans Patze im Auftrag der Historischen Kommission für Niedersachsen und Bremen*, ed. Dieter Brosius and Martin Last (Hildesheim, 1984), 26-41.

———. "Problem und Gestalt der ottonisch-salischen Reichskirchen," in *Reich und Kirche vor dem Investiturstreit: Gerd Tellenbach zum achzigsten Geburtstag*, ed. Karl Schmid (Sigmaringen, 1985), 83-98.

Flohrschutz, Günther. "Die freisinger Dienstmannen im 10. und 11. Jahrhundert," *Beiträge zur altbayerischen Kirchengeschichte* 25 (1967), 9-79.

Folkerts, Menso. "The Importance of Pseudo-Boethian *Geometria* during the Middle Ages," in *Boethius and the Liberal Arts: A Collection of Essays*, ed. Michael Masi (Bern, 1982), 187-209.

Fontaine, Jacques. *Isidore de Séville et la culture classique dans l'Espagne wisigothique* (Paris, 1959).

Freed, J. B. "The Formation of the Salzburg Ministerialage in the Tenth and Eleventh Centuries," *Viator* 9 (1978), 67-102.

Fried, Johannes. "Brunos Dedikationsgedicht," *Deutsches Archiv für Erforschung des Mittelalters* 43 (1987), 574-583.

———. "Die Kunst der Aktualisierung in der oralen Gesellschaft: Die Königserhebung Heinrichs I. als Exempel," *Geschichte in Wissenschaft und Unterricht* 44 (1993), 493-503.

———. "Die Königserhebung Heinrichs I. Erinnerung, Mündlichkeit und Traditionsbildung im 10. Jahrhundert," in *Mittelalterforschung nach der Wende 1989*, ed. Michael Borgolte (Munich, 1995), 267-318.

———. "Wissenschaft und Phantasie. Das Beispiel der Geschichte," *Historische Zeitschrift* 263 (1996) 291-316.

———. "Erinnerung und Vergessen. Die Gegenwart stiftet die Einheit der Vergangenheit," *Historische Zeitschrift* 273 (2001), 561-593.

———. *Die Schleier der Erinnerung: Grundzüge einer historischen Memorik* (Munich, 2004).

Friedmann, Bernhard. *Untersuchungen zur Geschichte des abodritischen Fürstentums bis zum Ende des 10. Jahrhunderts* (Berlin, 1986).

Friedrich, Reinhard. "Ottonenzeitliche Befestigungen im Rheinland und im Rhein-Main-Gebiet," *Europa im 10. Jahrhundert: Archäologie einer Aufbruchszeit*, ed. Joachim Henning (Mainz, 2002), 351-363.

Frolik, Jan. "Prag und die prager Burg im 10. Jahrhundert," *Europa im 10. Jahrhundert: Archäologie einer Aufbruchszeit*, ed. Joachim Henning (Mainz, 2002), 161-169.

Fuchs, Franz, and Peter Schmid (eds), *Kaiser Arnolf: Das ostfränkische Reich am Ende des 9. Jahrhunderts* (Munich, 2002)

Funkenstein, Amos. *Heilsplan und natürliche Entwicklung: Formen der Gegenwartsbestimmung im Geschichtsdenken des hohen Mittelalters* (Munich, 1965).

Gale, David A. "The Seax," in *Weapons and Warfare*, 71-84.

Gans, Paul. "The Medieval Horse Harness: Revolution or Evolution? A Case Study in Technological Change," in *Villard's Legacy: Studies in Medieval Technology, Science, and Art in Memory of Jean Gempel*, ed. Marie-Thérèse Zenner (Aldershot, 2004), 175-188.

Ganshof, F. L. "Benefice and Vassalage in the Age of Charlemagne," *Cambridge Historical Journal* 6 (1939), 147-175.

———. "Zur Entstehungsgeschichte und Bedeutung des Vertrages von Verdun (843)," *Deutsches Archiv* 12 (1956), 313-330.

———. "Charlemagne's Army," in *Frankish Institutions under Charlemagne*, trans. Bryce Lyon and Mary Lyon (Providence, RI, 1968), 59-68 and 151-161.

———. "The Genesis and Significance of the Treaty of Verdun (843)," *The Carolingians and the Frankish Monarchy: Studies in Carolingian History*, trans. Janet Sondheimer (London, 1971), 289-302.

Geary, Patrick. "Zusammenfassung," *Historiographie im frühen Mittelalter*, ed. Anton Scharer and Georg Scheibelreiter (Vienna, 1994), 539-542.

Geibig, Alfred. "Die Schwerter aus dem Hafen von Haithabu," *Berichte über die Ausgrabungen in Haithabu:Bericht 33*, ed. Kurt Schietzel (Neumünseter, 1999), 9-99.

Gericke, Helmuth. *Mathematik im Abendland: Von den römischen Feldmessern bis zu Descartes* (Berlin, 1990).

Giese, Martina. *Die Textfassungen der Lebensbeschreibung Bischof Bernwards von Hildesheim* (Hanover, 2006).

Giese, Wolfgang. *Heinrich I.: Begründer der ottonischen Herrschaft* (Darmstadt, 2008).

Gilliver, Catherine M. "The *De munitionibus castrorum*: Text and Translation," *Journal of Roman Military Equipment Studies* 4 (1993), 33-48.

Gillmor, Carroll. "The Introduction of the Traction Trebuchet into the Latin West," *Viator* 12 (1981), 1-8.

Glöckner, Karl. "Das Reichsgut im Rhein-Maingebiet," *Archiv für hessische Geschichte und Altertumskunde* nf 18 (1934), 195-216.

Gockel, Michael. *Karolingische Königshöfe am Mittelrhein* (Göttingen, 1970).

–––. "Die Bedeutung Treburs als Pfalzort," in *Deutsche Königspfalzen: Beiträge zur ihrer historischen und archäeologischen Erforschung*, vol. 3 (Göttingen, 1979), 86-110.

–––. "Allstedt," *Die deutschen Königspfalzen: Repertorium der Pfalzen, Königshöfe und übrigen Aufenthaltsorte der Könige im deutschen Reich des Mittelalters*, vol. II *Thüringien* (Göttingen, 2000), 1-38.

Godman, Peter. *Poetry of the Carolingian Renaissance* (London, 1985).

Goetz, Hans-Werner. "Die Wahrnehmung von 'Staat' und 'Herrschaft' im frühen Mittelalter," in *Staat im frühen Mittelalter*, ed. Stuart Airlie, Walter Pohl, and Helmut Reimitz (Vienna, 2006), 39-58.

Goffart, Walter. "Frankish Military Duty and the Fate of Roman Taxation," *Early Medieval Europe* 16 (2008), 166-190.

Goldberg, Eric J. *Struggle for Empire: Kingship and Conflict under Louis the German, 817–876* (Ithaca, NY, 2006).

Górecki, Janusz. "Waffen und Reiterausrüstungen von Ostrów Lednicki: Zur Geschichte des frühen polnischen Staates und seines Heeres," *Zeitschrift für Archäologie des Mittelalters* 29 (2001), 41-86.

Graham-Campbell, James. *Viking Artefacts: A Select Catalogue* (London, 1980).

Grebe, Klaus. "Ein Wallprofil vom Burgwall Reitwein und seine Auswertung für die Geschichte der Anlage," *Ausgrabungen und Funde* 27 (1982), 274-275.

Green, G. H. *Medieval Listening and Reading: The Primary Reception of German Literature 800–1300* (Cambridge, 1994).

Grenier, Albert. *Manuel d'archéologie gallo-romaine*, 6 vols. (Paris, 1924–1934).

Grewe, Holger, "Die bauliche Entwicklung der Pfalz Ingelheim im Hochmittelalter am Beispiel der Sakralarchitektur," in *Deutsche Königspfalzen: Beiträge zu ihrer historischen und archäologischen Erforschung* vol. 7: *Zentren herrschaftlicher Repräsentation im Hochmittelalter, Geschichte, Architektur und Zeremoniell*, ed. Caspar Ehlers, Jörg Jarnut and Matthias Wemhoff (Göttingen, 2007), 101-120.

Griffiths, W. B. "The Sling and its Place in the Roman Imperial Army," in *Roman Military Equipment: The Sources of Evidence, Proceedings of the Fifth Roman Military Equipment Conference, 1988*, ed. C. van Driel-Murray (Oxford, 1989), 255-279.

Grimm, Paul. *Handbuch vor-und frühgeschichtlicher Wall-und Wehranlagen Teil I: Die vor- und frühgeschichtlichen Burgwälle der Bezirke Halle und Magdeburg* (Berlin, 1958).

―――. "Fünf frühgeschichtliche Burgen bei Haina," *Studien aus Alteuropa* 2 (1965), 285-296.

―――. *Tilleda: Eine Königspfalz am Kyffhäuser, Teil I: Die Hauptburg* (Berlin, 1968).

―――. "Der Burghagen bei Reifenstein: Zur Funktion frühgeschichtlicher Befestigungen," *Ausgrabungen und Funde* 15 (1970), 285-291.

―――. "Drei Befestigungen der Ekkehardinger – Archäologische Beiträge zum Problem von Graf und Burg im 10. Jahrhundert," *Zeitschrift für Archäologie* 5 (1971), 60-80.

―――. "Zu ottonischen Märkten im westlichen Mittelelbe- und Saalegebiet," *Vor- und Frühformen der europäischen Stadt im Mittelalter: Bericht über ein Symposium in Reinhausen bei Göttingen in der Zeit von 18. bis 24. April 1972 Teil I*, ed. Herbert Jankuhn, Walter Schlesinger, and Heiko Steuer (Göttingen, 1973), 332-337.

―――. "Zu zwei Reichshöfen nahe der Pfalz Tilleda," *Ausgrabungen und Funde* 19 (1974), 266-273.

―――. "Zu Burgenproblem des 8.-10. Jh. Westliche der Saale," *Zeitschrift für Archäologie* 16 (1982), 203-210.

Hagen, Josef. *Römerstrassen der Rheinprovinz*, 2nd edn (Bonn, 1931).

Hägermann, Dieter. "Der Abt als Grundherr: Kloster und Wirtschaft im frühen Mittelalter," in *Herrschaft und Kirche: Beiträge zur Enstehung und Wirkungsweise episkopaler und monastischer Organisationsformen*, ed. Friedrich Prinz (Stuttgart, 1988), 345-385.

Haldon, John. *Warfare, State and Society in the Byzantine World 565-1204* (London, 1999).

Halsall, Guy. "Anthropology and the Study of Pre-Conquest Warfare and Society: The Ritual of War in Anglo-Saxon England," in *Weapons and Warfare*, 155-177.

―――. *Warfare and Society in the Barbarian West, 450–900* (London, 2003).

Hardt, Matthias. "Linien und Säume. Zonen und Räume an der Ostgrenze des Reiches im frühen und hohen Mittelalter," in *Grenze und Differenz im frühen Mittelalter*, ed. Walter Pohl and Helmut Reimitz (Vienna, 2000), 39-56.

―――. "Hesse, Elbe, Saale and the Frontiers of the Carolingian Empire," *The Transformation of Frontiers from Late Antiquity to the Carolingians*, ed. Walter Pohl, Ian Wood, and Helmut Reimitz (Leiden, Boston MA and Cologne, 2001), 219-232.

―――. "The *Limes Saxoniae* as Part of the Eastern Borderlands of the Frankish and Ottonian-Salian Empire," in *Borders, Barriers, and Ethnogenesis: Frontiers in Late Antiquity and the Middle Ages*, ed. Florin Curta (Turnhout, 2005), 35-50.

Hartmann, Martina, "Lothringen in Arnolfs Reich. Das Königtum Zwentibolds," in *Kaiser Arnolf: Das ostfränkische Reich am Ende des 9. Jahrhunderts*, ed. Franz Fuchs and Peter Schmid (eds), (Munich, 2002), 122-142.

Hauck, Karl. "Erzbischof Adalbert von Magdeburg als Geschichtsschreiber," in *Festschrift für Walter Schlesinger* vol. 2, ed. Helmut Beumann (Cologne, 1974), 276-353.

Hayen, Hajo. "Zwei hölzerne Moorwege aus dem Fundgebiet Ipwegermoor B, Kreis Ammerland," *Neue Ausgrabungen und Forchungen in Niedersachsen* 1 (1963), 113-131.

Henning, Joachim. "Archäologische Forschungen an Ringwällen in Nieder-ungslage: Die Niederlausitz als Burgenlandschaft der östlichen Mitteleuropas im frühen Mittelalter," in *Frühmittelalterliche Burgenbau in Mittel und Osteuropa*, ed. Joachim Henning and Alexander T. Ruttkay (Bonn, 1998), 9-29.

–––. "Der slawische Siedlungsraum und die ottonische Expansion östlich der Elbe: Ereignisgeschichte -Archäologie-Dendrochronlogie," *Europa im 10. Jahrhundert: Archäologie einer Aufbruchszeit*, ed. Joachim Henning (Mainz, 2002), 131-146.

–––, ed. *Europa im 10. Jahrhundert: Archäologie einer Aufbruchszeit* (Mainz, 2002). Ruttkay, Alexander T., eds. *Frühmittelalterliche Burgenbau in Mittel und Osteuropa* (Bonn, 1998).

Herrmann, Joachim. *Siedlung, Wirtschaft und gesellschaftliche Verhältnisse der slawischen Stämme zwischen Oder/Neiße und Elbe* (Berlin, 1968).

–––. "Reric-Ralswiek-Groß Raden. Seehandelplätze und Burgen an der südli-chen Ostseeküste," *Lübecker Schriften zur Archäologie und Kulturgeschichte* 9 (1984), 91-96.

–––. "Der Lutizenaufstand 983. Zu den geschichtlichen Voraussetzungen und den historischen Wirkungen," *Zeitschrift für Archäologie* 18 (1984), 9-17.

–––. "Herausbildung und Dynamik der germanisch-slawischen Siedlungsgrenze in Mitteleuropa," *Die Bayern und ihre Nachbarn: Berichte des Symposions der Kommission für Frühmittelalterforschung* (Vienna, 1985), 269-280.

–––. "Lorenzkirche, Markt des Burgwards Strehla im Daleminzergau der Mark Meißen," *Herbergen der Christenheit: Jahrbuch für deutsche Kirchengeschichte* 19 (1993), 17-27.

–––. "Belizi 997-Beltz-Belzig: Von der Slawenburg zur kursächsischen Festung zwischen Havelland und Fläming. Eine archäologisch-historische Topogra-phie," *Veröffentlichungen des brandenburgischen Landesmuseums für Ur-und Frühgeschichte* 28 (1994), 191-221.

Herrmann, Joachim, and Donat, Peter (eds). *Corpus archäologischer Quellen zur Frühgeschichte auf dem Gebiet der Deutschen Demokratischen Republik (7. bis 12. Jahrhundert)* (Berlin, 1973).

Herrmann, Joachim, and Hoffmann, Richard. "Neue Forschungen zum slawis-chen und frühdeutschen Burgwall 'Räuberberg' bei Phöben, Kr. Potsdam Land," *Ausgrabungen und Funde* 4 (1959), 294-306.

Herrmann, Volker. "Der 'Limes Sorabicus' und Halle im frühen Mittelalter," in *Siedlung, Kommunikation und Wirtschaft im westslawischen Raum: Beiträge der Sektion zur slawischen Frühgeschichte des 5. deutschen Archäologenkon-gresses in Frankfurt an der Oder* (2007), 133-143.

Heyen, F. J. *Reichsgut im Rheinland. Die Geschichte des königlichen Fiskus Boppard* (Bonn, 1956).

Hiestand, R. "Preßburg 907: Eine Wende in der Geschichte des ostfränkischen Reiches?" *Zeitschrift für bayerische Landesgeschichte* 57 (1994), 1-20.

Hill, D. H. "Siege-craft from the sixth to the tenth century," in *De Rebus Bellicis Part II*, ed. M. W. C Hassall (Oxford, 1979), 111-117.

Hill, David and Rumble R. Alexander, eds. *The Defense of Wessex: The Burghal Hidage and Anglo-Saxon Fortifications* (Manchester, 1996).

Hilton, R. H. and Sawyer, P. H. "Technological Determinism: the Stirrup and the Plough," *Past and Present* 24 (1963), 90-100.

Hirsch, H. "Der mittelalterliche Kaisergedanke in den liturgischen Gebeten," *MIÖG* 44 (1930), 1-20.

Hoffmann, Hartmut. *Buchkunst und Königtum im ottonischen und frühsalischen Reich*, MGH *Schriften* 30 (Stuttgart, 1986).

Hollister, C. Warren. "Norman Conquest and Genesis of English Feudalism," *American Historical Review* 66 (1961), 641-663.

———. *Anglo- Saxon Military Organization* (Oxford, 1962).

Holtzmann, Robert. *Geschichte der sächsischen Kaiserzeit,* third edit. (Munich, 1955).

Holzfurtner, Ludwig. *Gloriosus Dux. Studien zu Herzog Arnulf von Bayern (907-937)* (Munich, 2003).

Hooper, Nicholas. "The Anglo-Saxons at War," in *Weapons and Warfare in Anglo-Saxon England,* ed. S. Chadwick Hawkes (Oxford, 1989), 191-202.

Hubert, Jean. "Evolution de la topographie de l'aspect des villes de Gaule du Ve au Xe siècle," *Settimane di Studio del Centro Itaiano di studi sull'alto Medioevo,* 6 (1959), 529-558.

Hubinger, Paul Egon. "König Heinrich I. und der deutsche Westen," *Annalen des historischen Vereins für Niederrhein, insbesondere das alte Erzbistum Köln* 131 (1937), 1-23.

Hülle, Werner. *Westausbreitung und Wehranlagen der Slawen in Mitteldeutschland* (Leipzig, 1940).

Hüpper-Dröge, Dagmar. *Schild und Speer: Waffen und ihre Bezeichnungen im frühen Mittelalter* (Frankfurt, 1983).

Huth, J. J. "Die Burgwarde der Oberlausitz," *Letopis B* 28.2 (981), 132-161.

Illmer, Detlef. *Erziehung und Wissensvermittlung im frühen Mittelalter. Ein Beitrag zur Entstehungsgeschichte der Schule* (Kastellaun, 1979).

———. "Arithmetik in der gelehrten Arbeitsweise des frühen Mittelalters: Eine Studie zum Grundsatz "nisi enim nomen scieris, cognitio rerum perit." In *Institutionen, Kultur und Gesellschaft im Mittelalter: Festschrift für Josef Fleckenstein zu seinem 65. Geburtstag,* ed. Werner Rösener and Thomas Zotz (Sigmaringen, 1984), 35-58.

———. "Bruns Dedikationsgedicht als Zeugnis der karolingischen Renovatio unter Otto d. Gr.: Zu Carl Erdmanns neuer und Wilhelm Wattenbachs alter Deutung," *Deutsches Archiv* 11 (1954-1955), 219-226.

Innes, Matthew. *State and Society in the Early Middle Ages: The Middle Rhine Valley, 400–1000* (Cambridge, 2000).

–––. "Charlemagne's Government," in *Charlemagne: Empire and Society*, ed. Joanna Story (Manchester, 2005), 71-89.

Jaeger, Stephen C. *The Origins of Courtliness: Civilizing Trends and the Formation of Courtly Ideals 939–1210* (Phildalphia, 1985).

Jankuhn, H. "Ein Ulfberht-Schwert aus der Elbe bei Hamburg," in *Festschrift für Gustav Schantes zum 65. Geburtstag*, ed. K. Kersten (Neumünster, 1951), 212-229.

Jansen, Lutz. "Ausgrabungen in Oschatz und Altoschatz," *Archäologie aktuell im Freistaat Sachsen* 6 (1998), 176-179.

Johnson, Stephen. *Late Roman Fortifications* (Totowa, NJ, 1983).

Jones, A. H. M. "Military Chaplains in the Roman Army," *The Harvard Theological Review* 46 (1953), 239-240.

Kaeding, Susanne, Kümmerlen, Britta, and Seidel, Kerstin. "Heinrich I. – ein 'Freundschaftskönig'," *Concilium medii aevi* 3 (2000), 265-326.

Kaegi, Walter. "Byzantine Logistics: Problems and Perspectives," in *Feeding Mars: Logistics in Western Warfare from the Middle Ages to the Present* (Boulder, CO, 1993), 39-55.

Kasten, Brigitte. *Adalhard von Corbie* (Düsseldorf, 1986).

Keller, Hagen. "Zum Charakter der 'Staatlichkeit' zwischen karolingischer Reichsreform und hochmittelalterlichem Herrschaftsausbau," *Frühmittelalterliche Studien* 23 (1989), 248-264.

–––. "*Machabaeorum pugnae*: Zum Stellenwert eines biblischen Vorbilds in Widukinds Deutung der ottonischen Königsherrschaft," in *Iconographia sacra: Mythos, Bildkunst und Dichtung in der Religions-und Sozialgeschichte Alteuropas: Festschrift für Karl Hauck zum 75. Geburtstag* (Berlin, 1994), 417-437.

–––. "Entscheidungssituationen und Lernprozesse in den Anfängen der deutschen Geschichte: Die 'Italien und Kaiserpolitik' Ottos des Großen," *Frühmittelalterliche Studien* 33 (1999), 20-48.

Kellner, Mazimilian Georg. *Die Ungarneinfälle im Bild der Quellen bis 1150* (Munich, 1997).

Kempke, Torsten. "Bemerkungen zur Delvenau-Stecknitz-Route im frühen Mittelalter," *Hammaburg: Vor-und frühgeschichtliche Forschungen aus dem niederelbischen Raum* 9 (1989), 175-184.

–––. "Ringwälle und Waffen der Slawen in Deutschland," *Archäologie in Deutschland* 17 (2001), 24-27.

Kennecke, Heike. "Forschung Burg Lenzen, Wo Slawen gegen Sachsen kämpften," *Archäologie in Deutschland* 22 (2006), 8-13.

Kersting, Thomas. "Die Burg von Luckenwalde am niederen Fläming, Brandenburg: Bodendenkmalpflege und Landesgeschichte," *Cum grano salis: Beiträge zur europäischen Vor und Frühgeschichte: Festschrift für Volker Bierbrauer zum 65. Geburtstag* (Friedberg, 2005), 331-338.

Kirsch, Eberhard, and Mehner, Andreas. "Der Schloßberg von Lübbenau, Lkr.

Oberspreewald-Lausitz," *Veröffentlichungen zur brandenburgischen Landesarchäologie* 36/37 (2002-2003), 203-222.

Klebel, Ernst. "Herzogtümer und Marken bis 900," *Deutsches Archive für Geschichte des Mittelalters* 2 (1938), 1-53.

Köhler, G. *Die Entwicklung des Kriegswesens und der Kriegführung in der Ritterzeit von Mitte des II. Jahrhunderts bis zu den Hussitenkriegen* vol. 3 (Breslau, 1890).

Koehler, K. "Geflügelte Lanzenspitzen," *Zeitschrift für Ethnologie* 29 (1897), 214-221.

Koeniger, Michael. *Die Militärseelsorge der Karolingerzeit: Ihr Recht und ihre Praxis* (Munich, 1918).

Korfmann, M. "The Sling as a Weapon," *Scientific American* 229 (1973), 35-42.

Kottje, Raymond. "Die Tötung im Kriege: Ein moralisches und rechtliches Problem im frühen Mittlelalter," *Beiträge zur Friedensethik* 11 (1991), 1-21.

Kouril, Pavel. "Frühmittelalterliche Befestigungen in Schlesien und Nordmähren," in *Frühmittelalterliche Burgenbau*, 349-358.

Kraft, Rudolf. "Das Reichsgut von Oppenheim," *Hessisches Jahrbuch für Landesgeschichte* 11 (1964), 20-41.

Krahwinkler, Harald. *Friaul im Frühmittelalter: Geschichte einer Region vom Ende des fünten bis zum End des zehnten Jahrhunderts* (Vienna, 1992), 245-266.

Kreutz, Barbara M. *Before the Normans: Southern Italy in the Ninth and Tenth Centuries* (Philadelphia, 1991).

Krieger, Karl-Friedrich. "Obligatory Military Service and the Use of Mercenaries in Imperial Military Campaigns under the Hohenstaufen Emperors," in *England and Germany in the High Middle Ages*, ed. Alfred Haverkamp and Hanna Vollrath (Oxford, 1996), 151-167.

Küas, Herbert. "Wehrtürme und Wohntürme auf ausgegrabenen deutschen Burgen zu Leipzig, Meißen und Groitzch," *Sächsische Heimatblätter* 19 (1973), 145-155.

–––. "Die Leipziger Burg des 10. Jahrhunderts," *Arbeits und Forschungsberichte zur sächsischen Bodendenkmalspflege* 20/21 (1976), 299-332.

Kurasinksi, Tomasz. "Waffen im Zeichenkreis. Über die in den Gräbern auf den Gebieten des frühmittelalterlichen Polen vorgefundenen Flügellanzenspitzen," *Sprawozdania Archeologiczne* 57 (2005), 165-196.

Kurnatowska, Zofia. "The Organization of the Polish State—Possible Interpretations of Archaeological Sources," *Quaestiones Medii Aevi Novae* 1 (1996), 5-24.

Kurze, Dietrich. "Christianisierung und Kirchenorganisation zwischen Elbe und Oder," *Jahrbuch des Diözesangeschichtsvereins Berlin* 30/31 (1990-1991), 11-30.

Laistner, M. L. W. *Thought and Letters in Western Europe, A.D. 500–900*, 2nd. rev. edn. (London and Ithaca, NY, 1957).

Lake, Justin C. "Truth, Plausibility, and the Virtues of Narrative at the Millennium," *Journal of Medieval History* 35 (2009), 221-238.

Lammert, Friedrich. "Die antike Poliorketik und ihr Weiterwirken," *Klio* 31 (1938), 389-411.

Landes, Richard. *Relics, Apocalypse, and the Deceits of History: Ademar of Chabannes, 989–1034* (Cambridge, MA, 1995).

Langdon, John. *Horses, Oxen and Technological Innovation: The Use of Draught Animals in English Farming from 1066 to 1500* (Cambridge, 1986).

Laudage, Johannes. *Otto der Grosse (912-973): Eine Biographie* (Regensburg, 2001).

Lebuda, Gerhard. "Zur Gliederung der slawischen Stämme in der Mark Brandenburg (10.-12. Jahrhundert)," *Jahrbuch für die Geschichte Mittel und Ostdeutschland* 42 (1994) 103-139.

Lederer-Herkenhoff, Nicole. "Thietmar von Merseburg," in Ulrich Knefelkamp, ed., *Weltbild und Realität: Einführung in die mittelalterliche Geschichtsschreibung* (Bamberg 1992), 111-120.

Lehmann, Rudolf. "Zur Geschichte der Verkehrsstraßen in der Niederlausitz bis zum Ausgang des 18. Jahrhunderts," *Jahrbuch für brandenburgische Geschichte* 25 (1974), 49-93.

Leighton, Albert. *Transportation and Communication in Early Medival Europe* (Devon, 1972).

Leopold, Gerhard. "Archäologische Ausgrabungen an Stätten der ottonischen Herrscher," *Herrschaftsrepräsentation im Ottonischen Sachsen* (1998), 33-76.

Leyser, Karl. "The Battle at the Lech, 955: A Study in Tenth-Century Warfare," *History* 50 (1965), 1-25; reprinted in K. J. Leyser, *Medieval Germany and its Neighbours: 900–1250* (London, 1982), 43-67.

———. "Henry I and the Beginnings of the Saxon Empire," *The English Historical Review* 83 (1968), 1-32; reprinted in K. J. Leyser, *Medieval Germany and its Neighbours 900–1250* (London, 1982), 11-42.

———. "Early Medieval Canon Law and the Beginning of Knighthood," in *Institutionen, Kultur und Gesellschaft im Mittelalter. Festschrift für Josef Fleckenstein zu seinem 65. Geburtstag*, eds. Lutz Fenske, Werner Rösener, and Thomas Zotz (Sigmaringen, 1984), 549-566; reprinted in *Communications and Power in Medieval Europe: The Carolingian and Ottonian Centuries*, ed. Timothy Reuter (London and Rio Grande), 51-71.

———. "Ends and Means in Liudprand of Cremona," *Byzantinische Forschungen* 13 (1988), 119-143; reprinted in *Communications and Power in Medieval Europe: The Carolingian and Ottonian Centuries*, ed. Timothy Reuter (London, 1994), 125-142.

Liebeschuetz, J. H. W. G. *Decline and Fall of the Roman City* (Oxford, 2003).

Lies, J. "Baggerfunde der Jahre 1974/75 von Magdeburg-Fermersleben," *Ausgrabungen und Funde* 21 (1976), 137-244.

Lintzel, Martin. "Heinrich I. und das Herzogtum Schwaben," *Historische Vierteljahresschrift* 24 (1927), 1-17.

Lippelt, Helmut. *Thietmar von Merseburg: Reichsbischof und Chronist* (Cologne, 1973).

Loud, Graham. "Byzantium and Southern Italy (876–1000)," *The Cambridge History of the Byzantine Empire c. 500–1492* (Cambridge, 2008), 560-582.

Lourie, Elena. "A Society Organized for War: Medieval Spain," *in Past and Present* 35 (1966), 54-76.

Lowe, E. A. *Codices Latini Antiquiores: A Palaeographical Guide to Latin Manuscripts Prior to the Ninth Century*, 11 vols. (Oxford, 1934–1971).

Lubeck, Christian. "Die Äbte von Fulda als Politiker Ottos des Großen," *Historisches Jahrbuch* 71 (1952), 273-304.

Ludat, Herbert, "Böhmen und die Anfänge Ottos I.," *Politik, Gesellschaft, Geschichtsschreibung: Giessener Festgabe für Frantisek Graus zum 60. Geburtstag* (Cologne, 1982), 131-164.

Lüdke, Franz. *König Heinrich I.* (Berlin, 1936).

Lutwak, Edward N. *The Grand Strategy of the Roman Empire* (Baltimore, 1976, repr. London, 1999).

Macartney, C.A. *The Magyars in the Ninth Century*, 2nd edn (Cambridge, 1968).

MacCurdy, J. T. *The Structure of Morale* (Cambridge, 1943).

MacLean, Simon. *Politics in the Late Ninth Century: Charles the Fat and the End of the Carolingian Empire* (Cambridge, 2003).

–––. *History and Politics in Late Carolingian and Ottonian Europe: The Chronicle of Regino of Prüm and Adalbert of Magdeburg* (Manchester, 2009).

Maier-Bode, Wolfgang. "Liudprand von Cremona," in *Weltbild und Realität: Einführung in die mittelalterliche Geschichtsschreibung*, ed. Ulrich Knefelkamp (Pfaffenweiler, 1992), 93-101.

Marsden, W. *Greek and Roman Artillery: Historical Development* (Oxford, 1969).

Marshall, P. K. "Scriptores Historiae Augustae," in *Texts and Transmission*, 354-356.

–––. "Valerius Maximus," in *Texts and Transmission*, 428-430.

Mascher, Karlheinz, *Reichsgut und Komitat am Südharz im Hochmittelalter* (Cologne, 1957).

Mathisen, Ralph W. "Barbarian Bishops and the Churches 'in barbaricis gentibus' during Late Antiquity," *Speculum* 72 (1997), 664-697.

Mayr-Harting, Henry. *Ottonian Book Illumination: An Historical Study* (Oxford, 1991).

–––. "The Church of Magdeburg: Its Trade and Its Town in the Tenth and Early Eleventh Centuries," in *Church and City 1000–1500: Essays in Honour of Christopher Brooke*, ed. David Abulafia, Michael Franklin, and Miri Rubin (Cambridge, 1992), 129-150.

–––. *Church and Cosmos in Early Ottonian Germany: The View from Cologne* (Oxford, 2007).

McCleod, W. "The Range of the Ancient Bow," *Phoenix* 19 (1965), 1-14.

McCormick, Michael. "The Liturgy of War in the Early Middle Ages: Crisis Litanies, and the Carolingian Monarchy," *Viator* 15 (1984), 1-24.

–––. *Eternal Victory: Triumphal Rulership in Late Antiquity, Byzantium, and the Early Medieval West* (Cambridge, 1986).

–––. "Liturgie et guerre des carolingiens à la première croisade," in *'Militia*

Christi' e Crociata nei secoli XI-XIII: miscellanea del centro di studi medio-evali 13 (1992), 209-40.

———. *The Origins of the European Economy: Communications and Commerce, A.D. 300-900* (Cambridge, 2001).

McKeon, Richard. "Rhetoric in the Middle Ages," *Speculum* 17 (1942), 1-32.

McKitterick, Rosamond (Pierce). "The 'Frankish' Penitentials," *Studies in Church History* 11 (1975), 31-39.

McKitterick, Rosamond. "Charles the Bald (823–877) and His Library: The Patronage of Learning," *The English Historical Review* 95 (1980), 28-47; republished with the same pagination in Rosamond McKitterick, *The Frankish Kings and Culture in the Early Middle Ages* (Aldershot, 1995).

———. *The Frankish Kingdoms under the Carolingians: 751–987* (London, 1983).

———. "The Palace School of Charles the Bald," in *Charles the Bald: Court and Kingdom*, ed. Janet L. Nelson and Margaret T. Gibson (Aldershot, 1990), 326-339; reprinted with the same pagination in Rosamond McKitterick, *The Frankish Kings and Culture in the Early Middle Ages* (Aldershot, 1995).

———. "Continuity and Innovation in Tenth-Century Ottonian Culture," in *Intellectual Life in the Middle Ages: Essays Presented to Margaret Gibson*, ed. Lesley Smith and Benedicta Ward (London, 1992), 15-24; reprinted with the same pagination in Rosamond McKitterick, *The Frankish Kings and Culture in the Early Middle Ages* (Aldershot, 1995).

———. "The Written Word and Oral Communication: Rome's Legacy to the Franks," in *Latin Culture and Medieval Germanic Europe: Germania Latina I*, ed. Richard North and Tette Hofstra (Gröningen, 1992), 89-112; reprinted with the same pagination in Rosamond McKitterick, *The Frankish Kings and Culture in the Early Middle Ages* (Aldershot, 1995).

———. "Ottonian Intellectual Culture in the Tenth Century and the Role of Theophanu," *Early Medieval Europe* 2 (1993), 53-74.

———. "The Audience for Latin Historiography in the Early Middle Ages: Text Transmission and Manuscript Dissemination," in *Historiographie im frühen Mittelalter*, ed. Anton Scharer and Georg Scheibelreiter (Vienna, 1994), 96-114.

———. "Bischöfe und die handschriftlichen Überlieferung des Rechts im 10. Jahrhundert," in *Mönchtum-Kirche-Herrschaft 750-1000. Josef Semmler zum 65. Geburtstag*, ed. Dieter R. Bauer, Rudolf Hiestand, Brigitte Kasten and Sönke Lorenz (Sigmaringen, 1998), 231-242.

———. Political Ideology in Carolingian historiography," in *The Uses of the Past in the Early Middle Ages*, ed. Yitzhak Hen and Matthew Innes (Cambridge, 2000), 162-174.

———. "Ottonische Kultur und Bildung," in *Otto der Große. Magdeburg und Europa*, ed. Matthias Puhle (Mainz, 2001), I: 209-224.

———. *Charlemagne: The Formation of a European Identity* (Cambridge, 2008).

Meens, Rob. "The Frequency and Nature of Early Medieval Penance," in *Handling*

Sin: Confession in the Middle Ages, ed. Peter Biller and A. J. Minnis (York, 1998), 35-63.

Menghin, Wilfried. "Neue Inschriftenschwerter aus Süddeutschland und die Chronologie karolingischer Spathen auf dem Kontinent," in *Vorzeit zwischen Main und Donau: Neue archäologische Forschungen und Funde aus Franken und Altbayern*, ed. K. Spindler (Erlangen, 1980), 227-272.

———. *Das Schwert im frühen Mittelalter: Chronologische-typologischen Gräbern des 5. bis 7. Jahrhunderts* (Stuttgart, 1983).

Metz, Wolfgang. "Tafelgut, Königsstraße und Servitium Regis in Deutschland, vornehmlich im 10. und 11. Jahrhundert," *Historisches Jahrbuch* 91 (1971), 257-291.

———. *Zur Erforschung des karolingischen Reichsgutes* (Darmstadt, 1971).

Meulemeester, Johnny de. "Comment s'est défendu au IXe siècle?" *Acta Archaeologica Lovaniensia* 8 (1995), 371-385.

Mitterauer, Michael. "Burgbezirke und Burgwerkleistung in der babenbergischen Mark," *Jahrbuch für Landeskunde Niederösterreich* 38 (1970), 217-231.

Mohr, Walter. *König Heinrich I. (919-936): Eine kritische Studie zur Geschichtschreibung der letzten hundert Jahre* (Saarlouis, 1950).

———. *Geschichte des Herzogtums Groß-Lothringen (900-1048)* (Saarbrücken, 1974).

Moortel, Aleydis Van de. "A New Look at the Utrecht Ship," in *Boats, Ships, and Shipyards. Ninth International Symposium on Boat and Ship Archaeology, Venice 2000*, ed. C. Beltrame (Venice, 2003), 183-189.

———. "The Utrecht Type: Adaptation of an Inland Boatbuilding Tradition to Urbanization and Growing Maritime Contacts in Medieval Northern Europe," in *Between the Seas: Transfer and Exchange in Nautical Technology*, ed. Ronald Bockius (Mainz, 2009), 321-327.

———. "The Utrecht Ship Type: An Expanded Logboat Tradition in its Historical Context," in *Between the Seas: Transfer and Exchange in Nautical Technology*, ed. Ronald Bockius (Mainz, 2009), 329-336.

———. "Medieval Boats and Ships of Germany, the Low Countries, and Northeast France: Archaeological Evidence for Shipbuilding Traditions, Timber Resources, Trade and Communications," in *Settlement and Coastal Research in the Lower North Sea Region* (Köthen, 2011), 67-105.

Morillo, Stephen. *Warfare under the Anglo-Norman Kings 1066–1135* (Woodbridge, 1994).

Morrison, Karl F. "Widukind's Mirror for a Princess: An Exercise in Self-Knowledge," in *Forchungen zur Reichs-, Papst- und Landesgeschichte. Peter Herde zum 65. Geburtstag von Freunden, Schülern und Kollegen dargebracht*, 2 vols. ed. Karl Borchardt and Enno Bünz (Stuttgart, 1998), 49-71.

Mortet, V. "La mesure des colonnes à la fin de l'époque romaine d'après un très ancien formulaire," *Bibliothèque de l'Ecole des Chartes* 57 (1896), 289.

Müller, Adriaan von. "Der Burgwall von Berlin Spandau," *Europas Mitte um 1000*, ed. Alfried Wieczorek and Hans Hinz (Stuttgart, 2000), 278-281.

Müller-Wille, Michael. "Krieger und Reiter im Spiegel früh und hochmittelalterliche Funde Schleswig-Holsteins," *Offa: Berichte und Mitteilungen zur Urge-schichte, Frühgeschichte und Mittelalterarchäologie* 34 (1977), 40-74.

Murray, Alexander. "Religion among the Poor in Thirteenth-Century France: The Testimony of Humbert of Romans," *Traditio* 30 (1974), 285-324.

Mütherich, Florentine. "Der karolingische Agrimensoren-Codex in Rom," *Aachener Künstblätter* 45 (1974), 59-74.

Mystakides, B.A. *Byzantinische-Deutsche Beziehungen der Zeit der Ottonen* (Stutt-gart, 1891).

Naumann, Helmut. "Rätsel des letzten Aufstandes gegen Otto I. (953-954)," *Archiv für Kulturgeschichte* 46 (1964), 133-184.

Nelson, Janet. "The Church's Military Service in the Ninth Century: A Contem-porary View?" *Studies in Church History* 20 (1983), 15-30; reprinted in Janet Nelson. *Politics and Ritual in Early Medieval Europe* (London, 1986), 117-132.

–––. *Charles the Bald* (London, 1992).

–––. "Literacy in Carolingian Government," in *The Uses of Literacy in Early Medi-eval Europe*, ed. Rosamond McKitterick (Cambridge, 1990), 258-296.

–––. "Was Charlemagne's Court a Courtly Society?" in *Court Culture in the Early Middle Ages: The Proceedings of the First Alcuin Conference*, ed. Catherine Cubitt (Turnhout, 2003), 39-57.

–––. "The Henry Loyn Memorial Lecture for 2006: Henry Loyn and the Context of Anglo-Saxon England," *The Haskins Society Journal* 19 (2007), 154-169.

Nesbitt, J. W. "Rate of March for Crusading Armies in Europe: A Study in Computation," *Traditio* (1963), 167-182.

Neugebauer, Otto. *The Exact Sciences in Antiquity*, 2nd edn (Providence, RI, 1957).

Nickel, Ernst. "Magdeburg in karolingisch-ottonischer Zeit," *Zeitschrift für Archäologie* 7 (1973), 102-142.

Nicholas, David. *The Growth of the Medieval City from Late Antiquity to the Early Fourteenth Century* (New York, 1997).

Nightingale, John. "Bishop Gerard of Toul (963–94) and Attitudes to Episcopal Office," in *Warriors and Churchmen in the High Middle Ages: Essays Presented to Karl Leyser*, ed. Timothy Reuter (London, 1992), 41-62.

Noëttes, R. Lefebvre des. *L'attelage et le cheval de selle à travers les âges*, 2 vols (Paris, 1931).

Nonn, Ulrich. "Das Bild Karl Martells in mittelalterlichen Quellen," in *Karl Martel in seiner Zeit*, eds. Jörg Jarnut, Ulrich Nonn, and Michael Richter (Sigmaringen, 1994), 9-21.

Oexle, Judith. and Strobel, Michael. "Auf den Spuren der "urbs, quae dicitur Gana", der Hauptburg der Daleminizier. Erste archäologischer Untersuchungen in der slawischen Befestigung von Hof/Stauchitz," *Arbeits und Forschungsber-ichte zur sächsischen Bodendenkmalpflege* 46 (2004), 253-263.

Padberg, Lutz E von. "Geschichtsschreibung und kulterelles Gedächtnis: Formen der Vergangenheitswahrnehmung in der hochmittelalterlichen Historiog-raphie am Beispiel von Thietmar von Merseburg, Adam von Bremen und Helmold von Bosau," *Zeitschrift für Kirchengeschichte* 105 (1994), 156-177.

Panek, Jaroslav, and Tuma, Oldrich (eds). *A History of the Czech Lands* (Prague, 2009).

Parisot, Robert. *Le royaume de Lorraine sous les Carolingiens, 843-923* (Paris, 1899).

Partner, Nancy F. "The New Cornificius: Medieval History and the Artifice of Words," in *Classical Rhetoric and Medieval Historiography*, ed. E. Breisach (Kalamazoo, MI, 1985), 5-60.

Patzold, Steffan. "Die Bischöfe im karolingischen Staat: Praktisches Wissen über die politische Ordnung im Frankenreich des 9. Jahrhunderts," in *Staat im frühen Mittelalter*, ed. Stuart Airlie, Walter Pohl, and Helmut Reimitz (Vienna, 2006), 133-162.

Paulsen, Harm. "Pfeil und Bogen im Haithabu," in *Berichte über die Ausgrabungen in Haithabu: Bericht 33*, ed. Kurt Schietzel (Neumünseter, 1999), 93-147.

Paxton, Frederick S. *Christianizing Death: The Creation of a Ritual Process in Early Medieval Europe* (Ithaca, NY, 1990).

Pearson, Kathy L. "Nutrition and the Early-Medieval Diet," *Speculum*, 72 (1997), 1-32.

Petri, Franz. "Der Rhein in der europäischen Geschichte und den europäischen Raumbeziehungen von der Vorzeit bis zum Hochmittelalter," *Das 1. Jahrtausend, Textband 2* (Düsseldorf, 1964), 567-615.

Petry, Klaus. "Die Geldzinse im Prümer Urbar von 893: Bemerkungen zum spätkarolingischen Geldumlauf des Rhein-Maas-und Moselraumes im 9. Jahrhundert," *Rheinische Vierteljahresblätter* 52 (1988) 16-42.

Philipsen, Johannes P. W. "The Utrecht Ship," *Mariner's Mirror* 51 (1965), 35-46.

Popp, Christian. "Gründung und Frühzeit des Bistums Havelberg," *Mitteilungen des Vereins für Geschichte der Prignitz* 3 (2003), 6-82.

Poschmann, Bernard. *Buße und letzte Ölung* (Freiburg 1951).

– – –. *Penance and the Anointing of the Sick*, trans. and rev. Francis Courtney (New York, 1968).

Poupardin, René. *Le royaume de Bourgogne (888-1030)* (Paris, 1907).

Powers, James F. *A Society Organized for War: The Iberian Municipal Militias in the Central Middle Ages, 1000–1284* (Berkeley and Los Angeles, 1988).

Powicke, Michael. *Military Obligation in Medieval England* (Oxford, 1962).

Preston, S. H., McDaniel, A. and Grushka, C. "A New Model Life Table for High-Mortality Populations," *Historical Methods* 26 (1994), 149-159.

Purton, Peter. *A History of the Early Medieval Siege, c. 450–1200* (Woodbridge, 2010).

Radig, Werner. *Der Burgberg Meißen und der Slawengau Daleminzien* (Augsburg, 1929).

Ramackers, Johannes. "Die rheinischen Aufmarschstrassen in den Sachsenkriegen Karls des Grossen," *Annalen des historische Verein Westfallen* 142-143 (1943–1951), 1-27.

Rathgen, Bernard. *Das Geschütz im Mittelalter* (Berlin, 1928).

Ray, Roger. "Medieval Historiography through the Twelfth Century: Problems and Progress of Research," *Viator* 5 (1974) 33-60.

———. "Rhetorical Scepticism and Verisimilar Narrative in John of Salisbury's *Historia Pontificalis*," in *Classical Rhetoric and Medieval Historiography*, ed. E. Breisach (Kalamazoo, 1985), 61-102.

Reddé, Michel, *L'Architecture de la Gaule romaine. Les fortifications militaires, Documents d'archéologie française* 100, directed by Michel Reddé with the aid of Raymond Brulet, Rudolf Fellmann, Jan-Kees Haalebos, and Siegmar von Schnurbein (Paris and Bordeaux, 2006).

Reeve, Michael D. "Suetonius," *Texts and Transmission*, 399-406.

———. "The Transmission of Vegetius' *Epitoma Rei Militaris*," *Aevum* 74 (2000), 243-354.

Reimer, Hubert. "Der slawische Burgwall von Klietz, Kreis Havelberg – ein Vorbericht," *Jahresschrift für mitteldeutsche Vorgeschichte* 75 (1992), 325-345.

Reinecke, P. "Studien über Denkmäler des frühen Mittelalters," *Mitteilungen der anthropologischen Gesellschaft in Wien* 29 (1899), 35-52.

Renard, Étienne. "La politique militaire de Charlemagne et la paysannerie franque," *Francia* 36 (2009), 1-33.

Rentschler, Michael. *Liudprand von Cremona: Eine Studie zum ost-westlichen Kulturgefälle im Mittelalter* (Frankfurt am Main, 1981).

Reuling, Ulrich. "Quedlinburg: Königspfalz-Reichsstift-Markt," in *Deutsche Königspfalzen: Beiträge zu ihrer historischen und archäologischen Erforschung vierter Band: Pfalzen-Reichsgut-Königshöfe*, ed. Lutz Fenske (Göttingen, 1996), 184-247.

Reuter, Timothy. "The 'Imperial Church System' of the Ottonian and Salian Rulers: A Reconsideration," *Journal of Ecclesiastical History* 33 (1982), 347-374.

———. "Plunder and Tribute in the Carolingian Empire," *Transactions of the Royal Historical Society*, 5th series, 35 (1985), 75-94.

———. "The End of Carolingian Military Expansion," in *Charlemagne's Heir: New Perspectives on the Reign of Louis the Pious (814–840)*, ed. Peter Godman and Roger Collins (Oxford, 1990), 391-405.

———. *Germany in the Early Middle Ages c. 800–1056* (London, 1991).

———. "The Recruitment of Armies in the Early Middle Ages: What Can We Know?" in *Military Aspects of Scandinavian Society in a European Perspective, AD 1000–1300*, ed. A. Norgard Jorgensen and B. L. Clausen (National Museum, Copenhagen, 1997), 25-31.

———. "Carolingian and Ottonian Warfare," in *Medieval Warfare: A History*, ed. Maurice Keen (Oxford, 1999), 13-35.

Reynolds, L. D. "Ammianus Marcellinus," in *Texts and Transmission: A Survey of the Latin Classics*, ed. L. D. Reynolds and P. K. Marshall (Oxford, 1983), 6-8.

———. "Eutropius," *Texts and Transmission*, 159-162.

———. "Frontinus, Strategemata," *Texts and Transmission*, 171-174.

———. "Justinus," *Texts and Transmission*, 197-199.

———. "Livy," *Texts and Transmission*, 205-214.

———. "Sallust," *Texts and Transmission*, 341-349.

———. "Velleius Paterculus," *Texts and Transmission*, 431-433.

Richardot, Philippe. *Végèce et la culture militaire au moyen âge (Ve-Xe siècle)* (Paris, 1998).

Riché, Perre, *Education et culture dans l'Occident barbare, VIe-VIIIe siècles* (1962), translated by John Contreni as *Education and Culture in the Barbarian West, sixth through eighth centuries* (Columbia, SC, 1976).

———. "Les bibiothèques de trois aristocrates laïcs carolingiens," *Le moyen âge*, 69 (1963), 87-104.

Riehm, Karl. "Vom Solquell zum Solbrunnen: Eine topographische Studie zur Gründungsgeschichte der Stadt Halle," *Jahresschrift für mitteldeutsche Vorgeschichte* 57 (1973), 197-209.

Rihll, Tracey. *The Catapult: A History* (Yardley, PA, 2007).

Rittenbach, W. "Über die Grenzen des Bistums Meißen," *Jahrbuch für die Geschichte Mittel- und Ostdeutschlands* 19 (1970), 49-73.

Rittenbach, W., and Seifert, F. *Geschichte der Bischöfe von Meißen 968-1581* (Leipzig, 1965).

Rogers, Clifford J. "The Offensive/Defensive in Medieval Strategy," *XII Congreß der internationalen Kommission für Militärgeschichte* (Vienna, 1997), 158-171; reprinted with the same pagination in idem, *Essays on Medieval History: Strategy, Military Revolutions and the Hundred Years War* (Burlington, VT, 2010).

———. "Edward III and the Dialectics of Strategy, 1327–1360," *Transactions of the Royal Historical Society* 6.4 (1994), 265-283; reprinted with the same pagination in idem, *Essays on Medieval History: Strategy, Military Revolutions and the Hundred Years War* (Burlington, VT, 2010).

———. *Soldiers' Lives Through History: The Middle Ages* (Westport, CT, 2007).

Rogers, Randal. *Latin Siege Warfare in the Twelfth Century* (Oxford, 1992).

Rösler, Horst. "Ein altslawischer Burgwall mit frühdeutscher Überbauung von Groß Lübbenau, Kr. Calau," *Ausgrabungen und Funde* 28 (1983), 85-90.

Roth, Jonathan P. *The Logistics of the Roman Army at War (264–335)* (Leiden, 1999).

———. *Roman Warfare* (Cambridge, 2009).

Rouillard, Philippe. *Histoire de la penitence des origins à nos jours* (Paris, 1996), 43-48.

Ruttkay, Alexander. "The Organization of Troops, Warfare and Arms in the Period of the Great Moravian State," *Slovenska archeologia* 30 (1982), 165-198.

Sander, Erich. "Der Verfall der römischen Belagerungskunst," *Historische Zeitschrift* 149 (1934), 457-467.

———. "Die Heeresorganisation Heinrichs I.," *Historisches Jahrbuch* 59 (1939), 1-26.

Schäfer, D. "Die agrarii milites des Widukind," *Sitzungsberichte des königlichen preussischen Akademie der Wissenschaften* 27 (1905), 569-577.

Schalles-Fischer, Marianne. *Pfalz und Fiskus Frankfurt: Eine Untersuchung zur Verfassungsgeschichte des fränkischen-deutschen Königtums* (Göttingen, 1969).

Scharff, Thomas. *Die Kämpfe der Herrscher und der Heiligen: Krieg und historische Erinnerung in der Karolingerzeit* (Darmstadt, 2002).

Scherff, Bruno. *Studien zum Heer der Ottonen und der ersten Salier (919-1056)* (Bonn, 1985).

Schlesinger, Walter. "Burgen und Burgbezirke. Beobachtungen im mitteldeutschen Osten," *Von Land und Kultur, Festschrift für Rudolf Kötzschke*, ed. Werner Emmerich (1937), 77-105, and reprinted in idem, *Mitteldeutsche Beiträge zur deutschen Verfassungsgeschiche des Mittelalters* (Göttingen, 1961), 158-187

———. *Die Entstehung der Landesherrschaft, Teil I* (Dresden, 1941, revised 2nd edn Darmstadt, 1964).

———. "Die Pfalzen im Rhein-Main-Gebiet," *Geschichte in Wissenschaft und Unterricht* 16 (1965), 487-504.

Schmid, Karl. "Zur Amicitia zwischen Heinrich I. und dem westfränkischen König Robert im Jahre 923," *Francia* 12 (1984), 119-147.

———. "Die Urkunde König Heinrichs I. für Babo aus dem Jahre 920," *Singener Stadtgeschichte* 2 (1990), 30-42.

Schmid, Peter, *Regensburg: Stadt der Könige und Herzöge im Mittelalter* (Kallmünz, 1977).

Schmid-Hecklau, Arne. *Die archäologischen Ausgrabungen auf dem Burgberg in Meißen: Die Grabungen 1959-1963* (Dresden, 2004).

Schmidt, Berthold, and Nitzschke, Waldemar. "Untersuchungen in slawischen Burgen zwischen Saale und Fläming," *Ausgrabungen und Funde* 20 (1975), 43-51.

Schmidt, Volker. *Drense: Eine Hauptburg der Ukrane* (Berlin, 1989).

Schmitz, H. *Pfalz und Fiskus Ingelheim* (Marburg, 1974).

Schneider, Rudolf. *Die Artillerie des Mittelalters* (Berlin, 1910).

Schneidmüller, Bernd. "Französische Lothringenpolitik im 10. Jahrhundert," *Jahrbuch für westdeutsche Landesgeschichte* 5 (1979), 1-31.

Schoenfeld, Edward J. "Anglo-Saxon 'Burhs' and Continental 'Burgen': Early Medieval Fortifications in Constitutional Perspective," *The Haskins Society Journal* 6 (1994), 49-66.

Schramm, Percy Ernst. *Die deutschen Kaiser und Könige in Bildern ihrer Zeit* vol. 1 (Berlin, 1928).

Schramm, Percy Ernst. and Mütherich, Florentine. *Denkmale der deutschen Könige und Kaiser* (Munich, 1981).

Schwenk, Bernd. "Das Hundetragen. Ein Rechtsbrauch im Mittelalter," *Historisches Jahrbuch* 110 (1990), 289-308.

Scientific Change: Historical Studies in the Intellectual, Social, and Technological Invention from Antiquity to the Present, ed. A. C. Crombie (London, 1963).

Searle, John R. *The Construction of Social Reality* (New York 1995).

Sergi, Giuseppe. "The Kingdom of Italy," in *The New Cambridge Medieval History* volume 3, c. 900–c. 1024, ed. Timothy Reuter (Cambridge, 1999), 346-371.

Settia, Aldo A. "Infantry and Cavalry in Lombardy (11th–12th Centuries)," trans. Valerie Eads, *Journal of Medieval Military History* 6 (2008), 58-78.

Shopkow, Leah. *History and Community: Norman Historical Writing in the Eleventh and Twelfth Centuries* (Washington, DC, 1997).

Smith, Cyril Stanley. and Hawthorne, John G. "Mappae Clavicula: A Little Key to the World of Medieval Techniques," *Transactions of the American Philosophical Society* 64 (1974), 3-128.

Smith, Julia M. H. "Religion and lay society," *The New Cambridge Medieval History: volume 2, c. 700–900*, ed. Rosamond McKitterick (Cambridge 1995), 654-678.

Sonnlechner, Christoph. "The Establishment of New Units of Production in Carolingian Times: Making Early Medieval Sources Relevant for Environmental History," *Viator* 35 (2004), 21-48.

Sonnleitner, Käthe. "Der Konflikt zwischen Otto I. und seinem Sohn Liudolf als Problem der zeitgenössischen Geschichtsschreibung," in *Festschrift Gerhard Pferschy zum 70. Geburtstag*, ed. Alfred Ableitinger (Graz, 2000), 615-625.

Springer, Matthias. "Agrarii Milites," *Niedersächsisches Jahrbuch für Landesgeschicthe* 66 (1994), 129-166.

Sproemberg, Heinrich. "Die lothringische Politik Ottos des Großen," *Rheinische Vierteljahrsblätter* 11 (1941), 1-101.

Squire, A. *Aelred of Rievaulx* (Kalamazoo, MI, 1981).

Staab, Franz. "Zur Organisation des Früh-und Hochmittelalterlichen Reichsgutes an der Unteren Nahe," *Geschichtliche Landeskunde* 21 (1980), 1-29.

Stana, Cenek. "Prerov- eine Burg des Boleslav Chrobry in Mähren," in *Frühmittelalterliche Burgenbau*, 49-69.

Steinacker, C. "Die Flügellanze der Karolingerzeit. Jagdspieß, Fahnenlanze oder Reiterwaffe?," in *Archäologie als Sozialgeschichte. Studien zu Siedlung, Wirtschaft und Gesellschaft im frühgeschichtlichen Mit teleuropa. Festschrift für Heiko Steuer zum 60. Geburtstag* (Rahden, 1999), 119-126.

Stevens, Wesley. "Walafrid Strabo: A Student at Fulda," in *Historical Papers of the CHA for 1971*, ed. J. Atherton (Ottawa, 1972), 13-20; reprinted with the same pagination in idem, *Cycles of Time and Scientific Learning in Medieval Europe* (Aldershot, 1995).

———. "Compotistica et Astronomica in the Fulda School," in *Saints, Scholars, and Heroes: Studies in Medieval Culture in Honor of Charles W. Jones* (1979), 27-64.

———. *Bede's Scientific Achievement: Jarrow Lecture, 1985* (Jarrow, Durham, 1985).

———. "Cycles of Time: Calendrical and Astronomical Reckonings in Early Science," in *Time and Process: Interdisciplinary Issues, The Study of Time VII*, ed. J. T. Fraser and Lewis Rowell (Madison, CT, 1993), 27-51.

———. *Cycles of Time and Scientific Learning in Medieval Europe* (Aldershot, 1995).

———. "Field and Streams: Language and Practice of Arithmetic and Geometry in Early Medieval Schools," in *Word, Image, Number. Communication in the Middle Ages*, ed. John J. Contreni and Santa Casciani (Turnhout, 2002), 113-204.

Stolle, Franz. *Der Römische Legionär und sein Gepäck ('Mulus Marianus'): eine Abhandlung über den Mundvorrat, über den Mundvorrat, die Gepäcklast und den Tornister des römischen Legionärs* (Strasbourg, 1914).

Störmer, Wilhelm. "Zur Frage der Funktionen des kirchlichen Fernbesitzes im Gebiet der Ostalpen vom 8. bis zum 10. Jahrhundert," in *Die transalpinen*

Verbindungen der Bayern, Alemannen und Franken bis zum 10. Jahrhundert, ed. Helmut Beumann and Werner Schröder (Sigmaringen, 1987), 379-403.

Strezelczyk, Jerzy. "Bohemia and Poland: Two Examples of Successful Slavonic State Formation," *Cambridge Medieval History vol. 3, c. 900–c. 1024,* ed. Timothy Reuter (Cambridge, 1999), 514-535.

Strickland, Matthew, and Robert Hardy. *From Hastings to the* Mary Rose: *The Great Warbow* (Stroud, 2005).

Struve, K. W. *Die Burgen in Schleswig-Holstein* vol. 1 *Die Slawischen Burgen* (Neumünster, 1981).

Sutherland, John M. *Liudprand of Cremona, Bishop, Diplomat, Historian: Studies of the Man and his Age* (Spoleto, 1988).

Szabo, Thomas. "Der Übergang von der Antike zum Mittelalter am Beispiel des Straßennetzes," in *Europäische Technik im Mittelalter 800 bis 1400: Tradition und Innovation, Ein Handbuch,* ed. Uta Lindgren, 4th edn (Berlin, 1996), 25-43.

Szameit, Erik. "Karolingische Waffenfunde aus Österreich Teil II: Die Saxe und Lanzenspitzen," *Archaeologia austriaca* 71 (1987), 155-171.

–––. "Fränkische Reiter des 10. Jahrhunderts," in *Otto der Große. Magdeburg und Europa. Katalog zur Austellung 2,* ed. Matthias Puhle (Mainz, 2001), 254-261.

–––. "Gedanken zum ostfränkischen Kriegswesen des 9. und 10. Jahrhunderts," in *Schicksalsjahr 907: Die Schlacht bei Preßburg und das frühmittelalterliche Niederösterreich* (St. Pölten, 2007), 67-76.

Tarrant, R. J. "Lucan," *Texts and Transmission,* 215-218.

–––. "Tacitus," *Texts and Transmission,* 406-409.

Tarver, W. T. S. "The Traction Trebuchet: A Reconstruction of an Early Medieval Siege Engine," *Technology and Culture* 36 (1995), 136-167.

Terray, Emmanuel. "Contribution à une étude de l'armée assante," *Cahiers d'études africaines* 16 (1976), 297-356.

Thompson, E. A. "Introduction," in *A Roman Reformer and Inventor: Being a New Text of the Treatise* De rebus bellicis, ed. E.A. Thompson (Oxford, 1952).

Ullman, B. L. "Geometry in the Mediaeval Quadrivium," in *Studi dei bibliografia e die storia in onore di Tammaro de Marinis,* vol. 4 (1964), 263-285.

Ulrich, Jens. "Der Burgwall von Klempenow, Lkr. Demmin," *Archäologische Berichte aus Mecklenburg-Vorpommern* 11 (2004), 28-38.

Unversagt, Wilhelm, and Schuldt, Ewald. "Ausgrabungen in den frühgeschichtlichen Burgwällen von Teterow und Behren-Lübchen im Lande Mecklenburg," in Römisch-Germanische Kommission des deutschen Archäologischen Instituts (ed.) *Neue Ausgrabungen in Deutschland* (Berlin, 1958), 564-568.

Verbruggen, J. F. *The Art of Warfare in Western Europe during the Middle Ages from the Eighth Century to 1340,* 2nd ed., trans. S. Ward and R. W. Southern (Woodbridge, 1997).

–––. "The Role of Cavalry in Medieval Warfare," *Journal of Medieval Military History* 3 (2005), 46-71.

Verhein, Klaus. "Studien zu Quellen zum Reichsgut der Karolingerzeit," part 2, *Deutsches Archiv für Geschichte des Mittelalters* 10 (1954), 313-394.

———. Studien zu Quellen zum Reichsgut der Karolingerzeit," part 2, *Deutsches Archiv für Geschichte des Mittelalters* 11 (1955), 333-392.

Verhulst, Adriaan. "Karolingische Agrarpolitik: Das Capitulare de Villis und die Hungersnote von 792/93 und 805/6," *Zeitschrift für Agrargeschichte und Agrarsoziologie* 13 (1965), 175-189.

———. ed. *Le Grand domaine aux époques mérovingienne et carolingienne. Die Grundherrschaft im frühen Mittelalter* (Ghent, 1985).

———. "Economic Organization," in *The New Cambridge Medieval History, c. 700–c. 900*, vol. 2, ed. Rosamond McKitterick (Cambridge, 1995), 481-509.

———. *The Rise of Cities in North-West Europe* (Cambridge, 1999).

Vogel, Cyrille. "Les rituals de la penitence tarifée," in *Liturgica opera divina e umana, studi offerti à S. E. Mons A. Bugnini: Bibliotheca 'Ephemerides liturgicae' Subsidia* 26 (Rome, 1982), 419-427.

Vogt, Heinz-Joachim. "Archäologische Untersuchungen im Altstadtbereich von Torgau," *Ausgrabungen und Funde* 37 (1992), 46-53.

Voltmer, E. "Von der Bischofsstadt zur Reichsstadt. Speyer im Hoch-und Spätmittelalter (10. Bis Anfang 15. Jahrhundert," in *Geschichte der Stadt Speyer*, ed. W. Eger (Stuttgart, 1982), 249-368.

Voss, Rolf. "Der altslawische Tempelort Groß Raden in Mecklenburg," *Europas Mitte um 1000*, ed. Alfred Wieczorek and Hans Hinz (Stuttgart, 2000), 252-256.

Vyronis, Speros. "The Evolution of Slavic Society and the Slavic Invasions of Greece: The First Major Slavic Attack on Thessaloniki, A.D. 597," *Hespia* 50 (1981), 378-390.

Wachter, Berndt. "Dendrodaten zu frühmittellalterlichen Burgen im Hannoverschen Wendland," in *Frühmittelalterliche Burgenbau*, 235-247.

Waley, Daniel. *The Italian City-Republics*, 3rd edn (New York, 1988).

Wallach, L. "Alcuin on Virtues and Vices: A Manual for a Carolingian Soldier," *Harvard Theological Review*, 48 (1955), 175-195.

———. *Alcuin and Charlemagne: Studies in Carolingian History and Literature* (Ithaca, NY, 1959).

Wattenbach, Wilhelm, and Holtzmann, Robert. *Deutschlands Geschichtsquellen im Mittelalter: Die Zeit der Sachsen und Salier: Das Zeitalter des ottonischen Staates (900-1050)*, part one, vols. 1-2, ed. Franz-Josef Schmale (Cologne, 1967).

Weidemann, Konrad. "Die Topographie von Mainz in der Römerzeit und frühen Mittelalter," *Jahrbuch der Römisch-Germanischen Zentralmuseums Mainz* 15 (1969 appeared 1970), 146-199.

Weinrich, L. "Laurentius-Verehrung in ottonischer Zeit," *Jahrbuch für die Geschichte Mittel-und Ostdeutschlands* 21 (1972), 45-66.

Wenskus, R. "Die soziale Entwicklung im ottonischen Sachsen im Lichte der Königsurkunsden für das Erzstift Hamburg-Bremen," in *Institutionen*,

Kultur und Gesellschaft im Mittelalter: Festschrift für Josef Fleckenstein zu seinem 65. Geburtstag, ed. Lutz Fenske (Sigmaringen, 1984), 501-514.

Werner, Karl Ferdinand. "Heersorganization und Kriegsführung im deutschen Königreich des 10. und 11. Jahrhunderts," *Settimane di Studio de Centro Italiano Sull'alto Medievo* 15 (1968), 791-843.

Westphal, Herbert. "Zur Bewaffnung und Ausrüstung bei Sachsen und Franken: Gemeinsamkeiten und Unterschiede am Beispiel der Sachkultur" in *Kunst und Kultur der Karolingerzeit: Karl der Große und Papst Leo III. in Paderborn*, ed. Christoph Stiegemann and Matthias Wemhoff (Mainz, 1999), 323-327.

———. *Franken oder Sachsen? Untersuchungen an frühmittelalterliche Waffen* (Oldenburg, 2002).

Westphalen, Thomas. "Die frühen Burgen Leipzigs," in *Archäeologie und Architektur: Das frühe Leipzig*, ed. Wolfgang Hocquél (Leipzig, 2003), 43-50.

Wetzel, Günther. "Der erste slawische Burgwall des Kreises Bad Liebenwerda in Fichtenberg bei Mühlberg," *Ausgrabungen und Funde* 22 (1977), 76-85.

———. "Neue Erkentnisse zur Befestigung der Burg bei Gehren, Kr. Luckau," *Ausgrabungen und Funde* 35 (1990), 90-92.

White, Lynn T. *Medieval Technology and Social Change* (Oxford, 1962).

Wieder, Michael A., Smith, Carol, and Brackage, Cinthia, eds, *Essentials of Fire Fighting*, 3rd edn (Stillwater, OK, 1992).

Winkler, Friedemann. *Leipzigs Anfänge: Bekanntes, Neues, offene Fragen* (Beucha, 1998).

Winterbottom, M. "Caesar," *Texts and Transmission*, 35-36.

———. "Curtius Rufus," *Texts and Transmission*, 35-36.

Wittekind, Susanne. "Die Makkabäer als Vorbild des geistlichen Kampfes: Eine Kunsthistorische Deutung des Leidener Makkabäer-Codex Perizoni 17," *Frühmittelalterliche Studien* 37 (2003), 47-71.

Wolf, Gunther. "De Pactis Ottonis I.," *Archiv für Diplomatik* 37 (1991), 33-48.

———. "König Heinrichs I. Romzugsplan 935/936," *Zeitschrift für Kirchengeschichte* 103 (1992), 33-45.

Wolfram, Herwig. "Karl Martell und das fränkische Lehenswesen. Aufnahme eines Nichtbestandes," in *Karl Martel in seiner Zeit*, ed. Jörg Jarnut, Ulrich Nonn, and Michael Richter (Sigmaringen, 1994), 61-78.

Wood, Susan. *The Proprietary Church in the Medieval West* (Oxford, 2006).

Zernack, Klaus. "Otto der Große und die slawische Reiche," in *Otto der Große, Magdeburg und Europa* (Mainz, 2001), 517-524.

Zielinski, Herbert. "Der Weg Nach Rom: Otto der Große und die Anfänge der ottonischen Italienpolitik," in *Die Faszination der Papstgeschichte*, ed. Wilfrid Hartmann and Klaus Herkbers (Cologne, 2008), 97-107.

Zotz, Thomas. "Das Elsass-Ein Teil des Zwischenreichs?" in *Lotharingia: Eine Europäische Kernlandschaft um das Jahr 1000*, eds. Hans-Walter Herrmann and Reinhard Schneider (Saarbrücken, 1995), 49-70.

Index

Warfare in History

Bloodied Banners: Martial Display on the Medieval Battlefield, *Robert W. Jones*

Alfred's Wars: Sources and Interpretations of Anglo-Saxon Warfare in the Viking Age, *Ryan Lavelle*

The Dutch Army and the Military Revolutions, 1588–1688, *Olaf van Nimwegen*

In the Steps of the Black Prince: The Road to Poitiers, 1355–1356, *Peter Hoskins*

Norman Naval Operations in the Mediterranean, *Charles D. Stanton*

Shipping the Medieval Military: English Maritime Logistics in the Fourteenth Century, *Craig L. Lambert*

Edward III and the War at Sea: The English Navy, 1327–1377, *Graham Cushway*

The Soldier Experience in the Fourteenth Century, *edited by Adrian R. Bell and Anne Curry*

Warfare in Tenth-Century Germany, *David S. Bachrach*

Chivalry, Kingship and Crusade: The English Experience in the Fourteenth Century, *Timothy Guard*

The Norman Campaigns in the Balkans, 1081–1108 AD, *Georgios Theotokis*

Lightning Source UK Ltd.
Milton Keynes UK
UKHW02f1559230118
316698UK00003BA/113/P